ANALECTA BIBLICA
INVESTIGATIONES SCIENTIFICAE IN RES BIBLICAS

147

JAN LAMBRECHT, S.J.

COLLECTED STUDIES

on Pauline Literature
and on The Book of Revelation

EDITRICE PONTIFICIO ISTITUTO BIBLICO - ROMA 2001

IMPRIMI POTEST

Romae, die 29 martii 2001

R.P. ROBERT F. O'TOOLE, S.J.
Rector Pontificii Instituti Biblici

IMPRIMATUR

Dal Vicariato di Roma, 29 marzo 2001

✠ CESARE NOSIGLIA
Arcivescovo tit. di Vittoriana
Vicegerente di Roma

ISBN 88-7653-147-5
© E.P.I.B. – Roma – 2001

EDITRICE PONTIFICIO ISTITUTO BIBLICO
Piazza della Pilotta, 35 - 00187 Roma, Italia

Contents

II. THE BOOK OF REVELATION

Preface

The present volume is published on the occasion of my 75th birthday (April 23, 2001) and of the five years I have been an Invited Professor at the Pontificio Istituto Biblico in Rome. The book contains thirty studies, most of them written in Rome. In some of them attention is devoted to a philological problem, in most the interest goes to the line of thought and content of the biblical text. Some studies are full-fledged articles, other but brief notes. Two are presented in a translation from the Dutch (nos. 23 and 29) and three are previously unpublished (nos. 5, 21 and 25). The other essays have appeared in different journals and publications, as the list in the "Acknowledgments" shows. Bringing them together in one volume may prove useful.

The work consists of two parts. "Pauline and Deutero-Pauline Letters" is the larger one. For the homologoumena the order of presentation is that of the canon: Romans, 1 and 2 Corinthians, Galatians and 1 Thessalonians. Two Deutero-Pauline notes, one on Ephesians and the other on 2 Thessalonians, are included, as well as a note on 1 Peter, the letter which is claimed to betray Pauline influence. "The Book of Revelation" is the second part and presents a collection of five articles.

For previous publications on Paul reference may be made to *Studies on 2 Corinthians* (together with R. Bieringer) and to *Pauline Studies*, both volumes published in 1994 as nos. 112 and 115 of the series "Bibliotheca Ephemeridum Theologicarum Lovaniensium" (University Press and Peeters: Leuven). Insights present in the articles on Paul's second letter to the Corinthians are incorporated in my commentary *Second Corinthians* (Sacra Pagina; Liturgical Press: Collegeville 1999). In 1979 I was the president of the 30th "Colloquium Biblicum Lovaniense" which was devoted to the Book of Revelation and Apocalyptic in the New Testament. This meeting resulted in the publication of *L'Apocalypse johannique et l'Apocalyptique dans le Nouveau Testament* (ed. J. Lambrecht; BETL 53; Duculot–University Press: Gembloux–Leuven 1980).

I am most grateful to my confreres Robert O'Toole, Rector of the Biblicum, and Albert Vanhoye, Director of the series "Analecta Biblica", for their readiness to publish these essays. Dr. Veronica Koperski, S.F.C.C., my former student from Leuven, now Professor at Barry University, Miami Shores (Florida), has most generously and critically read nearly all these studies; she also corrected and refined the English. I am greatly indebted to her and want to express here my sincere gratitude. A special word of thanks to Dr. Holger Gzella for his suggestions with regard to some of the more recent studies and for his help in correcting the proofs.

I also thank the colleagues and students of the Biblicum and its Jesuit community. Before my final departure to Leuven (Belgium) I confess my fear that I will miss the qualities of Roman life which have made these last five years so enjoyable.

April 23, 2001

Jan Lambrecht, S.J.
Pontifical Biblical Institute, Rome

Acknowlegments

The following essays originally appeared in:

1. *The Journal of Biblical Literature* 119 (2000) 526-528. Copyright – The Society of Biblical Literature, Atlanta, GA.
2. *Gregorianum* 81 (2000) 441-451. Copyright – Editrice Pontificia Università Gregroriana, Rome.
3. *New Testament Studies* 45 (1999) 141-147. Copyright – Cambridge University Press, Cambridge.
4. *Novum Testamentum* 42 (2000) 257-261. Copyright – Koninklijke Brill, Leiden.
5. (Unpublished)
6. R. KAMPLING – T. SÖDING (eds.), *Ekklesiologie des Neuen Testaments. FS K. Kertelge* (Freiburg–Basel–Wien 1996) 316-335. Copyright – Verlag Herder, Freiburg.
7. *Gregorianum* 77 (1996) 333-339. Copyright – Editrice Pontificia Università Gregoriana, Rome.
8. *Bijdragen* 61 (2001). Copyright – Peeters Publishers, Leuven.
9. *Zeitschrift für die neutestamentliche Wissenschaft* 91 (2000) 143-145. Copyright – Walter de Gruyter, Berlin.
10. *Novum Testamentum* 40 (1998) 352-368. Copyright – Koninklijke Brill, Leiden.
11. R. BIERINGER (ed.), *The Corinthian Correspondence* (BETL 125; Leuven 1996) 325-346. From the 46th "Colloquium Biblicum Lovaniense (1994)". Copyright – Peeters Publishers, Leuven.
12. *Biblica* 77 (1996) 398-416. Copyright – Editrice Pontificio Istituto Biblico, Rome.
13. *New Testament Studies* 43 (1997) 285-290. Copyright – Cambridge University Press, Cambridge.
14. J.D.G. DUNN (ed.), *Paul and the Mosaic Law* (WUNT 89; Tübingen 1996) 53-74. From "The Third Durham–Tübingen Research Symposium on Earliest Christianity and Judaism (Durham, September 1994)". Copyright – J.B.C. Mohr (Paul Siebeck), Tübingen.
15. A. VANHOYE (ed.), *La foi agissant par l'amour (Galates 4,12–6,16)* (Benedictina 13; Rome 1996) 13-31. From the 14th "Colloquium

oecumenicum Paulinum (1994)". Copyright – Benedictina editrice, Farfa (RI).

16. *Biblica* 4 (1999) 525-536. Copyright – Editrice Pontificio Istituto Biblico, Rome.

17. *Novum Testamentum* 38 (1996) 237-241. Copyright – Koninklijke Brill, Leiden.

18. *Biblica* 79 (1998) 515-524. Copyright – Editrice Pontificio Istituto Biblico, Rome.

19. *Biblica* 78 (1997) 33-56. Copyright – Editrice Pontificio Biblico, Rome.

20. *Landas. Journal of Loyola School of Theology* (Manila) 15 (2001).

21. (Unpublished)

22. K.P. DONFRIED – J. BEUTLER (eds.), *The Thessalonians Debate. Methodological Discord or Methodological Synthesis?* (Grand Rapids – Cambridge 2000) 163-178. From the "Studiorum Novi Testamenti Societas Seminar on 'The Thessalonian Correspondence'" (Prague 1995 and Strasbourg 1996). Copyright – Wm.B. Eerdmans Publishing Co., Grand Rapids.

23. *Collationes* 27 (1997) 227-241. In Dutch: "Christus en de Kerk. Man en vrouw in Efeziërs 5,21-33".

24. *Ephemerides theologicae Lovanienses* 76 (2000) 435-441. Copyright – Peeters Publishers, Leuven.

25. (Unpublished)

26. *Ephemerides theologicae Lovanienses* 75 (1999) 421-429. Copyright – Peeters Publishers, Leuven.

27. R. BIERINGER, D. POLLEFEYT & F. VANNEUVILLE (eds.), *Anti-Judaism and the Fourth Gospel (Jewish and Christian Heritage)* (Assen 2001) 512-528. From the "Interdisciplinary Academic Seminar 'Anti-Judaism in the Fourth Gospel and the Jewish-Christian Dialogue'" (Leuven, January 2000). Copyright – Van Gorcum, Assen.

28. *Biblica* 79 (1998) 198-220. Copyright – Editrice Pontificio Istituto Biblico, Rome.

29. From the "Studiosorum Novi Testamenti Conventus" Jubilee Volume *Vroegchristelijke gemeenten tussen werkelijkheid en ideaal* (2001). In Dutch: "Het volk van God in de Openbaring van Johannes".

30. *Biblica* 81 (2000) 362-385. Copyright – Editrice Pontificio Istituto Biblico, Rome.

Thanks are hereby expressed to the editors and publishers who kindly granted us permission to reprint these studies.

Abbreviations

AB	Anchor Bible
AbNTC	Abingdon New Testament Commentaries
AnBib	Analecta biblica
AThANT	Abhandlungen zur Theologie des Neuen und Alten Testaments
AusBR	*Australian Biblical Research*
BA	*Biblical Archaeologist*
BDR	F. BLASS & A. DEBRUNNER. *Grammatik des neutestamentlichen Griechisch*, reworked by F. REHKOPF, Göttingen [17]1990.
BETL	Bibliotheca Ephemeridum theologicarum Lovaniensium
BHT	Beiträge zur historischen Theologie
Bib	*Biblica*
Bijdr	*Bijdragen*
BNTC	Black's New Testament Commentaries
BU	Biblische Untersuchungen
BulBR	*Bulletin Biblical Research*
BZ	*Biblische Zeitschrift*
BZNW	Beihefte zur ZNW
CB.NT	Coniectanea Biblica. New Testament Series
CBQ	*Catholic Biblical Quarterly*
CNT	Commentaire du Nouveau Testament
Coll	*Collationes*
EDNT	*Exegetical Dictionary of the New Testament*
EKK	Evangelisch-katholischer Kommentar zum Neuen Testament
EstBíb	Estudios bíblicos
EtB	Etudes bibliques
ETL	*Ephemerides theologicae Lovanienses*
EvT	*Evangelische Theologie*
ExpT	*Expository Times*
FilNeotest	*Filología neotestamentaria*
FRLANT	Forschungen zur Religion und Literatur des Alten und Neuen Testaments
FS	Festschrift
FzB	Forschung zur Bibel

GNS	Good News Studies
Greg	*Gregorianum*
GThA	Göttinger theologische Arbeiten
HNT	Handbuch zum Neuen Testament
HTKNT	Herders Theologischer Kommentar zum Neuen Testament
HTR	*Harvard Theological Review*
HUT	Hermeneutische Untersuchungen zur Theologie
ICC	International Critical Commentary
Interp	*Interpretation*
IVP	The InterVarsity Press New Testament Commentary Series
JBL	*Journal of Biblical Literature*
JETS	*Journal of the Evangelical Theological Society*
JSNT	*Journal for the Study of the New Testament*
JSNT.S	JSNT. Supplement Series
JSP.S	Journal for the Study of Pseudepigrapha. Supplement Series
JTS	*Journal of Theological Studies*
KEK	Kritisch-exegetischer Kommentar über das Neue Testament
LeDiv	Lectio divina
LouvSt	*Louvain Studies*
LouvTPM	Louvain Theological & Pastoral Monographs
MS.SNTS	Monograph Series. SNTS
MüThZ	*Münchener theologische Zeitschrift*
NCBC	New Century Bible Commentary
Neotest	*Neotestamentica*
NICNT	New International Commentary on the New Testament
NIGTC	New International Greek Text Commentary
NT	*Novum Testamentum*
NTA	Neutestamentliche Abhandlungen
NTS	*New Testament Studies*
NT.S	Supplements to Novum Testamentum
NTT	*Nederlands Theologisch Tijdschrift*
NTTheol	New Testament Theology
OBO	Orbis Biblicus et Orientalis
ÖTKNT	Ökumenischer Taschenbuch-Kommentar zum Neuen Testament
QD	Quaestiones disputatae
RB	*Revue biblique*
RechScR	*Recherches de science religieuse*
RHPR	*Revue d'histoire et de philosophie religieuses*
RivBib	*Rivista Biblica*
RivBib.S	Supplementi alla Rivista Biblica

RNT	Regensburger Neues Testament
SBL	Society for Biblical Literature
SBL.DS	SBL. Dissertation Series
SBL.SBS	SBL. Sources for Biblical Study
SBT	Studies in Biblical Theology
SJT	*Scottish Journal of Theology*
SNTS	Society for New Testament Studies
SNTU	*Studien zum Neuen Testament und seiner Umwelt*
SP	Sacra Pagina
StANT	Studien zum Alten und Neuen Testament
StBT	Studia biblica et theologica
StCHNT	Studia ad Corpus Hellenisticum Novi Testamenti
StRel	*Studies in Religion. Sciences religieuses*
StUNT	Studien zur Umwelt des Neuen Testaments
SvEÅ	*Svensk Exegetisk Årsbok*
TDNT	*Theological Dictionary of the New Testament*
ThF	Theologische Forschung
ThLZ	*Theologische Literaturzeitung*
THNT	Theologischer Handkommentar zum Neuen Testament
ThSt	Theologische Studien
ThSt	*Theological Studies*
ThQuart	*Theologische Quartalschrift*
ThZ	*Theologische Zeitschrift*
TrThZ	*Trierer theologische Zeitschrift*
TU	Texte und Untersuchungen
TynB	*Tyndale Bulletin*
WBC	Word Biblical Commentary
WMANT	Wissenschaftliche Monographien zum Alten und Neuen Testament
WUNT	Wissenschaftliche Untersuchungen zum Neuen Testament
ZaStNT	Zacchaeus Studies: New Testament
ZNW	*Zeitschrift für die neutestamentliche Wissenschaft*
ZThK	*Zeitschrift für Theologie und Kirche*
ZüBKNT	Zürcher Bibel-Kommentar zum Neuen Testament
ZWTh	*Zeitschrift für wissenschafliche Theologie*

PART ONE

PAULINE AND DEUTERO-PAULINE LETTERS

The Journal of Biblical Literature 119 (2000) 526-528

1

Paul's Logic in Romans 3,29-30

For the sake of our analysis the following rather literal translation of Rom 3,29-30 is proposed:

29a Or is he God of Jews only?
 b Is he not also God of Gentiles?
 c Yes, also of Gentiles,
30a if indeed God is one,
 b [the God] who will justify circumcision from faith and uncircumcision through the faith.

In Greek the two questions of v. 29ab and the beginning answer of v. 29c are elliptical: ἢ Ἰουδαίων ὁ θεὸς μόνον; οὐχὶ καὶ ἐθνῶν; ναὶ καὶ ἐθνῶν. Elements must be supplied from the context. Because of the inversion in the translation of εἷς ὁ θεός in v. 30a, one could repeat "the God" at the beginning of v. 30b; moreover, "is" must certainly be added in v. 30a since the grammatical function of "one" is that of predicate: "God is one". The relative clause of v. 30b qualifies the subject of v. 30a. If the future δικαιώσει in v. 30b is temporal, it probably is eschatological in the broad sense of this term, that is, referring to what God in Christ will do (and is already doing). But that future could be gnomic (pointing to an expected and customary action of God) or perhaps logical (God can be relied on to justify). The article in the phrase διὰ τῆς πίστεως at the end of v. 30b should be taken as anaphoric, that is, referring back to ἐκ πίστεως in this verse: through "that same" faith (in Christ, most probably). The majority of exegetes assume that the change from ἐκ to διά is but a stylistic variation[1]; yet one may ask whether there is no difference at all. This shift, however, as well as the exact nuance of the future verb, hardly affects the discussion of this brief note.

---

[1] Cf., e.g., J.A. FITZMYER, *Romans* (AB; New York 1992), 365-366.

1. The particle εἴπερ (v. 30a)[2] means "if indeed" or "if it be true" and refers to what is commonly accepted. It is more or less the equivalent of "since". In many explanations the relative clause v. 30b is somewhat separated from v. 30a. The RSV and NRSV translate v. 30: "since God is one; and he will justify ..."[3]. Verse 30b is sometimes called "a corollary" or an implication of v. 30a[4]. The justification of Jews and Gentiles alike follows from God's oneness. James D.G. Dunn explains: "if God is one ..., then he must be the God of all humankind"[5]. The implicit reasoning appears to be: because God is one he will justify .... According to this interpretation v. 30a not only grounds v. 29a (because God is one he is also the God of the Gentiles), but equally, and rather strangely, v. 30b (because God is one he will justify not only the Jews but also the Gentiles)[6].

2. As a matter of fact vv. 29c-30 constitute a conditional period with protasis and apodosis. A free — but, regarding the content, faithful — reconstruction is: "If indeed God is one, the God who will justify Jews and Gentiles alike [protasis, v. 30ab], then this God is also the God of Gentiles [apodosis, v. 29c]". The whole of v. 30 "conditions" and motivates the thesis of v. 29c. V. 30b is not a new insight provided by the oneness of God, that is, by Jewish monotheism; it is not a conclusion that Paul draws from what he says in v. 30a[7]. In v. 30b ὅς should not be taken as the equivalent of ὅστις with a causal ("inasmuch as") or a consecutive ("such as") nuance. The relative clause of v. 30b is solely descriptive and qualifies Paul's vision of God. This must also be the vision of his Roman addressees.

3. As far as content is concerned, v. 30b can be considered very close to the statement of v. 28: "For we maintain that a person is justified by

---

[2] A less probable variant reading has ἔπειπερ ("because indeed").

[3] Cf. C.E.B. CRANFIELD, *A Critical and Exegetical Commentary on the Epistle to the Romans* (ICC; Edinburgh 1975) 219: "seeing that God is one, and he will justify ...".

[4] Cf. CRANFIELD, *Romans,* 222: "The relative clause states what is for Paul the corollary to be drawn from the confession that God is one ..."; D.J. MOO, *The Epistle to the Romans* (NICNT; Grand Rapids–Cambridge 1996) 251: "In v. 30 Paul both explains why God must be God of the Gentiles as well as of the Jews and draws an implication from that truth", and p. 252: "Paul states this radical implication of monotheism in a relative clause ...".

[5] J.D.G. DUNN, *Romans 1–8* (WBC; Waco 1988) 193.

[6] For the second part of this sentence, see T.L. DONALDSON, *Paul and the Gentiles: Remapping the Apostle's Convictional World* (Minneapolis 1997) 84: "because God is one, God will justify circumcised and uncircumcised alike on the sole ground of faith".

[7] Cf. E. KÄSEMANN, *Commentary on Romans* (Grand Rapids 1980) 104: "The one God can only be the one who has a claim to all and who encounters all, not just as Creator, but also as he who establishes salvation". B. BYRNE, *Romans* (SP; Collegeville 1996) 135, translates: "God is one, which means that he will justify ...".

faith, apart from works of law". This statement too is not a new idea. Rather it is the basic insight that was reached by the lengthy exposition of Rom 1,16–3,26 and more particularly 3,21-26. This insight is used in the argument of 3,27-28 to prove (cf. γάρ in v. 28[8]) that boasting is ruled out διὰ νόμου πίστεως. The convictional statement of v. 28 grounds v. 27. In vv. 29-30 a very similar conviction is used to make clear that God is also the God of the Gentiles[9]. "A person is justified by faith" (v. 28) becomes: God "will justify the circumcised as well as the uncircumcised from or through faith (v. 30b)"[10].

4. One could be tempted to find in v. 30a Jewish monotheism and in v. 30b the Christian reply to Jewish election and its particularism[11]. Verse 30a would refer to God as the Creator of the universe and the whole of humankind (cf. 1 Cor 8,6); in v. 30b an equally universalistic salvation project would be indicated. Yet Paul does not seem to be employing here a two-step argument. His "one and the same God" is christologically active. God is qualified as the God who justifies through faith in Christ. That faith is the sole condition, equally for Jew and Gentile[12].

---

[8] See B.M. METZGER, *A Textual Commentary on the Greek New Testament* (New York [2]1994) 450: γάρ is to be preferred (with the letter B: "almost certain") over the reading οὖν.

[9] Cf. M.-J. LAGRANGE, *Epître aux Romains* (EtB; Paris 1916) 79-80: "Ce n'est ... pas un argument vraiment nouveau qui commence au v. 29. Ce qui établit l'égalité entre les hommes par rapport à Dieu, c'est encore qu'ils sont au même point touchant la foi en Christ".

[10] Because of Paul's explicitness in Rom 1,16–3,26 the logic of Paul's argument in 3,30b does not require "unexpressed minor" premises such as that defended by DONALDSON, *Paul and the Gentiles*, 84-85.

[11] Yet for the defense of Jewish universalism, see N. DAHL, *Studies in Paul: Theology for the Early Christian Mission* (Minneapolis 1977) 190-191; DONALDSON, *Paul and the Gentiles*.

[12] For a similar approach, cf. R.W. THOMPSON, "The Inclusion of the Gentiles in Rom 3,27-30", *Bib* 69 (1988) 343-346, esp. 345-346.

Gregorianum 81 (2000) 441-451

2

The Implied Exhortation in Romans 8,5-8

I. INTRODUCTION

In his recent commentary on Romans Douglas Moo claims that in Rom 8,5 and 8 the so-called equivalent expressions "being according to the flesh" and "being in the flesh" constitute a positional rather than a behavioral concept. In composing the contrasts in 8,1-13 Paul's purpose is not paraenetic; "he is not warning Christians about two different possibilities they face in order to encourage them to live according to the Spirit". "Being in the flesh" is not a possibility for the believer. "Paul's interest here is descriptive rather than hortatory"[1]. Moo considers flesh and Spirit in Rom 8 not as parts of a person, "nor even as impulses or powers within a person, but as the powers, or dominating features, of the two 'realms' of salvation history"[2]. For believers there has been the conversion, that is, the decisive transfer into the new age. In Rom 8,9 "being in the flesh" is not the Christians' condition of mortality nor their moral weakness or proneness to sin. "To be in the flesh" is to belong to the old age[3].

---

[1] D.J. Moo, *The Epistle to the Romans* (NICNT; Grand Rapids–Cambridge 1996) 486; cf., with much emphasis, G.D. Fee, *God's Empowering Presence* (Peabody, MA 1994) 519-559.

[2] Moo, *Romans*, 485. The contrast is between the old age of sin and death, a purely human situation, the world in rebellion against God on the one hand and on the other the new age of righteousness and life, "created and dominated by God's Spirit as his eschatological gift" (485).

[3] Moo, *Romans*, 489-490. On p. 490 he writes: "Subject to physical decay and death, prone to sin, tempted to let the flesh take control of us again we may be — but, to do justice to Paul, we must insist that the believer is freed from 'the law of sin and death' ..., 'dead to sin's power' ..., and no longer 'in the flesh'". Cf. Fee, *Presence*, 537-538. For a recent general treatment of the Christians' sinless existence, see H. Umbach, *In Christus getauft — von der Sünde befreit. Die Gemeinde als sündenfreier Raum bei Paulus* (FRLANT 181; Göttingen 1999).

One may ask, however, whether Rom 8,1-13 is only positional and descriptive without any exhortation. Does Paul in this paragraph not take into account the Christians' daily moral struggle, the possibility that they might be walking "according to flesh" and thus fatally regress to their former unconverted state of radically "being in the flesh"?

The Greek text of Rom 8,8 is οἱ δὲ ἐν σαρκὶ ὄντες θεῷ ἀρέσαι οὐ δύνανται. NRSV (= RSV) and NAB translate: "Those who are in the flesh cannot please God". At first sight it may seem that unregenerate people are meant here. The articular participle ("those who are") points to a class of persons, not to an attitude or an orientation in the individual person. The statement "cannot please" refers to a situation in which these people are. In 8,9a Christians are opposed to them: ὑμεῖς δὲ οὐκ ἐστὲ ἐν σαρκὶ ἀλλὰ ἐν πνεύματι ("but you are not in the flesh; you are in the Spirit"; NRSV[4]). In this last verse, moreover, the second person plural distinguishes, it would seem, Christians from non-Christians. Finally, the close parallel in 7,5a ("while we were in the flesh") could, if needed, confirm this view.

Rom 8,5 reads οἱ γὰρ κατὰ σάρκα ὄντες τὰ τῆς σαρκὸς φρονοῦσιν, οἱ δὲ κατὰ πνεῦμα τὰ τοῦ πνεύματος, which, rendered literally, reads: "for those who are according to the flesh set their minds on the things of the flesh, but those (who are) according to the Spirit set their minds on the things of the Spirit". According to J.A. Fitzmyer, Paul here also "refers to unregenerate human beings"[5]. The articular participle and the mention of "flesh" seem to support this opinion. Yet in v. 5a the expression is κατὰ σάρκα, not ἐν σαρκί as in v. 8. Just before v. 5 Paul writes: "so that the just requirement of the law might be fulfilled in us"; he adds τοῖς μὴ κατὰ σάρκα περιπατοῦσιν ἀλλὰ κατὰ πνεῦμα: (in us) "who walk not according to the flesh but according to the Spirit" (v. 4). Fitzmyer notes: "The Greek participle with the negative *mē* gives a proviso or conditional sense to the expression, 'provided we walk not according to the flesh'"[6]. There is, according to this interpretation, the possibility that Christians still conduct a fleshly life. Therefore the question can be raised

---

[4] NRSV does not translate ἀλλά; NAB has "on the contrary".

[5] J.A. FITZMYER, *Romans* (AB; New York 1992) 488.

[6] *Romans*, 488. Cf. U. WILCKENS, *Der Brief an die Römer* (EKK; Zürich–Neukirchen/Vluyn 1980) 129-130. However, according to M.-J. LAGRANGE, *Epître aux Romains* (EtB; Paris 1916) the participle indicates "plutôt le *fait* de notre collaboration qu'une *condition* requise" (195). So many others, e.g., C.E.B. CRANFIELD, *The Epistle to the Romans. Vol. I* (ICC; Edinburgh 1975) 385; FEE, *Presence*, 537: "For Paul this is simply a description of two mutually exclusive ways of life, not exhortation".

whether with κατὰ σάρκα verse 5a does not also refer to such "sinful" Christians rather than to unbelievers, that is, people before and outside of Christ. The general tenor of vv. 6-7, as well as the exhortations in 6,12-13 and in 8,12-13, in the last text with κατὰ σάρκα and ζῆν, may point in that direction indeed.

Hence one would like to know exactly what Paul's argument in 8,5-8 is. In between the direct address employed in v. 4 (ἐν ἡμῖν) and v. 9 (ὑμεῖς ... ἐν ὑμῖν), by using the third person throughout vv. 5-8 Paul keeps the reasoning on a fundamental and general level. The οἱ ... κατὰ σάρκα ὄντες of v. 5 corresponds with the οἱ ... κατὰ σάρκα ὄντες of v. 8 (and v. 9); these phrases appear to constitute the inclusion of this subdivision[7]. Is the text of 8,5-8 purely descriptive, positional, or should one postulate here the presence of paraenesis and warning[8]? Before attempting to answer this question, let us examine 7,4-6 and 8,1-4.

II. ANALYSIS

Rom 7,4-6 and 8,1-4

In Rom 7,4-5 Paul certainly refers to the earlier unregenerate condition of those who are now believers. Within vv. 5-6 there is the opposition of past and present, of ὅτε (v. 5) and νῦν (v. 6). The believers have died to the law through the body of Christ; they are discharged from it; they are no longer captives. In the past that law aroused the sinful passions which were at work in their members to bear fruit for death. Now as believers they belong to Christ in order to bear fruit for God. They are able to serve God; they are not under the old written code but possess the new life of the Spirit.

It would seem that in 8,1-3 that radical change and liberation is further explained: most aspects of 7,4-6 are repeated and elaborated. In 8,4, however, Paul emphasizes the fulfillment of the law's demand, the "bearing fruit for God" (cf. 7,4), i.e., it would seem, the necessary ethical life of the Christian.

In his monograph *Fleisch und Geist* Egon Brandenburger has shown that Paul's use of the flesh–Spirit antithesis can only be understood within

---

[7] Cf. H. PAULSEN, *Überlieferung und Auslegung in Römer 8* (WMANT 43; Neukirchen/Vluyn 1974) 33.

[8] Cf. FEE, *Presence*, 539 (on 8,5-8): "This is description, not exhortation".

the broader Hellenistic-Jewish context of dualistic wisdom, such as is present in Philo's writings (be it in somewhat differing concepts and vocabulary)[9]. In Paul there is an irreducible contrast between flesh and Spirit. Although "flesh" can still be used in a neutral sense, in its opposition to the Spirit "flesh" is not only weak but also sinful and, moreover, a cause of sin. While "flesh" can point to behavior ("Verhaltensaussage") it often appears as a substance ("Substanzaussage") and is more than once personified. Flesh and Spirit are powers which fight against one another. They both actively "desire" (ἐπιθυμέω, cf. Gal 5,17); they "set their minds" (φρονέω, φρόνημα, cf. Rom 8,5-7) on opposite things. They appear to be even more than substances when depicted as realms and spheres of power which surround and control human beings. People are "in the flesh" or "in the Spirit". However, as dominated by the Spirit Christians are not only surrounded by it; that Spirit is also said to dwell in them. The Spirit is an eschatological gift; it comes from God to bring salvation.

Obviously, two categories of persons should be distinguished, those in the flesh and those in the Spirit (cf. "those who are in Christ Jesus", Rom 8,1)[10]. There appears to be a "before" and an "after". In Rom 7,5-6 Paul clearly separates the past from the present: "when we were living in the flesh" and "now we are discharged from the law" (cf. 8,1: "there is ... now no condemnation for those who are in Christ Jesus"). The question, however, arises: is there not an overlapping of flesh and Spirit in the Christian? What does it mean to speak of Christians being still "in the flesh" (cf. 2 Cor 10,2-3) before death? Do they automatically walk according to the Spirit or can they still walk according to the flesh? Is there in them not a daily struggle and does Paul not point to it in Rom 8,4-9?

It would seem that in Rom 8,4 "flesh" and "Spirit" do not denote separate entities or parts of the human person. They rather represent two possibilities of human existence[11]. "Flesh" points to human weakness, tempta-

---

[9] E. BRANDENBURGER, *Fleisch und Geist. Paulus und die dualistische Weisheit* (WMANT 29; Neukirchen/Vluyn 1968). Cf. ID., *Das Böse. Eine biblisch-theologische Studie* (ThSt 132; Zürich 1986).

[10] In Rom 7,7-25 Paul deals with non-Christians and can therefore hardly mention the Spirit. Yet even in this passage Paul opposes "the law of my mind" to "the law of sin", both present in his "members" (v. 23). Cf. BRANDENBURGER, *Fleisch und Geist*, 172-173, on Paul's vocabulary and reasoning in Rom 7; more in general, J. LAMBRECHT, *The Wretched "I" and Its Liberation: Paul in Romans 7 and 8* (LouvTPM 14; Leuven 1992).

[11] Cf. B. BYRNE, *Romans* (SP; Collegeville 1996) 238 and 244. But see also D. ZELLER, *Der Brief an die Römer* (RNT; Regensburg 1985) 157: "Es sind den Menschen in seinem Dasein, aber auch in seinem ganzen Wollen beeinflussende Sphären, so dass sie im Wechsel von V. 5 zu V. 6 an die Stelle des menschlichen Subjekts treten können".

tion and proneness to sin. Walking or living "according to the flesh" is still a (negative) possibility for Christians. A first indication for a distinction of two categories of Christian people is probably to be found already at the end of 8,4: we, i.e., "those in Christ" (v. 1), who walk (τοῖς περιπατοῦσιν) not according to the flesh but according to the Spirit. We may quote J.D.G Dunn: "It should ... be noted that the initial formulation of the σάρξ-πνεῦμα antithesis is expressed not as mutually exclusive conditions, but more as an exhortation, as contrasting and opposed alternatives ..."[12]. If Christians do not walk according to the Spirit, they still are people who have been freed by Christ. Are all of them immediately separated from Christ? Are they irretrievably perishing or lost? Presumably not.

Rom 8,5-8

The presentation of the structured Greek text may prove helpful for our discussion:

5 οἱ γὰρ κατὰ σάρκα ὄντες τὰ τῆς σαρκὸς φρονοῦσιν,
   οἱ δὲ κατὰ πνεῦμα τὰ τοῦ πνεύματος.
6 τὸ γὰρ φρόνημα τῆς σαρκὸς θάνατος,
   τὸ δὲ φρόνημα τοῦ πνεύματος ζωὴ καὶ εἰρήνη·
7 διότι τὸ φρόνημα τῆς σαρκὸς ἔχθρα εἰς θεόν,
   τῷ γὰρ νόμῳ τοῦ θεοῦ οὐχ ὑποτάσσεται,
   οὐδὲ γὰρ δύναται·
8 οἱ δὲ ἐν σαρκὶ ὄντες θεῷ ἀρέσαι οὐ δύνανται.

In 8,5 Paul explains (γάρ) the end of v. 4; he depicts the two opposite possibilities. Using article and participle (οἱ ὄντες) and the same expressions as in v. 4 (κατὰ σάρκα and κατὰ πνεῦμα) he now contrasts the two groups[13]. He opposes the concerns of these groups by means of the same verb φρονοῦσιν: the ones set their minds on the things of the flesh; the others set their minds on the things of the Spirit. Together with the distinction of these two groups the characterization is generalized; verse 5b no longer speaks of "in us who walk ...". Both categories seem to point to con-

---

12 J.D.G. DUNN, *Romans 1–8* (WBC; Waco 1988) 425.

13 Cf. DUNN, *Romans 1–8*, 425: "In modern terms, the sociological category 'type' comes closer to Paul's meaning — the type as an abstracted, even idealized model to which individuals conform to greater or less degree, but rarely (if at all) completely". The opposite classes are also mentioned in Phil 3,17–4,1: note, above all, the expressions τοὺς οὕτω περιπατοῦντας καθώς ... in 3,17 and οἱ τὰ ἐπίγεια φρονοῦντες in 3,19.

crete possibilities. Christians can enter the first category, although, of course, they should belong to the second[14].

In 8,6 Paul's further explanation (a second γάρ) becomes even more abstract. "Flesh" and "Spirit" now are personified. The groups are no longer mentioned. By means of φρόνημα, a substantive derived from the verb φρονέω in v. 5, Paul now opposes two kinds of concern (τὸ φρόνημα τῆς σαρκός and τὸ φρόνημα τοῦ πνεύματος) and indicates what the respective final outcome will be: eschatological "death" on one side and on the other real "life and peace". The reason why Paul speaks in a more general way might be that both mind-sets are aspirations and strivings existing not only in two opposite groups but also within the Christian community itself. They seemingly can also be present in one and the same person[15].

Then, quite surprisingly, in 8,7 the positive side is no more spoken of. All attention is now devoted to the negative mind-set of the flesh. The personification of the flesh continues. Already in each of the verses 5 and 6 a γάρ manifests the explicative character of what comes after 8,4[16]. In 8,7 this clarification, now of v. 6, continues: διότι ("because") and two more γάρ's. The verse may be rendered freely as follows: "because the concern of the flesh is all but enmity with God, for the flesh does not submit to God's law[17], for the flesh simply cannot (οὐ δύναται) do this". If our understanding of v. 6 is correct, then in v. 7 Paul still increases his implicit warning.

Verse 8 is equally one-sided. The last statement of v. 7 is reinforced and verse 8 functions as a conclusion: "those who are in the flesh cannot (οὐ δύνανται) please God". The situation is helpless and desperate. In v. 8 Paul again refers to a class of people (οἱ ὄντες), but instead of κατὰ σάρκα

---

[14] Cf. BYRNE, *Romans*, 238-239 and ID., "Living out the Righteousness of God: The Contribution of Rom 6:1–8:13 to an Understanding of Paul's Ethical Presuppositions", *CBQ* (1991) 557-581, esp. 569.

[15] FEE, *Presence*, speaks of "two radically opposed kinds of existence" (540), "two basic alternatives" (543, on v. 9), but excludes a "basic struggle taking place in the believer's heart" (542, on vv. 7-8) and denies a reference to "two kinds of Christian life" (547) or to two warring, rival forces which both strive for control in the Christian's inmost being (cf. p. 539). For Fee, the believer's walking according to the Spirit is but the "evidence" of one's present position in Christ (cf. p. 554).

[16] MOO, *Romans*, 487, needlessly, it would seem, denies the explanatory character of both γάρ's in 8,5-6.

[17] See the plea of BYRNE, *Romans*, 244, for an understanding of "law" here in a sense broader than the law of Moses. He refers to 8,4 and contends that "the law of God" in 8,7 designates "God's will regarding human behavior". This interpretation is also preferred by MOO, *Romans*, 488.

as in v. 5 he now writes ἐν σαρκί. Apparently those people find themselves hopelessly situated "in" the flesh. "Flesh", of course, possesses here
the same negative sense as in 8,4-7[18]. After vv. 6-7 one is justified to doubt
that this conclusion is merely descriptive. It would seem that the implied
caution is still present: walking according to the flesh will ultimately bring
about a regression to "being in the flesh" and belonging to the unregenerate group.

Rom 8,9-11

One could insist that in 8,5-8, more specifically in v. 8, Paul has in
mind the "wretched" unregenerate people whom he depicted in 7,14-23
using the first person singular "I". We are tempted to think so since in 8,9
Paul switches to the second person plural and strongly opposes the category of people just mentioned: "but you are not in the flesh; you are in the
Spirit". Yet the protasis in v. 9b (εἴπερ: "if, indeed", "if, in fact") possesses a scarcely hidden adhortatory nuance: "if indeed (or: on the assumption
that) the Spirit dwells in you"[19]. This reminds the reader of Paul's main
concern: Christians might forget their moral obligations; they might
neglect their Spirit-filled life. Then, in v. 9cd, Paul again uses the third person and his "realis" sentence is more objective, without a reference to the
reality or truth of the if-clause[20]: if anyone does not have the Spirit of
Christ, he does not belong to him.

---

[18] One almost spontaneously thinks of 2 Cor 10,2-3 where Paul, however, contrasts a neutral ἐν σαρκί (cf. Gal 2,20 and Phil 1,22) with the negatively qualified κατὰ σάρκα.

[19] Cf. WILCKENS, *Römer*, 131. According to CRANFIELD, *Romans*, 388, however, the clause
"is not to be understood ... as a discreet warning ...". C.K. BARRETT, *A Commentary on the
Epistle to the Romans* (BNTC; London 1957) even translates: "if, as is indeed the case" (158).
MOO, *Romans*, 490-491, discusses Paul's conditional language: it could mean that Paul "is not
convinced that all his readers are truly indwelt by the Spirit" (490). MOO prefers, however, the
"since"–meaning: Paul assumes the reality of the Christian experience of the Spirit. Cf.
LAGRANGE, *Epître aux Romains*, 197-198, who contrasts "si tamen" ("si toutefois" which
implies an "avertissement") and "si quidem" ("puisque", "si, comme j'en ai la confiance"; but
he hesitates: "c'est peut-être forcer la note").

[20] Cf. S. BRODEUR, *The Holy Spirit's Agency in the Resurrection of the Dead. An
Exegetico-Theological Study of 1 Corinthians 15,44b-49 and Romans 8,9-13* (Tesi Gegoriana.
Ser. Teol. 14; Roma 1996) 170-172, who in view of the six conditional sentences in 8,9-13
summarizes recent grammatical studies on the Simple Condition (the so-called "realis"): "it
indicates a logical connection between protasis and apodosis without any reference to the reality, truth, or actuality of the statement itself" (171). But, of course, one has to take into
account the context and, moreover, in v. 9b the particle is εἴπερ, not εἰ.

The εἰ-clause of v. 10a (and that of v. 11a), however, may contain a nuance of reticence: the "if" possibly implies "on the condition that". Most probably the μέν-clause of v. 10b is concessive: "although the body is dead because of sin"[21]. This signifies that due to human sin we will die (see 5,12); we are and remain mortal (cf. 8,11b)[22]. So the main affirmation is to be found in the δέ-clause of v. 10c: "but the Spirit means life because of righteousness". It is not to be excluded that "righteousness" here takes on the sense of moral conduct[23]: the end-result of walking according to the Spirit, of righteousness, is eschatological life.

Verse 11 explains the future life as the Christians' resurrection. If the Spirit of God who raised Christ Jesus from the dead dwells in us, God will also make alive our mortal bodies and this will occur "through" or "because"[24] of the indwelling Spirit. However, this does not prevent Paul from emphasizing again the unacceptability of living according to the flesh in 8,12-13. Even Fee here speaks of an "imperatival application"[25].

Gal 5,16-18 and Rom 8,4-8

In Romans 8 one does not encounter grammatical imperatives. However, in what seems to be a parallel passage, Gal 5,13-24, imperatives are prominent: see 5,13 and 16 (and already 5,1). This passage from Galatians is decidedly hortatory[26].

A number of data underscore the similarity between Gal 5,16-18 and

---

[21] So, e.g., RSV (NRSV: "though"), REB and NAB. One can paraphrase this nuance as follows: it is true that the body is dead because of sin. Cf. LAGRANGE, *Epître aux Romains*, 198: "une sorte de concession", "s'il est toujours vrai de dire que ..."; FEE, *Presence*, 549-550: "even though".

[22] Cf. BYRNE, *Romans*, 245: "That *nekron* refers to physical death and has the sense of 'mortal' is confirmed by the reference to *thnēta sōmata* in the following verse". See also MOO, *Romans*, 491-492; ZELLER, *Römer*, 158: "Das Todeslos steht so fest, dass der 'Leib des Todes' (vgl. 7,24b) sogar wie in dualistischer Philosophie ... schon als Leichnam bezeichnet wird".

[23] BYRNE, *Romans*, 245, specifies: "the ethical righteousness created in believers through the operation of the Spirit". LAGRANGE, *Epître aux Romains*, 198-199, even distinguishes "l'action exercée antérieurement par la justice" and "la justice à pratiquer". However, many commentators see here a reference to the typical Pauline concept of justification: "this 'righteousness' being that 'imputed righteousness' which leads to life ..." (MOO, *Romans*, 492). Cf. also DUNN, *Romans 1–8*, 432; FEE, *Presence*, 551-552; the REB version: "yet the Spirit is your life because you have been justified".

[24] The text critical evidence is divided between διά with genitive or accusative. See the long discussion in FEE, *Presence*, 543, n. 205 (his own preference — a minority position — is διά with the accusative: "because"). Cf., e.g., CRANFIELD, *Romans*, 391-392: "we are fairly confident that the genitive reading is what Paul dictated" (391).

[25] *Presence, 539.*

[26] On might also refer to the similar passage of Phil 3,17–4,1.

Rom 8,4-8[27]: the contrast between flesh and Spirit, the mention of the law (cf. also Gal 5,14), the verb περιπατέω followed by πνεύματι (Gal 5,16; probably a dative of means) or κατὰ πνεῦμα (Rom 8,4). Moreover, ἐπιθυμία σαρκός (Gal 5,16) can, to a certain extent, be compared with φρόνημα τῆς σαρκός (Rom 8,6-7), as well as the verb ἐπιθυμέω (Gal 5,17)[28] with φρονέω (Rom 8,5). In Gal 5,16-17 "flesh" is personified; the same is true for Rom 8,6-7. Just as Paul expresses a general consideration by means of a more abstract language in Gal 5,17, so does he also in Rom 8,6-7. The absolute incompatibility between flesh and Spirit which is emphasized in Gal 5,17 finds in Rom 8,7-8 its equivalent in the flesh's impossibility to submit to the law of God and to please God[29].

From the larger context it is evident that in the exhortations of Galatians Paul deals with Christians who do not live up to a perfect behavior according to the Spirit, not only because of the lack of charity in the community referred to in 5,15, but also because of other sins such as those listed in 5,19-21 (cf. also 6,1-10). Although Paul is convinced of the liberation brought by Christ, Christians are living in the overlapping of the ages; they are still tempted by the flesh. As a matter of fact, some of them are living according to the flesh to some degree. In Galatians there is not only the distinction between past and present and not only the affirmation of the eschatological newness, but also the recognition of the existential daily struggle. Paul's negatively qualified "flesh" is not only the power which dominated the realm of the old age before and without Christ. With its strivings and impulses that "flesh" is still present, also in believers. To walk, to be led and to live by the Spirit involves a continuous fight not to gratify the desires of the flesh[30].

Since Gal 5,16-18 is thoroughly hortatory and at the same time so similar to Rom 8,4-8, the proposed interpretation of the last passage in an existential sense appears to be greatly supported by the thrust of the first.

---

[27] Cf. PAULSEN, *Römer 8*, 45-47, who tries to detect a pre-Pauline tradition for the σάρξ-πνεῦμα antithesis.

[28] Cf. J. LAMBRECHT, "The Right Things You Want to Do. A Note on Galatians 5,17d", *Bib* 49 (1998) 515-524.

[29] More similarities could be indicated if the whole of Gal 5,1–6,10 and of Rom 8,1-17 were taken into account. We just mention the theme of freedom from the law present in both text units and the remark by ZELLER, *Römer*, 157: "eine Konkretion zu V. 5 [= Rom 8,5] bieten die Kataloge Gal 5,19-23".

[30] One wonders how FEE, *Presence*, 424-425, can claim that the material in Gal 5,13-26 "is not just a series of exhortations: it is argument by way of exhortation" and that there "the concern from beginning to end is with Christian life in community, not with the interior life of the individual Christian" (in the same vein see pp. 427-438, more in particular on vv. 16-18).

In Romans 8 Paul most probably thinks of the behavioral life of his addressees. His language is not just the description of the two contrasting ages. In a hidden way his admittedly positional language in 8,1-11 is intensively paraenetic. He has in mind the concrete and endangered existence of the community as well as that of individual believer[31].

III. CONCLUSION

First of all one must recognize that the expression "those who are in the flesh" of Rom 8,8 is almost identical with "while we were in the flesh" of 7,5 and that the incapacity to submit to God's law and to please God of 8,7-8 cannot but remind the reader of the desperate unregenerate situation which Paul so pointedly describes in 7,14-23. The context in chapter 8, however, is basically different, especially because of the mention of the Spirit.

Yet in 8,4-8 Paul appears to focus on the concrete danger, that regenerate people begin and continue to walk according to the flesh. He sees — to make his concern explicit — the possibility of two categories of Christians: those who "are" according to the flesh and those who "are" according to the Spirit (cf. 8,5). Paul reflects on that danger; in vv. 6-7 his language becomes somewhat meditative and more abstract. He considers what τò φρόνημα τῆς σαρκός means and what it ultimately will bring about. We are left with the impression that, almost invisibly, shifts are taking place in the text: from walking according to the flesh (v. 4) to being according to the flesh (v. 5) to being in the flesh (v. 8)[32]. The situation seems to go from bad to worse.

---

[31] Without specifically referring to exhortation, BRANDENBURGER, *Fleisch und Geist*, 183, points to the fact that Philo, because of his dependence on "dualistische Weisheit" traditions, has to deal with the tension between "already" and "not yet", "ein analoges Problem wie bei Paulus": "Das Pneuma wohnt im Glaubenden, doch die Sarx ist noch als feindliche Macht wirksam (Röm 8; Gal 5); das sündige Soma ist vernichtet (Röm 6,6), und die Sarx mit ihren Leidenschaften und Begierden ist gekreuzigt (Gal 5,24), doch die Taten des Soma müssen noch getötet werden (Röm 8,13)".

[32] BYRNE, *Romans*, 234, translates the beginning of v. 8: "Those who 'really live' in the flesh". FITZMYER, *Romans*, 488, points to the difference between the expressions of v. 4 and v. 5 (Paul "probes more deeply"), but takes the beginning of v. 8, which he renders by "those who live 'by' the flesh", as "a repetition of the idea expressed in v. 5" (p. 489). DUNN, *Romans 1–8*, 427, too, calls the expression of v. 8 "clearly equivalent to" that of v. 5. CRANFIELD, *Romans*, 385, does not want to press the differences in vv. 4.5 and 8: Paul "has not developed a carefully fixed technical terminology".

Although the statement of v. 8 (they "cannot please God") is more radical than that of v. 5a (they "set their minds on the things of the flesh"), in both verses Paul may be most concerned with Christian people, not with the unbelievers. It would seem that Christians who are not living according to the Spirit are meant. Their utterly dangerous situation is described[33]. As verses 7-8 clearly indicate, this situation risks becoming the same as that of the still unregenerate people dealt with by Paul in 7,7-25. Therefore, although the style of 8,12 is awkward, its tone is unmistakably warning: "so then, brothers, we are debtors, not to the flesh, to live according to the flesh". We suggest that the same exhortative urgence is not absent from 8,5-8.

---

[33] Cf. the apparent position of DUNN, *Romans 1–8*, esp. 441-422.

New Testament Studies 45 (1999) 141-147

3

The Caesura Between Romans 9, 30-33 and 10, 1-4

Does Rom 10,1 constitute a caesura in Paul's argument?[1] "A matter of some dispute is the function of vv. 30-33 [of ch. 9] and whether 10.1 constitutes a significant break in the argument"[2]. Many commentators see 9,30–10,21 as the second of the three major sections in Romans 9–11[3]. The subject matter introduced by the question τί οὖν ἐροῦμεν of 9,30 is, according to them, so different from what precedes that it indicates a decisive transition point. One may ask, however, whether 9,30-33 is not better considered as the conclusion of that first stage.

Our short paper will investigate this — at first sight minor — problem in three steps: What reasons are there for considering 9,30–10,21 as a unit and for 9,30 therefore as a major break? Then, are there better reasons to defend the integrity of 9,6-33 and to take 10,1 as a caesura? Finally, to what extent are 9,30-33 and 10,2-4 parallel? We will see that in the third and last step the question of where and how Paul speaks of Israel's culpability cannot be avoided.

---

[1] An offered short paper, SNTS Birmingham 1997.

[2] Cf. J.D.G. DUNN, *Romans 9–16* (WBC; Waco 1989) 597. Dunn himself (p. 576) prefers to see 9,30 as the beginning of the second section.

[3] For example, M.-J. LAGRANGE, *Epître aux Romains* (EtB; Paris [4]1931) 248; C.E.B. CRANFIELD, *Epistle to the Romans* (ICC; Edinburgh 1979) 503; U. WILCKENS, *Der Brief an die Römer 6-11* (EKK; Zürich–Neukirchen/Vluyn 1980) 209-211; D. ZELLER, *Der Brief an die Römer* (RNT; Regensburg 1985) 183; J.A. FITZMYER, *Romans* (AB; New York 1996) 576; B. BYRNE, *Romans* (SP; Collegeville 1996) 307; D.J. MOO, *The Epistle to the Romans* (NICNT; Grand Rapids 1996) 616-617. E. KÄSEMANN, *An die Römer* (HNT; Tübingen [4]1980) writes unequivocally: "Trotz der neuen Einleitung in 10,1f. dürfen 9,30-33 nicht als Abschluss zu 26-29 gezogen werden .... Sie sind auch nicht bloss Überleitung ..., sondern geben die in c. 10 enfaltete und begründete These ..." (276). Among those who prefer 10,1-21 as the unit are O. MICHEL, *Der Brief an die Römer* (KEK; Göttingen [14]1978) 249; H. SCHLIER, *Der Römerbrief* (HTKNT; Freiburg [2]1979) 305. See also F. SIEGERT, *Argumentation bei Paulus gezeigt an Röm 9–11* (WUNT 34; Tübingen 1985) 115-116.141 and 148.

I. A BREAK BETWEEN ROM 9,30 AND 31?

Let us first listen to the arguments in favor a major break between vv. 29 and 30 in Romans 9.

The most important reason for finding a caesura in 9,30 and for connecting 9,30-33 closely with what follows in chapter 10, the change in subject matter, has already been mentioned. From 9,30 onwards, it is said, attention is no longer paid to God's free decision but to Israel's failure. Israel did not succeed in fulfilling the law of righteousness; Israel pursued righteousness as if it were based on works; the Israelites have stumbled over the stumbling stone (9,31-33). The same emphasis is present in 10,2-3. Although the Israelites had a zeal for God, that zeal was not enlightened; they were ignorant of the righteousness that comes from God and did not submit to it; they were seeking to establish their own righteousness[4]. Manifestly 9,30-33 and 10,1-4 belong together.

There are, moreover, a number of verbal and conceptional connections between 9,30-33 and 10,1-4. In both passages the term δικαιοσύνη occurs four (or three) times[5]. The opposition between faith and works in 9,30-31 returns in 10,3 with "God's righteousness" and "their own". The "one who believes" of 9,33 reappears in "every one who believes" of 10,4. The expression ὑπὲρ αὐτῶν in 10,1 (Paul's heartfelt prayer "for them" that they may be saved) takes up the implicit subject of the verb in 9,32: "'they' have stumbled". In view of all these correspondences — and there would be even more if 10,5-13 were added in the analysis — one could feel justified in believing that 9,30-33 is the beginning of the second section[6]. With Israel and Gentiles, with righteousness, faith, and works, the vocabulary and motifs from chapters 3–4 suddenly appear again, namely from 9,30 onwards.

For the defenders of this opinion the seemingly new start in 10,1 is easily explained. The verse "is actually an interjection into an argument that would otherwise flow smoothly from 9,30–10,4, an interjection representing Paul's emotional response to the stumbling of Israel described in

---

[4] This description employs the translation of the RSV and the NRSV.

[5] The term is omitted after "their own" in 10,3 by a part the manuscript tradition.

[6] One can also refer to 10,11b which resumes 9,33b: both verses constitute a sort of inclusion with regard to 9,30–10,13. Some commentators also see an inclusion in 9,30-32 and 10,20-21; yet there is almost no vocabulary correspondence between that alleged beginning and end.

9:32-33"[7]. So 10,1 does not constitute a new beginning nor a break; it is but an emotional interjection.

II. ROM 10,1 MARKS A CAESURA

A number of considerations, however, plead for the view that 9,30-31 is the conclusion of the first section in Romans 9–11[8] and that in 10,1 there is a new beginning.

First of all, 10,1 can hardly be downgraded to an emotional exclamation. The verse is too long to function properly as an interjection. Moreover, the first person singular continues in v. 2: "I bear them witness...". The address ἀδελφοί at the beginning of the verse certainly indicates the intensity of Paul's feeling, but perhaps also the presence of a major break[9]. The similarity of 10,1 to 9,1-5 and 11,1 is striking. Paul as a Jew three times gives expression to his personal concern for his people and introduces or interrupts his reasoning by using a confessional style in the first person singular[10]. Three times he does so in a passionate and straightforward way. It is difficult to maintain that Paul's second "outcry", with its μέν solitarium[11], does not function in the same manner as the other two, i.e., as an introduction to a significant shift in the argument.

---

[7] S.R. BECHTLER, "Christ, the Τέλος of the Law: The Goal of Romans 10:4", *CBQ* 56 (1994) 288-308, quotation on p. 291, n. 11.

[8] Cf. the brief remarks in L. DE LORENZI (ed.), *Die Israelfrage nach Röm 9–11* (Benedictina 3; Rome 1977) by R. PESCH (p. 86), W.C. VAN UNNIK (pp. 121-122) and C.K. BARRETT (p. 123: reply).

[9] Cf. SIEGERT, *Argumentation,* 116: One can "der herkömmlichen Kapiteleinteilung durchaus zustimmen, die mit 10,1 ἀδελφοί einen Neueinsatz annimmt. Direkte Anreden am Beginn eines Satzes sind ein starkes Gliederungssignal ...". However, the vocative "brothers" does not always mark a new start (see, e.g., Rom 1,13; 7,4; 8,12).

[10] The first person singular in 9,19 (ἐρεῖς μοι οὖν) can be neglected. But in ch. 11 that first person appears three more times: in 11,11 (λέγω οὖν), 11,13-14 ("Now I am speaking to you Gentiles. Inasmuch then as I am an apostle to the Gentiles, I magnify my ministry in order to make my fellow Jews jealous, and thus save some of them") and 11,25 ("Brothers, I want you to understand this mystery ..."). One sees that by repetitious use of the first person singular Paul's personal involvement continues to increase.

[11] BAUER–ALAND (*Wörterbuch zum Neuen Testament* [6th edn; Berlin 1988] 1019), comment on Rom 10,1 (and 1 Thess 2,18): "Der Hervorhebung des Subjektes dient μέν [i.e., *solitarium*] in Sätzen, die eine Mitteilung enthalten, welche der Redende über seinen eigenen Zustand macht".

A second reason is furnished by the brief diatribe–style question at the beginning of 9,30-33, namely τί οὖν ἐροῦμεν. 9,30 forms the last of four beginnings marking a subdivision within the larger section. To be sure, each of them is somewhat different. In the initial opening at 9,6, the question itself is not present, but it has to be mentally supplied in view of the statement–answer in the verse. The elective pattern of God's action is illustrated by Isaac and Jacob (vv. 6-13). The second beginning in 9,14 has τί οὖν ἐροῦμεν, a question identical to that in v. 30[12]; it is followed by another clarifying question: "Is there injustice on God's part?", to which the answer is negative. Paul here refers to God's merciful dealing with Moses and his hardening of Pharaoh (vv. 14-18). The third one in 9,19 has ἐρεῖς μοι οὖν, and is followed by a double question: "Why does he still find fault? For who can resist his will?" Paul first gives the example of the potter (vv. 20-21) and then speaks of God's call of the Gentiles (vv. 22-29). After τί οὖν ἐροῦμεν in 9,30, the fourth introduction, Paul presents his lengthy positive answer in vv. 30-31; it summarizes what is said in 9,22-29. The διὰ τί ("why") at the beginning of v. 32 asks for the reason for this state of affairs. Two reasons are given in vv. 32-33: the Israelites did not pursue it through faith; they stumbled over the stumbling stone. This diatribe–style of composing is no longer present in chapter 10. One cannot avoid the impression that the four introductions in chapter 9 should not be separated.

A third reason is provided by the quotation in 9,33 which, as we know, is a combination of Isa 28,16 and 8,14. The quotation appropriately concludes 9,30-33 (and the whole first section). It is introduced by καθὼς γέγραπται and highlights God's activity. The other subdivisions in chapter 9 are also rounded off by one or more OT quotations. It seems logical to assume that these four subdivisions belong together[13].

Fourth, there is more than the formal consistency to which the foregoing remarks witness. In the third subdivision (9,19-29), after the reference to Isaac and Jacob in vv. 6-13 and Moses and Pharaoh in vv. 14-18,

---

[12] According to Moo (*Romans*, 621, n. 18), in 9,14 "Paul uses the question to introduce teaching that responds to a possible objection to what he has been saying", while in 9,30 "the question introduces a summary or amplification of his teaching".

[13] A more speculative consideration, which concerns 9,33, may be added here. The same conflated quotation is also present in 1 Pet 2,6-8, and in that letter, moreover, we find an allusion to Hos 2,25 which is also quoted in Rom 9,25. This may reveal the existence of an early Christian chain of OT texts which both authors independently employed. If such is the case, this would somehow confirm the connection between 9,25 and 33, and thus between 9,19-29 and 9,30-33.

Paul first employs the image of the potter in vv. 20-21 and then finally but still in an abrupt manner and in the contorted sentence of vv. 22-23 arrives at God's free election of the Gentiles and the Jews. In v. 22 the "wrath" of God and the expression "the vessels of wrath" (= the Jews) suggest unfaithfulness and sin on the part of the Jews, but verse 23 contains the main purpose clause and speaks of God's intention with "the vessels of mercy" (= the Gentiles). In vv. 24-29 those who have been called "not only from the Jews but also from the Gentiles" (v. 24) are further dealt with. Therefore it would seem that in 9,30-31 Paul renders explicit what was pointed to in vv. 22-29 and what constitutes the main point of the whole first section: the Gentiles have attained righteousness, while Israel did not succeed in fulfilling the law of righteousness.

A fifth reason is to be found in the remarkable correspondence between 9,30-33 and 11,5-10. It is well known that in 11,1-10 Paul returns to the idea of God's free election which has been emphasized in chapter 9. In Rom 11,5-10, as in 9,30-33, failure is pointed to: "Israel failed to obtain what it sought". In both passages there is an opposition, in chapter 9 "Gentiles–Israel" and in chapter 11 "the elect–the rest"[14]. In both passages too, more particularly in the quotations, God's action is put forward in a one-sided way. Moreover, in 11,5-7 Paul takes up words and ideas from 9,6-29 and 30-33: see ἐκλογή (11,5.7 and 9,11); ἐξ ἔργων (11,6 and 9,12.32); the opposition grace–works in 11,6 reminds the reader of that of faith–works in 9,32 (cf. 9,11-12.16). The inference would seem to be that just as 11,5-10 is part of 11,1-10, so also 9,30-33 is part of 9,6-33. Both texts, chapter 9 as well as 11,1-10, offer a theodicy.

These five arguments, especially when taken together, make one tend to the conclusion that 9,30-33 is better considered as the final part of the first major section in Romans 9–11 and that 10,1 marks a caesura, just before the beginning of the second major section.

III. SHIFTS BETWEEN 9,30-33 AND 10,1-4

But what, then, should be said about the evident parallelism between 9,30-33 and 10,2-4? What precisely is the function of 10,2-4 over against

---

[14] The opposition is not completely the same. By "so too at the present time there is a 'remnant, chosen by grace'" in 11,5 Paul means the Gentile *and* Jewish Christians. Cf. already in 9,24: "even us whom he has called, not from the Jews only but also from the Gentiles".

9,30-33? As already stated, in both passages the emphasis lies on Israel's failure; moreover, verbal and conceptional connections are present. Three more points have recently been brought forward and must be discussed.

(1) In both passages, it is said, the law must be understood as leading to righteousness. In 9,31 δικαιοσύνης is a genitive of purpose or result: "not a righteous law but a law leading to righteousness is in view"[15]. This understanding of the law corresponds with the interpretation of 10,4: "Christ is said to be the τέλος, the goal toward which God intended the law to lead"[16], i.e., righteousness for everyone who believes.

The explanation of the genitive expression "the law of righteousness" in 9,31 is most probably correct. However, whether this interpretation of 9,31 favors the understanding of τέλος as "goal" in 10,4 is not clear to me; nor does this genitive as such, as far as I see, require the meaning of "end, termination" or that of "culmination"[17].

(2) It is put forward that ὡς ἐξ ἔργων in 9,32 must be explained in such a way that the expression does not refer to works–righteousness "but a particular mode of observing the Torah ... a defective kind of pursuit"[18]. While trying to keep the law Israel fails to accept Christ as universal savior; Israel stumbles over the stumbling stone. This point, too, it is claimed, finds its parallel in 10,2-4. Paul blames the Israelites, not because they have a zeal for God, but because they are ignorant and do not submit to God's

---

[15] BECHTLER, "Christ", 293. The author continues: "Whereas the Gentiles attained a righteousness they were not even pursuing, Paul says, Israel, although pursuing a law that was *to lead to*, or *result in* righteousness, 'did not attain the law'" (ibid.). Cf., e.g., C.E.B. CRANFIELD, "Some Notes on Romans 9.30-33", E.E. ELLIS & E. GRÄSSER (eds.), *Jesus und Paulus. FS W.G. Kümmel* (Göttingen 1975) 35-43, esp. 37-38.

[16] BECHTLER, "Christ", 302.

[17] As is well known, a growing number of authors interpret τέλος of 10,4 as "goal (of the law)", no longer as "end, termination (of the law)". Cf., more particularly, R. BADENAS, *Christ the End of the Law: Romans 10,4 in Pauline Perspective* (JSNT.S 10; Sheffield 1985). In his monograph the author not only analyses 10,4 within its context (in an often strained way), but also offers a history of the interpretation as well as a survey of the use of τέλος in biblical and cognate literature. See the severe criticism of Badenas by O. HOFIUS, "Gesetz und Evangelium nach 2. Korinthier 3", *Paulusstudien* (WUNT 51; Tübingen 1989) 75-120, esp. 110, n. 217. Yet see also the translation "culmination (of the law)" and its defense by MOO, *Romans*, 638-643.

[18] BECHTLER, "Christ", 295: "For Israel to imagine that it could disregard Christ and attain righteousness via Torah observance alone ... is not only to misunderstand God's act in Christ, but to misunderstand the nature of Torah observance itself. Such mistaken pursuit of Torah, Paul says, can only result in failure to attain Torah and the righteousness it proffers". Bechtler refers to Käsemann as the repsentative of the school of thought which sees in Rom 9,30–10,4 a Paul who blames Israel for its legalistic righteousness (see p. 297). Cf. also the defense of the same position by CRANFIELD, "Some Notes", 40-41, and MOO, *Romans*, 634-636.

righteousness, while they seek to establish their own (vv. 2-3). God wants the inclusion of the Gentiles apart from the works of the law, through faith in Christ; the gospel is a power to salvation to every one who believes, Jews but also Gentiles (cf. 1,16-17; 3,21-31). Seeking to establish their own righteousness[19] is the opposite of submitting to God's righteousness. "The problem described in 10,3, therefore, is not that Israel, by its meritorious efforts, is attempting to create its own righteousness, but that its zealous commitment to its exclusivistic view of the covenant precludes the possibility of God's offer of salvation to Gentiles outside the covenant"[20].

The second remark, which defends a nowadays fairly common corporate understanding (Israel *versus* Gentiles), can hardly be accepted here. In 9,30-33 Paul seems to deplore two "failures" with regard to Israel: "working", i.e., concretely speaking, striving to do the works of the law[21], and not accepting Jesus. The two failures are related, yet not identical. Working results in not believing (v. 32b) and not accepting Jesus (v. 32c). The first failure, this should be admitted, is probably not a legalistic observance of the law. It is clinging to human work and refusal of divine gift. The fact that notwithstanding its pursuit Israel did not "obtain the law" that leads to righteousness also means, it would seem, that Israel did not observe the law completely. The Jews were found to be sinners and, just like the Gentiles, in need of God's justification through Christ[22]. In 9,32-33 and 10,2-4 Paul does not appear to blame Israel because it wants to exclude the Gentiles.

(3) The third point is of special concern to this short paper. According to Bechtler and others[23], one more correspondence between 9,30-33 and 10,2-4 is constituted by the absence in both passages of the language of sin

---

[19] Cf. BECHTLER, "Christ", 292: the participle διώκων in 9,31 must be interpreted as concessive: "Pauls asks why Israel, *although pursuing* νόμον δικαιοσύνης, did not attain it".

[20] Cf. BECHTLER, "Christ", 295-298, quotation on p. 298. Israel's problem is not "that the nation sought to earn merit before God by virtue of its works" (305, n. 63).

[21] Cf. 9,12 and 11,6, where ἐξ ἔργων is used even more radically, without reference to the law.

[22] Cf. MOO, *Romans*, 626-627 and 634-635. It is true that v. 32c is an asyndeton; yet this is not a reason to consider v. 32b and c as one grounding clause. So recently W. REINHOLD, "Paulus und das Gesetz: Zur Exegese von Röm 9,30-33", *BZ* 38 (1994) 253-264: "Weil sie — nich aus Glauben, sondern in Werken befangen! — an den Stein des Anstosses anstiessen" (260). Assuming this so-called parenthesis would result in a quite different construction from that present in the parallel 9,11-12a.

[23] Cf. BECHTLER, "Christ", 297, n. 33. See also, e.g., M.A. GETTY, "Paul and the Salvation of Israel: A Perspective on Romans 9-11", *CBQ* 50 (1988) 456-499, esp. 459.462.463 and 467.

and culpability. To be sure, Israel's failure is stated in each of them: "they have stumbled" (9,32); "they did not submit" (10,3). There is misconception and a lack of knowledge on the part of the Israelites. But these commentators are inclined to think that Paul as yet[24] avoids the accusatory indication of their sinful attitude.

Let us consider the text. Rom 10,2-4 is not a pure repetition of 9,30-33. After the mention of his sorrow and his prayer for Israel's salvation in 10,1, Paul explains and specifies what he has just said in 9,30-33. He stresses that he himself is a witness to Israel's zeal for God. "Zeal" as well as "seeking to establish" are clarifications of "pursuing" of 9,31. "Establishing their own righteousness" is equally an explanation of the brief and cryptic expression "not of faith but as if of works" in 9,32. The righteousness mentioned in 9,30 and 31 is twice qualified in 10,3 as God's righteousness. From 10,4 one arrives at the certainty that "the stumbling stone" and the "rock of scandal" in 9,32 and 33 must be understood christologically. Finally, the rather neutral, matter-of-fact statement "they stumbled over the stumbling stone" of 9,32 becomes a seemingly morally qualified clause in 10,3: "they did not submit to God's righteousness".

This last specification brings us to the insight that in 10,1-4 a new approach to the problem of Israel has really been initiated. Although open and incriminating language still seems to be avoided in 10,1-4, οὐκ ὑπετάγησαν ("they did not submit") in 10,3 most probably points to culpability. A similar remark can be made regarding the clause "seeking to establish their own (righteousness)" in the same verse. Paul no longer simply states a fact, as he did in 9,31-32. Notwithstanding the admission of zeal in 10,2 and (perhaps) the excuse of ignorance in 10,2-3a[25], by "seeking to establish their own righteousness" Paul appears to emphasize Israel's stubborn, misguided and hence sinful enterprise, and by "they did not submit to God's righteousness" he refers to its culpable refusal. This is a shift in the rhetorical structure and logic. A second shift is linked with the first. In 9,32 there is the question, διὰ τί: "Why (did Israel not succeed)?" This question would seem to announce a transition from God's election to Israel's reaction and responsibility. But in v. 33a Paul returns to God's "predestination": God lays a stone that makes them stumble, a rock that makes them fall[26]. In 10,1-4 God is no longer spoken of as actor. The two

---

[24] This will occur at the end of the chapter. See 10,21: "a disobiedient and contrary people", and cf. 10,16: "they have not all obeyed the gospel".

[25] Cf. BECHTLER, "Christ", 307: "... in 10,2-3, Israel's ignorance did not necessarily entail the nations's culpability ...".

[26] It must be admitted: v. 33b ("he who believes in him ...") rather points to the human responsibility.

shifts together constitute the change from God's sovereign free initiative to Israel's inexcusable, sinful refusal, that is, from theodicy in chapter 9 to human failure and sin in chapter 10.

Paul's reference in 10,1-2a to his personal prayerful compassion as well as his witnessing involvement introduces this whole second section with due solemnity. Of course, just as in 10,19, with the quotation from Deuteronomy (ἐγὼ παραζηλώσω ὑμᾶς ἐπ' οὐκ ἔθνει ...), Paul will prepare the new argument of 11,11-32 (the salvation of the Gentiles makes Israel jealous), so also in 9,30-33, by the mention of Israel's failure, he announces what will be the main topic of chapter 10, i.e., the (one-sided) emphasis on Israel's refusal, on its responsibility and even culpability[27]. However, the fair recognition of such an announcement in 9,30-33 in no way endangers our view of its appurtenance to the first major section. Between 9,30-33 and 10,1-4 there is, so it appears to us, a significant break in the argument: in chapter 10 there is no longer diatribe–style, no longer theodicy; the focus lies on human responsibility and culpability. In 10,16 we read: "they have not all obeyed"; in 10,18 there is the question: "But I ask, have they not heard?" The explicit answer is given in 10,21: "All day long I have held out my hands to a disobedient and contrary people". But the sinful attitude of the Israelites was already pointed to, we think, in 10,3: "seeking their own, they did not submit to God's righteousness".

---

[27] Cf. LAGRANGE, *Epître aux Romains*, 249: "Il est vrai qu'ici [9,30] commence un nouvel aspect de la question, la responsabilité d'Israël, mais c'est en même temps le mot de la fin pour la péricope précédente, car en somme Paul n'avait pas encore dit clairement qu'Israël pour le plus grand nombre avait choppé".

Novum Testamentum 42 (2000) 257-261

4

Syntactical and Logical Remarks on Romans 15,8-9a

I. INTRODUCTION

Many people, if not all, will agree with C.E.B. Cranfield that Rom 15,9a "is specially difficult".[1] NA[27] presents the following Greek text of 15,8-9a:

8a λέγω γὰρ Χριστὸν διάκονον γεγενῆσθαι περιτομῆς ὑπὲρ ἀληθείας θεοῦ,

b εἰς τὸ βεβαιῶσαι τὰς ἐπαγγελίας τῶν πατέρων,

9a τὰ δὲ ἔθνη ὑπὲρ ἐλέους δοξάσαι τὸν θεόν.

This is the RSV translation:

8a For I tell you that Christ became a servant to the circumcised[2] to show God's truthfulness,

b in order to confirm the promises given to the patriarchs,

9a and in order that the Gentiles might glorify God for his mercy.

II. SOME SYNTACTICAL/LOGICAL REMARKS

1. There are three reasons which together make it very difficult to take

---

[1] C.E.B. CRANFIELD, *The Epistle to the Romans. Vol. II* (ICC; Edinburgh [2]1981) 742. J.D.G. DUNN, *Romans 9–16* (WBC; Waco 1989): "The precise articulation of the first clause of v. 9 with v. 8 is unclear, perhaps because Paul did not want to specify it more clearly ..." (852); one should "allow the translation to express the ambiguity ..." (848).

[2] According to M.-J. LAGRANGE, *Epître aux Romains* (EtB; Paris 1916) 346, "Paul ne met ... pas les Juifs en scène directement; il oppose plutôt une certaine économie de promesse à une économie de miséricorde". Yet it would appear that "circumcision" here is simply a way of denoting the Jews.

v. 9a as the strict parallel to v. 8b (the RSV adds in v. 9a "in order that")[3]. (1) While in v. 8b Christ is the implied grammatical subject of "to confirm", in v. 9a it is "the Gentiles"; such a change of subject does not favor the acceptance of a sort of symmetry[4]. (2) Paul appears to intend a contrast between ὑπὲρ ἀληθείας (v. 8a) and ὑπὲρ ἐλέους (v. 9a)[5]. The first phrase, however, does not belong to the εἰς τό clause of v. 8b. (3) Verse 8b functions as a clarification of God's truthfulness (end of v. 8a)[6]: God is truthful by confirming, i.e., by fulfulling[7] the promises given to the fathers. It is unlikely that the plural "promises" here refers to the specific promise given to Abraham, namely, that the Gentiles will be blessed in him (cf. Gal 3,8). The opposing δέ, referring to the Gentiles at the beginning of v. 9a, corroborates this view (RSV here has a less correct connecting "and")[8].

Yet reading v. 9a immediately after v. 8b suggests, it would seem, the presence of a nuance of purpose in v. 9a as well. Furthermore, just as the aorist infinitive βεβαιῶσαι almost certainly points to the future in relation to the verb on which it depends, so also does the aorist infinitive δοξάσαι[9].

2. The grammatical dependence of the infinitive "to glorify" (v. 9a) on

---

[3] D.J. Moo, *The Epistle to the Romans* (NICNT; Grand Rapids–Cambridge 1996) 876-877, defends this parallelism; he refers to a number of other exegetes. Cf. also T.L. Donaldson, *Paul and the Gentiles: Remapping the Apostle's Convictional World* (Minneapolis 1997) 95-99: "With most commentators ... I take vv. 8b and 9 as two parallel statements concerning the purpose of Christ's becoming a servant of the Jews" (97); Christ's ministry to Israel has two goals: "the confirming of the patriarchal promises (8b) and the creation of a situation where Gentiles would glorify God (v. 9)" (99). By means of a strained interpretation of both vocabulary and syntax S.K. Williams, "The 'Righteousness of God' in Romans", *JBL* 99 (1980) 241-299, esp. 285-289, even connects the two goals: "in order to confirm the promises to the fathers and so that, consequently, the Gentiles might glorify God for his mercy" (288).

[4] Cranfield, *Romans*, 743, stresses "the very strong objection that an εἰς τό clause extending over vv. 8b and 9a and containing an extraordinarily harsh change of subjects ... and further complicated by the fact that v. 9b is dependent on it, is a stylistic horror in Greek ...".

[5] Dunn, *Romans 9–16*, 848, along with others, is hardly justified in his appeal here to the Old Testament equivalents "mercy — or grace — and truth", which often function more or less as a hendiadys.

[6] The expression ὑπὲρ ἀληθείας is better not taken as an anticipation of v. 8b.

[7] Cf. Lagrange, *Epître aux Romains*, 346.

[8] In a less correct way, it would seem, J.A. Fitzmyer, *Romans* (AB; New York 1992) 706, considers "to confirm the promises made to the patriarchs" as the second purpose after "to show God's fidelity" and before the Gentiles' glorification of God; he also claims that the Gentiles are included in those promises; cf. Dunn, *Romans 9–16*, 848. Moo, *Romans*, 877-878, rightly prefers the application here to the Jewish people specifically. Cf. Donaldson, *Paul and the Gentiles*, 98: "Nowhere in Romans is the salvation of the Gentiles presented as a fulfillment of God's promises to Abraham" (with discussion of 4,16).

[9] Cranfield, *Romans*, 754, however, prefers a present action.

"I tell you" (at the beginning of v. 8a) is strained, not only because of the distance and the statement (v. 8b) that intervenes between them, but also because of the logic. The sentence "For I tell you that Christ became a servant to the circumcised to show God's truthfulness ... but that the Gentiles (must) glorify God for his mercy" scarcely makes sense[10]. Paul appears to be composing elliptically and to have omitted a specific statement[11]. One is as it were forced to repeat "I tell you" and to insert a verb which points to an action of Christ for the Gentiles similar to that in favor of the Jews[12].

In v. 7b Paul writes: "as Christ has received you". "You" most probably refers to the whole Roman community. The majority of the community, however, are Gentiles and in chapters 14–15 Paul urges the "strong" (Gentiles) to receive and welcome the "weak" (Jews): see, e.g., 14,1[13]. Hence the underlying line of thought in 15,8-9a would appear to be: (not only did Christ become a servant to the Jews) he also received and welcomed the Gentiles; (not only did he want to show his truthfulness to the promises) he also wanted to show his mercy to the Gentiles. These actions of Christ, becoming a servant to the Jews and receiving the Gentiles, are not the same. Nor were his aims the same: "for the sake of truthfulness" differs from "for the sake of mercy".

3. A closer look at v. 9a shows that elements of the unstated, implicit action for the Gentiles are taken up and explicitly mentioned in this verse. The reference to τὰ ἔθνη and the expression ὑπὲρ ἐλέους belong to this implied yet not expressed clause. However, with regard to that last expression a shift in meaning must be noted. The sense is no longer "for the sake of mercy" (or "in order to show his mercy"). No, the Gentiles must glorify God for the mercy manifested to them. In v. 9a mercy is no longer the prospective (or the aim) of Christ's action; it becomes the reason for the Gentiles glorifying God or perhaps even the object of their glorification.

---

[10] Can one with D. ZELLER, *Juden und Heiden in der Mission des Paulus. Studien zum Römerbrief* (FzB 8; Stuttgart ²1976) 219, simply state: "λέγω γάρ regiert zwei Akkusative mit Infinitiv"?

[11] Cf. CRANFIELD, *Romans*, who highlights the "remarkably perceptive comment" (743) by R. CORNELY (*Commentarius in S. Pauli Apostoli epistolas I*, Paris, 1898) and "his penetrating insight into the elliptical nature" (744) of vv. 8-9a. With regard to v. 9a, Cranfield summarizes as follows: Paul passes "over in silence the parallel thought to v. 8 (which was actually in his mind), namely, that Christ has called the Gentiles for the sake of God's mercy, in order to manifest His kindness ..." (753).

[12] Cf. B. BYRNE, *Romans* (SP; Collegeville 1996) 431; his addition in v. 9a is: "and (he [Christ] performed a similar function) in the case of the Gentiles that they might glorify God for the receipt of mercy". V. 9a forms "a parallel to the whole of v. 8".

[13] Cf., e.g., D. ZELLER, *Der Brief an die Römer* (RNT, Regensburg 1984) 231-232: V. 7b "apostrophiert" the Roman church as Gentile Christians.

4. It can hardly be accidental that in v. 9a the idea of "glorification" is present. In v. 6, at the end of the preceding pericope, Paul writes: "in order that together you may with one voice 'glorify' the God and Father of our Lord Jesus Christ". At the end of v. 7 by means of the coined formula he repeats the idea: "for the 'glory' of God" (εἰς δόξαν τοῦ θεοῦ)[14]. Admittedly, in vv. 6-7 all Christians in Rome are exhorted, but the specific attention to the Gentiles in v. 9a does not in the least eliminate the conscious repetition of the glorification theme; indeed, this theme is emphasized. One should take note of the fact that in v. 6 as well as in v. 7 glorifying God is seen as a final purpose. This strongly confirms the view that in v. 9a the Gentiles' glorification of God is also considered an aim, a purpose. Out of Christ's merciful action (the indicative) follows the Christians' task (the imperative) to extol and exalt God. Supporting reference can also be made to the quotation in v. 11 "Praise the Lord, all you Gentiles, and let all peoples sound his praise" (Ps 117,1).

5. A last syntactical point must not escape our analysis. Both the γάρ at the beginning of v. 8a[15] and the δέ at the beginning of v. 9a suggest that a hidden μέν may be present. As is well known, in a (μὲν) γὰρ ... δέ–construction the first clause is often concessive and points to what everybody would agree upon. A free restatement of the μέν–clause may begin with "although", "admittedly", or "it is true that ...". The real reason (γάρ) is to be found in the δέ-clause; this second clause is the main point of what the author wants to say.

Notwithstanding the explicative and interruptive addition of v. 8b — which gives weight to v. 8a — such a construction is probably present in vv. 8a.9a. A paraphrase of vv. 7 and 8a.9a runs as follows: "Receive and welcome one another, as Christ has received you[16], for the glory of God. For, I tell you, it is true that Christ became a servant of the Jews to show God's truthfulness, but in order to show his mercy Christ received the Gentiles so that they, too, may glorify God".[17]

---

[14] Cf. LAGRANGE, Epître aux Romains, 347.

[15] The variant reading δέ after λέγω is but weakly attested.

[16] Cf. B.M. METZGER, A Textual Commentary on the Greek New Testament (Stuttgart [2]1994) 473: "The reading ὑμᾶς, which has superior and more diversified support than the reading ἡμᾶς, is in harmony with the other instances of the second person plural in the context (verses 5-7)".

[17] Cf. LAGRANGE, Epître aux Romains, 346: "La phrase [v. 8] est permissive" and 347: "... la circoncison n'a été nommée que par une sorte de parenthèse"; ZELLER, Juden und Heiden, 220: "V. 8 [hat] ungeachtet der parataktischen Stellung sinngemäss eher hypotaktische Funktion"; BYRNE, Romans, 431-432: "... the statement about Christ's ministry to the Circumcision is introduced only as a foil to what Paul wants to say about the Gentiles in support of v. 7".

The four citations which follow in vv. 9b-12 prove that the emphasis lies on the content of v. 9a, not on that of 8a. Moreover, both the immediate and general context justifies this interpretation as well[18]. The (strong) Gentiles must realize that they are "vessels of mercy" (σκεύη ἐλέους, 9,23, and cf. 11,30-31: ἔλεος); they must not forget the astonishing "kindness" of God to them (χρηστότης, 11,22) and they must therefore welcome the weaker members (presumably Jewish Christians).

III. CONCLUSION

Thus these five syntactical or logical remarks may, I suggest, provide a better understanding of the difficult v. 9a: a lack of strict parallelism between v. 9a and 8b, Paul's elliptic style, a shift in meaning as far as the expression "for the sake of mercy" is concerned, the emphasis on the glorification of God, and a concessive nuance in v. 8a.

---

[18] Cf. CRANFIELD, *Romans*, 744; ZELLER, *Juden und Heiden*, 219-221; E. KÄSEMANN, *Commentary on Romans* (Grand Rapids 1980) 385-386.

Additional Note: See also J. ROSS WAGNER, "The Christ, Servant of Jew and Gentile: A Fresh Approach to Romans 15:8-9", *JBL* 116 (1997) 473.485. This study was unkown to me at the time when I wrote my contribution. Wagner's proposal, too, assumes an ellipse: "For I say that the Christ has become a servant of the circumcision on behalf of the truthfulness of God, in order to confirm the promises made for the patriarchs, and [a servant] with respect to the Gentiles on behalf of the mercy of God in order to glorify God". He strangely understands Christ as the grammatical subject of "to glorify" and "the Gentiles" as an accusative of respect.

5

The Power of God
A Note on the Connection Between 1 Cor 1,17 and 18

In 1 Cor 1,14-17 Paul emphasizes his minimal baptismal activity: "I thank God that I baptized none of you except .... For Christ did not send me to baptize but to proclaim the gospel ..." (vv. 14.17). The Greek text of verses 17-18 reads as follows:

17a οὐ γὰρ ἀπέστειλέν με Χριστὸς βαπτίζειν ἀλλὰ εὐαγγελί-
ζεσθαι, οὐκ ἐν σοφίᾳ λόγου,
b ἵνα μὴ κενωθῇ ὁ σταυρὸς τοῦ Χριστοῦ.
18a Ὁ λόγος γὰρ ὁ τοῦ σταυροῦ τοῖς μὲν ἀπολλυμένοις
μωρία ἐστίν,
b τοῖς δὲ σῳζομένοις ἡμῖν δύναμις θεοῦ ἐστιν.

How does Paul's thought progress from verse 17 to verse 18? This must be examined.

I. STATUS QUAESTIONIS

Three remarks can be made regarding verse 18. (1) Notwithstanding a postpositive γάρ in verse 18a and, therefore, its connection with verse 17, almost all commentaries and translations commence a new paragraph with verse 18[1]. (2) The expected antithetical term to foolishness is "wisdom", not "power". (3) It strikes the reader that in verse 18a Paul speaks of ὁ

---

[1] Cf. G.D. FEE, *The First Epistle to the Corinthians* (NICNT; Grand Rapids, MI 1987) 68: "The 'for' that begins this sentence [v. 18] ties it to v. 17 as an explanation of the final clause in that verse. Unfortunately our paragraph break and the limits of English tend to cause us to miss the subtle contrast that Paul intends".

λόγος ... ὁ τοῦ σταυροῦ while in the preceding verse 17b the expression is ὁ σταυρὸς τοῦ Χριστοῦ, without ὁ λόγος.

Verses 17-18 belong to the first major part of 1 Corinthians which can be entitled "Quarreling and Divisions in the Congregation" and extends from 1,10 to 4,21. Most exegetes rightly, it would seem, take 1,10-17 as a first unit of that part: "Quarrels in Corinth". Verse 18 is then the beginning of a second unit, 1,18–2,5: "Christ Crucified". This longer unit can be divided into three subdivisions: (a) a general exposition of the message about the cross (1,18-25), (b) an application to the Corinthians (1,26-31), and (c) an application to Paul (2,1-5). In (a) we meet the expression "Christ crucified" (1,23) and in (c) the slightly different phrase "Jesus and him crucified" (2,2). Each of the three subdivisions stresses God's initiative: see 1,20-21; 1,27-31 and 2,5. The first subdivision motivates the opening sentence with a quotation from Isa 29,14; the second concludes the rejection of mere human boasting with an abbrevation of Jer 9,22-23 (or 1 Sam 2,10). The unit begins and ends with the opposition between human folly or wisdom and God's power (δύναμις θεοῦ): compare 1,18 with 2,5[2].

What is the logical connection between 1,18 and 17, and hence between 1,18–2,5 and 1,10-17[3]? Why does Paul suddenly mention "the power of God" in 1,18b[4] and why is he speaking of "the word" of the cross in 1,18a?

---

[2] Cf. my "First Corinthians" in W.R. FARMER (ed.), *The International Bible Commentary* (Collegeville, MN 1998) 1601-32, esp. 1605-06. See also K. MÜLLER, "1 Kor. 1,28-25. Die eschatologisch-kritische Funktion der Verkündigung des Kreuzes", *BZ* 10 (1966) 246-272; R. PENNA, "The Gospel as 'Power of God' According to 1 Corinthians 1:18-25", in ID., *Paul the Apostle. I: Jew and Greek Alike,* Collegeville 1996, 169-180; U. HECKEL, *Kraft in Schwachheit. Untersuchungen zu 2. Kor 10–13* (WUNT II, 56; Tübingen 1993) 179-180, 199-200 and 289-295.

[3] Cf. J. KREMER, *Der Erste Brief an die Korinther* (RNT; Regensburg 1997) 36: "Mit V. 18 beginnt ein Abschnitt, der nicht direkt auf die Spaltungen in der Gemeinde eingeht, sondern ... an V. 17b ... anknüpft und das dort kurz angesprochene Thema entfaltet".

[4] Cf. FEE, *First Corinthians,* 69: "The contrast between 'foolishness' and 'power' is not precise, of course"; HECKEL, *Kraft in Schwachheit,* 200: "Schon in der Leitthese in 1,18 tritt der μωρία nicht — wie es sich nahelegen würde — die Weisheit der Glaubenden gegenüber, sondern die δύναμις θεοῦ, so dass es nicht einfach um ein Erkenntnisproblem und die Korrektur eines Missverständnisses auf Seiten des Menschen geht, sondern um die Heilswirksamkeit des Wortes vom Kreuz ... und das Widerfahrnis der rettenden Gotteskraft...". Does Heckel provide us with the full answer?

II. POWER AND DEPRIVATION OF POWER

By means of the expression "the word of the cross" in verse 18a Paul obviously, by way of a kind of anaphora, takes up "the cross (of Christ)" at the end of the preceding verse 17b. Commentators do not completely neglect the postpositive γάρ but, today even more so because of the influence of a rhetorical approach, they emphasize the function of verse 18 as a *propositio*, "an opening statement" or "thesis"[5]. Yet Johannes Weiss writes: "Nicht bloss V. 18 ist Begründung des paradoxen 17. Verses, sondern dieser ganze Abschnitt. Denn V. 17 ... wird im Grunde genommen erst in 2,5 wirklich erläutert"[6]. It may be better, however, not to isolate 2,5 but to compare 2,4-5 with 1,17-18 and not only with 1,18. "My speech (λόγος) and proclamation" of 2,4 recalls "to evangelize" in 1,17 and "the message (λόγος) of the cross" in 1,18. Both the expressions ἐν πειθοῖς σοφίας λόγοις in 2,4 and ἐν σοφίᾳ ἀνθρώπων in 2,5 correspond more or less in sense with ἐν σοφίᾳ λόγου of 1,17. Paul's proclamation "with a demonstration of the Spirit and power" of 2,4 reminds the reader of "the word of the cross" which to those who are being saved is "the power of God" of 1,18. Finally, the expression "power of God" is present in 2,5 as well as in 1,18[7].

The γάρ-connection between 1,17 and 1,18, however, should not be minimized. There is not only the anaphora of "the cross" and the pointed

---

[5] Cf. R.F. COLLINS, *First Corinthians* (SP 7; Collegeville, MN 2000), 90, but see also p. 101 on the explanatory "for"; H. CONZELMANN, *1 Corinthians* (Philadelphia 1975), 41 (first Paul "expounds the thesis"); KREMER, *1 Korinther*, 37 (v. 18 is "die These"); HECKEL, *Kraft in Schwachheit,* passim ("Leitthese", "Kernthese", "Leitsatz"); W. SCHRAGE, *Der erste Brief an die Korinther* (EKK VII/1; Zürich–Neukirchen/Vluyn 1991) 167, but see also p. 170: "V 18 greift das Stichwort σταυρός auf erläutert thetisch und in ,prägnanter Kürze V 17b". For J.S. VOS, "Die Argumentation des Paulus in 1 Kor 1,10–3,4", in R. BIERINGER (ed.), *The Corinthian Correspondence* (BETL 125; Leuven 1996) 87-119, 1,10 provides the *propositio* of 1,10–4,21 (p. 87) and 1,18 is "eine These über das Wesen" of the message of the cross (p. 97); on 1,17 see pp. 91-97.

[6] J. WEISS, *Der erste Korintherbrief* (KEK; Göttingen 1910) 24. Cf. further on the same page: "Da V. 18 nicht eigentlich die genaue Begründung fur V. 17b enthält, so ist γάρ hier nur ein Zeichen, dass eine längere, erläuternde Erörterung beginnt". Cf. Conzelmann, *1 Corinthians*, 41 ("too formalistic"); SCHRAGE, *Der erste Brief an die Korinther*, 170.

[7] Cf. COLLINS, *First Corinthians*, 119: "1:17b is prospective while 2:4-5 is retrospective". D. LIFTIN, *St. Paul's Theology of Proclamation. 1 Corinthians 1–4 and Greco-Roman Rhetoric* (SNTS MS 79; Cambridge 1994) 190, highlights the parallelism between 1,17 and 2,4-5. The ἵνα-clauses of 1,17b and 2,5 constitute the third element; yet their contents are quite different.

repetition of λόγος (with the sense of "message" in v. 18a, no longer that of "speech, rhetoric" as in v. 17a)[8]. The verb "to evangelize" of verse 17a, too, is taken up by "the word" in v. 18a. A preaching of gospel with eloquent wisdom and rhetorical skill would empty the cross of Christ of its power (cf. 1,17b: ἵνα μὴ κενωθῇ ὁ σταυρὸς τοῦ Χριστοῦ)[9]. Only a proclamation which avoids "plausible words of wisdom" (2,4) will keep safe "the power of God" (cf. 1,18b). The manifestation of δύναμις θεοῦ is the opposite of emptying or deprivation of power. One thus comes to understand why Paul in verse 18b must write "power", and not "wisdom", the contrast to "foolishness" of verse 18a. So "the power of God" (v. 18b) refers back to "lest the cross of Christ be emptied (of its power") (v. 17b).

There is still more to be said. "Commentators have often puzzled over the way in which matters of form could void the power of the cross"[10]. But does the phrase ἐν σοφίᾳ λόγου of v. 17a in the first place point to superficial rhetorical skill and oratorial techniques, more to form than content[11]? The phrase most probably implies oratorial techniques *and* logically sound, persuasive reasoning (cf. 2,4), where the latter seems to belong to "content" rather than "form". However, ἐν σοφίᾳ λόγου carries in itself the idea of power, i.e. "the dynamic of Graeco-Roman rhetoric"[12]. In verse 17 Paul seems to conceive of "two dynamics — that of the rhetor and that of the cross — as mutually exclusive" and he fears "that operating according to the rhetor's dynamic would hinder the working of the Gospel, effectively voiding the cross's own power to create belief"[13].

"Foolishness" (μωρία) in verse 18a certainly is meant as the opposite

---

[8] Cf. FEE, *First Corinthians*, 68.

[9] The verb κενόω means "to empty", "to render ineffective", "to make void", hence also "to empty of power", "to deprive of power".

[10] LIFTIN, *Paul's Theology of Proclamation*, 190. On pp. 188-189 Liftin writes: "It is tendentious to interpret οὐκ ἐν σοφίᾳ λόγου in vs. 17 primarily in terms of content, as if Paul is merely asserting that the ideas he preaches must not be those of human wisdom"; see also his discussion of the ten related constructions in 1 and 2 Corinthians (esp. 1 Cor 1,17; 2,1.4.5 and 13) on pp. 155-159. Cf. 2 Cor 10,10 and 11,6. See also T.H. LIM, "'Not in persuasive words of wisdom, but in the demonstration of the Spirit and power'", *NT* 29 (1987) 137-149, who in his examination of 2,4 claims that here, too, above all, "human techniques of eloquence" (p. 148) is meant. In the Greco-Roman world of rhetoric practice "σοφία ... is a term which is often used to describe the ability, skill or cleverness of an eloquent speaker" (p. 146).

[11] FEE, *First Corinthians*, 64, asks: "Is the emphasis on the content (wisdom) or the form (word), or perhaps on both?" He goes on: "In light of the contrastive purpose clause that follows, the genitive, 'of word,' is most likely descriptive, and means something like 'not with a kind of *sophia* characterized by rhetoric (or perhaps reason or logic)'". He concludes: "Thus the emphasis is first of all on content". Is this correct?

[12] LIFTIN, *Paul's Theology of Proclamation*, 191.

[13] LIFTIN, *Paul's Theology of Proclamation*, 192.

of human "wisdom" (σοφία) which uses rhetoric (v. 17a). Yet "foolishness" in verse 21 is no longer the complete opposite of the eloquent wisdom. It has become a paradox which refers to a more profound type of wisdom, true wisdom, the counterpart of "the wisdom of the wise" and "the discernment of the discerning" (v. 19), of "the wisdom of the world" (v. 20) and of "the wisdom of this age" (2,6). That human wisdom is much more sinister and fatal than human eloquence alone[14].

The appearance of "power" in verse 18b may be surprising at first, but the presence of that concept shows how verse 18 really motivates verse 17. "The power of God" (v. 18b) is opposed to the purely human power inherent in the eloquent wisdom of verse 17a and, at the same time, refers to the absence of power of which verse 17b speaks. The grounding function of verse 18 seems to be more notional than strictly causal. We may paraphrase: "since we know that the message of the cross is the power of God".

It cannot but strike the reader that at the end of the unit the same imprecise opposition between human wisdom and the power of God (not God's wisdom) twice recurs. In 2,4 we read οὐκ ἐν πειθοῖς σοφίας λόγοις ἀλλ᾽ ἐν ἀποδείξει πνεύματος καὶ δυνάμεως and in 2,5 (οὐκ) ἐν σοφίᾳ ἀνθρώπων ἀλλ᾽ ἐν δυνάμει θεοῦ. This shift may be intended by Paul to increase and complete the ring composition which the expression ἐν δυνάμει θεοῦ in 2,5 (cf. 1,18b) by itself brings about[15]. As in 1,18, "power" in 2,4-5 does not (or not so much) allude to the "signs, wonders, and miracles" mentioned in 2 Cor 12,12. Regarding Corinthian rhetoric and divine power we should also mention what Paul says at the end of the major section, 1 Cor 4,19-20: "... I will find out not the talk of these arrogant people but their power. For the kingdom of God depends not on talk but on power".

Commentaries rightly pay attention to the μέν ... δέ–opposition in verse 18, to the antithetical pairing of the two articular participles τοῖς ἀπολλυμένοις and τοῖς σῳζομένοις and to the repetition of ἐστιν. Moreover, the fact that both the addition of ἡμῖν and the longer δύναμις θεοῦ (over against the single noun μωρία) emphasize the second element

---

[14] Cf., e.g., C.K. BARRETT, *The First Epistle to the Corinthians* (BNTC; London 1968), 49 and 52, on the different senses of "wisdom".

[15] See also 1,24 and 2,4. Although the concept "power of God" is further referred to in 1,22 (σημεῖα), 25 (ἰσχυρότερον) and 26 (δυνατοί) and, of course, is present in the whole section, the more basic idea in 1,18–2,5 is God's wisdom (and "foolishness") over against human wisdom. Cf. also 1,30 and the way, e.g., FEE, *First Corinthians*, 85-86, explains 1,30: "True wisdom is to be understood in terms of the three illustrative metaphors [righteousness, sanctification and redemption, all grammatically in apposition to wisdom] which refer to the saving event of Christ" (86); see also VOS, "Argumentation", 102-103.

of the antithesis is duly recognized. Yet we may ask whether in this μὲν γὰρ ... δέ–construction the main reason or motivation (γάρ) is not given in verse 18b, while what stands in the first member (v. 18a) becomes somewhat concessive: "For, although the word of the cross is foolishness for those who are perishing, for those who are being saved, for us, it is the power of God"[16]. If this suggestion possesses any validity, then the positive verse 18b is more important than its negative parallel, verse 18a. It has to be admitted that in verse 19 Paul, by means of a quotation from Isaiah, proves as it were God's power and that Paul's attention goes to the negative side: "I will destroy the wisdom of the wise and the discernment of the discerning I will thwart". The destruction, however, is no longer a annihilation of humans, but a removal of their wisdom and cleverness. That rather general statement of verse 19 prepares, together with vv. 20-23, Paul's still hidden reproach of the "wise" Corinthians, his fellow Christians, not unbelievers: God decided, through the foolishness of Paul's proclamation, to save those mistaken brothers and sisters (cf. vv. 21 and 24-25, and the open attack in vv. 26-28). Furthermore, in 2,4-5 at the end of the unit Paul again, by way of inclusion, stresses God's positive, salvific power.

III. THE CROSS AND THE MESSAGE ABOUT THE CROSS

The transition from 1,17 to 1,18 is not without a shift. According to verse 17b the cross of Christ is power: it can be deprived and emptied of power. Yet in verse 18b it is the word of the cross that is the power of God[17]. Why does Paul bring about this shift? What is the relation between the cross and the message about the cross[18]?

---

[16] For this use and meaning of the construction, see M. ZERWICK, *Biblical Greek* (Rome 1963) nos. 474-477. The γάρ is called by X. Léon-Dufour "un γάρ à portée différée". A paraphrase may be offered: "I admit that to those who are perishing the message of the cross is foolishness, but to us it is the power of God".

[17] According to 1,23-24 Paul preaches Christ crucified who to those who are called is "the power or God and the wisdom of God". On the parallelism between 1,18 and 1,23-24, see PENNA, "Power of God", 175-177. The author also shows how God manifested his power by raising the crucified Christ, and how Christ himself thus became "the power of God" (173-174 and 176-178).

[18] HECKEL, *Kraft in Schwachheit*, 288-300, esp. 289-292; PENNA, "Power of God", 178-180. Cf. T. SÖDING, "Das Geheimnis Gottes im Kreuz Jesu (1Kor 2,1f. 7ff). Die paulinische

There can be no doubt that we have been justified by Jesus' death on the cross, that in Christ Jesus we have our redemption, that Christ died on the cross for the remission of our sins (cf., e.g., Rom 3,24-25 and 1 Cor 15,3). According to 1 Cor 1,24 Christ himself is "the power of God and the wisdom of God"; according to 1,30 he became for us "wisdom from God, and righteousness and sanctification and redemption". It was in the cross event that God's weakness was stronger than human strength (cf. 1,25). Of course, by way of a paradox, weakness can be called strength (cf. 2 Cor 12,10), just as wisdom is called foolishness in 1 Cor 1,21. But, as a matter of fact, weakness is not strength. God manifested his strength by raising Jesus from the dead. Christ "was crucified in weakness, but lives by the 'power of God'" (2 Cor 13,4).

On the other hand Paul is convinced that the message of the cross, too, contains God's power (cf. 1,18). In 2,4 he writes that his speech and proclamation occurred with a demonstration of the Spirit and power (cf. 2 Cor 4,7). The same was already indicated in 1 Thess 1,5: "our message of the gospel came to you not in word only, but also in power and in the Holy Spirit and with full conviction"; according to 2,13 Paul's word is not really a human word but God's word which is powerful and at work in the believers[19]. In Rom 1,16 Paul states that the gospel is "the power of God for salvation to everyone who has faith". In order to have faith one has to hear. How is one to believe without hearing the proclamation? So "faith comes from what is heard, and what is heard comes through the word of Christ" (Rom 10,17; cf. vv. 14-16). Thus God decided, through the foolishness of Paul's proclamation, to save those who believe (cf. 1 Cor 1,21). In Christ Jesus Paul became the father of the Corinthians through the gospel: διὰ τοῦ εὐαγγελίου ἐγὼ ὑμᾶς ἐγέννησα (1 Cor 4,15b)[20].

It also appears that Christ cannot be separated from God who always has the initiative and, furthermore, that the power of God is not different from his own Spirit, mentioned in 2,4 for the first time in this letter (cf. 1 Thess 1,5).

In conclusion: not only the shift from verse 17b to verse 18a but also the new content of 1,18–2,5 (with its basic contrast of human foolishness

---

Christologie im Spannungsfeld von Mythos und Kerygma", *BZ* 38 (1994) 174-194; "Erweis des Geistes und der Kraft. Der theologische Anspruch der paulinischen Evangeliumsverkündigung und die Anfänge der neutestamentlichen Kanon-Bildung", *Catholica* 47 (1993) 184-200. Both studies are reprinted in ID., *Das Wort vom Kreuzes. Studien zur paulinischen Theologie* (WUNT 93; Tübingen 1997) 71-92 and 196-221.

[19] HECKEL, *Kraft in Schwachheit,* 291, calls "die Verkündigung" (i.e., the word of the cross) "die vermittelnde Ursache".

[20] Of course, not only the spoken word but also Paul's apostolic lifestyle is meant.

and divine wisdom) legitimate its relative distinction from 1,10-17. However, a close consideration of the somewhat hidden logical connection between the two units, especially attention to the motivating function of verse 18, illustrates how, according to Paul, God was powerfully at work in both the cross event and the apostle's message. In verse 17b the purely human dynamic of eloquent wisdom is said to endanger the power of the cross.

6

Paul as example
A Study of 1 Corinthians 4,6-21

1 Cor 4,6-21 can be considered as the last unit of the first major section of the letter (1,10–4,21). Within this passage, a number of questions arise. What is the exact rendering of the verb μετεσχημάτισα in verse 6 and how must we interpret "nothing beyond what is written" in the same verse? Verses 9-13 contain a *peristasis* catalogue which functions quite differently from similar catalogues in 2 Corinthians. In verse 16 Paul calls the Corinthians to imitation of himself. Although this remains basically somewhat unusual, it is not the only time that self-imitation is mentioned in Paul's letters. But what specifically in Paul's conduct should be imitated in 1 Cor 4? Also, what is meant by "the ways of Paul in Christ" (v. 17) which Timothy is to recall to the Corinthian Christians? The threatening tone in verses 19-21, so soon after verses 14-15, is surprising, to say the least. Finally, is it possible to determine in what the Corinthians' realized eschatology did consist (cf. the double ἤδη and the verbs in v. 8)?

In a first reading this study will pay attention to the line of thought and the structure in this passage. In the second part three exegetical notes will be presented. The discussion of Paul's strategy in employing the catalogue of hardships and the appeal for imitation of himself is reserved for the final section.

I. LINE OF THOUGHT AND STRUCTURE

The expression "for your benefit" (δι᾽ ὑμᾶς) of verse 6 sets the tone: the Corinthians should learn from the example of the ministers. In this unit two subdivisions can be distinguished, verses 6-13 and 14-21. In verses 6-13 Paul contrasts community and apostles, puffed up Christians and despised apostles. Immediately afterwards in verses 14-21 he pleads with the Corinthians, his "beloved children" (τέκνα μου ἀγαπητά). He urges them to become imitators of him. For this reason he is sending Timothy who will remind them of his preaching; in addition Paul announces his own coming. The verb φυσιοῦμαι occurs at the beginning (v. 6; cf. καυχάομαι in v. 7 and the other verbs in v. 8) and at the end (vv. 18 and 19) of the unit. In the first subdivision we further segregate verses 6-8 and 9-13, in the second verses 14-17 and 18-21.

Line of Thought

Verses 6-8 begin with ταῦτα δέ, ἀδελφοί[1]. "These things" (ταῦτα) in verse 6 may point to the general principle that a servant of Christ is but a servant whose work will be judged (3,5-15) and of whom it is required to be found trustworthy (4,2). Paul has "transposed" (applied) this principle to Apollos and himself for the benefit of the Corinthian Christians: they should learn from their ministers' place in the plan of God that boasting on behalf of one servant at the expense of another does not make sense. Yet, verses 7-8 no longer explicitly mention boasting about others. Paul attacks the self-certain, self-centered mentality of the Corinthians. In verse 7 he asks pertinent questions about the origin of what they possess. In verse 8, with penetrating irony and biting sarcasm, he ridicules their feelings of over-realized superiority. It would appear that at the end of verse 8 the opposite conclusion to that of verse 6 is reached. The apostles are no longer the example for the community; no, the community is the ideal for the apostles! In verse 6 one clause remains obscure: that you may learn by us "not beyond what is written". Was this a well-known saying in Corinth? Is it an appeal to moderation, or to a basic fidelity to Scripture? Or is the clause, after all, a gloss?

Verses 9-13 provide us with the true, realistic picture of apostolic existence. Verse 9 and verse 13b can be considered as the inclusion of Paul's depiction of what the apostles are (vv. 10-13a). Both these verses say that the apostles have become a spectacle to the world, despised by all. Whereas in verse 9 this miserable condition is ascribed to God's action, in verse 13b it simply appears as the result of human treatment: "like the rubbish of the world, the dregs of all things"[2]. In verse 10 Paul contrasts the apostles and

---

[1] In 1 Cor 1,10–4,21 the vocative ἀδελφοί occurs five more times: 1,10.11.26; 2,1 and 3,1. — This study is dedicated to Karl Kertelge, since many years colleague and friend.

[2] H. MERKLEIN, *Der erste Brief an die Korinther, Kapitel 1-4* (ÖTKNT; Gütersloh–Würzburg 1992) 317, however, thinks that we may consider ἐγενήθημεν in verse

the Corinthians: "we are fools ..., you are wise ...". Verses 11-13a constitute one of the well-known lists of tribulations: Paul depicts the apostolic sufferings, dangers and trials[3]. The style of verses 12b-13a becomes once
more antithetical: "when reviled, we bless ...". Otherwise than in verses 8
and 10 the opposition now is between apostles and the non-Christian
world. "We labor" in verse 12a may point to Paul's apostolic care for other
Christians while the added participle "working" indicates the way he supports himself, or the two verbs refer to the same so-called ignominious
physical efforts.

In *verses 14-17* Paul switches from attacking severity to tender pleading. The affectionate tone is brought about by the 1st pers. sing. as well as
by the wording ("my beloved children"), the imagery ("I became your
father through the preaching of the gospel") and the considerate pleading
itself ("not to make you ashamed but to admonish you"). From this 1st
pers. sing. it also becomes probable that in verses 9-13 Paul was thinking
above all of his own apostolic life-style, not so much of that of his "brother
Sosthenes" (1,1) and the apostles generally. Then, in verse 16 Paul presents
himself explicitly as an example[4]. The Corinthians must imitate his con-

---

13b as a *passivum divinum*; this seems, however, somewhat far-fetched. Cf. K.T. KLEINKNECHT,
*Der leidende Gerechtfertigte. Die alttestamentlich-jüdische Tradition vom 'leidenden Gerechten'
und ihre Rezeption bei Paulus* (WUNT 2/13; Tübingen 1984) 232. Like Merklein (316-317) we
hesitate to find in verse 13b a sacrificial reference. Cf. C. SPICQ, *Notes de lexicographie néo-testa-
mentaire* (OBO 22/b; Fribourg–Göttingen 1978) 681-682: περικάθαρμα, περίψημα. Spicq first
states: "Nul doute que cette nuance d'abjection soit à retenir dans *I Cor.* IV, 13" (681). But there is
also the nuance of "rançon, victime expiatoire": "On ne peut exclure de *I Cor.* IV, 13 cette valeur de
sacrifice par lequel le censé-coupable expie et purifie ceux qui l'offrent. On comprendra donc que
saint Paul, méprisé et rejeté par les hommes, se sacrifie pour eux (*II Cor.* IV, 10sv., VI, 9; *Philip.* II,
17), il accepte d'être une victime expiatoire, et ce faisant il assimile sa fonction d'apôtre à celle du
Christ crucifié et rédempteur (*Gal.* VI, 17; *Col.* I, 24-25" (682).

[3] R. HODGSON, "Paul the Apostle and First Century Tribulation Lists", *ZNW* 74 (1983) 59-
80, counts eight such lists: Rom 8,35; 1 Cor 4,10-13a; 2 Cor 4,8-9; 6,4b-5; 6,8-10; 11,23b-29;
12,10; Phil 4,12. W. SCHRAGE, *Der erste Brief an die Korinther (1Kor 1,1–6,11)* (EKK;
Zürich–Neukirchen/Vluyn 1991) 345, comments on 1 Cor 4,10-13a: "Der Katalog ist ... zunächst eindeutig eine Korrektur der ἤδη-Sätze der Korinther und hat eine anti-enthusiastische
Spitze". For general remarks on the lists of hardships, see recently S.B. ANDREWS, "Too Weak
Not to Lead: The Form and Function of 2 Cor 11.23b-33", *NTS* 41 (1995) 263-276.

[4] The Pauline calls for self-imitation remain strange. Cf., e.g., D. STANLEY, "Imitation in
Paul's Letters: Its Significance for His Relationship to Jesus and His Own Christian
Foundation", P. RICHARDSON–J.C. HURD (eds.), *From Jesus to Paul. FS F.W. Beare* (Waterloo
[Ontario] 1984) 127-141: "... the novelty of the proposal that his hellenstic Christians imitate
himself is cause for surprise in one who repudiated the insinuation of his opponents that he was
seeking to make disciples for himself" (127; a citation of 2 Cor 4,5 follows). See also A.
REINHARTZ, "On the Meaning of the Pauline Exhortation: 'mimêtai mou ginesthe' - 'become
imitators of me'", *StRel* 16 (1987) 393-403, esp. 393-394.

duct and behavior (cf. 11,1: "be imitators of me, as I am of Christ"). In verse 17 Paul connects the sending of Timothy, his "beloved and faithful child in Christ", with his plea: "for this reason I sent you ..."[5]. Timothy will remind the Corinthians of Paul's ways in Christ as Paul teaches these ways everywhere in every church. Notwithstanding the verb "to teach", by "my ways in Christ" Paul probably means not primarily his spoken message but above all his apostolic conduct as it is depicted in verses 9-13.

The manner in which he announces his own proposed visit to Corinth in *verses 18-21* presumably reveals that some Corinthians misinterpreted Paul's absence as lack of courage[6]. The language is again severe and, moreover, not without threat against some arrogant Christians. By employing the verb "to become inflated" (vv. 18-19) and the noun "kingdom" (v. 20), Paul returns to the vocabulary which was prominent at the beginning of the unit (see v. 6 and v. 8). The very end of this paragraph and, at the same time, of the whole major section is rather abrupt: "What would you prefer? Am I to come with a stick, or with love in a spirit of gentleness?"[7]

Discussion of Structural Particularities

The inclusive character of the verb φυσιόω with regard to the whole passage has already been pointed to. In the analysis of style and line of thought one must, of course, pay attention to the presence of δέ and ἀλλά or οὐ... ἀλλά, γάρ and οὖν in several verses, the asyndeta and the nominal clauses.

The rhetorical ingredients of verses 7 and 8 should not go unnoticed. In verse 7 we have three questions, each with the verb in the 2nd pers. sing. and each with τίς or τί. The questions increase in length, one verb, two verbs, three verbs; their recriminative weight equally intensifies:

(1) τίς γάρ σε διακρίνει;
(2) τί δὲ ἔχεις ὃ οὐκ ἔλαβες;
(3) εἰ δὲ καὶ ἔλαβες, τί καυχᾶσαι ὡς μὴ λαβών;

---

[5] Otherwise K.E. BAILEY, "The Structure of I Corinthians and Paul's Theological Method with Special Reference to 4:17", *NT* 25 (1983) 152-181, esp. 160-163.

[6] Otherwise J.T. FITZGERALD, *Cracks in an Earthen Vessel: An Examination of the Catalogues of Hardships in the Corinthian Correspondence* (SBL.DS 99; Atlanta 1988) 127: "The statement ... has absolutely nothing to do with any 'charge' or 'accusation' by the Corinthians". This is hardly correct.

[7] G.D. FEE, *The First Epistle to the Corinthians* (NICNT; Grand Rapids 1987) 1992, sees this verse as "lead-in to the argument that follows".

In verse 7 Paul employs the verb λαμβάνω three times.

In verse 8abc there is a switch to the 2nd pers. plur.: again there are three clauses, the first two commencing with ἤδη, while the last two have an aorist tense. The third one makes explicit the opposition between the Corinthians and the apostles which is also present in the first two:

    (1) ἤδη κεκορεσμένοι ἐστέ·
    (2) ἤδη ἐπλουτήσατε·
    (3) χωρὶς ἡμῶν ἐβασιλεύσατε.

In verse 8de there is a rather devastating play on words:

    καὶ ὄφελόν γε ἐβασιλεύσατε,
    ἵνα καὶ ἡμεῖς ὑμῖν συμβασιλεύσωμεν.

The structural qualities of verses 9-13 are even more remarkable:

```
*       9   δοκῶ γάρ,
            ὁ θεὸς ἡμᾶς τοὺς ἀποστόλους ἐσχάτους ἀπέδειξεν
                ὡς ἐπιθανατίους,
            ὅτι θέατρον ἐγενήθημεν τῷ κόσμῳ
            καὶ ἀγγέλοις καὶ ἀνθρώποις.
a       10  (1) ἡμεῖς μωροὶ διὰ Χριστόν,
                ὑμεῖς δὲ φρόνιμοι ἐν Χριστῷ·
            (2) ἡμεῖς ἀσθενεῖς,                    (α)
                ὑμεῖς δὲ ἰσχυροί·                  (β)
            (3) ὑμεῖς ἔνδοξοι,                     (β)
                ἡμεῖς δὲ ἄτιμοι.                   (α)
b       11  ἄχρι τῆς ἄρτι ὥρας
            (1) καὶ πεινῶμεν       καὶ διψῶμεν
            (2) καὶ γυμνιτεύομεν   καὶ κολαφιζόμεθα
            (3) καὶ ἀστατοῦμεν
        12                        καὶ κοπιῶμεν
            ἐργαζόμενοι ταῖς ἰδίαις χερσίν·
c           (1) λοιδορούμενοι
                                    εὐλογοῦμεν,
            (2) διωκόμενοι
                                    ἀνεχόμεθα,
13a         (3) δυσφημούμενοι
                                    παρακαλοῦμεν·
*       13b ὡς περικαθάρματα τοῦ κόσμου ἐγενήθημεν,
            πάντων περίψημα,
            ἕως ἄρτι.[8]
```

---

[8] See the excellent structural analyses by K.A. PLANK, *Paul and the Irony of Affliction* (SBL Semeia Stud.; Atlanta 1987) 77-86 and FITZGERALD, *Cracks*, 129-132. Fitzgerald introduces his treatment as follows: "Of all Paul's Corinthian catalogues, it is the one in 1 Cor 4

Verses 9 and 13b frame this passage (see *). In verse 9 God is the subject; in verse 13b it is "we". In both verses there is the comparative particle ὡς and the noun κόσμος; in both the public character of the apostles' humble status is stressed. Verses 10-13a consist of three strophes (*a, b, c*), each of them containing a triad. In view of the triadic character of both verses 7 and 8 this is hardly accidental. Several more details should be noted.

In verse 10 (= *a*) Paul uses an antithetical style. Yet, otherwise than in 2 Corinthians 11, e.g., he does not contrast apostles and opponents but apostles and their Corinthian brothers and sisters. Paul indicates how the world judges both groups thus opposed. In (1) the διὰ Χριστόν points to the reason why the apostles are (and prefer to be) "fools". The ἐν Χριστῷ at the end should not mislead us; the Corinthians appear "wise in Christ", but only according to their own superficial opinion[9]. The reader remembers the previous verses, 7 and especially 8. Most probably the two Christ-expressions should mentally be supplied in (2) and (3)[10]. Note further the chiastic construction of (2) and (3). This makes the "we in disrepute" stand at the end of (3); it provides a good transition to the "we"-description of the following strophe[11].

The second and third strophes (*b* and *c*) deal with the apostolic style of life; the Corinthians have disappeared. Verses 11-13a constitute the real center of the *peristasis* catalogue. The beginning ἄχρι τῆς ἄρτι ὥρας (v. 11) — which contentwise belongs to all six following verbs — clearly corresponds with ἕως ἄρτι of verse 13b (end of *c*).

The verbs in verses 11-12a (= *b*) are best taken as three pairs. Hunger and thirst go together; nakedness and blows probably also (attention is given to the fragile body; moreover, the verbs are of equal length); unsettled life and labor are complementary[12.] One notices a shift at the end of the

---

whose structure is the most debated and the least appreciated" (129). See also SCHRAGE, *1 Korinther*, 331 (on 4,6-13): "Der ganze Abschnitt ist rhetorisch sehr kunst- und wirkungsvoll" (brief analysis on p. 333). KLEINKNECHT, *Gerechtfertigte,* Cf. already J. WEISS, "Beiträge zur Paulinischen Rhetorik", *Theologische Studien. FS B. Weiss* (Göttingen 1897) 165-247, esp. 209-210: "Die eindringliche Kraft dieses Passus kann nicht geschildert, sondern muss nachempfunden werden".

[9] Cf. SCHRAGE, *1 Korinther*, 343: "'in Christus' macht die Ironie noch bitterer". See Rom 11,25 and 12,16.

[10] So rightly FITZGERALD, *Cracks*, 130.

[11] Compare 2 Cor 6,8 (part of another *peristasis* catalogue): διὰ δόξης καὶ ἀτιμίας. Paul here applies both terms to himself. Also compare φρόνιμοι, ἰσχυροί, ἔνδοξοι in 1 Cor 4,10 with σοφοί, δυνατοί, εὐγενεῖς in 1 Cor 1,26. H. CONZELMANN, *1 Corinthians* (Hermeneia; Philadelphia 1975) 89, notes: "merely a rhetorical variation without inherent meaning".

[12] Otherwise FITZGERALD, *Cracks*, 132: his arrangement is not 2/2/2, but 3/3 (see also his footnote 38 on the same page).

list in the second strophe, not only regarding the form (added lengthy participle construction) but possibly also insofar as the content is concerned. Κοπιῶμεν is presumably no longer just a painful circumstance; the verb may point to apostolic commitment and much demanding care[13]. At the very least, this verb in the 1st pers. plur., together with the participial expression "working with our own hands", indicate activity. The rather active attitude of the third strophe is thus appropriately announced at the end of strophe *b*[14]. Moreover, the polysyndetic *b* (six καί's) is contrasted with the asyndetic style of *c*[15].

In verses 12b-13a (= *c*) the participles "reviled, persecuted, slandered" depict suffering; the main (personal) verbs refer to the paradoxical reaction of the apostles: "we bless, we endure, we try to conciliate". These personal verbs are more stressed than the participles. Yet "sosehr in den drei Antithesen die *verba finita* den Akzent tragen, sosehr zeigt der Abschluss von V 13, dass Paulus bei aller Betonung des Segnens, Aushaltens und Zuredens die Peristasen selbst als den roten Faden seiner Argumentation ansieht"[16]. As in the second strophe the opposition here lies between apostles and the hostile world. This world is mentioned in the conclusive verse 13b which itself is structured chiastically.

A last structural consideration concerns verses 14-21. In verse 14 Paul addresses the Corinthians as τέκνα μου ἀγαπητά, in verse 15 he explicitly claims to be their "father in Christ Jesus", since through the gospel he gave them new life. It is highly probable that the same father imagery is at the background of verse 21; Paul asks whether he must come to them with a stick or in a spirit of meekness. Both possible ways of acting could be characteristic of a father.

II. THREE EXEGETICAL NOTES

Here follows a brief discussion of three exegetical problems. Within

---

[13] Cf. C.K. BARRETT, *A Commentary on the First Epistle to the Corinthians* (BNTC; London 1968) 112: "We do our Christian service, and at the same time for our support engage in secular work".

[14] Cf. MERKLEIN, *1 Korinther*, 304: the apostolic existence is "durch die Gegenüberstellung von passivem Erleiden und aktivem Verhalten eindrucksvoll profiliert".

[15] Cf. PLANK, *Irony*, 83-84.

[16] SCHRAGE, *1 Korinther*, 348.

the framework of this study no exhaustive investigation can be offered; we limit ourselves to the presentation of a hopefully well-argued understanding of the text. A first consideration is the cluster of difficulties in verse 6. Then, something should be said about the "already" mentality of the Corinthians (see v. 8, but also vv. 6-7 and 10). In the third place we will inquire what it implies for Paul to be the "father" of the Corinthian Christians (see vv. 14-21).

Apostles and Christians

It is difficult to be certain whether the second ἵνα clause of verse 6 directly depends on the main verb of the sentence (μετεσχημάτισα) or is grammatically subordinate to the first ἵνα clause[17]. In the first case one could expect a καί between the two clauses, but its absence is not decisive. Whatever choice is made, we can consider the second clause as a clarification or a (partial) concretization of the first one. However, the two final clauses may be pointing to two somewhat differing, but not completely independent injunctions, regarding, e.g., the wrong personal attitude in verse 6b and the intra-communal strife in verse 6c. Furthermore, as already stated above, since Paul and Apollos have specifically been dealt with in 3,5–4,5, it would seem that in verse 6c Paul speaks not of boasting by one Corinthian against another, but by a Corinthian Christian (εἷς = τις) on behalf of one apostle (ὑπὲρ τοῦ ἑνός, e.g., Paul) at the expense of another (κατὰ τοῦ ἑτέρου, e.g., Apollos)[18].

The interpretation of the first ἵνα clause (v. 6b) cannot but remain uncertain[19]. The gloss hypothesis regarding τὸ μὴ ὑπὲρ ἃ γέγραπται is

---

[17] Cf., e.g., FITZGERALD, Cracks, 120, n. 16: both final clauses depend on the main verb. Otherwise M.D. HOOKER, "'Beyond the Things Which Are Written': An examination of 1 Cor. iv. 6", NTS 10 (1963-64) 127-132: "... we find that the second ἵνα clause appears to depend upon the first, rather than to be co-ordinate with it" (128).

[18] Cf. E.-B. ALLO, Première Epître aux Corinthiens (EtB; Paris [2]1956) 72; MERKLEIN, 1 Korinther, 308-309.

[19] Cf. SCHRAGE, 1 Korinther, 336: There "bleibt eine gewisse Ratlosigkeit"; W.P. DE BOER, The Imitation of Paul. An Exegetical Study (Kampen 1962) 142: "The significance of the phrase ... is most elusive and probably can not be recaptured with certainty by us who are so far removed from the original Corinthian readers". Some recent studies: HOOKER, "Beyond"; FITZGERALD, Cracks, 122-127; P. WALLIS, "Ein neuer Auslegungsversuch der Stelle I. Kor. 4,6", ThLZ 75 (1950) 506-508; A. LEGAULT, "'Beyond the Things Which Are Written' (1 Cor. iv. 6)", NTS 18 (1971-72) 227-231; J.M. ROSS, "Not Above What Is Written: A Note on 1 Cor 4:6", ExpT 82 (1970-71) 215-217; J. STRUGNELL, "A Plea for Conjectural Emendation in the New

best definitively rejected (no textual evidence)[20]. That this expression was a Corinthian "slogan" is unprovable, yet it may have been a "proverbial saying"[21]. We may assume, I think, that the verb γέγραπται refers to Scripture. Because of what the expression itself says ("not above what has been written") and given the proximity of 3,18-23 to 4,6, the two quotations in 3,19 and 20 must be taken into account: "He catches the wise in their craftiness" (Job 5,13) and: "The Lord knows the thoughts of the wise, that they are futile" (Ps 94,11). Of course, the quotations function as proof texts within 3,18-23. What Paul emphasizes in this passage and in 4,1-5 is that the Christians must not deceive themselves; if they think that they are wise in this age, they should become fools so that they may become wise (see 3,18). They should not boast about human leaders (see 3,21) and they should not pronounce judgments before the time, that is, before the Lord comes, who will disclose what is hidden (see 4,5). Therefore the "rule" of 4,6b appears to refer back to 3,18-23 (and, by implication, also to 4,1-5). Moreover, the expression ἐν ημῖν ("so that you may learn 'through me'") in the same verse 6b points to Paul and Apollos mentioned in verse 6a and, through this reference, to the whole preceding unit 3,5–4,5 where Paul reflects on the apostolic position and attitude of both together and each individually. The Christians of Corinth must learn from the example of Paul and Apollos as it is explained at length there. Of course, that unit in turn is connected contentwise with the whole of 1,10–3,4. Whether "what has been written" directly refers also to the more distant citations in that large section is not so certain[22].

What can be said about verse 6a itself and the meaning of ταῦτα and

---

Testament, with a Coda on 1 Cor 4:6", *CBQ* 36 (1974) 343-358; L.L. WELBORN, "A Conciliatory Principle in 1 Cor. 4:6", *NT* 29 (1987) 320-346; C. WOLFF, "'Nicht über das hinaus was geschrieben ist!' 1. Kor. 4,6 in der neueren Auslegungsgeschichte", H. SCHULTZE a.o. (eds.), "... *Das Tiefe Wort erneun*". *FS J. Henkys* (Berlin–Brandenburg 1989) 187-194.

[20] See, e.g., the discussion in WOLFF, "Nicht über das hinaus", 186-187.

[21] Cf. ALLO, *1 Corinthiens*: "une expression consacrée" (72); "un proverbe" and "un dicton" (73). See HOOKER, "Beyond", 132: the elliptical structure, the negative construction, and the introductory τό: these three features suggest "that Paul is here quoting some saying which is known to his readers". The saying is either coined by himself or it is "a misquotation, a deliberate denial of the maxim of others that one *should* go 'beyond the things which are written'".

[22] Otherwise HOOKER, "Beyond", 129. KLEINKNECHT, *Gerechtfertigte*, 224. M. MITCHELL, *Paul and the Rhetoric of Reconciliation: An Exegetical Investigation of the Language and Composition of 1 Corinthians* (HUT 28; Tübingen 1991) 220, n. 183, rightly dismisses two recent "inventive solutions ... for the exegetical crux": (1) according to WELBORN, "Principle", the clause of verse 6b is a conciliatory principle reflecting peace treaty formulae; (2) in the opinion of FITZGERALD, *Cracks*, 122-127, it refers to the ancient mode of tracing letters for learning the alphabet. Fitzgerald is also criticized by WOLLF, "Nicht über das hinaus", 191.

μετασχηματίζω? When we examine the other passages where Paul employs the verb μετασχηματίζω[23], a construction appears which is the opposite of what in verse 6a could be expected. It would run more or less as follows: I have changed myself and Apollos (= my situation and that of Apollos) into the metaphors of gardening and building (see 3,6-17). M.D. Hooker, however, remarks: "but of course Paul and Apollos did not in fact appear in these guises, and the changes are figurative ones. It is the metaphor, and not the outward appearance of Paul, which has been varied"[24]. This is basically correct. But does ταῦτα, the direct object of μετεσχημάτισα in verse 6a, refer to the metaphors alone? It would seem that the whole reasoning and exposition of 3,5–4,5 (and through it indirectly of 1,10–3,4 as well) is taken up by ταῦτα[25]. In the preceding unit Paul "has changed the appearance" of what he aims at "into himself and Apollos". For what as a matter of fact applies to the Corinthians (their factionality, their inflated sense of superiority) is illustrated by what Paul in 3,5–4,5 says about himself and Apollos. In 4,6a he then openly states that, for the benefit of the Corinthians, he "has transferred, transposed" that kind of problem to himself and Apollos, as if it were their own problem[26].

Our understanding differs therefore from the so-called "covert allusion" interpretation recently defended again by B. Fiore and D.R. Hall[27]. Paul would be replacing the names of the wisdom teachers by the names of

---

[23] See 2 Cor 11,13.14.15 and Phil 3,21.

[24] HOOKER, "Beyond", 131. Cf. FEE, *1 Corinthians*, 167: "The context and the emphatic position of 'these things' demand a meaning wherein the figures, not the persons are what have 'changed forms'". Yet Fee explains this as being "from metaphor to metaphor" and neglects, it would seem, the εἰς-construction.

[25] MERKLEIN, *1 Korinther*, 301-302, rather strangely sees in ταῦτα the content of 1,18–2,16 ("die richtige Einschätzung der Verkündiger") which in 3,5–4,5 (= "die Anwendung") has been applied to Paul and Apollos.

[26] Cf. J. WEISS, *Der erste Korintherbrief* (KEK; Göttingen 1910) 101: "Anstatt direkt die Verkehrtheit zu tadeln, die in dem Parteitreiben und in dem φυσιοῦσθαι liegt, und positiv zu schildern, wie die Gemeindeglieder mit einander verkehren sollen, hat er an dem Beispiel 'Paulus und Apollos' gezeigt, wie Christus-Leute in Wahrheit zu einander stehen sollen".

[27] B. FIORE, "'Covert Allusion' in 1 Corinthians 1–4", *CBQ* 47 (1985) 85-102 (Paul is "the prime metaphor" [93-94]); ID., *The Function of Personal Example in the Socratic and Pastoral Epistles* (AnBib 105; Rome 1986) 164-190; D.R. HALL, "A Disguise for the Wise: μετασχηματισμός in 1 Corinthians 4.6", *NTS* 40 (1994) 143-149. J.M. NÜTZEL, "art. μετασχηματίζω", *EDNT II* (1991) 419, rejects the meaning "say something figuratively", but for the wrong reason: "since no figure of speech appears in the preceding context". But the passage 3,6-17 still belongs to the context. Nützel's own hesitant yet hardly convincing proposal is: "say in an unusual way" (unusual because Paul has used himself and Apollos as examples). See also FITZGERALD, *Cracks*, 119-122.

the four heads of the (non existent!) parties: Paul, Peter, Apollos and Jesus[28]. But what he in 3,5–4,5 concretely says about himself and Apollos is, according to 4,6 (δι᾽ ὑμᾶς), meant for (the situation of) all Corinthians. In this sense the content of 3,5–4,5 is only alluding to the persons who in 4,6 are explicitly indicated (although, of course, the text of chapters 1–4 is interspersed with clear informative exhortations regarding the situation of the Corinthians).

Already

If our interpretation of verse 6c is correct (the Corinthians are puffed up in favor of one leader against the other), it must be noted that from verse 7 onward Paul no longer directly attacks the allegiance of the believers to himself or Apollos, but rather their personal attitude and conviction. Of course, factionalism is part and parcel of their conduct. In verses 7-10 Paul ironically and not without bitterness depicts their over-realized superiority. He explains how they are "puffed up", how they go beyond the rule of Scripture, that is, beyond what Scripture permits.

Due attention should be given to the confrontational tone of the questions in verse 7 (2nd pers. sing.). The Corinthians seem to be convinced that they possess special gifts[29]; they boast of them as if these gifts had not been received, not given by God. In verse 8 the "already" aspect of this mentality is attacked. The Corinthians are in the opinion of being already filled (ἤδη and perfect tense); they have become rich (ἤδη and ingressive

---

[28] Cf. HALL, "Disguise", 144: "... when Paul describes the relationship between himself and Apollos, what he is really concerned about is certain unnamed teachers who were at work in the church at Corinth, and competing for the allegiance of the church members". Already F. FIELD, *Notes on Select Passsages of the Greek Testament* (Otium Norvicens 3; Oxford 1881): "... Paul substitutes for the names of the actual parties concerned those of himself, Apollos ...";
A. ROBERTSON–A. PLUMMER, *First Corinthians* (ICC; Edinburgh ²1914) 80-81: "In the present passage there seems to be a reference to the *rhetorical* sense of σχῆμα (= *figura*) to denote a *veiled allusion*. The meaning will be, 'I have transferred these warnings to myself and Apollos for the purpose of a covert allusion, and that for your sakes, that in our persons you may get instruction'". See DE BOER, *Imitation*, 141, on a similar explanation of J.B. Lightfoot.

[29] The translation of verse 7a is: "Who does distinguish you (from your fellow Christians)?" BARRETT, *1 Corinthians*, 107-108, writes: "The answer may be 'no one; for in fact you are not different from your neigbour; you are and can be nothing more than a pardoned sinner'. Alternatively it could be, 'So far as you differ from your neighbour, by possessing special gifts, it is God (not you yourself) who made you differ, since the gifts were given by him; you have nothing therefore to boast of'. The former alternative seems to make better sense".

aorist); they have become kings (again ingressive aorist)[30]. Gifts, additional wisdom and spiritual riches: all this is Christian in essence; in and by itself it is not wrong. What cannot be right, however, is the illusion of being already in full possession. Some Corinthians must have thought that they had already reached perfection. Paul accuses them of holding a realized eschatology which is unwarranted[31].

In verse 10, by referring to them sarcastically as being wise in Christ, strong (in Christ), in honor (because of Christ) and by simultaneously presenting the apostles in the opposite form, Paul reminds the Corinthians of their humble origin as is depicted in 1,26: "not many of you were wise according to wordly standards, not many were powerful, not many were of noble birth"[32]. Seemingly, because of their confidence in false philosophical wisdom and rhetorical skills, they despise the message of the cross and so expose their lack of maturity; as a matter of fact they are still babes in Christ; they are still fleshly (cf. 3,1-4; and see in these verses, over against the ἤδη of 4,6, the "not yet" time indications: οὔπω, ἔτι νῦν and ἔτι). In 4,10 Paul thus again condemns their exaggerated sense of security. The sharp contrast with what the apostles are (4,9-13) cannot but negatively highlight the Corinthians' fallacious feeling of superiority.

---

[30] For the use of ἤδη (and λαμβάνω and compounds) in a context of realized eschatology, see also Phil 3,12: οὐχ ὅτι ἤδη ἔλαβον ἢ ἤδη τετελείωμαι ʿ...

[31] Cf. e.g., BARRETT, 1 Corinthians, 109: "The Corinthians are behaving as if the age to come were already consummated, as if the saints had already taken over the kingdom ...; for them there is no 'no yet' to qualify the 'already' of realized eschatology. In this they are simply mistaken". See ID. in the discussion after the paper of J. McHUGH, "Present and Future in the Life of the Community (1 Cor 4,6-13 in the Context of 1 Cor 4,6-21)", in L. DE LORENZI (ed.), Paolo a una chiesa divisa (1 Cor 1–4) (Benedictina 5; Rome 1980) 177-188 and the discussion on pp. 188-208, esp. 292; CONZELMANN, 1 Corinthians: "... the Corinthian exaltation Christology, in which the moment of receipt is left behind, replaced by the habitual possession of the benefits of salvation" (87); "... the claim to be already perfect" (87); "the Corinthians are convinced that they already have part in God's sovereignty ... in having part in the exalted Christ, i.e., in having the Spirit" (87-88); FEE, 1 Corinthians, 172-174. Cf. also PLANK, Irony, 26-30; A.C. THISELTON, "Realized Eschatology at Corinth", NTS 24 (1977-78) 510-526; A.J.M. WEDDERBURN, "The Problem of the Denial of the Resurrection in I Corinthians xv", NT 23 (1981) 229-241, esp. 233-236: "... if the phrase 'realized eschatology' begs too many questions, it can be claimed that the Corinthians were strongly conscious of being in possession of spiritual blessings now. The language in which that consciousness is expressed is, however, noteworthy" (234). Many exegetes want to localize this often termed "present, realized eschatology" in the Apollos party.

[32] Cf. e.g., PLANK, Irony, 47 and 59.

Paul as Father

The second subdivision (vv. 14-21) is most probably dominated by the father imagery in its entirety: Paul as a father with his admonition and plea in verses 14-17 and Paul as a father with a threatening warning in verses 18-21. On the part of Paul himself there is clearly a self-assertive tone. The father image follows that of servants of Christ and stewards (= the apostles; see 4,1-2; cf. 3,5). Paul's self-assurance has already come to the fore in the way in which he developed the metaphors of gardening and building in 3,6-15. In 3,6 Paul writes: "I planted, Apollos watered, but God gave the growth". In 3,10-11 the affirmation is even stronger: "According to the grace of God given to me, like a skilled master builder I laid a foundation, and another man is building upon it .... No other foundation can any one lay than that which is laid, which is Jesus Christ". Without doubt, Paul knows and says that he is the founder of the church in Corinth.

In 4,15 Paul very much stresses that he is the only father of the Corinthians: "you might have ten thousand guardians in Christ, you do not have many fathers. Indeed, in Christ Jesus I became your father through the gospel". Just as in 3,10 the qualification "according to the grace of God given to me" somewhat weakens Paul's expression of self-confidence, so also in 4,15 the phrases "in Christ Jesus" and "through the gospel" soften to a certain extent Paul's self-confident affirmation. Nonetheless he does not change his opinion: he is the true and only father of the Corinthians (see the emphatic ἐγώ in v. 15). Paul speaks of a begetting to supernatural life by the gospel which he preached. The proclamation caused his hearers to enter into an entirely new life: sanctification by the Spirit, incorporation in Christ, the promise of an eternal inheritance. Paul is a father because he has transmitted to the Corinthians a word of life, a seed which has transformed them into children of God-Father. The gospel message elicits in the hearers a filial response which testifies to the new beings that they have become[33].

Paul compares himself to a father in 1 Thess 2,11: He has exhorted the Thessalonians ὡς πατὴρ τέκνα ἑαυτοῦ[34]. This occurs again in Phil 2,22:

---

[33] Cf. M. SAILLARD, "C'est moi qui, par l'Evangile, vous ai enfantés dans le Christ Jésus (1 Cor 4,15)", *RechScR* 56 (1968) 5-41.

[34] 1 Thess 2,11 is part of one long sentence in the Greek text (vv. 10-12): "You are witnesses, and God also, how pure, upright, and blameless our conduct was toward you believers. As you know, we dealt with each one of you like a father with his children, urging and encouraging you and pleading that you lead a life worthy of God, who calls you into his own kingdom and glory".

Timothy served with me in the work of the gospel ὡς πατρὶ τέκνον ("like a son with a father")[35]. This last passage must strike us, since in 1 Cor 4,17 the same Timothy is called "my beloved and faithful child in the Lord"[36]. The adjective ἀγαπητός and the noun τέκνον are employed separately by Paul elsewhere in his letters[37], but Timothy alone receives the qualification of the combined terms.

In 1 Cor 4,15 Paul literally writes: "in Christ Jesus 'I begot' (ἐγέννησα) you through the gospel". We may compare this with Phlm 10: "I appeal to you for my child, Onesimus, ὃν ἐγέννησα in my imprisonment". One more passage must be mentioned here. In Gal 4,12-20 Paul becomes very emotional. In verses 13-14 he reminds the Galatians of his bodily ailment during the preaching of the gospel, "and though my condition was a trial to you, you did not scorn or despise me, but received me as an angel of God, as Christ Jesus". In verse 19 he then writes: τέκνα μου, οὓς πάλιν ὠδίνω μέχρις οὗ μορφωθῇ Χριστὸς ἐν ὑμῖν. Paul is again in travail; he sees himself as their mother! Paul, father and mother alike[38].

In 1 Cor 4,14-16 Paul links his call for imitation to the relationship of father and child. W.P. de Boer appropriately comments: "From this vantage point (cf. οὖν) Paul makes his great plea to the Corinthians: 'I beseech you, be ye imitators of me' (4,16). As my children, be what children ought to be: be my imitators. As children begotten (4,15), beloved (4,14), fed (3,2), taught (4,6), admonished (4,14) by me, reflect the kind of life you have come to know in your father"[39].

---

[35] In 1 Thess 3,2 Timothy is called τὸν ἀδελφὸν ἡμῶν καὶ συνεργὸν τοῦ θεοῦ.

[36] Cf. the mention of Timothy in 1 Cor 16,10-11.

[37] We may quote the very emphatic address in Phil 4,9: ἀδελφοί μου ἀγαπητοὶ καὶ ἐπιπόθητοι, χαρὰ καὶ στέφανός μου. The adjective ἀγαπητός is often employed in greetings for individual persons, not always combined with ἀδελφός(-οί). Cf. O. WISCHMEYER, "Das Adjektiv ἀγαπητός in den paulinischen Briefen. Eine traditionsgeschichtliche Miszelle", NTS 32 (1986) 476-480. For τέκνον see also 1 Thess 2,7; Gal 4,19; 2 Cor 6,13 and Phlm 10.

[38] See also 1 Thess 2,7. We examine Gal 4,12-20 (also in relation to 1 Cor 4,14-16) in "Like a Mother in the Pain of Childbirth Again: A Study of Galatians 4,12-10", in this volume, pp. 183-199.

[39] DE BOER, Imitation, 146; cf. 214, and also 153: "By imitation the child grows in his likeness to his parents. He catches and adopts something of the essence of his parents. The closer the relationship of parent and child, the more the similarities develop. And this closeness of the relationship is largely determined by the factor of love. Hence, it is not insignificant that Paul refers to the Corinthians as beloved children". For the cultural (Roman) background of the father imagery, see now also E.M. LASSEN, "The Use of the Father Image in Imperial Propaganda and 1 Corinthians 4:14-21", TynB 42 (1991) 127-136.

III. IMITATION

As is well known "imitation" (*Nachahmung*) is not identical to "following" (*Nachfolge*)[40]. The imitators attempt to pattern their life on an example; they are living in the same manner as (*leben wie*) the model. The followers share the life of a master; they are living with (*leben mit; Lebensgemeinschaft*) that person. The disciple never becomes the master; he/she remains a follower. The prepaschal following of Jesus is a paradigm for the postpaschal following of Christ. Such metaphorical following becomes imitation. In 11,1 Paul calls his Corinthian Christians: "Be imitators of me, as I am of Christ". In 4,16 the second christological part is lacking, but therefore, of course, not denied. How does the immediate context of chapter 4 characterize that imitation?

In Paul's second list of hardships, 2 Cor 4,8-9, the apostolic sufferings are seen as a consequence of the union with Christ: "always carrying in the body the death of Jesus, so that the life of Jesus may also be manifested in our bodies" (v. 10)[41]. One can hardly maintain that the same christological depth is present when Paul composes his first list in 1 Cor 4,9-13. Yet it cannot be said that 1 Cor 1–4 is lacking in profound theological meditation. Let us examine precisely how the first list functions in this context.

The Corinthians' Need of Correction

After the epistolary thanskgiving, Paul immediately writes: "I appeal to you, brothers, by the name of our Lord Jesus Christ, that all of you be in

---

[40] For the topic "imitation" in Paul (and the cultural background) see W. MICHAELIS, "art. μιμέομαι ...", *TDNT IV*, 659-674; D.M. STANLEY, "'Become imitators of me': The Pauline Conception of Apostolic Tradition", *Bib* 40 (1959) 859-877; A. SCHULZ, *Nachfolgen und nachahmen. Studien über das Verhältnis der neutestamentlichen Jüngerschaft zur urchristlichen Vorbildethik* (StANT 6; München 1962); DE BOER, *Imitation*; E. GÜTTGEMANNS, *Der leidende Apostel und sein Herr. Studien zur paulinischen Christologie* (FRLANT 90; Göttingen 1966) 190, n. 192 (bibliography). We may recommend De Boer's monograph for the overall treatment of imitation in Paul and its antecedents. The author also refutes the position of Michaelis who in his μιμέομαι-article in *TDNT* submerges the idea of imitation in that of obedience.

[41] Cf. J. LAMBRECHT, "The nekrōsis of Jesus: Ministry and Suffering in 2 Corinthians 4,7-15", R. BIERINGER–J. LAMBRECHT, *Studies on 2 Corinthians* (BETL 112; Leuven 1994) 309-333, esp. 324-332.

agreement and that there be no divisions among you, but that you be united in the same mind and the same purpose" (1 Cor 4,10). A correction is thus needed: mutual agreement, complete unity of mind and thought.

However, the factions and quarrels among the Corinthians betray a deeper evil, their "fleshly" mentality characterized by a wisdom that is thoroughly of this world[42]. Therefore, Paul must deal with the folly of the cross that is God's wisdom, and with the weakness of God that is stronger than merely human effort. Here above all, on this existential level, the Corinthians are in great need of correction. Since Christ died on the cross in weakness, the apostles who are preaching Christ crucified cannot preach that gospel with eloquent wisdom, "lest the cross of Christ be emptied of its power" (1,17). Paul decided to know nothing except Jesus Christ and him crucified, so that the faith of the Corinthians "might not rest on human wisdom but on the power of God" (2,5). Moreover, in 1,18-31 Paul stresses the paradoxical way of God's election. God chose what was foolish in this world, and what was weak, low and despised. So no place is left for any human pride in the presence of God. And in 3,18 he repeats: "Do not deceive yourselves. If you think that you are wise in this age, you should become fools so that you may become wise".

The Appeal to Imitate

In 1 Cor 4,6-21 another consideration is added. After Paul stated in verse 6 that his argument of 3,5–4,5 (and of what precedes) was carried out for the benefit of the Corinthians, that is, that they may learn by his example and that of Apollos not to go beyond what is written, he opposes in sharp, ironical terms "puffed up" Christians and despised ministers (4,7-13). However, immediately afterwards, not without deep emotion, he pleads with his "beloved children" (vv. 14-15) and appeals to them: "be imitators of me" (v. 16)[43]. The apostolic existence thus becomes the concrete example to be imitated by the Corinthians. It would seem that the catalogue of sufferings (vv. 9-13) is presented as exemplary conduct. It

---

[42] SCHRAGE, *1 Korinther*, 352, rightly remarks that we must pay attention not only to "die Parteiungen" but also to "die tiefer sitzende Desorientierung durch die Weisheitsüberschätzung ..., die auch die Überbewertung der Weisheitslehrer sowie eine Abwertung des Apostels nach sich zog". Cf. ID., "Das apostolische Amt des Paulus nach 1 Kor 4,14-17", A. VANHOYE (ed.), *L'apôtre Paul. Personnalité, style et conception du ministère*" (BETL 83; Leuven 1986) 103-119, esp. 103.

[43] Cf. B. SANDERS, "Imitating Paul: 1 Cor 4:16", *HTR* 74 (1981) 353-363.

must be asked whether this is its only or primary function. However, it is first necessary to make some clarifications and distinctions in regard to imitation in 4,6-21.

a) We can hear a first call to imitation in verse 6b: "that you may learn 'through us'". Due attention should be paid to the expression δι᾽ ὑμᾶς at the end of verse 6a and ἐν ἡμῖν at the beginning of verse 6b[44]. Despite the lack of imitation vocabulary the idea itself is nonetheless present. In verses 6-13 Paul employs the 1st pers. plur.[45] and in the first place refers to himself and Apollos, both explicitly mentioned in verse 6. The tone in these verses is — as we know — sarcastic, full of rebuke. Shaming, however, is not Paul's real aim (cf. v. 14). His intentions are clearly expressed by the double final clause in verse 6.

If it is now asked what, in the context of verses 6-13, the Corinthians must imitate, one is directed by the ταῦτα of verse 6a to Paul's exposé of 3,5–4,5. In this unit Paul explains what it means to be a servant and a steward (cf. 3,5: διάκονοι, and 4,1: ὑπερέτας Χριστοῦ καὶ οἰκονόμους θεοῦ). Not only must the Corinthians regard Paul and Apollos correctly, that is, as servants and stewards, they must also apply their insights on the true apostolic identity to themselves and imitate the apostolic way of life (see 3,18-23 and 4,6bc). To be sure, the picture which Paul draws of these ministers in 4,9-13 is firstly meant polemically, as a shaming counterpart of the arrogance which some Corinthians manifest. This *peristasis* category, however, cannot be separated from what Paul has explained in 3,5–4,5; it is, as it were, the concretization of the theory contained in that unit. Therefore, the list of hardships also possesses an exemplifying and admonitory function[46]. Paul presents himself and Apollos as examples. The Corinthians should learn from them and their concrete apostolic existence what is entailed by "not to go beyond what is written" (4,6b).

b) As already stated above, the tone of verses 14-21 is completely dif-

---

[44] Cf. FITZGERALD, *Cracks*, 147: Paul's "use of *synkrisis* serves to heighten the catalogue's admonitory function"; and: "The irony is profound, and it is designed to prompt the Corinthians to make a radical reassessment of their present status".

[45] See verses 6b and 8-13 (there is one 1st pers. sing. at the beginning, in v. 6a). In verse 6bc the "we" points to Paul and Apollos. But who are the "we-apostles" in verses 8-13? Apollos is certainly not included; he is never called an "apostle". According to MERKLEIN, *1 Korinther*, 312, one must "zunächst an Paulus selbst ... denken .... Das schliesst eine generalisierende Tendenz nicht aus .... Nicht das Individuum, sondern die apostolische Existenz steht im Vordergrund".

[46] Cf. FITZGERALD, *Cracks*, 122 and 147-148. HODGSON, "Paul", 65; MERKLEIN, *1 Korinther*, 306; SCHRAGE, *1 Korinther*, 333 and 341.

ferent[47]. Although ταῦτα in verse 14 most probably refers back to verses 6-13, there is a sudden shift in this verse. From now on Paul uses the 1st pers. sing. He clarifies his real intention and pleads with the Corinthians: "I am not writing this to make you ashamed, but to admonish you as my beloved children". In verse 15 he develops the father imagery and stresses: "in Christ Jesus I became your father through the gospel". He therefore is entitled to urge[48] them: μιμηταί μου γίνεσθε ("be and remain [present tense!] imitators of me", v. 16). That 1st pers. sing. cannot but strike the reader. Paul no longer includes Apollos or other apostles. He becomes very personal. The question must therefore be raised a second time as to how this imitation must be seen. What exactly in Paul must be imitated?

While reading verses 14-16 one has, of course not forgotten the catalogue of verses 9-13. Although the catalogue is composed in the 1st pers. plur., the reader suspects Paul's more personal autobiography. In writing those verses Paul had chiefly his own apostolic experiences and tribulations in mind. Now, in verse 16, he appeals to his beloved children to imitate that type of existence[49]. Yet, we may ask whether Paul only thinks of suffering, persecution and dishonor as a program to be imitated. Most probably not. In verse 17 he recalls his sending of Timothy who will "remind you of my ways in Christ, as I teach them everywhere in every church". By using the expression τὰς ὁδούς μου τὰς ἐν Χριστῷ and adding to it καθὼς πανταχοῦ ἐν πάσῃ ἐκκλησίᾳ διδάσκω Paul not only creates a certain tension between his personal exemplary life and a perhaps more general traditional teaching, he also as it were broadens the horizon. More is meant than specific difficulties encountered by the apostle in Corinth; it is the whole Christian way of life — the same taught in every church — which Paul puts forward as a model for conduct[50].

---

[47] MERKLEIN, *1 Korinther*, 323, however, argues that verse 14 does not bring a "Stimmungsumschlag". Yet the admonishing and urging in verses 14-16 are a tender pleading.

[48] Whether the presence of παρακαλῶ in verse 16 forms an inclusion with the same verb in 1,10 — as often is maintained — is not so certain. SCHRAGE, "Amt", 111, however, writes: "In 1 Kor 1,10 folgt auf das παρακαλῶ darum ἀδελφοί und hier sind eben τέκνα μου ἀγαπητά angeredet".

[49] Cf. MERKLEIN, *1 Korinther*, 327.

[50] Cf. FEE, *1 Corinthians*, 186-187; "... especially from what is said further in verse 17, the concern is now also being raised to the much broader level of their behavior in general, as is reflected throughout the rest of the letter". It would seem that in his explanation SCHRAGE, *1 Korinther*, 360, remains somewhat one-sided through his emphasis on the *theologia crucis*: "Die ὁδοί sind also, pointiert formuliert, Wegweisungen im Zeichen des Kreuzes, Konkretisierungen des Kreuzesweges in indikativischen wie imperativischen Ausformungen,

The Function of the List of Hardships

By way of conclusion we repeat that the *peristasis* catalogue of verses 9-13 has an exemplary function because of the two calls to imitation, the indirect one in verse 6 and the explicit other in verse 16. Of course, its primary function in the context of verses 6-13 is to offer a counter-picture of the apostles' existence over against that of the Corinthians; but this does not exclude a complementary paradigmatic use[51].

A second conclusion can be drawn. Although in both subdivisions, verses 6-13 and 14-21, Paul certainly intends this list also as model for imitation, in each of them the list is not the complete model. There is in two instances a widening, a broadening. In 3,5–4,5, the unit immediately preceding 4,6, Paul explains the very essence of the apostolic identity and its true "spirituality"; it is the example from which the Corinthians must learn. This is no doubt more inclusive than the paradigmatic program of the list. Similarly, in 4,17 Paul refers to what he has been teaching everywhere in all churches. This overall Christian lifestyle, not just the particular conduct of Paul and the apostles, has to be followed and adopted. Thus again an amplification is added to the list.

A final conclusion concerns Paul's threefold insistence. By means of the letter — its arguments and exhortations, its explicit appeals and pleas — Paul certainly wants to urge his call for imitation. The letter itself is his actual effort. He employs, however, a second means. He sends Timothy, his "beloved and faithful child in the Lord" as a personal substitute. Timothy must remind the Corinthians of Paul's ways in Christ; he must thus urge them to imitate the founder of their church (v. 17) A last means of insistence consists of Paul's announcement of his coming "soon". The tone in verses 18-21 is severe and threatening. In that visit there will be a decisive confrontation. Paul will find out what the power of those "puffed up" people really is. Yet, he leaves his future way of acting to their choice: "What would you prefer? Am I to come to you with a stick, or with love in a spir-

---

die 'in Christus Jesus' ihren Ort haben, weil sie vom Heilsgeschehen in Tod und Auferweckung Jesus Christi bestimmt sind (vgl. Röm 14,9 u.ö.)"; cf. ID., "Amt", 112-118. See also the good discussion in DE BOER, *Imitation*, 146-152: "Paul saw himself as teaching in the personal example which he set. Paul's ways are his personal conduct, the ways he lived as a Christian, the example of the Christian way of life which he set" (152). This author emphasizes — perhaps too much — Paul's personal experiences.

51 Although W.D. SPENCER, "The Power in Paul's Teaching (1 Cor 4:9-20)", *JETS* 32 (1989) 51-61, seems to simply identify suffering and power in Paul, he rightly stresses that "Paul uses his own example, his own afflicted body as didactic model ...".

it of gentleness?" (v. 21). The Corinthians should make up their mind[52].

God's wisdom and power has ordained that the apostles, like God's Son Christ-crucified himself, cannot use "fleshly" wisdom and power. And so, weakness, persecution and being despised belong intrinsically to the apostolic vocation. Yet —this should be duly recognized — in 4,6-21 Paul uses the catalogue of hardships not, it would seem, to prove his unity with Christ, but in the first place to shame the arrogant Christians and further also to provide them, his spiritual children, with an example. For Paul, that exemplarity apparently is an essential part of the comprehensive Christian lifestyle. Of course, in the final analysis imitation of Paul is no more than mediated imitation of Christ: "Be imitators of me, as I am of Christ" (1 Cor 11,1); or, even better, imitators of Paul *and* of the Lord (cf. 1 Thess 1,6).

---

[52] Cf. DE BOER, *Imitation*, 143.

Gregorianum 77 (1996) 333-339

7

Universalism in 1 Corinthians 8,1–11,1

In 1 Cor 8,1–11,1 we have the fourth major section in Paul's first letter to the Corinthians[1]. In these three chapters Paul deals with meat sacrificed to idols. The question was probably raised in the letter which is mentioned in 7,1. The concentric structure of this section is evident: A (ch. 8), B (ch. 9) and A' (ch. 10). In between units A and A', which both treat the issue itself, unit B (Paul's renunciation as example) is inserted[2].

Paul's basic position in this section is that Christians, because they know that idols do not exist (8,4-6), are free to eat consecrated meat (8,9; 10,27). Yet no matter how much knowledge and freedom are justly valued, love of the weak fellow believers may require a renunciation of rights (8,7-13; 10,28). As a matter of fact Paul deals with a double danger, not only the danger of lack of love through contempt for the scrupulous Christian, but also that of idolatry. True, idols do not exist, but demons do, and participation in the pagan cult constitutes idolatry, i.e., communion with demons (10,14.19-21).

---

[1] The first letter to the Corinthians begins with the usual salutation (1,1-3) and thanksgiving (1,4-9). It ends with exhortations and greetings (16,13-24). Within the body of the letter very divergent materials are discussed. A strictly conceptual development does not seem to underlie the composition. There is hardly any logical progression of thought and reasoning. Paul deals successively with a varied range of subjects. At least, this is our first impression. The following eight major sections can easily be distinguished: 1,10–4,21 (divisions); 5,1–6,20 (a case of immorality; lawsuits; laxity); 7,1-40 (marriage and unmarried life); 8,1–11,1 (the eating of food offered to idols); 11,2-34 (dress at public prayer; abuses at the Lord's supper); 12,1–14,40 (variety of spiritual gifts); 15,1-58: (the future bodily resurrection of Christians); 16,1-12 (the collection and travel plans).

[2] Regarding structure three notes may be added. (1) Already in 8,13 Paul epmloys the 1st pers. sing.; this verse prepares for chapter 9. (2) Next to the positive example of Paul one finds, in 10,1-13, the negative, warning example of Israel in the desert; one could, therefore, maintain that the B-part consists of the whole of 9,1–10,13. (3) At the very end of the exposé, in 10,33–11,1, Paul again utilizes the autobiographical 1st pers. sing. and calls for imitation.

Although the discussion is clearly intra-communal, some of Paul's incidental remarks reveal his view of the other religions as well as his missionary attitude. In this contribution we will first give a brief analysis of the text; then comes a reflection upon the data and, at the end, a conclusion.

I. ANALYSIS

In a first reading, describing the characteristics of the three main parts of the section, particular attention will be paid to those passages which are relevant to our topic.

8,1-13: Knowledge and Love

In this first unit (A) Paul's reasoning proceeds in three steps. First he opposes knowledge and love (vv. 1-3). Then he emphasizes the non-existence of idols as well as the existence of only one God and one Lord (vv. 4-6). Both these parts are introduced by a similar clause with "concerning", "food offered to idols" and "we know".

The longer third part (vv. 7-13) deals with the avoidance of scandal. The weak believers who do not possess sufficient knowledge can be led to fall by those who do possess knowledge and sit at table in an idol's temple (vv. 7-13).

Verses 4-6 deal with knowledge and faith-certainty. It is not at all certain, I think, that in verse 4 Corinthian slogans are cited. What is stated in this verse could quite probably be what Paul fully admits. If so, it already is part of his reaction: idols have no real existence; there is but one God. Paul qualifies that initial reaction in the long sentence consisting of verses 5-6.

Grammatically speaking verse 5a is a concessive clause: although there may be so-called gods ...; but in verse 5b Paul corrects what could be seen as a hesitation and adds: as indeed there are many gods and many lords. These gods and lords are, of course, not the idols; they are really existing demons (see 10,20-21). The addition of "lords" in verse 5 prepares for the naming of the "Lord, Jesus Christ" in the following verse.

Verse 6 contains the main clause. Paul here utilizes and combines traditional formulae from the creed or the baptismal confession. The parallelism between "one God, the Father" and "one Lord, Jesus Christ" is striking. Christ is proclaimed as the preexistent mediator of all things in creation as well as the mediator of "us (Christians)" in redemption[3].

9,1-27: Paul's Example

At first sight chapter 9 (= B) looks like an interruption, somewhat of a digression. Yet its function within the argument is to provide an example which can be compared with the renunciation that is asked from the "knowing" Corinthians. In Corinth Paul preached the gospel free of charge; he renounced his right to obtain a living by it. On the basis of content we distinguish two subdivisions, each introduced by the term "free": verses 1-18 (self-defence) and verses 19-27 (adaptation and personal salvation). In presenting himself as an example Paul offers a number of considerations which could be considered as somewhat deviating from the proper subject: the reasons in favor of living by the gospel (vv. 7-14), boasting and reward (vv. 15-18), the way Paul becomes all things to all (vv. 19-23), and the strict discipline which Paul imposes on himself in order not to be disqualified at the end (vv. 24-27). One might well ask: does Paul, in what appears to be a very personal self-defence, still have in view the concrete problem of the letter, i.e, meat offered to idols?

Verses 19-23 are of relevance to our theme. They may be taken together with verses 24-27, although the two passages are quite different. In the first passage Paul deals with his own missionary adaptation to specific situations; in the second, he speaks an exhortative language regarding the life of the Christian and that of himself. Yet verse 23b, the end of the first subdivision, constitutes a transition to the second: Paul has in mind his own salvation. Final salvation is the theme of verses 24-27[4].

The structure of verses 19-23 is very ingenious. Verse 19 corresponds with verse 22b and together they form an inclusion: see "all" in both verses, and compare "that I might win the more" (v. 19) with "that I might by all means save some" (v. 22b). Verse 19 announces Paul's main thesis of missionary adjustment: although I am free from all, I have made myself a slave of all, that I might win the more. Four concretizations follow and are

---

[3] Three times in verse 6 the first person plural is employed: "we Christians".

[4] What Paul states positively in verse 23b (that I may share in the blessings of the gospel) he expresses negatively in verse 27b (lest I myself should be disqualified). One should also notice that the idea of "slavery" in verse 19 (lit.: "I have enslaved myself") is taken up in verse 27 (lit.: "I lead my body into slavery").

elaborated: Jews, those under the law, those outside the law, and the weak (vv. 20-21). The category of "those under the law" after "Jews" is somewhat surprising (basically the same group!), but we must pay due attention to the typically Pauline added correction: "though not being myself under the law". A similarly important correction is also present in the following phrases: "not being without law toward God but under the law of Christ". The mention of "the weak", the fourth concretization, demonstrates that Paul has not forgotten the topic of the whole section (see the use of this term in ch. 8). Another remarkable stylistic characteristic is the presence of seven purpose clauses: the first five with the missionary verb "to win", the sixth with the more theological verb "to save". The seventh and last purpose clause ends on a sudden shift. The missionary aim is still explicit in verse 23a ("I do it all for the sake of the gospel"), but then, in verse 23b, Paul adverts to his own destiny, his participation in the blessings of the gospel[5].

10,1–11,1: No Partnership with Demons

In the first half of chapter 10 (= A') Paul pays attention to the dangers which threaten the Corinthian Christians, especially the "knowing" among them. Only in 10,23 does he return to the theme dealt with in chapter 8 (= A). Paul begins the chapter with a midrash on the negative example of the ancestors of Israel in the desert (vv. 1-13). Paul's main fear with regard to the Corinthian Christians is their (probably sacramental) overconfidence: "So if you think you are standing, watch out that you do not fall" (v. 12).

"Therefore, my beloved, flee from idolatry" (v. 14). Three times in verses 14-22 Paul appeals to the judgment of the Corinthians who are addressed as sensible, reasonable people: verse 15 ("judge for yourselves what I say"); verse 18 ("consider Israel 'according to the flesh'"); and

---

[5] This desire for participation in the blessings of the gospel makes Paul aware that final salvation will not be so easy. The body has to be disciplined; self-control is needed. Two athletic metaphors are employed in verses 24-27: running and boxing. The Corinthians must have been familiar with them since the Isthmian games took place in their region. From the 2nd pers. plur. in verse 24 ("do you not know .... So run that you may obtain the prize") Paul changes to the 1st pers. plur. in verse 25 ("we must receive an imperishable wreath"), and, in verse 26-27, to the autobiographical 1st pers. sing. In chapter 10, however, he will return to his addressees by means of the 2nd pers. plur., and an example which is taken from Israel's past. With "so that after proclaiming to others I myself should not be disqualified" (v. 27) the long self-defensive digression, the example of Paul, ends rather strangely.

verse 19 ("what do I say?" that is, "what do I mean, imply?"). They must consider and compare the eucharist, the Jewish sacrifices, the pagan worship. What is going on in these rites? The basic concept which Paul brings forward here is participation, partnership through sharing in worship. Partaking creates communion, either with Christ (and the other Christians) or with the demons. A compromise is impossible. Just as he did in 8,4-5, so also in verse 19 Paul stresses the nonexistence of idols. Yet, although the other gods are but demons, demons really exist: "What do I imply then? ... that an idol is anything? No, I imply that what pagans sacrifice, they sacrifice to demons and not to God" (vv. 19-20)[6]. The final questions in verse 22a contain a serious warning: we should not provoke God by idolatrous behavior.

10,23–11,1 constitutes the conclusion of the three chapters. Verses 23-24 and verses 32-33 form an inclusion of the unit: compare their content and also the wording (beneficial, to seek not one's own good but the benefit of the other/the many). Verse 23 repeats a saying (a slogan in Corinth?) which we already know from 6,12. Paul's comment pleads for consideration for the scrupulous believers. Yet in what follows he also strongly emphasizes the freedom of those who possess knowledge and judge correctly. Two situations are brought forward: one buys food (v. 25) and one is invited for a meal by an unbeliever (in his house?) (v. 27). Twice it is clearly stated: "eat ... without raising any question on the ground of conscience". Verse 26 adduces a citation from Ps 24,1 as motivation. In verses 28-29a Paul deals with the possible exception: your action scandalizes the conscience of either the unbeliever or the weak believer. But in verses 29b-30 Paul, employing the 1st pers. sing., again reflects upon Christian freedom and defends it against the objections of the weak. Then verses 31-32 conclude beautifully with a generalization containing the double rule: God's glory (cf. 6,20b) in freedom, yet no offence against the other! In 10,33–11,1 there is a rather surprising addition. Paul returns to the topic of his own behavior which he has depicted in chapter 9; he expresses once more his missionary consideration for "the many, that they may be saved" (v. 33). His appeal is daring, almost provocative: "Be imitators of me, as I am of Christ" (11,1)[7].

In this large, variegated section devoted to "meat offered to idols" the

---

[6] In chapter 8 the term δαιμόνιον is not employed. It occurs four times in 10,20-21, never elsewhere in the undisputed letters of Paul.

[7] We have the first part of this appeal in 4,16 (cf. Gal 4,12; Phil 3,17; 1 Thess 1,6 and 2,14).

knowledge of the mature Christians is fully recognized, but what is stressed is that it has to give way to love of the weak fellow believer. Love is more important, it builds up (cf. 8,1).

II. REFLECTION

From our first reading two items require further comment: Paul's negative vision of the pagan religions and his apostolic zeal to save as many people as possible. The first item is clearly present in 8,4-6, the second more specifically in 9,19-23. Both items recur in chapter 10, especially in verses 14-22, 26-27 and 32-33.

The Danger of Idolatry

In 8,4-6 Paul distinguishes between idols and "so-called gods in heaven and earth". Idols have no "real" existence; they are nothing. This basic insight functions in Paul's defence of the freedom of Christians. Yet there are many gods and lords; they are demons (see 10,19-20). One cannot doubt the nefarious existence of demons. Paul stresses that for Christians there is only one God and Father, beginning and end of their life (cf. 10,26: "the earth is the Lord's, and everything in it"). There is only one Lord, Jesus Christ, the mediator in creation and redemption. That is the Christians' fundamental belief and confession. Christian monotheism and pagan worship of gods (who in fact are demons) and lords cannot go together.

Not only is Christian faith here defined over against gentile superstition, but the Old Testament confession of the one God–Creator is also expanded. For Christians Jesus Christ is the one Lord–Mediator in the creation of the whole universe, as well as in our personal ongoing existence. This renewed, typically Christian confession is decidedly universalistic in outlook.

In 10,1-22 Paul warns his Corinthian Christians against idolatry. During their wandering in the desert some of the Israelites have become idolaters. Scripture portrays the events and in this way instructs us: the Israelites serve as an example. "So if you think you are standing, watch out that you do not fall" (v. 12); "flee from the worship of idols" (v. 14). Paul has not forgotten what he had stated in chapter 8; he repeats: idols do not really exist; they are nothing (10,19). But the danger is communion with the really existing demons: "I do not want you to be partners with demons. You cannot drink the cup of the Lord and the cup of demons. You cannot partake of the table of the Lord and the table of demons". Moreover, idolatry is not simply cult. Just as in the case of those Israelites in the desert (see 10,8-10), so also for us worship of idols would lead to immorality and testing of God. Paul asks in 10,22: "Shall we provoke the Lord to jealousy?"

Paul's evaluation of gentile religion is thus thoroughly negative. For Christians, "on whom the end of the ages have come" (10,11), there is no compromise possible. Becoming a believer involves a radical and definitive separation. Christians have said goodbye to their gentile past. They should be sensible people: worshiping the Father and Jesus Christ excludes partnership with the demons (cf. 10,20-21).

Paul the Missionary

In chapter 9 Paul explains that he did not use his apostolic rights to earn his living by the gospel. In Corinth he worked with his own hands. In depicting this behavior Paul presents himself as an example for the Corinthians. For the sake of love of the weak fellow Christians they, too, should give up part of their freedom and, in certain circumstances, not eat meat sacrificed to idols. Then, in 9,19, Paul suddenly broadens the horizon: "Though I am free with respect to all, I have made myself a slave to all, so that I might win more of them". Paul visibly is and remains the apostle of the Gentiles. His missionary vocation brings with it a far-reaching adaptation: "I have become all things to all people, that I might by all means save some. I do it all for the sake of the gospel ..." (vv. 22-23). Paul is convinced that his call possesses a universalistic dimension.

In 10,31-33 he returns to the same theme. The reference to his exemplary conduct is not absent, but here he begins with an exhortation: "Whether you eat or drink or whatever you do, do everything for the glory of God. Give no offense to Jews or to Greeks or to the church of God, just as I try to please everyone in everything I do, not seeking my own advantage, but that of many, so that they may be saved". The conclusion of this passage reminds us of the last clauses of 9,19 and 22. Of course, in chapter 10 Paul's main concern is that the Corinthians should not become idolaters and that the "weak" should not be scandalized and destroyed by those "who know". Yet almost spontaneously his missionary zeal comes to the forefront.

In 10,32 Paul refers to the existence of Jews, Greeks and Christians. This awareness, however, is neither a static approval of this situation of diversity nor, even less, any recognition whatsoever of another way of salvation. In him lives an irresistible dynamism of evangelization. He is "called to be an apostle of Christ Jesus by the will of God" (1,1). For Paul, salvation is by definition universal; it is meant for the whole of humankind. Yet salvation occurs through Christ, and through Christ alone. For Paul, Christ is the unique Savior and only the believers, that is, those who have become Christians, constitute the universal, worldwide "church of God" (10,32).

III. CONCLUSION

In 1 Cor 8–10 Paul's vision no doubt is universalistic, but his universalism is decidedly "Christian". All peoples are called to belong to Christ and so, through Christ, secure their salvation. This is Paul's innermost conviction.

Our conclusion can be brief. For a balanced evaluation of Paul's position today three important considerations should be kept in mind. Firstly, what Paul is writing in this major section of 1 Corinthians is addressed to fellow Christians, not to Gentiles. Moreover, Paul is a Christian missionary full of zeal, completely given to his evangelizing vocation. Can we presume that, in proclaiming the gospel to the Gentiles, the real Paul has been as "open-minded" as the Lukan Paul in Acts 17,16-34? Our analysis of the text does not rule out that view.

Secondly, although in this section Paul strongly defends Christian liberty and although his stand regarding meat offered to idols is surprisingly liberal, Paul's legitimate fear is that Corinthian Christians may eventually, through sacrifice in pagan cult, become partners with demons and, even though their knowledge is genuine, they may be lacking in love and without consideration for the conscience of "weak" fellow Christians. Paul reminds his readers of the right principle: "Knowledge puffs up, but love builds up" (8,1).

Thirdly, neither the question concerning the salvific value of other authentic religions nor that of the salvation of innumerable people (in past, present and future times) without knowledge of Christ were actually asked by Paul. These questions simply did not enter his horizon; they should, however, duly be investigated in theology today. Much more than before many Christians realize their minority position and, confronted with the existence of other religions, are in doubt about the ways of their God who desires everyone to be saved (cf. 1 Tim 2,4).

8

Three Brief Notes on 1 Corinthians 15

Several questions arise with regard to the beginning and ending of 1 Corinthians 15. Paul first focuses his attention on Christ's past resurrection in order to ground the future resurrection of the departed Christians which is discussed further in the chapter. A double question must be asked. Did the Christians in Corinth believe in Christ's resurrection without any doubt? What most likely is the nature of the denial of future resurrection to which Paul refers? At the end of the chapter Paul appears to assume that he himself and others will not die before the parousia. Does the attention to the living reflect a shift in his thought and is there a common destiny for the dead and the living at the second coming of Christ?

Far from constituting a complete treatment of these questions this contribution provides only three brief notes. They are also meant to be "simple" in the sense that they will be uncomplicated and easily understood. They present modest positions which try to avoid excessive reconstructions and overly speculative hypotheses. The bibliographical references are in no way exhaustive. The first note re-reads 15,1-11 and deals with the Corinthians' faith in the resurrection of Christ. The second note will consider 15,12 once more and ask what the denial of the resurrection of the dead most probably signifies. In the third note, by directing our attention especially to 15,50-58, we will look at the future which Paul indicates for those Christians who are still alive at the parousia[1].

I. THE RESURRECTION OF CHRIST

Paul deals with the past resurrection of Christ in vv. 1-11 and employs

---

[1] The biblical quotations in these Notes are taken from the Revised Standard Version, more literal than most other modern translations.

it as the ground for asserting the future resurrection of the dead. It is commonly assumed that faith in Christ's resurrection was a solid fact in Corinth; it had only to be recalled. But was there no doubt about Christ's resurrection? Did all Christians in Corinth really (and easily) believe that Christ had been raised? Some details of chapter 15 may indicate that Paul had to defend the traditional faith. We bring together here reflections already made by different authors.

Wavering Faith?

A Christian who claims that there is no resurrection of the dead (cf. v. 12) could possibly include Christ among the dead or will probably sooner or later begin to doubt the past resurrection of Christ.

By means of the long list of witnesses in vv. 6-8 Paul seems to want to prove the reality of Christ's resurrection[2]. Verse 6 merits a special mention: Christ appeared to more than 500 brothers at one time; most of them are still alive, though some have fallen asleep[3]. One is tempted to assume that Paul implies: you yourselves can still ask them. Is all this not pointing to the Corinthians' lack of faith in the resurrection of Christ[4]?

---

[2] See W. SCHRAGE, "I. Korinther 15:1-11", in L. DE LORENZI (ed.), *Résurrection du Christ et des chrétiens (1 Cor 15)* (Benedictina 8; Rome 1985) 21-45: "Nur wenn nach Meinung des Paulus die Auferstehung Jesu in Korinth *nicht* mehr über allen Zweifel erhaben ist, erhält nach meinen Verständnis auch die Erweiterung der Zeugenliste in V. 6ff durch Paulus ihre Plausibilität und ihren Sinn" (25), and: "Mir scheint ..., dass Paulus den Glauben an die Auferstehung Jesu keineswegs so unumstösslich voraussetzt, wie meist angenommen wird" (26; see also p. 42). Cf. R.F. COLLINS, *First Corinthians* (SP; Collegeville 1999) 526: "Some of those who denied the resurrection of the dead may also have denied the resurrection of Jesus" (but also see p. 542).

[3] The last clause of v. 6 (lit.: "but some have fallen asleep") is corrective but hardly constitutes the main point. The comment on v. 6ab by J. KREMER, *Der erste Brief an die Korinther* (RNT; Regensburg 1997) appears somewhat far-fetched: "Da es ähnliche (freilich jüngere) jüdische Beteuerungsformeln gibt ..., stellt sich die Frage, ob dieser Zusatz bloss eine rhetorische Formel ist, um damals auf eine für den heutigen Leser sehr ungewöhnliche Weise die Wahrheit der Erscheinung selbst zu betonen" (331).

[4] B. SPÖRLEIN, *Die Leugnung der Auferstehung. Eine historisch-kritische Untersuchung zu 1 Kor 15* (BU 7; Regensburg 1971), 55-63, examines the data of the preceding two paragraphs and, moreover, the fact that in v. 12 "is preached" is used and not "you believe" (cf. our fourth paragraph on Sider). Although he writes "diese Beobachtungen zusammengenommen lassen es tatsächlich als möglich erscheinen, dass eine Gruppe innerhalb der korinthischen Christengemeinde mit der allgemeinen Totenauferstehung auch die Tatsächlichkeit einer

A. Robertson and A. Plummer comment on γνωρίζω in v. 1: "There is a gentle reproach in the word. He [= Paul] has to begin again and teach them an elementary fact, which they had already accepted"[5]. Do they still accept that fact, one is led to ask. Within the context of vv. 1-2 the meaning of γνωρίζω is not "to make known" but "to remind", perhaps with the nuance of "to confirm". The "use of the present indicative to describe" this act of speaking "narrowly focuses on the present moment"[6].

R.J. Sider points to four more features which probably intimate the wavering of the Corinthians' faith[7]. (1) In v. 2 we read: If you retain the gospel in the sense in which I preached it to you. This seems to imply that not everybody in Corinth understood Paul's preaching correctly. (2) The same verse ends with "unless you believed in vain". The reader has the impression that some may have abandoned elements of the faith which Paul is going to repeat by means of the creedal formula. (3) In v. 11 the verb κηρύσσομεν is in the present tense and ἐπιστεύσατε is in the aorist[8]. That aorist may intimate that the faith is no longer present in all Corinthians. (4) In vv. 12-19 Paul argues: since Christ *is preached* as raised from the dead (v. 12), you must agree that the believers will also be raised. In v. 12 he does not say: since *you believe* that Christ is risen. This again seems to be a hint as to the uncertain faith of the Corinthians, to their doubts.

Auferstehung des Christus aus den Toten verneinte" (57), his final conclusion is negative. Yet on p. 62 he states that in 15,1-12 Paul wants to make sure Christ's resurrection "einerseits um seine spätere Argumentation auf eine unumstössliche Basis zu stellen und andererseits wohl auch um mögliche Zweifeln, welche auch die Auferweckung des Christus aus den Toten betreffen könnten, zuvorzukommen".

[5] A. ROBERTSON–A. PLUMMER, *The First Epistle of St Paul to the Corinthians* (ICC; Edinburgh [2]1914) 331.

[6] B.M. FANNING, *Verbal Aspect in New Testament Greek* (Oxford 1990) 189-190, 189. He further comments: "The emphasis on the present time compresses the viewpoint of the present and reduces any possible durative and continuing sense" (189).

[7] R.J. SIDER, "St. Paul's Understanding of the Nature and Significance of the Resurrection in 1 Corinthians XV 1-19", *NT* 19 (1977) 124-141. We may quote Sider's comment on v. 12: "It is precisely this preaching to which, Paul fears, the Corinthians are no longer clinging (v. 2). It is not at all indisputable that Paul assumes a common belief in verse 12. He may simply be arguing from the fact of the kerygma, which, he assumes, ought to be authoritative for Christians" (131). C.M. TUCKETT, "The Corinthians Who Say 'There is no resurrection of the dead' (1 Cor 15,12)", R. BIERINGER (ed.), *The Corinthian Correspondence* (BETL 125; Leuven 1996) 247-275, rejects Sider's arguments (see 256) but, it seems to me, not in a convincing way.

[8] The aorist is probably inceptive ("you became believers"); or does it perhaps "take a summary view of the entire situation ... and denote the (past) *existence*" of the Corinthians in the state of believers? See FANNING, *Verbal Aspect*, 138.

Conclusion

Both the number and convergence of these indications do not allow us to simply dismiss the probability of a lack of faith in Christ's resurrection among the Christians at Corinth[9]. This is, of course, a supposition, but one that can hardly be avoided. We do not know whether that lack of faith was already unbelief or just a beginning doubt. We do not know the number of those people nor is it certain that all of the group referred to in v. 12 belong to them. Yet one may be tempted to go further in the reconstruction of that unbelief: was it complete in the sense that some Corinthians no longer believed in Christ's resurrection at all? Or did the doubt perhaps consist in a qualification of the resurrection idea itself, e.g., a minimization of Christ's bodily resurrection, an underestimation of his physical death, a reduction of resurrection to spiritual survival? Yet hypotheses such as the last ones inevitably become speculative. Their persuasive force should not be taken for granted.

It would seem that in vv. 1-11 Paul tries to "prove" the reality of Christ's resurrection and that he has to do it because the faith in that resurrection was doubted by some Corinthians.

II. THERE IS NO RESURRECTION OF THE DEAD

In 15,12 Paul exclaims: "Now if Christ is proclaimed as raised from the dead, how can some of you say there is no resurrection of the dead?" One may exclude that Paul misunderstood the content of the denial of some Corinthians. This does not mean, however, that their negative statement has been interpreted in the same way by all commentators.

Different Interpretations

The three basic positions are well known. Some Corinthians claim that

---

[9] I wonder whether 1 Cor 15,3-11 can appropriately be called a *narratio*, and, even if so, whether it is true that "comme *narratio*, ces versets montrent que le problème des Corinthiens n'est pas la foi en la résurrection du Christ". See J.-N. ALETTI, "La *dispositio* rhétorique dans les épîtres pauliniennes", *NTS* 38 (1992) 385-401, 396.

there is no resurrection at all. Death is the end of everything; life after death does not exist. This is the first position which is supported, it would seem, by the very wording of v. 12b.

A second interpretation holds that in the Greek (or Hellenistic) society of Corinth the immortality of the soul cannot have been denied radically. Hence, "no resurrection" must be understood as "no bodily resurrection". A *post mortem* existence there certainly is, but only due to the immortality of the soul. Justin Martyr mentions this position in his *Dialogue with Trypho* 80,4.

The third understanding puts the resurrection reality before death and interprets v. 12b as claiming: there is no future resurrection. This third position appears to be the most commonly held today. Nuances, however, are numerous. Some speak of a realized eschatology, others of a spirit-filled, sacramentally overconscious existence of a gnostic type[10]. In support of these views reference is often made to the "pneumatikoi" of chapters 1–4 and to the "pneumatic" gifts of chapters 12–14[11], and more in particular to 4,8; "Already you are filled! Already you have become rich! Without me you have become kings!" and to the slogan of 6,12 and 10,23: "All things are lawful (for me)". Christians already live a "risen" life. In 2 Tim 2,17-18 it is stated explicitly: Hymenaeus and Philetus swerve "from the truth by holding that the resurrection is past already. They are upsetting the faith of some". According to the third position the denial is not of the resurrection as such but of the futurity of the resurrection[12].

No Resurrection at All

It is probable that, after all, the first interpretation is the correct one.

---

[10] Cf. J. KREMER, *1 Korinther*, 318; M.C. DE BOER, *The Defeat of Death. Apocalyptic Eschatology in 1 Corinthians 15 and Romans 5* (JSNT.S 22; Sheffield 1988) 96-105: "... the claim that 'there is no resurrection of the dead' ... on the part of the Corinthians was an outgrowth of their appropriation of the baptismal motif of dying and rising with Christ in accordance with their gnostic anthropological presuppositions and pneumatic experience" (104).

[11] Cf., e.g., C. WOLFF, *Der erste Brief des Paulus an die Korinther* (THNT; Berlin ²1982) 149: "Das korinthische (Miss-)Verständnis der Auferstehung ... gründet ... ebenfalls in Überbewertung des Pneumatischen"; G. BARTH, "Zur Frage nach der in 1Korinther 15 bekämpften Auferstehungsleugnung", ZNW (1992) 187-201: "... Geistenthusiasten ..., die meinten, durch den sakramental empfangenen und garantierten Geist schon jetzt himmlisches Leben zu besitzen..." (192).

[12] Cf. the overview of the three categories by TUCKETT, "No Resurrection of the Dead", 251-261. But in monographs (cf., e.g., SPÖRLEIN, *Leugnung*) and commentaries there are proposals with four or five (and even more) distinctions. So it has been held that, just as in Thessalonica, so also some in Corinth thought that only those who were alive at the parousia would be saved, not the dead.

Let me first give some general considerations. One can safely propound that unbelief regarding afterlife and resurrection existed and exists in all times and among all peoples. Faith in the resurrection or life after death is not generally attested in the Jewish diaspora of Paul's time[13]. The Christian community of Corinth was not that large, maybe between 200 and 300 members. It was composed of a majority of simple people (cf. 1 Cor 1,26: not many were wise and powerful or of noble birth). They were surrounded by a society which to a certain extent and perhaps more often in the upper classes can be characterized as materialistic, if not immoral. Belief in a future bodily resurrection goes counter to what everybody in town daily sees and experiences: death, burial, definitive separation from friends, disappearance of loved ones. Belief in a resurrection of the body is not seldom ridiculed by referring to the decomposition of the corpses. Several data in 1 Cor 15 appear to confirm that a radical denial of the bodily resurrection by some Christians is in view.

What we find in v. 12b is in its literal form clear enough: some Corinthians say that there is no resurrection. The straightforward understanding of this clause recommends itself. In v. 12 Paul employs an indignant question within a conditional period: "if Christ has been raised, ... how can some of you say ...?" One easily recognizes the basic reasoning which commands that question: Christ is risen from the dead, thus there will also be a resurrection of the dead. It can be assumed that in v. 12a Paul took over the verb ἐγήγερται from the creedal formula in v. 4b and that he himself added the expression ἐκ τῶν νεκρῶν ("*from the dead*"), referring not to Christ being "raised from death itself but from among those who have died"[14], precisely because of the denial of the Corinthians: the resurrection *of the dead*. The conclusion cannot be avoided: just as Christ's past resurrection was bodily, so the future raising of the believers will be a bodily resurrection. This future bodily resurrection appears to have been rejected by Christian people in Corinth. One should note that Paul says "some of you", not all. Of course, these few may have had a negative influence on the whole Corinthian community[15]. Yet even more is to be said. Just as in vv. 1-11, because of the sudden perfect tense ἐγήγερται in

---

[13] Cf. the brief summary of the findings in BARTH, "Auferstehungsleugnung", 195-200.

[14] G.D. FEE, *The First Epistle to the Corinthians* (NICNT; Grand Rapids 1987) 704-741. Cf. DE BOER, *The Defeat of Death*, 107.

[15] In chapter 15 Paul addresses the whole community, also after v. 12. However, this does not legitimate the conclusion "dass es sich bei der Auferstehungsleugnung um eine für die korinthische Gemeinde typische Grundhaltung handelte". So WOLFF, *1 Korinther*, 173.

v. 4, the emphasis is upon the present significance of Jesus' past resurrection, so also in vv. 12-19 where the perfect of this verb is repeated five times[16] and once more in v. 20: Christ has been raised; he is the first fruits of those who have fallen asleep. The focus is on his present condition and its relevance for the dead. "How can some of you say that there is no resurrection of the dead?" (v. 12b). Both resurrections are linked; both are bodily.

In v. 18 Paul's inference from "if the dead are not raised" and, therefore, from "if Christ has not been raised" (vv. 16-17) is that "also those ... who have fallen asleep in Christ have perished". The consecutive particle ἄρα in v. 18 does not refer to the consequences expressed in v. 17 ("your faith is futile and you are still in your sins"). The destruction mentioned in v. 18 is not the eschatological damnation because of unforgiven sins. No, we have to assume that Paul intends to say: the deceased believers are lost; they are completely destroyed; they no longer exist. No resurrection equals postmortal nonexistence.

In v. 19 Paul writes: "If for (lit.: 'in, during') this life only we have hoped in Christ, we are of all people most to be pitied". Such an utterance seems to refer to the position that death is the end. Admittedly, the grammar of the protasis is somewhat strange. In the periphrastic construction the word order of ἠλπικότες ἐσμὲν μόνον "would indicate 'only hope' but the argument requires 'only in this life'"[17]. If there is no resurrection, there is nothing to hope and to wait for after death; death is the absolute end. C.K. Barrett comments: "It may be that this is rhetorical exaggeration .... It is more probable however that Paul means exactly what he says"[18].

When Paul in v. 29 asks what people in Corinth could mean by being baptized on behalf of the dead if the dead are not raised, he most likely supposes the claim of some that there will be no resurrection, no afterlife at all. It is, however, not certain that "those who are baptized on behalf of the dead" are the same people as the deniers. One should not easily assume that a contradiction between v. 12 (no resurrection of the dead) and v. 29 (a baptism which betrays a faith in the survival of the dead) forces us to qualify the denial of v. 12.

---

[16] Cf. FANNING, *Verbal Aspect*, 301-302. For an aorist of the same verb "with a clear reference ... to the past act alone apart from implications in the verb itself about the present", see v. 15.

[17] M. ZERWICK–M. GROSVENOR, *A Grammatical Analysis of the Greek New Testament* (Rome 1981) 529. Cf. *2 Apoc. Bar.* 21,13: "For if only this life exists which everyone possesses here, nothing could be more bitter than this".

[18] C.K. BARRETT, *The First Epistle to the Corinthians* (BNTC; London 1968) 350.

In vv. 30-32 Paul depicts his apostolic dangers and states: "I die every day". Paul thus intimates that he would not conduct such a life if there is only this life before death and no resurrection life after death, as some in Corinth claim[19].

At the end of v. 32 the popular saying "let us eat and drink for tomorrow we die" is applied to those who hold the position which Paul wants to refute. This clearly indicates that for such people there is only life on earth, life which should be fully enjoyed in a down-to-earth way, since death is the irremediable end. The exhortation of vv. 33-34 shows that some Christians, too, live in that way. In the clause "some have no knowledge of God" (v. 34), knowledge most probably points to that of the God who raised Christ and will raise those who are of Christ. The pronoun τινές in v. 34 may refer to the τινές of v. 12 and point to the same deniers.

Conclusion

We can conclude this second note. Verses 12-19 and 29-32, as well as the exhortation in vv. 33-34, refer to people who by denying the resurrection of the dead appear to deny life after death *simpliciter*. The existence of this category of Christians in Corinth — some of them without good morals, sinners (cf. vv. 32-34) — does not therefore negate the existence of another category of Christians, namely those who think they are spiritual (cf. chs. 2–4). The identification of these two categories cannot but remain extremely difficult, not only theoretically[20], but also, we think, because of what is written rather plainly in 15,12-34. Paul is contending against deniers. In vv. 32b-34 he depicts them as materialists. He himself stresses so much the future bodily resurrection of the deceased Christians that the denial of any kind of life after death must have been the claim of an opposite front[21].

---

[19] The fact that what Paul says about himself in vv. 19 and 30-32 seems to have been well-known topoi "im Hellenismus wie im hellenistischen Judentum" (cf. BARTH, "Auferstehungsleugnung", 193-195), does not diminish its autobiographical value and veracity. See also K. MÜLLER, "Die Leiblichkeit des Heils. 1Kor 15,35-58", L. DE LORENZI (ed.), *Résurrection du Christ et des chrétiens (1 Co 15)*, (Benedictina 8; Rome 1985), 171-255, esp. 173-176, for a forced reasoning which concludes that vv. 30-32 as well as v. 19 do not refer to "blosse Annihilation" but to the absence of salvation without a bodily resurrection. "Leiblosigkeit" in immortality after death is "Heilsverlust".

[20] Of course, one can speculate about the existence of two opposite movements within the same "gnostic" belief: asceticism and libertinism (the body does not matter any longer).

[21] Although the existence of those deniers is not assumed by BARTH,

III. THE DEAD AND THE LIVING

In 15,22a Paul writes "all die" (πάντες ἀποθνῄσκουσιν), in 15,51b "we shall not all sleep" (πάντες οὐ κοιμηθησόμεθα). In v. 22a "to die" points foremost to physical death; in the context of this chapter "to sleep" also means to die physically (see vv. 6.18 and 20 and cf. 1 Thess 4,13.14 and 15). How should one understand these seemingly contradictory statements "all" and "not all"?

In 1 Cor 15,22 "all die" is part of a comparative sentence: "For as in Adam all die, so also in Christ shall all be made alive". Because of Adam's sin all die, all must die, all will die, all have become mortal (cf. Rom 5,12). Because of Christ' redemption all will be brought to life again; they will be raised. "All" in v. 22a is truly universal: the whole of humanity. This, however, cannot be said of "all" in v. 22b since Paul here means the Christians: "those who belong to Christ" (v. 23: οἱ τοῦ Χριστοῦ)[22]. Even this second "all" has to be further qualified: not only those who believe in Christ but also those whose faith is working through love (cf. Gal 5,6). The exhortations and warnings in vv. 33-34 and 58 require the second implication. Of course, in v. 22b Paul's focus is not on these limitations, but they are by no means absent. The parousia of Christ (v. 23; cf. vv. 52-53) will contain a judgment. The first universal "all" of v. 22a possesses its own, though not expressed, limitation as will become evident from v. 51.

The statement in 15,51b belongs to a sentence which is introduced solemnly by "Lo! I tell you a mystery" (v. 51a): "We shall not all sleep, but we shall all be changed, in a moment, in the twinkling of an eye, at the last trumpet" (vv. 51bc.52a)[23]. Its content is further explained by v. 52bc and v. 53, two grounding verses each introduced by γάρ. The reference is clearly to the end of time, the day of judgment, although the condemnation of wrongdoers is not mentioned.

"Auferstehungsleugnung", he concludes: Paul "benutzt ... den konkreten Anlass des korinthischen Enthusiasmus mit seiner Spiritualisierung der Eschatologie, um nicht nur die korinthische Art von Auferstehungsleugnung zu korrigieren, sondern darüber hinaus — gewissermassen mit einem Seitenhieb — den Auferstehungsglauben überhaupt zu verteidigen und einzuschärfen" (201).

[22] Yet DE BOER, *The Defeat of Death*, 112, and S. HILLERT, *Limited and Universal Salvation. A Text-Oriented and Hermeneutical Study of Two Perspectives in Paul* (CB.NT 31; Stockholm 1999), e.g., defend the vision of a universal salvation in Paul.

[23] For a discussion of the variant readings, see the commentaries.

Can a comparison of statements in vv. 20-49 and vv. 50-58 teach us something about the reasoning of Paul? How are the two opposite clauses of vv. 22a and 51b to be understood?

The Dead Will Be Raised

In 15,19 Paul writes: "If for this life only we have hoped in Christ, we are of all men most to be pitied". Paul utilizes the first person plural here and, at first sight, the immediate context suggests that he looks forward to his own resurrection[24]. Yet it would seem that in the whole of 15,12-49 he deals with the resurrection of those Christians who have already died, i.e., with the resurrection of the dead. Paul repeatedly employs the expressions ἀνάστασις τῶν νεκρῶν (vv. 12.13.21.42) and ἐγείρονται οἱ νεκροί (vv. 15.16.29.32.35 and 52: ἐγερθήσονται). Of course, it is Christ who died who is said to have been "raised on the third day" (v. 4) and to "have been raised ἐκ νεκρῶν" (vv. 12.20, verb in the perfect tense: ἐγήγερται). The term νεκρός occurs once more in v. 29. Moreover, the verb ζῳοποιέω ("to make live" one who died) is present in vv. 22 and 45 (cf v. 36) and the verb κοιμάομαι ("to sleep", to die), as already stated, is used in vv. 6.18.20 and 51. With this in mind five remarks can be made:

(1) In vv. 23-24 Paul states that the resurrection will occur in an ordered temporal sequence: "Christ the first fruits, then at his coming those who belong to Christ. Then comes τὸ τέλος...". As is generally accepted, τὸ τέλος does not point to another group; it means "the end". Those who will still be alive at the moment of the parousia are simply not mentioned. This means that the destruction of personified Death referred to in v. 26 is here the equivalent of the resurrection of the dead and not, at least not explicitly, the transformation of the living.

(2) In v. 29 Paul is again focusing on those who have died: "What do people mean by being baptized on behalf of the dead? If the dead are not raised at all, why are people baptized on their behalf?"

(3) In vv. 30-32a Paul points to his own perils. He lives "in danger (of death) every hour" (v. 30). He exclaims: "I die every day!" (v. 31a). "Dying" here is, of course, employed metaphorically. But physical death is apparently not so far away. Such a continual facing of death would have been impossible for him without faith in the resurrection of the dead.

---

[24] See also 15,30-32 and cf., e.g., 4,14 and 1 Cor 6,14.

(4) The illustration of a bodily resurrection by means of what happens to the seed of v. 36 again shows that death is thought of: "What you sow does not come to life 'unless it dies'" (ἐὰν μὴ ἀποθάνῃ, v. 36). This implies: death is, as it were, the condition for being brought to life.

(5) Although in v. 49 Paul changes to the first person plural, the contrast between aorist indicative (ἐφορέσαμεν) and future indicative (φορέσομεν) intimates that in between those two types of "wearing the likeness (as clothes)" death is to be assumed: "Just as (before death) we have borne the image τοῦ χοϊκοῦ, so (after death) we shall also bear the image τοῦ ἐπουρανίου. The "we" here seems to refer to Christians in general and, we believe, not so much to Paul himself.

The conclusion to be drawn from this analysis is that according to Paul those Corinthians who are saying "there is no resurrection of the dead" (v. 12) appear to be thinking less of their own resurrection and more of that of their deceased brothers and sisters (cf. 1 Thess 4,13-18). In the same way Paul's own attention is, one might say, solely directed to this question from 15,12 until 15,49. Yet a shift seems to occur in what follows in this chapter.

The Living Too Will Be Changed

From vv. 51-52 it becomes evident that Paul is of the opinion that he himself (and other believers) will be alive at the parousia of Christ: "... we shall not all sleep, but we shall all be changed ... the dead will be raised imperishable, and we shall be changed". The grammatical subject of the second ἀλλαγησόμεθα (at the end of v. 52) is no longer "we (without ἡμεῖς) ... all" but only "we = ἡμεῖς". Again, several observations can be made:

(1) Most probably the "mystery" announced in v. 51a is to be found in vv. 51bc-52a and is then further explained in vv. 52b-53. It is often claimed that the emphasis in vv. 51-52a lies on "we shall all be changed". This is true but should be interpreted in a correct way. Paul's reasoning can be reconstructed, it would seem, as follows: although not all will die, yet all, i.e., the still living included, will be changed at the parousia of Christ. Verses 52bcd can equally be paraphrased in the same line of thought: "For the trumpet will sound, and — surely — the dead will be raised imperishable, but we, the still living, we shall be changed as well". The transformation of those who will still be alive at the judgment day also seems to be focused upon. Perhaps we should say that the "mystery" (v. 51) which Paul reveals contains no less than five elements: (a) change (b) of all (not only of the

deceased believers) (c) effected by God ("will be changed", divine passive) (d) at the coming of Christ (e) in a moment. Of course, the focus is on change, i.e., transformation.

(2) Verse 50 with τοῦτο δέ φημι, ἀδελφοί (v. 50a) clearly constitutes a new start and, therefore, belongs to the text unit of vv. 50-57. That in Semitic thought the expression "flesh and blood" applies to living persons only, not to the dead, is generally accepted[25]. There may be some nuances in answering the question to what extent "flesh" and "blood" in v. 50b receive separate attention, but by "flesh and blood" Paul points to the living insofar as their present body is still subject to decay and death and, therefore, not fit for the kingdom of God. In v. 50, however, Paul cannot have forgotten his consideration of the dead. In this verse he formulates a general truth about all human beings, living and dead. Yet a shift of attention, from dead to living, appears at this juncture. Most likely the more abstract v. 50c repeats what precedes. If, then, v. 50c is a synonymous parallel of v. 50b, ἡ φθορά does not point to the corrupted bodies of the deceased[26] but the corruptible condition of living persons (cf. σπείρεται ἐν φθορᾷ, v. 42b). Paul, already in the whole of v. 50, directs his attention also to those Christians who are still alive and to himself. They all look forward to Christ's return. In Paul's days the number of departed Christians could hardly have been bigger than that of the living ones. So the latter category must also be dealt with in this chapter.

(3) As already said, in vv. 21-23 those still living at the parousia have not been mentioned; only the risen Christ and the dead in Christ who will be raised are enumerated. In v. 52, however, the two categories of the dead Christians and the living Christians are put one next to the other: "For

---

[25] J. JEREMIAS, "'Flesh and blood cannot inherit the Kingdom of God' (1 Cor. xx. 50), *NTS* 2 (1955-56) 151-159, esp. 152-154. This study in reprinted in ID., *Abba. Studien zur neutestamentlichen Theologie und Zeitgeschichte* (Göttingen 1966) 298-307.

[26] Otherwise JEREMIAS, "Flesh and blood", 152: "corpses in decomposition". According to this author "in *vv.* 50-54 Paul makes use of chiasmus; for *vv.* 50-51 have the sequence: the living/the dead; whereas *vv.* 52-54 have the opposite sequence: the dead/the living" (154). See the discussion by J. GILLMAN, "Transformation in 1 Cor 15,50-53", *ETL* 58 (1982) 309-333, esp. 309-322; Gillman defends a synonymous parallelism in v. 50 as well as in v. 53 and propounds a cyclical structure for the subunit vv. 50-53: a (v. 50), b (vv. 51-52) and a' (v. 53) (see pp. 320-321). Cf. ID., "A Thematic Comparison: 1 Cor 15:50-57 an 2 Cor 5:1-5", *JBL* (1988) 439-454, esp. 442-445; J. PLEVNIK, *Paul and the Parousia. An Exegetical and Theological Investigation* (Peabody, MA 1997) 145-169, esp. 147-155; FEE, *1 Corinthians*, 798-800; MÜLLER, "Leiblichkeit", 227-239. Regarding φθορά see BAUER–ALAND: "Zustand der Vergänglichkeit" (1 Cor 15,42); "auch konkret 'das, was sich im Zustand der Vergänglichkeit befindet, das Vergängliche'" (15,50), and T. HOLZ, in *EWNT III*, 423: "in v. 50 φθορά parallels 'flesh and blood,' referring to a person in this earthly confinement".

(γάρ) the trumpet will sound, and 'the dead' will be raised imperishable, and 'we' [i.e., the living ones] shall be changed". In v. 53 Paul explains (γάρ) further: "For this perishable nature must put on the imperishable, and this mortal nature must put on immortality". When this has happened, the last enemy will have been destroyed, i.e., death will have been swallowed up in victory (v. 54)[27]. At first sight it would seem that τὸ φθαρτὸν τοῦτο (lit.: "this corruptible [being or nature]) in v. 53 (and v. 54) refers back to ἄφθαρτοι in v. 52 and as such indicates only the dead, while τὸ θνητὸν τοῦτο would point to "us" who will be changed[28]. Yet it is more likely that contentwise v. 53b repeats v. 53a, just as v. 54b is the equivalent of v. 54a (cf. v. 50c over against v. 50b). Both verses 53 and 54ab are expressed in synonymous parallelism; in their four clauses they appear to depict the global event which includes the resurrection of the dead, as well as the transformation of the living.

By themselves, however, the expressions τὸ φθαρτὸν τοῦτο (cf. ἡ φθορά in v. 50c) and τὸ θνητὸν τοῦτο point rather to still existing and living persons[29]. Perhaps something similar can be said about the verb ἐνδύομαι that Paul uses four times in vv. 53-54: it is not so much the dead but rather the living persons who "will put on" imperishable and immortal bodies. In 1 Cor 15 the verb ἐκδύομαι ("to die") does not appear. Although in 15,53-54 the double compound verb ἐπενδύομαι of 2 Cor 5,2.4 is also missing, the frequent use of "to put on" intimates that more attention is devoted to the living Christians than to the dead.

(4) In our search for Paul's way of reasoning many elements in this second part cannot but remain highly hypothetical. Because of the explicit mention of the dead and their resurrection in v. 52, the κοιμηθέντες or νεκροί are not forgotten and by no means excluded by Paul in vv. 50-55. Therefore, it is not an either-or situation but a question of less and more attention. However, that at the end of 1 Cor 15 Paul seems to be more concerned with those who are still living is not only suggested by our analysis of vv. 50-53 (and 54) but also supported by the content of vv. 56-58. The reflexive statement in v. 56, the use of the present tense (διδόντι) and first person plural in v. 57, and the exhortation in v. 58 to steadfastness and abounding labor for the Lord: all this shows Paul's particular apostolic care for his still living fel-

---

[27] With citation of Isa 25,8 and furthermore, in v. 55, of Hos 13,14.

[28] So JEREMIAS, "Flesh and Blood".

[29] Cf. COLLINS, *1 Corinthians*, 581: "The perishable/mortal being ... to whom Paul refers is not himself, but the human being insofar as the human, *in its present condition* [my italics], is perishable and mortal".

low believers. Moreover, Paul does not motivate this appeal by a consideration of their approaching death and future resurrection.

Conclusions

Three conclusions may be drawn from this last note. Admittedly, the
first two are by no means original.

First a terminological remark merits repeating. In v. 51 the verb ἀλ-
λάσσομαι ("to be changed") is employed in a more general sense for both
those who will be raised imperishable and those who will still be alive at
the parousia and whose bodies then will be transformed. At the end of v.
52, however, this verb is used only for the second category. In 1 Thess 4,17
the verb applied to them was ἁρπάζομαι ("to be caught up"). In Phil 3,21
the change of the mortal body is more appropriately expressed by means of
μετασχηματίζω ("to transform") and the adjective σύμμορφον
("conform"): Christ will transform our lowly bodies so that they will be
like his glorious body.

Second, the twofold "all" in v. 22 must be differently qualified: "For
as in Adam all die, so also in Christ shall all be made alive". The second
"all" (v. 22b) refers to Christians alone. Since "resurrection" in 1 Cor 15
is a positive reality and not a neutral event, the term in this context does
not refer to a general coming to life before the last judgment.
"Resurrection" is rising to a glorified, eternal life with Christ. Yet those
Christians who have become unfaithful or are conducting an immoral life
will not be raised to that life (cf. 6,9-10). The first "all" (v. 22a) is limited
differently by v. 51: Christians who will be alive at the return of Christ
shall not first die; they will be changed and put on immortality. While writing 1 Corinthians Paul (still) thinks that he belongs to this category.

The third conclusion concerns the dead and the living. It would seem
that in 15,12-49 Paul's attention is devoted exclusively to the dead believers and their resurrection. Only from v. 50 onwards do those still living
come into focus[30]. To what extent they constitute Paul's main concern there
is not easy to say. Yet we have seen that several indicia appear to confirm
the opinion that Paul's attention has somewhat shifted from the dead to the
living. Many commentators divide the third major section of 1 Cor 15,

---

[30] Perhaps one might point out a trajectory from attention to the dead Christians in 1 Thess
4 to equal treatment of dead and living in 1 Cor 15 to an almost unique concern to the living in
2 Cor 5 (and Phil 3,20-21?). See also B.F. MEYER, "Did Paul's View of the Resurrection of the
Dead Undergo Development?" *ThSt* 47 (1986) 363-387, 379 (also on v. 50).

namely vv. 35-58, into two subdivisions: after the questions in v. 35, Paul first argues, in vv. 36-49, for the possibility of a bodily resurrection; in vv. 50-58 his argumentation then defends the necessary transformation of the perishable body. We may claim that in this second subdivision Paul has in mind the still living Christians no less than the deceased believers.

GENERAL OUTLOOK

Let me summarize the main content of the three notes. 1) In Corinth belief in Christ's resurrection may have been less certain than is commonly assumed. 2) In denying a future resurrection some Christians probably denied the possibility of life after death. 3) At the end of the discussion of the bodily resurrection of departed Christians, Paul almost spontaneously also deals with the future transformation of those who will be still alive at the parousia of the Lord. Needless to say, these remarks in no way diminish the coherence and depth of Paul's thought in his famous resurrection chapter.

Zeitschrift für die neutestamentliche Wissenschaft 91 (2000) 143-145

9

Just a Possibility?
A Reply to Johan S. Vos on 1 Corinthians 15,12-20

In 1 Cor 15,12 Paul writes "Now if Christ is proclaimed as raised from the dead, how can some of you say there is no resurrection of the dead?" (NSRV). After 15,1-11 Paul begins with an emotional, indignant question; the indignation indicates that in his opinion the if-clause is closely connected with the question itself. In what sense, only logically or also contentwise? Does Johan S. Vos provide us with an answer in *Die Logik des Paulus in 1 Kor 15,12-20*, an article recently published in this journal[1]?

Out of verse 12 a less complex conditional period can be reconstructed, one which more clearly shows Paul's reasoning: "If Christ is risen (protasis), there will be a resurrection of the dead (apodosis)". This implication, consisting of an antecedent and a consequent, functions as the "major" of Paul's argumentation which, however, is left uncompleted. The "minor" can easily be taken from the preceding section: "now, as a matter of fact, Christ is risen". The conclusion then follows: "thus, there will be a resurrection of the dead"[2].

Three problems will be dealt with in this brief note. (1) Is, according to verse 12, through Christ's resurrection, the future resurrection of the dead just a possibility[3] or a future certain reality? (2) What is the function of verse 12 within its context, more in particular in relation to the following verses 13-19? (3) What kind of logic does Paul use in verse 12 and the whole unit? A critical look at the study of J.S. Vos may help us in tackling these problems.

---

[1] J.S. Vos, "Die Logik des Paulus in 1 Kor 15,12-20", ZNW 90 (1999) 78-97.

[2] Cf. J. Lambrecht, "Paul's Christological Use of Scripture in 1 Corinthians 15,20-28", *NTS* 28 (1982) 502-527, also in: Id., *Pauline Studies* (BETL 115; Leuven 1994) 125-149, esp. 126-127.

[3] It is often claimed that in Paul's reasoning the logic is: "If Christ is risen, then a resurrection of the dead is not excluded".

I. THE CONTRIBUTION OF JOHAN S. VOS

In his valuable article Vos critically discusses the theses brought forward by Th.G. Bucher in a number of studies[4]. Vos examines how ancient and modern authors define the logic in 1 Cor 15,12-20 and, in a careful and balanced way, presents his personal views. The following are his main conclusions:

(a) Verse 12 belongs to the text unit which continues up to verse 19 (or verse 20) (see p. 89).

(b) When verse 12 is rightly taken as the starting point of the argumentation, it contains the major premiss of a hypothetical syllogism. The minor ("Christ is risen from the dead") can be supplied from verses 1-11 and is explicitly expressed in verse 20. Therefore, verse 12 is written in the category of the *modus ponens*[5] (see p. 89).

(c) One can consider verses 13-19 as an indirect proof, a *probatio ad absurdum*. This category, however, is not incompatible with the ground structure, i.e., the *modus tollens*[6] in verses 13-19 (see pp. 89-90).

(d) Vos hesitates to find in verse 12 an implication of future reality. He asks whether the resurrection of Christ can be called the *causa exemplaris* of the resurrection of the other dead[7]. The fact that Christ is risen proves perhaps only the possibility of the others' resurrection (see pp. 91 and 96).

(e) The *modus tollens* structure of verses 13-19 does not obstruct the analysis of verse 13 according to Aristotelian syllogistic (see p. 94).

(f) The *argumentum ad hominem*, understood as based on *pathos* more than on *logos*, is best limited to verses 14 and 17-19[8]. The presence of this category, however, does not exclude nor diminish the formal-logical character of the unit as a whole (see pp. 96-97).

II. PAUL'S REASONING

1. There are no particular problems with (a), (b) and (c). Against (d)

---

[4] For the publications of Th.G. BUCHER, see VOS, "Die Logik", 78, n. 1.

[5] The "minor" is confirmed: If A, then B; now A is present; thus also B.

[6] The "minor" is negated: If A, then B; now B is *not* present; thus neither A is present.

[7] Cf. p. 91: "Anfechtbar bleibt die von mehreren Auslegern vertretene These, die Schlüssigkeit von V. 12 beruhe auf der Tatsache, dass Christus die *causa exemplaris* der Auferstehung der anderen Toten sei, dass die Gläubigen die Glieder seines Leibes seien, oder dass Paulus schon in V. 12 den ganzen Gedanken von V. 20 vor Augen habe".

[8] The premisses are not universally accepted nor objectively demonstrable.

(more than a possibility?[9]) it would seem that for Paul Christ's resurrection constitutes the basis for that of the Christians. To show this one has not to refer to texts outside 1 Cor 15. In verses 1-11 Paul emphasizes the facticity of Christ's resurrection. Not only verse 20 but the whole of verses 20-22 and 23-28 (esp. v. 25) as well as verses 44-49 (esp. vv. 44d and 49b) should convince us that already in verse 12 Paul holds that the future resurrection of Christians will be brought about by that of Christ. The implied connection in verse 12 is causal: If Christ is really risen, then the dead will rise. In this chapter Paul does not speak of a general resurrection. Christians will be made alive in Christ, through Christ. He is the first fruits; all those who belong to him will follow as soon as the last enemy, death, will have been destroyed (cf. vv. 23-28).

2. To what extent was an independent syllogism really present in Paul's mind when he composed the hypothetical sentence of verse 13 (cf. e)? In order to prove that the statement of verse 13a ("there is no resurrection of the dead") is false, he will hardly have reasoned according to the following syllogism: The dead do not rise; Christ has died; thus Christ is not risen[10]. Nor will Paul have argued according to a strict formal line: one exception (Christ's resurrection) invalidates a general statement (there is no universal resurrection of the dead). No, Paul takes his starting-point in verse 12: Christ's new life influences the fate of all who are joined with him.

In 15,12-19 verse 12 is clearly the main sentence: if Christ is risen, one cannot say there is no resurrection of the dead Christians. Twice in this unit Paul formulates the opposite, almost identically, in verse 13: "If there is no resurrection of the dead (= Christians), then Christ has not been raised", and in verse 16: "if the dead (= Christians) are not raised, then Christ has not been raised". The negation of the "then" clause is the not expressed minor: but, as a matter of fact, Christ is risen. The implicit conclusion is that the content of the if-clause ("there is no resurrection of the dead") is false. So we have here the *modus tollens*.

Twice, in verses 14-15 as well as 17-18, immediately after verses 13 and 16, Paul provides the proof of his not expressed minor by means of an indirect reasoning, a so-called *reductio ad absurdum*. He points out what the untenable consequences for the Christians would be "if Christ has not been raised". Paul's kerygma would be in vain (v. 14b); the Corinthians' faith would be in vain (v. 14c); Paul would have been a false witness (v.

---

[9] See esp. H. Grotius on p. 92 and C.L. Bauer on p. 93.

[10] cf. p. 92 within the discussion of Grotius.

15); the Corinthians' faith would be futile (v. 17b); they would be still in their sins (v. 17c); the Christians who have died in Christ would have perished (v. 18). Evidently (for Christians) all these consequences cannot be true; thus Christ has been raised.

Finally, in verse 19, Paul concludes the series by means of a last conditional sentence. If hope is confined to this life, then "we — Paul and the Corinthians, it would seem — are of all people most to be pitied". Verse 19a ("If for this life only we have hoped in Christ") is the equivalent of verse 13a and 16a (if Christ is not risen)[11].

Verse 20, I think, does not belong to the passage; it is better taken as the beginning of a new unit (vv. 20-28)[12].

3. A last remark concerns the *argumentum ad hominem* (f). If the usual definition be accepted which implies that this kind of argument lacks logical stringency and gives way to so-called rhetoric and psychology, Paul would most probably deny the presence of such a kind of reasoning in verses 12-19. Anyone feels, of course, the *pathos* in this passage, but the *logos* is by no means absent.

Most probably, however, Paul would protest against the motivation of Vos: "Weil ... die Prämissen weder objektiv nachprüfbar noch allgemein akzeptiert sind, ja auch für einen Teil der korinthischen Gemeinde nicht selbstverständlich gewesen sein dürften"[13]. Of course, Paul addresses Corinthian Christians, not unbelievers. Yet, for him what he writes in 15,1-11 and 12-19 — and in the whole chapter — is universally valid and undoubtedly meant for every human being, a matter of saving reality and established truth. So the application of the category *argumentum ad hominem*, even if limited to verses 14 and 17-19, must not take place without the necessary qualifications.

---

[11] For this structural analysis of verses 12-19 see especially pp. 82 (Thomas Aquinas), 84-85 (H. Bullinger) and 88-89 (G. Estius, R. Cornely, C.L. Bauer, J.E. Osiander). Vos himself appears to be in favor of it as well.

[12] See LAMBRECHT, *Pauline Studies*, 125-130.

[13] P. 96.

Novum Testamentum 40 (1998) 352-368

10

Paul's Boasting About the Corinthians
A Study of 2 Corinthians 8,24–9,5

According to 2 Cor 9,2 Paul is boasting to the Macedonians about the eagerness of Achaia with regard to the collection for Jerusalem. Paul most probably writes from Macedonia. It is possible that in this verse he literally repeats what he is saying to the Christians of that province: "Achaia is prepared since last year" (9,2)[1]. Furthermore, according to 8,24 Titus and the two Macedonian "brothers" have heard of that boasting (see "our boasting about you to them") and from 9,4 it is clear that those Macedonians who might come with Paul to Corinth are also acquainted with it. Thus in 8,24–9,5 Paul refers to that boasting three times, once at the end of chapter 8 and twice in the first verses of chapter 9.

Chapter 9 begins with a rather stereotypical formula: "it is superfluous for me to write": περισσόν μοί ἐστιν τὸ γράφειν. Put in isolation, one would easily expect that Paul is introducing a new topic, i.e., the collection (cf. "about [περί] the service for the saints"). Yet chapter 8 has just dealt with that very collection. How should this be understood? Moreover, the sentence in 9,1 is introduced by the particles μὲν γάρ. Does one have to assume, especially because of γάρ, a connection with the preceding chapter?

---

[1] Or: "has been prepared". The verb is a perfect passive. Text and context make clear that "being prepared" is not the same as "having completed" or "being ready". Cf. H.D. BETZ, *2 Corinthians 8 and 9: A Commentary on Two Administrative Letters of the Apostle Paul* (Hermeneia; Philadelphia 1985) 92: "What is implied is ... that Achaia was prepared to undertake the final phase of the collection .... The verb περισκευάζειν ('to prepare') reinforces the interpretation: it is, in the first place, a military term describing preparation for military action but not its completion". Cf. 8,10: "you have begun last year".

I. THE STATE OF THE QUESTION

Stanley K. Stowers

In his 1990 article "Περὶ μὲν γάρ and the Integrity of 2 Cor. 8 and 9", Stanley K. Stowers has proved, it would seem, that 2 Cor 9,1-5 is logically connected with 8,24[2]. "The most important argument for treating" the collection chapters 8 and 9 as fragments of separate letters "has always been based on the expression περὶ μὲν γάρ which introduces 9,1. It is the only argument ... which is susceptible to anything resembling 'objective' verification or falsification"[3]. This argument has been demonstrated to be unconvincing, so Stowers concludes at the end of his study, and rightly, we may claim.

Stowers has investigated and compared ninety textually certain instances of this phrase in the existing Greek literature[4]. The main instances are brought forward and discussed in the article. The author defends the thesis that περὶ μὲν γάρ always "expresses a close relationship — a reason, warrant, explanation, subtopic — to what precedes"[5]. The standard introductory clause "the writing is superfluous" in 9,1 cannot change this state of affairs; by means of this formula Paul proceeds to elaborate on the collection[6]. Neither does the presence of a coordinating δέ in 9,3 remove the connective force of μὲν γάρ[7].

Stowers then very briefly examines the content of chapter 8. He explains how verses 16-23 (the sending of the delegates) constitute the basis for the exhortation in v. 24 and how 9,1-4 provide a warrant and explanation for it[8]. He paraphrases 8,24–9,4 as follows. "Justify my boasting by receiving the delegates and being prepared. For although I do have a basic confidence in your willingness to help the saints (of which is I have boasted to the Macedonians that you are ready since last year), I think it necessary to send these delegates lest you are not ready and we should be

---

[2] S.K. STOWERS, "Περὶ μὲν γάρ and the Intregity of 2 Cor. 8 and 9", *NT* 32 (1990) 340-348.
[3] STOWERS, "*Peri men gar*", 340.
[4] The only other place in the New Testament where the expression is found is Acts 28,22. See STOWERS, "*Peri men gar*", 341: The expression here introduces something new (reference to "this new sect") and "yet connects with what precedes ...".
[5] STOWERS, "*Peri men gar*", 345.
[6] Cf. STOWERS, "*Peri men gar*", 344-345.
[7] Cf. STOWERS, "*Peri men gar*", 345.
[8] Cf. STOWERS, "*Peri men gar*", 346.

shamed"[9]. Because of the connection between 9,1-5 and 8,24, Stowers' final conclusion is that it is "most implausible to think of chapter 8 and 9 as fragments of two letters"[10]. These insights, I think, can be reinforced by an even more careful investigation of 8,24–9,5 and a more sustained consideration of the line of thought in the whole of the two chapters.

Other Authors and Theories

But first a word about some recent opinions of a different kind. For three decades the publication of G. Bornkamm and D. Georgi[11] have heavily influenced those who see chapters 8 and 9 as separate letters. Three more recent works may be briefly mentioned here, that of Hans Dieter Betz[12], against which Stowers is reacting, and those of Verlyn D. Verbrugge[13] and Margaret E. Thrall[14], the last two being quite dissimilar.

In the first chapter of his influential commentary on 2 Cor 8 and 9 Betz presents an extended overview of the history of New Testament scholarship regarding the two chapters[15]. Among other things he deplores "the complete lack of methodological reflection"[16]. The arguments against or in favor of seeing the chapters as independent units mostly remain speculative. He himself finds the interpretation of περὶ μὲν γάρ in 9,1 crucial for a correct evaluation of chapter 9. Moreover, the fact that he is able to detect in each of the chapters a rhetorical division and to identify the literary genre and function of each confirms the hypothesis of separate composi-

---

[9] STOWERS, "*Peri men gar*", 347.

[10] STOWERS, "*Peri men gar*", 348.

[11] G. BORNKAMM, *Die Vorgeschichte des sogenannten Zweiten Korintherbriefes*, first published in 1961, available in ID., *Geschichte und Glaube II* (= *Gesammelte Aufsätze IV*) (Munich 1971) 162-194 and also in ID., *Studien zum Neuen Testament* (Munich 1985) 237-269; for an abbreviated version, see ID., "The History of the Origin of the So-called Second Letter to the Corinthians", *NTS* 8 (1961-62) 258-263; D. GEORGI, *Die Geschichte der Kollekte des Paulus für Jerusalem* (ThF 38; Hamburg/Bergstedt 1965); English translation: *Remembering the Poor: The History of Paul's Collection for Jerusalem* (Nashville 1992). Cf. also K.F. NICKLE, *The Collection: A Study in Paul's Strategy* (SBT 48; London 1966).

[12] See n. 1.

[13] V.D. VERBRUGGE, *Paul's Style of Church Leadership Illustrated by His Instruction to the Corinthians on the Collection: To Command or Not to Command* (San Francisco 1992).

[14] M.E. THRALL, *The Second Epistle to the Corinthians. Volume I: Introduction and Commentary on II Corinthians I–VII* (ICC; Edinburgh 1994).

[15] See BETZ, *2 Corinthians 8 and 9*, 3-36.

[16] BETZ, *2 Corinthians 8 and 9*, 25.

tions. Betz calls 2 Cor 8 a letter fragment (= the letter-body) of the so-called mixed type; it belongs to the administrative category of Paul's corre-spondence[17]. The rhetoric in its first part is deliberative: exordium (vv. 1-5), narratio (v. 6); propositio (vv. 7-8); threefold probatio ("the honorable", "the expedient", "equality", vv. 9-15). In its second part the rhetoric is jurid-ical: commendation of the delegates (vv. 16-22); authorization of the dele-gates (v. 23). V. 24 is the peroratio[18]. In Betz's view 2 Cor 9 is the body of an independent advisory letter[19] with exordium (vv. 1-2), narratio (vv. 3-5a), propositio (v. 5b-c), probatio (vv. 6-14) and peroratio (v. 15). Epistolary prescript and postscript are, of course, omitted by the editor who combined the fragments[20].

The work of V.D. Verbruggge is a doctoral dissertation defended in 1989 at the University of Notre Dame. The 1992 publication "Paul's Style of Church Leadership Illustrated by His Instructions to the Corinthians on the Collection: To Command or Not to Command" is its revised form. In this monograph much attention is given to a comparison of Paul's three alleged collection letters (1 Cor 16,1-2; 2 Cor 8 and 2 Cor 9) with possible Greco-Roman parallels. Relatively little space is devoted to the Pauline text itself. Verbrugge writes: "a strong case can be made that these two chapters (2 Cor 8 and 9) did not originally belong together as one contin-uous unit"[21] Five reasons are put forward which are for the most part well known. The first one is the beginning in 9,1 with περὶ μὲν γάρ which sug-gests "an independent thought-unit". Yet chapter 8 deals with the same theme. Hence the hypothesis that the two chapters were originally sepa-rate. For Verbrugge γάρ in 9,1 is most likely redactional[22]. A second reason

---

[17] BETZ 2 Corinthians 8 and 9, 139.

[18] Cf. BETZ, 2 Corinthians 8 and 9. It would seem that serious reservations must be made, not only regarding the independent letter theory and the classification ("adminstrative letter"), but also as far as the delineation and identification of the sections in chapter 8 (and subsections in vv. 6-15) are concerned. For further criticism, see THRALL, Second Corinthians, 37-38 and, in a more general way, J.T. REED, A Discourse Analysis of Philippians: Method and Rhetoric in the Debate over Literary Integrity (JSNT.S 136; Sheffield 1997) 156-168.173-178 and 442-454. See also C.J. CLASSEN, "Paulus und die antike Rhetorik", ZNW 82 (1991) 1-13.

[19] Cf. BETZ, 2 Corinthians 8 and 9, 139.

[20] Cf. BETZ, 2 Corinthians 8 and 9, 88-90. Besides having justified doubts regarding the general view — chapter 9 a separate letter and arranged as a classical discourse — one should not take v. 5bc as a propositio nor accept the division of vv. 6-14 into a thesis and five distinct proofs. Moreover, few scholars would be willing to see v. 15 as Paul's intonation of a thanks-giving, i.e., the first line of a hymn which, at the reading of the letter, the Corinthians will spontaneously continue. Cf. THRALL, 2 Corinthians, 41-42.

[21] VERBRUGGE, Paul's Style, 100.

[22] Cf. VERBRUGGE, Paul's Style, 100-101.

is the oddity for Paul to say, after a preceding pericope such as 8,1-15, that it is superfluous to write about the collection (9,1), as if it were a new theme[23]. The third reason is the term Ἀχαΐα in 9,2, which seems to indicate a wider audience than in chapter 8[24]. The fourth one is the fact that 8,24 does not possess a personal main verb, only a participle. According to Verbrugge "this participle is best interpreted as a somewhat typical way to end a letter"[25]. Lastly Verbrugge accepts Betz's rhetorical analysis: chapters 8 and 9 "each have a separate rhetorical structure"[26]. This again suggests two compositions independent from each other.

While three major commentaries — those of V. Furnish (1984), M. Carrez (1986) and C. Wolff (1989)[27] — are of the opinion that chapters 8 and 9 belong together and are an integral part of a Pauline letter (i.e., chs. 1–9), the more recent commentary, that of M.E. Thrall (1994), prefers to see chapter 9 as separate from chapter 8 (which itself belong to chs. 1–7) and as an independent letter[28]. To be fair, we must immediately add that Thrall reaches this conclusion after an extended discussion of the arguments in favor and those against the partition[29] and that she qualifies her preference: "with some hesitation"[30]. The two reasons which have influenced her preference are: "the full description of the διακονία" in 9,1 (cf. 8,4)[31]; and "the absence — in that expression 'the service of the poor' — of a qualifying demonstrative pronoun" (if chapter 9 follows chapter 8, one expects in 9,1 "'that' service", i.e., the service already spoken of in the preceding chapter)[32]. In her opinion, too, the γάρ of 9,1 "could well be redactional. It is one of the most obvious transitional particles for an editor to use ..."[33].

The authors succinctly presented here show that in our days the hypothesis of the separation of chapter 9 from chapter 8 — whether they

---

[23] Cf. VERBRUGGE, Paul's Style, 101.

[24] Cf. VERBRUGGE, Paul's Style, 101.

[25] VERBRUGGE, Paul's Style, 101. See the extensive treatment of 8,24 on pp. 254-258.

[26] VERBRUGGE, Paul's Style, 101.

[27] V.P. FURNISH, II Corinthians (AB; Garden City, NY 1984)); M. CARREZ, La deuxième épître aux Corinthiens (CNT; Geneva 1986); C. WOLFF, Der zweite Brief des Paulus an die Korinther (THNT; Berlin 1989).

[28] Cf. THRALL, Second Corinthians, 36-43.

[29] THRALL, Second Corinthians, 42: "most ... are finely-balanced". One has to remember that only the first volume of her commentary has appeared; chapters 8 and 9 are not yet fully explained.

[30] THRALL, Second Corinthians, 42.

[31] THRALL, Second Corinthians, 42.

[32] Cf. THRALL, Second Corinthians, 42.

[33] THRALL, Second Corinthians, 42.

are independent letters or not — is still seriously defended[34]. Betz more than once repeats that the opinion which sees 2 Corinthians as one integral letter is as hypothetical as the partition theories: one "cannot rely on the naive assumption that unity is the natural state of the letter"[35]. He also claims that "the surest position of the historical critic, the *ars nesciendi*"[36], i.e., resignation in the face of ignorance, restraint in view of lack of information, must be considered as a too easy attitude[37]. We should therefore repeat his question: "What sort of evidence can be adduced to demonstrate the extent and the kind of redaction in this letter?"[38]

II. THE TEXT

The relation between chapter 8 and chapter 9 has been explained in different ways. Are these chapters written by Paul as part of a longer letter? Did they originally belong together? If not, which of the two was the first[39]? As already stated, some exegetes are of the opinion that chapter 9 constituted a (later) separate fragment or letter. To be sure, this chapter appears to be, to a certain extent, a repetition of what is found in chapter 8. In 9,2 Paul mentions "Achaia"; one could ask whether the addressees are still the same as those in chapter 8, Christians of Corinth. Is the audience perhaps wider? In 8,1-6 Paul praises the Macedonians before the Corinthians, while according to 9,1-4 he has been and is boasting to the Macedonians about "Achaia". This also seems rather strange. Furthermore,

---

[34] Cf. recently R.S. Ascough, "The Completion of a Religious Duty: The Background of 2 Cor. 8.1-15", *NTS* 42 (1996) 584-599. 2 Cor 8 is more likely "part of a separate letter" (585, n. 5).

[35] Betz, *2 Corinthians 8 and 9*, 28.

[36] Betz, *2 Corinthians 8 and 9*, 30.

[37] Cf. Betz, *2 Corinthians 8 and 9*, 14 and 28. On pp. 31-32 he discusses W.G. Kümmel who is of the opinion that Paul's tortured reasoning is thoroughly understandable in his position with regard to a newly reconciled community: "This sort of argument seeks to circumvent the observations of critical scholars by appealing to credulity and preference for the status quo" (32).

[38] Betz, *2 Corinthians 8 and 9*, 35.

[39] For a good survey of the arguments and the positions, see R. Bieringer, "Teilungshypothesen zum 2. Korintherbrief. Ein Forschungsüberblick", in R. Bieringer–J. Lambrecht, *Studies on 2 Corinthians* (BETL 112; Leuven 1994) 67-115, esp. 98-103 and chart on p. 104.

at first sight 9,1, with its stock sentence, presents itself as introducing something new (the beginning of a letter?).

Yet a number of data indicates that chapter 9 is not a second letter but the continuation of the previous chapter. Let us first analyze 8,24–9,5. It would seem that no less than seven points in favor a logical connection between 9,1-5 and 8,24 must be taken into account.

(1) The explaining or grounding γάρ ("for") in 9,1 clearly links chapter 9 with what precedes. There is no valid reason to doubt the causal or explanatory force of the particle and to consider it as a transitional δέ[40]. The hypothesis that γάρ is editorial (cf., e.g., Verbrugge and Thrall) is but a stopgap-solution needed for those who already assume that the two chapters were composed independently of each other.

(2) In 9,1 Paul employs a figure of style, a *praeteritio*: "it is superfluous to me to write about...". Betz comments on this type of introduction and puts forward the idea that the Christians of Achaia "had grown tired of hearing of" the collection. "Rhetorically speaking, the collection had become a matter of 'boredom' or 'weariness' (*taedium*). To relieve the tiresomeness of the subject, Paul employed a contemporary epistolary tag, a variation on the basic notion that 'though I have nothing to say to you, I am writing to you all the same'. A denial of this kind was, and remains, one of the simplest devices for beginning a letter that introduces a subject which has grown tiresome to its readers"[41]. Betz's reconstruction appears somewhat far-fetched. Did the Christians of Achaia really hear so often and so much of the collection? A more convincing explanation is to see its function in connection with our third and fourth remarks.

(3) In 9,1 we read "it is superfluous for me" and then the present infinitive γράφειν, preceded by the anaphoric article τό ("the, i.e., 'this' writing"). The meaning of this construction should probably be rendered as follows: "there is no need for me to go on writing"[42]. Moreover, the article τῆς before "service for the saints" may also be anaphoric ("this service", i.e., the collection). If so, it refers back to the subject matter of chapter 8.

---

[40] Cf., e.g., the lexicon of BAUER–ALAND, col. 303: γάρ, no. 4: "Anknüpfend und fortführend" (but 2 Cor 9,1 is not mentioned).

[41] BETZ, *2 Corinthians 8 and 9*, 90-91.

[42] However, in 1 Thess 4,9 and 5,1 Paul employs γράφειν without a nuance of duration or continuity; yet see Phil 3,1b: τὰ αὐτὰ γράφειν ἐμοὶ μὲν οὐκ ὀκνηρόν, ὑμῖν δὲ ἀσφαλές, and cf. REED, *Discourse Analysis*, 228-265, esp. 242-256. As to the article, we must not omit to mention BDR, no. 399.2: τό in 2 Cor 9,1 is "wenig deutlich anaphorisch (der Artikel bezeichnet etwas Naheliegendes, das geschehen könnte)".

The use of the full expression as in 8,4 most likely occurs for the sake of emphasis[43].

(4) Notwithstanding the distance between the two particles, it seems likely that in v. 1 the μέν ("on the one hand") at the beginning is to be connected with the δέ ("on the other hand") of v. 3. As is well known that in such a μὲν γὰρ ... δέ construction the grounding γάρ is often a "γάρ à portée différée". This means that in that case the reason or motivation is to be found in the δέ clause and that the μέν clause then is concessive: "for although ... yet"[44]. In a paraphrase the line of thought in 9,1-3 would then be as follows: "*For, although* it is superfluous to go on writing to you about this collection — since I know your desire of which I am boasting to the people of Macedonia — *yet* I still want to explain the implication of the sending of the brothers beforehand". It would seem that in chapter 8 Paul has not given all his reasons for that mission (see 8,20-21). Now he adds: I am sending the brothers ahead of me (and possibly some Macedonians), lest my boast about you may prove empty, lest we — I myself and you — may be put to shame. This understanding of 9,1-4 makes the hypothesis of a "γάρ à portée différée" in 9,1 recommendable.

(5) This brings us to the theme of boasting in 8,24–9,3. "Boasting" in 9,2-3 almost certainly refers back to "boasting" in 8,24[45]. One should admit without further ado that after the command: "show the proof of your love", the addition of "and of our boasting about you" in 8,24 is rather unexpected and grammatically strange. So Paul now must concretize what the content of that boasting about the Corinthians is: their preparedness since last year. Above all, he wants to point out the implications of that boasting: if at the arrival of Paul and perhaps of some Macedonians with him the collection is not ready, the boasting will prove empty; both Paul and the Corinthians will be disgraced[46]. Obviously, 8,24 and 9,1-5 belong together.

(6) The absence of any qualification of "the brothers" in 9,3 and 5 forces us to suppose that there is a reference to 8,16-23 where Titus and the two brothers are recommended and briefly qualified. The order which Paul

---

[43] Cf. THRALL, *Second Corinthians*, 40;

[44] Cf., e.g., M. ZERWICK, *Biblical Greek* (Rome 1963) nos. 474-477.

[45] Cf. STOWERS, "*Peri men gar*", 347: "Paul's boasting about the Corinthians is a theme that connects the two chapters (8:24; 9:2-3; cf. 8:22)".

[46] In 7,14 the verbs καυχάομαι (cf. 8,2) and καταισχύνομαι (cf. 9,4) were employed. In that verse, however, Paul dealt with his boasting to the Corinthians about Titus' Christian and apostolic qualities. Yet a vocabulary connection between chapter 7 and chapters 8-9 should be admitted. This could perhaps even be a small indication that all belong to the same writing.

then gives in 8,24 cannot be separated from these verses. Yet there is still more to be said. Why did Paul send those brothers, who are meant to be his companions regarding the collection, ahead of him? The answer to this question can be found in 9,5: "I thought it necessary to urge the brothers to go to you ahead of me and arrange beforehand the already promised generous gift, so that it would be ready ..."[47]. So once again we see how 9,1-5 explains and complements data mentioned in 8,16-24.

(7) The name of the Roman province "Achaia" in 9,2 is probably mentioned because of the reference to the "Macedonians", Macedonia being another Roman province. We have the same connection in 11,9 and 10 (cf. 1 Thess 1,7-8, twice, and Rom 15,26). "Corinth" may be meant, or, at least, included by the naming of "Achaia". On the other hand, some Christians must have lived outside that city, in the province (cf. the addressees mentioned in 2 Cor 1,1). There is no need to postulate an audience for chapter 9 different from that for chapter 8. Moreover, the "to you" at the end of 9,1 points back to the grammatical subject contained in the participle ἐνδεικνύμενοι of 8,24.

Taken together, these seven considerations would seem to establish beyond reasonable doubt that 9,1-5 is connected with 8,24, as well as that Paul wrote 9,1-5 immediately after 8,24. Can this view of connection be expanded to the entire chapters 8 and 9?

III. THE CONTEXT

The mention of Achaia in 9,2, as already stated, can hardly be taken as a change of addressees, from Corinthians to Achaians. Chapters 8 and 9 appear to have the same audience as indicated in 1,1: "to the church of God which is at Corinth, with all the saints who are in the whole of Achaia".

Three Specific Items

When chapter 9 is compared with chapter 8 three items are often pointed to, which, at first sight, appear to betray their difference and even inde-

---

[47] In 9,3 Paul writes ἔπεμψα, clearly a resumption of συνεπέμψαμεν in 8,18 and 22. Compare 9,5 with Phil 2,25: ἀναγκαῖον δὲ ἡγησάμην ... πέμψαι πρὸς ὑμᾶς.

pendence: contradiction, repetitions and shifts in the language. Before putting 8,24–9,5 within the broader context of the collection, i.e., chapters 8–9, these three specific items must first be dealt with.

What about *contradiction*? It has been asked how in the same letter Paul could first present the Macedonians as an example to the Corinthians (8,1-5) and then declare that the Corinthians (Achaia) have been and still are an example for the Macedonians (9,1-5). Is this not, if not contradictory, at the least inconsistent? Four remarks can make clear that this is not necessarily so.

There is first the difference of time. Paul boasted about the Macedonians to the Corinthians last year[48] and at that time the Corinthians' zeal stirred up most of the Macedonian Christians. Paul now, while writing the letter, refers to the generosity of the Macedonians and depicts them as an example to the Corinthians.

Second, there is a difference of subject as well. Paul spoke of the Corinthians' preparedness as far as the collection is concerned, while he now mentions the way in which the Macedonians completed their participation in this undertaking. Completion (final stage) is not the same as preparation (resolve, first steps).

Third, one should not lose sight of the difference in rhetorical function. What the Macedonians have done is employed as an exhortative example. Their joy and generosity, their spontaneous and free gesture should spur the Corinthians to a similar completion of the collection. Apparently Paul wants to test the genuineness of the Corinthians' love by pointing to the zeal of the Macedonians (cf. 8,8). The mention, however, of the past and present boasting about the Corinthians to the Macedonians has a quite dissimilar aim. To be sure, it equally has an exhortative function, but only indirectly and negatively as it were, i.e., only because that boasting could prove wrong and cause shame both to Paul and the Corinthians.

Fourth, no doubt, in 8,1-5 the recent completion of the collection of the Macedonians is an example. Yet in front of this greater zeal the Corinthians may have felt humbled somewhat. Can 9,2 perhaps (also) be seen as a kind of counterweight which will please the addressees? It was their preparedness which initially stimulated the Macedonians.

So, because of all these differences, it is clear that no contradiction whatsoever between these two exemplary behaviors should be assumed.

---

[48] According to 9,2 ("For I know your eagerness about which I boast to the Macedonians") Paul is still boasting (present tense). There is, however, no reason for assuming that there was no boasting long ago. Cf. "prepared since last year" in 9,2.

What about *repetitions*? In both chapters Paul insists upon the completion of the collection. Although in 8,8 he states that he will not give a command and in 8,10 consequently he presents only advice, one should not miss the urgency and the insistence in 8,11: "now then, also complete that work ..."[49]. An inviting, even commanding tone is also present in 9,7: "(Let) each (give) according to (what) has been decided in his heart ...". Moreover, Paul appears to insist on giving willingly (ch. 8) and on free decision (ch. 9: no constraint). There is scarcely a difference between these qualifications. Do these exhortations not constitute a repetition and should, therefore, the question not be raised if two such similar "commands" can stand in the same writing.

Yet, on closer inspection, what is asked for is not exactly the same. In chapter 8 Paul emphasizes completing willingly, and furthermore also the idea of equality is present, whereas in chapter 9, in addition to attempting to stimulate the Corinthians to carry on with the collection, he makes a plea for liberality and generosity. The two insistences are not repetitious; they may be termed complementary[50].

Shifts in Language? It has been said that in between chapter 8 and chapter 9 there is a shift from first person plural to first person singular, from narration to exhortation, from the collection as χάρις ("grace", hence "gracious work") to collection as εὐλογία ("blessing", hence "generous gift").

But these so-called shifts are not so evident nor so radical. There is a mixture of plural and singular within the two chapters, more use of the plural in chapter 8, somewhat more use of the singular at the beginning of chapter 9[51]. One can hardly maintain the distinction between narration and exhortation: elements of the two genres are present in both chapters. It is true that the collection is no longer called χάρις in chapter 9 and that εὐλογία is not used in chapter 8. Yet in 8,4 as well as in 9,1 Paul employs the same phrase for the collection: "the service for the saints". It is rather striking that within chapters 8 and 9 no "neutral" word is employed for the collection[52]. In chapter 8 he calls it mostly χάρις (see vv. 1.6-7 and 19). In

---

[49] According to ASCOUGH, "The Completion", in 2 Cor 8,6 and 11 the verb ἐπιτελέω has the sense of the fulfilment of a religious duty.

[50] Cf. THRALL, *Second Corinthians*, who on p. 39 cites more cases but judges: "The alleged repetition may be more apparent than real: chap. 9 deals with the same situation as chap. 8, but does not repeat its contents" (40-41).

[51] Yet see first person singular in 8,8 and 23, and first person plural in 9,3.4 and 11.

[52] Such as λογεία in 1 Cor 16,1. Cf. ASCOUGH, "The Completion", 593: "In fact, Paul uses a number of different words in the context of the collection, many with theological or religious significance".

chapter 9 one finds the terms διακονία ("service"; see vv. 1 and 12-13"; cf. 8,4) and εὐλογία ("blessing"; see vv. 5-6); he refers to it also as δικαιοσύνη ("righteousness"; see vv. 9-10) and ἁπλότης ("simplicity"; see vv. 11 and 13). Such data do not appear to allow a conclusion regarding an independent composition of each chapter.

Moreover, the vocabulary contacts between the two chapters are numerous[53]. We have already mentioned in 9,1-5 "the service for the saints" (cf. 8,4), "boasting" (cf. 8,24) and the sending and urging of the brothers (cf. 8,6.16 and 22). Furthermore, "desire" or "eagerness" occur in 9,2 and 8,11-12, the expression "since last year" in 9,2 and 8,10. We may also refer to "riches" in 9,11 and 8,2.9; to δοκιμή or/and δοκιμάζω in 9,13 and 8,2.22; and to περισσεύω and περίσσευμα in 9,8.12 and 8,2.7.14. It could, of course, be maintained that two letters written about the same time and regarding the same topic can very well contain identical concepts and partly the same vocabulary. But in the light of the overwhelming evidence for their belonging together presented in this study, the verbal and conceptual links between the two chapters constitute, it would seem, a reinforcement of that evidence.

Finally, just as in 8,1 Paul employs the phrase "the grace of God" in 9,14 as well. Although the meaning of the phrase in 8,1, concretely referring to the collection, is more restricted than that in 9,14, where it points to the whole of God's salvation, it seems reasonable to consider the two uses as an inclusion which frames the two chapters.

The Line of Thought

What is, then, Paul's reasoning and what is the line of thought in this lengthy treatment of the collection which consists of two chapters?

Within *chapter 8* one best distinguishes three sections: vv. 1-6 (the example of the churches in Macedonia); vv. 7-15 (the appeal proper); and vv. 16-24 (the recommendation of Titus and two other persons).

In 8,1-6, Paul is stressing that the great fervor of the Macedonian churches regarding the collection spurred him on to send Titus to Corinth in order to complete the collection there. His praise of the Macedonians is quite imposing and no doubt also tactical, meant as a forceful exhortation for the Corinthians.

---

[53] See, e.g., WOLFF, *Zweiter Korintherbrief*, 163-164.

In 8,7-15, Paul urges the Corinthians to bring the collection, which had already been begun last year, to a successful conclusion. However, he cannot give a strict command, only an advice. Yet he can point out what Jesus' incarnation signifies; he can equally remind the Corinthians of the fact that last year they willingly began this undertaking; he can cleverly emphasize that one should only give according to what one possesses. Furthermore, he brings forward that equality should be the aim, which means that the Corinthians must now help Jerusalem, but also — should the poor people there later have plenty — that Jerusalem will have to help the Corinthians in case they will be in need.

In this second section, the appeal itself, he is very prudent. He does not want to order, yet he gives advice: it is better for you to finish what you began last year. The collection is presented as a test of the genuineness of their love. And, having mentioned the exemplary conduct of the Macedonian Christians rather circumstantially, Paul in one solemn sentence refers to the example ("the grace") of Jesus Christ: rich though he was, he made himself poor for your sake, in order to make you rich by means of his poverty. At this point a threefold shift in the reasoning has to be noted. In a surprising way, while insisting on a completion which should be qualified by the Corinthians' free will — a first shift — he suddenly brings in two more shifts within his argument. He states that one has only to give according to one's means; and he also deals with the idea of equality. The conclusion of the appeal is formed by a quotation from Exod 16,18, a saying about the gathering of the manna: the person who gathered much did not have too much, the one who gathered little did not have too little.

In 8,16-24, then, Paul finishes, it would seem, with a heartfelt recommendation of his partner Titus and of two other Christians, one appointed by the churches, the other chosen by Paul himself. The addressees are told that by sending those persons to Corinth Paul intends to be careful with regard to financial matters, for the collection could easily stir up insinuations against him. At all costs Paul wants to avoid any blame against his own person. The brothers will be present during the handling of the collection. They will be able to witness that the whole enterprise is honorable not only in the sight of the Lord but also in that of the Christians. Therefore, Paul urges the Christians in Corinth: by receiving those brothers demonstrate your love and — again a shift — see to it that our boasting about you may prove reliable and genuine.

Paul's style in this chapter presents the typical characteristics which we find elsewhere in 2 Corinthians, e.g., the repetitious use of the same or related words in close context. We may equally mention the frequent occurrence of χάρις in its varying nuances of a gracious work done either by Christ or by Christians, as well as the presence of the "fervor" terminology. Furthermore, twice, in vv. 3-6 and vv. 10-11, the grammatical construction is complicated, constrained. True, one is still able to understand what Paul intends to say, but a literal translation is hardly feasible. The tortuous character of these sentences is likely caused by the delicate content to be expressed[54].

Was it Paul's first idea to end his appeal with the recommendation of the brothers? This cannot be excluded. Yet what might perhaps be called an accidental addition in v. 24 ("and our boasting about you to them") forces Paul to continue or to begin again. The discussion of the connection between 9,1-5 and 8,24 in part II of this study would seem to plead for their unity and, through the coherence of 8,24–9,5, for considering 8,16–9,5 as a textual unit[55]. Yet, as we have seen, the end of 8,24 is but loosely attached to what precedes and the argument within 9,1-5 is too weighty and autonomous to make it subservient to the recommendation of the brothers. Moreover, the *praeteritio* in 9,1 constitutes a break and a sort of new beginning.

In *chapter 9*, Paul's continued appeal, three sections can be distinguished: vv. 1-5 (do not put me to shame); vv. 6-9 (give liberally); and vv. 10-15 (thanksgivings will accompany your gift). The end of v. 5 announces the theme of the second section, and this second section is finished off beautifully by the psalm quotation of v. 9[56].

In 9,1-5 Paul informs his addressees about what he has told the Macedonians of them: Achaia has been ready since last year. Yet, since some Macedonians could come with him to Corinth, Paul fears that he (and the Corinthians) might be put to shame if it becomes evident that, as a matter of fact, the "promised" collection is not ready. Therefore, by way of precaution, he has sent "the brothers" ahead of him. One can hardly miss the point: this first section already contains an implicit exhortation to complete the collection.

This exhortation, then, becomes more explicit in the second section (9,6-9). Paul urges the Corinthians to give in a generous way. He uses the

---

[54] For more about Paul's strategy, cf S.J. JOUBERT, "Behind the Mask of Rhetoric: 2 Corinthians 8 and the Intra-Textual Relation between Paul and the Corinthians", *Neotest* 26 (1992) 101-112.

[55] Cf. FURNISH, *II Corinthians*, 420, who takes 8,16–9,5 as a unit: "Commendation of the Representatives".

[56] 2 Cor 8–9 contains two explicit citations from the Old Testament, both ending a subdivision and both introduced by καθὼς γέγραπται: 8,15 (Exod 16,18: equality) and 9,9 (Ps 111,9, LXX: liberality).

image of sowing and reaping; he emphasizes that God will lavishly provide the Corinthians with all kinds of gifts and will take care of them, so that there will be enough of everything for an independent, self-sufficient life, enough also for doing even more good works. Their generosity, Paul adds by citing the psalm, will be remembered for ever.

In the third section (9,10-15), God is the central figure. God creates, as it were, the generosity of the Corinthians. The result is that their liberality will bring with it much thanksgiving on the part of those who receive the collection, i.e., "the saints" of Jerusalem. If "the saints" of v. 12 are the grammatical subject of the verb δοξάζοντες ("glorifying") in v. 13, Paul further deals with their actions: these saints will glorify God for the Corinthians' obedient Christian life and their generosity, and they will pray for them and even long for them because of God's surpassing grace given them. Yet, according to a perhaps more defensible grammatical analysis, the Corinthians themselves are the ones who will glorify God by their obedience to the gospel and also, of course, by their generous giving. Paul then announces that the Jerusalem Christians, in their prayer, will long for the Gentile Christians, because of the grace of God, i.e., the salvation, which is also given to them. Paul thanks God for this inexpressible gift. One sees how — in both interpretations — this third section becomes more general, almost all-embracing.

Just as in certain places in chapter 8, the style in 9,3-4.5.10-11 and 13-14 is heavy. One cannot avoid the impression that to a certain extent such a constrained way of writing is intentional. When the two collection chapters are taken together, Paul's inventiveness in exhorting his Christians to renewed and generous giving arrests the attention. He refers to the example of the churches of Macedonia and, quite unexpectedly, even to the example of the Lord Jesus Christ becoming poor though he was rich. He appeals the Corinthians' well-known eagerness and fervor. He announces that he is going to "test" the genuineness of their love. He tells his readers that, in front of the Macedonians, he is boasting of their project: since last year it has been prepared. This, however, is an overzealous statement, not without danger; Paul immediately adds that, out of fear of being shamed, he has sent ahead of him Titus and the other two brothers to "arrange" the collection "before" his arrival. Above all, he speaks of God who is the creative source of their generosity and who himself is continually giving in abundance; God who will be glorified by the Corinthians' obedience to the gospel and by the collection itself; God, finally, who also will exceedingly be thanked by "the saints" for what they, the Corinthians, are doing, for the grace given to them.

From the last verses of these two chapters a great expectation emerges, the grandiose dream of Paul. The collection as such has nothing to do with the payment of the temple tax. The collection is certainly more than a charitable gathering of money; it means more than purely material help to the poor. Not only is Paul certain that "the saints" of Jerusalem will thank God for what they receive, he also inwardly hopes that, through their reception of this collection, his apostolic work among the Gentiles will be fully recognized. It is a dream of final reconciliation and mutual appreciation; it is a vision of the sealed union between Jewish and Gentile Christians, of Christian love and prayer and longing for one another. For Paul, therefore, that collection is the implementation of the agreement with the "three pillars" (cf. Gal 2,10). Above all the collection must be seen as a demonstrative sign of unity between Gentile Christians and the Jewish Christians of Jerusalem. In its way, the collection even achieves that union without endangering the equal status of the Gentiles. According to Paul, the material gesture is not without spiritual dimensions, that of genuine love, a communion which for Paul is the very stamp of Christianity[57].

CONCLUSION

Although it is better to avoid seeing chapter 9 as a doublet of chapter 8 and although the connections, conceptual and verbal, between the two chapters are numerous indeed, we hesitate to assume a pre-established outline in Paul's mind for their composition. We are left with the impression that most likely chapter 8 has its pre-arranged structure (example, appeal, recommendation), but that chapter 9, after all, has rather been "added": a new beginning which explains the danger of Paul's boasting, a renewed motivated insistence (now on generosity), a second Old Testament citation, and with the thanksgiving a final broadening of the horizon. This lengthy addition is probably occasioned by the unexpected mention of boasting in 8,24. Of course, characterizing chapter 9 as an "addition" in no way diminishes its content value. Nor does such a view make chapter 9 independent. No, from the beginning the two chapters have belonged together.

---

[57] Cf. GEORGI, *Die Geschichte der Kollekte*; NICKLE, *The Collection*; K. BERGER, "Almosen für Israel", *NTS* 23 (1976-77) 180-204, esp. 195-204.

11

Dangerous Boasting
Paul's Self-Commendation in 2 Corinthians 10–13

In 2 Cor 12,7-9 Paul exclaims that he had three times appealed to the Lord that the messenger of Satan would no longer torment him, that the thorn in the flesh might be removed. The answer of the risen Lord was: "My grace is sufficient for you, for power is made perfect in weakness". Paul briefly comments on this saying and, at the end, asserts: "Whenever I am weak, then I am strong" (12,10). For listener or reader, such seemingly paradoxical language is both disturbing and attractive. It is not easy to understand, and this can lead to frustration. On the other had, driven by the initial obscurity of the apparent paradox, some may postulate a hidden profound truth. Thus it has been maintained that however difficult it is logically to grasp what Paul means, his weakness is strength. The two contradictory terms must be identified. For such a position we can refer to, e.g., Ernst Käsemann, Erhardt Güttgemanns and Jacob Jervell[1].

Two recent publications strongly and, it appears to me, rightly[2] argue against this view: the 1990 article by Scott Hafemann, "'Self-Commendation' and Apostolic Legitimacy"[3], and the 1993 monograph by Ulrich Heckel, "Kraft in Schwachheit"[4]. According to these studies, for Paul,

---

[1] See the discussion of this position in my "The Nekrōsis of Jesus. Ministry and Suffering in 2 Cor 4,7-15", A. Vanhoye (ed.), *L'apôtre Paul. Personnalité, style et conception du ministère* (BETL 73; Leuven 1986) 120-143, esp. 128-143; published also in R. Bieringer–J. Lambrecht, *Studies in 2 Corinthians* (BETL 112; Leuven 1994) 309-333. — For a good survey of opinions concerning 2 Cor 12,9-10, see V.S. Nicdao, *Power in Weakness in 2 Corinthians 12,9-10. A History of Recent Interpretations* (unpubl. licentiate thesis, Katholieke Universiteit Leuven 1991).

[2] Cf. Lambrecht, "Nekrōsis", 131: "Weakness itself is not power, neither is suffering glory, nor death life".

[3] S. Hafemann, "'Self-Commendation' and Apostolic Legitimacy in 2 Corinthians: A Pauline Dialectic" *NTS* 36 (1990) 66-88.

[4] U. Heckel, *Kraft in Schwachheit. Untersuchungen zu 2. Kor 10–13* (WUNT 2/56; Tübingen 1993).

as for us, weakness cannot simply coincide with strength. In order to understand Paul's paradoxical statement some distinctions must be made.

In common speech self-commendation need not necessarily be understood as boasting. In commending oneself, a person often intends his or her self-praise as a justification or legitimation. Boasting for the most part misses that nuance: in boasting one publicly speaks of status and achievements with justifiable or unjustifiable pride. Yet in 2 Cor 10,17-18 Paul connects the terms boasting and self-commendation. He first freely cites part of Jer 9,22-23: "Let the one who boasts, boast in the Lord"[5] and then adds his own reflection: "For it is not those who commend themselves that are approved, but those whom the Lord commends". Moreover, at first sight Paul here seems to disapprove of self-commendation as well as of boasting of oneself. We are led, it would seem, to conclude that the one who commends him/herself does not boast in the Lord, and this is greatly reprehensible. Therefore we understand Paul's hesitation in the same chapter: "Even if I boast a little too much of our authority, which the Lord gave for building you up and not for tearing you down, I will not be ashamed of it" (10,8). Nevertheless, according to Paul, in this verse boasting is not radically excluded nor can it always be avoided. Further in the letter, Paul will boast "as a fool", he will boast "according to the flesh, not according to the Lord", and he will also boast of his weaknesses. Moreover, he sometimes boasts of his apostolic attitude and achievements. So a number of questions arise. When and why does boasting and self-commendation become wrong? Is all boasting perhaps in a certain sense foolish? Is it always dangerous? What type of self-commendation does Paul use? What type is permitted?

It would seem that within the delicate, confusing complex of Paul's statements three aspects must be kept in mind: there certainly is such a thing as legitimate boasting: all boasting, however, is dangerous; and boasting concretely functions in Paul's defensive self-commendation.

---

[5] Paul has already cited this text in 1 Cor 1,31 where he formally introduces it as a Scripture quotation by "as it is written". See the study by J. SCHREINER, "Jeremias 9,22.23 als Hintergrund des paulinischen 'Sich-Rühmens'", J. GNILKA (ed.), Neues Testament und Kirche. FS R. Schnackenburg (Freiburg– Basel–Wien 1974) 530-542; HECKEL, Kraft in Schwachheit, 172-182. Cf. also K. WONG, "'Lord' in 2 Corinthians 10:17", LouvSt 17 (1992) 243-245: the "Lord" in 2 Cor 10,17-18 is God (cf. v. 13), not Christ. C. WOLFF, Der zweite Brief des Paulus an die Korinther (THNT; Berlin 1989) 207, maintains — unconvincingly, it would seem — that not Jer 9,23-24 but the Septuagint text of 1 Sam 2,10 forms the basis of this so-called citation because of the context in 1 Sam and the early church's acquaintance with the song of Hanna (1 Sam 2,1-10).

I. LEGITIMATE BOASTING

Paul is convinced that only boasting in the Lord is acceptable boasting[6]. By commending themselves and taking pride in the work of others, Paul's opponents give in to wrongful boasting; they do not boast in the Lord. But what must we say about Paul's own self-commendation, the boasting of his authority and his apostolic successes? Is this boasting legitimate? Is this perhaps "boasting in the Lord"?

No doubt Paul feels uneasy with self-commendation. In 2 Cor 3,1 he asks: "Are we beginning to commend ourselves again?" and in 5,12 he stresses: "We are not commending ourselves again". Yet in 3,2-3 Paul openly claims that by itself the existence of the Corinthian church is the equivalent of a letter of recommendation: a letter "written on our hearts, to be known and read by all ..., a letter of Christ". In 4,2 he writes: "by the open statement of the truth we commend ourselves to the conscience of everyone in the sight of God". And in 6,3-10 he even maintains that no obstacle is put in anyone's way, so that no fault may be found with his ministry; as a servant of God he has commended himself in every way (then follows a list of tribulations). 2 Cor 10 provides us with an impressive example of Paul's legitimate boasting.

The Structure of 2 Corinthians 10

Chapters 10–13 of 2 Corinthians can be taken as a unity, with a style and tone all of their own which distinguish them from the rest of the letter.

---

[6] Cf. the seminar paper of C.K. BARRETT, "Boasting (καυχᾶσθαι, κτλ) in the Pauline Epistles", A. VANHOYE (ed.), *L'Apôtre Paul*, 363-368; J. SÁNCHEZ BOSCH, "L'apologie apostolique — 2 Cor 10–11 comme réponse de Paul à ses adversaires", E. LOHSE (ed.), *Verteidigung und Begründung des apostolischen Amtes (2 Kor 10–13)* (Benedictina 11; Rome 1992) 43-63. We just mention a few recent studies: J. SÁNCHEZ BOSCH, *"Gloriarse" segun San Pablo. Sentido y teologia de 'καυχάομαι'* (AnBib 40; Rome 1970); E.A. JUDGE, "Paul's Boasting in Relation to Contemporary Professional Practice", *AusBR* 16 (1968) 37-50; C. FORBES, "Comparison, Self-Praise and Irony. Paul's Boasting and the Conventions of Hellenistic Rhetoric", *NTS* 32 (1986) 1-30; H.D. BETZ, "De laude ipsius (Masalia 539A-547F)", ID. (ed.) *Plutarch's Ethical Writings and Early Christian Literature* (StCHNT 4; Leiden 1978) 367-393 (on Paul: 378-381). For boasting as a divisive force within the Corinthian community, see the analysis of 1 Cor 1–4 by M.M. MITCHEL, *Paul and the Rhetoric of Reconciliation. An Exegetical Investigation of the Language and Composition of 1 Corinthians* (HUT 28; Tübingen 1991) 91-95; for 2 Cor 10–13 see H.D. BETZ, *Der Apostel Paulus und die sokratische Tradition* (BHT 45; Tübingen 1972) 70-100.

The style is vivid and emotional: pleading and parenesis, biting irony, bitter sarcasm, threat and condemnation go hand-in-hand. The tone is both apologetic (self-defense vis-à-vis the faithful of Corinth) and, indirectly, polemical (attack against the opponents, the intruders). Moreover, Paul's way or reasoning in these chapters has paradoxical — if not contradictory — features about it. In 10,12, Paul states that he does not wish to compare himself with some of those who rate themselves so highly[7] but, as a matter of a fact, already in 10,13-16 and again in chapters 11 and 12, he does compare himself with his opponents. Again, Paul stresses that boasting is foolish; and yet, he must boast; he is compelled to do it. But then, paradoxically it would seem, what he ultimately boasts of is his weaknesses. Is this still "foolish" boasting? Further, the majority of the sections in chapters 10–13 can be regarded as apologies, and indeed they are apologies, but Paul himself protests in 12,19: "Have you been thinking all along that we have been defending ourselves before you? We are speaking in Christ before God. Everything we do, beloved, is for the sake of building you up".

Although no strict, obvious division can be discovered within chapter 10, two subunits present themselves: verses 1-11 and verses 12-18[8]. The first one is held together by the motif of Paul's future coming (see v. 2 and v. 11) and by the reproaches referred to or quoted in verse 1b and verse 10. The second subunit, although connected to the preceding by γάρ in verse 12, which probably refers back to verse 8, forms a kind of excursus, a seemingly independent consideration in which the themes of commendation (vv. 12 and 18) and boasting (vv. 13, 15, 16 and 17) are developed by Paul by means of an explanation of how he envisages his apostolic authority in relation to the field of his work. This second pericope is, moreover, clearly related to chapters 11 and 12 by its motif of boasting.

With a very emphatic expression Paul begins a new section in 10,1: Αὐτὸς δὲ ἐγὼ Παῦλος παρακαλῶ ὑμᾶς ... This sentence, however, remains incomplete. Probably, the phrase δέομαι δέ of verse 2, which constitutes a new beginning after the relative clause of verse 1b, takes up the idea present in the verb παρακαλῶ. If so, what is said in verse 2-6 can be considered as the explication of what Paul already had in mind in writing

---

[7] Of course, Paul's statement of v. 12 also has somewhat the character of a rhetorical device. Recently two authors have reconstructed the identity of Paul's opponents in Corinth by means of data from 2 Corintians 10–13: R. PENNA, "La présence des adversaires de Paul en 2 Cor 10–13", LOHSE (éd.), Verteidigung, 7-41; G. STRECKER, "Die Legitimität des paulinischen Apostolates nach 2 Kor 10–13", ibid., 107-128, esp. 112-114 (= NTS 38 [1992] 566-586).

[8] For a discussion of the "delimitation of the pericope 2 Cor 10,12-18", see WONG, "Lord", 244-246.

verse 1a. After verse 6 another topic is introduced. A number of data, however, does not sustain the view that the line of thought of 10,1-11 is simply twofold. Verses 9-11 clearly point back to verses 1-6, so that these two sets of verses can be spoken of as corresponding parts.

The parallelism between verses 1-6 and 9-11 involves four elements. (1) In both units the opposition between Paul's behavior when he is present at Corinth and when he is absent is mentioned: see the verbs πάρειμι (or the noun παρουσία) and ἄπειμι in verses 1-2 and 11, and compare ταπεινὸς κατὰ σάρκα and θαρρῶ in verse 1 with ἀσθενής–ἐξουθενημένος and βαρύς–ἰσχυρός in verse 10. (2) When Paul is away he is said to be bold. In verses 1-3 it is not explicitly stated that this boldness appears in his letters. But most probably we have to explain the reference to Paul's boldness in these verses in this way in light of the threefold mention of "letters" in verses 9, 10 and 11. (3) In both passages Paul seems to anticipate a future visit to Corinth. Such a visit is undoubtedly referred to in verse 2 (see also vv. 4b-6) and most probably in verse 11 (cf. the affirmation of his future boldness and confidence). (4) Just as verses 2a and 3-6 can be considered as Paul's apologetic answer to the reproach implied in verse 1b and 2b, so verse 11 can be seen as Paul's defense against the accusation quoted in verse 10. In view of all these correspondences[9], one cannot avoid the impression that the accusation concerning his so-called difference in attitude is the center of Paul attention in both sets of verses.

Concerning the inner structure of chapter 10 an important feature must still be noted, namely the introductory function of verse 8 in relation to verses 12-18. In verse 8 (and perhaps already in verse 7) Paul speaks of the apostolic authority given to him by the Lord. He prepares the reader for the "boasting" which follows. He will use his building up of the Corinthians as the basis of his self-commendation. The same three themes of authority, boasting and commendation are then explicitly dealt with in verses 12-18. We may also refer to the following parallelism of both vocabulary and motif:

---

[9] Nonetheless, the parallelism between vv. 1-6 and 9-11 is not perfect. Therefore it would hardly be appropriate to characterize the structure of 10,1-11 as intentionally concentric. The somewhat cyclic feature is, rather, the casual result of Paul's emotional way of writing here. Moreover, grammatically speaking, the ἵνα-clause of v. 9 may still belong to the sentence that begins in v. 8. The differences between vv. 1-6 and 9-11 are also worth noting: (a) Only in vv. 1-6 do we find Paul's entreating and pleading (cf. the introductory verbs in the first person singular in vv. 1 and 2); only here too does Paul explain, by means of a brief apology, the source of his boldness (vv. 4b-6). (b) The mention of the letters in vv. 9-11 and the quotation of v. 10 specify and concretize the reproach which is only alluded to in vv. 1b and 2b; in v. 11 there is, moreover, an appeal to the person(s) who made the accusation.

verse 8	verses 12-18
περισσότερόν τι	οὐκ εἰς τὰ ἄμετρα (vv. 13, 15)
καυχήσωμαι	καυχησόμεθα (v. 13)
ἐξουσία	μέτρον τοῦ κανόνος (v. 13; cf. v. 15)
ἔδωκεν ὁ κύριος	ἐμέρισεν ... ὁ θεός (v. 13)
the building up	evangelization (vv. 14-16)
οὐχ αἰσχυνθήσομαι	ὃν (also Paul) ὁ κύριος συνίστησιν (v. 18).

It would seem, then, that the annunciatory function of verse 8 (and v. 7) cannot be denied. But this, in turn, entails that verses 9-11 now appear as a kind of interruption.

We find in 2 Corinthians thus two main points in the argument. In this chapter Paul first and foremost defends himself against the claim that he is bold and strong only when absent, that is, in his letters. His so-called timidity, however, must not be misinterpreted. If necessary, he will "show boldness" when present: see verses 1-6 and 9-11. Within verses 7-8 and 12-18, a second point appears. Here Paul deals with what he really is (he belongs to Christ, v. 7) and with the authority the Lord has given him (v. 8); he deals with his apostolic prerogatives in Corinth (vv. 13-16); he boasts. And so, if our structural analysis is correct, the line of thought in 2 Corinthians 10 can be visualized in terms of the following "back and forth" or symmetric pattern:

a		vv. 1-6	Paul's attitude (humble–bold)
	b	vv. 7-8	boasting
a		vv. 9-11	Paul's attitude (weak–strong)
	b	vv. 12-18	boasting

One more characteristic of 2 Corinthians should not be overlooked: its relation with 12,14–13,10. As in 12,14–13,10 Paul begins in chapter 10 by exhorting the Corinthians. Something has to be done by them before his coming. In both sections Paul also announces his future (third) visit[10].

---

[10] Chapters 10 and 13 can be considered, to some degree, as framing and including the middle chapters 11 and 12.

a) A number of motifs are present in both chapter 10 and chapter 13: Paul speaks of his absence and presence at Corinth (10,1-2.11 and 13,2.10) and of his future (third) coming (10,2.4-6.11 and 13,1.2.10). In both chapters, he threatens to show boldness, to be severe and not to spare anyone at this coming (10,2.11 and 13,2.10). The motif of obedience–disobedience on the part of the Corinthians which is explicitly spoken of in 10,6 also seems present in 13,1-2.5.9-10. Paul mentions in 10,9-11, but equally in 13,10, his earlier letters and/or his actual writing. In both chapters Paul opposes the themes of weakness and power. Moreover, in 10,8 and 13,10, by means of an almost identical wording, he points to the auhority which the Lord has given him for building up

Moreover, we cannot avoid the impression that already in chapter 10 Paul has been thinking of bringing his letter to a close. He wishes to express a final concern, to give a last exhortation. The Corinthians should no longer suspect him of being a poor, weak apostle. They should, rather, become obedient, avoid disorder and sin. They should examine and test themselves! The connection of chapter 10 with 12,14–13,10 suggests that all Paul's boasting — his apology and polemics, his speaking of himself and his self-commendation — can be considered as a sort of digression. Is not the whole of 10,7–12,13 a long insertion in between 10,6 and 12,14, analogous to the way in which 2,14–7,4 interrupts Paul's account of his plans in 1,12–2,13 and 7,5-16[11]?

Paul's Reasoning in 2 Cor 10,12-18

Verses 13-16 comprise the core of the pericope, surrounded by verse

---

and not for tearing down. In 10,18 we meet the motif of "tested and approved" which is dominant in chapter 13 (see vv. 3.5-7). "To belong to Christ" in 10,7 recurs in slightly different expressions in 13,5: "to be in the faith; Christ Jesus is in you" (cf. 13,3: "Christ is speakinig in me").

b) In light of the presence in both chapters of these common motifs, it should not surprise us that there is a similarity in their respective vocabularies as well. We compare

	ch. 10	with	*13,1-10*	
1	ταπεινός		(cf. 12,21: ταπεινώσει)	
	ἀπών (11 ἀπόντες)		2.10	ἀπών
2	παρών (11 παρόντες)		2.10	παρών
4	δυνατός		3	δυνατέω, 4 δύναμις, 9 δυνατός
6	ἐν ἑτοίμῳ ἔχοντες		(cf. 12,14: ἑτοίμως ἔχω)	
7	Χριστοῦ εἶναι		5	Χριστὸς Ἰησοῦς ἐν ὑμῖν
8	περὶ τῆς ἐξουσίας		10	κατὰ τὴν ἐξουσίαν
	ἧς ἔδωκεν ὁ κύριος			ἣν ὁ κύριος ἔδωκέν μοι
	εἰς οἰκοδομήν			εἰς οἰκοδομήν (cf. 12,19: ὑπὲρ τῆς ὑμῶν οἰκοδομῆς)
	καὶ οὐκ εἰς καθαίρεσιν			καὶ οὐκ εἰς καθαίρεσιν
9-11	ἐπιστολαί		10	γράφων
15	πίστις		5	πίστις
18	δόκιμος		7	δόκιμος, 3 δοκιμή
			5	δοκιμάζω, 5.6.7. ἀδόκιμος

Given all these parallels, E.-B. ALLO, *Seconde épître aux Corinthiens* (EtB; Paris ²1956) 240, can affirm: "L''apologie' des 4 chapitres font un tout très harmonique, où la fin rejoint le commencement". Cf. also M.-A. CHEVALLIER, "L'argumentation de Paul dans II Corinthiens 10 à 13", *RHPR* 70 (1990) 3-15, esp. 13-14.

[11] Cf. HECKEL, *Kraft in Schwachheit*, 6-51: 10,1-6 is "der Eingangsappell", 10,7–12,13 "der apologetische Vergleich mit dem Selbstruhm der Gegner", 12,14–13,10 "die Ankündigung für den dritten Besuch", and 13,11-13 "der Briefschluss".

12 and verses 17-18[12]. In this middle part Paul speaks of himself, of what he has done and what he hopes to do. He does not boast of work which is not his own. In stating what he is doing and not doing, he is defending himself and, in a veiled and polemic way, compares himself with others, his opponents. They are explicitly referred to in verse 12 and the allusion to them in verses 17-18 can hardly be missed. The framing verses 12 and 17-18[13] contain Paul's counter attack; he accuses his opponents of self-commendation and comparison with one another; he stresses the non-sense, the worthlessness of such an attitude. The wrong sort of boasting and commendation (vv. 17-18; cf. v. 13a) consists precisely in the fact that the opponents measure themselves by themselves and compare themselves with one another. How does the argumentation proceed?

Verse 12: Οὐ γὰρ τολμῶμεν ἐγκρῖναι ἢ συγκρῖναι ἑαυτούς τισιν τῶν ἑαυτοὺς συνιστανόντων, ἀλλὰ αὐτοὶ ἐν ἑαυτοῖς ἑαυτοὺς μετροῦντες καὶ συγκρίνοντες ἑαυτοὺς ἑαυτοῖς οὐ συνιᾶσιν. If is it correct to see verse 12 linked by its γάρ to verse 8, then Paul intends to begin the boasting of his authority which he announced in that verse. His boasting will not, however, take the form of a comparison with his opponents who commend themselves, for their self-commendation consists in reciprocal measuring and comparing and all this leads to boasting beyond measure (see v. 13a).

Verses 13-16: 13 ἡμεῖς δὲ οὐκ εἰς τὰ ἄμετρα καυχησόμεθα ἀλλὰ κατὰ τὸ μέτρον τοῦ κανόνος οὗ ἐμέρισεν ἡμῖν ὁ θεὸς μέτρου, ἐφικέσθαι ἄχρι καὶ ὑμῶν. 14 οὐ γὰρ ὡς μὴ ἐφικνούμενοι εἰς ὑμᾶς ὑπερεκτείνομεν ἑαυτούς, ἄχρι γὰρ καὶ ὑμῶν ἐφθάσαμεν ἐν τῷ εὐαγγελίῳ τοῦ Χριστοῦ, 15 οὐκ εἰς τὰ ἄμετρα καυχώμενοι ἐν ἀλλοτρίοις κόποις, ἐλπίδα δὲ ἔχοντες αὐξανομένης τῆς πίστεως ὑμῶν ἐν ὑμῖν μεγαλυνθῆναι κατὰ τὸν κανόνα ἡμῶν εἰς περισσείαν 16 εἰς τὰ ὑπερέκεινα ὑμῶν εὐαγγελίσασθαι, οὐκ ἐν ἀλλοτρίῳ κανόνι εἰς τὰ

---

[12] For a defense of the longer reading in vv. 12-13, see B. METZGER, *A Textual Commentary on the Greek New Testament* (London–New York 1985) 583: "The absence of οὐ συνιᾶσιν. ἡμεῖς δέ ... is doubtless the result of an accident in transcription, when the eye of a copyist passed from οὐ to οὐκ and omitted the intervening words".

[13] See the terminological elements of what could perhaps be called an inclusion: τῶν ἑαυτοὺς συνιστανόντων in v. 12 and ὁ ἑαυτὸν συνιστάνων in v. 18, as well as the correspondence in content between two negative assertions: οὐ συνιᾶσιν in v. 12 and οὐ ... δόκιμος in v. 18. We say "perhaps", since other elements militate against too sharp a division. In v. 12 Paul begins with the first person plural (see the emphatic ἡμεῖς δέ at the beginning of v. 13 over against αὐτοί at the beginning of v. 12b). Moreover, in vv. 13-16 he indirectly attacks his opponents while, in vv. 17-18, he has in mind both himself and the opponents. There is, no doubt, a cyclic structure, but it should not be pressed too strongly.

ἕτοιμα καυχήσασθαι. Paul's standard of boasting is the auhority given to him by God. In the unfolding of verses 13-16, it becomes clearer how Paul concretely understands that authority. It is a sphere assigned to him by God, consisting of the regions where Paul has to proclaim the gospel and is entitled to do so. Corinth belongs to these regions. Paul has not exceeded his legitimate measure and he has not taken credit for what others have done. Both verse 14 and verse 15a are a repetition of verse 13[14], but, at the same time, each of them goes a step further in the concretization:

V. 13: We will not boast "without measure"[15],

but according to the measure of our "canon" (i.e. to reach you)[16].

V. 14: For we are not overextending ourselves

for we were the first to come to you with the gospel of Christ.

V. 15a: We are not boasting "without measure", i.e., in other men's labors ...

In verses 15b-16 the rather static and apologetic reference to his past missionary activity in Corinth (vv. 13-15a) gives way toward a glance to the future. Paul cherishes the hope of preaching the gospel in regions beyond the Corinthians[17], once their faith is increased[18].

---

[14] If v. 13a can be taken as a resumption of v. 12a (cf. negation, first person plural, similar content), the parallelism between vv. 13a, 14a, 15a (and 16a) is even more striking. All these clauses are negatively formulated and in the first person plural. All contain the theme "without measure" (vv. 13a and 15a) or a ὑπέρ-construction (vv. 14a and 16a). See also the term ἀλλότριος in v. 15a and v. 16b. The negation in vv. 13a, 14a and 16a is followed each time by a positive corrective or explanatory assertion.

[15] Cf. HAFEMANN, "Self-Commendation", 78: "Literally, εἰς τὰ ἄμετρα could ... be translated 'things without a measure' or 'beyond proper limits' or even 'extravagantly'". Taking into account the two uses of μέτρον in the same verse and the specific emphasis in vv. 13-16, a literal translation recommends itself: "ἄμετρος can be rendered as the simple negation of μέτρον, which figuratively would represent the idea of 'extravagance', i.e., something measured which goes beyond the norm" (ibid.).

[16] The grammar of v. 13 is notoriously difficult and the meaning or nuance of κανών in vv. 13 and 16 is disputed. According to HAFEMANN, "Self-Commendation", 76-80, "canon" here has no local sense: it retains "its normal concrete meaning of 'standard of judgment' or 'norm'" (78). He critically discusses the short contribution of J.F. STRANGE, "2 Corinthians 10:13-16 Illuminated by a Recently Published Inscription", BA 46 (1983) 176-168, who thinks to have found in this inscription a witness for the local meaning of "canon"; so also E.E. JUDGE, "The Regional 'Kanōn' for the Requisitioned Transport", G.H.R. HORSLEY (ed.), New Documents Illustrating Early Christianity (North Ryde 1989) 36-45. Cf. STRECKER, "Die Legitimität", 115-116.

[17] Cf. 1 Cor 1,17: "Christ did not send me to baptize, but to proclaim the gospel". With regard to Paul's missionary planning, cf. Rom 15,15-21. See also PENNA, "La présence des adversaires", 20: "Il ne faut pas exclure qu'en 10,13-16, il y ait une allusion à la convention de Jérusalem (cf. Gal 2,6-10), qui reconnaissait à Paul une compétence missionnaire auprès des païens, et dont les adversaires, au contraire, ne disposaient pas".

[18] Compare the idea of growth in 10,6: "when your obedience is complete".

Verses 17-18: 17 Ὁ δὲ καυχώμενος ἐν κυρίῳ καυχάσθω· 18 οὐ γὰρ ὁ ἑαυτὸν συνιστάνων, ἐκεῖνός ἐστιν δόκιμος, ἀλλὰ ὃν ὁ κύριος συνίστησιν. After verse 16 Paul concludes. The thesis-sentences are put in the third person, but Paul certainly has himself in mind as well as his opponents. By measuring themselves against one another and by boasting of others' work and commending themselves, the opponents show their lack of "good sense" (v. 12); they will not be approved. The addressees of the letter should compare Paul with the intruders and draw the appropriate conclusion. For "it is not the man who commends himself that is accepted, but the man whom the Lord commends" (v. 18, RSV)[19].

Boasting in 2 Cor 10,8 and 12-18

The situation in Corinth is most critical for Paul. He is said to be weak when present. His speech is contemptible; only his letters are weighty and strong, but when writing, of course, he is absent. Apparently other missionaries display more strength, more rhetorical skill. Paul's authority in Corinth is no longer beyond dispute. For his own part, Paul does not want to show boldness, but he will be ready to punish every disobedience at his future coming.

In 10,8 and 10,13-16 Paul refers to the authority which the Lord himself has given him. He mentions his personal commission, the evangelization of the Gentiles, and this commission includes his work among the Corinthians. He was the founder of their Christian community; he was the first to reach Corinth with the gospel of Christ. So he is not overstretching his "measure". On the contrary, the very existence of the Corinthian church, the fruit of his missionary work, is his true recommendation and his rightful, legitimate boast (cf. also 3,2-3)[20].

Paul's emphatic argumentation in 2 Cor 10 brings us to the obvious

---

[19] Apparently in order to avoid exclusive language the NRSV translation changed singular into plural: "For it is not those who commend themselves that are approved, but those whom the Lord commends". The NEB version has: "For it is not *the one* who recommends himself, but *the one* whom the Lord recommends, who is to be accepted". Here the end is surprising: "is to be accepted" renders ἐστιν δόκιμος.

[20] Cf. HAFEMANN, "Self-Commendation", 80: "Paul's assertion in v. 13 makes it clear that the contrast between Paul's boast and the boast of his opponents described in v. 12 is based on the unexpressed premise that his 'founding function' is the only appropriate, divinely appointed 'canon' according to which apostolic authority in a particular church can be determined". As we will see further on, "only" is exaggerated.

conclusion that not all self-commendation, not all boasting of personal achievement, is wrong. We cannot but apply what is said by Paul in verses 17-18 also to Paul himself. Because in Corinth he has built under God's commission, the work he did was God's work. His boasting of the faith of the Corinthians as the result of his efforts is at the same time a boasting in the Lord. Through his accomplishment he is recommended by the Lord. Self-commendation and recommendation by God here coincide. Scott Hafemann comments: Paul's "boast concerning his authority is, in reality, merely the appropriate human counterpart to the 'Lord's commendation' upon which one's approval ultimately rests"[21]. God's commission provided Paul with authority; that commission was carried out by Paul and resulted in a visible church. The Corinthian church, therefore, legitimates the apostle. True, Paul does not like to boast of that authority (see 10,8); true, his boasting is forced upon him through the critical and sad situation in Corinth (see 10,13-16); true, verses 17-18 are meant in the first place as a charge against the unjustified boasting of his opponents. Yet according to 2 Cor 10,8.12-18, since the Lord commends him Paul is approved[22]. He can boast of his authority and achievements in a legitimate way.

II. IS ALL BOASTING DANGEROUS?

In Rom 3,28 "Paul states that (Jewish) boasting is excluded because one (every Christian) is justified by faith apart from works prescribed by the law. In chapter 4 he illustrates this basic thesis by means of the example of Abraham. Our ancestor Abraham believed God, and this was reckoned to him as righteousness. In 4,4-5 a "general" principle is clearly pointed out: "to one who works, wages are not reckoned as a gift but as something due. But to one who without works trusts him [= God] who justifies the ungodly, such faith is reckoned as righteousness". So in Paul's

---

[21] HAFEMANN, "Self-Commendation", 75. See also p. 82: "'To boast in the Lord' is to boast in what God in Christ has actually done through one's life; or expressed actively, to boast in what one has accomplished him/herself in Christ". The thesis of FORBES, "Comparison, Self-Praise and Irony", is too radical: "For Paul *self*-praise is never legitimate" (20). It seems to me that J.A. LOUBSER, "A New Look at Paradox and Irony in 2 Corinthians 10–13", *Neotest* 26 (1992) 507-523, overstates the ironical character of 2 Cor 10–13.

[22] WONG, "Lord", 252, rightly stresses that "boasting in the Lord (= God)" (2 Cor 10,17) must not be simply identified with Paul's boasting in the cross of Jesus Christ (Gal 6,14).

view: the beginning of Christian life, initial justification, comes about "by God's grace as a gift, through the redemption that is in Christ Jesus" (3,24) and, as far as the human subject is concerned, God's righteousness is given "apart from law ... through faith in Jesus Christ for all who believe" (3,21). Therefore, in regard to justification, boasting of personal merit is radically excluded. Therefore, let us boast in God alone (cf. 2 Cor 10,17); may we "never boast of anything except the cross of our Lord Jesus Christ" (Gal 6,14).

We must ask: does this position also apply to the life after justification, our Christian life as justified people who want to reach final salvation? Many answer this question positively, without any hesitation[23]. Yet this may lead, I think, to a less correct understanding of Paul. The apostle, we have seen, does not absolutely reject legitimate boasting and self-commendation, for he himself boasts of his fruitful missionary achievement in Corinth. In his opinion this boasting coincides with boasting in the Lord. To be sure, we also saw that not all boasting is legitimate, certainly not that of his opponents. There is therefore an opposition between sinful, ungodly boasting[24] and rightful, legitimate boasting. But what can be said about Paul's famous "foolish" boasting in 2 Cor 11–12? Does it belong to the category of wrongful, sinful boasting? Probably not.

Wise Versus Foolish Boasting?

In this context, a distinction is usually made between boasting foolishly, i.e., according to the flesh, not according to the Lord (cf. 11,17-18), and boasting that is wise and permitted, i.e., boasting in the Lord. In 2 Cor 11,1, Paul pleads that his readers tolerate him, even when he is a little foolish. In 11,16, he repeats: no one should think that he (Paul) is a fool, but if they do, then they must accept him as a fool, so that he too may boast a little. For since there are so many who boast κατὰ σάρκα, he will do the same (cf. 11,18). What exactly will he do? Since the Corinthians so gladly tolerate fools, he too will act as a fool, he will boast of his Jewish pedigree;

---

[23] See, e.g., R.H. GUNDRY, "Grace, Works, and Staying Saved in Paul", *Bib* 66 (1985) 1-38 (very strongly against E.P. Sanders).

[24] In Rom 2,17-24 Paul seems to have no quarrel with Jewish boasting in and of itself, boasting in God, boasting in the law, boasting in the Jewish privileges. Boasting becomes illegitimate and unacceptable if one dishonors the law. See J. LAMBRECHT–R.W. THOMPSON, *Justification by Faith: The Implication of Romans 3:27-31* (ZaStNT; Collegeville 1989) 13-30.

like his opponents he is a Hebrew, an Israelite, a descendant of Abraham
(11,19-22). He then goes on: "Are they ministers of Christ? — I am talking
like a madman — I am a better one: with far greater labors, far more impri-
sonments, with countless flogging, and often near death" (11,23).

In 11,24-29 he goes on with a list of hardships: tribulations, persecutions and difficulties undergone. It is often said that, within this list, almost
imperceptibly a shift takes place; Paul no longer mentions his glorious
accomplishments but insists upon absence of power, upon utter weakness
and misery. Therefore, in 11,30 he is able to state: "If I must boast, I will
boast of the things that show my weakness". This verse may point to the
shameful escape from Damascus which he is about to narrate in 11,32-33,
but, as is evident from 12,10a, it also refers back to the list of hardships in
11,23b-29. All this would seem another type of boasting than the "foolish"
boasting of origin and works in 11,22-23b.

Then in 12,1-4, somewhat unexpectedly, Paul begins again: "it is
necessary to boast; nothing is to be gained by it, but I will go on to visions
and revelations of the Lord" (v. 1). Apparently this is, anew, a boasting in
foolishness. However, in 12,5 he repeats: "on my own behalf I will not
boast, except of my weaknesses" and he deals then with "the thorn in his
flesh", the messenger of Satan who torments him (12,7-8). Because the
Lord has revealed that his grace is sufficient and that his power is strongest
when the apostle is weak, Paul even proclaims: "I will boast all the more
gladly of my weaknesses ..." (12,10). Thus twice, in chapter 11 as well as
in chapter 12, foolish boasting gives way to "wise" boasting of weakness.

The question, however, must be raised whether, for Paul, there are
really two types of boasting, wise and unwise. Is there, for Paul, besides
the foolish boasting also a natural, matter-of-course, legitimate boasting
which is wise and not foolish at all? Is such legitimate boasting above all
the paradoxical boasting of weakness[25]? I do not think so. It appears to me
that Paul considers *all* boasting in a certain sense foolish and also dangerous. In 10,8 we have already detected some uneasiness or hesitation in the
formulation of the verse: "Now, even if I boast a little too much of our
authority ..., I will not be ashamed of it". In 11,30, too, there is a sort of
reluctance, also with regard to boasting of weakness: "If I must boast (εἰ
καυχᾶσθαι δεῖ), I will boast of the things that show my weakness". The

---

[25] For FORBES, "Comparison, Self-Praise and Irony", 16-22, Paul's boasting in foolishness is a "deliberate self-derision", ironical throughout. Is this so? Forbes claims that boasting
as such is rejected by Paul; only the paradoxical boasting of weakness is valid. A similar critical evaluation of BETZ, *Der Apostel Paulus*, is needed.

fact that in 12,9 Paul will "rather[26] boast most gladly" of his weaknesses most probably does not mean that he sees this boasting as normal and free of danger. After all, in regard to his boasting in 2 Cor 10–12, that on origin and privileges as well as that on weaknesses, he confesses: "I have been a fool! You forced me to it" (12,11).

Therefore, we are brought to the conclusion that, as a matter of fact, all boasting, whether of status and accomplishment or of poor condition, is foolish and not without danger. To be sure, there certainly is a gradation in foolishness and there are different sorts of boasting and, consequently, different degrees of danger. Moreover, if after all Paul must boast and is forced to do it, he clearly expresses his preference. However, one cannot but assume that some danger of ungodly self-praise and self-exaltation is present in each type of boasting. Yet, despite what must be called again and again God's manifold assistance, Paul was certainly not just a passive idle and "weak" subject.

Boasting of Weakness

This brings us back to the delicate problem of Paul's boasting of weakness. Is he only boasting of his human lack of power, his radical incapacity, his weakness as such? We must here keep in mind Paul's "treasure in clay jars, so that it may be made clear that this extraordinary power belongs to God and does not come from" the apostle himself (4,7). Moreover, there can be no doubt that in 11,23b-33 as in 12,7-8 Paul emphasizes the absence of powerful glory and success. Yet it would be wrong, it seems to me, to eliminate each nuance of Paul's faithful, active endurance. Of course, just as Paul stresses "by the grace of God I am what I am" in 1 Cor 15,10, so it is also by God's grace that Paul can endure. However, the grace that God gave him was not without effect. Through that grace Paul was admirably, heroically strong[27]! We may refer here to 4,8-10 and 16: "We are

---

[26] It would seem that the comparative μᾶλλον determines καυχήσομαι and retains its comparative force. Cf. A. PLUMMER, *A Critical and Exegetical Commentary on the Second Epistle of St Paul to the Corinthians* (ICC; Edinburgh 1915) 335: "Most gladly therefore (because of the Lord's reply) will I rather glory in my weaknesses (than pray that they may be removed). The order of the words is important. It is not μᾶλλον ἐν ταῖς ἀσθενείαις καυχ., and we must not interpret 'will I glory in weaknesses rather than in the revelations granted to me'". I do not agree with HECKEL, *Kraft in Schwachheit*, 101-102, who rejects the comparative sense of μᾶλλον.

[27] Cf. G.G. O'COLLINS, "Power Made Perfect in Weakness: 2 Cor 12:9-10", *CBQ* 33

afflicted in every way, but not crushed; perplexed, but not driven to despair; persecuted, but not forsaken; struck down, but not destroyed .... Even though our outer nature is wasting away, our inner nature is being renewed day by day"[28]; and 6,8-11: "We are treated ... as dying, and see — we are alive ...".

In 12,9-10a the distinction between Paul's weakness and the power of Christ is very evident. The Lord said to Paul: "'My grace is sufficient for you, for power is made perfect in weakness'. So, I will boast all the more gladly of my weaknesses, so that the power of Christ may dwell in me. Therefore I am content with weaknesses, insults, hardships, persecutions, and calamities for the sake of Christ"[29]. The distinction, however, disappears in the paradoxical language of 12,10b: "For whenever I am weak, then I am strong". Of course, we should keep in mind that "paradoxical language intends to be provocative. A paradox mentions only the antithesis and does not offer a complete presentation of the case. The paradox is not absolute. Weakness is not strength. The paradox ought to lead to reflection and by reflection the good listener or reader should find the way out"[30]. So we can paraphrase verse 10b: "For whenever as creature and sinner I am weak, then the strength of Christ is strong in me".

But this paraphrase may appear an understatement and, moreover, it runs the risk of being misunderstood. It is Paul himself who in Christ and through Christ is also humanly strong notwithstanding his weakness. It is

---

(1971) 528-537: Christ's triumphant power is 'effective' in the concrete circumstances of Paul's life, and hence is visibly revealed" (537). See also the lengthy treatment in HECKEL, *Kraft in Schwachheit*, 215-300. One wonders, however, whether Heckel sufficiently appreciates the 'human' God-given strength in the midst of all these weaknesses. An expression such as "die göttliche Kraftentfaltung gerade *in* seiner menschlichen Schwachheit" (298) seems to neglect this aspect. Is it true that "die Vollmacht des Herrn ... seiner Verkündigung *unabhängig von seiner menschlichen Schwachheit* ihre rettende Kraft verleiht" (297; italics mine)? Hardly.

[28] Cf. LAMBRECHT, "Nekrōsis", 131. Weakness and strength go together: "... over and over again Paul here [in 2 Cor 4,7-18] emphasizes that his misery is not total. He distinguishes between suffering and that which follows, deliverance. Both occur in his life. Death is not complete; life triumphs .... Paul ... points to the simultaneous wasting away and renewal, every day .... One should not misunderstand or radicalize the 'invisible' character of the daily renewal. As for Paul, his apostolic life, with its work, suffering and persecution, even now manifests in a visible way in the midst of weakness and dying much victory, power and glory".

[29] Most probably ὑπὲρ Χριστοῦ is to be linked with the tribulations which are "endured" for Christ. The NRSV ("... calamities [endured] for the sake of Christ" corrects the RSV ("for the sake of Christ, then, I am content ..."). The interpretation of HECKEL, *Kraft in Schwachheit*, 111, is forced: "um (der Kraft) Christi willen" (the "präpositionale Wendung begründet ... Wohlgefallen ...").

[30] LAMBRECHT, "Nekrōsis", 131.

precisely of that strength — though it is not explicitly mentioned in 11,23-33 and 12,7-8 — that Paul, I presume, is also boasting, legitimately yet foolishly and dangerously boasting in the Lord. The danger will entirely disappear only in the eschaton. In 1,13-14 Paul writes: "I hope you will understand until the end — as you have already understood us in part — that on the day of the Lord Jesus we are your boast even as you are our boast"[31].

III. BOASTING AS COMMENDATION

In 2 Cor 12,12, Paul speaks of "the signs of the true apostle". In 13,3, he says to the Corinthians: "you desire a proof that Christ is speaking in me". What is it that truly commends an apostle? How is the authentic apostle identifiable and recognizable for the Christians, distinguishable from the false one? Nowhere else has Paul brought together so many elements of this proof as he has done in 2 Corinthians. They are authenticating signs of his apostolate. The objective signs, visible and verifiable, constitute, of course, equally the commendation of the apostle and, at the same time, his legitimate boast. However, it goes without saying that the interpretation of these signs by the Christians is no easy matter. This discernment requires the assistance of the Spirit and will in the end hardly produce a "mathematical", once and for all certainty.

Several Proofs

We have seen in our first section that Paul for his legitimation refers to the visible results of his apostolic work, to the very existence of the Corinthian community: see 10,12-18. Gerd Theissen states the rule in simple terms: "Wo immer Paulus angegriffen wird, verweist er auf sein 'Werk'. Dies weist ihn als legitimen Apostel aus"[32]. The Corinthians are his boast, not only on the day of the Lord Jesus (cf. 1,14); they are his work in the Lord (1 Cor 9). They are his true "letter of recommendation", writ-

---

[31] Cf. 1 Thess 2,19-20 and Phil 2,16.

[32] G. THEISSEN, *Studien zur Soziologie des Urchristentums* (WUNT 19; Tübingen ²1983) 223; see also p. 225. Cf. HECKEL, *Kraft in Schwachheit*, e.g., 295.

ten on his heart, "known and read by all", "a letter of Christ" prepared by Paul (2 Cor 3,2-3). The children for whom Paul was in the pain of childbirth again until Christ was formed in them (cf. Gal 4,19) "prove" the authority which the Lord gave him, the authenticity of his commission[33].

More than once Paul also mentions his complete openness: "We ourselves are well known to God, and I hope that we are also well known to your consciences" (2 Cor 5,11). There can be no doubt, Paul is certain that his honest, straightforward attitude pleads for the genuineness of his apostleship: "We have renounced the shameful things that one hides; we refuse to practice cunning or to falsify God's word; but by the open statement of the truth we commend ourselves to the conscience of everyone in the sight of God" (4,2; cf. 2,17 and see also 12,14-18).

Paul is, moreover, innerly convinced that his way of life and moral conduct are of vital importance for his missionary work: "We are putting no obstacle in anyone's way, so that no fault may be found with our ministry, but as servants of God we have commended ourselves in every way: through great endurance, in afflictions, hardships, calamities ..." (2 Cor 6,3-4 and see the whole list of hardships up to 6,10)[34]. "Indeed, this is our boast, the testimony of our conscience: we have behaved in the world with frankness and godly sincerity, not by earthly wisdom but by the grace of God — and all the more toward you" (1,12). The integrity of his personal conduct provides a proof for the veracity of his message.

It would seem that Paul speaks but incidentally of "the signs of the true apostle" which were performed in Corinth "with utmost patience, signs and wonders and mighty works" (12,12)[35]. Nonetheless, one must not deny that

---

[33] Cf. BETZ, *Der Apostel Paulus*, 118-137; HAFEMANN, "Self-Commendation", 79: "Paul's arrival in Corinth and the ensuing birth of the church are thus the *divinely* appointed indication and objective evidence that Paul's claim to authority in Corinth is valid". WONG, "Lord", 252-253, maintains: "boasting of the Lord" is for Paul "boasting of one's missionary achievement done in one's mission field which is assigned by God" (252).

[34] A special aspect of this behavior is Paul's "Armut und Heimatlosigkeit", his "Niedrigkeitsexistenz": "Sie weist ihn als wahren Diener Christi aus (2 Kor 11,23) bzw. als Diener Gottes (6,4) ... als Apostel (1 Kor 4,9)". So C. WOLFF, "Niedrigkeit und Verzicht in Wort und Weg Jesu und in der apostolischen Existenz des Paulus", *NTS* 34 (1988) 183-196 (citation on p. 183).

[35] The construction of this sentence is unusual. Paul twice employs the term σημεῖα, yet with a different grammatical function (and different meaning? See, e.g., BETZ, *Der Apostel Paulus*, 70). The possibly triumphalistic ring in the mention of these supernatural phenomena is subdued not only by the fact that Paul rarely speaks of them but also, in 12,12, by the addition of the expression ἐν πολλῇ ὑπομονῇ.

for Paul these signs and wonders do possess an authenticating value[36]. In Rom 15,15-17 he states that the grace has been given him by God to be a minister of Christ Jesus to the Gentiles in the priestly service of the gospel of God. He has reason to boast of his work for God. In this letter he also mentions the "signs": "I will not venture to speak of anything except what Christ has accomplished through me to win obedience from the Gentiles, by word and deed, by the power of signs and wonders, by the power of the Spirit of God ..." (15,18-19). Again, it is evident to Paul's mind that both work and wonders authenticate the apostle.

It must have been Paul's heart-felt desire that the fact of proclaiming the gospel to the Corinthians free of charge be an undeniable proof of the purity and veracity of this apostolic endeavor. But, as far as we can surmise, this criterion has not been recognized at Corinth; it was not received with gratitude; it was even misinterpreted (see 11,7-12 and 12,13-19). Yet, Paul emphasizes his making no use of an apostle's right to get a living by the gospel: no one will deprive him of this ground for boasting (see 1 Cor 9,6-18)!

Weaknesses and Privileges

According to Paul it is most of all the weakness of the apostle which proves the genuineness of his apostleship[37]. After he has abundantly pointed out his weakness, he goes on to write: "I hope you will find out that we have not failed" (13,6). That the apostles "are treated as impostors, and yet are true; as unknown, and yet not killed; as sorrowful, yet always rejoicing; as poor, yet making many rich; as having nothing, and yet possessing everything" (6,9-10) is indeed a most convincing proof of apostolic authenticity and godly recommendation. In this way it is made clear "that this extraordinary power belongs to God and does not come" from the apos-

---

[36] Cf., e.g., C.K. BARRETT, *The Second Letter to the Corinthians* (BNTC; London 1973) 335: "The power of Christ became visible in miracles ..." (with reference to 2 Cor 12,12; Rom 15,19 and Gal 3,5). Otherwise HAFEMANN, "Self-Commendation", 87: wonders and mighty works "do not in and of themselves verify the apstolic ministry"; THEISSEN, *Studien*, 224-225: Paul "legitimiert sich nicht durch sie [= wonders]" (225). STRECKER, "Legitimität", 119, is more prudent in his judgment.

[37] By paying special attention to 1 Thessalonians J.L. SUMNEY, "Paul's 'Weakness': an Integral Part of His Conception of Apostleship", *JSNT* 52 (1993) 71-91, argues that weakness conditioned Paul's understanding of his apostleship much earlier than his controversy with the opponents in Corinth.

tles themselves (4,7). The Lord himself has revealed to Paul that, paradoxically, power is made perfect in weakness (cf. 12,9a). Therefore, Paul
adds in a personal reflection: "I will rather boast most gladly of my weaknesses, so that the power of Christ may dwell in me. Therefore I am content with weaknesses, insults, hardships, persecutions, and calamities for
the sake of Christ; for whenever I am weak, then I am strong" (12,9b-10)[38].

But what is to be said about Paul's "foolish" boasting of his Jewish
origins (11,21-22; cf. Rom 11,1 and Phil 3,3-6), of his "greater labors" than
those of the other apostles (2 Cor 11,23-29[39]; cf. 1 Cor 15,10), of his
visions and revelations of the Lord (2 Cor 12,1-5)? Does all this also
belong to his credentials? In 12,6 he denies the foolishness of this action of
boasting: "If I wish to boast, I will not be a fool, for I will be speaking the
truth. But I refrain from it ...". To be sure, in 12,1 he remarks that "nothing
is to be gained" (οὐ συμφέρον) by this sort of boasting and in 12,2-3 and
5 he regards God's extraordinary gifts as not given to him but, as it were,
to a different person (οἶδα ἄνθρωπον ...). Nevertheless, despite all that, he
does boast of such things, more than once; and he emphasizes that he
speaks the truth. Therefore, it appears to me that this specific boasting in
foolishness — more foolish than other boasting which, as we saw, is
always to a certain extent foolish — is not necessarily wrong[40], although it
may be particularly dangerous and not so useful for the legitimation process itself[41]. Yet, in the concrete Corinthian circumstances, this boasting

---

[38] WOLFF, "Niedrigkeit und Verzicht", rightly underlines that not only Paul but every
Christian has to suffer: "Ein Qualitätsunterschied besteht nicht, es sind grundsätzlich 'diesel-
ben Leiden' (2 Kor 1. 6; vgl. 1 Thess 1. 6; Phil 1. 30), jeder Glaubende ist also durch die
Gemeinschaft mit Christus in dynamischer Weise in die Leiden Christi miteinbezogen. Aber
für den Apostel ist das *besondere Ausmass* der Leiden kennzeichnend (1 Kor 4. 9a; 2 Kor 1. 5;
11. 23), das seine umfassende missionarische Tätigkeit mit sich brachte. Durch diese einzigar-
tige Nähe zur Passion Jesu ist er in unverwechselbarer Weise der Bevollmächtigte, Gesandte
des Christus" (190).

[39] In 2 Cor 11,23-33, SÁNCHEZ BOSCH, "L'apologie apostolique", 53-57, distinguishes
"trois types d'expériences (les souffrances extérieures [vv. 23-27], les souffrances intérieures
[vv. 28-29] et la 'faiblesse' [vv. 30-33]) derrière lesquelles Paul voit toujours le doigt de Dieu
qui l'identifie comme Apôtre" (57).

[40] From Rom 2,17 too it appears that Jews may rely on the law and boast of their relationship to God, on the condition that they do not "dishonor God by breaking the law" (2,23);
and, above all, on the condition that their unenlightened zeal is not regarded as the basis of their
own righteousness, ignoring that from God which was manifested in Jesus Christ (cf.
9,30–10,4). See also note 24 above.

[41] Paul's emphasis on the fact that his "ecstasy" (5,13) and his visions and revelations
(12,1) are not meant for the public world and may therefore be of no avail in proving the
authenticity of his ministry should probably not be interpreted too literally.

could be of some positive help for recognizing his valid ministry (cf. 11,5 and 12,11: "In nothing did I prove inferior to those super-apostles, even if I am a nobody").

Anticipative Resurrection Power

One most important credential has not yet been mentioned, i.e., Paul's strength (often in the midst of weakness). Paul does not deny that his letters are "weighty and strong" (10,10), that he is bold towards the Corinthians when he is away. But he adds: "what we say by letter when absent, we will also do when present" (10,11). Although he does not seem to favor such an intervention, he intends, if needed, to show boldness and to punish every disobedience in Corinth. Since his power is not human but divine, it will be irresistible (cf. 10,1-6).

As far as Paul's human–divine strength is concerned, one passage in 2 Corinthians deserves our special attention: 13,1-4[42]. Paul announces his third coming. The main affirmation lies at the end of verse 2: "I warned those who sinned previously and all the others, and I warn them now while absent, as I did when present on my second visit, that if I come again, 'I will not be lenient'". Verse 3a provides a motivation for this warning: "since you desire proof that Christ is speaking in me". 'Christ' is then further explained by means of a relative clause: "Christ, who is not weak in dealing with you, but powerful in you" (v. 3bc). Paul continues in verse 4: "For he was crucified in weakness, but lives by the power of God. For we are weak in him, but in dealing with you we will live with him by the power of God". The symmetry of the two sentences within verse 4 is very striking, indeed:

a   καὶ γὰρ ἐσταυρώθη ἐξ ἀσθενείας,

b   ἀλλὰ ζῇ ἐκ δυνάμεως θεοῦ.

c   καὶ γὰρ ἡμεῖς ἀσθενοῦμεν ἐν αὐτῷ,

d   ἀλλὰ ζήσομεν σὺν αὐτῷ ἐκ δυνάμεως θεοῦ εἰς ὑμᾶς.

The whole of verse 4 "proves" what is said in verse 3. More specifically, verse 4d repeats and grounds verse 3a (δοκιμὴν ζητεῖτε τοῦ ἐν ἐμοὶ λαλοῦντος Χριστοῦ) and, through it, the warning threat at the end of

---

[42] For a more thorough analysis I may refer here to my "Philological and Exegetical Notes on 2 Corinthians 13,4" in R. BIERINGER–J. LAMBRECHT, *Studies*, 589-598. Sections of this article are utilized here.

verse 2 (οὐ φείσομαι). The formal parallelism between verse 4ab and 4cd should in no way deceive us. Paul is not making two separate statements, one about Christ and one about himself. He is not even comparing himself with Christ ("so Christ, so we too"). His conviction that Christ speaks in him, and that as an apostle he is weak in Christ and with Christ will prove powerful, filled with life, sufficiently shows that behind this parataxis lies an implication concerning Christ and Paul. Out of Christ's death and life comes Paul's weakness and strength. The argumentation behind the symmetric composition requires a consecutive second sentence: "For indeed Christ was crucified in weakness but lives by the power of God, *so that* we too are weak in him but shall live with him by the power of God in dealing with you"[43].

The two sentences, moreover, possess a γάρ-ἀλλά construction which, most probably, is the equivalent of the well-known μὲν γὰρ ... δέ construction in which the μέν-clause has a concessive nuance and the real reason is found in the δέ-clause. The particle μέν is often missing. In verse 4ab Paul expresses the motivation for the fact that Christ is mighty in the midst of the Corinthians (see v. 3bc). The logical sense can be brought out by means of a paraphrase: "for indeed, although *Christ* was crucified because of weakness, he *certainly* lives because of God's power". In verse 4cd Paul gives the motivation for his own firm decision not to spare the Corinthians at his third coming (see the end of v. 2): "For *although* we too are weak in him, in dealing with you we shall *certainly* live with him because of God's power". In both sentences (v. 4ab and 4 cd) the first clause (a and c) refers to supposedly common Christian knowledge, evidence upon which all readers agree and which, therefore, can easily be conceded. In both sentences it is the second clause (b and d) that is the motivation properly speaking.

Moreover, in 13,3-4 there is a remarkable and theologically most interesting use of the tenses of the verbs:

Christ is actually speaking through Paul (v. 3a):	*present continuous*
he is not weak now but mighty with regard to the Corinthians (v. 3bc):	*present continuous*
the Corinthians know very well that Christ was crucified (4a):	*narrative aorist*

---

[43] The outward symmetry is also broken by the different meaning of the καί in v. 4a (= applies to the whole sentence: "indeed") and that in v. 4c (= emphasizes only ἡμεῖς: "we too").

but they should also realize
that he is now living (4b):   *present continuous*

Paul admits
that the same Corinthians experience
that he himself is weak (v. 4c):   *present continuous*

but he stresses that they must also believe
that he will deal with them
in a life-filled, powerful way (v. 4d): *future*

In verse 4 the movement from past to present and from present to future
should not go unnoticed; one meets here all three temporal dimensions.
Thus once more the formal parallelism in verse 4 is broken, now by Paul's
wording itself. The differences in time indicate the limits of the real inclusion of Paul in Christ. Christ was crucified long ago; yet, the apostle still
suffers. Christ is living his resurrection life; in Paul that life is already present but its future manifestation before the Corinthians, forceful as it will be,
is but a weak anticipation of the fullness of life after death[44].

Paul's human–divine apostolic strength has been and will be experienced by the Corinthians. This anticipative resurrection power[45] is, of course,
Paul's credential par excellence. In its own way it constitutes a visible proof
of authenticity which all believers encounter.

Conclusion

We may thus conclude that Paul appears to have quite a number of legitimacy proofs which at the same time are good apostolic reasons to be proud:
the existence of the Corinthian church, his openness, his moral conduct, the
signs and wonders, his preaching free of charge, his weakness, the privileges,
and the anticipative manifestation of Christ's resurrection power.

---

[44] Although the language used in v. 4d is certainly that of resurrection life after death of
all Christians alike, because of the specific context of 13,1-4 and of the striking addition of εἰς
ὑμᾶς, we may claim, I think, that, in the first place, in ζήσομεν the first person plural points
to Paul and "life" to his future powerful action in Corinth. For the metaphorical use of resurrection language, cf. also 1,10.

[45] Cf. WOLFF, "Niedrigkeit und Verzicht", 192: "Paulus selbst verstand sich als von der
Niedrigkeit des Gekreuzigten und — proleptisch — von der Kraft des Auferstandenen geprägt ...".

Not all boasting, however, is equally useful, but if — as for Paul — self-praise coincides with boasting in the Lord, the Giver of all good, then this boasting, although never without danger and to a certain degree always foolish, is positive. It functions in his rightful self-defense and helps his Christians to identify the true apostle. What Paul in 2 Cor 10–13 explains in great length regarding apostolic boasting, no doubt applies analogously to the self-commendation and boasting of every Christian[46].

The analysis of 2 Cor 10,1-6 (cf. pp. 109-113) is further elaborated in the following study of this volume (nr. 12).

---

[46] Cf., e.g., 1 Thess 1,6-10, a passage which mentions grounds for Christian boasting. See also notes 24 and 40 above.

Biblica 77 (1996) 398-416

12

Paul's Appeal and the Obedience to Christ
The Line of Thought in 2 Corinthians 10,1-6

The second part of the main title "the obedience to Christ" is taken from 2 Cor 10,5b: "and we take every thought captive to obey Christ (εἰς τὴν ὑπακοὴν τοῦ Χριστοῦ). The question is whether and how that obedience to Christ can be linked with the appeal present in 10,1a: "I myself, Paul, appeal to you (παρακαλῶ ὑμᾶς) by the meekness and gentleness of Christ". Most interpreters assume that the sentence in v. 1a is not complete. The relative clause of v. 1b interrupts what Paul originally intended to say. With "I who am humble when face to face with you, but bold toward you when I am away!" Paul reflects on what some report on him. One expects, however, that his appeal will receive a concretization and, therefore, it is often said that 10,2, with the verb δέομαι, takes up the idea of παρακαλῶ: "I ask that when I am present I need not show boldness by daring to oppose those who think we are acting according to human standards". According to this view, verse 2 provides the content of Paul's appeal[1]. Yet in v. 1a the expression "by the meekness and gentleness of Christ" suggests that Christ is in one way or another an example. But verses 2-6 do not point to such items of ethical behavior. They are not exhortation in the strict sense of the term.

Another problem, which could be referred to as epistolary, must also be mentioned. Those who take 2 Corinthians as an integral letter could be tempted to see in 10,1 the beginning of the hortatory section of that letter. Yet the content of chs. 10–13 is hardly straight moral exhortation. Others who consider the chapters as (part of) a separate letter must explain Paul's appeal at the beginning of these chapters.

---

[1] Cf., e.g., E.B.-ALLO, *Seconde épître aux Corinthiens* (EtB; Paris ²1956) 241: "On attend comme régime un mot qui ne vient pas, car la phrase est interrompue par une parenthèse, et l'idée de παρακαλῶ est reprise par un autre verbe, δέομαι".

The precise question which the present study considers is twofold. Is it possible to plausibly reconstruct what Paul intended to add as a further qualification of the verb παρακαλῶ at the moment that he wrote 10,1a? Does the answer to this first question, together with a better insight into Paul's reasoning in 10,1-6, confirm or weaken the position of the integrity of 2 Corinthians? The procedure of this study will be as follows. First, in a close reading, Paul's train of thought in 10,1-6 will be investigated. Then three special items regarding Paul's parenesis must be elucidated. The final step will examine the formula "by the meekness and gentleness of Christ" in connection with Paul's appeal to the Corinthians and their obedience to Christ.

I. THE LINE OF THOUGHT

Within chapter 10 and, more in particular, 10,1-11, the verses 1-6 form a small tightly knit unit. Yet a first reading already indicates that the line of thought is complex.

Verse 1

A. Plummer comments on v. 1: "The appeal reads somewhat strangely as a prelude to one of the most bitter and vehement paragraphs in the writings of St Paul"[2]. The relative pronoun ὅς in v. 1 certainly has Paul as its antecedent, Christ's "virtues", i.e., his meekness and gentleness mentioned in v. 1a, bring Paul to think of his own attitude or, better, to what some people in Corinth report of him. So in v. 1b Paul qualifies himself; yet the whole of the relative clause refers to a reproach, the content of which will become clearer in v. 2 and especially in v. 10. The REB translates v. 1b: "I who am so timid (you say) when face to face with you, so courageous when I am away from you". The addition "you say (i.e., you Corinthians)" is probably not a completely correct interpretation: "you intruders as well as you Corinthian critics" might be preferred; The qualification of Paul in v. 1b, a

---

[2] A. PLUMMER, *A Critical and Exegetical Commentary on the Second Epistle of St Paul to the Corinthians* (ICC; Edinburg 1915) 273.

parenthesis, should not necessarily have constituted an anacolouthon nor an absolute interruption. The main reasoning could easily have been resumed in v. 2. Whether this is the case should become apparent in the ensuing discussion.

Verse 2

The (over)literal translation of v. 2a runs as follows: "But I ask not when present to be bold with the confidence". One has mentally to insert a ὑμᾶς after "I ask" (or "I beg") and add the εἰς ὑμᾶς from the end of v. 1: I beg (you) not to force me to be bold (with you) when present". It is not at all certain that the verb δέομαι is an equivalent of παρακαλῶ and takes up the train of thought of v. 1a. Verse 2 appears to react to v. 1b, not to continue v. 1a. The implicit reproach is countered: Paul says that he could easily show boldness toward the Corinthians and that he is planning to do so toward his opponents. Verse 2 even contains a barely hidden threat. If necessary, he will use his daring confidence. We find here also an indirect reference to a future visit (cf. 12,20 and 13,1). The particle δέ at the beginning of the sentence points to an opposition between the accusation and the reaction of Paul. The vocabulary in v. 2 (παρών and θαρρῆσαι) recalls that of v. 1b (ἀπών and θαρρῶ). In v. 2 we may further point to the synonym of θαρρῆσαι, namely τολμῆσαι[3], and to the double use of λογίζομαι: Paul thinks (= counts, plans) and some think (= are of the opinion, accuse). The "some who think" are most probably mainly Paul's opponents, but also the Corinthian critics.

One could detect at the beginning of v. 2 a kind of moral appeal to the Corinthians: "I beg (you to behave in such a way) that I am not forced to be bold (with you)"[4]. At any rate, in v. 2 Paul no longer has in mind the specific (or more general) exhortation which was announced in v. 1a. This constitutes a major shift in the line of thought. It is also worthwhile to note

---

[3] Yet according to PLUMMER, *2 Corinthians*, 274, the verbs are presumably not synonyms: "The change of word is probably neither accidental nor merely for the sake of variety, but marks the difference between the feigned courage [θαρρῶ] which his critics attributed to him and the uncompromising boldness [τολμῆσαι] which he is confident of exhibiting if his opponents render it necessary".

[4] C.K. BARRETT, *A Commentary on the Second Epistle to the Corinthians* (BNTC; London ²1979) 249, does not admit this reconstruction: Paul "does not say (though it would have been easy to do so), I ask *you* to repent, that I may not have to show this bold front against *you*". It is not clear to me why not.

that Paul has begun this section with the first person singular, very much emphasized (αὐτὸς ... ἐγὼ Παυλός v. 1a); in v. 2 that singular is still present, but toward the end of the verse a first person plural appears — one might say almost unnoticed: ἡμᾶς ... περιπατοῦντας. This plural will continue through verse 7.

The last expression of v. 2 was: "as if we are walking κατὰ σάρκα". Paul's opponents and critics falsely (cf. ὡς) assume that his way of acting is dictated by worldly or human standards. As far as we can judge, the expression here is not referring to a sinful egocentric conduct but to Paul's lack of power, to his humble and timid condition when he was face to face with the Corinthians (cf. v. 1)[5]. That this interpretation is correct becomes evident from v. 3.

Verse 3

V. 3 is introduced by γάρ and explicates the phrase "walking according to the flesh". As often occurs in a γάρ-sentence, the first clause is concessive: "to be sure", or "true", or "indeed, we are in the flesh", that is, we are limited, fragile human beings. Due consideration must be given to the change of preposition: ἐν σαρκί. The second clause, then, categorically negates a κατὰ σάρκα way of action: "we do not wage war according to human (or worldly) standards"[6]. The verb περιπατέω is replaced by στρατεύομαι and thus the military imagery is introduced, "by far the most elaborate instance" of this use in the Pauline letters"[7]. It looks as if Paul is somewhat captivated by it.

Verse 4a

This verse contains a second γάρ-sentence and forms a real parenthesis within this context. Paul wants to clarify what he means by a battle that is not "according to the flesh (κατὰ σάρκα)". Attention is given solely to the (metaphorical) weapons Paul is using: they are not σαρκικά. The vocab-

---

[5] Cf., e.g., ALLO, *2 Corinthiens*, 243-244. C. WOLFF, *Der zweite Brief des Paulus an die Korinther* (THNT; Berlin 1989) 197, defends the ethical sense.

[6] Cf. V. FURNISH, *2 Corinthians* (AB; Garden City, NY 1984) 257, who rightly states: "In both formulations *sarx* ("flesh") stands for what is finite, worldly, limited, and limiting".

[7] FURNISH, *2 Corinthians*, 457. Cf. WOLFF, *2 Korinther*, 195: "In den Kampfaussagen nimmt Paulus die Vorstellung von der geistlichen Waffenrüstung auf, die er wiederholt verwendet, 6,7; 1. Thess. 5,8; Röm. 6,13; 13,12; vgl auch Phil. 2,25 und Philem. 2".

ulary is basically the same as in v. 3: compare σαρκικός and στρατεία with στρατεύομαι.

The negative οὐ σαρκικά is now positively filled: Paul's weapons are "powerful to God"; i.e., God can use them; or: they have divine power; they are "mightily effective"[8]. They have the power to destroy strongholds.

Verses 4b-6a

After the parenthesis concerning the weapons, Paul returns to the battle itself. As is well known, strictly speaking, the three participles (nominative, plural) of vv. 4b-6a could still depend on the personal verb "we wage war" of v. 3b. However, because of the parenthesis of v. 4a one easily loses sight of this verb. So the participles are perhaps better taken as nominatives absolute, no longer having any grammatical connection with v. 3. The first verb (καθαιροῦντες) takes up the idea present in the expression πρὸς καθαίρεσιν in the same verse 4, and thus it becomes clear that verses 4b-6a will depict in ample detail what "weapons, powerful for God and able to destroy strongholds" can do.

Metaphorical and realistic expressions are intermingled. Compare ὕψωμα ἐπαιρόμενον and αἰχμαλωτίζοντες on the one hand with λογισμούς, γνῶσιν τοῦ θεοῦ, πᾶν νόημα εἰς τὴν ὑπακοὴν τοῦ Χριστοῦ and the whole of v. 6a on the other hand. The readers may have the impression that by this rather strange war imagery Paul presents a general depiction of his forceful apostolate: past, present and future, applied to friend and enemy alike. Yet the images betray Paul's awareness of opposition against him. A nuance of threat in his speech cannot go unnoticed. The phrase "being ready" of v. 6a, moreover, contains another allusion to a future visit to Corinth by Paul. We are reminded of v. 2b: Paul's decision to be bold with those who slander him is now referred to as his readiness to punish every disobedience.

Verse 6b

This last verse surprises the reader for two reasons. (1) While in v. 5 Paul sees the obedience to Christ of all as the final aim of his apostolic

---

[8] FURNISH, *2 Corinthians*, 454.

endeavor (every mind has to obey Christ), in v. 6b the obedience of the addressees alone is emphasized: ὑμῶν ὑπακοή. One must ask, therefore, whether the concept of "obedience" of v. 6b is still exactly the same as that which is present in the expression of v. 5[9]. (2) A careful consideration of the tense in the construction of v. 6b (ὅταν πληρωθῇ) recognizes the anteriority *vis-à-vis* the action spoken of in v. 6a. Paul will eventually punish every disobedience "after that" the obedience of the Corinthians "will have been completed", i.e., "once your obedience will be complete"[10]. One has the impression that just as in v. 2a Paul was implicitly requesting from the Corinthians an adequate behavior towards himself, so also in v. 6b the obedience asked for contains a reference not only to Christ (cf. v. 5), but also to his person[11]. This again implies a change of direction in Paul's argumentation.

Conclusion

The preceding brief analysis can be summarized as follows. In 10,1-6 there is a substantial shift with regard to more than one aspect. Paul appears to announce a moral exhortation. He mentions Christ who is the basis of his authority and whose qualities of meekness and gentleness are exemplary for Christians (and Paul himself) — at least that is our impression. But from v. 1b onwards he speaks of an accusation brought forward against him and he defends himself; he denies what the opponents say.

Inimical intruders and critics of his person have entered the scene; this is manifest in v. 2b. At the beginning of the pericope one expects that the Corinthians would be exhorted to a better Christian life. But, certainly from v. 2b onwards, Paul seems to be very much occupied with himself and his enemies; he indicates how he himself acts and will act as an apostle. Paul is able to show that he does not lack boldness; he will oppose his enemies and demolish their arguments and pretension; his weapons will prove powerful for God. Only at the very end, in v. 6b, do the addressees come

---

[9] WOLFF, *2 Korinther*, 199, does not see any difference between the two uses.

[10] Cf. BARRETT, *2 Corinthians*, 253-254: "When he has achieved this goal [the obedience of the Corinthians], his next step will be to punish the intruders ..."; and the excellent comment by FURNISH, *2 Corinthians*, 464.

[11] For "obedience to Paul", see with ὑπακοή Phlm 21 and 2 Cor 7,15 (to Titus; and Paul?), with ὑπήκοος 2 Cor 2,9 (cf. the use of παρακαλῶ in v. 8), with ὑπακούω Phil 2,12 ("as you have always obeyed" [most probably: "to me"]; here also the alternation of presence and absence).

back to the forefront; their obedience must reach completion before Paul can effectively deal with the opposition. Yet one wonders whether that obedience of the Corinthians in v. 6b is still the same obedience to Christ mentioned in v. 5.

II. THREE SPECIAL ITEMS

Three factors remain to be dealt with. What exactly does the use of παρακαλῶ suggest? What does Paul mean by "his authority to build up" the Corinthians (cf. v. 8)? And can a consideration of Paul's exhortation at the end of the letter help us to better understand the appeal at the beginning of chapter 10?

"Parakalō" in Paul

Paul employs the verb παρακαλῶ frequently. As is well known the range of meanings of this verb is wide: from exhorting and appealing to comforting and consoling[12]. Besides 2 Cor 10,1, Paul employs παρακαλῶ four more times with the preposition διά followed by a genitive: Rom 12,1 and 15,30; 1 Cor 1,10 and 2 Cor 5,20[13].

In 2 Cor 5,20 God is the grammatical subject of the genitive absolute

---

[12] Cf. D. LÜHRMANN, "Freundschaftsbrief trotz Spannungen. Zu Gattung und Aufbau des ersten Korintherbriefs", W. SCHRAGE (ed.), *Studien zum Text und zur Ethik des Neuen Testaments. FS H. Greeven* (BZNW 47; Berlin–New York 1986) 296-314. For the study of παρακαλῶ see C.J. BJERKELUND, *Parakalō Form, Funktion und Sinn der parakalō-Sätze in den paulinischen Briefen* (Bibl. Theol. Norv. 1; Oslo 1967); T.Y MULLINS, "Petition as a Literary Form", *NT* 5 (1962) 46-54; H. SCHLIER, "Die Eigenart der christlichen Mahnung nach dem Apostel Paulus", ID., *Besinnung auf das Neue Testament* (Freiburg–Basel–Wien 1964) 340-357; J. THOMAS, παρακαλέω, παράκλησις, *EDNT III*, 23-27.

[13] Phlm 9 has a διά + acc. construction: διὰ τὴν ἀγάπην ... παρακαλῶ. The Pauline uses of παρακαλῶ in the sense of "appealing" can be divided with regard to grammar as follows: a) with infinitive construction: Rom 16,17; 2 Cor 2,8; 6,1; Phil 4,2; 1 Thess 4,10 (and 3,2: infinitive preceded by τό); b) with ἵνα-clause: 1 Cor 16,12; 16,15-16 (probably); 2 Cor 8,6; 9,5; 12,8; 1 Thess 4,1 (and 2,12: with εἰς τό + infinitive construction); c) followed by an imperative: 1 Cor 4,16; 1 Thess 5,14; d) absolute, but the context provides the content of the appeal: 2 Cor 12,18; 1 Thess 2,12; Phlm 9 and 10. What about 2 Cor 10,1a? Cf. the thorough discussion in LÜHRMANN, "Freundschaftsbrief", 300-304.

and the apostles are the agents through whom God acts: ὡς θεοῦ παρακαλοῦντος δι᾽ ἡμῶν ("seeing that God is making his appeal through us")[14].
5,20, however, is not a real parallel to the other texts precisely because God
and not Paul is the subject and, moreover, because the instrumental use of
διά with a human person as genitive ("through us") is not present in the
other passages. Yet the clause is interesting with regard to 2 Cor 10,1-2
since in 5,20, too, the verb παρακαλοῦντος is resumed by δεόμεθα: "we
beseech you". The content of the appeal of God in 5,20 is concretized by
that of Paul's beseeching: "reconcile yourselves to God"[15]. However, we
have already expressed doubt that 10,2 with its non-resumptive δέομαι can
be considered as a concretization of the content of παρακαλῶ in 10,1. This,
of course, weakens even more the similarity between 5,20 and 10,1-2[16].

In 1 Cor 1,10 the text reads: παρακαλῶ δὲ ὑμᾶς, ἀδελφοί, διὰ τοῦ
ὀνόματος κυρίου ἡμῶν ᾿Ιησοῦ Χριστοῦ, ἵνα τὸ αὐτὸ λέγητε πάντες
... ("I appeal to you, brothers, by the name of our Lord Jesus Christ, that all
of you speak with one voice ..."). Paul is the subject, the Christians (in
Corinth) are the addressees and the vocative "brothers" is employed. The
content of the appeal is expressed by means of a ἵνα-clause; in classical
Greek an infinitive construction would be utilized. "By the name of our
Lord Jesus Christ" points to the authority with which Paul wants to enforce
his appeal. This last item is not present in the same way in the other
instances, although the appropriation of God's authority is not, it would
seem, completely absent.

In Rom 12,1 Paul clearly begins a new section of his lengthy letter.
This reminds us of 2 Cor 10,1 where we have a similar situation if 2
Corinthians is assumed to be one letter. The text runs as follows:
Παρακαλῶ οὖν ὑμᾶς, ἀδελφοί, διὰ τῶν οἰκτιρμῶν τοῦ θεοῦ παραστῆ-

---

[14] Cf. PLUMMER, 2 Corinthians, 185: "The ὡς always gives a subjective view of what is
stated by the genitive absolute, but that subjective view may be shown by the context to be
either right or wrong". In 2 Cor 5,20, it must be understood as "right". Does the REB version,
e.g., perhaps prefer a "wrong" understanding: "It is as if God were appealing to you ..."?

[15] For this active translation see my "Reconcile yourselves ...': A Reading of 2
Corinthians 5,11-21", in R. BIERINGER–J. LAMBRECHT, Studies on 2 Corinthians (BETL 112;
Leuven 1994) 363-412; esp. 390-391.

[16] PLUMMER, 2 Corinthians, 274, claims that in 10,1-2 there is a difference of meaning
between παρακαλῶ and δέομαι: "The appeal to the meekness and gentleness of Christ influences the Apostle himself, and he drops from magisterial exhortation to earnest entreaty". He
detects in παρακαλῶ almost a minatory tone"; it "is here 'exhort' rather than 'entreat'" (273).
These kinds of remarks are not made by the author with regard to 5,20 (see pp. 185-186). It
would seem that in 5,20 the two verbs are used almost as synonyms. Cf. also BJERKELUND,
Parakalõ, 154-155.

σαι τὰ σώματα ὑμῶν θυσίαν ζῶσαν ἁγίαν εὐάρεστον τῷ θεῷ ... ("I appeal to you therefore, brothers, by the mercies of God, to present your bodies as a living sacrifice, holy and acceptable to God ..."). Again, Paul is the subject, the Christians (in Rome) are the addressees, and the vocative "brothers" is used. The content of the appeal is now expressed by means of a classical infinitive construction[17]. The διά-phrase most probably does not go with the infinitive, but with παρακαλῶ[18]. "By God's mercies" indicates the reason why Paul can appeal to the Romans to offer their bodies. The plural "mercies" and the particle "therefore" refer back to the preceding chapters wherein Paul dealt with God's acts of merciful goodness manifested to Jews and Greeks alike[19]. This reference enhances Paul's authority, as well as making the appeal more compelling. The question, however, must also be asked: is a merciful God at the same time not an example for the Christian way of life which Paul is going to recommend in Rom 12–15?

The text of Rom 15,30 is: Παρακαλῶ δὲ ὑμᾶς, ἀδελφοί, διὰ τοῦ κυρίου ἡμῶν Ἰησοῦ Χριστοῦ καὶ διὰ τῆς ἀγάπης τοῦ πνεύματος συναγωνίσασθαί μοι ἐν ταῖς προσευχαῖς ... ("I appeal to you, brothers, by our Lord Jesus Christ and by the love of the Spirit, to strive together with me in your prayers ..."). Once again, we have Paul, the Christians (in Rome), the vocative "brothers"[20], and an infinitive construction. The phrase "by our Lord Jesus Christ" can be compared with that of 1 Cor 1,10 "by the name of our Lord Jesus Christ". In both passages the authoritative appeal is strengthened through a reference to "our Lord Jesus Christ". The addition "(and) by the love of the Spirit" resembles "by the meekness and gentleness of Christ" of 2 Cor 10,1 and "by the mercies of God" of Rom 12,1. To be sure, there is already ground and motivation present in the phrases "by Christ" or "by the name of Christ"; Paul can appeal because of Christ. But the motivation of the other expressions possesses a moral and exemplary nuance as well: because Christ is meek and gentle, because the Spirit loves us, because God is merciful, because of all this the Christians must act and behave as Paul is going to ask.

We may bring together the results of this brief overview. In three passages — 1 Cor 1,10, Rom 12,1 and 15,30 — seven items are similar: (1) a connective particle (δέ or οὖν), (2) the subject of appeal (Paul), (3) the addressees (Christians), (4) the vocative address ("brothers"), (5) the διά

---

[17] Cf. BLASS–DEBRUNNER-FUNK, no. 408.
[18] J.A. FITZMYER, *Romans* (AB; New York 1993) 639.
[19] FITZMYER, *Romans*, 639.
[20] p[46] and b omit ἀδελφοί.

plus genitive phrase which through this reference to God or Christ grounds the appeal, (6) an infinitive construction (or the koiné substitute with ἵνα) and (7) the "moral" content of the appeal. Regarding that content, in 1 Cor 1,10 Paul exhorts the Christians to be united; in Rom 12,1-2 he urges them to conduct a Christian ethical life; and in Rom 15,30-32 he makes the more specific appeal to strive together with him in prayer for the good outcome of his plans for the future. As far as 2 Cor 10,1 is concerned, not so much the absence of "brothers" or the presence of the emphasis αὐτὸς ... ἐγὼ Παῦλος, but the brusque interruption at the end of v. 1a is striking: no infinitive construction, no indication of the content of the appeal[21]. And this notwithstanding the fact that the διά plus genitive phrase of 10,1a is very much like that of Rom 12,1 and 15,30 (second half) where it contains both a grounding and exemplary function.

It would seem, therefore, that at the beginning of 2 Cor 10,1 Paul intends to do what he does elsewhere, namely to formulate an exhortation to moral Christian life. But while writing "by the meekness and gentleness of Christ" his attention seems to be diverted; he remembers the slanders against his person which his opponents and critics are spreading. The "humble" Paul of v. 1b, as well as the Paul "walking according to the flesh" of v. 2b, was their misrepresentation of him; he must have realized that their way of portraying him was, against their own intention but as matter of fact, a caricature of Christ being meek and gentle.

What Paul asks of his Christians in Corinth in v. 2 is certainly a change of attitude and behavior. They should conduct themselves in such a way that he is not forced to show against them the same boldness which he counts on showing against the intruders. But is this the content of the appeal which he had in mind when he wrote v. 1a? Hardly! One cannot but assume that what is actually requested from the Corinthians in v. 2 has a narrower scope; it becomes focused on the struggle between Paul and the opponents, and, of course, also on the sides which some Corinthians are taking. It is no longer the exhortation he originally intended to give when he composed v. 1a.

In 13,11 Paul employs the verb in the passive: παρακαλεῖσθε, which must be translated by a paraphrase such as "heed my appeal, listen to my appeal, take my appeal to heart". The verb itself does not indicate the con-

---

[21] Cf. LÜHRMANN, "Freundschaftsbrief", 302-303: "παρακαλῶ-Sätze enthalten nun mit Ausnahme allein von 2Kor 10,1 immer eine Aufforderung zu einem bestimmten Verhalten ..., münden also in Paränese in einem sehr allgemeinen Sinn" (302).

tent of that appeal, but the other imperatives in the immediate context provide very clearly what is requested from the Corinthians: "mend your ways, (heed my appeal), agree with one another, live in peace"[22]. Is this perhaps the kind of moral exhortation which we were entitled to expect at 10,1[23]?

Paul's "Exousia" to Build Up

The second item to be considered is found in 10,8. There we read: "Now, even if I boast a little too much of our authority, which the Lord gave for building you up and not for tearing you down, I will not be ashamed of it". We encounter in this verse the first of many occurrences of the verb "to boast" within chapters 10–13. The whole of v. 8 looks to the future (cf. the ἐάν + subj. construction). Verse 8a, specifically, refers to what Paul is going to do in these chapters. A. Plummer notes: Paul "begins with an 'if', but he ends with a confident assertion (+ οὐκ αἰσχυνθήσομαι, v. 8c)"[24]. Περισσότερόν τι can mean either "somewhat abundantly" or "more abundantly". If there is a real comparison "more than", the question should be asked whether the phrase refers to vv. 3-6, where Paul is already somewhat boasting, or to v. 7, as C.K. Barrett comments: "a further boast, that is, beyond that of being .... 'Christ's'"[25]. The first interpretation may perhaps be preferred.

With ἐξουσία Paul refers to his "authority to preach the gospel and to command and discipline the members of the congregation"[26]. The ἐξουσία is "die apostolische Vollmacht"[27]. Paul seemingly refers to his apostolic vocation (see Gal 1,15-16). The metaphor οἰκοδομή here points to the process of building (not to the result, the building as product). As to καθαίρε-

---

[22] In 13,11 Paul continues: "and the God of love and peace will be with you". "Live in peace" and "the God of ... peace" no doubt point back to 12,20: "quarreling, jealousy, anger, selfishness, slander, gossip, conceit, and disorder". It is peace with one another (cf. Rom 12,18: μετὰ πάντων ἀνθρώπων εἰρηνεύοντες) that Paul has in mind. In Rom 5,1 peace with God is mentioned (cf. 2 Cor 5,20: "reconcile yourselves with God"; see also Rom 5,10). The boader context of 2 Corinthians allows us to suppose also an appeal to peace with Paul.

[23] For a description of what parenesis aims at, see F. HAHN, "Die christologische Begründung urchristlicher Paränese", ZNW 72 (1981) 88-99.

[24] PLUMMER, 2 Corinthians, 280.

[25] BARRETT, 2 Corinthians, 258.

[26] FURNISH, 2 Corinthians, 477.

[27] R. BULTMANN, Der zweite Brief an die Korinther (ed. E. DINKLER) (KEK; Göttingen [2]1987) 191.

οις we cannot but remember its use already in v. 4. But Paul appears to allude to the prophet Jeremiah, and perhaps more specifically to Jer 1,10: "See, today I appoint you over nations and over kingdoms, to pluck up and to pull down, to destroy and to overthrow, to build and to plant". If so, we should note Paul's rewriting: not to destroy, only to build up[28]. Moreover, we must also take into account that with "and not for tearing you down" Paul may be alluding to the destructive work of his opponents[29]. Have we to take αἰσχυνθήσομαι as a theological passive and to understand "by God" (cf. v. 18: ὁ κύριος συνίστησιν)? A positive answer to this question is not certain. The change from the first person plural to singular within v. 8 should be noted (the opposite occurred in v. 1).

The building up (οἰκοδομή) of the Corinthians is no doubt more than their renewed obedience to Paul and their simultaneous rejection of the opponents. The whole Christian life must be expanded and come to an adult, morally responsible stature. Paul means a complete obedience to Christ (cf. 10,5); he has in mind the perfection of his Christians (cf. 10,6b; but what is here "complete obedience"?), their improvement ("what we pray for is your improvement, τὴν ὑμῶν κατάρτισιν", 13,9; cf. καταρτί-ζεσθε in 13,11). His ἐξουσία to reach this goal will manifest itself in his confidence and boldness (10,2), in the use of weapons which have divine power to destroy strongholds (10,4), in his future presence in Corinth "with actions" (τῷ ἔργῳ; 10,11) and, if needed, with severity (cf. ἀποτόμως, 13,10). God is speaking in Paul (cf. 13,3). In fact, this apostolic authority is qualified by God's power, i.e., by the resurrection power to which he explicitly refers in 13,3-4[30].

The "Paraklēsis" Given in 2 Cor 12,19–13,11

At the end of the letter Paul is, in one way or another, exhorting the Corinthian Christians. In 12,19 he emphasizes that all his fighting and plead-ing in the letter has been done "for the upbuilding" of his beloved

---

[28] See J. DUPONT, *Gnosis. La connaissance religieuse dans les épîtres de Saint Paul* (Brugge–Paris 1949) 241. Dupont perhaps pays too much attention to Jer 1,10 alone. There are other passages in Jeremiah with a closer resemblance of vocabulary. See WOLFF, *2 Korinther*, 201-202.

[29] WOLFF, *2 Korinther*, 210: "Damit teilt er einen Seitenhieb an seine Widersacher aus".

[30] Cf. my study "Philological and Exegetical Notes on 2 Corinthians 13,4, BIERINGER–LAMBRECHT, *Studies on 2 Corinthians*, 589-598.

Corinthians. Alas, the moral situation in the church of Corinth is not as Paul wishes it to be. He fears that he "may have to mourn over many of those who sinned before and have not repented of the impurity, immorality, and licentiousness which they have practiced" (12,21). The Corinthians must examine and test themselves (cf. 13,5). Just as in 10,8, so also in 13,10 Paul speaks of the "authority which the Lord has given (him) for building up and not for tearing down". The final exhortative verse is 13,11 and reads as follows: "aim for perfection, listen to my appeal (παρακαλεῖ-σθε), be of one mind, live in peace".

To be sure, in this final passage there is still an amount of self-defense on the part of Paul and there are allusions to what the opponents are doing. One should also bear in mind that Paul is, above all, trying to win over his Corinthians, to have them reconciled with him. Yet the παράκλησις in the section is wider, more comprehensive. It is the quality of Christian life in its entirety which is put before the Corinthians: the fight against sin, the presence of God's effective love, the agreement with one another and peace in the Christian community. Once more we are brought to the same hypothesis. We ask ourselves: was all that also not the initial, yet unspoken content of Paul's παρακαλῶ in 10,1a, and does all that not belong to what he coins in 10,5 by means of the expression "obedience to Christ"[31]? When we realize how carefully Paul, by means of many correlations, composes 12,19–13,11 as an inclusion with 10,1-11[32], there should be no surprise that the content of both occurrences of παρακαλῶ (10,1 and 13,11) can be assumed to be identical.

III. THE MEEKNESS AND GENTLENESS OF CHRIST

R. Leivestad's remark on 10,1 is to the point: "An appeal to the 'meekness and gentleness of Christ' is hardly in keeping with the harsh and forthright tone of the following argument, in which the apostle asserts his right

---

[31] I think that there is more in 10,1-2 — implicitly in v. 1a — than PLUMMER, *2 Corinthians*, detects: "Three elements which are conspicuous in the four chapters find expression in these two introductory verses: the strong personal feeling, indignation at the calumnies of his opponents, and the intimation that, if the opposition continues, he will not spare" (272).

[32] Cf. my "Dangerous Boasting: Paul's Self-Commendation in 2 Corinthians 10–13" in this volume, 107-129, esp. note 10 on p. 112-113.

and his determination to show no lenience"[33]. Moreover, the meaning and function of the expression "by the meekness and gentleness of Christ" in 10,1 are not immediately evident. Does the expression refer to "virtues" of the earthly Jesus? What is the precise meaning here of the preposition διά followed by the genitive[34]? Is Christ presented as an example and, if so, is he imitated by Paul who appeals and begs? Or is he rather to be imitated by the Corinthians who should respond to Paul's request? It would seem that above all the last two questions are important regarding the topic of this study, i.e., the probable content that Paul originally had in mind when he wrote παρακαλῶ in v. 1a[35].

Paul Humble and Bold

E. Güttgemanns[36] points to the fact that verse 1b is connected in a rather strange way to the preceding clause. The relative pronoun ὅς has Paul as its antecedent. However, three factors taken together give the impression that verse 1b is almost the beginning of a Christological hymn: (1) Χριστός, not Jesus, standing immediately before ὅς, (2) the so-called qualifications πραΰτης and ἐπιείκεια, and (3) the ὅς-introduction itself. These observations must confirm Güttgemanns' thesis that, here as elsewhere, Paul underlines the main characteristic of the apostolic existence. The apostle is the epiphany of Christ: "Der durch 'Leiden' qualifizierte 'Leib' des Apostels ist der 'Ort', wo die Macht des Kyrios epiphan wird"[37]. All this, however, remains highly speculative[38].

H.D. Betz, from another point of view, asks whether verse 1b is simply an anticipation of the accusation explicitly quoted in v. 10. Through his investigation Betz comes to the conclusion – rightly, it would seem – that

---

[33] R. Leivestad, "'The Meekness and Gentleness of Christ' II Cor X. 1", *NTS* 12 (1965-66) 156-164, esp. 156. Cf. the quotation from Plummer on p. 399. See also Bjerkelund, *Parakalō*, 148, for his comment on 10,1a with regard to Paul's use of παρακαλῶ.

[34] Cf. e.g., Leivestad's interpretaton of διά in "The Meekness and Gentleness of Christ", 156: In 10,1 "διά is most likely used in the same way as πρός (cf. Latin 'per') to introduce an invocation or an adjuration". This gramatical explanation is hardly correct.

[35] Cf. our analysis of similar παρακαλῶ-expressions in Paul on pp. 137-141.

[36] E. Güttgemanns, *Der leidende Apostel und sein Herr. Studien zur paulinischen Christologie* (FRLANT 90; Göttingen 1966) 135-141.

[37] Güttgemanns, *Der leidende Apostel*, 140. Cf. the basically positive evaluation by Barrett, *2 Corinthians*, 247-248.

[38] See my critical remarks in "The Nekrōsis of Jesus: Ministry and Suffering in 2 Corinthians 4,7-15", Bieringer–Lambrecht, *Studies on 2 Corinthians*, 309-333, esp. 317-321.

in v. 1b Paul is already answering the accusation and defending himself. Paul acknowledges the data which gave rise to that accusation, but he cannot accept the accusatory interpretation of that data. That Paul, however, defends his apostolic ministry in this way is obviously connected with the example of Christ, as well as his reflection upon it, his Christology[39].

Jesus Meek and Gentle

Among others Leivestad very much stresses that in 10,1a Paul wants his readers to recognize a correspondence between Christ and himself, but Christ should not be taken here as the earthly Jesus. "Paul is not referring to the lenience and indulgence of the heavenly judge (= Christ), nor even to his mild and gracious attitude during his earthly life; he is alluding to the fact of the kenosis, the literal weakness and lowliness of the Lord"[40]. For this view, one could refer to 8,9 in the same letter and, evidently, also to Phil 2,6-7. V. Furnish, following Leivestad, similarly rejects the suggestion that in v. 1a Paul "is revealing his knowledge of the 'character' of the earthly Jesus .... It is much more likely that Paul is thinking of the pre-existent Lord who, in the gracious condescension of his incarnate life, became lowly, weak, and poor"[41].

Certain criticisms, however, must be leveled here against such an interpretation. That Christ is not seen here as king or judge seems to be correct[42]. But are we to exclude all references to Jesus' behavior during his

---

[39] Cf. H.D. Betz, *Der Apostel Paulus und die sokratische Tradition. Eine exegetische Untersuchung zu einer "Apologie". 2 Korinther 10–13* (BHT 45; Tübingen 1972) 51-52. In addition to his christological explanation, Betz points to a number of factors in the hellenistic world which probably also influenced Paul's expression here. Paul defends himself in more or less the same way as, e.g., a (poor, humble) Cynic-Stoic philosopher would answer the accusation of a (rich and eloquent) Sophist.

[40] Leivestad, "The Meekness and Gentleness of Christ", 163. We may also add the following passage: "The ταπεινότης of the apostle is the consequence, an imitation and a continuation of the kenosis of Christ, of the paradoxical demonstration of divine δύναμις working through human ἀσθένεια" (164).

[41] Furnish, *2 Corinthians*, 460.

[42] Leivestad rightly disagrees with Harnack who stated "that the LXX knows of no other meaning of the term than 'die Huld des Herrschers'" (quotation in "The Meekness and Gentleness of Christ", 158). In his *Analysis philologica Novi Testamenti graeci* (Rome [3]1966) 407, M. Zerwick explains ἐπι-είκεια by "moderation, aequitas (opp. severitati ...), virtus quae seposito rigore iustitiae id quod aequum est (ὃ ἔ-οικεν = τὸ εἰκός) prosequitur". We may also refer to C. Spicq, "Bénignité, mansuétude, clémence" *RB* 54 (1947) 321-339, esp. 333, and his *Notes de lexicographie néotestamentaire I* (OBO 22/1; Fribourg–Göttingen 1978) 263-267.

earthly life? To be sure, in the first half of the Christological hymn of Phil 2,6-11 the stress is on the incarnation itself as a "kenosis". Further, in 2 Cor 8,9 the same kenotic idea is formulated: ὅτι δι᾽ ὑμᾶς ἐπτώχευσεν πλού-σιος ὤν. The use of "Christ", not "Jesus", in 2 Cor 10,1a (in Phil 2,5: Christ Jesus; in 2,11: Jesus Christ) is also rightly mentioned. Moreover, the fact that in his letters Paul does not provide us with many data about the earthly life of Jesus may point away from a possible reference to Jesus' attitude on earth.

Yet, on the other hand, in reading the formula of 2 Cor 10,1a one spon-taneously thinks of Matt 11,29: ὅτι πραΰς εἰμι καὶ ταπεινὸς τῇ καρδίᾳ (cf. Zech 9,9: "Lo, your king comes to you; triumphant and victorious is he, humble and riding on a donkey, on a colt, the foal of a donkey)". Although it certainly is not advisable to assume that Paul is referring here to this saying of the Matthean Jesus, is he, therefore, in no way pointing to Jesus' earthly life? Barrett's remark concerning the "kenotic" theory is worth noting: "There is something to be said for this view, but it would have been impossible as theology had it been known that the behavior of Jesus had been marked by arrogance and violence ..."[43].

One can, it would seem, safely conclude that Paul in 2 Cor 10,1a has also concretely in mind the manner in which Jesus acted and behaved during his life on earth, after birth and before death.

And the Corinthians?

We may first recall the remarks of Plummer and Leivestad that the mention of Christ's meekness and gentleness remains strange at the begin-ning of four chapters where Paul is certainly not soft and lenient[44]. It is, moreover, unlikely that before writing 10,1a Paul had planned to employ the expression "by the meekness and gentleness of Christ" in order to point to the opponents' reproach of his own so-called weakness when he was present in Corinth (in v. 1b). It is only afterwards, i.e., while writing this very expression, that he came to think of that reproach. At that point, he may also have seen the meek and gentle Christ as an example for his apos-tolic behavior.

But what can be said about the Corinthians? Within 10,1-11 and 12,19–13,11 he urges the Corinthians to change their attitudes so that he

---

[43] BARRETT, *2 Corinthians*, 246.
[44] See pp. 132-134.

himself will not have to be bold and severe during the announced third visit. But just as he most probably did not consider the absence of his eventual future severity as an imitation of Christ's meekness and gentleness, so also can the Corinthians' change of attitude towards Paul hardly be seen as such an imitation. What he concretely begs of the Corinthians in 10,2 is not meekness and gentleness. It has to do with a rejection of their adherence to the opponents and their again becoming "obedient" to the apostle. Paul tries to win them over. He cannot live without their reconciliation with himself.

A much more probable interpretation of the function of the expression in 10,1a is that — besides being employed as ground for Paul's authority — it is put forward as an example for what he was going to ask from the Corinthians, but as a matter of fact did not ask. We could call such a "meekness and gentleness" an anticipation of the content of παρακαλῶ. This confirms our earlier assumption that the ὑπακοὴ τοῦ Χριστοῦ of v. 5 and the οἰκοδομή of v. 8 are broader than the specific return of sympathy for Paul on the part of the Corinthians. These two concepts point to the whole lifestyle of a Christian. The comprehensive content of "the obedience to Christ", or several aspects of it, is probably what Paul would have added after the παρακαλῶ of v. 1a. The way Paul exhorts the Corinthians in 12,19–13,11 suggests that this view is correct. Barrett appropriately writes: "The existence of Christians is determined both theologically and ethically by Jesus"[45]. It would appear that the mention of these characteristics of Jesus Christ in 10,1a was intended as grounding Paul's appeal and providing an example for the Corinthians. They, too, not only Paul, should adopt these virtues.

CONCLUSIONS

Five conclusions, I think, can been drawn from this study:

(1) If our reasoning is correct, it appears that at the end of 10,1a there is an interruption which is *not* resumed by v. 2. In v. 1b there is a shift in the line of thought which continues within vv. 2-6.

---

[45] BARRETT, *2 Corinthians*, 246. Cf. H. WINDISCH, *Der zweite Korintherbrief* (KEK; Göttingen [9]1924) 291: "Mit einem παρακαλῶ ὑμᾶς διὰ τῆς πραΰτητος τοῦ Χριστοῦ wird Paulus gern seine Hörer dazu vermahnt haben dem Herrn in der πραΰτης nachzufolgen ...".

(2) Most probably Paul's original intention while writing v. 1a was to begin an exhortative section which may have contained diverse items, but which all could have constituted an imitation of Christ' meekness and gentleness. In any case that appeal or exhortation would have meant more than just a begging of Paul for "obedience" to himself[46].

(3) On the other hand, reconciliation with God (cf. 5,20 and 6,1-2) and peace with one another (cf. 13,11) certainly imply reconciliation of the Corinthians with Paul and their obedience to him (10,6; cf., e.g., 7,3-4).

(4) In view of Paul's return to that exhortation in 12,19–13,11, the whole of 10,1b–13,10 (or 10,1b–12,18) should perhaps be considered as a kind of lengthy excursus. Is 10,1b–13,10 (or 10,1b–12,18), therefore, as an excursus not somewhat analogous to the equally major (but, of course, quite differing) excursus of 2,14–7,4?

(5) One is, finally, also tempted to compare 10,1a with Rom 12,1 and 1 Thess 4,1. Was 2 Cor 10,1a not originally intended as the beginning of the final parenetical section of the letter, just like those two verses? Of course, this is but one more, admittedly quite hypothetical, element in the argumentation for the unity of the letter[47].

---

[46] The comment of FURNISH, *2 Corinthians*, is but partly correct: "It is only in v. 6 that Paul identifies that for which he is appealing — the *obedience* of the Corinhtians; but this is implicit in v. 2, where the reason for the urgency of the appeal is given" (461).

[47] For a recent survey of the whole discussion and a plea of the letter's integrity, see the three sudies of R. BIERINGER in BIERINGER–LAMBRECHT, *Studies on 2 Corinthians*, 67-105: "Teilungshypothesen zum 2. Korintherbrief. Ein Forschungsüberblick"; 107-130: "Der 2. Korintherbrief als ursprüngliche Einheit. Ein Forschungsüberblick"; and 131-179: "Plädoyer für die Einheitlichkeit des 2. Korintherbriefes. Literarkritische und inhaltliche Argumente".

New Testament Studies 43 (1997) 285-290

13

Strength in Weakness
An Answer to Scott B. Andrews on 2 Cor 11,23b-33

In Volume 41 of *New Testament Studies* (1995) Scott B. Andrews published an article entitled "Too Weak Not to Lead: The Form and Function of 2 Cor 11.23b-33"[1]. This somewhat provocative title refers to the main thesis of the contribution. Paul willingly submits to hardships; he lowers himself socially. Precisely by being weak as a populist who accomodates the people, he claims leadership of the Corinthian Christians. He tries to win them over; they should follow him, not the opponents with their so-called high socal status.

One wonders, however, whether "being too weak not to lead" is really the point of Paul's *peristasis* catalogue in 2 Cor 11,23b-33. In this note we first summarize the position of Andrews and then critically discuss several items of his exegesis. We will conclude with a consideration of the function of the catalogue within 2 Cor 10–13.

I. THE POSITION OF SCOTT B. ANDREWS

Examples taken from rhetoricians and ancient philosophical literature show that the basic form of a catalogue of hardships contains the following three elements: (1) the items of hardship, (2) the reaction to the hardships, and (3) the resulting implication for one's status. Enduring and overcoming hardships provides one with a noble social status; succumbing to hardships and being overcome by them results in a lowly status. Andrews adds the remark that the second and third elements do not need to be stated explicitly in order to complete the form[2].

---

[1] *NTS* 41 (1995) 263-276.
[2] See pp. 264-269.

In 2 Cor 11,23b-33 all three elements are found. (1) In vv. 23b-28 (and 32) there is an expanded list of hardships; (2) in v. 30, as well as in v. 33, one finds Paul's reaction to the hardships; (3) in v. 29 the resulting status is indicated[3]. Andrews' particular exegesis of vv. 29-33 should be noted in more detail. In his opinion verse 29 does not contain further hardships; it "is filled with status implications that result from Paul's inability to master his difficult circumstances"[4]. In v. 29a ("Who is weak, and am I not weak?"), Paul uses the verb "being weak" to mark himself "as one of low social status who is able to sympathize with others who find themselves in a slavish and powerless position"[5]. Andrews translates 29b as follows: "Who has been entrapped, and am I not burnt up?"[6]. "Being entrapped" connotes persons who are considered of weak status; "being burnt up" implies Paul's own lowly status "because he cannot survive the test of strength"[7]. In v. 30 Paul utters his intention to boast of weakness; this reaction reveals his low status again. The oath of v. 31 confirms the sincerity of this reaction. What is told in v. 32 about the governor of Aretas who guards Damascus in order to seize the apostle is one more hardship. Verse 33 shows Paul's reaction; it is "that of a coward who ... escapes Damascus by hiding in a basket that was lowered from the city wall"[8].

What is, then, the function of this *peristasis* catalogue within the broader context of 2 Cor 10–13[9]? Chapters 10–13 depict Paul in the midst of a debate with his opponents about the criteria for leadership. The jury is the Christian community at Corinth. In 11,23b-28 Paul claims that he has performed more labors and encountered more hardships. Yet "in 11,29-33 the comparsion with the opponents takes a sharp turn"[10]. It is not endurance, courage or noble status and the upper class ideal which, according to Paul, are the determining criteria for leadership, but a weak and ignoble status, i.e., the result of submitting to adverse circumstances and being overcome by hardships. So, e.g., in Damascus "the apostle exhibits cowardice and yet claims that he should be the head of the Corinthian Christian community"[11]. Of course, in suffering Paul follows the example of the crucified

---

[3] See pp. 269-273.
[4] P. 271.
[5] P. 270.
[6] P. 271.
[7] Ibid.
[8] P. 272.
[9] See pp. 273-276.
[10] P. 274.
[11] Ibid.

Christ. At the same time, however, "the Corinthians would have viewed Paul as portraying himself as a populist leader or demagogue"[12]. Just as Odysseus was a person of lowly status (because of "his temple-robbing, his initial unwillingness to attack Troy, and his secret attack in the guise of slave"[13]) and yet more worthy than Ajax, so also Paul who "lacks the bodily presence of a strong man and does not speak with great skill (cf. 10,10; 11,6)"[14], who, moreover, submits to and is overcome by hardships, is more worthy than his opponents. Thus the *peristasis* catalogue of 11,23b-33 "functions to place" Paul "in the role of populist leader or dema-gogue"[15]. He "willingly accepts this position of dishonour to express his empathy with the weak ones and his hope that the Corinthians will decide to follow him"[16]. For, Andrews maintains, Paul is too weak not to lead.

II. CRITICAL REMARKS

Is the above interpretation of Paul's text acceptable? Let us first con-sider the catalogue and its immediate context[17]. We begin with 11,21b. Here Paul announces, once more (cf. vv. 16-18), what he is going to do: "But whatever anyone dares to boast of — I am speaking as a fool — I also dare to boast of that". We note the interruption within v. 21b: "I am speaking as a fool". In vv. 22-23a Paul then compares himself with the opponents: Are they Hebrews, Israelites, descendants of Abraham, minis-ters of Christ? So am I; I am even a better minister of Christ. Within v. 23a, just before the catalogue proper starts, there is a second interruption which recalls that of v. 21b: "I am talking like a madman". In vv. 23b-29 we have the long list of hardships. Verses 30-31 contain a reflection. In v. 30 it is the first time within chapters 10–13 that Paul speaks of boasting of "weakness"[18]; he announces that he is going to do it. In v. 31 he even refers

---

[12] Cf. pp. 274-275.

[13] P. 275. Andrews refers to "the positive descriptions of the populist or demagogic model" in Nicolaus of Damascus's account of Cyrus and also in Antisthenes' report of the discussion before the army between Ajax and Odysseus: who of them "is more worthy of receiv-ing the weapons of the deceased Achilles?" He admits, however, that the form of populist lead-ership "is viewed unfavourably in the majority of ancient Greco-Roman sources" (ibid.).

[14] P. 276.

[15] Ibid.

[16] Ibid.

[17] In this note we refrain from using references to commentaries and other publications.

[18] See the second time in 12,5. In both verses we have the same future tense. Compare τὰ τῆς ἀσθενείας καυχήσομαι (11,30) with οὐ καυχήσομαι εἰ μὴ ἐν ταῖς ἀσθενείαις (12,5).

"to the God and Father of Jesus Christ" so as to stress that he is not lying. Verses 32-33 then follow with an example of weakness, another and — for the moment — last hardship: Paul's flight from the danger in Damascus; it is narrated as a brief story, no longer simply "listed".

In no way can verse 29 be separated from the foregoing hardships. True, already in verse 28 the bare enumeration is disappearing, but v. 29 is not the so-called third element which indicates Paul's lowly status. "Being weak" and "being indignant" are reactions to the conditions of his Christians, but for Paul himself they constitute strained, difficult attitudes in his own apostolic life. In the catalogue of 2 Cor 11, verse 29 concretizes what in v. 28 is said about the daily pressure and Paul's anxiety for all the churches. Of course, Paul's voluntary, faith-inspired weakness in v. 29a is not exactly the same as the varied kinds of weaknesses of his Christians, but it manifestly points to his compassion and empathy. It is rather strange that Andrews does not refer to 1 Cor 9,22: "To the weak I became weak, so that I might win the weak". Paul's weakness is, above all, apostolic adaptation.

Andrews' translation of v. 29b ("who has been entrapped, and am I not burnt up") cannot be accepted for several reasons. First of all, the present tense is not respected sufficiently[19]. A literal version should read as follows: "who is being made to stumble (or: being led to sin), and I am not indignant?" One could, if need be, assume that "being entrapped" — Andrews' defendable translation of the passive σκανδαλίζομαι — "connotes persons who are considered of low or 'weak' status"[20]. We cannot accept, however, his interpretation of the second clause of verse 29b regarding Paul. In this specific context καὶ οὐκ ἐγὼ πυροῦμαι does not mean "and am I not burnt up?" and does not imply that Paul "is of 'weak' status because he cannot survive the test of strength"[21]. The metaphorical sense of the verb πυροῦμαι differs from that of the literal πῦρ in 1 Cor 3,13-15[22]. There can hardly be any doubt that here again Paul mentions his personal reaction, i.e., his indignation. For Paul, "being indignant" in verse 29b is

---

[19] On p. 271 Andrew uses a perfect tense: "Who has been entrapped?", but also a present: "Who is entrapped?". On p. 270 equally he writes a perfect: Paul "has been burnt up", but elsewhere a present: "I am burnt up".

[20] P. 271.

[21] Ibid.

[22] On p. 271, Andrews speaks of "the same word in 1 Cor 3,15", but the verb is κατακαήσεται ("will be burned up") and only the noun πῦρ is present in v. 15 (as in v. 13). The verb is used in 7,9 in the sense of "to burn with desire", "to be inflamed".

one of the painful, but nonetheless apostolic experiences, just as "being weak" is in verse 29a. Paul's indignation is his fiery reaction to the fact that Christians are led to sin. Thus in the whole of verse 29 there is, I think, not the slightest indication of a Paul being overcome by hardships, either those of others or his own. Paul masters the situation and, out of his apostolic concern, speaks of his compassion and anger.

What Paul, perhaps with a touch of irony, depicts in vv. 32-33 is another hardship, a *peristasis* which he, as an apostle, had to undergo. It consists of danger and persecution in the city, as well as of the humiliating and troublesome flight from it. By hiding in a basket which is let down through a window Paul escapes the hands of the governor. One can perhaps claim that Paul lacks courage and that his reaction to the hardship is not the most heroic one[23]. Is he, therefore, "a coward who neither faces troubles nor endures the difficult circumstances"[24]? Hardly. Yet it would seem that by this incident Paul gives extreme emphasis to his weakness and human powerlessness.

III. PAUL'S ATTITUDE OF STRENGTH IN WEAKNESS

In the catalogue of 2 Cor 11,23b-29 no explicit mention is made of the second element postulated by Andrews: a reaction whereby one either endures or succumbs. As said above, even verse 33 does not properly function as a (submissive) "reaction" in the technical sense of the term, nor can verse 30, I think, be explained in that way. Yet Paul's reaction is nonetheless implicitly present in the text, not only in vv. 23b-28, but also in vv. 29-33, one and the same positive attitude. Paul is filled with endurance, courage and fortitude in the midst of tribulations, of all kinds of difficulties, labor and persecution. Of course, it is by the grace of God that Paul is what he is, and that grace toward him was not in vain (cf. 1 Cor 15,10). One wonders how Andrews can possibly speak of Paul succumbing to and being overcome by hardships so that the result is a lowly status which deserves blame (third element). Would it not be better to hold that Paul's real lowly status — despised by unbelievers and perhaps partly also by the opponents — is the first element itself, i.e., nothing but the harships, afflictions, anxiety and pressure? In verse 30 Paul reflects on his boasting: "If I

·

---

[23] Cf. pp. 272-273.
[24] P. 272.

must boast, I will boast of the things that show my weakness". Andrews is right where he writes: "the apostle boasts of hardships that reveal his weak status"[25], but the added contention that Paul does not boast "of the fact that he has overcome or endured the hardships"[26] cannot be substantiated. True, Paul has not overcome the hardships in the sense that he removed them, but he certainly endured them.

It should be noted that boasting itself is not a primary, immediate reaction, but only a secondary and later one, upon reflection. Boasting can hardly be called Paul's permanent attitude toward hardships. Yet, with regard to Paul's boasting one should pay due attention to the three shifts within 11:16-33: at vv. 23b, 27 and 30. These shifts provide us, it would seem, with four types of boasting defined by the object Paul boasts about. (1) In vv. 22-23a, while comparing himself with his opponents and enumerating his Jewish and Christian titles, he visibly boasts κατὰ σάρκα (verse 18). (2) Within the *peristasis* list itself, in vv. 23b-26, Paul proves his superiority by listing outward hardships, adverse circumstances. (3) Within the same list, however, from verse 27 to verse 29, he points to his own toils and labors, his personal "active" attitude. (4) Finally, in vv. 32-33 a situation is depicted where Paul's utter weakness, i.e., the absence of his own power is emphasized. Although all boasting is foolish, there are grades: the boasting of type (1) is most foolish; that of type (4) less foolish and dangerous[27].

In a footnote Andrews remarks that the catalogue of chapter 11 differs greatly from other catalogues in Paul and he refers to those of 1 Cor 4,9-13; 2 Cor 4,7-12; and 6,3-10[28]. "In these previous lists, a reference to some

---

[25] P. 272.

[26] Ibid.

[27] Within 12,1-10, one can compare vv. 2-4 with (2), the second type of boasting, and vv. 5b and 7-9ab with (4), the fourth type.

In chapters 10–13 the verb ἀσθενέω occurs 7x, the noun ἀσθένεια 6x, and the adjective ἀσθενής 1x (10,10: Paul's bodily presence). There are several nuances in the use of this terminology in chs. 10–13. Paul speaks of the weaknesses of his Christians (11,29a), the weakness of Christ (13,3b and 4a) and, above all, of his own weakness. In 11,21 and 29b the verb indicates his positive apostolic attitude. Elsewhere, i.e., from 11,30 onward, Paul wants to underline the absence of personal human strength (in 11,30 and 12,5 he refers to events which illustrate his utmost powerlessness; they are respectively narrated in 11,32-33 and 12,7-9). I do not think that in this context Paul points to his "moral" weakness. It would seem that the use of the verb in 11,29 suggested him the noun (with a different nuance) in 11,30.

[28] See note 43 on p. 273. It is doubtful that the second members of the antithetical sentences in 2 Cor 4,8-9 indicate Paul's reactions: "afflicted, but *not crushed*; perplexed, but *not driven to despair*; persecuted, but *not forsaken*; struck down, but *not destroyed*". Rather it is God's assistance and intervention which are emphasized in them.

type of battle against or endurance of the hardships is evident"[29]. Andrews notes: "no such embattlement or endurance is found in 2 Cor 11,23b-33 where Paul's submission to hardships reveals the extreme manner in which the apostle is willing to argue ... for his place as a leader of the Corinthian Christians against the opponents"[30]. This statement, however, simply neglects the implicit, but unmistakable presence in this catalogue of Paul's endurance and, especially in vv. 27-29, his positive stand. Andrews gives to boasting in the whole of vv. 23b-33 a secular populist interpretation — despite his acknowledgement of Paul's christological view. Thought-provoking this may be as a thesis, but does it merit acceptance?

In Corinth both opponents and people most probably said that Paul was humble face to face (10,1), that his bodily presence was weak (10,10b), and that he was untrained in speech (11,6). Yet in chapter 13 Paul announces his third visit and warns the Corinthians: "if I come again, I will not be lenient" (13,2) and "in dealing with you" I will be strong by the resurrection power (13,4; cf. 10,2 and 11)[31]. He writes this letter, he says at the very end, "so that when I come, I may not have to be severe in using the authority that the Lord has given me for building up and not for tearing down" (13,10; cf. 10,8). Notwithstanding various handicaps of body and spirit — they are part of his hardships! — as an apostle Paul is not without strength. Although Paul "is walking" in weak and mortal flesh, he does not battle according to that flesh (see 10,3).

How then does the catalogue function in 2 Cor 10–13? Paul is convinced that in the midst of his weakness and while suffering afflictions and tribulations God's extraordinary power and the life of Jesus are made visible in him (cf. 4,7-11). Paul does not like to boast of that mysterious reality; boasting makes him uneasy. He realizes that such boasting is foolish and dangerous, although it is not against the truth (cf. 12,6)[32]. Yet in his attitude toward the difficulties Paul is in no way following a populist model or using demagogic tactics. By no means he is "too weak not to lead". It is not only the oddity of this last expression which irritates; it is Andrews' very view on the form and function of the catalogue in chapter 11 which cannot be true.

---

[29] Ibid.

[30] Ibid.

[31] Cf. J. LAMBRECHT, "Philological and Exegetical Notes on 2 Corinthians 13,4", in R. BIERINGER – J. LAMBRECHT, *Studies on 2 Corinthians* (BETL, 112; Leuven 1994) 589-598.

[32] See J. LAMBRECHT, "Dangerous Boasting: Paul's Self-Commendation in 2 Corinthians 10-13", in this volume, pp. 107-129.

Paul himself writes in 12,10: "Whenever I am weak, then I am strong". This paradoxical statement fully applies to the "weak" situations mentioned by Paul in 11,23b-33. No doubt, in origin his strength is not his own, but "the power of Christ" dwelling in him (12,9). In the final analysis, however, being an apostle and possessing authority for leadership cannot exist without strength, mostly hidden in the inner self (cf. 4,16), but not completely invisible. To be sure, it is strength according to Christian standards, God-given strength in weakness.

14

Paul's Reasoning in Galatians 2,11-21

This discussion paper deals with Gal 2,11-21*. In a first preliminary remark I would like to point out some delineations. This work will not address problems such as whether Galatia is the territory — my position — or the (Roman) province. The comparison between Galatians and Acts regarding historical exactitude will be omitted and thus it will not be necessary to reconstruct, e.g., the number and the dates of Paul's journeys to Jerusalem. The questions concerning the apostolic Decree of the so-called Jerusalem council which are mentioned in Acts 15 but do not appear in Galatians 2 also need not detain us too long. The view that the incident of Antioch occurred not before but after the Jerusalem council, as is suggested by Paul himself in Galatians, seems preferable. The letter to the Galatians may have been written not so long before Romans, about six or seven years after the Antioch incident.

My second preliminary remark concerns methodological procedure. I will try to avoid unwarranted hypotheses and reconstructions. The main question to be asked is: what does the text tell us? Perhaps the text itself does not provide us with sufficient information regarding numerous items about which we are curious.

The paper will consist of three parts. In the first part, through an initial reading, I will present my own understanding of Gal 2,11-21, occasionally using exegetical notes taken from previous publications[1]. The second section will consider the specific characteristics of Paul's argument, again

---

* This text is an expanded version of the paper read at the Third Durham–Tübingen Research Symposium on Earliest Christianity and Judaism (Durham, September, 1994).

[1] J. LAMBRECHT, "The Line of Thought in Galatians 2.14b-21", *NTS* 24 (1977-78) 484-495; "Once Again Galatians 2,17-18 and 3,21", *ETL* 63 (1987) 148-153; and "Transgressor by Nullifying God's Grace. A Study of Galatians 2,18-21", *Bib* 72 (1991) 217-236. The three articles are republished in J. LAMBRECHT, *Pauline Studies* (BETL 115; Leuven 1994) 193-204, 205-209, and 211-230.

with he help of a previous study[2]. The third part will contain a presentation and discussion of positions suggested or defended in some recent studies.

I. EXEGESIS

The passage consisting of Gal 2,11-21 belongs to the first major section of the letter, Paul's autobiographical report from the days of his persecution of the church of God until the incident of Antioch (1,11–2,21). The pericope itself can be dived into two parts: the description of the incident (2,11-14a) and Paul's spoken reaction at the time, his address to Peter (2,14b-21). Although verses 15-21 cannot be considered as a literal report of the words pronounced by Paul at Antioch and partly function as a more general statement meant in the first place for the recipients of the letter, they are connected with v. 14b and together they are presented by Paul as a small but impressive discourse.

Verses 11-14a

Paul is interiorly convinced that he preaches God's gospel. He has not received it from a human source but through a revelation of Jesus Christ (1,11-12). After the first test case, Titus and the question of whether he must be circumcised (2,1-10) — a case which found an adequate solution agreed upon in Jerusalem — there has now arisen a second case, the incident at Antioch with regard to table fellowship and/or the Jewish dietary prescriptions (2,11-14a). In his address to Peter Paul intends to prove that he is right, that his missionary work is consistent with "the truth of the gospel" (v. 14a).

Verse 11 provides us with the anticipatory summary of the report. In vv. 12-13 Paul explains why Peter stands self-condemned. This is taken up by the statement in v. 14a: "when I saw that they were not straightforward

---

[2] J. LAMBRECHT, "Unity and Diversity in Galatians 1–2", *Unité et diversité dans L'Eglise* (Commission Biblique Pontificale; Città del Vaticano 1989) 127-142; republished in LAMBRECHT, *Pauline Studies*, 177-192. — The reader is referred to the bibliogaphy used in the four articles mentioned in notes 1 and 2.

about the truth of the gospel". In the same verse 14a the clause "I said to Cephas before all" repeats what is meant by "I opposed him to his face". Most probably the third person plural ἦλθον in v. 12 is the reading to be preferred. We notice that in vv. 12-13 it is Cephas who begins with the separation; he is joined by the rest of the Jewish Christians; finally even Barnabas is carried away. Peter's withdrawal is qualified by the term "hypocrisy"; he is not only not straightforward about the truth of the gospel, but, what is worse, he knows that what he is doing is wrong. Peter and his followers are insincere. Their behavior has to do with table fellowship: first eating with the Gentile Christians, then separating themselves from them. It is not all that clear whether those meals included the Eucharist (probably not) nor is it evident that in this association with the Gentiles the prescriptions of the apostolic Decree of Acts 15 were already observed (probably not).

"The people from James" (v. 12) are not the same as the "false brothers" of 2,4. The two cases are different: circumcision and table fellowship. Moreover, "the people from James" are not called "false" and it would appear from 2,3-10 that the three pillars, Peter, John and also James, have not given in to "the false brothers", whereas "the people from James" seem to be to a certain degree the delegates of James. It is not plainly stated what their objections to the situation of Antioch were. Are they only scandalized because Jewish Christians eat with Gentiles, or can they also not understand how converted Gentiles do not observe the Jewish dietary laws[3]?

Verse 14b

Paul's address can be divided into three sections, unequal in regard to length: (1) verse 14b (second person singular, "you"): the introductory question; (2) verses 15-17 (first person plural, "we"): the profound reflection

---

[3] For supporting argumentation for these choices and for a more extensive study of Gal 2,11-14a, see A. WECHSLER, *Geschichtsbild und Apostelstreit. Eine forschungsgeschichtliche und exegetische Studie über den antiochenischen Zwischenfall (Gal 2,11-14)* (BZNW 62; Berlin–New York 1991), esp. 296-348 (e.g. ὅτε (δέ) in v. 11, the disputed reading in v. 12 — ἦλθεν or ἦλθον — and the implications of the meaning of ὑπόκρισις in v. 13, and that of ὀρθοποδέω in v. 14a). Cf. also D.J. VERSEPUT, "Paul's Gentile Mission and the Jewish Christian Community: A Study of the Narrative in Galatians 1 and 2", *NTS* 39 (1993) 36-58, esp. 51-57. M. STOWASSER, "Konflikte und Konfliktlösungen nach Gal 1–2", *TrThZ* 103 (1994) 56-79, esp. 72-77.

in which the ultimate reason for the Christian behavior is given; for a moment the speech forgets, as it were, the incident reported in vv. 10-14a; (3) verses 18-21 (first person singular, "I"): Paul returns to the concrete difficulty in Antioch and begins a second train of thought.

The question of v. 14b, in fact a conditional period, contains a sharp personal reprimand. Paul says to Peter: you should not do what you are doing; how can you compel the Gentiles to live like Jews? With the verb ἰουδαΐζω one rightly thinks of the Jewish way of life, the Jewish customs, especially circumcision, Sabbath observance, and the food laws. Yet in this specific context (cf. 2,1-10), Paul can no longer refer to circumcision; he has in mind the discriminating dietary prescriptions. In what sense does Peter compel the Gentiles? The answer to this question is not immediately obvious. The pressure on the Gentiles should presumably be explained as follows. If the Gentile Christians want to be fully accepted by their fellow Jewish Christians, they must adopt the Jewish lifestyle and "live like Jews". It is an indirect compulsion.

In the protasis Paul says: "If you, though a Jew, live like a Gentile and not like a Jew". By these words, notwithstanding the use of the present tense ζῆς, he refers to Peter's behavior before the withdrawal; but at the same time he may implicitly appeal to what Peter is still believing. The apodosis then wants to reveal an inconsistency between Peter's supposedly persisting Christian conviction and his changed present behavior. Peter, Paul asks with probing insistence, how is this possible, how can you?[4]

Verses 15-17

Verses 15-16 together form one long repetitious sentence. The main clause stands in the middle of v. 16 and begins with the statement "even we — you Peter and I Paul, Jews by birth — have believed in Jesus Christ". One should probably link v. 15 with v. 16a; both qualify the subject of the main clause. We may consider the δέ at the beginning of v. 16 as authentic and also mentally add in v. 15 ὄντες μέν so that the parallel character of both participial clauses becomes evident: on the one hand, on the other. As often in a μὲν ... δέ construction, the first clause (v. 15) possesses a concessive nuance: it is true, everybody knows, all agree that we are Jews by birth and not Gentile sinners. The emphasis, then, lies on the second clau-

---

[4] See WECHSLER, *Geschichtsbild*, 349-364.

se (v. 16a): yet we know, i.e., we fully realize that a person is justified not by works of the law but through faith in Jesus Christ.

The expression "works of the law" means "works done in obedience to the law" and comprises, it would seem, all such works, not only those in obedience to the ceremonial or dietary law. In view of the main clause with πιστεύω εἰς ... the genitive in πίστις Ἰησοῦ Χριστοῦ is almost certainly objective. In v. 16 three times the same three elements recur: the verb "to justify", the expression "by the works of the law" and the noun "(Jesus) Christ"; thus three times the same idea is put forward. First the motivation is clearly enunciated (because we know ...), then the act and its aim are indicated (we have believed ... in order that ...), and finally a Scripture quotation is added (because ...; cf. Ps 143,2).

The term ἁμαρτωλοί in the clause εἰ δὲ ζητοῦντες δικαιωθῆναι ἐν Χριστῷ εὑρέθημεν καὶ αὐτοὶ ἁμαρτωλοί (v. 17a) has been interpreted in many ways. Two important though mutually exclusive understandings may be helpful for our further discussion. First: through and since our becoming Christians we were found to be sinners because we started to live like the Gentiles (cf. v. 14), not observing the law, eating with the Gentiles: sinners because of post-conversional acts. Second: already before we believed in Jesus Christ we were sinners, just like the Gentiles (cf. v. 15): sinners because of pre-conversional acts.

According to the first interpretation, we, i.e., Paul and Peter (and the Jewish Christians in general), were found to be sinners because, having become Christians, we no longer observe the law (or certain portions of it). We are, therefore, on a par with the Gentiles. Our eating with them is an instance of disobedience to the law. Since our faith in Christ, i.e., our endeavor to be justified in him, is the cause of this disobedient behavior, the question arises whether Christ does not promote infidelity, whether he is not an agent of sin. Paul counters this question with an indignant μὴ γέ-νοιτο. In this interpretation, verse 17ab can easily be understood as an objection raised by the Judaizers against the Pauline thesis of v. 16. These Judaizers are convinced that the Jewish Christians should continue to observe the law.

The second interpretation connects the phrase "we ourselves were found to be sinners" with the situation of the Jewish Christians (and particularly Paul and Peter) prior to their becoming Christians. The decision of these Jewish Christians to believe in Jesus Christ manifests their conviction that they too, like the Gentiles, are sinners and in need of redemption, and that, as sinners, they can reach justification only through faith in Christ, not through works of the law. But how, in this second interpretation, can the conclusion be drawn from the Jewish Christians' recognition of themselves as sinners and their seeking to be justified in Christ that Christ is a minister of sin? He cannot be so designated simply on the grounds that it is their faith in Christ which has brought the Jewish Christians to the recognition of their sinfulness. How then should we understand the text? By taking to himself sinners alone — and before God all are sinners — and by justifying them by grace, without works of the law, Christ promotes sin, because there has to be sin if there are to be sinners for him to justify and because the sinners know that they can obtain remission of sins in Christ apart from the works of the law. We have presumably before us then the well-known accusation that Christ (or, better, Paul's christology) furthers antinomianism, that Christ' free remission of sin removes the restraints on sin and even approves and promotes sin. And so, one understands Paul's vehement reaction: μὴ γένοιτο — Christ is not an agent of sin; that is not my christology.

Which of the two interpretations is more probably correct? Perhaps a careful consideration of vv. 18-21 can help us in our choice. But let us first analyze v. 17 in more detail. Verse 17b, the apodosis of the conditional period, is best taken as a question: "Is Christ an agent of sin?" The protasis (v. 17a) is presumably not a condition contrary to fact. Our view on this point is not in the first place based on the absence of an ἄν in the apodosis — for this absence could, if necessary, be explained in terms of a transition from the "irrealis" in the protasis to a "realis" in the apodosis — or by the lack of a verb in the apodosis-question. It is rather the train of thought and, above all, a comparison with Paul's way of reasoning elsewhere which lead us to consider v. 17a as a simple condition, a "realis". In this case, just as in all other instances in Paul, the objection would contain a premise (here the conditional protasis of v. 17a) with which Paul agrees, and a question (here the apodosis of v. 17b) which draws an illegitimate, wrong conclusion from that premise. It is this conclusion, not the premise, which Paul radically rejects, here as elsewhere, by means of the μὴ γένοιτο.

In the protasis the verb εὑρέθημεν means "we were found to be". This happened (past tense) while we were seeking (present participle: possibly a causal nuance is present here: because we were seeking) to be justified in Christ. Most probably, ἁμαρτωλοί does not point to the sinful conduct of those who had become Christians (i.e., their post-conversional sins), but rather refers back to that fundamental sinfulness which in v. 15 is said to be characteristic of the Gentiles: we too, as Jews, before we believed in Christ, were sinners (i.e., by pre-conversional sins) just like the Gentiles. Precisely because we realized that nobody is justified by works of the law, even we Jews came to believe in Christ Jesus (v. 16).

The Judaizers concluded that this typically Pauline view entails that

Christ promotes sin. It would appear that the ἁμαρτία in v. 17b designates the same radical idea of sinfulness as the ἁμαρτωλοί in v. 17a (and v. 15). It is Christ's promotion of sin in this sense which is dramatically negated by Paul in v. 17c. In the opponents' objection, ἁμαρτία includes, of course, actions which for Paul are no longer real "sin", e.g., eating with the Gentiles. And, therefore, one could say that a certain ambiguity is present in the term ἁμαρτία in v. 17b. Such passages as 5,13 and Rom 3,7-8 and 6,1.15 show, however, that in the objection about promoting sin — an objection raised more than once by Paul's opponents — "sin" is to be taken in its most radical sense: Paul's system leads to antinominianism and immorality.

It will be noted that our understanding of v. 17 is basically in agreement with the second interpretation set out above.

Verses 18-21

It appears that after v. 17 there is a kind of break, a caesura. The γάρ at the beginning of v. 18 comes close to meaning "but". After his reflection on what happened at the time of justification Paul comes back to the concrete Antioch incident which manifested Peter's behavior of restoring what was pulled down. Of course, one could argue that between v. 17 and v. 18 something is missing, that in his emotion Paul has omitted the necessary logical link. So one may conjecture that Paul, after v. 17 and before writing v. 18, thought: "Not Christ is an agent of sin, *but* we may become promoters of sin, *for* if I build up again ...". This hypothetical intervening thought fulfills more or less the same logical function as our hypothetically slightly adversative γάρ which introduces a new idea.

The break between v. 17 and v. 18 is evident from the time references (in v. 17a: conversion; in v. 18: Antioch incident and now), and also from the sudden appearance of "I". Already in vv. 15-17 Paul, out of rhetorical skill as well as tactful concern, has associated himself with Peter. Peter must also be aimed at in v. 18, yet Paul equally reflects on what would be the consequences of his own eventual action. "But if I build up again those things which I tore down, then I prove myself a transgressor". Notwithstanding the caesura the term "transgressor" is somewhat related to "sinners" and "sin" in the preceding verse 17.

Verse 19ab motivates v. 18, more specifically the idea of transgressing: we have a normal explanatory γάρ. Since through the law Paul died to the law, he transgresses by building up that law. He should not work nor live any longer for the law; he must live for Christ. Some elements of this statement remain for the moment mysterious. The general flow of thought, however, can hardly be doubted. Verse 19c repeats and clarifies v. 19a. The way Paul died was the death on the cross: he has been crucified with Christ. By this complementary information we now know where, when and how Paul died. The perfect tense points to an enduring state.

In the light of v. 19c the lengthy verse 20 resumes and corrects v. 19ab as well as combining it with v. 19c; verse 20 opens with an opposing δέ. As a matter of fact Paul's actual life is no longer his own life, but hat of Christ. His present bodily life is lived in faith in the Son of God. Christ loved Paul personally and delivered himself for him. The reader will note that up till now the train of thought which came to a halt at the end of v. 18 has not been further developed. What Paul adds in vv. 19 and 20 is first motivation (v. 19ab), then clarification (v. 19c) and finally concretization of that motivation (v. 20).

With its negative content verse 21a probably resumes the idea of v. 18a (here in the form of a protasis). "I do not nullify the grace of God" seems to paraphrase "I am not going to build up again those things which I tore down". If this reading is correct Paul would become a transgressor by nullifying God's grace, by building up again. In v. 21bc there is another explanatory γάρ. A verb is lacking in the protasis of this conditional period and, moreover, there is no ἄν in the apodosis. So one may wonder whether instead of an "irrealis" (a condition contrary to fact) the grammatical form is not a "realis" (a "simple condition"). The form of a condition of fact is indifferent to the fulfillment or non-fulfillment of what is stated. What we have is no more than the stringent logical connection. The reasoning is: If A, then B. In v. 21bc this reads literally: "if justification is through the law, then Christ died in vain". Thus, to the question "Why does Paul nullify God's grace?" the answer is: "Because, if justification is through the law, then Christ died to no purpose". Verse 21b corresponds regarding its content to v. 18a: if the law is in force (again); if it is built up again. Verse 21c draws the conclusion: then the death of Christ has been in vain. Verse 21bc explains why, in such case, Paul destroys the grace of God.

At the end of this reading of vv. 18-21 we may once more point to Paul's way of reasoning. The train of thought comes to a standstill, as it were, after v. 18 and is then resumed in v. 21. Verses 19-20 motivate, explain and concretize v. 18. In v. 21a Paul denies the idea to which the hypothetical content of v. 18a leads, namely, that he is going to destroy the grace of God. Does verse 18b, therefore, not also contain that idea? Verse 21bc explain the statement of v. 21a; as in v. 18 we have a conditional period. Grammatically speaking verse 21b corresponds with v. 18a (twice a protasis with εἰ γάρ), and verse 21c with v. 18b (twice an apodosis, a "then"-clause). What must be said about their content, more in particular that of v.

18b ("then I prove myself a transgressor")? A further analysis is needed.

Further Analysis of Verses 18-21

Verse 18. The conditional sentence of v. 18 is a "realis", a condition of fact. In the protasis we have the opposition between καταλύω and οἰκοδο-μέω. Paul often uses antitheses. At first sight it does not make much difference if συνιστάνω ἐμαυτόν in the apodosis has the somewhat weaker sense "I show, I demonstrate, I prove myself" or the stronger one "I establish, I constitute myself". Pauline passages such as 2 Cor 7,11; Rom 3,5 and 5,8, however, seem to point to the weaker sense. Paul proves himself to be a transgressor. What does this mean?

The noun παραβάτης is not followed by an objective genitive, the presence of which would have indicated what Paul is actually transgressing. We shall have to look at the context to discover the implied direct object of "transgressing". The aorist tense κατέλυσα contains a reference to the time when Paul became a Christian. The adverb πάλιν and the verb οἰκοδομέω point the reader to the hypothetical step of Paul (and the actual step of Peter) "to live again like a Jew" (cf. 2,14). With ἅ and ταῦτα we must think in the first place of eating with the Gentiles, and, further, of calendar prescriptions (4,10), and circumcision (5,2-3). All this pertains to the Jewish law. But it should be duly noted that νόμος itself is not mentioned in v. 18a. If that had been the case one would have been brought, almost inevitably, to understand the ensuing παραβάτης in v. 18b as "transgressor of the law".

Many interpreters, however, do mentally supply "of the law" after "transgressor". How does Paul then show himself a transgressor of the law? There are two possibilities: either his previous pulling down of the law was a transgression of the law, or Paul, after having built up, will out of necessity sin in the future by not keeping all its commandments (see 3,10 and cf. 5,3). Because of the absence of νόμος in v. 18 and even more because of the line of thought in vv. 19-21, neither of these interpretations seems satisfactory.

Verse 19. The personal pronoun ἐγώ at the beginning of v. 19 is very emphatic. In view of the fact that θεῷ in v. 19b is best understood as a dative of interest and because of the correspondence between the opposing verbs ἀπέθανεν and ζήσω, the dative νόμῳ in v. 19a is probably a dative of disadvantage: through the law I died "to the law" so that it has no longer any power over me. There is no qualification of either use of "law" in v. 19a, but they must point to the same Jewish law (cf. also vv. 16 and 21).

The dative νόμῳ is preceded by the genitive expression διὰ νόμου. What is the meaning of this expression?

In order to find a sense for the puzzling διὰ νόμου in v. 19a one must, it would seem, take a lead from v. 19c and, through it, from 3,13. Why has Christ been crucified? According to 3,13 Christ became a curse, i.e., cursed by the law, because he hung on the cross; and so he redeemed us from that same curse of the law which we incurred through our sins. Paul appears here to be reasoning by means of categories such as reparatory substitution and atoning sacrifice. Christ died for us, on our behalf. Paul more specifically thinks in cultic terms of salvation through death. Christ has taken over the identity of us sinners; he died the death to which the law had condemned us and so redeemed and blessed us (cf. 3,13-14). Of course, the cultic terms are meant here metaphorically.

According to 2,19a Paul dies. Through the identification of Paul–sinner and Christ who on the cross became a curse, Paul was present and dying at the moment Jesus died on the cross. This death by the law was his redemption; it was at the same time a death *to* the law. Through this death Paul is no longer ὑπὸ νόμον (cf. 4,21). Henceforth he must live for God (2,19b; cf. Rom 7,4 and 6). Paul can even say in Gal 2,19c: I have been crucified with Christ. "This is a bold statement from one who was not even present at Calvary!" (G. Berényi). But Paul was present; this is his firm conviction. There and then, Paul died to the law. One realizes both the metaphorical and paradoxical qualities of the verb συσταυροῦμαι which is not found in extant literature before Paul. It is quite possible that Paul created this metaphor. The paradoxical character of v. 19c should be duly reflected upon: nothing is common between death on a cross and new life; moreover, both death and life are conceived of as through and together with Christ! The perfect tense συνεσταύρωμαι is not accidental.

Verse 20. This is the longest verse of the unit (vv. 18-21), much discussed because of the christological content of v. 20d which is often thought to go back to a traditional *Dahingabe-Formel*. Paul continues to speak a paradoxical language: no longer his own life, Christ's life in him; Christ delivers himself up for Paul. There are, moreover, two sharp antitheses: in v. 20ab "I–Christ", in v. 20cd "flesh–faith". The initial δέ in v. 20a corrects what Paul has just said in v. 19b about his living for God. As a matter of fact (again a δέ in v. 20b, now opposing), it is Christ who lives in him. We note the change of subject. In v. 20a and b we have before us two short clauses of equal length, beginning respectively with ζῶ δέ and ζῇ δέ and ending antithetically — the second as it were excluding the first — with ἐγώ and Χριστός. We may refer to 1 Cor 15,10 for a similar affirmation and negation: "I worked harder than any of them, though it was not I, but the grace of God which is with me".

Yet in v. 20cd, by means of a third and opposing δέ Paul must return to the first person singular, to his own life "now". He cannot deny it completely. It is, moreover, a life in the flesh. This human life is still (νῦν) bodily, creaturely fragile; it is not yet an eschatological existence. Nonetheless, already now that life in the flesh is simultaneously a life in the faith of the Son of God who loved Paul and delivered himself for him. The clause "what I now live" (v. 20c) is the direct object of the same verb of v. 20d: "(what I now live) I live ...". The relative pronoun ἅ may be limitative; it then suggests, as it were, a lesser form of life: "So far as I live now in the flesh". "I live" is qualified not only by "now" (over against the eschatological future) but also by "in the flesh" (over against a life which will be spiritual, heavenly, immortal and incorruptible — see 1 Cor 15,48-54).

In v. 20d υἱοῦ τοῦ θεοῦ is an objective genitive just as Ἰησοῦ Χριστοῦ in v. 16 which genitive is immediately explained in the same verse 16 by "even we have believed in Christ". G. Berényi has shown that verse 20d is not a stereotyped and traditional formula. Both wording and content come from Paul. Verse 20d is a Pauline creation. A comparison with the undoubtedly traditional formula in 1 Cor 15,3 Χριστός (traditional?) ἀπέθανεν ὑπὲρ τῶν ἁμαρτιῶν ἡμῶν might prove instructive. Three Pauline particularities vis-à-vis 1 Cor 15,3 must be stressed. (1) Instead of Χριστός we have in v. 20d υἱοῦ τοῦ θεοῦ. The title "Son of God" is "rarely used by Paul. With its solemnity this title underlines the contrast with 'me' and therefore contributes to the paradoxical character of the verse" (Berényi). (2) Παραδίδωμι is different from δίδωμι. Παραδίδωμι with personal object (here reflexive pronoun) possesses a negative meaning; it "implies that the person is delivering himself up to a hostile treatment" (Berényi). Moreover, "... the expression ... with παραδίδωμι and the reflexive pronoun is a creation of Paul himself" (Berényi). (3) The typical and original use of ἀγαπάω by Paul is confirmed by passages such as Rom 5,6-8 and 8,32-39 which both possess a similar context. This verb "provides the motivation and accounts for the efficacy of the Son of God's act of delivering himself up" (Berényi). Without love Christ would not have done this; without love his action would have no result.

Verse 21. "This sentence" is "abruptly introduced, without connective" (Burton). In the verb ἀθετέω of v. 21a there is most probably a modal nuance: I am not going or I am not willing or I am not allowed to cancel (to render invalid, to nullify) the grace of God. In v. 20 Paul had beautifully indicated what riches are contained in the expression ἡ χάρις τοῦ θεοῦ (subjective genitive): God's grace is basically the gift of Christ, his person and all that he did, especially his dying out of love. While in v. 20d Christ himself is the active subject, here in v. 21a God has the initiative. We may refer to Rom 8,35 and 39: in v. 35 Paul writes: "Who shall separate us from the love of *Christ*?" (cf. v. 37), while in v. 39 he has: nobody and nothing "will be able to separate us from the love of *God* in Christ Jesus our Lord". Thus, without any difficulty Paul can move from Christ to God and from God to Christ. "In this expression 'the love of God in Christ Jesus' Paul makes a synthesis and shows that in reality God's love and Christ's love are the same thing" (Berényi). How could Paul nullify God's grace? The context refers us back to v. 18a: by building up again what I pulled down, i.e., the prescriptions of the law.

Verse 21bc repeats that idea of clinging to the law by means of a more general formulation. The conditional period of v. 21bc is most probably in form again a "simple supposition" not an "irrealis". The translation of the protasis should then be: "If justification *is* through the law". Of course, Paul is convinced of the opposite, but the grammatical form as such does not indicate this; it only stresses the logical connection between protasis and apodosis, between justification through the law and its consequence, the useless death of Christ.

The expression διὰ νόμου of v. 21b has already appeared in v. 19a. The meaning here, however, is quite different. In v. 19 Paul speaks of his death together with Christ on the cross. Why in v 19a did he write: "through the law"? We may briefly comment on what we have already stated in our analysis of v. 19. Since Christ died on the cross, he became a curse through the law and so redeemed us from the curse of that law (see 3,13). Most probably Paul's reasoning in 3,10-14 implies that through not observing the law we are sinners and, therefore, cursed by the law (see 3,10); we cannot be justified by it. Only Christ, by becoming a curse and thus taking our place, brings redemption. In 2,19a Paul writes that the law caused his death and in 19c that he has been crucified with Christ. This seems to imply that in some sense Christ's death as well is caused by the law. This is true not because Christ violated the law, but because he had to become cursed by the law in order to redeem us from the curse of law. Admittedly, Paul writes in a very concise way. "Through the law" in 2,19a contains, most likely, the negative connotation that Paul, like all humankind, does not keep that law.

In the protasis of v. 21b, however, the supposition is that there is justification διὰ νόμου, that is, through observing the law, through doing the works of the law — which, of course, is impossible according to Paul. Verse 21b formulates as a hypothesis something that is denied three times within v. 16, namely, that nobody is justified by works of the law. Suppose, Paul says in v. 21bc, that justification as a matter of fact occurs through the law, then Christ's death is no longer needed, Christ died in vain. The expressions "by works of the law" (v. 16) and "through the law" (v. 21b) certainly point to observation and "doing". Yet doing itself is not wrong. On the contrary, it is "not keeping God's law", the non-observation of that law, that makes us all sinners (see Rom 3,23) so that we are in need of justification and redemption through Christ (and no longer through the law).

Verse 21c draws the conclusion from v. 21b. "The argument of the sentence is from a Christian point of view a *reductio ad absurdum*, and is adduced as proof of the preceding statement" (Burton). Verse 21c can be considered as a comment upon v. 21a, its elaboration; verse 21c is therefore also connected with v. 18b.

We may conclude this long analysis: By building up again the prescriptions of the law (v. 18a) Paul would nullify God's grace (v. 21a). He would be acting as if there is justification through the law (v. 21b). If there is such justification, then Christ died in vain (v. 21c). In v. 18, however, Paul adds after the protasis "if I restore those prescriptions" the apodosis "I show myself a transgressor".

Transgressor of What? (v. 18b)

Leaving aside 2,18, Paul five times uses παραβαίνω and παραβάτης with the meaning "transgressing the law" (Rom 2,23.25.27; 4,15; Gal 3,19), and once to refer to Adam's transgression of a commandment (Rom 5,14). The conclusion cannot be avoided: Pauline usage as well as the context of Gal 2,18 impel us to postulate after παραβάτης a legal concept: the Torah or some kind of commandment or law. Can we now determine in what Paul's transgression consists? Three possibilities must be taken into account.

a) Could Paul prove himself a transgressor because by becoming a Christian he destroyed the law? We must then paraphrase as follows: "But if build up again those things which I tore down, I recognize now that by my previous eating with the Gentiles I have violated the law and have been a transgressor of that law". "Those things" are the food laws, calendar prescriptions, and circumcision. One could easily enough understand such a reasoning on the part of Paul's Jewish-Christian opponents. For them καταλύω was a negative, sinful action. Building up again, then, implies a retraction which manifests and confesses the wrong nature of the previous destruction.

Yet three reasons plea against this understanding. First, too much remains implicit, unsaid, in such a train of thought, more particularly the transition from "I show (now) that (then) I was a transgressor". Second, συνιστάνω does not elsewhere in Paul's letters have the nuance of "I recognize, I confess", although this verb occurs therein twelve more times. Third, one cannot see how the γάρ sentence of v. 19 explains and motivates v. 18 when this interpretation is accepted.

b) In view of the difficulties with this first proposal an alternative interpretation connected with law presents itself. If Paul builds up again what he has torn down, then, i.e., afterwards, by subsequent actions, he will prove himself a transgressor of that restored law. As arguments in favor of this proposal we mention: οἰκοδομῶ is the main verb of the protasis; it stands at the end; it corresponds in tense with συνιστάνω. The idea which is supposed to be present is very Pauline. In the same letter to the Galatians, in 3,10, Paul states that all who rely on the works of the law are under a curse because they do not keep all prescriptions of that law. In 3,19 Paul states that the law is added τῶν παραβάσεων χάριν till the offspring should come. If this verse is compared with 3,22 it appears that in Paul's view the law concretely functions as a factor which does not limit but possibly even increases sin. Moreover, an oppositional connection between "Christ, an agent of sin" (v. 17) and "Paul, future transgressor (of the law)" becomes evident.

Several factors, however, make us hesitate with regard to this second proposal as well. In the first proposal there could be no doubt about what Paul has transgressed: the law which contains the food prescriptions pointed to in v. 18a. In this second interpretation, however, the link between the object of transgressing in v. 18b and the ταῦτα ἃ κατέλυσα in v. 18a is not so clear since Paul is thinking in v. 18b of radical moral sin (cf. sinners and sin in vv. 15 and 17), not of breaking ceremonial or dietary prescriptions. Further, although theoretically speaking a future sense could be read into συνιστάνω, the reference to future transgressions is not so easy to accept in v. 18b. Moreover, it would have then the unusual sense "I will constitute myself". Finally, the logical connection between v. 18 and v. 19 is equally difficult.

c) To be sure, because of the Pauline use of παραβάτης and because of the specific content of v. 18a (restoration of law prescriptions) one expects after "transgressor" the objective genitive "law"; one tends spontaneously to supply its absence. Yet, immediately afterwards, verse 19a points to a new situation: Paul is dead to the law; and in v. 19b there is the ἵνα-clause which formulates the new command: a Christian must live for God. Does the transgression of v. 18b not precisely consist in the building up again of the law which would make obedience to that new command no longer possible? The transgressor does violence to the will of God as clearly revealed in Christ. In the second proposal above the restoration was not the transgression: the restoration would inevitably lead to transgressions of the law. Here in our third proposal it is the restoration itself which also transgresses the new command to live solely for God.

Yet one still hesitates and persists in asking whether it is not too far-fetched to look at "living to God" in v. 19a as a command that can be transgressed. Moreover, we have to admit, the content parallelism between v. 18a and v. 21b as well as between v. 18b and v. 21a is not perfect. On the other hand, three more remarks seem to corroborate the third interpretation. (1) Within this tentative interpretation the motivating sentence of v. 19 works nicely in a logical way. The underlying idea is that I am not permitted to re-establish the law because I died to it by becoming a Christian. I am not permitted to transgress the life-command that results from that death. (2) Just as the noun παραβάτης, the verb ἀθετέω is also a legal term. After this verb one expects as direct object a command, an agreement or a law. Just as in v. 18b the object in v. 21a is not the Torah; otherwise than in v. 18b, however, the object is mentioned: God's grace. (3) The idea of refusing and rejecting God's grace is present in other passages of Paul's letters as well. We may refer to the letter to the Galatians itself where Paul in 1,6 expresses his astonishment: "you are so quickly moving away from (μετα-τίθεσθε ἀπό) him who called you in the grace of God". In 5,4 he writes: "You are severed from (κατηργήθητε ἀπό) Christ, you who would be justified by the law, you have fallen away from grace (τῆς χάριτος ἐξε-πέσατε)", and in 5,11 he states that the preaching of circumcision would mean that the stumbling block of the cross has been removed (κατήργη-ται). The most vigorous passage, however, is Rom 9,30–10,4 where Paul in 9,32 says about Israel that they have stumbled over (προσέκοψαν) the stumbling stone, in 10,2 that their zeal is not enlightened (οὐ κατ᾽ ἐπί-γνωσιν), and in 10,3 that they were ignorant (ἀγνοοῦντες) of God's righteousness and did not submit (οὐχ ὑπετάγησαν) to it (see also 10,21: λαὸς ἀπειθοῦν καὶ ἀντιλέγων).

Of course, all these remarks do not directly prove that in Gal 2,18b Paul had in mind a transgressor of God's new initiative in Christ and the command it implies, but at least they indicate for Paul the possibility of that idea. If our own proposal possesses any value, as we think it does, then one will notice that there is a kind of identification between nullifying (v. 21a) and transgressing (v. 18b), in so far as one who nullifies God's grace by the same token transgresses the life command it contains. As a matter of fact, by the restoration of the law Paul would destroy God's grace and become ipso facto a transgressor of that new command to live for God. What further commends this third understanding of παραβάτης is the fact that in it verses 18-21 form a small unit, framed by v. 18b and v. 21a, expressing the same idea: I am not going to be a transgressor, I am not going to nullify God's grace. In the final analysis Paul does not want to become a transgressor by nullifying the grace of God!

II. ARGUMENT

It would seem that the center of Paul's reasoning in the whole letter is given in 2,16. Nobody is justified by works of the law but through faith in Jesus Christ. Paul put forwards his basic conviction; he formulates the essence of what he believes: justification through faith. With this one argument he defends his apostolate and the concrete way he preached the gospel among the Gentiles. For Paul and for Peter, for Gentile and Jewish Christians alike, this faith is the same. In Paul's mind, "justification by faith" applies to all Christians. This conviction of Paul, moreover, is his sole apology.

One Gospel

In the letter to the Galatians Paul's emphasis on the "gospel of Christ" (see 1,6-10) is no doubt remarkable. True, Paul stresses the fact that this is precisely the gospel which he himself preached to the Galatians and which they received (see 1,8 and 9). But there is no alternative gospel (see 1,7), he argues. It is universal, the same for all Christians and meant for all humankind. This "catholic" character is also evident from the fact that the gospel which was preached by Paul is not a human gospel; he received it not from any human being but through a revelation of Jesus Christ (cf. 1,11-12). Because of this sameness of the gospel, Paul can say in 2,14b that Peter and the others in refusing table fellowship with the Gentile Christians were not straightforward about the truth of the gospel. On referring to this universally valid gospel in 1,23 Paul uses the singular expression εὐαγγελίζομαι τὴν πίστιν.

Yet Two Different Gospels?

It cannot but strike the readers of Galatians that after 1,6-12, with its stress on the one gospel, Paul distinguishes in 2,7-10 between two gospels: τὸ εὐαγγέλιον τῆς περιτομῆς and τὸ εὐαγγέλιον τῆς ἀκροβυστίας (v. 7), equally between to "apostolates" or missions (v. 8) and, implicitly, between two graces (v. 9). Can each of these gospels be characterized? As far as the text of Galatians 1-2 goes, three factors which make Paul's own gospel different may be listed. (1) Paul does not require that Gentile Christians be circumcised (cf. 2,3-5: Titus as "test-case"; see also, e.g., 5,3.11 and 6,13). (2) Paul's Gentile Christians do not observe the Jewish food laws (cf. 2,11-13). (3) And Paul, in a more general way, does not "compel the Gentiles to live like Jews" (2,14b). Obviously at least some works of the law can be neglected by the Gentile Christians, not only circumcision and food laws but, as 4,10-11 seems to say, also Jewish feast-days.

In 2,7-9 Paul apparently defends the good rights of both gospels. He himself "had been entrusted with the gospel to the uncircumcised, just as Peter had been entrusted with the gospel to the circumcised" (v. 7). The God who worked through Peter for the mission to the circumcised also worked through Paul for the Gentiles (cf. v. 8). The grace is given to Paul (just as it was given to others, we could add; cf. v. 9).

Yet, it would go too far, I think, if we infer from this evident parallelism that in Paul's mind God himself wants to seal or perpetuate the specific differences between the two gospels. In the reasoning of vv. 7-9 Paul defends his apostolate and his own way of acting, i.e., mainly the freedom of his Gentile Christians. What he says regarding Peter is but the point of departure for that focus. A specific "gospel to the Jews" is as it were taken for granted or, better, for the time being conceded by Paul. Therefore, we must not assume that in Paul's conception God really sanctions the Jewish distinctive particularities.

Paul's Way of Reasoning

When Paul wrote his letter to the Galatians, the situation in Galatia was analogous to that of about six or seven years earlier. Paul could therefore refer to the Jerusalem council and use that past conflict to clarify the new difficulties. Yet three specific factors must be pointed out. (1) In Galatia also there are those who cause trouble; according to Paul they preach another, a different gospel; they block, he says, the gospel of Christ (cf.

1,6-9). Most probably they are Jewish Christians. Do they come from Jerusalem? How far do they rely on James (as those in 2,12 do)? This is not clear. (2) Further, Paul is full of anxiety because he fears that his Galatian Christians will be led astray. Throughout the whole letter he pleads and tries to convince them or to win them back. It can be presumed .that the same danger and fear also existed in the earlier period. But this poignant character is very prominent in the letter. Moreover, Paul must defend himself. He stresses that he really is God's apostle and does not seek human favor. (3) In this letter Paul uses a rather strange, somewhat sarcastic vocabulary where he refers, now after six or seven years, to the Jerusalem authorities. In 2,2 he writes: οἱ δοκοῦντες, they who are of repute. In 2,6 he explains: οἱ δοκοῦντες εἶναί τι, they who were reputed to be something, and he adds: "what they were makes no difference to me; God shows no partiality". Further, in 2,9, he calls them οἱ δοκοῦντες στῦλοι εἶναι, they who were reputed to be pillars. The language is obviously not without a bitter tone.

Paul is deeply convinced that he preached the pure gospel of Christ to the Galatians (see 1,7). Judging from Gal 1,4 its kernel is "redemption". Jesus gave himself for our sins to deliver us from the present evil age. There is no alternative gospel. If other missionaries, even if an angel from heaven should bring a gospel contrary to that which Paul preached to the Galatians, let them be accursed.

With such a conviction how can Paul then in 2,7 distinguish between the gospel τῆς ἀκροβυστίας and that τῆς περιτομῆς? Paul certainly understands these expressions as pointing to the addressees: the gospel to the uncircumcised and that to the circumcised. Verses 8 and 9 corroborate such an understanding: in v. 8 "the apostolate εἰς τὰ ἔθνη" corresponds to "the apostolate τῆς περιτομῆς", and in v. 9 we encounter in parallel construction ἡμεῖς εἰς τὰ ἔθνη and αὐτοὶ δὲ εἰς τὴν περιτομήν. However, these gospels are not completely the same. The whole context teaches us that Jewish Christians still observe the law. As far as we can judge, their Jewish way of life (with circumcision, food laws and Sabbath) is not experienced as contrary to their faith in Christ.

The surprising feature now appears to be that the different gospel put forward by both the troublemakers in Galatia and, years earlier, but the people from James in Antioch, and in 1,6-9 so vehemently rejected by Paul, is precisely that εὐαγγέλιον τῆς περιτομῆς which he accepts without any difficulty in 2,7-9. What is then wrong with it? At first one would like to state that the point of friction lies only in the fact that Jewish Christian missionaries compel Gentile Christians to live as Jews. Under no condition can Paul accept this interference. Paul's fight for freedom is thus certainly a fight for a "Gentile" gospel which no longer contains those Jewish "identity markers".

But as we continue to read the letter we detect that that liberation is far from being just an external matter. Paul reflects on the implications; he reasons and tries to convince the others. In 2,14b-21 and elsewhere in Galatians (and in Romans) he grounds his position. Nobody is justified by works of the law. Redemption occurred through Jesus crucified. The Spirit is given through faith in Christ. It would seem that Jewish Christians spontaneously still attach salvific effect to these "identity markers". Such an understanding of their εὐαγγέλιον τῆς περιτομῆς is intrinsically vitiated.

In Gal 4,3 Paul reminds his Galatian Christians in passing that by becoming believers they were liberated from slavery to the former pagan regulations (τὰ στοιχεῖα τοῦ κόσμου). Their freedom is thus twice negatively defined, namely vis-à-vis the Jewish particularities and vis-à-vis their own Gentile past. As far as Galatians is concerned no word is spoken of a new, "Gentile" inculturation or contextualisation, more or less analogous to characteristics of the gospel τῆς περιτομῆς. On the contrary, Paul's whole attention is apparently focused on the essential content and the liberating effect of Christ's gospel.

III. THREE POINTS OF DISCUSSION

In this third section explicit attention is given only to the second part of the pericope, Paul's address. Even within this address we must omit a discussion of v. 16 and vv. 19-20; moreover, within the actual treatment of the three points only certain aspects of their problems will be dealt with.

Before we begin our discussion a word may be said about our proposed threefold structure of 2,14-21 (see pp. 159-160). Michael Bachmann has devoted large sections of his monograph to the analysis of the structure of 2,15-21[5], while Andreas Wechsler appears more or less to adopt our pro-

---

[5] M. BACHMANN, *Sünder oder Übertreter. Studien zur Argumentation in Gal 2,15ff.* (WUNT 59; Tübingen 1992) 25-54: "Zu Struktur und Intention von 2,15-21"; and 55-83: "Architektonisches". Two remarks are in order. (1) Verse 14b is omitted in this analysis. (2) Verse 17 receives a special treatment in regard to its strucural status: it stands "zwischen dem ersten ... und den zweiten Teil" (85). According to Bachmann, Gal 2,15-21 is "eine wohlüberlegte Komposition" (ibid.). V. JEGHER-BUCHER, *Der Galaterbrief auf dem Hintergrund antiker Epistolographie und Rhetorik* (AThANT 78; Zürich 1991) proposes a division which separates 2,17–3,5 ("Transitio") from 1,13–2,16 ("Argumentationseinheit"); this proposal is unconvincing.

posal[6]. In his comment Wechsler even confirms this view on structure by pointing to the fact that both main sections of that address (vv. 15-17 and vv. 18-21, "zwei Gedankenlinien") end in a conditional period "dessen Apodosis eine unmögliche Aussage über Christus enthält"[7]. He adds: "Die beiden ARA-Sätze enthalten also jeweils eine Absurdität in sich [Christ agent of sin; Christ's death in vain] und treffen voll in die Galatische Krise, weil sie die gegenseitigen Vorwürfe markieren"[8]. Wechsler also mentions that the caesura at v. 18 is after all not so strange: "Der Bruch nach μὴ γένοιτο erklärt sich am besten aus der blasphemischen Ungeheuerlichkeit von V. 17b [Christ agent of sin], die freilich in dem nicht weniger herausfordernden ἄρα Χριστὸς δωρεὰν ἀπέθανεν gekontert wird"[9].

Verse 14b

What does Peter's "living like a Gentile" mean? The position of Paul Bötgger is extreme and hardly deserves much attention[10]. The fact that Peter separates himself from the Gentile Christians and takes up the Jewish way of life would paradoxically make him a Gentile sinner: "Gerade der zum orthodoxen Judentum zurückkehren wollende Petrus hat dies paradoxerweise völlig verfehlt und ist auf die Stufe des Heidentums zurückgesunken ..."[11]. And again: "Indem Petrus ὑπὸ νόμον zurückgekehrt ist ..., steht er im Bereich seiner in die Sünde führenden und deswegen von Gott trennenden und verurteilenden Macht"[12].

More interesting are the brief perhaps somewhat forced remarks which Martin Karrer devotes to Gal 1–2 in his article "Petrus im paulinischen Gemeindekreis"[13]. From 1,18 and 2,10 one can deduce that for Paul Peter is the highly respected "Zentralgestalt"[14]. The Antioch incident is the anti-

---

[6] WECHSLER, *Geschichtsbild*, 394-395.

[7] Ibid., 395.

[8] Ibid. Yet BACHMANN, *Sünder*, 57, rightly warns us that there is no strict parallelism between v. 17ab (with its rhetorical question) and v. 21bc. As has already been mentioned in this paper, verse 18 corresponds with v. 21bc. See also pp. 73-74.

[9] *Geschichtsbild*, p. 395.

[10] P.C. BÖTTGER, "Paulus und Petrus in Antiochien. Zum Verständnis von Galater 2. 11-21", *NTS* 37 (1991) 77-100, esp. 79-82.

[11] Ibid., 81

[12] Ibid., 81-82.

[13] M. KARRER, "Petrus im paulinischen Gemeindekreis", *ZNW* 80 (1989) 210-231, esp. 213-221.

[14] Ibid., 214-216.

climax to this. Peter stands condemned (by God) because he yields to human pressure. The passage "demonstriert die Richtigkeit der 1,10 vorangestellten These, dass Paulus sich durch Menschen nicht bestimmen lasse, im Unterschied zum grossen Petrus. Paulus widersteht, Petrus aber erliegt"[15]. Yet, according to Karrer, Peter was certainly not a "Judaizer". The Antioch incident was an exception to his behavior. The present tense ζῆς in 2,14b (as well as Acts 10,1–11,18) shows his basic attitude. "Er passt sich, obwohl jüdischer Herkunft und mit dem Apostolat unter den Beschnittenen beauftragt, grundsätzlich und in der Dauer seines Wirkens den Lebensgewohnheiten der 'Völker' an. Im Bruch der Tischgemeinschaft in Antiochien bricht er ... seine eigene Regel"[16].

The new proposal by James Dunn is put forward with great emphasis[17]. He first mentions the double problem: the present tense of the verb (ζῆς; is Peter still living like a Gentile when Paul speaks?) and the force of the expression itself ("does Paul imply that Peter had totally abandoned all characteristic and distinctive Jewish practices?"[18]). To maintain that Peter still continues to live like a Gentile in other matters than table fellowship is no good solution since the Jewish way of life is an indivisible whole. Equally, to maintain that the phrase "to live like a Gentile" can objectively be used for a minimum of Torah observance like that required by the apostolic Decree — Dunn here refers to his own earlier thesis — is also hardly acceptable[19]. Dunn now proposes as "the key to the most plausible solution" that Paul is "probably picking up the actual words used by the James group in their rebuke of Peter, 'How can you, Peter, a Jew, live like a Gentile?'"[20]. It is "*not* the language of objective description but ... the language of inter-Jewish factional dispute"[21]. Conservative Jews denounce every failure to conform to their positions as complete treason, as a following of the Gentile way of life.

Dunn' suggestion that we have here an "an echo of intra-Jewish polem-

---

[15] Ibid., 217.

[16] Ibid. 219. Cf., e.g. STOWASSER, "Konflikte", 76.

[17] J.D.G. DUNN, "Echos of Intra-Jewish Polemic in Paul's Letter to the Galatians", *JBL* 112 (1993) 459-477. On 2,14 see also ID., *The Epistle to the Galatians* (BNTC; Peabody, MA 1993) 126-130.

[18] "Echoes", 468.

[19] Cf. ibid.

[20] Ibid., 469. See also ID., *The Theology of Paul's Letter to the Galatians* (NTTheol; Cambridge 1993) 74: "In the eyes of the James' group Peter has been 'living like a Gentile and not as a Jew' (2.14); he had been behaving like 'Gentile sinners' (2.15)".

[21] "Echoes", 469.

ic", however attractive, remains quite hypothetical. To be fair, in his study he discusses two more echoes in Gal 2,15-16 ("Jews by nature, not Gentile sinners" and "works of the law") and possible hints in 2,11-17 (furthermore also the calendar piety mentioned in 4,10 and Paul's accusation in 4,17). Yet, it appears to me that the number of so-called instances scarcely increases the probability of Dunn's proposal. Moreover, there is still his hardly provable thesis that table fellowship at Antioch showed "respect for the principal Jewish scruples against, say, eating blood and pork"[22] (cf. the apostolic Decree of Acts 15) and, therefore, did not mean completely free association between Christian Jews and Gentiles[23].

Verses 17-18

For Dunn 2,17 is seemingly an "irrealis", a statement not accepted by Paul but brought forward by the people from James. "Evidently the James faction's insistence that the Gentile believers at Antioch were still to be categorized as 'sinners' drew the corollary, obvious to all the Jewish factions represented, that those Jews who consorted with such 'sinners' and thus conducted themselves in ways repugnant to Torah loyalists would find themselves regarded by the Jewish 'righteous' as equally 'sinners'"[24]. Moreover, it is Dunn's opinion that 'sinner' in v. 17a (and v. 17b) has the same meaning as that in v. 15 and is an echo of the language used by the group from James. Gentiles are sinners "by nature" because they are outside the law. Table fellowship is one of the great sins. According to this

---

[22] Ibid., 468.

[23] See J.D.G. DUNN, "The Incident at Antioch" *JSNT* 18 (1983) 3-57, e.g., 25; republished in ID., *Jesus, Paul and the Law. Studies in Mark and Galatians* (London 1990) 127-174, and Additional Note on pp. 174-182. Cf. the critical discussion by WECHSLER, *Geschichtsbild*, 353-355. We may also quote VERSEPUT, "Gentile Mission", 532, n. 34: Dunn "may be correct in his historical assessment that the Gentiles [= Gentile Christians] in Antioch were already observing some of the basic food laws and that Peter's action served only to raise the ritual barriers surrounding table-fellowship. Paul, however, ignores this fact in the present context and concentrates wholly on the reality that Gentiles were being denied such fellowship".

[24] "Echoes", 465; see also ID., *Galatians*, 141 and *Theology*, 75. Cf. in the same vein J.M.G. BARCLAY, *Obeying the Truth: A Study of Paul's Ethics in Galatians* (Edinburgh 1988), 77-80. Dunn's understanding can be compared with the somewhat differing position of R.N. LONGENECKER, *Galatians* (WBC; Dallas, TX 1990) 88-90: "... in saying 'we are found to be sinners' Paul is responding to a charge of his opponents and granting the truth of their underlying observation: that Christians, though claiming a higher standard for living, yet sin" (90). In v. 17a Paul would be pointing to the Galatians' libertinism.

interpretation, in v. 17 Paul particularly thinks of that type of sin after becoming a Christian[25].

For the refutation of this exegesis we not only can refer to the first part of this paper (pp. 160-163) and the studies on which it relies, but also to the two already mentioned recent monographs. Wechsler accepts our three main decisions regarding v. 17: (1) Vers 17a is a "realis" (Paul agrees with its content); (2) in v. 17a "sinners" refers to the pre-conversional situation of the Jewish Christians and possesses a more radical sense (cf., e.g., Rom 3,23) than Dunn seems to suppose; (3) verse 17b (Christ agent of sin) should be explained according to what Paul says in Rom 3,8; 6,1 and 15: a law-free gospel provokes libertinism[26]. Moreover, Wechsler also assumes that after v. 17, notwithstanding the γάρ in v. 18, there is a break in the line of argument. There is, as it were, a new start; Paul returns to the Antioch incident[27].

Bachmann has not been able to use the work of Wechsler. He himself also considers v. 17a as a "realis"[28]. Verse 17a "repeats" what is said in vv. 15-16; all verses refer to "die Zeit des Gläubigwerdens"[29]. He very much and rightly underlines the fact that in v. 17 a shift occurs, "ein gewisser Bruch zwischen V. 17a und V. 17b"[30]. While in v. 17a the sinful condition at the time of the conversion is pointed to, in v. 17b (and the following verses) Christian life is envisaged[31]. For Bachmann, too, sinner and sin in v. 17 have a radical sense, although in Paul's view not sin but the Christ-event is dominant[32]. The author, however, does not see a break between v. 17 and v. 18[33].

---

[25] "Echoes", 462-465. Cf. F.J. MATERA, *Galatians* (SP; Collegeville, MN 1992) 95: "Faith in Christ results in ethnic Jews living as Gentile sinners, because they no longer practice legal works such as the dietary laws".

[26] WECHSLER, *Geschichtsbild*, 380-383. Cf. T. SÖDING, "Die Gegner des Apostels Paulus in Galatien. Beobachtungen zu ihrer Evangeliumsverkündigung und ihrem Konflikt mit Paulus", *MüThZ* 24 (1991) 305-321, esp. 313-314. VERSEPUT, "Gentile Mission", 54-55 and n. 44.

[27] WECHSLER, *Geschichtsbild*, 386. Cf. VERSEPUT, "Gentile Mission", 35 and n. 46, as well as n. 48 (in v. 18 there is no reference to the behavior of Peter).

[28] *Sünder*, e.g., 40 and 56. His conclusion is made on the basis of a lengthy investigation of all μὴ γένοιτο passages in Paul (30-54).

[29] Ibid., 38.

[30] Ibid., 40.

[31] Ibid., 37-40. His claim is that "die inhaltliche Verschiebung von V. 17a zu V. 17b bringe das christliche Leben ins Spiel, das dann jedenfalls in den nachfolgenden Versen im Zentrum steht" (62).

[32] See, e.g., ibid., 81-83.88.90 and 101-102. Regarding the function of Christ for Christian life cf., e.g., pp. 64 and 68.

[33] Ibid., 53-54. "Die ... Protasis V. 18a ... [vermittelt] zwischen V. 17b and V. 18b" (53). Cf. also pp. 32-33.

Verses 18 and 21

One of the most important results of Bachmann's monograph is, I think, the way he explains παραβάτης of v. 18b. There can be no doubt about the negative character of "the building up again" (not of "the tearing down") in the protasis of v. 18a[34]. From his thorough "diachronic" analysis of παραβάτης, παραβαίνω and παράβασις Bachmann draws the conclusion that "transgressing" is not always linked with the law but may in particular cases refer to a "grundsätzliche Verfehlung des Willens Gottes"[35]. In v. 18b we must understand it "als einen fundamentalen Verstoss gegen Gottes Heilswillen und -handeln"[36]. He detects a "ringkompositorische, chiastische, sachliche Korrespondenz" between the conditional periods of v. 18 and v. 21bc[37]. All this can be seen as a corroboration and further clarification of what I myself proposed, especially in my study of 1991 (cf. pp. 165-172 of this paper)[38].

The treatment we find in Wechsler is much more concise[39]. Yet he, too, sees the transgression concretized in ταῦτα πάλιν οἰκοδομῶ (v. 18a). The transgressor who builds up the law again does not transgress that law but is "einer, der dem Rechtfertigungsgeschehen in Christus zuwider handelt"[40]. Like Bachmann, Wechsler also sees a parallelism between v. 18 and v. 21, but he equally refers to v. 14a: "to be not straightforward about the truth of the gospel". Verse 18 must therefore be interpreted in accor-

---

[34] Ibid., 56.

[35] Ibid., 73-77 (quoted phrase on p. 77). Compare LONGENECKER, *Galatians*, 91, who maintains that the term παραβάτης means "violator of the law", "law-breaker": "It has to do with not just breaking a specific statute of the law but with setting aside the law's real intent .... So here in v. 18 Paul insists that to revert to the Mosaic law as a Christian is what really constitutes breaking the law, for then the law's true intent is nullified".

[36] BACHMANN, *Sünder*, 56. Cf., e.g., pp. 53.67.69.83 and 85: "παραβάτης, freilich nicht 'Übertreter' (lediglich) einer Einzelvorschrift des Gesetzes, vielmehr des heilvollen Wollens und Handelns Gottes in Christus, des Christusgeschehens". Otherwise recently VERSEPUT, "Gentile Mission", 55-56: "... παραβάτης is most naturally understood in relationship to the idea of covenant Law or command, in this context to the 'unjustified' status of the Jew outside of Christ .... Any return to the Law-service meant confinement in the role of transgressor".

[37] BACHMANN, *Sünder*, 62-70.

[38] See the reference in n. 2. Cf. the mention of that study by BACHMANN, *Sünder*, p. VII of the "Vorwort".

[39] *Geschichtsbild*, 390-393.

[40] Ibid., 391. He continues: "Der kausale Anschluss von V. 19 wäre dann folgendermassen zu paraphrasieren: 'Weil ich durch das Gesetz dem Gesetz gestorben bin, ist die Wiederaufrichtung des Gesetzes eine aktive Übertretung meines neuen christlichen Standorts'". Wechsler calls it also: a transgression of the "neuen Christus-Existenz" (392).

dance with these two framing verses: 14 ("Verstoss gegen die Wahrheit des Evangeliums") and 21 ("Verstoss gegen die Gnade Gottes")[41].

In his monograph Wechsler[42] refers to an old contribution by Richard Lipsius[43] where the same interpretation of "transgressor" is already put forward. By way of conclusion we may quote from the related passage of this 1861 article. Lipsius states that for Jewish Christians "transgression" "ist die Übertretung ausdrücklicher Vorschriften des Mosaischen Gesetzes"[44]. This sense, however, is unacceptable for Gal 2,18. Yet "transgression" is also "die Übertretung einer feierlich anerkannten Lebensnorm überhaupt; auch innerhalb der Sphäre des christlichen Glaubensprincips gibt es eine παράβασις, und grade dieser hat sich Petrus schuldig gemacht"[45]. When Peter builds up again the things which he tore down, "so handelt er nicht nur inconsequent, sondern gibt zugleich die neue christliche Lebensnorm wieder auf, und eben dies ist zunächst seine παράβασις"[46].

The readers of this paper may judge the degree to which recent publications demonstrate the soundness of our exposition of Gal 2,14b-21 with its numerous sensitive issues.

---

[41] Ibid., 393.
[42] Ibid., 387, n. 501, and p. 390, n. 524.
[43] R.A. LIPSIUS, "Über Gal. 2,17 ff.", ZWTh 4 (1861) 72-82.
[44] Ibid., 79.
[45] Ibid.
[46] Ibid., 79-80.

15

Like a Mother in the Pain of Childbirth Again
A Study of Galatians 4,12-20

Gal 4,12-20 can be regarded as part of the lengthy middle section of Paul's letter (3,1–5,12). The pericope is a fairly well delineated unit. It is distinguished from its immediate context by Paul's emotional tone, by the autobiographical data, and by the comparison which is made between the Galatians' former attitude and their changed behavior versus Paul, as well as by Paul's begging and his plea[1]. At the beginning of the passage the apostle calls for a reciprocal attitude: "become like me, for I also (have become) like you" (v. 12). In the pericope itself he highlights his former personal, excellent relationship with the Galatians, while at the end he expresses the estrangement he feels now: "my children, for whom I am again in the pain of childbirth until Christ is formed in you" (v. 19). Is there a call for imitation of Paul and is there a connection between this call and his position as a mother twice suffering in birth-pains, as founder of the churches of Galatia?

In a first reading we will consider the structure and the line of thought

---

[1] On the various approaches of the rhetorical analysis of Paul's letter to the Galatians, see A. PITTA, *Disposizione e messaggio della lettera ai Galati. Analisi retorico-letteraria* (AnBib 131; Rome 1992). In regard to "the rhetorical character of the passage" Gal 4,12-20 we refer to the numerous remarks of H.D. BETZ, *Galatians* (Hermeneia; Philadelphia 1979) within pp. 220-237. Betz points out: "What Paul offers in the section is a string of topoi belonging to the theme of 'friendship' (περὶ φιλίας)" (221), and: "A personal appeal to friendship is entirely in conformity with Hellenistic style, which calls for change between heavy and light sections and which would require an emotional and personal approach to offset the impression of mere abstractions" (ibid.). We may also quote B. CORSANI, *Lettera ai Galati* (Genova, 1990): "... sappiamo da Quintilliano che nella parte dimostrativa di orazioni e di lettere era commune, ad un certo punto, inserire del materiale relativo al *topos* περὶ φιλίας. L'appello all' amicizia o al commune sentire ... serviva ad allentare la tensione e permetteva di riprendere l'argomentazione più profonda con nuove bordate logiche o polemiche". R.N. LONGENECKER, *Galatians* (WBC; Dallas 1990) 184-187, remarks on a shift from forensic to deliberative rhetoric; but it is questionable whether such a distinction is here to the point.

of the pericope. The second part of this paper will be devoted to a brief exegetical analysis. In the third and last section particular attention will be paid to the significance of Paul's apostolic authority and his example.

I. STRUCTURE AND LINE OF THOUGHT

There decidedly is a caesura after 4,20. A new paragraph begins with λέγετέ μοι in verse 21. However, this is probably also the case at 4,12: Paul begins with an imperative and stresses both the 1st pers. sing. and the 2nd pers. plur., i.e., himself and his addressees: γίνεσθε ὡς ἐγώ, ὅτι κἀγὼ ὡς ὑμεῖς. He employs the vocative ἀδελφοί (cf. the vocative τέκνα μου in v. 19). The call "become as I (am)" introduces a topic different from that in the preceding verses 8-11[2]. So we should have no doubt about the introductory value of verse 12: it provides a fresh start; it constitutes the beginning of a new pericope. Nevertheless one may be tempted to regard verse 11 as likewise belonging to our pericope: here, too, the 1st pers. sing. and 2nd pers. plur. are employed; the verb κεκοπίακα points to the past which will be treated in verses 13-15; moreover, in content φοβοῦμαι somewhat corresponds to ἀποροῦμαι of verse 20. All this is true, but verse 11 nonetheless looks back to verses 8-10 and provides Paul's conclusion of that small unit. It is, therefore, better to consider Gal 4,12-20 as a pericope on its own which deals with Paul's personal relationship with the Galatians.

Within the passage, three unequal parts can be distinguished: verses 12, 13-16 and 17-20[3].

Verse 12 begins with an imperative, an appeal: "Become as I (am)". The verse contains four brief clauses. The last one, verse 12d (οὐδέν με ἠδικήσατε), functions as a kind of motivation, as if Paul were saying: I am in a position to beseech you (v. 12c), *since* you did me no wrong. With the aorist indicative ἠδικήσατε Paul refers back to a former period of time. Therefore, the clause also prepares for what follows (vv. 13-16).

In verses 13-16 the past is contrasted with the present. In this subdivision we find two long sentences which recall the (first?) arrival of Paul in

---

[2] Some exegetes consider Gal 4,8-20 as a unit. Cf., e.g., W. GROSSOUW, *De brief van Paulus aan de Galaten* (Bussum 1974) 166, and the *Traduction oecuménique de la Bible*.

[3] For another division see, e.g., F.J. MATERA, *Galatians* (SP; Collegeville 1992) 163.

Galatia. The first one, verses 13-14, is introduced by the formula οἴδατε δὲ ὅτι, the second, verse 15b, by the equally set phrase μαρτυρῶ γὰρ ὅτι. After each sentence there is a brief rhetorical question. With these two questions Paul refers to the present: "What has become (ποῦ οὖν) of the good will, the happiness you felt?" (v. 15a), and: "So now, have I become (ὥστε γέγονα) your enemy by telling you the truth?" (v. 16; but is this, grammatically speaking, a question?). The broad description of the past as well as the incisive questions regarding the present provide this part with a somewhat melancholy and reproachful character.

Verses 17-20 are best taken together as one subunit. There is in verses 17-18 the play on the verb ζηλόω which occurs three times; verses 18-19 most probably constitute one long sentence[4]. Verse 20 is connected with verse 18 by the identical phrase παρεῖναι (...) πρὸς ὑμᾶς In these four verses Paul reveals the intentions of the opponents; he contrasts his own concern and love with their "zeal"[5]. Implicitly verse 20 contains an exhortation: if he could have been present he certainly would have admonished them so that Christ be formed in them (cf. v. 19); he would also have repeated the order of verse 12, namely, to become as he is. Contentwise, therefore, verse 12 and verse 20 together form the inclusion, the frame of the whole pericope. The confession at the end of verse 20 betrays a helpless confusion: "for I am perplexed about you". The clause motivates the expressed desire ("I could wish ...") and somehow recalls the anxiety present in verse 11: "I am afraid that my work for you may have been wasted".

As already stated, the autobiographical, emotional 1st pers. sing. is

---

[4] Cf. E. DEWITT BURTON, *The Epistle to the Galatians* (Edinburgh 1921): Verse 19 is "probably to be attached to the preceding verse".

[5] On the identification of Paul's opponents in Galatia, see, e.g., T. SÖDING, "Die Gegner des Paulus in Galatien. Beobachtungen zu ihrer Evangeliumsverkündigung und ihrem Konflikt mit Paulus", in *MüThZ* 52 (1991) 305-321. We may quote what is recently written by F. THIELMAN *Paul and the Law: A Contextual Approach* (Downes Groves, IL 1994) 123: "The [Galatian] agitators ... appear to have been Jewish Christians who traveled to Paul's churches in order to convince them that faith in Jesus Christ was only a first step. The faith of the Galatians needed to be completed (Gal 3,3) by acceptance of the Mosaic law and full conversion to Judaism, including circumcision. The agitators were not content, however, to let matters rest in the realm of theological ideas. Instead, they accompanied the positive proclamation of their own gospel with an attempt to discredit Paul himself (4,12-28; compare 1,10; 5,11) and a policy of excluding from fellowship any Galatian believers who did not conform to their requirements (4,17; compare 2,11-14). The tactic of social exclusion would have been especially painful for members of the congregation who were already considered outcasts by friends and family because of their abandonment of the traditional religions (4,8).

very prominent in this pericope. The 2nd pers. plur. with which Paul addresses his Galatian Christians is equally very much present. There is only one verse with the 3rd pers. plur., verse 17. It depicts the action of the agitators; in this verse Paul reveals and sharply criticizes their tactics.

II. EXEGETICAL NOTES

In presenting a few notes of detailed exegesis we follow the order of the three subunits.

Verse 12

The Revised English Bible translates verse 12 freely: "Put yourselves in my place, my friends, I beg you, as I put myself in yours". This reminds us of the invitation to reciprocity in 2 Cor 6,11-13. One also thinks of 1 Thess 3,6: you long to see us, as we long to see you. Is Gal 4,12 just a moving appeal to a more cordial attitude?

It has been maintained that verse 12 has nothing to do with imitation. Even the terminology is missing, it is said. However, a fairly common clarification of the elliptical first two clauses (v. 12ab) adds the following verbs: γίνεσθε ὡς ἐγώ εἰμι, ὅτι κἀγὼ ἐγενόμην ὡς ὑμεῖς ἦτε[6]. A. Oepke, e.g., prefers not to supplement the verb εἰμι twice and proposes as the meaning of verse 12ab: behave (or: be) as I, since I behave (or am: γίνομαι) as you. It is a call for mutual understanding. Moreover, in his opinion the idea of imitation can hardly be present in verse 12b. Paul did not imitate the Galatians in the same way as he is supposed to require the Galatians' imitation of himself[7].

---

[6] Cf., e.g., W.P. DE BOER, *The Imitation of Paul: An Exegetical Study* (Kampen 1962) 191, and, for the whole discussion of Gal 4,12, pp. 188-196. The comparison in Gal 4,12b necessarily remains somewhat vague. M. ZERWICK–M. GROSVENOR, *A Grammatical Analysis of the Greek New Testament* (Rome 1981) 572, add at the end of verse 12b: "(as you) were when I first came, not seeking salvation through observance of the Law". For a brief discussion of various proposals, see R.N. LONGENECKER, *Galatians*, who furthermore comments on p. 189: "The imperative γίνεσθε ὡς κἀγώ ... assumes, of course, that the Galatian Christians were not like Paul, for they were beginnning to observe the Jewish calendar and dietary laws as necessary for a proper Christian lifestyle and they were contemplating circumcision as requisite for a true biblical faith...".

[7] A. OEPKE, *Der Brief des Paulus an die Galater* (THNT; Berlin ²1960) 104-105: "eine

Yet it would seem that in verse 12ab Paul is pointing to more than behavior and reciprocal feelings. The "becoming" which Paul demands must be understood in the light of the preceding context of the letter[8]. In v. 12b Paul is most probably referring to the fact that he, as a Jew, realized that he was not better than the Gentile sinners and needed justification by faith in Christ Jesus, not by works of the law (see 2,16). Therefore, the Galatians should take an example from him; they should turn away from the works of the law which they are already observing or want to observe[9]. There is a difference of time between verse 12a and verse 12b. The first clause is "a present call for action; the other is a statement of a past fact"[10]. Moreover, the present tense verb in verse 12a does not point to a new attitude. It can almost be understood as "remain in the state in which you now are". Based on the γίνομαι terminology there is, however, a well-balanced parallelism: "Become [= remain] as I [= free from bondage to the law], since I (became) as you [= free from bondage to the law]". In verse 12b Paul appears to mean more than the accommodation which he mentions in 1 Cor 9,21[11].

However, in verse 12ab the μιμέομαι vocabulary is missing, indeed. Yet the imitation idea is not altogether absent. The Galatian Christians have to imitate Paul, but Paul, of course, never completely imitated the Gentile way

---

allgemeine Bitte um Verständigung" (104). BETZ, *Galatians*, who translates: "Remain as I am because also I have become as you are" (220), comments: "The underlying idea is the topos from popular philosophy that 'true friendship' is possible only among equals" (p. 222). Cf., e.g., also J. SMIT, *Opbouw en gedachtengang van de brief aan de Galaten* (Nijmegen 1986) 96, n. 14.

[8] Cf. DE BOER, *Imitation*, 191: "... the most natural way is to fill the elliptical phrases with content which is already in mind from what Paul has been saying".

[9] In Gal 4,12a Paul requires from his Christian Galatians a "conversion" different from that which is implored of God in Acts 26,29: Paul replies to Agrippa: "... I pray to God that not only you but also all who are listening to me today might become such as I am (ὁποῖος καὶ ἐγώ εἰμι). Cf. DE BOER, *Imitation*, 195; B.R. GAVENTA, "Galatians 1 and 2: Autobiography as Paradigm", *NT* 28 (1986) 309-326, esp. 319-322 and 326: "Thus, 'become as I' means that the Galatians are to imitate Paul by rejecting all that threatens to remove them from an exclusive relationship to the gospel. 'For also I as you' means that one reason for their imitation of Paul is that Paul has already rejected his zeal for the Law and the tradition (321)"; "What the Galatians can imitate is Paul's single-minded response to the gospel that was revealed to him" (322); "To become as Paul means to allow Christ to live in oneself (cf. 2,20) to the exclusion of the Law or of any other tradition or category (cf. 3,27-28)" (ibid.).

[10] DE BOER, *Imitation*, 193. Cf. CORSANI, *Galati*, 280: "La prima frase è un' esortazione apostolica, la seconda è la citazione di un' esperanza personale di Paolo avvenuta in passato...".

[11] Cf. DE BOER, *Imitation*, 191-192. De Boer appropriately notes on verse 12a: "Paul is not asking for any kind of accommodation in regard to the law on the part of the Galatians".

of life[12]. The topic of imitation occurs more than once in Paul, and, moreover, in different (undisputed) Pauline letters. We quote five important parallel passages:

1 Thess 1,6-7: Καὶ ὑμεῖς μιμηταὶ ἡμῶν ἐγενήθητε καὶ τοῦ κυρίου, δεξάμενοι τὸν λόγον ἐν θλίψει πολλῇ μετὰ χαρᾶς πνεύματος ἁγίου, ὥστε γενέσθαι ὑμᾶς τύπον πᾶσιν τοῖς πιστεύουσιν ἐν τῇ Μακεδονίᾳ καὶ ἐν τῇ Ἀχαΐᾳ.

1 Thess 2,14: ῾Υμεῖς γὰρ μιμηταὶ ἐγενήθητε, ἀδελφοί, τῶν ἐκκλησιῶν τοῦ θεοῦ τῶν οὐσῶν ἐν τῇ Ἰουδαίᾳ ἐν Χριστῷ Ἰησοῦ, ὅτι τὰ αὐτὰ ἐπάθετε καὶ ὑμεῖς ὑπὸ τῶν ἰδίων συμφυλετῶν καθὼς καὶ αὐτοὶ ὑπὸ τῶν Ἰουδαίων,

1 Cor 4,16: Παρακαλῶ οὖν ὑμᾶς, μιμηταί μου γίνεσθε.

1 Cor 11,1: Μιμηταί μου γίνεσθε καθὼς κἀγὼ Χριστοῦ.

Phil 3,17: Συμμιμηταί μου γίνεσθε, ἀδελφοί, καὶ σκοπεῖτε τοὺς οὕτω περιπατοῦντας, καθὼς ἔχετε τύπον ἡμᾶς (cf. 4,9).

From these five passages and Gal 4,12 it appears that Christians must imitate Paul (as well as other good Christians, Phil 3,17); they must also follow the Lord (1 Thess 1,6). The Thessalonians became imitators of Paul and the churches in Judea, and so they in turn became examples. Paul himself imitates Christ. Imitating Paul involves more than simply a one-time following him in his sufferings; rather, it would seem that his whole lifestyle is included. Besides μιμητής (συμμιμητής), present in the five passages cited, we should also take note of the term τύπος ("example") in 1 Thess 1,7 and Phil 3,17. Moreover, in both Gal 4 and Phil 3 the "mimesis" idea appears in close proximity to the μορφή terminology: see Gal 4,19 and Phil 3,10. It also strikes us that Paul asks for imitation of himself only from churches which he has founded[13].

Verse 12c, δέομαι ὑμῶν, reinforces the preceding imperative. As already said, verse 12d seems to function as some sort of motivation. It is not clear whether by "you did me no wrong" Paul is referring to a particular incident or to events which he does not want to overemphasize[14]. Or is he just (ironically?) saying the opposite of what he is going to stress in verses 13-16, specifically in verse 15a and verse 16?

---

[12] See the discussion in CORSANI, *Galati*, 279-281.

[13] Cf., e.g., DE BOER, *Imitation*, 206.

[14] LONGENECKER, *Galatians*, 190, paraphrases: "I grant, whatever your views and proposed actions, that I have not been personally wronged by what has gone on among Christians in Galatia".

Verses 13-16

By means of the phrase "you know" of verse 13 Paul reminds the Galatians of their first encounter with him. Does τὸ πρότερον distinguish between a first and a second time? In N.T. Greek it can also mean "at first" without reference to a second previous visit[15]. The verb εὐαγγελίζομαι points to Paul's proclamation of the gospel. Almost spontaneously, 1 Cor 1,17 comes to mind: God did not send me to baptize, but to proclaim the gospel. Obviously Paul had not planned this evangelization in Galatia. It was his illness which occasioned it: δι᾽ ἀσθένειαν τῆς σαρκός[16]. What kind of illness? We do not know, although because of verse 15b (to tear out the eyes) and 6,11 ("see what large letters I make when I am writing in my own hand"), an eye ailment is not improbable[17]. Anyone is acquainted with the other Pauline letters will also reflect upon the mysterious "thorn in the flesh" of 2 Cor 12,7.

In the expression τὸν πειρασμὸν ὑμῶν of verse 14 the genitive is probably objective: trial for the Galatians caused by Paul's physical condition, his human frailty (ἐν τῇ σαρκί μου). The verb ἐκπτύω (to spit out) is most likely employed here in a figurative sense of "to despise, to reject"[18]. It is not sure whether the translation of ὡς ἄγγελος θεοῦ is here "as a messenger of God" of (more probably) "as an angel of God". The second ὡς phrase is no doubt meant as a climax: even as Christ Jesus himself. The one sent is as the one sending. Whether in view of Paul's bodily illness we must think here of Christ crucified is not clear.

Verse 15 begins with a rhetorical question. It is necessary to mentally supply a "now". "Therefore where is 'now' your happiness?" Paul does not

---

[15] Cf. 2 Cor 1,15.

[16] For E. GÜTTGEMANNS, *Der leidende Apostel und sein Herr. Studien zur paulinischen Christologie* (FRLANT 90; Göttingen 1966) 170-194, διά + accusative is here the equivalent of διά + genitive. Paul proclaimed the gospel *through* his ailment, his suffering. Yet this "suffering" of Paul is no longer accepted by the gnosticizing Galatians (see esp. pp. 173-177). Güttgemanns' whole treatment of Gal 4,12-20 is vitiated by audacious and far-fetched hypotheses.

[17] See, e.g., H. SCHLIER, *Der Brief an die Galater* (KEK; Göttingen [13]1965) 211; F. MUSSNER, *Der Brief an die Galater* (HTKNT), Freiburg–Basel–Wien, 309; J.D.G. DUNN, *The Epistle to the Galatians* (BNTC; Peabody, MA 1993) 236. Or was it epilepsy or headache? Cf. J. BLIGH, "Comment on Gal. 4,15", F.L. CROSS (ed.), *Studia evangelica, IV* (TU 102; Berlin 1968) 382-383.

[18] A literal understanding of the verb would make us think of a gesture of disdain or part of an apotropaic rite. Cf., e.g., GROSSOUW, *Galaten*, 171; CORSANI, *Galati*, 283-284; DUNN, *Galatians*, 234.

see it any longer; it has disappeared and he does not understand why and how (see the γάρ in v. 15b). The expressions ὁ πειρασμὸς ὑμῶν (v. 14) and ὁ μακαρισμὸς ὑμῶν (v. 15a) appear to be parallel. Is this by accident? Yet while the first ὑμῶν is probably an objective genitive[19], the second seems to be subjective[20]. The Galatians were happy with Paul's presence. Where is their happiness now? In verse 13 Paul wrote "*you* know"; in verse 15b he now writes: "*I* can bear you witness". Whether the language of the irrealis period of verse 15b is purely metaphorical is not so certain. A verb must be supplied in the protasis: εἰ (ἦν) δυνατόν (if it had been possible), and classical Greek would normally require an ἄν after the verb in the apodosis (I would have given).

Is a second rhetorical question present in verse 16? Most probably. The verse is introduced by ὥστε but, because of the content, it can hardly be grammatically dependent on verse 15. We must paraphrase: Is the result of all this that I have become (and 'now' am) an enemy to you[21]? Here, too, a 'now' must be supplied mentally. The participle ἀληθεύων (by speaking the truth) refers to Paul's proclamation of the "truth of the gospel" (2,5 and 14) 'then'; this proclamation has been and is still being attacked by the agitators. The mention of "I = your enemy" causes Paul to speak in verse 17 of the real enemies of the Galatian Christians, his opponents.

Verses 17-20

Not everything is clear in verses 17-20. We see that Paul plays on the verb ζηλόω, employed twice in verse 17 (in the active voice) and once more in verse 18 (in the passive voice). Three times, too, we encounter an

---

[19] LONGENECKER, *Galatians*, 191, translates: "Though my illness was a temptation for you [to reject me])". There exists a variant reading with μου (so, e.g., P[46]). But the better attested and more difficult reading ὑμῶν is no doubt original.

[20] Cf., e.g., BURTON, *Galatians*, 243; and the discussion in CORSANI, *Galati*, 285. LONGENECKER, *Galatians*, 192, prefers a possessive genitive: "Where, then, is your [former state of] blessedness?" On the difficulties of rendering the expression, see also DUNN, *Galatians*, 230, n. 4.

[21] A number of exegetes claim that the clause is not a question but an indignant exclamation. See, e.g., BURTON, *Galatians*, 245; LONGENECKER, *Galatians*, 193; R.Y.K. FUNG, *The Epistle to the Galatians* (NICNT; Grand Rapids 1988) 199 (a statement). One should also pay attention to γέγονα (perfect tense: "I have become and am now") and to the more or less antithetical parallellism: ἐχθρὸς ὑμῶν ... ἀληθεύων ὑμῖν. Fung assumes for ἐχθρός an active sense: The Galatians "now regarded Paul as someone with hostile intentions towards them" (ibid.).

expression with καλ-: οὐ καλῶς (v. 17), καλὸν δέ (ἐστιν) and ἐν καλῷ in verse 18.

Paul suddenly employs the third person plural. The expression ζηλόω καλῶς τινά in verse 17 means "to show interest for someone (or: to run after a person, to make much of a person), and this in the right way (or: for a good purpose)". The subject of the verb in verse 17a is expressed only in the verb; however, it clearly refers to the agitators; they run after the Galatians for no good purpose: οὐ καλῶς. Concretely speaking, they have a double intention. First they want to isolate the Galatian Christians from their fellow Christians (or from Paul?)[22]. The second, underlying purpose, however, is that the Galatian Christians ("you") "should run after" the agitators.

Verse 18a begins with the impersonal construction "it is good (it is a fine thing)" which is followed by an infinitive clause. Yet the subject of the infinitive passive, ζηλοῦσθαι, is not expressed. The sentence sounds like a general principle. Most probably, however, the Galatians are the unnamed subject of ζηλοῦσθαι. J. Rohde gives a paraphrase with the verb in the active: "Es sei gut für die Galater, dass sich immer jemand um sie bemüht mit Eifer ..., doch müssten diese Bemühungen im Bereich des Guten ... liegen"[23]. In this paraphrase the agent is "jemand", somebody.

One could wonder, however, whether Paul himself is not this unnamed agent[24]. Two reasons seem to plead for this view. In verse 18b Paul is the subject of the verb παρεῖναι, and verse 19 can easily be understood as a concretization of this particular attention, this constant care. According to this proposal Paul claims that he always cares for the Galatians, not only when he is present with them[25]. One could refer to 2 Cor 11,2: ζηλοῶ γὰρ

---

[22] The explanation of verse 17 by DUNN, *Galatians*, 237-239, is difficult to follow and its logic appears somewhat forced. The missionaries want "to exclude all Gentiles other than proselytes from Christ, the Jewish Messiah, and from the eschatological community" (238). They point out that without the works of the law the Gentiles Christians are still outside the boundaries as laid down by the Torah. Yet, by showing this kind of zeal with regard to the Galatians, the missionaries hope that they will "come to show a similar zeal with regard to them" (ibid.); through doing the works of the law they enter the community. The exclusion aims at inclusion!

We may also mention here the rather idiosyncratic proposal by F.R.M. HITCHCOCK, "The Meaning of ἐκλείειν in Galatians IV 17", *JTS* 40 (1939) 149-151. The verb means "to hatch out" and points to "the process by which the chick leaves the egg" (p. 150). He renders verse 17 freely as follows: "They are cultivating you but not for an honourable purpose, for it is their intention to bring you out to exploit you, so that you may cultivate them" (ibid.).

[23] J. ROHDE, *Der Brief des Paulus an die Galater* (THNT; Berlin 1989) 189.

[24] F. SIEFFERT, *Der Brief an die Galater* (KEK; Göttingen [8]1894, 274. See FUNG, *Galatians*, 210-202, for the rejection of Paul as grammatical subject of ζηλοῦσθαι (so J.B. Lightfoot).

[25] Cf. M.-J. LAGRANGE, *Epître aux Galates* (EtB; Paris, [2]1925) 116.

ὑμᾶς θεοῦ ζήλῳ. Yet Gal 4,18a is perhaps too general a saying (lit.: "good is always to be courted in a good way") for the interpretation with Paul as the unnamed agent.

Therefore, it might seem better to leave verse 18a vague or, perhaps even more appropriate, to suppose a reference to the opponents. Paul is still thinking of the agitators' action. In verse 18b Paul qualifies the last word of verse 18a, "always" by means of "not only when I am present with you". It is here, in verse 18b and not earlier, that Paul speaks of himself. So, from what he writes in verse 18, we are forced, by implication, to assume that Paul appears to be convinced that his opponents will not be able to exercise their negative influence during his presence but can only do so when he is absent. With this second interpretation of verse 18 we can easily understand what Paul desires in verse 20: he very much wants to be present with them. Moreover, we clearly see why in verse 19 he expresses his existential care and concern. Yet the choice between the two interpretations remains difficult.

N[26] and a number of translations put a full stop after verse 18 and regard verse 19 as a new sentence[26]. In this view we have in verse 19 an exclamation "my children"[27] and a relative clause, but no main verb nor main clause. It is preferable, I think, to link the vocative τέκνα μου to the immediately preceding ὑμᾶς and regard verses 18-19 as one long sentence. The emotional and intimate "my children" is somewhat surprising after the more usual ἀδελφοί of verse 12, and the imagery which comes after that expression is no less startling. Paul presents himself as a mother who is, a second time, suffering "birth-pains" for the Galatians (οὓς πάλιν ὠδίνω)[28]. Paul strangely adds: that process of travail will continue "until Christ is formed" in his Christians.

Do we have to see Christ as a developing, growing embryo in the womb of those Christians? "The maternal imagery employed here ... is complex. Instead of saying that he gave birth to the community, Paul tells the Galatians that he is again suffering the pangs of birth ... until Christ is formed in or among them .... Thus Christ, like an embryo, takes shape among the Galatians, but Paul suffers the pains of childbirth..."[29]. It is

---

[26] Or, better, an anacolouthon. See, e.g., the RSV: "... and not only when I am present with you. My little children, with whom I am again in travail until Christ be formed in you!"

[27] For the reasons why LONGENECKER prefers the poorly attested variant τεκνία, see his *Galatians*, 195.

[28] See BURTON, *Galatians*, 248: "The figure of speech involved in ὠδίνω, though startling to modern ears, is unambiguously clear".

[29] MATERA, *Galatians*, 166. On μορφόω, as used for the growing of a foetus, see BURTON, *Galatians*, 248-249; HITCHCOCK, *Meaning*, 150.

perhaps better not to press the image[30]. Moreover, the expression ἐν ὑμῖν, which recurs at the end of verse 20, may already in verse 19 have a collective sense ("among you"; not: "in each of you"), just as it does in verse 20 ("about you")[31]. But in view of Gal 2,20 this last point remains uncertain. Some take both senses together[32].

The imperfect ἤθελον at the beginning of verse 20 replaces a potential optative (= "I could wish") and indicates that it is now (ἄρτι) not possible for Paul to go to Galatia and be present with the Christians there[33]. However, he very much desires to be there so that he could "change" his voice, i.e., the tone of his speaking. One almost spontaneously thinks of a speaking in a pleading, loving and affectionate way[34], though perhaps Paul

---

[30] Cf. LAGRANGE, *Galates*, 117: "... la comparaison ne peut être serrée de près, car, dans la nature, les douleurs, précédant la naissance, suivent la formation complète de l'enfant dans le sein de sa mère". If Paul thinks of a developing embryo, his imagery is rather confusing. The mother (= Paul) is again in travail, and within his womb are the Galatians who themselves are with child (= Christ). See R. HERMANN, "Über den Sinn des Μορφοῦσθαι Χριστὸν ἐν ὑμῖν in Gal. 4,19", in *ThLZ* 80 (1955) 713-726: "Paulus hat Geburtswehen, und die Galater scheinen gebären zu sollen; denn in ihnen gewinnt Christus Gestalt, vergleichbar dem menschlichen Embryo" (col. 713). But also see CORSANI, *Galati*, 289: "... Paolo non si cura della coerenza: dopo aver menzionato se stesso come chi soffre le doglie del parto, ecco che nel verso 19b a portare a termine la gravidanza spirituale sono i Galati, nei quali si forma o finisce di formarsi il Cristo".

[31] So R. HERMANN, "Über den Sinn", col. 717; LONGENECKER, *Galatians*, 195. Cf. MATERA, *Galatians*, 166-167: "While the modern reader thinks of Christ being formed in the individual, it is more likely that Paul has the entire community, as a corporate body, in mind" (166). The 2d pers. plur. in the preceding verses could seem to recommend the collective understanding of the expression. For the whole of verse 19, see B.R. GAVENTA, "The Maternity of Paul: An Exegetical Study of Galatians 4,19", R.T. FORTNA & B.R. GAVENTA (eds.), *The Conversation Continues: Studies in Paul and John. FS J.L. Martyn* (Nashville 1990) 189-201.

[32] Cf. BETZ, *Galatians*, 234; ROHDE, *Galater*, 190: "Die beiden ... Deutungen sollten nicht als sich einander ausschliessend angesehen werden: Christus muss sowohl in dem Denken der einzelnen galatischen Christen Gestalt annehmen als auch in den galatischen Gemeinden insgesamt...;" DUNN, *Galatians*, 241: "The corporate sense of 'Christ in you or among you (as the body of Christ)' is not excluded".

[33] Cf. 1 Thess 2,17-18.

[34] The voice of a caring mother! See a brief overview of the expression's interpretation in ancient and modern times in G. WILHELMI, "καὶ ἀλλάξαι τὴν φωνήν μου", *ZNW* 65 (1974) 151-154. His own proposal is grammatically strained and, moreover, far-fetched: "Könnte ich doch jetzt ... von Ephesus aus bei auch sein und könnte ich jetzt von Ephesus aus meine Stimme verändern — so, dass ihr sie hören könnt" (153). "Verändern" means here change into a louder voice. Cf. the criticism by CORSANI, *Galati*, 291. We also wonder whether the sense "exchange" is correct here. It is mentioned by BETZ, *Galatians*, 236, and adopted by LONGENECKER, *Galatians*, 196: "exchange my voice [for the letter]"; also by DUNN, *Galatians*, 241.

intends to say that, when present, he would be able to judge the concrete circumstances and through change "adapt" his language to the needs of the actual situation[35]. Paul gives the reason why he desires to be present with them: he is perplexed, he is at a loss, he is at his wit's end about his Galatian Christians. The clause ἀποροῦμαι ἐν ὑμῖν corresponds rather strikingly to φοβοῦμαι ὑμᾶς μή ... of verse 11. We might recall: the same expression παρεῖναι πρὸς ὑμᾶς is present in verse 18; likewise ἐν ὑμῖν occurs at the end of the verse, just as at the end of verse 19.

III. THE IMITATION OF PAUL

Among the rather numerous passages in which Paul, by way of commandment or statement, refers to imitation of himself, one text presents itself for a more thorough comparison with Gal 4,12-20. Just as in our pericope so also in 1 Cor 4,14-16 the two themes of imitating Paul and Paul's parenthood[36] are present. A more detailed analysis of both passages will no doubt be profitable since there are a number of similarities between them but also not a few differences[37]. All this may help us to better understand Paul both as apostle and example[38].

Similarities between Gal 4,12-20 and 1 Cor 4,14-16

We may begin with the vocabulary. A list of identical (or similar) words and expressions can be discerned:

---

[35] Cf. ROHDE, *Galater*, 190-191: "Bei einer persönlichen Anwesenheit würde er eher merken, welcher Ton anzuschlagen wäre, um die Galater wieder auf seine Seite zu ziehen" (191).

[36] For Paul as father see also 1 Thess 2,11-12 and Philemon 10. Cf. 2 Cor 6,13 (children); 12,14 (children and parents); Phil 2,22 (Timothy his child).

[37] Cf. J. LAMBRECHT, "Paul as Example: A Study of 1 Corinthians 4,6-21", R. KAMPLING & T. SÖDING (eds.), *Ekklesiologie des Neuen Testaments. FS K. Kertelge* (Freiburg–Basel–Wien 1996) 316-335; also in this volume, pp. 43-62.

[38] For the topic "imitation" in Paul (and the cultural background) see W. MICHAELIS, μιμέομαι, in *TDNT IV*, 659-674; D.M. STANLEY, "'Become imitators of me': The Pauline Conception of Apostolic Tradition'", *Bib* 40 (1959) 859-877; A. SCHULZ, *Nachfolgen und Nachahmen. Studien über das Verhältnis der neutestamentlichen Jüngerschaft zur urchristlichen Vorbildethik* (StANT 6; München 1962); DE BOER, *Imitation*.

	1 Cor 4		*Gal 4*
14	τέκνα μου ἀγαπητά	19	τέκνα μου
	(cf. also 16: ἀδελφοί)		(cf. also 12: ἀδελφοί)
	οὐκ ἐντρέπων	cf.	content of 12d and 20d
15	parent	19	parent
	ἐν Χριστῷ, ἐν Χριστῷ ᾿Ιησοῦ	14	ὡς Χριστὸν ᾿Ιησοῦν
		19	Χριστός
	διὰ τοῦ εὐαγγελίου	13	εὐηγγελισάμην
16	παρακαλῶ οὖν ὑμᾶς	12	δέομαι ὑμᾶς
	μιμηταί μου γίνεσθε	12	γίνεσθε ὡς ἐγώ

Such a list is already by itself impressive. Moreover, a significant factor is the presence in both passages of the call to imitate Paul as well as of the emphasis of being the father or mother of the Christians in Corinth or in Galatia. We should notice that in the two texts Paul 'softens' as it were the idea of parenthood through additions: compare the begetting occurring "in Christ Jesus through the gospel" in 1 Cor 4,15 with the giving birth in pain "until Christ is formed in you" in Gal 4,19. A third element is rather implicit but no less real. From both passages and their respective contexts one has the impression that the relationship between Paul and the believers has become strained; there is a tension between them; Paul tries to win them over, to restore the relationship.

Differences between Gal 4,12-20 and 1 Cor 4,14-16

The major difference is the image itself: father in 1 Cor 4 and mother in Gal 4 with the appropriate verbs (γεννάω and ὠδίνω). In 1 Cor 4 the parenthood is only mentioned before the call for imitation; in Gal 4 Paul speaks about it at the end of the passage, at a certain distance from that call. In 1 Cor 4 Paul points to this past begetting (no repetition is spoken of); in Gal 4 Paul states that he has to suffer the birth-pains a second time (πά-λιν). In 1 Cor Paul opposes himself as the only "father" to the countless παιδαγωγοί; in 1 Gal 4 he contrasts his motherly care and the birth pangs of the second birth with the insincere "zeal" of the opponents, the agitators.

The call for imitation also differs. In 1 Cor 4 we have the noun μιμη-ταί; in Gal 4 the noun is lacking but there is the particle of comparison ὡς. In 1 Cor 4 the imperative remains isolated (only one clause), but the attentive readers of the letter will point ahead to 11,1 where after the command Paul refers to his imitation of Christ: (μιμηταί μου γίνεσθε) καθὼς κἀγὼ

Χριστοῦ; in Gal 4 the second clause also contains a comparison but within a motivation: ὅτι κἀγὼ ὡς ὑμεῖς, and this motivation consists of Paul's reciprocal having become as the Galatians[39].

There also are differing nuances regarding what exactly must be imitated. In the context of 1 Cor 4 Paul certainly has the apostolic sufferings in mind (cf. vv. 9-13), but imitation of Paul most probably involves his whole exemplary lifestyle (cf. v. 17: "my ways in Christ, as I teach them everywhere in every church")[40]; in Gal 4 and its broader context Paul deals with justification without the works of the law and the temptation of the Galatians to accept the Jewish way of life: the Galatians have to imitate Paul as a person who through his conversion became as they themselves as non-Jewish Christians were and are, i.e., without obedience to the law.

In 1 Cor 4 Paul mentions the sending of his beloved child Timothy who will remind them of the manner in which they must imitate the apostle (v. 17), and Paul announces his impending coming to Corinth (vv. 18-21); in Gal 4 there is neither Timothy nor any other co-worker, and Paul can only speak of his intense but unrealizable desire to be present with the Galatians, not of a planned journey to their region.

The most intriguing aspect of all is the seemingly different function of Paul's parenthood. In 1 Cor 4 Paul emphasizes the "begetting", him being the only father, in order to legitimate his call for imitation. In Gal 4 this legitimization idea is not explicitly worked out; there is but the separate presence of both motifs. The question to be asked, however, is whether this presence itself within the same pericope is not enough to constitute an implicit link between the two motifs, i.e., whether Paul's being the mother of the Galatians and being in travail a second time (v. 19) does not provide the basic ground for his preceding imitation call (v. 12).

The Appeal of a Mother

Betz writes: "Gal 4,19 should be dealt with as a conglomerate of concepts all belonging to the complex of rebirth"[41.] Verse 19 strikes the readers in at least six aspects: (1) the sudden intimate address in the vocative τέκνα μου; (2) Paul seeing himself as a mother in travail; (3) the fact that

---

[39] The idea of Paul's imitation of Christ is not completely absent in Gal 4,12-20 since it is said in verse 14 that the Galatians received Paul "as Christ Jesus".

[40] Cf. LAMBRECHT, "Paul as an Example", 45-46.

[41] *Galatians*, 235.

second birth pangs are pointed to: "again" (but not for another child); (4) the rather unexpected mention of Christ; (5) the shift within the same imagery which now metaphorically speaks of the formation of Christ in the womb of either the individual Galatians or their Christian communities; and (6), finally, the strange result of this depiction in regard to the birth-pains that precede the delivery: the labor continues "until" the completion of the formation[42].

The pericope Gal 4,12-20 no doubt is an emotional text. Therefore grammatical links and strictly logical development may be lacking. Paul compares the past and present of his relationship with the Galatians. He accuses his opponents of insincere intentions. He presents himself as their mother[43] who is again in travail until Christ is really formed in them[44]. He feels deeply sorry that he cannot be present with them. By means of this passage he invites and commands them to become as he is, free from the law, not bound again in slavery. Listening carefully to this passage we realize that Paul employs the image of his being a mother, again in the pains of childbirth, as a ground, i.e., as an authoritative basis for his command. Being the mother of the Galatians is being the founder of their churches[45]. It is, of course, with the founder's authority and the mother's love that he admonishes and pleads.

Gal 4,12-20 functions within Paul's rhetorical strategy. After the long argumentation within 2,15–4,11 it is an additional but important argument to convince the Galatians of the dangerous way which the agitators put before them.

The comparison with 1 Cor 4,14-16 provides a welcome confirmation of our view of the link between call and parental authority. In this last text Paul's fatherhood explicitly grounds his call for imitation in his being the founder of the church in Corinth. Because Paul is the only father, he is justified to require imitation from his children. In Gal 4 there is a distance

---

[42] See footnote 30.

[43] Cf. 1 Thess 2,7. HITCHCOCK, "Sinn", 150, stresses that τρόφος means mother, not nurse, "for a nurse is gentle to other people's children". We may also refer to Jesus' comparison in Matt 23,37 = Luke 13,34: ὄρνις (a hen or "the mother bird").

[44] We may compare verse 19 with 2 Cor 4,12 and its even more radical expression: "Death is at work in us, but life in you". See J. LAMBRECHT, "The nekrōsis of Jesus: Ministry and Suffering in 2 Corinthians 4,7-15", A. VANHOYE (ed.), L'apôtre Paul. Personnalité, style et conception du ministère (BETL 73; Leuven 1986) 120-143; republished in R. BIERINGER–J. LAMBRECHT, Studies on 2 Corinthians (BETL 112; Leuven 1994) 309-333.

[45] One here reflects on passages such as Gal 1,8; 1 Cor 1,13-16; 3,5-15; 2 Cor 4,5; 5,18-21; 10,12-18, where Paul stresses that he is only a servant, an ambassador of Christ but equally emphasizes his special position as founder of churches.

between the two motifs and, otherwise than in 1 Cor 4, the call precedes the image of parenthood and is, moreover, motivated by the immediately following comparison "for I also (have become) like you". Therefore, the same basic connection between parental authority and exhortation to imitate the parent is not so evident; it must be postulated. But in our opinion this can be rightly done. Because Paul is the mother of the Galatians, because he is again in pain and travail until Christ is formed in them, Paul is entitled, more than all others, to order: "become as I am"[46].

Notwithstanding this comment one might still be tempted to consider the two motifs of Paul's call to imitation and his motherhood (as well as its link) in a less profound way. Is "imitating Paul", after all, not just being free from the Jewish identity markers, from the Jewish style of life? Is Paul being a mother in travail anymore than a bold image? While it might appear so, the clause "until Christ is formed in you" (v. 19) should prevent a too formal understanding. This clause manifests in a certain sense the very depth of Paul's own "conformity" with Christ (cf. Phil 3,10: συμμορφιζόμενος). In Gal 2,20 Paul states autobiographically: "I have been crucified with Christ; it is no longer I who live, but Christ who lives in me, ζῆ ἐν ἐμοὶ Χριστός"[47]. It is this Christ that must take shape in the Galatians (cf. 2 Cor 3,18)[48]. It is decidedly a Christ-like Paul that must be imitated. Even if ἐν ὑμῖν of Gal 4,19 means "among you", a formation of Christ in the community, to be sure, requires for its authenticity no less than the spiritual formation of Christ crucified within each of the members.

The same clause "until Christ is formed in you" qualifies Paul as being a mother of the Galatians in a still different but equally unexpected way. In Gal 3,7 it is stated that the Gentile Christians of Galatia are "sons of Abraham"; in 3,26 Paul writes "in Christ you are all υἱοὶ θεοῦ, through faith" (cf. 3,29). In 4,4-7, almost just before our pericope, Paul explains how all Christians become adopted sons of God, able to cry "Abba! Father!" According to Paul, it is evident that God is the real Father of all Christians; therefore, the apostle's "motherhood" has only a mediating function.

---

[46] Cf. GÜTTGEMANNS, *Der leidende Apostel*, 193-194, who suggests a "sachlicher Zusammenhang" (194) between verse 12ab and verse 19.

[47] Cf. J. LAMBRECHT, "Transgressor by Nullifying God's Grace: A Study of Galatians 2,18-21", *Bib* 72 (1991) 217-236; republished in ID., *Pauline Studies* (BETL 115; Leuven 1994) 211-230.

[48] Cf. J. LAMBRECHT, "Transformation in 2 Corinthians 3,18", *Bib* 64 (1983) 243-254; republished in BIERINGER–LAMBRECHT, *Studies on 2 Corinthians*, 295-307. This transformation, i.e., "the very process of spiritual birth", is called by DUNN, *Galatians*, 240, "a long-drawn-out affair", "a life-long process".

It might be good also to look at what comes after our pericope. In 4,26 Paul audaciously states that Jerusalem is μήτηρ ἡμῶν. "So then, brothers, we are sons not of the slave but of the free woman. For freedom Christ has set us free. Stand firm, therefore, and do not submit again to a yoke of slavery" (4,31–5,1). From this passage it is clear, again, that Paul as "mother" of the Galatians must be understood, of course, metaphorically. Paul wants to express his sincere concern for the Galatians; he has played the decisive role of founder of their churches and, therefore, he can call the Galatian Christians his "spiritual" children.

Biblica 80 (1999) 525-536

16

Abraham and His Offspring
A Comparison of Galatians 5,1 with 3,13

These notes do not pretend to offer a full christology of Paul's letter to the Galatians. Nor do they claim to treat the figure of Abraham in Galatians (and Romans) exhaustively. In view of an often unnoticed similarity between Gal 5,1 and 3,13 the two verses will be compared and their respective contexts brought into that comparison. Just as after the Abraham passage of 3,6-12 Christ is mentioned in 3,13 quite unexpectedly, so also after 4,21-31, Paul's so-called allegory which deals with the wives and sons of Abraham, the sudden statement about Christ in 5,1 cannot but surprise the reader[1]. Although the word order differs, both vocabulary and content of parts of 3,13a and 5,1a are identical or at least similar: Χριστὸς ἡμᾶς ἐξηγόρησεν..., and ... ἡμᾶς Χριστὸς ἠλευθέρωσεν. In 5,2-6 Christ is mentioned three more times (see vv. 2.4 and 6)[2]; one can also point to the christological terms "grace" (v. 4) and "faith" (vv. 5 and 6). This attention to Christ is striking. One more introductory remark is called for. In this study the name "Abraham" is taken in a wider sense: not only Abraham himself, but also Sarah and Hagar, and equally Isaac and Ishmael ("Abraham had two sons, one by a slave and one by a free woman", 4,22).

I. THOSE OF FAITH WITH ABRAHAM WHO HAD FAITH

Gal 3,1-14 forms the first pericope of the middle section of the letter,

---

[1] On Gal 5,1 see A. OEPKE, *Der Brief des Paulus an die Galater* (THNT; Berlin ²1960) 117: "Der abgehackte Einsatz hat etwas Befremdliches".

[2] Cf. F. PASTOR RAMOS, *La libertad en la carta a los Gálatas*. Estudio exegético-teológico (Madrid 1977) 91: "la palabra 'Cristo' ... que no aparecía desde 4,19".

3,1-5,12, a lengthy discussion concerning the Mosaic law and Christian freedom. Within that pericope there is the comparison with Abraham (3,6-9)[3]. After his invective question in verse 1 Paul speaks in verses 2-5 about the Galatians' experiences of the Spirit. Twice, in verse 2 and verse 5, Paul interpellates: did you receive and do you possess that Spirit thanks to works of the law or thanks to your hearing with faith? The answer is not given, but it is clear from the context that one has to choose the second alternative: through listening and believing. The comparison with Abraham then follows: he also "believed God, and it was reckoned to him as righteousness" (v. 6; quoting Gen 15,6). Therefore, faith is surely a matter which is common to Abraham and the Galatians. But is this the only such matter? What is the relationship between the Spirit experiences of the Galatians and the righteousness of Abraham? Both are guaranteed on the ground of faith. Are the two simply identical?

The conclusion in verse 7 has far-reaching implications: "Therefore know [probably an imperative] that it is the people of faith who are the children of Abraham". Why can this conclusion be drawn? According to Paul faith is so important that it constitutes the basis for a connection between Abraham and the others, a connection so strong that the believing Galatians can be called children of Abraham. Verse 6 quotes Gen 15,6, where Abraham's faith and righteousness are mentioned. In verse 8 a further citation is present: "All the Gentiles shall be blessed in you" (probably a conflation of Gen 18,8 and 12,3). It would be wrong to understand this blessing of all the Gentiles as a kind of reward for Abraham's faith; Paul's reflections run in another direction. He emphasizes the parallel between father and children, and thereby also between his righteousness and their blessing. It also becomes evident that for the Gentiles righteousness (v. 8a) and blessing (v. 8b) are identical. All this was planned by God; scripture foresaw it (προϊδοῦσα) and proclaimed it beforehand as gospel (προευηγγελίσατο) to Abraham.

In verse 9 one more conclusion is indicated: "So then, those who believe are blessed with Abraham who believed". Gentiles believe and are blessed together with Abraham who had faith. A small change in comparison with verse 8 is worthy of note: "in" Abraham becomes "with" Abraham. According to verse 9 Abraham not only believes (and not only receives the

---

[3] This first paragraph is an edited version of sections of "Curse and Blessing: A Study of Galatians 3,10-14", in J. LAMBRECHT, *Pauline Studies* (BETL 115; Leuven 1994) 271-298, cf. 277-279 and 287.

scriptural promise of the Gentiles' future blessing), but he himself is also blessed, like the Gentiles. For Abraham, too, righteousness is the same as blessing. Moreover, blessing refers to the Spirit. Although Paul could hardly say that Abraham already possessed the Spirit, through the two purpose clauses in verse 14 one understands that the blessing of Abraham is the promise of the Spirit. The second clause explains the first.

In Gal 3,2-9 Paul very much stresses the decisive importance of faith. By hearing with faith the Galatians have received and experienced the Spirit. This corresponds with scripture: Abraham is justified through faith; in him all nations, all the Gentiles will be blessed. Those who believe are his children; together with him they are blessed. One would think that faith is the only condition. Being blessed through faith is being justified through faith, and this implies the possession of the Spirit.

This reading, however, has not yet considered the sudden mention of Christ in 3,13-14. "Christ redeemed us from the curse of the law, having become a curse for us" (v. 13a)[4], "in order that in Christ Jesus the blessing of Abraham might come upon the Gentiles" (v. 14a). By these verses the insight is forced upon the reader that the parallel between Abraham and the Gentiles is in the end not so simple. The sequence "faith–blessing" may have been possible for Abraham. Without the intervention of Christ, however, it remains impossible for his children. Previously there was blessing thanks to faith; now Christ must first redeem humanity from the curse of sin.

Yet it should be realized that this qualification is not completely correct, since for Paul redemption by Christ is certainly more than a first step, more than as it were a necessary condition before justification can take place. Redemption by Christ is the justification itself. The needed faith is specifically faith in Christ. In Christ Jesus the blessing of Abraham comes upon the Gentiles (v. 14a) and through faith in Christ all Christians — Gentiles as well as Jews — receive the promise of the Spirit (v. 14b). One must, however, nuance these considerations once more. Strictly speaking, Abraham's faith too was not without a "christological" content. For he

---

[4] For an understanding of "us" (= Jews) in 3,13a as referring only to the Jewish Christians, see especially T.L. DONALDSON, "The 'Curse of the Law' and the Inclusion of the Gentiles: Galatians 3. 13-14", in *NTS* 32 (1986) 94-112. So F.J. MATERA, *Galatians* (Sacra Pagina; Collegeville 1992) 120, writes: "The pronoun *hēmas* ('us') refers to Jewish believers who have lived under the curse of the Law. The redemption of the Jew precedes that of the Gentile". This interpretation, however, is not generally accepted. See, e.g., recently S.K. WILLIAMS, *Galatians* (AbNTC; Nashville 1997) 92: by us in 3,13a "Paul does not refer narrowly to himself and other Christian Jews".

believed in God's promise which attained its realization and fulfillment precisely in Jesus Christ. This means that Abraham's faith and that of the Galatians may not be radically distinguished. Just as his children, Abraham too had to believe in God's new initiative of salvation in order to be justified. For Abraham that initiative was still a promise; for the Galatians it has become reality.

II. LIKE ISAAC CHILDREN OF THE PROMISE

Gal 3 is full of Old Testament quotations and references. It is understandable that Paul, writing this letter to a community consisting for the most part of Gentile Christians, introduces "a human example" in 3,15: "no one annuls even a man's will, or adds to it, once it has been ratified". But immediately afterwards, he resumes his reasoning with data taken from scripture. In 4,1-2 the profane humane reality, well-known to the Galatians, is once more brought forward: "I mean that the heir, as long as he is a child, is no better than a slave, though he is the owner of all the estate; but he is under guardians and trustees until the date set by the father". The application of this is worked out in 4,3-7. Paul's exclamation "how can you turn back again ..." is the center of 4,8-11, a brief passage in which he also expresses his fear: "I am afraid I have labored over you in vain" (v. 11). Then there follows in 4,12-20 a personal pleading in which Paul reminds the Galatians of their mutual loving relations. He also accuses his opponents: "they make much of you, but for no good purpose" (v. 17). This last pericope ends on a pathetic note: "I could wish to be present with you now and to change my tone, for I am perplexed about you" (v. 20).

Gal 4,21-31

In Gal 4,21-31[5] Paul returns to Scripture: "Tell me, you who desire to be under law, do you not hear the law?" "Law" is evidently used here in a double sense, referring first to the Torah as law and then to the Torah as scrip-

---

[5] For our comment on the different passages of Galatians we may refer to the major classic commentaries. That of R.N. LONGENECKER, *Galatians* (WBC; Dallas 1990), provides an extensive bibliography for each pericope.

ture. The formula "it is written" does not introduce a literal quotation. Paul summarizes several sections from Genesis, the stories of Hagar and Sarah and their sons (cf. Gen 16–25). Special attention is given to the status of the two mothers (slave and free) and to the way their respective children are born (according to the flesh and through promise). So a radical opposition prevails in the entire pericope.

The mothers are two covenants. Hagar is the covenant of Mount Sinai. It is the covenant of the law which entails lack of freedom, slavery. With this covenant Paul connects, in v. 25b, the present Jerusalem, which is in bondage with her children, the non-Christian Jews. The second part of the so-called allegory is not worked out. One is invited to supply: the other covenant is from Mount Zion; Sarah is Mount Zion, which corresponds to the Jerusalem above; she is in freedom with her children, the Christians (cf. v. 26). "Above" disrupts the expected temporal antithesis "present–future". The idea of a heavenly, already existent Jerusalem stems from apocalyptic Judaism. Paul, however, may also have chosen the new spatial image because he was convinced that the "future" is no longer completely future; it is somehow present now. That the two cities are seen as "mothers" (cf. vv. 25-26) can best be understood in connection with the two mothers, Hagar and Sarah.

The time factor complicates the allegory. It is not improbable that, in Paul's opinion, both covenants can be said to be existing in the history of Hagar and of Sarah. But the data concerning the Patriarchs point, above all, to two opposing realities: law (Sinai) and fulfilment of the promise, flesh and Spirit, slavery and freedom. The first covenant was inaugurated on Mount Sinai but it is still alive in the present Jerusalem; the new covenant, however, is only brought about by Jesus, now, in these days. The Hagar-line has three time moments: Hagar–Ishmael, law–Sinai, and present Jerusalem. The Sarah-line has only two such moments: Sarah–Isaac, and new covenant–Jerusalem above.

Twice, in verses 28 and 31, the vocative "brothers" occurs, twice also the term "children". The Galatians (cf. "you" in v. 28), Paul included (cf. "we are" in v. 31), are children of promise "after the manner of Isaac" who himself was a child of promise (cf. v. 23); they are children not of the slave girl but of the free woman. The two verses, 28 and 31, clearly form an "inclusio". Yet verse 31 also refers back to verses 21-22. There, "under law" suggests lack of freedom, bondage; there, too, the two terms παιδίο-κη and ἐλευθέρα are used for the first time. From these literary data one is able to conclude that in 4,21-31 Paul wants to prove that the Galatians as Christians are free, free from the law. They alone, not the non-Christian Jews, are the heirs (cf. v. 30).

The allegory of Gal 4,21-31 stands out in its fierce language. Three data should be noted. (1) The allegorizing of the unfree Hagar as Mount Sinai must have been particularly odious for non-Christian Jews. It implies a clear depreciation of the giving of the law. This is confirmed by the opposition of the two covenants in which Sinai is said to bear children for slavery. (2) No less offensive is Paul's treatment of his contemporary fellow-Jews. The present Jerusalem, the mother of the non-Christian Jews, is sharply criticized. The present Jerusalem corresponds to Mount Sinai (and the slave girl Hagar); the city is in bondage with her children; she persecutes the believers. She will be cast out and rejected; she will not have an inheritance. (3) The fact that Paul appropriates Sarah and Isaac, promise and heritage, Spirit and the Jerusalem above, i.e., all Israel's glory and her privileges for the church and thus also for the Gentile majority in that church, must certainly have been not less offensive to his fellow-Jews.

In Rom 9,6-13 Paul stresses the idea of God's free election. This applies to the call of Isaac and to that of Jacob. Not the children of the flesh are the children of God; only the children of the promise are reckoned as descendants (cf. v. 8). In Gal 4,21-31 it is underscored that Isaac is the son of Sarah through promise (cf. v. 23) and that he was born according to the Spirit (cf. v. 29). At the end of the pericope Paul very strongly affirms: "So, brothers, we are not children of the slave but of the free woman" (v. 11). Like Isaac we are children of the promise. Can one suppose that on the part of the Galatians nothing good or bad has been done and that God's purpose of election must continue, not because of works but because of his call (cf. Rom 9,11)? Since faith is not mentioned, one may have the impression that absolutely nothing is needed. The right descent meets with all the conditions: through promise, according to the Spirit. Christ does not enter on the scene; in fact, he is not even mentioned in Gal 4,21-31[6]. Yet just as in 3,13a Christ all at once appears in 5,1a: Τῇ ἐλευθερίᾳ ἡμᾶς Χριστὸς ἠλευθέρωσεν.

Gal 5,1

We can assume that Paul has composed 5,1a still under the influence of what he had just written in 4,31, without referring to contemporary prac-

---

[6] Cf. PASTOR RAMOS, *La Liberdad*, 139: "Hasta este momento no había habido ninguna alusión a Cristo en toda la tipología".

tices of slave emancipation[7]. Yet, as is well known, the problems regarding Gal 5,1 are legion. First of all, there are a number of variant readings. Furthermore, the question whether this verse still belongs to the allegory or can be seen as a new beginning[8] is not solved; therefore, many prefer a compromise: the verse constitutes a transition. This question is related to the other, namely whether the major parenetical part of Galatians begins with 5,1 or rather with 5,13. Much attention is also devoted to the connection between the two clauses, the indicative in verse 1a and the imperative in verse 1b. Commentators also ask how the dative at the beginning of the verse has to be taken: is it instrumental or is it the equivalent of a Hebrew absolute infinitive or, more probably, a dative of advantage? All these problems[9] may have caused the lack of attention given to the sudden appearance of Christ in 5,1a[10].

"For freedom Christ has set us free" (5,1). A survey of parallel affirmations in the letter to the Galatians reveals both the kernel of Paul's thought and the possible variations and images[11]. In 1,4 it is said that Christ "gave himself (δόντος ἑαυτόν) for our sins to deliver (ὅπως ἐξέληται) us from the present evil age"[12]. The verb used in 2,16 for that which is produced through or by faith in Christ (cf. 2,17: "in Christ") is, of course, δικαιοῦμαι. As stated already, in 3,13a Paul maintains that "Christ redeemed (ἐξηγόρασεν) us from the curse of the law, having become a curse for

---

[7] Paul does not seem to allude here to the hellenistic sacral manumission nor to the Jewish redemption of slaves. F. MUSSNER, *Der Galaterbrief* (HTKNT; Freiburg–Basel–Wien 1974) 345, concludes his discussion as follows: "Die Formulierung ... macht ... den Eindruck, dass sie von Paulus ad hoc aus dem von ihm besonders in 4,31 Vorgelegten geschaffen worden ist".

[8] M.-J. LAGRANGE, *Epître aux Galates* (EtB; Paris 1918), 132-133, sees in 4,31 (with διό, ἀδελφοί...) the beginning of a new pericope (4,31–5,12).

[9] Cf. the discussion and choices in, e.g., LONGENECKER, *Galatians*, 220 and 223-225; PASTOR RAMOS, *La libertad*, 89-92.

[10] A. VANHOYE, *La lettera ai Galati*. Seconda parte, Roma ³1997, is an exception: the affirmation "corregge l'impressione che poteva lasciare la tipologia precedente, cioè che dobbiamo la nostra libertà a una astrazione, la seconda *diathēkē*, o a una realtà celeste collettiva, la Gerusalemme di lassù. Non è così! La nostra libertà la dobbiamo a un intervento di Cristo, intervento preciso, storico, espresso con un aoristo: *eleutherōsen*" (213). Regarding the verb, see also MUSSNER, *Galaterbrief*, 343: the aorist "schaut auf das historische Kreuzesgeschehen zurück" (with reference to the similar aorist in 3,13a).

[11] Cf. PASTOR RAMOS, *La libertad*, 235-242.

[12] At first sight Paul's reflection in 2,20: "... the Son of God, who loved me and gave himself (παραδόντος ἑαυτόν) for me" appears to be very similar to the tradition in 1,4a . Yet G. BERÉNYI, "Gal 2,20: a Pre-Pauline or a Pauline Text?", *Bib* 65 (1984) 490-537, convincingly, it would seem, defends the Pauline character of 2,20. The author highlights three Pauline particularities: the title Son of God; the verb παραδίδωμι and the reflexive pronoun; the typical and original use of ἀγαπάω.

us". One may, finally, also refer to 4,5 in which the same verb occurs: When the time has come, God sent his son "to redeem (ἵνα ... ἐξαγορά-ση) those who were under the law". Consequently, that Christ gave himself for our sins can be expressed equally well by justification, by deliverance from the evil age, by redemption from the curse of the law, and by libera-tion, i.e. setting us free from the slavery of the law. In each case, Christ is the agent of these actions. On 5,1a E. Burton writes: "The sentence is, in fact, an epitome of the contention of the whole letter"[13].

The similarities between 5,1a and 3,13a are very impressive: absence of a connecting particle and presence of "Christ", "us" and a verb in the aorist. In both clauses the verb indicates an act by Christ which saves us out of a negative situation. Further, just as "curse" in 3,13a takes up that term from 3,10, so also the "freedom" terminology links 5,1a with 4,30-31.26 and 22-23. One should, however, not keep silent about the differen-ces. The metaphorical language is after all not the same: redemption from the curse of the law in 3,13a over against liberation (from slavery) in 5,1a. In 3,13a Christ is said to have become a curse for us; a similar statement which points to his vicarious death on the cross is missing in 5,1a. In 3,13a the position "Christ" at the beginning of the clause is very prominent; in 5,1a "Christ" comes only as the fourth word. One could be tempted to say that in 5,1a Christ is mentioned almost unintentionally. Yet the threefold repetition of "Christ" in 5,2-6 hardly occurs by accident; it betrays Paul's design.

The phrase "for freedom Christ has set us free" obtains most empha-sis: by the position of τῇ ἐλευθερίᾳ in front of the clause and immediately after τῆς ἐλευθέρας at the end of the preceding verse (4,31)[14]; by the re-iteration of the theme by means of the verb ἐλευθερόω in the same clause; by the reference back to the whole of 4,21-31 (cf. Sarah the free woman of whom the Galatians are the children, and the free Jerusalem above); by the repetition of the same idea in 5,13 ("for you, to freedom you were called, brothers"); and, not in the least, also by its negative counterpart, the slav-ery, in the imperatival clause of 5,1b. Although in 5,1a the noun "free-dom" probably possesses a positive nuance, Paul sees the verb "setting free" in the first place negatively, i.e., as a being freed from the slavery of the Sinai covenant and the law. In 4,21 he addresses the Galatians who

---

13 E. DE WITT BURTON, *The Epistle to the Galatians* (ICC; Edinburgh 1921) 270.
14 Cf. F. SIEFFERT, *Der Brief an die Galater* (KEK; Göttingen ⁹1899) 297: the emphasis does not lie on Christ but on freedom which follows immediately on "the free woman" in 4,31.

desire to be "under the law"[15]. In 5,1b he says to them "stand fast and do not submit again (πάλιν) to a yoke of slavery". In 4,9 he already expressed the same warning: "how can you turn back again (πάλιν) to the weak στοι-χεῖα, whose slaves you want to be once more (πάλιν)?" He will stress this warning again in 5,7-11 and also in 6,12-13 at the very end of his letter. This is the freedom which Paul has in Christ (2,4: τὴν ἐλευθερίαν ἡμῶν ἣν ἔχομεν ἐν Χριστῷ Ἰησοῦ: in Jerusalem the false brothers slipped in to spy out the freedom of Paul and Barnabas in order to bring them into bondage or slavery).

Gal 5,2-12

Whether or not Gal 5,1 structurally belongs to what follows, the first five conspicuous and authoritative words of 5,2 (Ἴδε ἐγὼ Παῦλος λέγω ὑμῖν) mark, it would seem, a new beginning[16]. They function to emphasize Paul's worry and fear. In verses 1-6 the name Christ is present four times in an accumulated way. By itself this frequency somewhat distinguishes these verses from the next subdivision (vv. 7-12)[17]. Paul points to what he considers the great danger in Galatia: Christians desire to live as Jews (cf. 2,14). Circumcision is closely linked with the law and all its command-ments (see 5,3-4). Two systems are diametrically opposed: justification by faith and so-called justification by the law. They are alternatives, indeed. If the Galatians are going to choose the law, then Christ will be of no advan-tage to them; they will be severed from him; they will have fallen away from grace (cf. vv. 2 and 4). Over against those supposedly judaizing Galatians Paul in verse 5 puts the authentically Christian "we" (ἡμεῖς). The Christian situation is one of eagerly expecting the final, eschatological righteousness, a life of being in Christ, of having a faith which works and expresses itself through love (cf. vv. 5-6).

In verses 7-12 Paul explicitly addresses the Galatians: "You were run-ning well; who hindered you from obeying the truth?" (v. 7). He attacks and accuses the opponents. They cause trouble, they unsettle the Galatians.

---

[15] Cf. D. LÜHRMANN, Der Brief an die Galater (ZBK; Zurich 1978) 80; H. SCHLIER, Der Brief an die Galater (KEK; Göttingen ⁵1971) 229-230: "Freiheit vom Gesetz ... Freiheit von der Sünde ... Freiheit vom Tode". Yet: "Man wird nicht behaupten dürfen, dass Paulus diese Bestimmungen in dem Satz 5,1 alle gegenwärtig sind".

[16] Cf. MUSSNER, Galaterbrief, 344-345, for highlighting the authoritative character of these words.

[17] See, however, 5,11 with its mention of the cross (of Christ, cf. 6,12 and 14).

Paul announces their condemnation at the day of judgment; in an outburst, he even expresses the wish that they should mutilate themselves. Then, Paul once more refers to himself. No, he does not preach circumcision; he does not remove the scandal of the cross.

Apparently the whole of 5,2-12 is needed in order to correctly explain the freedom for which Christ has set us free. Paul's pleading, his severe attacks, his protestation and self-presentation: all his arguing testifies to the fear that the Galatians may listen to the "different gospel" (1,6) which ultimately means slavery and absence of freedom.

III. CHRIST AND THOSE OF CHRIST: ABRAHAM'S OFFSPRING

In between 3,1-14 and 4,21–5,12 there occurs the lengthy section 3,15–4,20, by no means a strictly unified text. No doubt, the rest of chapter three, with the mention of Abraham and his offspring (σπέρμα) in 3,16, as well as in 3,29, forms a unit: 3,15-29. What follows in 4,1-7 seems still to be connected with it, a kind of supplementary pericope. Because of Paul's airing of his fear for the Galatians and because of his warning against judaizing practices, the differing passages 4,7-11 and 4,12-20 can be considered together. The first subdivision 3,15-29 requires a careful reading in view of the presence of references to Abraham and Christ; Paul's type of reasoning is no longer the same here.

Gal 3,15-29

After 3,14 Paul writes "brothers" and announces a human example (κατὰ ἄνθρωπον λέγω): no one annuls a will (διαθήκην) which has been ratified, or adds to it (v. 15). The term διαθήκη is used again in v. 17, in the same sense of will or testament[18]. For Paul the reality of that will is the promise (or promises) made to Abraham. The noun ἐπαγγελία has already occurred in 3,14 ("the promise of the Spirit"). The promise terminology reappears in vv. 16.17.18.19.21.22 and 29. It will become obvious that the content of the promise is Abraham's blessing, is the inheritance, life, righteousness and the Spirit.

---

[18] Cf. WILLIAMS, *Galatians*, 95-96.

With reference to Gen 13,15, verse 16 states that "the promises were made to Abraham and to his offspring". In a curious way Paul modifies the originally collective meaning of "offspring" (σπέρμα). Since the term is in the singular, he claims that it points to one only, and this one is Christ. As said above, the sudden mention of Christ in 3,13 was unexpected. In 3,16 that identification of Abraham's offspring with Christ alone is not only unexpected but utterly confusing. Moreover, the time period between Abraham and Christ would seem to be suppressed. Do we have, then, a phenomenon which should be compared with that of 3,13 and 5,1? Yet after the statement in 3,7 that only those of faith are the children of Abraham, Paul can hardly hold in 3,16 that unbelieving Jews continue to be offspring or descendants of Abraham. Sooner than one might have anticipated, from verse 17 onward, the time argument emerges in all clarity; its treatment makes Paul's reasoning in 3,15-29 different from that in 3,1-14 and 4,21-5,12. The law comes in. The lawgiving stands in between Abraham and Christ; it is later than the promise and earlier than the fulfillment. Yet, the law is powerless, its role is not positive.

The first negative feature of the law is a temporal one: the law came later, four hundred and thirty years after the promise. Therefore, it cannot nullify or destroy the promise (cf. v. 17). At the end of verse 19 Paul states that the law was ordained by angels through a mediator. "Mediator" here most probably points to Moses, not so much as an intermediary agent between two groups — angels and humans — but as the representative of the many angels[19]. In contrast God spoke the promise directly to Abraham, without angels and without an intermediary–representative. Again, law appears to be inferior. There is, moreover, a second temporal feature, equally negative, pointing not to the past but to the future. The function of the law is limited in time. Already in verse 19 it is said that the law will last (only) "till the offspring should come to whom the promise had been made". This temporal limitation is worked out very clearly in the

---

[19.] H.D. BETZ, *Galatians* (Hermeneia; Philadelphia 1979) 171-172, e.g., retains the idea of mediating: "... as a go-between related to two parties, the mediator is defined merely in contrast with the oneness of God, that is, as the representative of a plurality. It is not at all necessary to identify this plurality as the angels in 3:19d, or as the people in the Sinai tradition" (171). Cf. also J.D.G. DUNN, *The Epistle to the Galatians* (BNTC; London 1993) 191: "Paul was probably attempting a not very successful ... epigrammatic play-off between the thought of God's oneness and the fact that mediation implies more than one (between whom to mediate"). A. VANHOYE, "Un médiateur des anges en Ga 3,19-20", *Bib* 59 (1978) 403-411, defends the less likely position that an angel is the representative of the multitude of angels mentioned in v. 19.

somewhat simplistic survey of salvation history given in verses 22-25. Two periods of time are distinguished, that of the law and that of faith (or: that of sin and that of Christ). When the second arrives, the first disappears.

Promise and faith are so closely linked that in 3,18 promise even takes the place of faith in the opposition to the law: "for if the inheritance is by the law, it is no longer by promise" (cf. the end of v. 29: "heirs according to promise"). One notes the same radical tone as with faith. In diatribe style Paul asks in verse 21: "Is the law then against the promises of God?" "Certainly not" is the expected first emotional reaction. In fact, the real answer is not given afterwards; it must be supplied. Perhaps one may reconstruct it as follows: although the law is not against the promise and is holy, just and good (cf. Rom 7,12), yet through it sin works death (cf. Rom 7,13). What Paul eventually says after "certainly not" explains this answer: "for if a law had been given which could make alive, then righteousness would indeed be by the law" (v. 21). The negative stand regarding the law prevails, the same as in 3,10-12. Even if verse 19 does not mean that the law's function is to increase sin but to limit it, one should not consider such a role as constructive. This is obvious from what is stated in verse 23: "before faith came, we were confined under the law, kept under restraint until faith should be revealed". The time of the law is characterized by Paul as lacking in freedom (cf. v. 22: scripture consigned all things to sin). In verses 24-25 Paul understands the responsibility of the "custodian" (παι-δαγωγός) probably not as pedagogic in a positive sense but only as restric-tive, in any case as provisional. In these verses Paul employs the first per-son plural and thus speaks to the Galatians in a trusting tone. Therefore, it would be un-Pauline to find in the law a preparation "unto Christ"[20]. The law is opposed to both the promise (past) and its fulfillment (future).

Promise itself points to fulfillment. In verse 16 the offspring of Abraham is strangely identified as being one person, Christ. In verse 19 the future coming of that offspring is mentioned again; verse 22 speaks of the future giving of what was promised and verse 23 of the coming of faith and its being revealed. Verse 24 points to the coming of Christ and verse 25, again, to the coming of faith. This frequency of remarks which look forward to Christ explodes, as it were, in verses 26-29. Already in verses 21-25 righteousness and life are mentioned. Yet in verses 26-29 one encounters the climax in expressions which all indicate the fulfillment of

---

[20] The question remains, however, whether a positive nuance is completely absent in the clauses which contain ἄχρις οὗ (3,19), εἰς τὴν μέλλουσαν πίστιν (3,24) and εἰς Χριστόν (3,25).

the promise: sons of God, faith in Christ, baptism and putting on of Christ, all one in Christ, finally, by way of intended inclusion: "if you are Christ's, then you are Abraham's offspring, heirs according to promise" (v. 29). In verse 16 the uniqueness of Abraham's offspring was affirmed and underscored in a forced manner (cf. also v. 19); at the end of the passage, in verse 29, all believers are one in Christ and so they are collectively Abraham's offspring, his children (cf. v. 7). While in verse 23-25 the first person plural is used, in verses 26-29 Paul changes to the second person plural; he thus addresses the Galatians with great emphasis.

Twice, in 3,6-12 and in 4,21-31, the reader might be brought to the suspicion that belonging to Abraham or his family is sufficient. Abraham's children must believe, just as Abraham was one who believed; like Isaac, born according to the Spirit, they are children of the promise. Yet in 3,13 as well as in 5,1 Christ appears on the scene, without warning; a misunderstanding is no longer possible. The faith that is needed is faith in Christ crucified who redeemed us from the curse; the Spirit is the Spirit of Christ who has set us free from the law. In 3,15-29, however, nothing looks abrupt, nothing unexpected. Christ is explicitly present from verse 16 onward. His coming is repeatedly referred to in verses 19-25 and the fulfillment he brought is broadly depicted in verses 26-29. Paul's argumentation here by means of the promise to Abraham, the intervening law and the coming of Christ manifests his view of salvation history.

Gal 4,1-20

One should consider Gal 4,1-7 as a sort of complement to 3,15-29. With λέγω δέ Paul introduces a second human example connected with the first (cf. 3,15): the child–heir is not better than a slave "until the date set by the father" (4,1-2). In the application of this example ("so with us", 4,3), it would seem that all Christians in Galatia have been slaves to elemental principles, either in their pagan past or kept in slavery under the Jewish law. In 4,4-7 Paul explains — broadly as in 3,26-29 — what has happened "when the fullness of time came": God sent his Son, born of a woman and born under the law, in order to redeem those under the law so that all might become children by adoption. God sent his Spirit into our hearts, crying "Abba, Father". Therefore, we are no longer slaves but children and heirs. Apparently the same salvation historical pattern of argument is present, be it without explicit mention of the promise: first the period of slavery and then the fullness of time with Christ. Yet the unfree condition before Christ is not only that of restriction under the law but also the pagan enslavement to beings "that are by nature no gods" (4,8).

In 4,8-11 Paul, once more in a strange way, compares and even identifies the pre-Christian condition of the Gentile believers with the judaizing
lifestyle proposed by the opponents: you were in bondage to "no gods",
how can you turn back "again" to the weak and poor elemental spirits?
Why do you wish to enslave yourselves to them "again"? As it happens
Paul twice uses the term πάλιν. In verse 11 he then complains: "I am afraid
I have labored over you in vain".

The same fear can be felt in the emotional and pleading pericope
which follows in 4,12-20. Paul reminds the Galatians of their previous
loving attitude with regard to himself: "Have I become an enemy by telling
you the truth?" (v. 16). Paul continues to warn them against the dishonest
"courting" of the opponents. From the preceding context one knows that
they want to bring the Galatians "under the law" (cf. 4,21). It is a law
which restricts and condemns, a law which is incapable of providing life
(cf. 3,22).

CONCLUSION

The reading of Gal 3,15-29 and 4,1-7 cannot but show us Paul's heavily christological emphasis. Christ is both the apex and center in the argument. One final question remains with regard to 3,13 and 5,1. While it cannot be denied that in both verses Paul, rather unexpectedly, brings in a most
forceful statement about Christ, should one speak here of a conscious correction on the part of the author, or of an important complement? Neither
of these options seems likely. In 3,13 and 5,1 Paul mentions Christ, it
would seem, spontaneously, not as a correction[21] or complement, but out
of the fullness of his personal conviction, out of his most profound vision
of salvation history. Yet both 3,7-9 and 4,21-31 reveal to us how easily Paul
is taken up, almost completely, in the presentation of Abraham and his
family. That Genesis material provides him not only with an illustration. A
promise was made to Abraham and he believed God; this faith was reckoned to him as righteousness. According to Paul, Abraham's faith was
already, by way of anticipation, Christian faith. Moreover, for Paul οἱ ἐκ
πίστεως in 3,7 and 9 implicitly are believers in Christ. This also applies to

---

[21] Cf. note 10.

4,26. The children of ἡ ἄνω ᾽Ιερουσαλήμ are free because they belong to Christ, even if in v. 26 this is not (yet) explicitly stated. God promised an inheritance to Abraham. Through their belonging to Christ Christians have become, not by law but according to that promise, the heirs (cf. 3,29)[22].

Abraham's offspring is Christ; that offspring at the same time consists of all those who have faith in Christ[23]. Therefore, a seemingly brusque but easy transition from Abraham to Christ should not disturb the reader too much.

---

[22] Cf. DUNN, *Galatians*, 208.

[23] Cf. WILLIAMS, *Galatians*, 92: Paul's "insistence on the incompability of faith and the Law are grounded in yet more fundamental convictions about the eschatological import of Jesus' death and resurrection".

Novum Testamentum 38 (1996) 237-241

17

Is Galatians 5,11b a Parenthesis?
A Response to T. Baarda

The RSV translates the three lines of Gal 5,11 quite literally as follows:
(1) But if I, brethren, still preach circumcision,
(2) why am I still persecuted?
(3) In that case (ἄρα) the stumbling block of the cross has been removed.

In 1992 T. Baarda published a brief study on the verse in this journal[1]. His main thesis is twofold: verse 11c constitutes the apodosis of the conditional period; verse 11b is but a parenthesis. In this note I shall first summarize the argumentation of Baarda, then put forward my own understanding of the verse and end by drawing conclusions from this investigation.

I. THE POSITION OF T. BAARDA

It would seem that the argumentation of Baarda can be condensed under three headings: the logic, the difference between v. 11b and v. 11c, and the function of v. 11b.

Gal 5,11c (line 3) begins with ἄρα. Most probably this ἄρα is an inferential particle. One expects that "it introduces in some way or another an apodosis of the conditional phrase, in order to emphasize the fatal effect. But the effect of what? Not of the idea expressed in lines 1-2, but *only* of

---

[1] T. BAARDA, "Τί ἔτι διώκομαι in Gal. 5:11: Apodosis or Parenthesis?" *NT* 34 (1992) 250-256.

the suggestion made in line 1"[2]. An apodosis introduced by an inferential ἄρα can be found, e.g., in 2,21 and 3,29; 2 Cor 5,14; 1 Cor 15,14 and 17-18.

The last reference to 1 Corinthians is not without interest. Just as in Gal 5,11, so also in 1 Cor 15,17-18 "the particle ἄρα is found at a later stage in an argumentation"[3]:

(1) If Christ has not been raised,
(2) your faith is futile,
(3) and you are still in your sins;
(4) then (ἄρα) those also who have fallen asleep in Christ have perished.

Yet the two passages differ. In 1 Cor 5,17-18 "all the lines (2-4) after the conditional clause express, in various wordings, the *same* consequence .... But this is not so in Gal 5,11"[4]. In this last verse line 2 (persecution of Paul) and line 3 (fatal effect) "are of a quite different character"[5].

Verse 11b (line 2) functions as a proof that Paul does not preach circumcision[6]. It is but a parenthesis and not what Paul wants to underscore. By using a conditional sentence with v. 11a (line 1) as protasis and v. 11c (line 3) as apodosis Paul wishes to emphasize "that *any* preaching of circumcision as requirement for salvation nullifies the message of the gospel"[7].

To end this presentation, I may quote Baarda's paraphrase of what "Paul actually says":

> *But for me, brothers,* in contrast with those who now embarrass you with their requirement of circumcision for the incorporation in the true Israel, *if I were still preaching circumcision* as such a requirement — and you know that I do not preach circumcision, *why else would I still be persecuted?* — *then* the ground for the Gospel, *the skandalon of the cross would have fallen away*[8].

---

[2] BAARDA, "Gal. 5:11", 250. Cf. p. 251: "... one cannot see how this inference could be drawn from lines 1-2, in which Paul emphatically denies that he is preaching circumcision. It could be only a conclusion of line 1, 'if I still preach circumcision'".

[3] BAARDA, "Gal. 5:11", 251.

[4] BAARDA, "Gal. 5:11", 252.

[5] BAARDA, "Gal. 5:11", 252.

[6] Cf. BAARDA, "Gal. 5:11", e.g., 255: "Τί ἔτι διώκομαι is not an inference ..., but a sufficient *proof* of the fact that Paul did not preach circumcision".

[7] BAARDA, "Gal. 5:11", 255.

[8] BAARDA, "Gal. 5:11", 254.

II. RENEWED ANALYSIS

Complete certainty about Paul's way of organizing his thoughts in Gal 5,11 can hardly be attained. Two factors in this verse cause difficulties in our understanding of Paul's reasoning. The protasis (εἰ ... κηρύσσω) is grammatically speaking a so-called "realis", a simple condition, but one expects here an irrealis, a condition contrary to fact: "if I were still preaching circumcision"[9]. There can be no doubt, since his becoming a Christian Paul does no longer[10] preach circumcision. Notwithstanding the simple condition of this protasis Paul refers to an irreal hypothesis, a condition contrary to fact. The second factor even contains a double irregularity: immediately after the protasis Paul employs a question — "a sign of the vividness"[11] of his speech — instead of an apodosis in statement form. And, otherwise than in the preceding protasis, with this question Paul points to his actual situation of persecution, not to an irreal fact.

It would seem, however, that all these bewildering features do not destroy the underlying logic. In v. 11ab Paul wants to express the following idea: "If I were still preaching circumcision, I would not be persecuted". Verse 11b, therefore, must be considered as a true apodosis. The question replaces a "normal" apodosis. We may refer to 1 Cor 15,12 where, just as in Gal 5,11b, the apodosis is put in a question form: "Now if Christ is preached as risen from the dead, how can some of you say that there is no resurrection of the dead?" We can simplify this sentence, transform the question into a statement and reconstruct Paul's reasoning as follows: "If Christ is risen (protasis), then there will also be a resurrection of the dead (apodosis)"[12]. In Paul's mind the question in 1 Cor 15,12 certainly functions as the

---

[9.] Cf., e.g., the paraphrasis by Baarda which we just quoted.

[10.] Within the framework of this note a discussion of the meaning of the two ἔτι's can be omitted.

[11.] BAARDA, "Gal. 5:11", 254. Cf. E. DE WITT BURTON, *The Epistle to the Galatians* (ICC; Edinburgh 1921) 286: "The conditional clause εἰ ... κηρύσσω, though having the form of a simple present supposition, evidently expresses an unfulfilled condition". J. ROHDE, *Der Brief des Paulus an die Galater* (THNT; Berlin 1989), is correct, I think, in not finding in v. 11a a reference to what the opponents say. He, too, stresses the irreal character and considers v. 11ab as a unit: "Der Vordersatz εἰ περιτομὴν ἔτι κηρύσσω nimmt ... nicht eine gegnerische Behauptung auf, sondern Paulus setzt selbst den schlechthin unwirklichen Fall als wirklich, er predige noch die Beschneidung und weist dann durch die Frage τί ἔτι διώκομαι daraufhin, dass kein Grund zu seiner Verfolgung vorliegen würde" (223).

[12.] Cf. J. LAMBRECHT, "Paul's Christological Use of Scripture in 1 Cor. 15.20-28", *NTS* 28 (1982) 502-527, esp. 503; also in ID., *Pauline Studies* (BETL 115; Leuven 1994) 125-149, esp. 126-127.

apodosis in the conditional sentence. The same, it would seem, applies to Gal 5,11ab.

Taking v. 11b as (the equivalent of) an apodosis does not diminish the apodosis character of v. 11c as well. In v. 11c we have a second apodosis, equally depending on v. 11a. However, the grammatical and logical difficulties within v. 11ab, more in particular the fact that Paul shifts to a question in v. 11b, causes the reader to experience a sort of break at the end of v. 11b and requires mentally a repetition of the protasis of v. 11a (RSV: "in that case"[13]) before continuing with v. 11c. I do not see why Paul could not have in mind two rather different but not unconnected types of apodosis: absence of persecution and removal of the scandal.

III. CONCLUSION

The conclusion of this short note is threefold.

Most probably Gal 5,11b is not simply a parenthesis[14] and, as such, not an interruption of Paul's reasoning. Hidden within the question form lies the apodosis which depends on the protasis of v. 11a: if I were still preaching circumcision, there would be no reason why I should be persecuted. Of course, further reasoning can extract a proof from v. 11b: Paul's actual being persecuted is a proof of the fact that he no longer preaches circumcision. Yet, by itself, the protasis of v. 11a expects an apodosis, and a first apodosis is present in v. 11b.

Verse 11c, introduced by ἄρα, provides us with a second apodosis,

---

[13.] Cf. REB: "to do that" (i.e., to preach the circumcision).

[14.] Cf. BAARDA, "Gal. 5:11", 255: verse 11b "in fact is merely said *en parenthèse*". This author finds another parenthesis in Galatians, namely within 1,11-12. In his opinion the phrase ἀλλὰ δι᾽ ἀποκαλύψεως Ἰησοῦ Χριστοῦ (v. 12) is the continuation of ὅτι οὐκ ἔστιν κατὰ ἄνθρωπον (v. 11b). Consequently, "for I did not receive it from man, nor was I taught it" (v. 12) is but a parenthesis. See T. BAARDA, "Openbaring — Traditie en Didachè. Paulus' zelfstandigheid in het licht van Galaten 1,11-12", F.H. KUIPER–J.J. VAN NIJEN–J.C. SCHREUDER (eds.), *Zelfstandig geloven. FS J. Firet* (Kampen 1987) 152-167, esp. 152-159. Yet most probably the phrase at the end of v. 12 is an integral part of the motivating clause of v. 12. It stands in opposition to παρὰ ἀνθρώπου in this verse and grammatically depends on the same verb παρέλαβον. One must, I think, consider οὔτε ἐδιδάχθην as a somewhat interrupting, clarifying addition. Cf. also the critique by J. VOS, "Die Argumentation des Paulus in Galater 1,1–2,10", J. LAMBRECHT (ed.), *The Truth of the Gospel (Galatians 1:1–4:11)* (Benedictina 12; Rome 1993) 27, n. 62.

equally depending on the protasis of v. 11a[15]. Of course, since verse 11b is not a statement but a question and, moreover, points to Paul's present situation, this second apodosis with its irrealis character[16] does not follow smoothly. One must first repeat, as it were, the protasis of v. 11a.

Verse 11b and verse 11c offer two different inferences which are drawn from the irreal supposition "if I were still preaching circumcision" (v. 11a, formulated, however, in the form of a simple condition: if I preach). The first apodosis points to Paul himself and is, therefore, rather subjective. In a more objective way the second apodosis refers to the fatal consequence as regards the gospel message. One should not consider the mention of these two aspects, one next to the other, as impossible or improbable[17]. In this verse, Paul does not link them contentwise[18]. Elsewhere in his letters, however, he does not hesitate to do this: persecuted he carries in his body the death of Jesus, so that the life of Jesus may be manifested (cf. 2 Cor 4,7-12).

[15.] Otherwise F. MUSSNER, *Der Galaterbrief* (HTKNT; Freiburg–Basel–Wien 1974) 363: "... V 11c [ist] für den Apostel die notwendige Schlussfolge aus V 11a und b".

[16.] The verb in v. 11c — κατήργηται (perfect tense) — is a "realis", but one expects an irrealis (ἄν with an imperfect): the scandal would be removed.

[17.] Cf. the presence of both aspects in the conditional periods of 1 Cor 15,12-19 and 29-32.

[18.] Cf., e.g., MUSSNER, *Galaterbrief*, 360; also on p. 362: "Die Verfolgung des Apostels hängt ursächlich zusammen mit seiner Predigt, in der er das Ärgernis des Kreuzes für Juden und Heiden zur Geltung bringt ...". See the critique by BAARDA, "Gal. 5:11", 255.

Biblica 79 (1998) 514-524

18

The Right Things You Want to Do
A Note on Galatians 5,17d

Gal 5,13–6,10 is usually taken as the parenetic section of the letter. Verses 13-24 of chapter 5 can be considered as its first unit. In v. 13a ("For you were called to freedom") Paul more or less repeats what he has already said in v. 1a: "For freedom Christ has set us free". In v. 1 he had continued: "Stand fast, therefore, and do not submit again to a yoke of slavery", i.e., do not become subject to the law (cf. 4,21). The continuation in v. 13, however, is different, although the freedom's opposite, the theme of "slavery", is likewise repeated: "only do not use your freedom as an opportunity for the flesh; but through love become slaves to one another". The term "flesh" appears, and mutual service, love of neighbor is seen as a curb on any kind of wrongly-understood freedom. In vv. 14-15, then, this love of neighbor is further inculcated. In vv. 16-24 Paul calls for a life by the Spirit; he radically opposes "flesh" and "Spirit" (cf. 4,29 and, more especially, 3,3b: "Having started with the Spirit, are you now ending with the flesh?").

As is well known, within Gal 5,16-18 verse 17 defies any easy interpretation. This is the literal translation of the passage:

16 But I say, walk by the Spirit, and you will not fulfil the lust of the flesh.

17 For the flesh lusts against the Spirit, but the Spirit against the flesh; for these are opposed to each other, to prevent you from doing whatever you would.

18 But if you are led by the Spirit, you are not under the law.

According to v. 17 flesh and Spirit are at war; their desires are opposed to each other. This situation seems to cause a stalemate "so that you cannot do whatever you want". Yet in v. 16 Paul is definitely urging the Galatians; he visibly takes for granted the possibility of the Christians' choice for a life guided by the Spirit: you certainly will not (οὐ μή: strong negation) yield to the covetousness of the flesh. The same applies to v. 18. How then must verse 17 be understood within its immediate context? Not so long ago John M.G. Barclay wrote: "In fact this clause is generally acknowledged to be one of the most difficult in the whole letter"[1].

I. A FIRST COMPARISON

Several solutions to the difficulties in v. 17 have been proposed. However, before presenting a survey of the main interpretations, it may prove useful initially to compare Gal 5,17 with the somewhat similar passage Rom 7,15b-16[2].

Gal 5,17

17a	ἡ γὰρ σὰρξ ἐπιθυμεῖ κατὰ τοῦ πνεύματος,
17b	τὸ δὲ πνεῦμα κατὰ τῆς σαρκός,
17c	ταῦτα γὰρ ἀλλήλοις ἀντίκειται,
17d	ἵνα μὴ ἃ ἐὰν θέλητε ταῦτα ποιῆτε.

Rom 7,15bc-16ab

15b	οὐ γὰρ ὃ θέλω τοῦτο πράσσω,
15c	ἀλλ' ὃ μισῶ τοῦτο ποιῶ.
16a	εἰ δὲ ὃ οὐ θέλω τοῦτο ποιῶ,
16b	σύμφημι τῷ νόμῳ ὅτι καλός.

---

[1] J.M.G. BARCLAY, *Obeying the Truth. A Study of Paul's Ethics in Galatians* (Studies of the New Testament and its World; Edinburgh 1988) 122. Cf. In-Gyu HONG, *The Law in Galatians* (JSNT.S 81; Sheffield 1993) 185: "This verse has been a vexing problem to many interpreters. Here scholarly opinions differ considerably". Regarding the context Hong notes: "The flesh appears to be a personified power that works against the Spirit .... For Paul, existence under the flesh is compatible with existence under the law ..., for subjection to the flesh causes man to break the law and thereby brings him under the bondage of the law" (87; cf. 166 and 175-176). According to J. BLIGH, *Galatians. A Discussion of St Paul's Epistle* (London 1966) 446, verse 16 is the equivalent of a conditional sentence ("If you walk by the Spirit, you will not fulfil the lust of the flesh") and is clearly parallel to v. 18 ("If you are led by the Spirit, you are not under the law").

[2] For a comparison see, e.g., P. ALTHAUS, "'... Dass ihr nicht tut, was ihr wollt' (Zur Auslegung von Gal. 5,17)", *ThLZ* 76 (1951) 15-18; O. MODALSKI, "Gal. 2,19-21; 5,16-18 und Röm. 7,7-24", *ThZ* 21 (1965) 22-37, esp. 29-37; and, in a rather original way, H.D. BETZ, *Galatians* (Hermeneia; Philadelphia 1979), 278-281 (see our note 5).

As can be seen Gal 5,17d is very similar to Rom 7,15b. Both clauses have a negation: see μή and οὐ. Both display a similar construction: ἃ ... ταῦτα and ὃ ... τοῦτο. In each the resumptive demonstrative pronoun[3] takes up the preceding relative pronoun which lacks determination. Moreover, the two clauses utilize the verb θέλω in a relative subclause. Finally, the verb ποιέω in Gal 5,17d is almost certainly the equivalent of πράσσω in Rom 7,15b (cf. 7,16a.19 and 20 with ποιέω).

There are, of course, major differences, too. In Gal 5,17d the negative clause introduced by ἵνα μή depends on v. 17c and thus completes this clause which itself explains (γάρ) v. 17ab. The γάρ-clause of Rom 7,15b, however, is the first half of a co-ordinated sentence (οὐ ἀλλά) that rounds off v. 14: "I am carnal, sold under sin". Moreover, in Gal 5,17d the subjunctive (ἃ ἐὰν θέλητε) points to a general possibility, a future eventuality "what you would" of — better? — "whatever you would"). In Rom 7,15b, however, by means of an indicative Paul speaks of what actually happens in the present (I do not do "what I want": ὃ θέλω). We should also mention the use of the first person singular in Rom 7,15b-16b whereas in Gal 5,17 the third person is employed in the three first clauses while in the fourth (v. 17d), quite suddenly, the second person plural appears and is found throughout the surrounding verses 16 and 18.

The main difference, however, is the function of these clauses in their respective context, i.e., in the line of thought. In Rom 7,13-25 Paul depicts the inner split in the "I". This "I" knows what is good, wants to do what is right and in its inmost self delights in the law of God. But evil lies close at hand; the "I" does the very thing it hates. The "I" does not understand its own actions. In utter powerlessness and despair Paul exclaims: "Wretched man that I am! Who will rescue me from this body of death?" (v. 24). In Romans 7 he most probably depicts the pre-Christian situation, the unredeemed state of the Jew and perhaps anyone's condition without Christ[4]. In Gal 5,13–6,10, on the other hand, Paul addresses his Christians in Galatia; he exhorts them. In 5,17d he does not explicitly say whether it is good or evil — or both — that they are unable to do; at any rate, they appear to be incapable of performing a desired act. The opposition between flesh and Spirit seems to aim at this: (literally) "in order that whatever you want (to do), these things you do not do"[5].

---

[3] In German: "anaphorisches Demonstrativ".

[4] Cf. J. LAMBRECHT, *The Wretched "I" and Its Liberation* (LouvTPM 14; Leuven 1992).

[5] BETZ, *Galatians*, 279-280, detects two "wills" in Rom 7 and in Gal 5,17 even three (the

Up to this point our findings are rather disturbing. In the context of Rom 7, where a preconversion situation is described, Paul admits that the inmost self of the human person wants to do what is right (vv. 18-23) and that his mind agrees that the law is good (v. 25), although this person is sold under sin (v. 14) and as matter of fact serves "the law of sin" (v. 25). In Gal 5–6, in a context of parenesis meant for the Christians in Galatia, the reader quite unexpectedly comes across 5,17 in which verse, if the above interpretation is accepted, Paul points to a hopeless blind alley, a dead-end. Within the Christian there is, according to v. 17, a fierce opposition put up by the lusting flesh and a Spirit which is just as insistent; there appears to be no way out. The reader asks: does the Spirit, after all, not prevail?

II. SEVERAL PROPOSALS

In Gal 5,17c ("for these are opposed to each other") ταῦτα resumes the desiring of the flesh and that of the Spirit (see v. 17ab). Flesh and the Spirit, or more concretely, their desires, are in conflict with each other. The aim of that conflict, or its result, is that "you Galatians" cannot do whatever you wish to do (v. 17d). In recent exegesis four main lines of interpretation can be distinguished[6].

A Stalemate Between Flesh and Spirit

According to this interpretation, the most obvious sense of v. 17d taken in itself is, it would seem, that one is unable to follow either the

---

"I", the "Spirit" and the "flesh"). For Betz the anthropological theory in Gal 5,17 — basically pre-Pauline in origin — is not integrated into the soteriological context of vv. 16 and 18 and, therefore, "it must be taken for what it says: the human body is a battefield on which the powers of the flesh and the Spirit fight against each other, so that the human will is disabled from carrying out its intentions" (280-281). Furthermore, Rom 7 is not simply the working out of Gal 5,17: "... we should assume that Paul's theological thinking did not stop between the letters, that because of new situations he encountered and new insights he gained, new efforts were required to state his position" (280).

[6] For a more detailed survey and bibliographical references, see BARCLAY, *Obeying the Truth*, 110-119; cf. also F.J. MATERA, *Galatians* (SP; Collegeville 1992) 206-207.

urging of the flesh or that of the Spirit. Flesh and Spirit frustrate each another; the consequence is a stalemate; no possibility of acting according to either one of these powers, of really and fully obeying either the flesh or the Spirit[7]. Yet for a Christian such a stalemate is the admission of defeat; there can be, after all, no victory of the Spirit over the flesh.

Verse 17, however, should not be isolated; it cannot be explained without its context. So most commentators consider what Paul says in this verse as an exaggeration for the sake of warning. Paul entreats the Galatians: "Walk by the Spirit and you will not gratify the desires of the flesh" (v. 16). The Christians, however, should not be naive; as long as they are in the body and live on earth the struggle will prove difficult. In each Christian, flesh and Spirit are diametrically opposed and do battle with each other. Therefore, the Galatians should take into account the all too real "not yet" of the eschatological reservation. What they can be assured of, however, is the fact that if they allow themselves to be led by the Spirit, they will not be under the domination of the law (cf. v. 18)[8]. Quite the contrary, through love of neighbor they will fulfil the whole law (cf. v. 14). True, according to this explanation the content of "whatever you would" in v. 17d is both good and evil; in its very wording the verse indicates a blockage. It is claimed, however, that one should not take v. 17d literally. What Paul says here is meant to emphasize the dangers of Christian moral life in this world and to add a motivating force to his exhortation, forceful as it is.

For M.-J. Lagrange πνεῦμα in v. 17 is not the Spirit of God (cf. 4,6) but the renewed spirit, i.e., the human spirit transformed by the divine

---

[7] Cf. E. DE WITT BURTON, *The Epistle to the Galatians* (ICC; Edinburgh 1921) 300-302: "Does the man choose evil, the Spirit opposes him; does he choose good, the flesh hinders him" (302); BETZ, *Galatians*, 279-281 (but see note 5); J. ROHDE, *Der Brief des Paulus an die Galater* (THNT; Berlin 1989) 234-235; R.N. LONGENECKER, *Galatians* (WBC; Dallas 1990) 245-246; A. VANHOYE, *Lettera ai Galati. Seconda parte* (Rome [3]1997) 221-222 (see our quotation in note 23); J.D.G. DUNN, *The Epistle to the Galatians* (BNTC; London 1993) 297-300: "... those things you want are associated with the desirings of *both* flesh *and* Spirit" (299). See also ALTHAUS, "... Dass ihr nicht tut, was ihr wollt", 15-16, who clearly describes (but rejects) "das jeweilige Wollen des Menschen" (15) and lists German exegetes who defend this majority opinion (Bengel, B. Weiss, Zahn, Schlatter, Oepke, Lietzmann, Schlier).

[8] Cf. F. MUSSNER, *Der Galaterbrief* (HTKNT; Freiburg–Basel–Wien 1974) 375-378: The flesh and the Spirit "kämpfen im Menschen um den Menschen. Der Mensch ist jedoch den beiden Mächten nicht einfach ausgeliefert; das 'Begehren' des Geistes bzw. des Fleisches stellt ihn vielmehr in eine Entscheidungssituation, in der er jeweils aufgerufen ist, 'das zu tun', wozu er getrieben wird. Wäre der Mensch machtlos zwischen beide Mächte gestellt und wäre er das nur passive Kampffeld zwischen Fleisch und Geist, dann hätten der Imperativ des Apostels in V 16 ... und die Aussage des V 18 keinen Sinn" (377-378).

Spirit. The contrast between flesh and spirit is a contrast within the human being; the opposition must be situated on the same level. In Catholic theology that spirit is termed "grace". In people on earth, Christian people included, too, fleshly tendencies and spiritual aspirations are continually in conflict[9]. A difficulty with this proposal is that it assumes a change from God's Spirit as described in 4,6 (and probably also in 5,16.18.22 and 25) to the human spirit in 5,17, although, of course, the presence of the Spirit in us cannot but transform our spirit[10].

Fleshly Desires

A number of interpreters prefer to take the expression "whatever you would" as pointing to the evil desires of the flesh: even Christians are tempted over and over again; even they may want to follow the cravings of the flesh. Paul does not repeat the verb ἐπιθυμεῖ in v. 17b. This verb, it is argued, should not be supplied since in v. 17a it is used in a negative sense ("to lust"). As in Rom 7,7-8 it most probably refers to fleshly sinful "covetousness"[11]. The presence of the Spirit in the Christians strongly opposes the flesh. This opposing drive frustrates those fleshly desires on the condition, of course, that one "walks by the Spirit" or "is guided by the Spirit": see vv. 16 and 18[12].

It must be recognized that this understanding does fit the context of 5,13-24. In v. 17 itself, however, there is nothing which indicates the victorious action of the Spirit. The verb ἐπιθυμέω of v. 17a is mentally supplied almost spontaneously in v. 17b[13] and, therefore, in both clauses its meaning is most probably neutral ("to desire"). Moreover, it would be rather strange that what the Galatian Christians want is always evil and

---

[9] M.-J. LAGRANGE *Epître aux Galates* (EtB; Paris 1918) 147-148: "Il y a donc entre les facultés humaines et l'Esprit de Dieu ce moyen terme qui est l'esprit participé, et que la théologie catholique nomme la grâce. C'est ici le sens le plus naturel, puisque les puissances sont affrontées dans l'homme" (147).

[10] For the human spirit, see the closing verse "your spirit" (Gal 6,18).

[11] Cf., e.g., B. CORSANI, *Lettera ai Galati* (Genova 1990) 353: "Sarebbe per lo meno singolare che Paolo usasse questo verbo per un soggetto come τὸ πνεῦμα".

[12] G.W. HANSEN, *Galatians* (IVP; Downers Grove, IL 1993) 170-171: Spirit-led Christians do not indulge their sinful nature (v. 13) nor gratify its desires (v. 16); they do not do the evil things they want to do; they are not "left without moral direction to do whatever they want" (171). This would also seem to be the position of CORSANI, *Galati*, 353-366 (esp. 355).

[13] DUNN, *Galatians*, 297: "to supply 'fights' ... is unwarranted".

wrong. Are we, therefore, left with the mutual opposition of flesh and Spirit as defended in the first proposal? The answer is: not necessarily.

Spirit-Inspired Wishes

Some commentators take the expression "whatever you would" the other way round: it perhaps refers to the good desires, to the urging of the Spirit. In their view Paul can hardly assume that, with its opposite desires, the flesh makes the activity of the Spirit unsuccessful since the immediate context militates against such an understanding. The repeated exhortations force us to suppose that a life guided by the Spirit must and can be lived in a Christian community[14].

But then the question should be asked again: does this approach take into account the outright opposition present in v. 17?

A Structureless Existence

In his valuable monograph "Obeying the Truth" John M.G. Barclay proposes to understand ἃ ἐὰν θέλητε as "(doing) whatever you want". By this expression Paul means a "structureless existence"[15]. However, since the Christians "are caught up into a warfare which determines their moral choices" such an existence is no longer possible. The Galatians cannot go from the flesh to the Spirit and back from the Spirit to the flesh. They must take sides. Or better, "they are already committed *to* some forms of activity (the Spirit) and *against* others (the flesh)"[16]. More than the written context it is Christian life itself that shows the way out.

---

[14] See more particularly, ALTHAUS, "... Dass ihr nicht tut, was ihr wollt" (with references to Luther and Calvin). R. BULTMANN, "Christus des Gesetzes Ende" (1940), ID., *Glauben und Verstehen II* (Tübingen 1952) 46, n. 6 (this interpretation "ist wohl vorzuziehen"); MODALSKI, "Gal. 2,19-21; 5,16-18", 30; D. LÜHRMANN, *Der Brief an die Galater* (ZBK; Zurich 1978) 88-89, translates: "was ihr (eigentlich) wollt" (88) and comments: "Über das Gesetz kommt der Mensch gerade nicht zur erhofften Identität mit sich selbst" (89). U. BORSE, *Der Brief an die Galater* (RNT; Regensburg 1984) 194-196, provides a rather loose paraphrase as translation: "damit ihr (eben) das tut, was ihr nicht wollt" (194); he explains and defends his version by referring to Rom 7 (195-196).

[15] BARCLAY, *Obeying the Truth*, 115. The Christians are not free "to live however they like", "to do whatever they want" (112). Cf. MATERA, *Galatians*, 207: "the dangerous position of libertinism, doing whatever they want".

[16] BARCLAY, *Obeying the Truth*, 115. "The warfare imagery is invoked not to indicate that the two sides are evenly balanced" (ibid.). Cf. MATERA, *Galatians*, 199-200 and 206-207; HANSEN, *Galatians*, 168-172 (but see also note 12); HONG, *The Law*, 185-186.

This interpretation brings us back to the comprehensive understanding of "whatever you would" in v. 17d: "structureless" means good or evil, right or wrong. However, the point of difference is that Barclay interprets the whole of v. 17 in a positive way.

III. WHAT YOU WANT TO DO

In Gal 5,16b the οὐ μή construction is almost certainly not the equivalent of an imperative[17]. With this emphatic negative the construction expresses the result if the imperative of v. 16a is obeyed: walk by the Spirit, and thus you will in no way yield to the desires of the flesh. Verse 17 contains two γάρ-clauses. The first one ("for the flesh desires against the Spirit", v. 17a) grounds the whole of v. 16; more specifically, by pointing to the "desiring" activity of the flesh, it provides the reason why the Galatians must "walk by the Spirit"[18]. Verse 17b adds the antithetic remark introduced with δέ: "but the Spirit against the flesh". The second γάρ-clause (v. 17cd)[19] further explains v. 17ab: for these (i.e., flesh and Spirit) oppose each other lest you do whatever you wish[20]. It would seem that the ἵνα μή+ subjunctive clause (v. 17d) directly depends on v. 17c, not on the whole of v. 17abc. It is not immediately clear whether verse 17d still possesses a purpose force ("in order that") or, more probably, simply points to the result ("so that")[21]. Verse 18 consists of a conditional period: "but if you are led by the Spirit, you are not under the law". This last expression, ὑπὸ νόμου, probably indicates the law obligations which, according to Paul, no

---

[17] BARCLAY, *Obeying the Truth*, 111, n. 10.

[18] In this reading the causal (and warning) force of γάρ is expressed in the first clause and not, as often in a μὲν γὰρ ... δέ–construction, in the second clause. Cf. M. ZERWICK, *Biblical Greek* (Rome 1963) nos. 474-477.

[19] The variant reading δέ for this second γάρ is almost certainly secondary. According to MUSSNER, *Galaterbrief*, 176, n. 16, γάρ is "sicher ursprünglich".

[20] See LONGENECKER, *Galatians*, 245: "The neutral plural pronoun ταῦτα ('these things,' 'entities') refers back to 'the flesh' and 'the Spirit,' treating them now more as 'things' or 'entities' than personal forces".

[21] See ZERWICK, *Biblical Greek*, no. 352; BARCLAY, *Obeying the Truth*, 112, who quotes C.F.D. MOULE, *An Idiom Book of New Testament Greek* (Cambrige ²1959) 142, describing the "Semitic mind" as "notoriously unwilling to draw a sharp dividing line between purpose and consequence". Often the terms "telic" and "ecbatic" are used. To see in v. 17d a divine intention, as ROHDE, *Galater*, 234, does ("von Gott her bezweckt"), is most probably misguided.

one is able to carry out and which therefore lead to transgressions and sin, condemnation and curse (cf. e.g., 3,10 and Rom 3,19-20 and 23)[22].

A. Vanhoye stresses that ὃ ἐὰν θέλητε means "'whatever' you would"[23]. He explains the content of such a "wanting" as containing both good and evil: "il nostro sogno sarebbe di poter soddisfare tutti i nostri impulsi successivi, il desiderio di vivere comodamente e il desiderio di essere generosi, il desiderio dei piaceri di ogni genere, sessuali, sensuali, e il desiderio della gioia spirituale e dell'amore puro"[24]. One is inclined, however, to ask whether the claim regarding the ἄν (or ἐάν) with the subjunctive can be pressed here. True, by itself such a construction points to the future[25] and, therefore, the matter remains indeterminate and universal. Does it necessarily mean "whatever" or "whatsoever"? To be sure, the relative pronoun ἅ is without antecedent. Moreover, the resumptive demonstrative pronoun ταῦτα does not exclude a possible universal sense in the previous clause. However, in addition to Rom 7,15c, Paul employs the construction with an indeterminate relative pronoun and subjunctive, followed by a resumptive pronoun, in two more passages, namely in Gal 6,7: ὃ ἐὰν σπείρῃ, τοῦτο καὶ θερίσει, and in 1 Cor 16,3: οὓς ἐὰν δοκιμάσητε, ... τούτους πέμψω. "Whatever" and "whoever" may be a correct rendering, yet in both cases the indeterminate and general character of the relative pronoun should not be unduly emphasized. The translation "what" (or "that which") in Gal 6,7[26] and "(those) who" in 1 Cor 6,7 is equally appropriate. The same, I presume, applies to Gal 5,17d[27].

---

[22] See, e.g., J. LAMBRECHT, *Pauline Studies* (BETL 115; Leuven 1994) 271-298: "Curse and Blessing: A Study of Galatians 3,10-14".

[23] VANHOYE, *Galati*, 221-222: "occorre tradurre con precisione *ha ean thelēte*; non significa semplicemente 'ciò che volete', ma 'tutto ciò che vorreste' (*an* con il congiuntivo ha questo senso)" (221). No doubt "vorreste" is the correct translation of the construction. In Paul's text, however, there is neither πάντα ("tutto") nor ἅτινα (cf. 5,19).

[24] Ibid., 221.

[25] Cf. J.H. MOULTON, *A Grammar of New Testament Greek. Vol. III: Syntax* (by N. TURNER; Edinburgh 1963) 106-110; A.T. ROBERTSON, *A Grammar of the Greek New Testament in the Light of Historical Research* (London 1914) 957: "The subjunctive with the indefinite relative ... is futuristic", and hence indeterminate and universal.

[26] See the opposition between "sowing to the flesh" and "sowing to the Spirit" in Gal 6,8, but there is no stalemate. The two results are indicated: "reaping corruption" and "reaping eternal life". Compare the indicative in Gal 6,12: ὅσοι θέλουσιν ..., οὗτοι ἀναγκάζουσιν ....

[27] MATERA, *Galatians*, 109, translates: "so that you cannot do whatever you want". He brings together five English translations: "to prevent you from doing what you would" (RSV); "to prevent you from doing what you want" (NRSV); "so that you may not do what you want" (NAB); "so that what you will do you cannot do" (NEB); "so that you cannot do what you want" (REB) (109-200). All have "what". Equally the *Lutherbibel* translates: "so dass ihr nicht tut, 'was' ihr wollt", and the *Einheitsübersetzung*: "so dass ihr nicht imstande seid, das zu tun, 'was' ihr wollt".

The content of ἅ in v. 17d remains general and vague, even if, as we believe, that content is positive. Moreover, the present tense of the verb in the subjunctive (ἅ ἐὰν) θέλητε points to continuation in the future; by itself the verb θέλω may have either a neutral or a negative or a positive direct object. All this is true. In Gal 5,17d, however, Paul speaks to the Galatians in the second person plural: "what you want". One can, it would seem, correctly assume that as Christians they want and wish to do what is right, not "whatsoever they would".

This is confirmed by the parallel passage in Rom 7, even though here the "I" is not yet a Christian. There can be no doubt that in Rom 7,15.18.19 and 21 the "I" wants what is good and right: see ἀγαθόν (v. 19) and τὸ καλόν (v. 21). The "I" delights in the law of God (v. 22). With regard to evil (κακόν, v. 21) Paul explicitly states that he does not want it: see οὐ θέλω in vv. 16.19 and 20. Because of the presence of the relative pronoun taken up by the determinative pronoun (see also γάρ) Rom 7,19 is very instructive: οὐ γὰρ ὃ θέλω ποιῶ ἀγαθόν, ἀλλὰ ὃ οὐ θέλω κακὸν τοῦτο πράσσω[28]. Even the preconversion "I" only wants to do what is good[29]. Earlier, in Rom 7,15-16, the context fills the double indeterminate ὃ unequivocally with two opposing ideas: wanting what is good, not wanting what is wrong. The "I" wants only what is good and right.

What is then the flow of thought in Gal 5,16-18? After the commandment and the ensuing assurance of v. 16, the grounding clause of v. 17a emphasizes the fact that in their Christian existence, as long as they live in the body, the desires of the flesh remain dangerously active[30]. Verse 17b then completes the one-sided picture of v. 17a: there is, of course, also the contrastive urging of the indwelling Spirit. In v. 17cd Paul adds: the opposition of flesh and Spirit is so strong that — without a determined resolution[31] — "you Galatians" would not be able to do the good you want to do.

---

[28] Cf. also Gal 2,18: εἰ γὰρ ἃ κατέλυσα ταῦτα πάλιν οἰκοδομῶ. K. BEYER, Semitische Syntax des Neuen Testaments (StUNT 1; Göttingen 1962) 171, writes about the resumptive demonstrative pronoun in the accusative: "Hier handelt es sich wohl um einen Gräzismus, da dies im Semitischen ganz selten ist" (see also p. 175).

[29] On the difference between Rom 7 and Gal 5, see J.M.S. BALJON, Exegetisch-kritische verhandeling over den brief van Paulus aan de Galaten (Leiden 1889) 243: "Daar is de νοῦς gebonden onder de macht van de σάρξ. Hier evenwel niet. Hier is alleen strijd". Cf. ALTHAUS, "... Dass ihr nicht tut, was ihr wollt", 16-18: "Das Subjekt des 'was ihr wollt' ist der von Gott geschaffener Mensch .... Die Erlösung des Menschen durch den Geist Jesu Christi knüpft an die Schöpfung ... an" (18).

[30] Paul seems to refer to the deficiencies in the Galatian churches (see, e.g., 5,15), but any Christian reader of this text recognizes the inner conflicts and the all too frequent moral defeats.

[31] The idea is not to be found in v. 17 but must be mentally supplied because of the immediate context.

However, if you are really led by the Spirit, you are not under the law and everything will be all right (cf. v. 18 with δέ at the beginning).

According to this paraphrase verse 17 functions as a stern warning. The motivating clause of v. 17a introduces a rather abstract anthropological consideration which is further worked out in v. 17bc. For a moment, as it were, Paul forgets the Christian moral choice which the Galatians are supposed to renew. Just as in 6,8, so also in 5,17abc the third person is used. It is only at v. 17d that Paul returns to the second person and makes the Galatians realize what would happen without a positive choice and the necessary inward discipline, without the personally accepted effective guidance of the Spirit: you would be unable to do the good you — even as ordinary human beings, but certainly as Christians — want to do[32].

In sum, I think that the third proposal of part II of this note should be explained along the lines suggested in part III[33]. We can be permitted, I believe, to suppose that the Spirit-filled Christians in Galatia want to do the right things. To be sure, they are in need of admonition and exhortation. In a realistic way Paul reminds them of their somewhat fragile condition. He points to the eschatological tension between the "already" and the "not yet", between the indicative and the imperative. They are still in the body; they yet live in this world. Some of these Gentile Christians are attracted to the "works of the law". But, as Paul has been arguing at great length in this letter, that is not a solution. On the contrary, the Spirit alone constitutes the really "empowering presence"[34]. Therefore, "if we live by the Spirit, let us also walk by the Spirit" (v. 25). It would seem that Gal 5,17, properly understood, fits very well into this context of admonition.

---

[32] Cf. A. OEPKE, "Irrwege in der neueren Paulusforschung", *ThLZ* 77 (1952) 449-458, answering Althaus (see our note 2): As long as one remains between the two forces one does not do what one "eigentlich, seiner schöpfungsgemäss gesetzten und vom Geist erneuerten Natur nach" (458) wills. See also the rather free rendering in the *Gute Nachricht Bibel*: "so dass ihr von euch aus das Gute nicht tun könnt, das ihr doch eigentlich wollt". H.M. RIDDERBOS, *The Epistle of Paul to the Churches of Galatia* (NICNT; Grand Rapids 1953) 203-204, likewise sees the content of "what you want to do" as positive ("by virtue of the new man" in the Christians). Yet as far as v. 17 is concerned he speaks of "an irreconcilable conflict", of the fact that Christian life, too, "is subject to a penetrating, internal dualism. Still, this is not the last thing that can be said of the matter. It is not passivity but action that is in order ...". Ridderbos then refers to vv. 16 and 18.

[33] See note 14 (cf. especially the strong defense by Althaus almost 50 years ago).

[34] Cf. the title of G. FEE's book: *God's Empowering Presence. The Holy Spirit in the Letters of Paul* (Peabody, MA 1994).

Additional Note:

See now also the remarks by J. KILGALLEN, "The Strivings of the Flesh ... (Galatians 5,17)", *Bib* 80 (1999) 113-114.

Biblica 78 (1997) 33-56

19

Paul's Coherent Admonition in Galatians 6,1-6
Mutual Help and Individual Attentiveness

A number of publications have explained the short passage Galatians 6,1-6 in quite different ways. What are the main difficulties in this text and how should one proceed to find a way out of the problems and come to a well-founded understanding of this passage? Let us first give a working translation of these six verses, as literally as possible.

1a   Brothers, if a person is overtaken in some transgression,
 b   you who are spiritual, you must restore such [a person] in a spirit of gentleness,
 c   while looking to yourselves, so that you too may not be tempted.
2a   Bear one another's burdens,
 b   and so you will fulfil the law of Christ.
3a   For if anyone thinks that he is something, when [in fact] he is nothing,
 b   he deludes himself.
4a   But let each put his own work to the test,
 b   and then he will have a matter for boasting only regarding himself and not regarding the other.
5   For each must bear his own load.
6   However, let the one who is taught the Word share in all good things with the one who teaches.

The first part of this study will point out, with the aid of recent approaches, three serious problems. In the second part, an analysis of the text will be offered. The third part will try to indicate Paul's coherent reasoning in this passage.

I. THREE DIFFICULTIES

There is a double restriction in this study. First, only Gal 6,1-6 is dealt with and not, e.g., the whole of the pericope 5,25–6,10 (or the even larger unit 5,13–6,10)[1]. Second, within this subunit not all items will be treated[2]. We limit ourselves to three of them because they seem to be important and, moreover, they have quite lately been approached in a way which can hardly be agreed upon.

No Coherent Argument in Gal 6,1-6?

It is generally assumed that in many of his exhortations Paul is not pointing to particular situations existing in the churches addressed, but is rather using traditional, although not specifically Christian, material[3.] Because of the absence of actual concerns, little coherent reasoning or train of thought can be expected in such exhortative passages. It would seem, moreover, that in Gal 6,1-6 several aphorisms are present. In his commentary H.D. Betz gathered a wealth of *non verbatim* parallels from Greco-Roman literature[4]. How could one suppose a strictly logical connection or a sustained train of thought in such a combination of sayings? Betz finds in 5,25–6,10 a "collection of *sententiae*"[5]. He sees some structure but no coherent, unitary argumentation[6]. Paul has assembled sayings which are

---

[1] Cf., e.g., the recently published study of W. SCHRAGE, "Probleme paulinischer Ethik anhand von Gal 5,25–6,10", A. VANHOYE (ed.), *La foi qui par l'amour agit. Galates 4,1–6,16* (Benedictina 13; Rome 1996) 155-194 and "Diskussion" on pp. 194-200. On pp. 166-169 the author discusses "Gliederung und Abgrenzung".

[2] Our study is, therefore, very different from that of, e.g., R.B. HAYS, "Christology and Ethics in Galatians: The Law of Christ", *CBQ* 49 (1987) 268-290. For an even more general treatment, see J.G. BARCLAY, *Obeying the Truth: A Study of Paul's Ethics in Galatians* (Edinburgh 1988); regarding 5,26–6,10, see esp. 146-177.

[3] For a good presentation of "usuelle und aktuelle Paränese" in Paul (beginning with M. Dibelius), see SCHRAGE, "Probleme", 160-166.

[4] H.D. BETZ, *Galatians. A Commentary on Paul's Letter to the Churches in Galatia* (Hermeneia; Philadelphia 1979). For Gal 6,1-6, see 295-306. In each verse of this brief pericope Betz finds a maxim (or *sententia* or 'gnome'). Often this saying stands on its own and little of it is specifically Christian. Paul conforms his position to the ethical thought of his contempories (no exaggerated or extreme behavior), although, of course, all is taken up within the Christian context of Paul's letter (see 292-293).

[5] *Galatians*, 291. Betz constantly refers to contemporary Jewish and especially Hellenistic traditions and to the *topoi* of diatribe literature. Cf. BARCLAY, *Obeying the Truth*, 147-148 and 170-172. In his book Barclay also discusses briefly the influence of Dibelius and his views on parenesis.

[6] *Galatians*, 292: "The sequence is neither uncoordinated nor overly systematized; some connection is provided by language and logic". Cf., e.g., F.J. MATERA, *Galatians* (SP; Collegeville 1992) 217: "The internal structure of this material [in 6,1-10] presents a problem.

but loosely related to one another[7]. As is well known, Betz' commentary has influenced a great number of exegetes.

In his 1995 study, "The Holy Spirit and the Human Spirit in Galatians (Gal 5,17)", J.C. O'Neill takes Betz's view to the extreme[8]. To be sure, the main point of O'Neill's article is the claim that in 5,13–6,10 Paul refers to the Holy Spirit less often than is usually thought. He is convinced that "this section was originally a Jewish collection of moral aphorisms that was later incorporated into Paul's epistle"[9]. In the 24 verses he (now) detects no less than 25 "originally separate sayings"[10]. They are connected by catchwords, not by structured argument[11]. "The place where this can be seen most clearly is in Gal 6,2 and 6,5. Two true proverbs, each superficially contradicting the other, are simply plonked down without any attempt at explanation: 'Bear one another's burdens' and 'Let each bear one's own burden'"[12]. O'Neill insists that we read such verses as though they stood isolated and alone; they are not related by logic. So, there is no connected, coherent argument in 5,13–6,10. The unavoidable consequence of this is that the context cannot help the exegete in trying to understand the particular verse, i.e., the aphorism. "Each saying must be taken by itself if it is to yield its secret"[13].

This is our first major question: Is it true that in 6,1-6 Paul is but a col-

---

While it is apparent that this unit contains a number of maxims, it is not clear how or if these maxims are related to each other".

[7] Cf., e.g., F. MUSSNER, *Der Galaterbrief* (HTKNT; Freiburg 1974), 396: What life according to the Spirit means "wird ... an ... lose miteinander zusammenhängenden Paränesen und Beispielen gezeigt ..." (but see the opposite conclusion on 402: "Es zeigt sich zurückschauend, dass 5,26–6,5 einen zusammengehörenden Komplex darstellt ..."; T. SÖDING, *Das Liebesgebot bei Paulus. Die Mahnung zur Agape im Rahmen der paulinischen Ethik* (NTA 26; Münster 1995) 192: "die lockere Disposition" of 5,13–6,10. B. CORSANI, *Lettera ai Galati* (Genova 1990) 378, comes to the same opinion, be it in a somewhat different way. — For a thoroughly citical discussion of Betz, see BARCLAY, *Obeying the Truth*, 170-177; cf. G.D. FEE, *God's Empowering Presence: The Holy Spirit in the Letters of Paul* (Peabody, MA 1994) 459-460.

[8] J.C. O'NEILL, "The Holy Spirit and the Human Spirit in Galatians (Gal 5,17)", *ETL* 71 (1995) 107-120.

[9] O'NEILL, "The Holy Spirit", 117.

[10] O'NEILL, "The Holy Spirit", 112. See Table I on 119-120. In *The Recovery of Paul's Letter to the Galatians* (London 1972), O'Neill found but 19 sayings. For a critque of this publication, see BARCLAY, *Obeying the Truth*, 9-10 and 147. Cf. also A. VANHOYE, "Paraclèse et doctrine pauliniennes: désaccord ou accord?", ID. (ed.), *La foi qui par l'amour agit*, 201-218, esp. 205.

[11] See the numbered catchwords in Tables I and II of O'NEILL, "The Holy Spirit", 119-121.

[12] O'NEILL, "The Holy Spirit", 112.

[13] O'NEILL, "The Holy Spirit", 112.

lector pasting together sentences — warnings, words of encouragement, counsels — and that Paul is not really an author who mounts an argument and writes connectedly?[14].

No Boasting in Verse 4?

The second major difficulty concerns v. 4 and, more in particular, the theme of boasting. Having read this verse, one immediately asks how Paul can write that, after putting to the test one's own work, a Christian will have a matter for boasting while in 6,14 the same Paul speaks of himself and declares: "far be it from me to boast except in the cross of our Lord Jesus Christ". Is all boasting, except for that in God and Christ and in his cross, not to be rejected? We must, however, add at once that in v. 4 there is not only the mention of a previous condition, namely the testing of one's own work, but also the limitation εἰς ἑαυτὸν μόνον ... καὶ οὐκ εἰς τὸν ἕτερον, and admit that the meaning of these last phrases is not clear at all.

But does Paul consider the possibility of boasting of one's own work? In his 1986 contribution to the *Festschrift* for Heinrich Greeven, "Werkruhm und Christusruhm im Galaterbrief", G. Klein vehemently denies this possibility[15]. His admittedly complex opinion[16] is clear: "Dass Paulus ... jedwedem Ruhm der Werke als Gipfel der Blasphemie widerstanden hat, wird durch Gal 6,4 nicht dementiert, sondern bestätigt"[17].

Klein sees verses 1-5 as a text unit and thus disagrees here with Betz. Yet, what in v. 1a appears to be an isolated case ("if anyone ...") is broadened in vv. 2-5 to the whole Christian community. Moreover, "lest you be tempted" in v. 1c is only a secondary topic, while in vv. 2-5 the human sinful condition becomes the main theme[18]. According to Klein, between v. 1

---

[14] O'NEILL, "The Holy Spirit", 116-117, is even of the opinion that it was not Paul himself but "librarians of the communities" in the Jewish diaspora who added that kind of material to Paul's authentic letters. But here one must pause and ask: Is this still a sound exegetical approach or have we entered into speculations and pure fantasy?

[15] G. KLEIN, "Werkruhm und Christusruhm im Galaterbrief und die Frage nach einer Entwicklung des Paulus. Ein hermeneutischer und exegetischer Zwischenruf", W. SCHRAGE (ed.), *Studien zum Text und zur Ethik des Neuen Testaments. Fs. H. Greeven* (BZNW 47; Berlin 1986) 196-211.

[16] We cannot deal here with the position of H. Hübner which Klein wants to refute. Cf. H. HÜBNER, *Das Gesetz bei Paulus. Ein Beitrag zum Werden der paulinischen Theologie* (FRLANT 119; Göttingen ³1982).

[17] KLEIN, "Werkruhm", 211; for the whole treatment of Gal 6,4, see esp. 202-209.

[18] Cf. KLEIN, "Werkruhm", 203: "Das, was v. 1 einleitend am Einzelfall vor Augen rückt, erscheint in v. 2ff. mit gewisser Akzentverlagerung ins Grundsätzliche erhoben".

and v. 2 there is a qualitative change, "ein qualitativer Sprung", from sinful actions to radical sinfulness which, before possible deeds, already perverts the roots of human nature themselves[19]. In v. 2 one must assume that for Paul all Christians have their "burdens". It would be wrong to refer to v. 1 and, because of its *eventualis* form ("only in case that"), speculate about the possibility that some Christians are without sin and do not need the help of their fellow Christians. If Paul in v. 2 commits every Christian to mutual help, this means that every Christian has some "burden" (of sinfulness) and is, therefore, in need of help of others[20].

Hence, Klein strongly opposes a conditional interpretation of the participial clause μηδὲν ὤν in v. 3a. There is no way of understanding this clause so as to permit exceptions ("in the case that one is nothing"), as if there could be some Christians (or, for that matter, some human beings) who before God "are something". No, everyone, as soon as he thinks he is something, deceives himself, since in fact he is nothing. "To be nothing" points to "eine Grundbefindlichkeit ..., die den Christen wie jeden Menschen prägt"[21].

But how does Klein then understand the "work" of v. 4a and "the (reason or ground or basis for) boasting" of v. 4b? He maintains that the text of the first half of this verse does not allow one to supply the condition "and if the result of the testing is positive, then ...". According to Paul, each testing will, as it were, automatically lead to boasting[22]. Yet that boasting will take place "before, in front of" the boasting person alone (εἰς ἑαυτὸν μόνον), not before or in front of the other (οὐκ εἰς τὸν ἕτερον), i.e., not by comparison with the work of the other[23]. The double εἰς-construction does not point to the object of boasting, but to the "forum" for which the boasting occurs[24]. Now, in Klein's opinion, since boasting in itself implies

---

[19] A more extended quotation may prove useful: "indem Paulus ... ein zunächst moralisch geprägten Sündenverständnis hinter sich lässt, steuert er die gerade für Christen stets aktuelle Einsicht an, dass Sünde sich nicht in der Untat ... erschöpft, ja erst dort endgültig triumphiert, wo sie nicht bloss einzelne Taten, sondern das Sein des Menschen entstellt" (KLEIN, "Werkruhm", 205).

[20] Cf. KLEIN, "Werkruhm", 205: "der Terminus τὰ βάρη hat ... als Oberbegriff zu gelten, der die unmoralische zusammen mit der moralischen Spielart der Sünde unter sich befasst".

[21] KLEIN, "Werkruhm", 206. Cf. SCHRAGE, "Probleme", 190: "Paulus sagt ..., dass überhaupt kein Mensch von sich aus etwas ist. Das konzessive μηδὲν ὤν gilt also grundsätzlich".

[22] Cf. KLEIN, "Werkruhm", 208.

[23] Cf. KLEIN, "Werkruhm", 205: not "durch einen der eigenen Korrektheit gewissen Vergleich mit den anderen".

[24] KLEIN, "Werkruhm", 209: "das καύχημα gilt vor dem Forum des Gerichtstages". See Phil 2,16.

a public forum of others, the testing of one's own work cannot provide a real ground of boasting. Thus, within this line of reasoning, even in v. 4 boasting of one's work is radically excluded. Klein's explanation of v. 4 rejoins that of v. 3: "ein frommes εἶναί τι bleibt allemal imaginär"[25].

One should not wonder, therefore, that "kein ἔργον je ein wirkliches καύχημα verschafft" to the individual Christian[26]. Through self-testing each Christian reaches a consciousness of nothingness; each also realizes that everyone has to carry his or her own load (v. 5). So it becomes equally evident how in their sinfulness all Christians need the help of their fellow Christians (cf. v. 2).

After listening critically to this subtle and specious explanation one cannot but ask whether an interpretation which declares that in v. 4 — against the obvious meaning — all boasting is excluded still respects the text, and what Paul means by it. Yet the difficulty of how to understand Paul's words in this verse remains, especially in view of the clearly opposite statement in v. 14.

Not Everyday Worries in Verse 5?

The third difficulty is called by D.W. Kuck in his recent study a "relatively modest *crux*" which is, however, "bound up closely with one's understanding of all of Gal 6.1-5, the rhetorical logic of which has been far from clear to interpreters"[27]. Kuck vigorously defends the eschatological interpretation of v. 5. Each person will bring his or her own work to God and God will judge it on the last day. He defends this position with the following five points.

(1) This understanding is not new. Other exegetes, probably a slight majority, have chosen this interpretation[28]. Augustine, too, read the verse in this way. (2) With its mention of the presentation of one's own work (=

---

[25] KLEIN, "Werkruhm", 209. Cf. W. HARNISCH, "Einübung des neuen Seins. Paulinische Paränese am Beispiel des Galaterbriefes", *ZThK* 84 (1987) 279-296, esp. 295 (independently from Klein, see n. 45). According to Harnisch, verse 4 has "einen unverkennbaren *ironischen Klang*". Boasting without a forum is impossible. Verse 4 is a "contradictio in adiecto" (n. 45).

[26] KLEIN, "Werkruhm", 209.

[27] D.W. KUCK, "'Each will bear his own burden': Paul's Creative Use of an Apocalyptic Motif", *NTS* 40 (1994) 289-298, quotation on p. 289.

[28] KUCK, "Burden", 289, n. 2 (the defenders of the non-eschatological meaning are also mentioned in this note).

burden) to God, verse 5 provides a climactic motivation against boasting in the community[29]. (3) There are a number of Jewish and Christian texts which stress final individual judgment (over against a mistaken confidence in belonging to the community). 4 Ezra 7.104-5 is a striking passage, indeed, since it has "both a parallel to the 'burden-bearing' language referring to God's judgment and an example of tendency to see final judgment in individual rather than corporate terms"[30]. (4) Within the immediate context of Gal 6,5, Paul speaks of the final individual judgment (see 5,21 and 6,7-9). Even more telling is that in 5,10 he announces the future judgment of troublemakers and employs the same verb βαστάζω, also in the future tense[31]. (5) Finally, the "emphasis on the judgement of individual Christians on the basis of their work in the Lord's church comes up frequently in Paul"[32]. In particular, Kuck draws attention to two longer passages, Rom 14,1-12 and 1 Cor 3,5–4,5, and briefly analyzes them[33].

According to Kuck, in vv. 4-5 Paul refers to an individual's work, which involves personal pride but cannot be used for boasting by a comparison with the work of others; it is at the same time a "load" or "burden" to be presented to God for evaluation and judgment. Yet, is verse 5 strictly eschatological, and are "work" (v. 4) and "load" (v. 5) identical?

II. ANALYSIS OF THE TEXT

A twofold analysis is to be done. Can a first general consideration of the text and the context already point to a certain coherence of 6,1-6? In view of the difficulties mentioned in the first part, what are the exegetical data of the individual verses?

---

[29] Cf. KUCK, "Burden", 294: "The principal argument in favour of taking Gal 6.5 as a reference to the eschatological judgment of God is that the flow of thought leads to this climax".

[30] KUCK, "Burden", 295.

[31] Cf. KUCK, "Burden", 295-296.

[32] KUCK, "Burden", 296.

[33] KUCK, "Burden", 297, concludes as follows: "Each [passage] is a reflection by Paul on the theme of the dynamics between the self-regard of the individual Christian and the harmony of the community. In each case, Paul grounds the individual attitude in the promise and threat of a particular judgment of one's Christian work, with appropriate rewards or loss of rewards".

The Passage 6,1-6

The exhortation in 5,16, "walk by the Spirit and do not gratify the desires of the flesh", is followed in vv. 17-23 by an exposition which depicts two opposite ways of life. Verse 24 concludes this passage: "Those who belong to Christ Jesus have crucified the flesh with its passions and desires".

The admonition starts again in v. 25: "If we live by the Spirit, let us also walk by the Spirit". This is a quite general injunction. Verse 26, however, provides a first (negative) application: "Let us have no self-conceit, no provoking of one another, no envy of one another". In 6,1, it would seem that Paul presents the positive alternative: "(But,) brothers, let us, in a spirit of gentleness, (rather) restore a fellow Christian who is overtaken by some transgression". One could call this verse a second application or concretization of 5,25[34]. It is introduced, not without emphasis, by the vocative "brothers"[35]. 6,6 constitutes then a third command: "Let him who is taught the Word share all good things with him who teaches". The fourth exhortation, "be not deceived", in v. 7 is general and so is the fifth one in 6,9-10, which is, as it were, all-encompassing: "Let us not grow weary in well-doing ... let us do good to all ...". But is this enumeration the appropriate method for reaching a global view of the pericope?

Not everything in 5,25–6,10 is an exhortation. Some verses contain a clarification and then a reflection or motivation[36]. One can refer to the eschatologically oriented considerations in 6,7b-8. But it would seem that also within 6,2-6 a clarifying development of the injunction of mutual assistance is presented. Verse 2a takes up and generalizes the order of v. 1b.

---

[34] According to E. DE WITT BURTON, *The Epistle to the Galatians* (ICC; Edinburgh 1921) 326, the (ἐάν) καί ("nevertheless") of v. 1a also connects with what precedes: "the case of one who should nevertheless fail to obey this injunction" (= v. 26).

[35] Cf. BETZ, *Galatians*, 295.

[36] It may be interesting to have a look at the persons and their arrangement:

5,25-26	first plural
6,1-2	second plural (third sing. in 1a; sec. sing. in 1c)
6,3-6	third singular
6,7a	second plural
6,7b-8	third singular
6,9-10	first plural

"Plural" points to "corporate responsibility", "singular" to "individual accountability". Cf. a similar presentation by BARCLAY, *Obeying the Truth*, 149-150; taken over by G.F. WESSELS, "The Call to Responsible Freedom in Paul's Persuasive Strategy. Galatians 5:13–6,10", *Neotest* 26 (1992) 461-473, esp. 470-471.

Verse 3, introduced by "for", appears to resume and reflect upon the warning of v. 1c. In its own way, verse 4a offers by means of a specific precept an alternative behavior, opposite to that of v. 3a; it is introduced by "but". Although we do not see immediately how verse 5 is logically connected with what precedes it[37], the verb "to bear" is the same as in v. 2 and "load" indicates the generic category of which "burdens" (= heavy loads, weights) in v. 2 are but a specification. There seems to be a contradiction between these two verses as far as content is concerned, but the data just mentioned, together with the motivating γάρ in v. 5, strongly suggest that this last verse belongs to the text unit which begins at 6,1. Although verse 6, with its expression "to teach the Word" and its double use of κατηχέω, sounds more specifically Christian, it is connected to v. 5 by δέ and presents itself as a further qualification.

The presence of at least some logical coherence within 6,1-6 is thus intimated by this first analysis of the argument[38]. The coherence is confirmed by several factors: the vocative "brothers" at the beginning of v. 1; the causal particle γάρ in both v. 3 and v. 5; the possible oppositional particle δέ in v. 4 as well as in v. 6. Furthermore there is what seems to be an *inclusio* by means of the verb βαστάζω, as well as "burdens" and load", in v. 2 and v. 5 respectively. And we have, moreover, a new beginning in v. 7, a quite general and negative injunction. Yet a more detailed exegesis of the individual verses is needed.

Exegesis of the Individual Verses

The following explanation of Gal 6,1-6 will not be exhaustive. A more detailed comment should be given only in so far as it is helpful for the solution of the three problems indicated in the first part of this study, i.e., the line of thought in this pericope, Paul's boasting, and the so-called eschatological reference in v. 5.

Verse 1. In Paul, the vocative "brothers" does not always stand at the beginning of a passage, but it certainly manifests here an insistence on the

---

[37] Cf. BETZ, *Galatians*, 303. But see FEE, *God's Empowering Presence*, 461-462, and his defense of the meaning of "Spirit-led Galatians" (cf. 5,18).

[38] Even BETZ writes about 5,25–6,10: "At first sight the collection appears confused, but it is not without organization and structure. Most likely Paul himself is the composer of the individual *sententiae*, a fact which demonstrates his abilities as a gnomic poet" (*Galatians*, 291).

injunction which follows. The new start of 6,1 is but a relative or a minor one[39]. For Paul's use of πνευματικοί[40] and ἐν πνεύματι πραΰτητος connects this verse with 5,25 where the "Spirit" is mentioned twice. Moreover, as already stated, there may be a conscious link which, in a slight paraphrase of 5,26–6,1, runs as follows: "You, Spirit-filled people, must not be vainglorious, not provoke nor envy one another; you should rather restore the brother who is overtaken by a transgression"[41]. Of course, the word "rather" is not expressed. Yet, the injunction of mutual help as an alternative to provocation and envy does make sense; it was probably present in Paul's mind. This would confirm the view that "brothers" does not function as a completely new beginning.

In v. 1a the protasis (ἐάν plus the subjunctive) is an *eventualis* form: "in the case that". By means of it Paul points to the possibility — if not to the probability — of transgressions in the Galatian churches. The verb of v. 1b, "restore", is an imperative present and reflects a rule that is to be observed always. "Surprisingly, Paul does no seem overly concerned with the offense itself, but his concern is more with the possibility that the handling of such a case might become a source of evil for those who administer it" (see v. 1c)[42]. It is worth noting that, formally speaking, the participle of v. 1c should have been in the plural. Paul suddenly changes to the second person singular: σκοπῶν σεαυτὸν μὴ καὶ σὺ πειρασθῇς. That second person singular is emphatic and, through it, every Christian in Galatia is being addressed[43]. The third person singular will predominate in vv. 3-6: anyone, each one, his own work. One rightly tends to think that the temptation of which v. 1c speaks refers to the same fault as that which is supposed in v. 1a[44].

Verse 2. There is no connecting particle between v. 1 and v. 2. This asyndetic construction is not a real break but supposes a logical link with

---

[39] Cf., e.g., BETZ, *Galatians*, 295; SCHRAGE, "Probleme", 168-169.

[40] Cf. the overview of possible meanings of πνευματικοί in J.D.G. DUNN, *The Epistle to the Galatians* (BNTC; London 1993) 319-320.

[41] Cf. FEE, *God's Empowering Presence*, 460, n. 321. The verb προλαμβάνομαι here presumably means "to be taken by surpise" by the fault (BURTON, *Galatians*, 326-327) or "entrapped by sin". Dunn and others prefer "to be detected": "has been discovered (unexpectedly) in the act of some 'transgression'" by fellow Christians (DUNN, *Galatians*, 319).

[42] BETZ, *Galatians*, 291; cf. DUNN, *Galatians*, 321; HARNISCH, "Einübung", 293.

[43] See SCHRAGE, "Probleme", 165, n. 19 (cf. Calvin and Erasmus).

[44] Otherwise, e.g., BETZ, *Galatians*, 298, who thinks of self-righteousness; this is also the preference of MATERA, *Galatians*, 241. But see, e.g., R.N. LONGENECKER, *Galatians* (WBC; Dallas 1990) 274; BARCLAY, *Obeying the Truth*, 158-159; CORSANI, *Galati*, 382-383; DUNN, *Galatians*, 321.

what precedes[45]; it is all the more understandable when one takes into account the added warning in v. 1c which constitutes an interruption in the argument. Strictly speaking, verse 2 resumes v. 1b; it should not be connected with v. 1c. Most commentators agree that the "bearing of burdens (τὰ βάρη)" of v. 2 concretizes the mutual help to be given (cf. v. 1b). The (heavy) burdens are to be seen as related in some way or another to that eventual transgression. They are, it is often said, the consequences of sin: the contrition, the depression, the culpability on the side of the sinner, the compassionate yet difficult taking care of others. However, one may ask whether "bearing one another's burdens" is not a generalization *vis-à-vis* the "restoring" of v. 1b. True, the burdensome amendment commanded in v. 1b remains in the forefront, but "burdens" sounds somewhat broader than what is suggested there. The term seems to refer to all kinds of "heavy weights", of difficulties[46]. Another shift should not be overlooked: in v. 1 the "sinner" is placed over against the "Spirit people"; in v. 2 there is a complete reciprocity, since the bearing of burdens is mutual[47].

It must be stated against Klein that between v. 1 and v. 2 there is no qualitative shift from actual sin to a most profound sinful condition (*Grundbefindlichkeit*). That action of bearing manifests the "spirit of gentleness" of which verse 1b speaks. As far as the content of v. 2 is concerned[48], it remains somewhat strange for the reader that the fulfilment of the law of Christ ("and 'so' you will fulfil ...") consists in this one line of action[49], even if the mutual bearing of burdens is a very comprehensive rule and even if it may be granted that its primary relation to sin is to a certain degree overcome.

---

[45] Cf. MUSSNER, *Galater*, 398: "Der Vers is asyndetisch angeschlossen, was, wie wiederholt in Gal, ein Zeichen für einen gedanklichen Zusammenhang mit dem Vorausgehenden ist".

[46] Cf. BURTON, *Galatians*, 329; H. SCHLIER, *Der Brief an die Galater* (KEK; Göttingen 1971) 371; BARCLAY, *Obeying the Truth*, 132; SCHRAGE, "Probleme", 188-189; SÖDING, *Liebesgebot*, 193-194; BETZ, *Galatians*, 299. Cf. Rom 15,1 and 1 Cor 12,36. The verb and the noun are present in the parable of the workers in the vineyard, see Matt 20,13. Cf. also Luke 14,27: "to 'bear' the cross". A specific reference to financial support for Jerusalem, as defended by J.G. STRELAN, "Burden-Bearing and the Law of Christ: A Re-Examination of Galatians 6:2", *JBL* 94 (1975) 266-276, is not evident. See the critique by, e.g., E.M. YOUNG, "'Fulfill the Law of Christ': An Examination of Galatians 6:2"; *StBT* 7 (1977) no. 2, 31-42.

[47] HAYS, "Christology and Ethics", 286-288, appropriately criticizes Betz for his explanation of v. 2a by means of the friendship *topos* in the Socratic tradition and parallel texts.

[48] Regarding the variant reading in v. 2b (aorist imperative instead of the future tense) it may suffice to refer to B.M. METZGER, *A Textual Commentary on the Greek New Testament* (Stuttgart ²1994) 530.

[49] Cf. CORSANI, *Galati*, 384.

By using in Gal 6,2b the paradoxical phrase "the law of Christ", Paul undoubtedly refers to 5,14 (in both verses: law, (ἀνα)πληρόω, and the concept of "love of neighbor")[50]. The phrase was most probably not a slogan of the opponents nor is it referring to a new "messianic torah". By "the law of Christ" Paul means both the replacement and reinterpretation of the torah[51]. He refers to "the pattern of action (or 'structure of existence') exemplified by the Christ who bore the burdens of others in becoming a curse 'for us'. Therein lies the fundamental paradigm for Christian ethics"[52].

Verse 3. For J.M.G. Barclay verses 3-5 form a cluster: "thematically they belong closely together"[53]. The short conditional period in this verse is a "realis" construction, a condition of fact or, better, a simple condition. By this construction itself nothing is said about the reality of the protasis; only the logical connection between protasis and apodosis is expressed: "if this, then that" (compare with the "eventualis" construction in v. 1a). Verse 3 provides a sort of further reflection, a comment on the warning of v. 1c; it may even constitute the grounding of that clause. The γάρ of v. 3 is most likely to be lined not with v. 2 but with v. 1c[54]. Yet the connection is not explicitly expressed. A Christian must take care of himself, so that he, too, may not be tempted (v. 1c). Why? Because he, too, is but a fragile and weak human creature. That weakness, however, is not the main point in v. 3, although it is present in the phrase "whereas [in fact] he is nothing".

The participial clause μηδὲν ὤν is best taken concessively: "although as a matter of fact he is nothing". This is, of course, exaggerated language which should not be explained literally as is done, e.g., by G. Klein.

---

[50] Gal 6,2a recalls 5,13c: "through love be servants/slaves of one another". Burden-bearing is the work of a slave; the two clauses underline the reciprocity; and, in both, concrete mutual love is their command.

[51] Cf. BARCLAY, *Obeying the Truth*, 143-145. See also pp. 138-142 where Barclay contends that Paul avoids the terms for observance of the law and uses instead the "ambiguous" fulfilment terminology (Rom 8,4; 13,8.10; Gal 5,14; 6,2): "Christians do not 'observe' the law, they 'fulfil' it, and they fulfil it through the one love-command and as it is redefined as 'the law of Christ'" (142).

[52] HAYS, "Christology and Ethics", 286-287. For the different possible meanings of "the law of Christ", cf. e.g., DUNN, *Galatians*, 322-324; MATERA, *Galatians*, 219-221; LONGENECKER, *Galatians*, 275-276; SCHRAGE, "Probleme", 164-165 and 183-188.

[53] *Obeying the Truth*, 159.

[54] Otherwise BURTON, *Galatians*, 330 (with v. 2b). LONGENECKER, *Galatians*, who puts v. 3 and v. 5 between quotation marks, is of the opinion that the postpositive particle γάρ, in both verses, signals a traditional maxim of the Greco-Roman world (see 268, 271 and 276-277).

Christians are something; they are God's creation, they are forgiven and justified persons. To be sure, when a comparison is made between the Creator and a creature, or the Redeemer and a sinner, the distance between them is immense. Yet, Christians are more than "nothing".

Verse 3, however, in no way describes all Christians (nor, for that matter, all human beings). What Paul intends to say is somewhat hidden behind his radicalized expressions and the brevity of his style. We may paraphrase the verse as follows: "If one thinks himself somebody without recognizing that all he is and possesses comes from God, i.e., if one thinks of himself as if he were not created and not a forgiven sinner, if one considers something as if it were not a gift (cf. 1 Cor 3,18-21 and 4,7), then he really deceives himself". Thus the participial phrase μηδὲν ὤν, with its concessive nuance, applies to the Christian who mistakenly and wrongly thinks that he is something. One final remark: in v. 1c a temptation to sin is meant while in v. 3b Paul only speaks of self-deception, although in v. 3a the boasting is wrong and sinful.

By means of a paraphrase such as the one given above, we suddenly see more clearly how verse 3 prepares v. 4, not only by its vocabulary, namely the reflexive pronoun ἑαυτόν, but also and even more so by the presence of the idea of "thinking to be something" (in the wrong way). The idea of boasting appears explicitly in v. 4.

Verse 4. The adversative particle δέ marks an antithesis to what precedes[55]. Verse 4 is the opposite parallel of v. 3, even more so than is usually assumed. Of course, a forceful imperative (v. 4a) is not an if-clause (v. 3a). Yet, together with the second clause of v. 4b, which explains what will happen once the instruction is obeyed, the imperative δοκιμαζέτω in v. 4a can be regarded as almost the equivalent of a conditional protasis "*If* one puts his own work to the test, then ..."[56]. By this conversion into an if-clause, the second clause becomes the apodosis and stresses the legitimacy of boasting. In v. 3a the protasis indicates a wrong action: if anyone thinks that he is something, being nothing (almost = if he boasts in the wrong way); the implied protasis of v. 4a proposes and demands the right behavior by

---

[55] Cf. BARCLAY, *Obeying the Truth*, 160; CORSANI, *Galati*, 387; LONGENECKER, *Galatians*, 276-277. Compare, however, the opinion of BETZ, *Galatians*, 303: "Another maxim follows, perhaps connected with v. 3 by the catchword (δοκ-). The saying, however, is independent".

[56] The same operation could be applied to 6,2: "If you bear one another's burdens, (then) you will fulfil the law of Christ", and 5,13: "if you walk by the Spirit, (then) you will not gratify the desires of the flesh".

requiring a prior examination of one's own work[57]. In v. 3b the self-deception is put forward because there is really nothing to be proud of; in v. 4b
an evidently correct and legitimate boasting is conceded: "that person will
have a ground for boasting"[58].

In view of this parallelism with v. 3, one cannot but suppose that the
outcome of the testing in v. 4a must be positive; this is implied by the line
of reasoning[59]. Only with a "good" work will there be a ground for boasting. By means of the temporal adverb τότε, Paul also emphasizes that the
exercise of self-examination has to be done first: after that exercise (and its
positive outcome) "then" that person will have a real ground for boasting.
It could be that, in Paul's mind, τὸ ἔργον ἑαυτοῦ is still in some way related to the "burdens" of v. 2a and, through them, to the restoration work of
v. 1b. Yet, since the distance between v. 2 and v. 4 is considerable and
Paul's thought has been progressing, a wider interpretation of "his own
work" is probable. "Work" is, then, a term which points to all that which
can be done during the life of a Christian[60]. If the result of that self-examination is positive, we are brought to assume — against G. Klein — that
such a Christian is allowed to think that he "is something" (cf. v. 3); moreover, Paul explicitly states in v. 4b that this Christian has a ground for
boasting[61]. The word καύχημα in v. 4b indicates not the act itself of
boasting, but the ground for boasting; in this context, it is identical with the
"work" (v. 4a).

However, by the phrase "with reference to himself only", i.e., "in
respect to himself alone", there is a limit to that legitimate boasting. One
should notice at once that the restriction is not given afterwards, as if first
the boasting is conceded and only then the limitation added. No, the Greek

---

[57] Cf. MATERA, *Galatians*, 221: "The antidote to self-deception is to test oneself".

[58] Neither in v. 4 nor in v. 3 does Paul speak of actual boasting.

[59] Cf. BURTON, *Galatians*, 332: "A protasis may be mentally supplied, 'if his work shall
be proved good'".

[60] "Work" means more than "conduct or actions" (so DUNN, *Galatians*, 325); it is the
work done, the achievements. BARCLAY, *Obeying the Truth*, 161, too, comments less correctly,
I think: "the basic character of a person's existence". — As is well known, a number of exegetes claim that there is a Pauline distinction between the negative plural ("works of the law")
and the positive singular ("work").

[61] MUSSNER, *Galater*, 401, strangely writes: "Leider zeigt eine ehrliche Selbstprüfung,
dass 'das eigene Werk' meist mit Sünde behaftet ist, so dass jegliches Sich-Rühmen nur κενο-
δοξία ist". But this is not the point in v. 4. For "boasting" in Paul, see J. LAMBRECHT,
"Dangerous Boasting. Paul's Self-Commendation in 2 Cor 10–13", R. BIERINGER (ed.),
The Corinthian Correspondence (BETL 125; Leuven 1996) 325-346; also in this volume,
pp. 107-129.

text, almost simultaneously, says that such a person "then, regarding himself only (τότε εἰς ἑαυτὸν μόνον), will have[62] a ground for boasting". The phrases "regarding *himself*" and "*his own* work" clearly correspond to one another.

The opposition follows: "and not regarding the other (καὶ οὐκ εἰς τὸν ἕτερον)". What does this last expression mean? The most probable solution to this problem must come from the fact that Paul is thinking here of a comparison. One must, therefore, mentally supply the following: "and not through comparison with the work of another Christian"[63]. This further implies, it would seem: "not through despising the other or holding the other in contempt". If this interpretation is correct, Paul almost imperceptibly reverts to an earlier injunction: a virtuous Christian must avoid vainglory as well as provocation (cf. 5,26).

There is still another point. Our understanding of v. 4 assumes that the position of Klein (see pp. 238-240) can hardly be accepted. He rightly stresses that the εἰς + the accusative construction does not indicate the object of boasting. Yet his own interpretation "before, in front of" is most likely incorrect here[64]. Moreover, the question could indeed be asked what boasting "before, in front of oneself" means. However, boasting in respect to oneself, not by comparison with others — their presence is not excluded by v. 4 — is perfectly possible.

Verse 5. Paul continues to speak in v. 5 with more or less the same vocabulary or with analogous concepts[65]. There can be no doubt that the

---

[62] Cf. BURTON, *Galatians*, 332. The future "will have" is not eschatological; otherwise CORSANI, *Galati*, 381 ("probabilmente escatologica"); MUSSNER, *Galater*, 401.

[63] Cf., e.g., SCHLIER, *Galater*, 274; M.-J. LAGRANGE, *Epître aux Galates* (EtB; Paris 1926) 157; DUNN, *Galatians*, 325; SCHRAGE, "Probleme", 191. For "boasting in front of" or "before", see Rom 4,2 and 15,7 (πρὸς θεόν); 1 Cor 1,29 (ἐνώπιον τοῦ θεοῦ); 2 Cor 7,14 (ἐπὶ Τίτου).

[64] "Before" is present in 2 Cor 8,24: ἡμῶν καυχήσεως ὑπὲρ ὑμῶν εἰς αὐτούς) ("of our boasting about you 'to', i.e., before, in front of them"). The most interesting parallel to Gal 6,4 is no doubt Rom 4,2, where the noun "ground for boasting" and the verb "have" are present: εἰ γὰρ Ἀβραὰμ ἐξ ἔργων ἐδικαιώθη, ἔχει καύχημα, ἀλλ᾽ οὐ πρὸς θεόν. Abraham would have a ground for boasting (namely if he were justified by works), but not before God. Yet πρός ("before") in Rom 4,2 and εἰς ("regarding") in Gal 6,4 are different. For a study of Rom 4,2, see J. LAMBRECHT, "Why is Boasting Excluded? A Note on Romans 3,27 and 4,2", ID., *Pauline Studies* (BETL 115; Leuven 1994) 27-31.

BARCLAY, *Obeying the Truth*, translates Gal 6,4b: "and then he will direct his boast to himself alone and not to his neighbour" (160) and comments: "after testing one's own work one must not flaunt it before others but keep one's boast to oneself" (161). But does the Greek allow such an interpetation?

[65] For ἕκαστος, see v. 4; for βαστάζω, see v. 2a; for τὸ ἴδιον, cf. ἑαυτοῦ in v. 4a; for the generic term φορτίον, cf. the specific term βάρη in v. 2a.

verse is integrated in the passage. Verse 5, introduced by γάρ, gives the motivation. But what precisely is "grounded" by this clause[66]? Again one must try to render explicit what is implied. In v. 5 Paul presumably gives a reason why one should not compare oneself with another. That reason is contained in the saying, "each one will bear his own load"[67]. The somewhat hidden meaning is that each Christian is "loaded" by his own difficulties. In v. 4b the future tense is employed indicatively (that person "will have"); in v. 5, however, the future is most likely imperatival: "each one will have to bear, each one must bear his own load". This may be preferable to seeing it as a gnomic future, i.e., a future often found in aphorisms[68].

If the reconstructed line of thought is still correct, Paul is referring to the very life of all Christians ("each one"), not to the day of final judgment. Like "burdens" in v. 2a, "load" in v. 5 points to the negative aspects of everyday life. In v. 2a the connection of "burdens" with sin still had to be accepted. Here, in v. 5, the meaning of the generic term "load" is almost certainly much wider; it may point to any adverse circumstance and tribulation, but also to personal shortcomings, sin and shame[69]. However, the command to mutual help in 6,2 forbids us to add to "will bear his own load" in v. 5 the nuance "completely alone". This negative load that must be carried (v. 5) is opposed to the positive work of v. 4a which constitutes a ground for boasting. Even the Christian with plenty of good "work" will have to bear "his own load"! There can be no doubt that the bearing as well as the boasting occur in daily life before the final judgment[70].

---

[66] Cf. BETZ, *Galatians*, 303-304. Yet Betz takes the particle as having no motivating force — just indicating continuation — and thinks that the implicit idea is that "one should avoid taking on more than one can handle" (304). But within the context of Gal 6,1-6 this is hardly the point.

[67] LAGRANGE, *Galates*, 157, says that Paul "laisse entrevoir ici qu'il y a un revers à la médaille". Regarding v. 2 and v. 5, he notes: "... la prétendue contradiction n'est qu'un aspect piquant et paradoxal sous lequel sont présentées les choses. Car c'est précisément parce que chacun a quelque chose à porter qu'on doit s'aider les uns les autres" (158). Cf. BURTON, *Galatians*, 334: "The paradoxical antithesis to v. 2a is doubtless conscious and intentional".

[68] SCHRAGE, "Probleme", 192, considers the possibility of an eschatological future, but adds: "das Futur kann gnomisch sein".

[69] Otherwise but less correct, I think, BARCLAY, *Obeying the Truth*, 161-162: load "seems to represent the weight not of suffering or sin but of responsibility before God" (162). The opinion of SCHLIER, *Galater*, 274, is to be rejected: "Φορτίον ist kaum von ἔργον unterschieden". The same applies to HARNISCH, "Einübung", 295 (one's own load = "das ruhmreiche Werk").

[70] Is there a reference to 5,10, where the same verb in the same future tense is found and the meaning is clearly eschatological? If so, then 6,5 must also be eschatological. But this deduction is unlikely since the verb in 5,10 is followed by τὸ κρίμα which indicates that the expression by itself connotes the final judgment. The other "data" put forward by Kuck with regard to the climactic position of the verse and to the parallel texts are equally insufficient to confer an eschatological meaning to 6,5.

Verse 6. Even this verse is called a "maxim" by Betz[71]. The third person singular continues, but now Paul addresses "the one who is taught the Word". That person must share (perhaps: "must continue to share") in all good things with "the one who teaches". The vocabulary in the sentence points explicitly to a specifically Christian context[72]. By the particle δέ (again adversative, cf. v. 4) this appeal is added, one is tempted to say, as an afterthought, a correction of v. 5. Paul "hastens to qualify his last exhortation"[73]. For a Christian could go too far in taking care only of his own worries. There is the community as well and, more in particular, those who are so involved in teaching the gospel that they do not have enough to live. They must be helped. A Christian must share with them "in all good things". It would seem that Paul, in the first place (but not exclusively), points to material, financial support[74].

III. THE COHERENCE OF 6,1-6

The results of this long analysis have to be brought together. However, before we attempt to reconstruct the line of thought within 6,1-6, it can already be stated that in Paul's reasoning there are shifts (see, e.g., v. 1c) More than once, the elements of the argument remain hidden or must be supplied (see, e.g., at the end of v. 4 and in v. 5). It happens that Paul returns to an idea which was no longer focused upon in the immediately preceding context (see, e.g., v. 2 and v. 3). Some concepts are taken up by different terms, but a broadening of their meaning may be assumed (see, e.g., "burdens" in v. 2a over against "transgression" in v. 1a, and "load" in v. 5 over against "burdens" in v. 2a). To claim that all this occurs because Paul is stringing together well-known maxims or aphorisms is at best only

---

[71] BETZ, *Galatians*, 304, emphasizes its independence: "The δέ ("but") provides a loose connection with the preceding, simply indicating that this saying follows v. 5. The meaning of the saying must, therefore, be established first on its own terms".

[72] Otherwise BETZ, *Galatians*, 305: "Again, the content is not specifically Christian". Yet "Word" refers to the gospel message. For Paul's use of this type of κοινων-terminology, cf. esp. Rom 12,13; 15,27 and Phil 4,15.

[73] DUNN, *Galatians*, 326.

[74] Cf. BURTON, *Galatians*, 338-339; SCHRAGE, "Probleme", 192-193; LONGENECKER, *Galatians*, 279. See also the long discussion of this verse in J. HAINZ, *Koinonia. "Kirche" als Gemeinschaft bei Paulus* (BU 16; Regensburg 1982) 62-89.

a part of the explanation. These data are certainly also due to the spontaneous or emotional, yet logically not "unconnected", manner in which many people often speak, and write. Paul was no exception.

Before a final survey of the themes, we will try to indicate the flow of thought in Paul's argument within 6,1-6[75]. That such a reconstruction is to a certain degree hypothetical will easily be conceded.

Line of Thought

The injunction of v. 1 to restore someone who might have been overtaken in some transgression appears to be connected with 5,25 by the qualification "(brothers) you who are spiritual" and the mention of a "spirit of gentleness" but, it would seem, also with 5,26. After the first particular instruction in 5,26, we have in 6,1 what could be called a second concretization of the general command "let us walk by the Spirit" (5,25). Yet this command to restore in a spirit of gentleness appears to be the opposite of what is to be avoided according to 5,26: self-conceit, provocation and envy. In 6,1c, at the end of the sentence, a new idea suddenly appears: you yourself may be tempted. The second person singular, not the plural, is used emphatically.

The command "bear one another's burdens" of 6,2a does not continue the warning of 6,1c; it repeats asyndetically, again in the plural, the injunction of v. 1b. Although "burdens" certainly sums up the heavy cost of "restoring" a transgressor, that term may have other and wider connotations as well: all kinds of troubles which are present in the daily life of Christians, their struggles and pressures on them. In 6,2b it is stated, with much emphasis and with a view to the whole of Christian existence, thatin this way, i.e., through a mutual carrying of the burdens, "the law of Christ" is fulfilled. Different from that in v. 1b, the helping is now reciprocal.

Yet if a Christian wrongly thinks that he is something, he deludes himself. Verse 3 probably motivates (γάρ) not v. 2 but v. 1c. The danger of temptation is real. While helping one's brother, who in his weakness is overtaken by a transgression, a Christian may become imprudent and wrongly think that he is somebody; this, however, is pure self-deception. Here, too, a shift in the argumentation has occurred. In v. 1c, one sponta-

---

[75] Cf. VANHOYE, "Paraclèse et doctrine pauliniennes", 207-209, on Paul's "incohérence du langage et cohérence de la pensée" with, on p. 208, special attention to Gal 6,1-6.

neously assumes that the Christian who "restores" may be tempted to sin in the same (or an analogous) way as the sinner. In v. 3b, Paul no longer mentions sin as such; he calls that wrong (and sinful) action "self-deceit".

The "anyone" of v. 3a becomes "each one" in v. 4. This verse offers, as it were, the key to the correct attitude of the Christian. Incorrect self-esteem is self-deceit (v. 3), but (δέ) let each one examine his own work and then, if that work proves to be valid, there may be room and ground for proper and legitimate boasting. Yet Paul's formulation is careful: the boasting concerns only that person himself, not the other. The cryptic expression "not regarding the other" presumably means that comparison with the other (and his work) has in any case to be avoided so that no contempt or provocation take place.

In v. 5 an explicit reason (γάρ) is now provided for moderation in boasting and avoiding pride which would despise the other: "Each one must bear his own load". The preceding context invites us to interpret "load" as the weaknesses and culpability of each Christian individually, as well as all kinds of difficulties and troubles. The bearing of this weight of adversities must take place in everyday life. Verse 5 is not eschatological in the strict sense of the term.

In v. 6 Paul adds a corrective (δέ) and, rather unexpectedly, points to the specific duty of the Christian community to provide the material necessities of life and all kinds of assistance for those who teach the Word.

In this brief passage one notes a movement from mutual help to individual attentiveness, from the second person plural to the second and third person singular, and from "one another" to "each one". Verses 1-6 "develop the two main themes of personal accountability and corporate responsibility which constantly balance each other throughout this section"[76]. There does not appear to be an eschatological climax in v. 5. The pericope proper ends at v. 10 and vv. 7-10 are eschatological indeed. The contradiction between v. 2 and v. 5 is more apparent than real. Mutual help evidently does not dispense one from personal responsibility; even with the help of others, every one still has to carry his own load.

Survey of Themes

In Gal 6,1-6 there is obviously more than the twofold emphasis on

---

[76] BARCLAY, *Obeying the Truth*, 167.

mutual help and individual attentiveness. The consideration of the line of thought has shown us how coherent and direct Paul's reasoning is, whatever traditional material he may have employed. A thematic survey can point out a whole list of particular accents, all of them Pauline insights, warning and guidelines. Our thematic approach will not so much point to the truths of time-less sayings. This final part of the study simply lists the surprisingly numerous concerns which a careful reading detects in this short passage.

(1) For Paul, sin is not absent in Christian life. He reckons with pos-sible transgressions. He refers to the eventuality that a Christian may "be overtaken" by a transgression; he may have purposely avoided an expres-sion which would indicate outright sinning.

(2) A Christian who falls into sin should not be left alone; such a per-son has to be restored by the community. Restoration, amendment and gen-tle solicitude are called for; no word of condemnation or punishment or banishment of the sinner is heard here.

(3) In an commonsensical way Paul states that, in restoring the other, one has to be prudent and careful. He, too, can be tempted to sin just as the sinner. Although Christians are "Spirit-led people" (cf. 5,18), their abiding frailty is realistically acknowledged.

(4) The instruction to bear one another's burdens is very impressive. In a community of Christians mutual help is a strict commandment, addressed to all members; it is a constant rule. Paul repeats what he already said in 5,13b.

(5) Much emphasis is put on what follows: καὶ οὕτως ("and so, in this way"). Burden-bearing is the fulfilment of the law of Christ. In 5,14 Paul states that in one clause, "loving one's neighbor as oneself", the whole (Mosaic) law is fulfilled. In 6,2, two things become evident: for a follower of Christ, bearing the burdens of others is the essential part and, indeed, the whole of loving one's neighbor as oneself; and such a fulfilment of the redefined (Mosaic) law is at the same time the fulfilment of the law of Christ. To be sure, Paul is not only thinking of what Christ demands; he also implicitly refers to Christ's example of bearing our burdens through his incarnation and his death on the cross.

(6) Paul realistically reckons with the possibility that a Christian might wrongly think that he is something (cf. 1 Cor 1,26-31). It is stated very plainly that such a person deludes himself.

(7) It may surprise us that Paul, immediately afterwards, admits a ground for legitimate boasting. Such a boasting, however, is only possible after a positive evaluation of one's own "work"; moreover, this can only occur with regard to oneself.

(8) Avoidance of comparison with others is an added theme which is (most likely) hinted at by Paul (cf. 2 Cor 10,12). Boasting is by its nature

public; yet it should never be accompanied by despising or provoking one's fellow Christian.

(9) Paul shows a realistic insight into the moral identity of each Christian. In addition to qualities or virtues and a valid "work", there is also always the individual "load" — the daily struggle of life, all kinds of pressures, even weaknesses and sin — which each must bear, not losing heart while doing good as long as one has the opportunity (cf. 6,9-10).

(10) Paul's last thought in this brief passage concerns a practical problem in the Christian community: because teachers of the Word are not able to make a decent living, they must be given a share "in all good things" by those who are taught.

One is struck by the multitude and variety of themes in 6,1-6. In a few sentences Paul succeeds in offering (not a complete, yet) a balanced concretization of Christian spirituality and behavior. All ten themes in this list have to do either with community life or personal behavior. They are guidelines and directives which are meant for instruction or for application to the concrete daily life of Galatian Christians[77].

Gal 6,1-6 is part of the major parenetical section 5,13–6,10. Christ has set us free from the law; we should not allow ourselves to become slaves again (5,1-12). Yet this freedom cannot be an excuse for living according to the flesh. We who belong to Christ and live by the Spirit have to follow the lead of the Spirit. We must love one another, bear one another's burdens and so fulfil the law of Christ. At the same time, however, each of us must take care of himself and test his own work. We should not delude ourselves: God cannot be cheated. Let us not become tired of doing good. Let us sow in the field of the Spirit; God is the master of the eschatological harvest.

Within Gal 5,13–6,10 the subunit 6,1-6 contains a very coherent argument. The unifying factor is the interweaving of mutual help and individual attentiveness, two complementary injunctions which throughout the manifold themes dominate Paul's parenesis in these verses. To be sure, various originally non-Christian ethical sayings are present. But Paul integrates them in a strict flow of thought. J. Dunn appropriately stresses that whatever their origin may be, "the source of motivation (the Spirit — 5,25) and the norm of behaviour (Christ — 6,2) are distinctively Christian"[78].

---

[77] For the relevance of Paul's moral instruction, see BARCLAY, *Obeying the Truth*, esp. 22-23, 36-74, 150-155, 167-170 and 217-218. Barclay duly cautions about the dangers connected with "mirror-reading". However, in view of 5,15 and 5,26, as well as the eight vices in 5,19-21 pointing to infighting, he notes "that there is sufficient evidence for communal strife in the Galatian churches and that this may well be the best context in which to understand the various maxims gathered in 5.25–6.10" (154).

[78] *Galatians*, 316.

20

Second Thoughts
Some Reflections on the Law in Galatians

The aim of this brief article is to reflect upon Paul's conception of the law as it is present in his letter to the Galatians. Although I have taught this letter during many years and published a number of studies on different texts, a settled certainty about Paul's vision of the law has not yet been completely attained. Doubts and hesitations remain. This article intends to explain some of the major difficulties and, at the same time, to indicate my choices and preferences. The reflections are offered by way of second thoughts, if not retraction. Some content criticism, be it dangerous and delicate, will not be absent.

The division is thematic but also commanded by the text of Galatians. First I will once again consider Gal 2,14b-21; the main topic will be the meaning of sin. A second part deals with 3,6-14 and will center its discussion on faith. In a third part the whole of the letter is reflected upon in an attempt to follow Paul's reasoning on the law.

I. GALATIANS 2,14b-21

Paul's spoken reaction to Peter in Antioch comprises the whole of Gal 2,14b-21, although, of course, the Galatian situation some seven years later influenced its composition at that time. The division into three unequal parts can be accepted: v. 14b (second person singular); vv. 15-17 (first person plural); and vv. 18-21 (first person singular). Not only are the persons significant, but also the content. It would seem that in vv. 15-17 Paul's consideration becomes more general and that in v. 18 he refers back to the Antioch incident.

Reasoning in 2,15-17

The first main point in vv. 15-17 can be rendered as follows: "Peter

(Paul says), although we as Jews are not Gentile sinners, yet, knowing that a person is not justified by the works of the law, we too have come to believe in Christ Jesus and in this manner we realize that we too are sinners". This reconstruction of Paul's line of thought assumes that "sinners" and "sin" in these verses point to real sin in the full religious and moral sense of that terminology. This in turn implies that in v. 15 "Gentile sinners" is not meant as a simple characterization of non-Jews, which would take "sinners", as it were, in a weakened sense, and, moreover, that according to v. 17 Paul and Peter recognize that they have been "sinners" in their pre-conversion life; therefore, they too, like the Gentiles, were in need of justification by faith in Christ.

In v. 16 the expression "by works of the law" is repeated three times. One can hardly doubt that Paul refers back to the works done in obedience to the law which are mentioned in 2,1-14: circumcision and the observance of the purity laws. Yet Paul most probably also has in mind the works not done. Because of those transgressions and omissions of the law, Paul and Peter, and all Jews, are real sinners who must be redeemed by Christ. In Rom 3,20 Paul repeats that no human being is justified by deeds prescribed by the law, that is, by works of the law, and in 3,9-18 he demonstrates how the Jews are not better off than the Greeks; they, too, are under the power of sin. In 3,23 he writes: "all have sinned and fall short of the glory of God".

Verse 17 contains a conditional period, most probably a "realis". The if-clause, the protasis, provides the common ground accepted by opponents and Paul alike. The opponents' attack that Paul must repel lies in the apodosis. In the rhetorical question "Is Christ then a servant of sin?" Paul points to Christ as an agent of sin not, I think, because through him those who believe no longer live like Jews. No, the insinuating question appears to refer to the kind of accusation that is found in Rom 3,8: some people slander Paul by saying that he says, "Let us do evil so that good may come", or to his own reflection in 6,1: "should we continue in sin in order that grace may abound?" A Messiah or Christ who justifies by grace through faith, not by the works of the law, must have been represented as potentially increasing sin: "should we sin because we are not under law but under grace?" (Rom 6,15). The answer to this type of charge is everywhere: "by no means".

Reasoning in 2,18-21

What is the connection of v. 18 with v. 17? The Greek has the particle γάρ ("for"), but I have defended a soft caesura between the two verses because of the change of person and the shift in the reasoning in v. 18. In a similar approach the New Standard Revised Version renders "but" rather than "for". Yet it could be that a motivating "for" is to be preferred after all. Paul reacts to the question "is Christ then a servant of sin?" with "certainly not" (v. 17). In v. 18 he continues: "for (not Christ but I would be such a servant, since) if I build up again the very things that I once tore down, then I demonstrate that I am a transgressor". Yet in this proposal we have to clarify the train of thought by adding a clause. The "I" in v. 18 is Paul but even more Peter, since Peter is building up again the Jewish way of life. Paul says to Peter: by building up you are going to become once again a transgressor of the law, i.e., a sinner as we were before our belief in Christ (cf. Rom 3).

The first person singular is also present in vv. 19-20, but what Paul writes here indicates most likely that he is above all reflecting upon his own personal condition as a Christian. That he died through the law to the law can be explained only by his reference to Christ and the cross event. As is evident from 3,13 Christ is cursed as a "sinner" according to the law; it can be held that the law crucified him. So Christ redeemed us from sin and the law. Paul is in Christ and was crucified with him: through the law Paul died to the law in order to live to God.

By means of "I do not nullify 'the grace of God'" (v. 21a) Paul refers back to that specific act of the Son of God who loved Paul and gave himself for Paul (cf. v. 20). While Paul here is primarily referring to his own experience of Christ, other passages make clear that what he says applies to all Christians. In previous studies I have been claiming that the "transgression" of v. 18b is identical with "nullification" of v. 21a. Paul would be saying: by building up once again the law I transgress not the law but God's salvific ordinance; I nullify his grace manifested in Christ. Yet this interpretation cannot but remain uncertain and, according to many, it is too specious.

It is not all clear that the conditional sentence in v. 21bc is an irrealis. If verse 21bc contains an irrealis, a condition contrary to fact, the translation must be: "for if justification were through the law, then Christ would have died for nothing". But a verb is missing in the protasis and, more significantly, there is the absence of the particle ἄν in the apodosis. So the construction could be, as in v. 17ab, a "realis" or, better, a "simple condition" (i.e., no more than the logical connection: if this, then that). In that case the literal translation is: "if justification through law, then Christ died in vain". We note the motivating or explicative γάρ ("for"). Believing that justification comes through the law effectively nullifies God's grace, i.e., it says that Christ's death is in vain, that it does not bring salvation.

In v. 16, at first the clause "no justification by works of the law" appears somewhat strange. But one can easily interpret "not by works of the law" as meaning: although some works of the law are done, other are not, and given the universal incomplete observance of the law all Jews too are sinners. In v. 21bc, however, the assertion is even more radical. One is brought to assume that there is no justification even if one keeps the law; otherwise, Paul says, Christ died in vain. It is difficult to accept such a statement. In the final analysis there can be no opposition between God's law and God's justification. Doing what God demands brings life. How then did Paul come to use such exaggerated, less than accurate language? The answer may be found in his meeting with Christ. The Christ event as well as life in Christ puts the rest in the background. Paul appears to denigrate the law, at least to some extent.

II. GALATIANS 3,6-14

Gal 3,6 introduces the second member of a comparison: "Just as (καθώς) Abraham believed God and it was reckoned to him as righteousness". The content of the first member, not indicated as such (no ὡς), is given in 3,1-5. So 3,6 is linked with the preceding verses. What the believing Galatians experienced can be compared with what happened to Abraham. But the Christians' relationship with Abraham is much more than that of a likeness or similarity.

Reasoning in 3,6-9

Those who believe are the descendants of Abraham; they are blessed in him. Those who believe are blessed with Abraham who believed. Abraham's faith was in God and his promises. That of the Galatians, of course, in Christ. Although in 3,1 Paul speaks of Jesus Christ emphatically as the one who "was publicly exhibited as crucified before the eyes" of the Galatians (and in 3,2-5 refers to the Spirit three times), in vv. 6-12 faith becomes, as it were, less determined; for the time being Christ is no longer mentioned. The reader may be tempted to ask if "faith in God", such as that of Abraham, is sufficient to be justified and blessed in Abraham.

The connection between vv. 9 and 10 is not clear logically speaking.

Verse 10 begins with a motivating clause: "'For' all who rely on the works of the law are under a curse". How does this ground v. 9: "Those who believe are blessed with Abraham who believed"? I have proposed a mental supplement after v. 9. Over against οἱ ἐκ πίστεως ("those out of faith", that is, those whose life is determined by faith) one may have expected the opposite expression οἱ ἐκ νόμου ("those out of the law", that is, those whose life is determined by the law) and, more importantly, the statement that the people of the law are not blessed. Verse 10 explains why those people cannot be blessed.

Reasoning in 3,10-12

In v. 10a Paul writes ὅσοι γὰρ ἐξ ἔργων νόμου εἰσίν, ὑπὸ κατάραν εἰσίν. "All those who rely on (the observance of) the works of the law" sounds decidedly positive. They try to do what the law prescribes, yet they "are under a curse". This last clause most probably means more than "they are only threatened by the law, not yet actually cursed". Although "to be under the law" looks somewhat different and less harsh than the explicit "cursed", the difference is not very great. To be under a curse signifies that one is under the power of a curse, is affected and ruled by curse. The ensuing v. 10b makes clear that this understanding is correct.

One could ask whether the statement of v. 10a is not paradoxical. This would be so in a reading without the γάρ-clause v. 10b: "For cursed is everyone who does not observe and obey all the things written in the book of the law". This second clause indicates that, just as in 2,16, Paul's thought is as follows: they rely on the law and do some works of the law, but other things written in the book of the law are not done and, therefore, they are cursed. "All" in the quotation from Deuteronomy can hardly be neglected. The people of the law are cursed because of their non-observance of the law.

Paul's explanatory considerations in vv. 11-12 take the form of general principles. We are brought to remember the same movement in the radical assertions of 2,16. Righteousness rests on faith; the law does not rest on faith; thus the law cannot justify. Both contrast and parallelism between the citation in v. 11b (Hab 2,4) and that in v. 12b (Lev 18,5) must be noted. Two principles are contrasted: believing and doing. "The one who is righteous by faith" (ὁ δίκαιος ἐκ πίστεως) is opposed to "whoever does the works of the law" (ὁ ποιήσας αὐτά); the two mentions of "will live" (ζήσεται in both clauses, in v. 12b emphasized by ἐν αὐτοῖς) correspond with one another and have the same meaning. In v. 12b Paul seems to assume that perfect obedience to the law would lead to "life", i.e., to final salvation. So, if we ask why it is, according to v. 11a, evident that no one is justified by the law, the complete answer is not that faith alone justifies. In view of v. 10b and v. 12b one must assume that Paul still thinks of a *de facto* lack of observance. Of course, after the Christ event, keeping to the law, holding fast to the law, becomes absurd. Faith in Christ is the only way. As in 2,21bc, this idea appears to be also present in 3,11-12. An attack on legalistic works-righteousness, however, cannot be detected.

Reasoning in 3,13-14

That according to Paul Christ has become "a curse" for us must be understood in the sense that Christ has become "sin" (2 Cor 5,21) and, because of that, condemned, crucified and, as "hanging on a tree", cursed. The expression "for us" is to be taken in the sense of "to our advantage", but the nuance "instead of us" can reasonably be postulated here in the argument of Paul.

In v. 13a Paul employs the first person plural twice: Christ redeemed us; he has become a curse for us. The reasons for the inclusive sense, "us" meaning all believers, both Jews and Gentiles, are well known: in his letter Paul addresses the Galatians the majority of whom are Gentile Christians; the formulaic character of v. 13a; and the fact that in v. 14b "that we might receive" is most probably inclusive. Yet in vv. 10-13 Paul explicitly deals with the Jewish law; in v. 14a he mentions the "Gentiles"; a widening to an inclusive horizon in v. 14b should not be considered as impossible; similar shifts can be found in 4,4-6: from Jewish-Christians (v. 4-5a) to Gentile-Christians (v. 5b) to the inclusive all (v. 6). Therefore, the exclusive sense in v. 13a, "us" meaning the Israelites, should probably be preferred. The Messiah comes from to Israel (cf. Rom 9,5); in between God and the Gentiles there is the promise to Abraham and his offspring, who is Christ (cf. Gal 3,16).

After the rather vague faith of Abraham and his descendants the sudden christological emphasis in vv. 13-14 cannot be missed. Christian faith is believing in Christ who redeemed the Jews by becoming a curse in a vicarious way. The justification of Jews and Gentiles alike occurs by faith in Christ; the same applies to the blessing of Abraham and the promise of the Spirit.

III. THE LAW IN GALATIANS

Paul writes his letter to the Galatians because they are so quickly deserting the one who has called them in the grace of Christ and are turning to a different gospel (1,6). By their different gospel the opponents compel the Gentiles to live like Jews and observe the Jewish law. In his writing Paul emphasizes that one is not justified by doing what the law prescribes but only by faith in Christ. The question arises: why is there no righteousness by works of the law (2,16) or why are all who rely on the works of the law under a curse (3,10a)? It would seem that Paul in Galatians provides various elements for an answer.

The Non-Observance of the Law

Paul is convinced that he himself and Peter (and all Jews) are sinners and, just as the Gentiles, in need of justification by believing in Christ Jesus. Most Jews strive for righteousness and try to fulfill the law. They certainly observe many commandments of the law. However, as Paul explains at great length in Rom 2–3, those Jews also transgress the law. In Gal 3,10b he quotes Deut 27,26 that everyone who does not obey all the things written in the book of the law is cursed. "Even the circumcised do not themselves obey the law" (Gal 6,13), although "every man who lets himself be circumcised ... is obliged to obey the entire law" (5,3).

There are some statements which by themselves suggest that the law was never meant to justify and provide "life". We read, as if it were self-evident: "Law does not rest on faith" (3,12a) and: "If a law had been given that could make alive, then righteousness would indeed come through the law" (3,21). Yet in 3,21 Paul has just affirmed that the law is certainly not against the promises (cf. Rom 7,12: "the law is holy, and the commandment is holy and just and good"). Therefore, we can hardly believe that according to Paul — notwithstanding assertions to the contrary — the law in God's plan of salvation was never meant to justify. The negative predicament is a matter of human fact, not a matter of divine principle. Paul's explicit reasoning about the law is forced at several points and should be balanced by referring to his more positive statements about the law.

The Nature of the Law

Scripture clearly states that Abraham has been justified by believing in God, not by (a not yet existing) law. That law came four hundred thirty years later than the promise. Moreover, it was not directly given by God but was ordained through angels by a mediator. Law has been promulgated "because of transgressions" (3,19). Its purpose is to reveal God's will so that people might recognize their transgressions. Paul perhaps also intends to say that law produces and increases the transgressions (cf. Rom 5,20).

Until Christ came scripture had imprisoned all things under the power of sin (3,22); we, Jewish-Christians, were guarded under the law (3,23). "Therefore the law was our disciplinarian" (5,24); we were subject to his discipline. Before the coming of faith we were enslaved to the law as to the cosmic powers controlling the universe (the στοιχεῖα τοῦ κόσμου, 4,3 and cf. 4,9). We were under the law, children of the slave woman, citizens of the present Jerusalem, a mother who is in slavery with her children (4,21-31).

Paul further characterizes life under the law as life under a curse, since the law curses all who transgress its commandments. Life under the law and subject to the law is necessarily a life according to the flesh, not according to the Spirit (3,3-4 and 5,13.16-18). It is a life which does not exclude sin (cf. 2,17; 3,22). Christ became "curse" (3,13) and "sin" (2 Cor 5,21) in order to save us who as sinners are cursed.

"For freedom Christ has set us free" (5,1a)

Through Christ we have become free children of the free woman, the Jerusalem above. The yoke of slavery from which we are set free is that of the law (5,1b). We are called to freedom and should not use that freedom as an opportunity for the flesh (5,13). For Paul, the Christ event is God's new initiative that completely overshadows the law. Christ died for our sins, i.e., for our transgressions of the law. From now on, even the positive striving to obey the law no longer makes sense. It implies seeking to establish our own righteousness by means of "works of the law" and, by this very fact, stumbling over the stumbling stone which is Christ (cf. Rom 9,30–10,4).

The Lord Jesus Christ "gave himself for our sins to set us free from the present evil age" (1,4: cf. 2,20: Christ loved Paul and "handed himself over" for Paul). "Christ redeemed us from the curse of the law by becoming a curse for us" (3,13a). In the fullness of time God sent his Son who redeemed those who were under the law so that all, Jews and Gentiles, might receive adoption as children (4,4-6). All are baptized in Christ and have clothed themselves with Christ. In Christ Jesus all are children of God through faith, Abraham's offspring, heirs according to the promise (3,26-29).

At the end of the letter Paul writes: "May I never boast of anything except the cross of our Lord Jesus Christ, by which the world has been crucified to me, and I to the world" (6,14). He carries "the marks of Jesus branded" on his body (6,17). That revolutionary encounter with Christ, that life in Christ, is the ultimate reason why for Paul righteousness is not, and cannot be, by the works of the law. With this in mind we are able to understand, interpret and even correct such polemical and radical statements as 3,21b: "If a law had been given that could make alive, then righteousness would indeed come through the law". Through faith in Christ the Galatians — and all Christians — have become "a new creation" and "the Israel of God" (6,15 and 16).

21

Connection of Disjunction?
A Note on 1 Thessalonians 2,13 Within 1,2–3,13

In his 1990 commentary Charles A Wanamaker refers to 1 Thess 2,13-16 as a "digression within the *narratio*"[1]. He comments that the transitional phrase καὶ διὰ τοῦτο in v. 13 "may either refer to what has preceded in the discussion or forward to the topic to be introduced" but adds that "the latter seems the better interpretation" since the ὅτι-clause which follows "expresses the reason for thanksgiving to God"[2]. Earl J. Richard renders the phrase: "for the following reason also"[3] and the NRSV translates v. 13a as follows: "And we also thank God constantly for this, that ...". The latter two versions clearly interpret τοῦτο as referring forward[4]. The opinion of Béda Rigaux in his major commentary is nuanced: the phrase "a toujours une relation à ce qui précède...; cependant très souvent la locution introduit un motif spécial et l'ajoute au général déjà mentioné"[5] and this occurs here by means of the ὅτι-clause. One would like to ask: is there between 2,12 and 2,13 a disjunction or a connection?

This grammatical and exegetical note does not directly deal with the question whether (the whole of) 2,13-16 belongs to the original letter — I think it does — nor with its strong anti-judaistic character. Our aim in these pages is to reconstruct as carefully as possible the line of thought within 1

---

[1] C.A. WANAMAKER, *The Epistles to the Thessalonians* (NIGTC; Grand Rapids – Exeter 1990) 108. This expression was introduced by Wilhelm Wuelner in 1987.

[2] WANAMAKER, *Thessalonians*, 110.

[3] E.J. RICHARD, *First and Second Thessalonians* (SP; Collegeville 1995) 111. According to Richard the expression is non-Pauline: "In reading the canonical, edited text, a forward-directed meaning is preferable, since 2:13 offers not a summary of what precedes (renewed thanks) but new content (thanks for an added reason — such is further indicated by the following 'because' clause)" (112).

[4] Cf. also, e.g., F.F. BRUCE, *1 & 2 Thessalonians* (WBC; Waco 1982) 44: the ὅτι-clause supplies the reason ("we give thanks that").

[5] B. RIGAUX, *Les Epîtres aux Thessaloniciens* (EtB; Paris–Gembloux 1956) 437. For A. ROOSEN, *De brieven van Paulus aan de Tessalonicenzen* (Roermond 1971), the phrase διὰ τοῦτο fulfills "zowel een prospectieve als een retrospectieve functie" (62, n. 56).

Thess 1,2–3,13. It would seem that the answer to the question about disjunction or connection is not without importance for such an undertaking.

Two preliminary remarks may be formulated. First, from the outset this analysis does not claim to be "epistolary" or "rhetorical". We shall use such terms as thanksgiving, apology (self-defense), narration (report), digression or theme (topos) in a non-technical manner[6]. Second, although we realize that every division risks neglecting some subtle shifts or allusions in the reasoning, at the end a tentative structure will be proposed.

I. A CONNECTING PHRASE

It is well known that in New Testament Greek the demonstrative pronoun οὗτος is no longer used exclusively to refer to what precedes[7]. While in 1 Thess 5,18 τοῦτο points back to what has just been said ("give thanks in all circumstances; for 'this' [is] the will of God"), in 4,3 the same pronoun refers to something which follows: "For this is the will of God, your sanctification, to abstain from unchastity". A similar reference forward is also present in 4,15: "For this we declare to you by the word of the Lord, that we who are alive ... shall not precede those who have fallen asleep". But what can be said about διὰ τοῦτο in 2,13?

The Phrase

The phrase διὰ τοῦτο occurs three times in 1 Thessalonians: 2,13; 3,5 and 3,7 (cf. 2 Thess 2,11)[8]. Is Rigaux correct in stating that διὰ τοῦτο always refers to something which precedes? If one takes into account all cases in Paul's undisputed letters, this appears not to be the case. There are twelve occurences besides those in 1 Thessalonians[9]. In three of them Paul

---

[6] Cf. K.P. DONFRIED – J. BEUTLER (eds.), *The Thessalonians Debate: Methodological Discord or Methodological Synthesis?* (Grand Rapids 2000). Some contributors to this recent volume apply the epistolary or rhetorical approach, I think, too narrowly and too technically.

[7] Cf., e.g., M. ZERWICK, *Biblical Greek* (Rome 1963) nr. 213.

[8] Cf. διό in 1 Thess 3,1 and 5,11 and the motivating διότι (= διὰ τοῦτο ὅτι) in 2,8.18 and 4,6.

[9] Rom 1,26; 4,16; 5,12; 13,6; 15,9; 1 Cor 4,17; 11,10.30; 2 Cor 4,1; 7,13; 13,10; Phlm 15.

clearly employs the phrase to announce what follows: see Rom 4,16 (διὰ τοῦτο ἐκ πίστεως: "This is why it depends on faith, in order that the promise may rest on grace only ..."); Phlm 15 ("Perhaps this is why he was parted from you for a while, that you might have him back for ever"); and 2 Cor 13,10, together with an announcing τοῦτο in 13,9b: τοῦτο καὶ εὐχόμεθα, τὴν ὑμῶν κατάρτισιν. Διὰ τοῦτο ταῦτα ἀπὼν γράφω, ἵνα παρὼν μὴ ἀποτόμως χρήσωμαι ... ("This is what we pray for, that you may become perfect. This is why I write these things while I am away from you, in order that when I come, I may not have to be severe in using ...")[10]. A reference forward always implies some break with the preceding context.

With its two καί's 1 Thess 2,13 has an even more mysterious beginning: καὶ διὰ τοῦτο καὶ ἡμεῖς εὐχαριστοῦμεν .... "Die überladene Ausrucksweise läst eine komplizierte Gedankenführung erkennen"[11].

Referring Back

Notwithstanding the fact that Paul thus more than once uses διὰ τοῦτο in a non-classical way, the phrase in 1 Thess 2,13 most probably refers to what precedes. Three converging reasons suggest this; each of them provides some evidence on its own. (1) Although not everywhere, Paul uses the phrase with a reference backward in the majority of cases; (2) the καί before διὰ τοῦτο seems to connect this phrase (and the whole clause) with what precedes; (3) the line of thought within the context appears to plead for such an understanding. The third reason must be expounded, of course. But two things will be done first: a comparison of 1 Thess 2,13 with 3,7-8 and a brief discussion of the meaning of 2,13ab if διὰ τοῦτο refers to what precedes.

A Comparison with 3,7-8

The Greek text of 3,7-8 reads as follows: 7 διὰ τοῦτο παρεκλήθημεν, ἀδελφοί, ἐφ' ὑμῖν ἐπὶ πάσῃ τῇ ἀνάγκῃ καὶ θλίψει ἡμῶν διὰ τῆς ὑμῶν

---

[10] One could hesitate with regard to 1 Cor 4,17.

[11] T. HOLTZ, *Der erste Brief an die Thessalonicher* (EKK; Zürich – Neukirchen/Vluyn 1986) 97. Cf. E. VON DOBSCHÜTZ, *Die Thessalonicher-Briefe* (KEK; Göttingen 1909) 103: "die etwas schwülstige ['swollen'] Einführung".

πίστεως, 8 ὅτι νῦν ζῶμεν ἐὰν ὑμεῖς στήκετε ἐν κυρίῳ. Just as in 2,13 we have a διὰ τοῦτο phrase, a main verb and also a ὅτι-clause. Yet the motivating clause in 3,8 ("for now we live") does denote the reason why Paul is comforted; the clause repeats and explains what it means to be comforted. Paul is consoled and encouraged because of the wonderful content of Timothy's report (cf. 3,6).

Of course, the verb "to be comforted" in 3,7 differs from "we thank" in 2,13 and there are more lexical discrepancies between the two texts. In both cases, however, it remains striking not only that διὰ τοῦτο is a connecting phrase, referring to what precedes, but also that this phrase is taken up or, as it were, concretized by what follows. In 3,7 this is demonstrated in the expressions ἐφ᾽ ὑμῖν and διὰ τῆς ὑμῶν πίστεως (we have been comforted "because of you" and "through your faith"), in 2,13, one may be tempted to say, in the ὅτι-clause. Yet the peculiar nuances of this last verse must now be indicated.

Exegesis of 2,13ab

At this stage it is not necessary to explain the entire sentence consisting of 2,13. We will consider the main elements of v. 13ab: καὶ διὰ τοῦτο καὶ ἡμεῖς εὐχαριστοῦμεν τῷ θεῷ ἀδιαλείπτως, ὅτι παραλαβόντες λόγον ἀκοῆς παρ᾽ ἡμῶν τοῦ θεοῦ ἐδέξασθε οὐ λόγον ἀνθρώπων ἀλλὰ ... λόγον θεοῦ .... The first καί, at the beginning of the verse, connects what follows with what has just been written. The διὰ τοῦτο phrase possesses its normal meaning; it refers back to the content of the preceding passage, namely 2,1-12[12]. "And for this reason" means: because of Paul's courage and honesty, his irreproachable behavior and manifest love during his ministry at Thessalonica as reported in 2,1-12. God is his witness and the Thessalonians know it; they remember all of it. Paul not only wants to recall his past ministry; he also (second καί)[13] wants to thank God constantly on account of it.

The ὅτι-clause of v. 13b, however, is not a repetition of what is

---

[12] Cf. VON DOBSCHÜTZ, *Thessalonicher-Briefe*, 103-104. This author considers v. 13 as still belonging to the unit 2,1-13 and calls it "der letzte Trumpf" (103) in Paul's apology.

[13] On the uncertainty regarding this second καί see, e.g., RIGAUX, *Thessaloniciens*, 437-438; E. BEST, *A Commentary on the First and Second Epistles to the Thessalonians* (BNTC; London 1972) 110. Cf. ZERWICK, *Biblical Greek*, nr. 462, who discusses the fact that after διό and διὰ τοῦτο the καί "is sometimes to be found in a stereotyped manner"; it may not belong to the pronoun (in 1 Thess 2,13: ἡμεῖς), "but to the verb (or rather, to the whole clause)".

expounded in 2,1-12 nor, strictly speaking, its concretization[14]. There appears to be a shift in the middle of verse 13. Paul adds a supplementary reason for thanking God, namely because "when you received the word of God that you heard from us, you accepted it not as a human word but as ... God's word ... ". This new reason is not so different from the content of the thanksgiving in 1,2-5; moreover, in 1,6 Paul already used the expression δεξάμενοι τὸν λόγον. Of course, because of the way Paul preached the gospel in Thessalonica and because of his apostolic lifestyle (cf. 2,1-12) the Christians must have realized that Paul's message was the word of God, not merely a human word (v. 13b); they must have experienced that this word of God was at work in them in the midst of suffering (vv. 13c-14)[15]. Yet between 2,13a and 13b there appears to be a shift in Paul's reasoning.

To conclude this first part, in the renewed thanksgiving of 2,13ab Paul seems to be offering a twofold reason for his thanking: first the description of his past ministry and exemplary behavior is pointed to in a retrospective way (καὶ διὰ τοῦτο), then the praiseworthy manner in which the Thessalonians received the gospel (the ὅτι-clause) is mentioned[16].

II. THE LINE OF THOUGHT IN 1,2–3,13

How does 1 Thess 2,13 function within its broader context? In order to answer this question the whole of the first half of the letter must be briefly analyzed.

1,2-10

After the salutation in 1,1 Paul[17] expresses thanksgiving to God. He

---

[14] We take this ὅτι as causal, not as introducing an object clause. For BEST, *Thessalonians*, e.g., 2,13b is an object clause: "we thank God that ..." (109).

[15] For a quite different interpretation of 2,13ab, see J.E. FRAME, *The Epistles of St. Paul to the Thessalonians* (ECC; Edinburgh 1912) 106: διὰ τοῦτο refers to 2,1-4; ὅτι is resumptive; the second καί qualifies "we". He translates the text as follows: "And for this reason, we too as well as you thank God continually, namely, because ...".

[16] HOLTZ, *Thessalonicher*, renders: "Und auch deswegen danken wir God unablässig" (96) and comments: "Paulus nimmt ausdrücklich den Eingangsdank wieder auf, bindet ihn an das soeben über sein Auftreten in Thessalonich Gesagte und erläutert das in dem Begründungssatz näher" (97). Two minor critical questions: Is "auch" in the translation in the right position and is the verb "erläutert" in the commentary well chosen?

[17] On the following pages we omit discussion as to whether or not the plural may include Paul's fellow-workers, especially Silvanus (cf. 1,1).

remembers the generous response of the Thessalonians to the gospel (v. 3); he remembers their election by God, the proof of God's love (v. 4). In v. 5a, a description of the Spirit-filled arrival of the gospel message is given; in v. 5b, a reference to the apostle is added "just as you know what kind of persons we proved to be among you for your sake". Paul's praise of the Thessalonians continues in vv. 6-10: they became imitators of Paul and of the Lord; they received the word with joy in spite of persecutions (v. 6); they became an example to all believers in Macedonia and Achaia (v. 7); their faith became known, and so the gospel rang out everywhere in those regions (v. 8). People there reported about Paul and his reception in Thessalonica; they reported the conversion of the Thessalonians, their life as believers, and their waiting for the coming of the risen Lord Jesus (vv. 9-10).

Whereas verses 2-5 constitute one lengthy sentence of thanksgiving, verses 6-10 consist of three independent sentences. Thanking is remembering and while remembering Paul praises the Thessalonians. The whole passage is full of that praise. The initial thanksgiving (v. 2) yields, as it were, to a laudatory remembrance of what occurred and of what is still present, i.e., of the Thessalonians' conversion and their Christian lifestyle. Most probably, however, the thanking itself is not forgotten in v. 5 and even not in vv. 6-10. Yet with its abundant praise the passage as a whole also functions as a *captatio benevolentiae*. Paul's full attention is devoted to the recipients of the letter. This does not obscure Paul's presence: he is the grammatical subject of the opening verb in v. 2; in v. 5a he shows himself as the preacher of the gospel and in v. 5b — rather surprisingly but with determination ("just as you know") — he refers to his apostolic conduct; he mentions himself also at the end of v. 8 as well as in v. 9a. However, notwithstanding these references to Paul, 1,2-10 deals with God's election and the Thessalonians' conversion in the recent past and, above all, with their continuing positive response and exemplary life up to the present.

2,1-12

The passage 2,1-12 is introduced by a connective γάρ and the term εἴσοδος of 1,9 is repeated in 2,1. Here, however, Paul will speak of himself at great length; he will remind the Thessalonians of his founding visit and the style of his apostleship then.

In vv. 1-8 he uses an οὐ ... ἀλλά construction three times. His coming was *not* in vain, *but*, notwithstanding previous sufferings in Philippi and opposition in Thessalonica, he preached the gospel with courage (vv. 1-2).

His appeal did *not* spring from deceit, *but* his preaching aimed at pleasing God (vv. 3-4). His apostolic action was *not* motivated by flattery or greed or looking for praise, *but* he behaved gently as a nursing mother[18]; he loved the Thessalonians so much that he was willing to share with them not only the gospel but his own self (vv. 5-8). Then, in vv. 9-12, Paul recalls how he worked day and night not to burden them, how his behavior was holy, upright and blameless, and how he dealt with each of them as a father does with his own children, urging them to lead lives worthy of God.

This passage can hardly be called a *narratio* in the strict sense. In this autobiographical report Paul gives evidence of what the Thessalonians already know; six times he points to that knowledge (vv. 1.2.5.9.10 and 11) and twice God is referred to as witness (vv. 5 and 10). This very personal testimony has been rightly called a mirror for future church leaders. Paul's behavior was exemplary indeed. Yet given the eschatological context of those days and the expectation of a not too far-off parousia, did Paul intend to present himself as a model for future preachers and authorities? Was he not rather defending himself? Most probably. It is true, we do not know who was attacking him, but the tone no doubt is apologetic[19].

2,1-12 is clearly different from 1,2-10. No longer the Thessalonians but Paul himself is the main subject matter of the pericope, his courage and pure intention, the loving care of a mother, the responsible encouragement of a father. The conversion of the Thessalonians and their commendable Christian life are no longer spoken of. All attention is now devoted to the period of Paul's stay in Thessalonica. The passage contains an intimate testimony in writing.

2,13-16

The first half of verse 13 has already been analyzed: the connecting

---

[18] Literally: "like a wet-nurse taking care of her own children" (2,7).

[19] Otherwise recently C.A. WANAMAKER, "Epistolary vs. Rhetorical Analysis: Is a Synthesis Possible?", in: DONFRIED – BEUTLER (eds.), *The Thessalonians Debate*, 255-286, esp. 265; cf. in the same volume the anti-apologetic approch of K.P. Donfried, R. Hoppe, J.S. Vos, O. Merk, J. Schoon-Janssen and F.W. Hughes. Yet see T. HOLTZ, "On the Background of 1 Thessalonians 2:12", ibid., 69-80, esp. 77-80: "It is not difficult to imagine how ... angry relatives and friends opposed those who had let themselves be misled into baptism through the proclamation of Paul and his coworkers ..." (78-79) and Paul "had to reckon with the fact that a negative propaganda campaign that aimed to destroy his work by attacking his person could have grave consequences" (79), and also the balanced study of J.A.D. WEIMA, "The Function of 1 Thessalonians 2:1-12 and the Use of Rhetorical Criticism: A Response to Otto Merk", ibid. 114-131.

character of "and therefore" which refers to what precedes and the renewed thanking in v. 13a, furthermore the shift in Paul's remembrance which becomes evident through the reason given in the ὅτι-clause of v. 13b. In that last clause Paul emphasizes the adequateness of the Thessalonians' response to his gospel: they accepted it not as human words but as what it really is, God's word. Then he adds that this word is at work in the Thessalonians who believe (v. 13c). The beginning of v. 14 is similar to 1,6: they became imitators, but here the imitation is that of the churches in Judea: "you suffered from your own countrymen the same things those churches suffered from the Jews". The description of what the Jews have done and of their fate in vv. 15-16 diverts the readers from the imitation theme in v. 14 and even more from the thanksgiving in v. 13. Therefore, verses 15-16 are rightly called a digression within Paul's reasoning.

Verses 13-14 prove that Paul has not forgotten the themes he was dealing with in 1,2-10. He comes back to thanksgiving and to praising the Thessalonians for their strong faith. His praise in vv. 13bc and 14 provides a reason to thank God, but the same applies to 2,1-12. The expression καὶ διὰ τοῦτο of v. 13a shows that Paul's apologetic testimony is subsumed by the verb "we give thanks to God". Moreover, it would seem that 2,13-16 functions as a closing to the report of Paul's founding visit to Thessalonica. Because of all this the passage as a whole is better not seen as a digression within the narrative nor as an emotional interruption of the lengthy report of chapters 2–3.

2,17–3,8

The section of 2,17–3,8 offers an interim-report. Paul here narrates what happened between his departure from Thessalonica and the writing of the letter. In 2,17-18 he tells the Thessalonians about the fact that he has been longing to see them and has tried more than once to visit them. In vv. 19-20 Paul poignantly expresses what the Thessalonians really mean to him: they are his hope and joy, his crown of boasting before the Lord Jesus at his parousia, his glory. A higher praise can hardly be imagined. Then, in 3,1-5, Paul deals with the mission of Timothy. The readers also get more information about Paul's intentions and fear. The Thessalonians are in danger; they must be strengthened in the midst of persecutions. Finally, verses 6-8 contain what happened at Timothy's return. Timothy brought good news about the Thessalonians' faith and about their love of Paul. Notwithstanding all distress Paul now, as it were, lives again or lives really, since he knows that they stand firm in the Lord.

The content of 2,17–3,8 differs from that in 2,1-12; the periods that are described are not the same. Yet the two reports are similar. Paul himself is the center in both autobiographical texts. In the second, no less than in the first, he manifests his tender love of the Christians in Thessalonica. If the whole of 1,2–3,8 is taken into consideration, one cannot but notice the movement from Thessalonians (1,2-10: thanksgiving and praise) to Paul (2,1-12: autobiographical report), then back to the Thessalonians (2,13-16: thanksgiving and praise) and again to Paul (2,17–3,8: autobiographical report). To be sure, as we stated above, praise of the Thessalonians is not absent in the Paul-sections, nor references to Paul's preaching in the thanksgiving sections. Yet the basic shifts are obvious.

3,9-10 and 3,11-13

In 3,9 Paul again mentions a thanksgiving; the theme appears a third and last time. Whereas in 1,2 and 2,13 he writes "we thank God" (and visibly is actually thanking while writing), in 3,9 he speaks of thanking by means of a rhetorical question: "How can we thank God enough for you in return...?" The connection of 3,9 with 2,17–3,8 is obvious: the theme of χάρα is repeated from 2,19 and, in a more peculiar way, "joy" here refers to the rejoicing at the good news brought by Timothy (3,6-8). The exclamation of 3,9 at the end of this report is climactic.

In 3,10, within the same grammatical sentence, Paul adds the particle δεόμενοι ("while we are praying") and so the remembering gives way to petitioning. A twofold intention concerning the future is expressed, that of Paul's seeing the Thessalonians face to face and that of supplying what is lacking in their faith.

In 3,11-13 Paul's petitioning becomes an explicit wish-prayer. In v. 11 he repeats the first intention of v. 10. In v. 12 he asks that the Lord may increase the Thessalonians' love for each other and for all, "just as we (love) you". The third petition, that in v. 13, is eschatological: that they may be blameless before God at the parousia of the Lord Jesus.

A thanksgiving supposes the remembering of the past (and the present); a prayer of petition looks to the future. In the thanksgivings of 1,2-10 and 2,13-16 Paul was at the same time praising the Thessalonians. In that of 3,9-10 the praise is still there — cf. the joy that he feels before the Lord because of them — but that remembering and praise give way to the expression of his longing to see them and the mention of his apostolic care. It should not be doubted that the content of 3,10 and 3,12-13 anticipates the hortatory and doctrinal sections of the second part of the letter.

III. CONCLUSIONS

By way of summary three conclusions can be drawn from our analysis.

First, just as 3,9 is subsuming what precedes in order to thank God for his benefactions, so also the initial resumptive clause of 2,13a (καὶ διὰ τοῦτο καὶ ἡμεῖς εὐχαριστοῦμεν ἀδιαλείπτως) has a connecting function. The phrase καὶ διὰ τοῦτο refers to Paul's autobiographical confession or testimony in 2,1-12; that testimony is a reason for thanking. Yet within 2,13 there is a shift. The ὅτι-clause of 2,13b, as well as the two other thanksgivings, indicate that Paul's main concern is the perseverance of the Thessalonians. Their continuing faith and love, their "standing fast in the Lord" (3,8) is the real cause of Paul's joy; for this he thanks God. The report sections of 2,1-12 and 2,17–3,8 may be more or less independent, but they find their climax in the thanksgiving sections of 2,13-16 and 3,9-10.

Second, it is well known that at the beginning of 1 Corinthians, Romans, Philippians and Philemon Paul uses a rather stereotyped thanksgiving[20]. For this he may be depending on hellenistic epistolography. In Paul's thanksgiving three elements come to the forefront: his actual thanking, his remembering of the past and, at the end, his petitioning for the future. Strikingly these three elements are also present in 1 Thessalonians 1–3, be it in a repeated, separate and still loose way: the thanking and remembering in the three thanksgivings, the petition in the third one as well as in the ensuing wish-prayer. Perhaps we may conclude that what has become a more fixed and typically Pauline formula in later letters is, in the early writing to the Thessalonians, still in the process of formative maturation.

Third, given the subtle shifts in Paul's mind, one could hesitate to propose a structure for 1 Thess 1,2–3,13. As we stated as the beginning of this note, there is the risk that a division will harden or unduly simplify Paul's spontaneity. Yet in the text we have noticed the movement from Thessalonians to Paul and back, i.e., the change from thanksgiving (praise) to autobiographical report (self-defense, personal testimony) and back, not once but twice. Therefore, an overall presentation in five (or six) sections

---

[20] For these second and third conclusions, cf. my study "Thanksgivings in 1 Thessalonians 1–3", in DONFRIED – BEUTLER (eds.), *The Thessalonians Debate*, 135-162, which first appeared in R.E. COLLINS (ed.), *The Thessalonian Correspondence* (BETL 87; Leuven 1990) 183-205.

may perhaps be helpful for further exegesis. In the following outline "a" points to thanksgiving (Thessalonians) and "b" to autobiographical report (Paul):

    a: 1,2-10
       b: 2,1-12
    a: 2,13-16
       b: 2,17–3,8
    a: 3,9-10
    3,11-13 (wish-prayer)[21].

In its combination of thanksgiving and report, 1 Thess 1,2–3,13 is certainly more than an introductory thanksgiving; it is best taken as the first part of the letter body itself.

---

[21] Cf. LAMBRECHT, "Thanksgivings", 157.

Additional Note: This article was written before I could consult the excellent commentary of A.B. MALHERBE, *The Letters to the Thessalonians* (AB; New York 2000). For this author 1 Thessalonians "is written in a paraenetic style, of which philophronesis was itself a part, which Paul uses for pastoral purposes" (105). The passage 2,1-12 is not apologetic; it is the "center-piece" of Paul's "self-presentation" (chs. 1-3) which "forms the basis for the practical advice Paul will give in chapters 4 and 5" (84). On 2,13 Malherbe comments: "The [first] *kai* connects v 13 to v 12, and continues the thought of that verse while adding something new.... The reason (*dia touto*) for this thanksgiving is that God continues to call them (v 12), to which he will add another reason, that they had received the word" (165).

22

A Structural Analysis of 1 Thessalonians 4–5

The title for the first day of this SNTS seminar is "Toward a form-critical/epistolary analysis of 1 Thessalonians". The leaders of the seminar have specified the aim of the day: The primary presenter should also make an attempt to link this analysis to rhetorical theory. In the letter through which I received the invitation I read: "We assume that your article 'Thanksgivings in 1 Thessalonians 1–3' of 1990[1] could serve as the basis for your presentation". The purpose of the present study, therefore, is not to rewrite that article but to add a consideration of the second part of 1 Thessalonians as well as to try to link my approach to rhetorical theory.

I. INTRODUCTION

In my 1990 article much attention is given to the epistolary thanksgi-

---

[1] J. LAMBRECHT, "Thanksgivings in 1 Thessalonians 1–3", R.F. COLLINS (ed.), *The Thessalonian Correspondence* (BETL 87; Leuven 1990) 183-205; also in J. LAMBRECHT, *Pauline Studies* (BETL 115; Leuven 1994) 319-141.

Five studies in *The Thessalonian Correspondence* are of particular interest to our topic: J. CHAPA, "Consolatory Patterns? 1 Thes 4,13.18; 5,11", 220-228; F.W. HUGHES, "The Rhetoric of 1 Thessalonians", 94-116; R. KIEFFER, "L'eschatologie en 1 Thessaloniciens dans une perspective rhétorique", 206-218; A. VANHOYE, "La composition de 1 Thessaloniciens", 73-86; W. WUELLNER, "The Argumentative Structure of 1 Thessalonians as Paradoxical Encomium", 117-136.

On 1 Thessalonians 1–3, see now also J. SCHOON-JANSSEN, *Umstrittene 'Apologien' in den Paulusbriefen. Studien zur rhetorischen Situation des 1. Thessalonicherbriefes, des Galaterbriefes und des Philipperbriefes* (GThA 45; Göttingen 1991); P. ARTZ, "The 'Epistolary Introductory Thanksgiving' in the Papyri and in Paul", *NT* 36 (1994) 29-46: "The combination of a report of a prayer and/or the μνεία-motif with a thankgiving to God for the addressees derives from Paul's personal intention and not from a common epistolary convention" (45). Compare this with my conclusions in "Thanksgivings", 192-194: "One must realize that 1 Thessalonians is Paul's first letter and that Paul is here probably in the process of 'creating' his structured thanksgiving" (193). Cf. J. MURPHY-O'CONNOR, *Paul the Letter-Writer: His World, His Options, His Skills* (GNS 41; Collegeville 1995) 55-64.

ving in 1 Thess 1–3 and a brief discussion is offered of items such as "body" of the letter, "apostolic *parousia*" and "epistolary recommendation". In the evaluation I stated: the delineation of the thanksgivings and the detection of the beginning of new sections, "the gathering of striking parallels in Pauline and non-Pauline letters, the careful study of topics with regard to apology and travelogue, the search for stereotyped formulae as well as the determination of their function, the discussion of different aspects of apostolic presence, and even the naming of newly found literary genres: all these efforts, and many more, may be helpful in our understanding of Paul"[2].

In addition I stated: "The danger, however, lies in exaggeration, in increasingly inventive speciousness, in too much, often far-fetched and strained, genre hunting. One might wonder whether Paul consciously starts in 2,1 the body of his letter, deliberately composes in 2,17–3,13 an apostolic *parousia* or really intends in 2,1-12 and 2,17–3,8 a twofold epistolary recommendation. Even to attribute to Paul a more or less spontaneous, subconscious following of pre-existing patterns may constitute here an unwarranted postulate"[3].

The proposal I made there concerning the structure of 1 Thess 1–3 is based on a combination of epistolary and thematic criteria. The same combination will now apply to the examination of the second part of the letter, chapters 4 and 5. I will inquire the "surface" structure, utilizing Paul's development of thought, often revealed by formal elements and by use of different literary genres.

II. ANALYSIS OF 1 THESSALONIANS 4–5

There is an almost general consensus which distinguishes the paraenetic sections 4,1-12 and 5,12-22 from the eschatological middle section 4,13–5,11[4]. I may quote here B.C. Johanson who is convinced that in 1

---

[2] LAMBRECHT, "Thanksgivings", 198-199.

[3] Ibid., 199.

[4] Cf., e.g., I.H. MARSHALL, *1 and 2 Thessalonians* (NCBC; Grand Rapids 1983) 10-11, distinguishes three areas: general morality (sexual morality and idleness); teaching about the parousia; and life together. His division is: 4,1-12 (Exhortation to Ethical Progress); 4,13–5,11 (Instruction and Exhortation about the Parousia); and 5,12-24 (Instruction for Life in the Church).

Thessalonians "the main 'point' of the communication lies in the ... major text-sequence of 4,1–5,24"[5]. He puts forward the ring-composition "A= 4,1-12, B= 4,13–5,11 and A'= 5,12-24"[6]. He compares 4,13-18 with 5,1-11, but at the same time stresses the differences of these passages vis-à-vis the framing ones (4,1-12 and 5,12-22): "Both subsequences formally close with an admonition beginning with the lexical recurrence of παρακαλεῖτε ἀλλήλους. Abundant use of apocalyptic motifs is made in both sections in contrast to what precedes and follows and both make use of creedal material, viz., ὅτι Ἰησοῦς ἀπέθανεν καὶ ἀνέστη (4,14); Ἰησοῦ Χριστοῦ τοῦ ἀποθανόντος ὑπὲρ ἡμῶν (5,9-10). There is also the general conceptual recurrence of σὺν κυρίῳ ἐσόμεθα (4,17) in ἅμα σὺν αὐτῷ ζήσομεν (5,10) with the references to the οἱ κομώμενοι, οἱ νεκροί – οἱ ζῶντες, οἱ περιλειπόμενοι of the former sequence echoed in the word-play in εἴτε γρηγορῶμεν εἴτε καθεύδωμεν ἅμα σὺν αὐτῷ ζήσομεν in 5,10"[7].

The end of the letter consists of a last prayer (5,23-24) and the final recommendations (5,25-28). Because of the parallelism in both content and wording of the prayer with the one at the end of the first part, 3,11-13, it seems better also to consider *5,23-24*, this second eschatological wish-prayer — almost a benediction — as a kind of conclusion of what precedes, not yet the beginning of the formal ending[8]. Regarding 5,23 verse 24

---

[5] B.C. JOHANSON, *To All the Brethren. A Text-Linguistic and Rhetorical Approach to 1 Thessalonians* (CB.NT 16; Stockholm 1987) 160. For an evaluation of this important monograph, see, e.g., KIEFFER, "Eschatologie", 208-209, and VANHOYE, "Composition". This last author fully recognizes the merits of Johanson's text-centered analyses. Yet he remains severe in his overall judgment: "Devenue plus technique, l'étude de la composition s'exprime en un langage esotérique, hérissé de néologismes et d'abréviations, ce qui, assurément, ne rend pas facile le processus de communication entre le lecteur et le commentateur. Un effort démesuré est nécessaire pour comprendre le 'métalangage' utilisé par ce dernier et pour vérifier si l'analyse exprimée dans le métalangage correspond réellement à des données du texte. Le métalangage donne à toute affirmation une apparence d'infaillibilité scientifique. Il rend plus difficile la tâche de démasquer les erreurs possibles" (74). Moreover, among other points, Vanhoye thoroughly criticizes also Johanson's qualification of the function of chs. 1–3 as (only) a preparatory *captatio benevolentiae*: "Il me semble qu'il faut reconnaître, au contraire, que 1 Thessaloniciens est avant tout une lettre, où 'la fonction épistolaire de contact' est prédominante" (86). The first part of 1 Thess is much more than a preparation for the second (82-86).

[6] JOHANSON, *To All the Brethren*, 143.

[7] Ibid., 118-119 (quotation on 118). He mentions also the "common emphasis on not being like οἱ λοιποί who grieve without hope (4,13) and who are spiritually asleep (5,6)" (118-119).

[8] In both prayers we have the introductory expression αὐτὸς δὲ ὁ θεός and the term ἀμέμπτους or ἀμέμπτως. The Thessalonians should be blameless at the day of Jesus' parousia (in each prayer: ἡ παρουσία τοῦ κυρίου ἡμῶν Ἰησοῦ (Χριστοῦ)). The two prayers are manifestly eschatological. Cf. P.-E. LANGEVIN, "L'intervention de Dieu selon 1 Thes 5,23-24", COLLINS (ed.) *Thessalonian Correspondence*, 236-256; J.A.D. WEIMA, "The Pauline Letter Closings: Analysis and Hermeneutical Significance", *BulBR* 5 (1995) 177-197.

functions as a motivating clause: such a prayer can be formulated since we are sure that the God who calls us will also do what we pray for[9]. This verse is thus connected with the prayer; verses 23-24 belong together.

In 5,25 we have with ἀδελφοί the beginning of *5,25-28*. Just as Paul has been praying for the Thessalonians so also the Thessalonians must pray for him: "pray for us". To a certain extent, therefore, verse 25 is also still linked with verses 23-24[10]. A letter appropriately ends with final requests and greetings. In verses 26-28 there are three sentences: Greet the brothers with a holy kiss; I adjure you by the Lord that this letter be read to all the brothers; the grace of our Lord Jesus Christ be with you. So this small unit contains an admonition (v. 26), an adjuration (v. 27)[11], and a final greeting (v. 28).

Paraenesis

The two sections which I called paraenetic, 4,1-12 and 5,12-22, correspond to one another by the genre itself: accumulations of exhortation. Moreover, it is hardly accidental that a number of terms are the same, especially at each beginning. In 4,1 as well as in 5,12 we have a petition formula and, within it, the verb ἐρωτῶμεν, the personal pronoun ὑμᾶς, the vocative ἀδελφοί; furthermore the expression ἐν κυρίῳ ('Ιησοῦ). We may add the presence of παρακαλοῦμεν in 4,1 and 5,14, and the remarkable

---

[9] Cf., e.g., LANGEVIN, "Intervention", 246.

[10] JOHANSON, *To All the Brethren*, 65-66: "... not only is there a thematic shift at 5,25 ..., but also a shift from a predominantly persuasive-exhortational ... to a predominantly phatic communicative function. The transition is, however, not abrupt, but has soft features in that the request for prayer follows naturally upon Paul's immediately preceding wish-prayer for the addressees".

[11] E.R. RICHARDS, *The Secretary in the Letters of Paul* (WUNT II/42; Tübingen 1991) 179-181, points to the first person singular in verse 27: "Throughout the letter, the stereotyped formulae are always in the plural. After the final greetings, however, in verse 26, there is a request in the singular (v. 27) .... Moreover, the previous requests have been rather abstract and 'spiritual', but this request is very pragmatic and stands in contrast to the rest of the epistle. Perhaps it is an indication of Paul taking the pen to affix a closing greeting (v. 28) and adding a personal request as well" (179-180). This may then reveal secretarial assistance in the writing of 1 Thessalonians. See also H. BINDER, "Paulus und die Thessalonicherbriefe", COLLINS (ed.) *Thessalonian Correspondence*, 87-93, who defends a co-authorship in the two letters to the Thessalonians (Paul and esp. Silvanus, "der 'zweite Mann'", who represented "den Autoritätsanspruch Jerusalems", 88) and speaks of "a häufiger Autorenwechsel" (91); MURPHY-O'CONNOR, *Paul the Letter-Writer*, esp. 16-20.

repetition of τοῦτο γὰρ ... θήλημα θεοῦ in 4,3 and 5,18[12]. To be sure, the sections also differ. In the second section the sentences are mostly shorter and, as it were, more nervous. While in 4,1-12 general moral admonitions are given, in 5,12-22 community life is focused upon.

Περὶ δέ in 4,9 indicates a new start, but the division within *4,1-12* is almost completely topical. After the very emphatic opening of the verses 1-2 which introduce the second part in its entirety[13], three warnings are dealt with: warning against unchastity (vv. 3-8: dangers which come from the pagan past of the converts), the love commandment (vv. 9-10: the flower of Christianity) and the admonition concerning quiet and honest work (vv. 11-12: apocalyptic complacency, a danger which may have its origin in Christians' expectation of the imminent return of their Lord and could scandalize τοὺς ἔξω)[14]. Lexical elements in verses 1-2 and verses 10-12 reveal an inclusion: ἀδελφοί, ὑμεῖς, παρακαλέω, περισσεύω μᾶλλον in 4,1 and 4,10; περιπατέω in 4,1 and 4,12; and παραγγελία in 4,2 and παραγγέλλω in 4,11[15].

---

[12] We may also point to the presence of ἀπέχομαι in 4,3 and 5,22 and of πνεῦμα in 4,8 and 5,19. JOHANSON, *To All the Brethren*, 143, moreover, mentions "ἁγιασμός, ἁγιασμῷ, ἁγιάσαι (4,3, 7; 5,23), ἐκάλεσεν ὑμᾶς or καλῶν ὑμᾶς (4,7; 5,24)".

[13] The phrase λοιπὸν οὖν, ἀδελφοί ("finally therefore, brothers") in 4,1 might seem to announce the end. Cf. 2 Cor 13,11: λοιπόν, ἀδελφοί and Phil 4,8: τὸ λοιπόν, ἀδελφοί. Yet by itself it is not. Cf. JOHANSON, *To All the Brethren*, 112: "Here in I Thess 4,1 the evidence is seen to support taking λοιπὸν οὖν as generally inferential ('then' or 'and so') in relation to 1,2–3,13 in view of its exordial-like character [?]. Thus it seems to mark a major text-sequential transition to the text-sequence containing the main message of the letter". U. SCHNELLE, "Die Ethik des 1. Thessalonicherbriefes", COLLINS (ed.), *Thessalonian Correspondence*, 295-305, esp. 302, stresses that the transition is linked (οὖν) with the eschatological content of 3,13 which just precedes.

[14] As is well known, not all exegetes would agree that in verses 3-8 Paul only deals with unchastity; some claim that honesty in business is spoken of in verse 6 (τὸ μὴ ὑπερβαίνειν καὶ πλεονεκτεῖν ἐν τῷ πράγματι τὸν ἀδελφὸν αὐτοῦ). Yet verse 7 with (a) ἐκάλεσεν ... ὁ θεός, (b) ἐν ἁγιασμῷ and (c) ἐπὶ ἀκαθαρίᾳ constitutes an inclusion with verse 3 with (a) θέλημα τοῦ θεοῦ, (b) ὁ ἁγιασμός and (c) πορνεία. Is it therefore not better to explain verse 6 according to the overall theme of verses 3-8?

Another point of discussion is the question to what extent Paul's exhortations refer to a concretely existing situation in Thessalonica (cf. the distinction between "aktuell" and "usuell"). See J. LAMBRECHT, "A Call to Witness by All. Evangelisation in 1 Thessalonians", ID., *Pauline Studies*, 343-359, esp. 352-355 (bibliography on 360-361); U. SCHNELLE "Ethik", 295-305 ("usuell"); JOHANSON, *To All the Brethren*, e.g., 113-118.

On 4,9-12, see the recent study of J. S. KLOPPENBORG, "ΦΙΛΑΔΕΛΦΙΑ, ΘΕΟΔΙΔΑΚΤΟΣ and the Dioscuri: Rhetorical Engagement in 1 Thessalonians 4.9-12", *NTS* 39 (1993) 265-289 (περὶ δέ is an epistolary shorthand introducing a matter of common concern; φιλαδελφία is known in Thessalonica as the near proverbial virtue of the divine twins Castor and Polyceudes; θεοδίδακτος is a term probably coined by Paul himself to convey the idea of divine instruction).

I see three small subdivisions in *5,12-22:* verses 12-13; verses 14-15; and verses 16-22. Verse 12 begins with ἐρωτῶμεν δὲ ὑμᾶς, ἀδελφοί and verse 14 with the parallel παρακαλοῦμεν δὲ ὑμᾶς, ἀδελφοί; the brief clauses in verses 16-18a, after the long sentence of verse 15, in their own manner indicate a new beginning[16]. While in verse 12 the address "brothers" refers to all fellow Christians in Thessalonica, the terms "you, brothers" in verse 14 presumably point to those who may become or are, I would say, the first local church leaders; their specific duties towards Christians and non-Christians (εἰς πάντας, v. 15) are envisaged. It would seem that from verse 16 onward the second person plural is again directed to all Thessalonians. If this way of interpreting is valid we would have an a-b-a' composition: all Christians–leaders–all Christians. The unit a' begins with three imperatives (brief clauses); then follows the emphatic motivation: "for this is the will of God in Christ Jesus for you" (cf. 4,3); finally there are five imperatives (a "pentad", five brief clauses which together treat in a delicate manner the way in which the working of the Spirit has to be judged)[17]. One may perhaps consider εἰρηνεύετε (end of v. 13) and (ὁ θεός) τῆς εἰρήνης (v. 23) as a inclusion.

Eschatology

The central eschatological section, 4,13–5,11, requires careful consideration. We will do so in four steps.

(1) Because of the threefold presence of the preposition περί in 4,9, 4,13 and 5,1 one could be tempted to underestimate the structural qualities of the text. Does περί not indicate a loose sequence of themes and topics? Such a question is strengthened by the strikingly similar outlook of 4,9 and 5,1-2:

> 4,9: περὶ δὲ τῆς φιλαδελφίας
>> 5,1-2: περὶ δὲ τῶν χρόνων καὶ τῶν καιρῶν
> 4,9: οὐ χρείαν ἔχετε γράφειν ὑμῖν
>> 5,1-2: οὐ χρείαν ἔχετε ὑμῖν γράφεσθαι
> 4,9: αὐτοὶ γὰρ ὑμεῖς θεοδίδακτοί ἐστε
>> 5,1-2: αὐτοὶ γὰρ ἀκριβῶς οἴδατε

In both passages the δέ is progressive and announces a new theme

---

[15] Cf. JOHANSON, *To All the Brethren*, 113.
[16] Cf. ibid., 136-139.
[17] Cf. LAMBRECHT, "A Call to Witness", 356-357.

("now concerning ..."). In both passages Paul stresses that the Thessalonians do not need to have anything written to them; they already know.

Yet in 4,13 the caesura is much greater and the situation appears to be different. The preposition περί does not stand at the beginning of the sentence; the tone is more personal: Paul deals no longer with "virtues" but with information about the future of deceased Christians. That is a matter which the Thessalonians do not yet seem to know[18].

(2) The beginning and the end of the section correspond to each other as far as content and vocabulary are concerned. We may compare the following elements from *5,9-11* and *4,13-18*:

5,9:	ὁ θεός	4,14: ὁ θεός
	The Lord Jesus Christ4,	14.15.16.17
5,10:	ἀποθανόντος	4,14: ἀπέθανεν
	wake, sleep	4,13.15-17: alive, asleep
	ἅμα	4,17: ἅμα
	σὺν αὐτῷ	4,17: σὺν αὐτῷ
	"we"	4,17: ἐσόμεθα
5,11:	διὸ παρακαλεῖτε	4,18: ὥστε παρακαλεῖτε
	ἀλλήλους	ἀλλήλους

Just as in 4,13-18 Paul deals in 5,9-11 with the final destination of all Christians, dead and living alike. Both passages provide information which must make possible the mutual consolation. It would seem that we can understand the particle ὅτι of 5,9 in a pregnant way: for (this we should know, namely, that) God has destined us .... If the two passages are thus corresponding to one another, then (1) from 5,10 (τοῦ ἀποθανόντος ὑπὲρ ἡμῶν ἵνα ... σὺν αὐτῷ ζήσωμεν) we may conclude that in 4,14 the same strict causal connection between Christ's death and our resurrection is implicitly present, and (2) from 4,16-18 we know that ζήσωμεν in 5,10 (= σωτηρία, 5,9) imply both resurrection (4,16) and the "being always with the Lord" (4,17).

The paraenetic character of both passages is the same: because

---

[18] For the disclosure formula "we would not have you ignorant" in 4,13, see also Rom 1,13; 11,25; 1 Cor 10,1; 12,1; 2 Cor 1,8. Cf. JOHANSON, *To All the Brethren*, 120: The formula "not only serves to signal a transition to a different topic but also the introduction of new information, as indicated by θέλομεν together with the noetic verb".

Christians are aware of their eschatological future — no destination for wrath but vocation to obtain salvation through the Lord Jesus Christ, i.e., lasting life with him — they must not grieve (4,13), they must comfort and encourage one another (4,18 and 5,11).

Moreover, the passages 4,13-18[19] and 5,9-11 constitute together an inclusion. This confirms the correctness of the general assumption that 4,13–5,11 is a coherent section, a large thematic unity.

(3) The remaining verses, *5,1-8*, are different. There is another type of information and exhortation. Paul here stresses something that the Thessalonians are supposed to know already: the sudden, unexpected and imminent coming of the Lord, "as a thief in the night" (v. 2). Paul also emphasizes that Christians are not in darkness (they know and, morally speaking, they are children of light and day); therefore the coming day should not surprise them. Paul here distinguishes, not between dead and living (i.e., between two kinds of Christians) as in the two framing passages, but between Christians and the other people who say "there is peace and security"; sudden destruction will come upon those people and there will be no escape. See "you yourselves" (v. 2) and "when they say" (v. 3; cf. οἱ λοιποί, v. 6)[20].

The exhortation is no longer to console one another but: "keep awake and be sober" (v. 6). Verses 7-8 give the motivation and repeat that admonition: "For those who sleep sleep at night, and those who are drunk get drunk at night. But, since we belong to the day, let us be sober, and put on the breastplate of faith and love, and for a helmet the hope of salvation". Moreover, the exhortation is "given a particularly gentle pastoral tone due to the hortatory subjunctives used only in the whole letter"[21].

One more difference between 5,1-8 and the framing units. In verses 6-

---

[19] Cf. J. DELOBEL, "The Fate of the Dead according to 1 Thessalonians 4 and 1 Corinthians 15", COLLINS (ed.), *Thessalonian Correspondence*, 340-347. According to J.-N ALETTI, "Paul et la rhétorique. Etat de la question et propositions", J. SCHLOSSER (ed.), *Paul de Tarse* (LeDiv 165; Paris 1996) 27-50: "Paul combine très souvent les parallélismes et le cadre conceptuel de la rhétorique argumentative" (33). For the "micro-unité" 4,13-18, he indicates the "parallèles lexicaux", as well as the "composition discursive": A = *introduction* (v. 13: annonce du thème); B = *propositio* (l'apodose v. 14b); C = *preuves* (v. 15-17); D = *conclusion* (v. 18: exhortation) (33-34).

[20] However, this distinction, together with the expression οἱ λοιποί (5,6), occurs already in 4,13: οἱ λοιποὶ οἱ μὴ ἔχοντες ἐλπίδα.

[21] JOHANSON, *To All the Brethren*, 133. The concentric structure proposed by C. FOCANT, "Les fils du Jour (1 Thes 5,5)", COLLINS (ed.), *Thessalonian Correspondence*, 348-355, esp. 350-353, is hardly convincing.

8 the verbs καθεύδω and γρηγορέω are employed metaphorically[22], just as "night" and "darkness", and "day" and "light" in verses 4-8. There occurs a rather strange shift in 5,9-10: here the equally metaphorical sense of καθεύδω is "to be dead" (cf. κοιμάομαι in 4,13-15), and that of γρηγορέω "to be (still) alive" (cf. ζάω in 4,15 and 17).

(4) The conclusion of this structural analysis can now be drawn. It appears that 4,13-5,11 consists of three units, of which the third corresponds to the first; there is thus a concentric feature in this section:

> a: 4,13-18: because of the future resurrection comfort one another;
> b: 5,1-8: because of the near but uncertain date be sober and awake;
> a':   5,9-11: because of the final salvation encourage one another.

Of course, contentwise the three units are not so different; they are linked together. Moreover, verses 9-10 of chapter 5 function as a motivation for the exhortation to keep awake and to be sober (cf. ὅτι at the beginning of v. 9)[23]. Finally, the very last verse, 5,11, is probably more than the exhortation which follows from 5,9-10. In some way it functions as the conclusion of the whole section 4,13-5,11 (cf. the introductory διό in 5,11). It is also quite possible that παρακαλεῖτε in verse 11 differs in meaning from the same imperative in 4,18: no longer consolation of those who grief because of their deceased fellow Christians, but encouragement and "upbuilding" or, more concretely, exhortation to vigilance as in 5,6-8. The addition of both καὶ οἰκοδομεῖτε εἰς τὸν ἕνα and καθὼς καὶ ποεῖτε in 5,11 confirms this suggestion for a shift of meaning. One might even compare this last expression with καθὼς καὶ περιπατεῖτε at the beginning of the second half of the letter, 4,1.

Structure

We can hardly put forward that Paul wanted to give to the second part

---

[22] Cf. μεθύω ("to get drunk", 5,7) and νήφω ("to be sober", 5,6 and 8). In verse 7a the sense of καθεύδω is most probably literal ("to sleep").

[23] Cf. T. Söding, "Der Erste Thessalonicherbrief und die frühe paulinische Evangeliumsverkündigung. Zur Frage einer Entwicklung der paulinischen Theologie", *BZ* 35 (1991) 180-203: "Dass Glaube, Liebe und Hoffnung zur eschatologischen Rettung führen, folgt nach dem 1 Thess aus dem Heilshandeln Gottes in Jesus Christus" (197). See n. 49 on ὅτι "als Verbindung zwischen 5,8 und 5,9". Johanson, *To All the Brethren*, 134, however, nuances: Verses 9-10b "should not be seen so much as giving the motivation for the exhortations to sober vigilance as giving the theological-christological basis of their status".

of his letter to the Thessalonians a structure similar to that of the first part. Yet, if our analysis has any value, there exists a striking similarity; like chapters 1–3 chapters 4–5 mainly consist of five internally related units and a wish-prayer[24]:

4,1-2: introductory paraenesis
    a 4,3-12: paraenesis
        b 4,13-18: final destiny of Christians
    a 5,1-8: paraenesis
        b 5,9-11: final destiny of Christians
    a 5,12-22: paraenesis
5,23-24: eschatological wish-prayer

The paraenesis in the a-units contains moral exhortation and admonishments. The exhortation present at the end of the b-units asks for mutual consolation and encouragement. Of course the movement of paraenesis (a) to information (b) should not eclipse the distinct eschatological character of the three middle units, 4,13–5,11. Moreover, all paraenesis in 1 Thessalonians serves an eschatological purpose[25]. Finally, the surprising similarity in structure between 1 Thess 1–3 and 1 Thess 4–5 should not cover up the great differences of content: thanksgiving is not paraenesis and autobiographical apology is not eschatological information.

III. METHODOLOGICAL REFLECTONS

At the end of our analysis I may come back to a reflection on the method[26]. Three items require a brief comment. What is the relevancy of

---

[24] Compare the differing chiastic and alternating patterns in JOHANSON, *To All the Brethren*, 151.

[25] For the connection between paraenesis and eschatology, see, e.g., SÖDING, "Der Erste Thessalonicherbrief", 188: "Die Paraklese zielt auf die Vorbereitung der Glaubenden für den 'Tag des Herrn' (5,2), an dem sie heilig und untadelig dastehen sollen (3,12f; 4,3-8; 5,23)"; and 193: "Die gesamte Paraklese des 1Thess steht im Zeichen der Vorbereitung auf die Parusie des Kyrios ...".

[26] Cf. LAMBRECHT, "Thanksgivings", 192-194 and 198-202. For broad and balanced methodological reflections, see JOHANSON, *To All the Brethren*, with regard to rhetorics esp. 157-172; Aletti, "Paul et la rhétorique"; MURPHY-O'CONNOR, *Paul the Letter-Writer*, esp. 65-98; and my more general study "Rhetorical Criticism and the New Testament", *Bijdr* 50 (1989) 239-253.

content in each proposal of structure? What type of letter is 1
Thessalonians? What are the main characteristics of this particular letter,
the first written by Paul?

The Relevancy of Content

In his discussion of the rhetoric of the Thessalonian letters, Jewett
writes: "Prior to the appearance of the rhetorical studies ..., the research
that has been done on the structure ... fell in two general categories: analyses of the logical or thematic development, and analyses of the epistolary
form"[27]. One gets the impression that there are three types of structure:
thematic, epistolary and rhetorical.

Yet we have only to look further than the main divisions of both the
epistolary form (e.g., salutation, thanksgiving, body, greetings) and the
rhetorical pattern (e.g., exordium, narratio, probatio, peroratio) in order to
see immediately the entrance of the content considerations[28]. This is a first
remark. The second concerns the possible identification of sections of the
letter. So one would be willing to qualify the report of 2,1-12 and 2,17–3,8
as a *narratio* and the thanksgiving of 1,2-10 as an *exordium*, but one can
hardly call 4,1–5,22 a *probatio*. There is the danger of forcing a text into
the straitjacket of a so-called common pattern[29]. This brings us to a third

---

[27] R. JEWETT, *The Thessalonian Correspondence. Pauline Rhetoric and Millenarian Piety*
(Foundations and Facets; Philadelphia 1986), 63-78 and charts on 216-221; cited text on 68.
Cf., e.g., the rhetorical approach by C.A. WANAMAKER, *The Epistles to the Thessalonians*
(NIGTC; Grand Rapids 1990) 45-50 (for a critical discussion, see ALETTI, "Paul et la rhéto-
rique", 35-36).

[28] We may refer to the divisions within the "body" of the letter and quote JEWETT,
Thessalonian Correspondence, 70: "There is usually a proper identification of the epistolary
prescript and postscript as well as a portion of the thanksgiving. But such categories are interspersed with topical titles ...". Is this, however, not equally true of what Jewett himself does on,
e.g., p. 75, regarding 4,9-12? These verses are part of the "probatio" and constitute "the second
proof concerning the communal ethic". The division is as follows: 1. Reiteration of previous
grounding and accomplishment of the love ethic (4,9-10a); 2. The admonitions 4,10b-12: a.
Continue in the ethic (v. 10b), b. Live quietly (v. 11a), c. Be self-supporting (v. 11b), Gain
public respect (v. 12a), e. Be independent (v. 12b). The same applies to HUGHES, "Rhetoric",
109-116 (= "A Rhetorical Summary of 1 Thessalonians", extremely detailed).

[29] Cf. VANHOYE, "Composition", 82 and 78-79: The rhetorical patterns "s'efforcent de
faire entrer le texte de l'épître dans le lit de Procuste que la rhétorique classique a défini pour
les discours et non pour les lettres". See also the careful remarks of JOHANSON, *To All the
Brethren*, 141-142, regarding 5,12-24 as *peroratio*. His conclusion: "While these observations
do not qualify 5,12-24 as a *peroratio* characteristic of orations as such, there are nevertheless

remark. Although an author can sometimes follow a given form, a literary genre, almost unconsciously, a more sophisticated pattern supposes an intended effort. In order to conclude to the presence of such a pattern formal and topical indications are needed. It would seem to me that they are lacking in 1 Thessalonians as far as the proposed rhetorical structure is concerned. Our fourth remark: with regard to the "body" of the letter and its arrangement two factors are of much more importance than a given pattern. First, attention must be given to the situation in Thessalonica with on the one hand the praiseworthy conduct of Christians and on the other their specific difficulties regarding moral life and doctrine. Second, the free and creative talent of Paul as writer should not be underestimated. There is a final remark. One should also bear in mind that a so-called thematic structure must not neglect the formal criteria. In all structural analyses form and content cannot be separated.

What Kind of Letter?

I will try to answer two questions. The first is: should we consider 1 Thessalonians as a letter of consolation? In two recent studies Juan Chapa took up this question in his reaction to K. Donfried and A. Smith who attempted to interpret 1 Thessalonians as such a letter[30]. Chapa first exam-

---

sufficient peroration-like characteristics to justify taking 5,12-24 as a whole to function as the conclusion not merely of the text-sequence 4,1–5,24, but of the whole letter-body (1,2–5,24)" (142). For the whole of 4,1–5,24, see 72-74, 78 and 161-163. Cf. Johanson's reflection at the beginning of his monograph: a "text-centered analysis is necessary in order to be able to judge the extent to which conventional influence has controlled individual expression or to which the individual author has bent and shaped the conventional into something new and appropriate to the situation in hand" (6).

30 J. CHAPA, "Is First Thessalonians a Letter of Consolation?" *NTS* 40 (1994) 150-160 and "Consolatory Patterns"; A. SMITH, *The Social and Ethical Implications of the Pauline Rhetoric in 1 Thessalonians* (Diss. Vanderbilt Univ.; Ann Arbor, Univ. Microfilms Intern. 1989), 170; K. DONFRIED, "The Theology of 1 Thessalonians as a Reflection of Its Purpose", M.P. HORGAN, P.J. KOBELSKI (eds.), *To Touch the Text. FS J.A. Fitzmyer* (New York 1989) 243-260, esp. 243-244 and 259-260: "... we understand 1 Thessalonians not primarily as a 'paraenetic' letter but as a 'paracletic' letter, as a *consolatio*" (243-244); "1 Thessalonians is a λόγος παραμυθητικός to a Christian church suffering the effects of persecution. ... an encouragement to the discouraged" (260). See also DONFRIED, "1 Thessalonians, Acts and Early Paul", COLLINS (ed.), *Thessalonian Correspondence*, 3-26. For an introduction in ancient letter writing see, e.g., A. M. MALHERBE, *Ancient Epistolary Theorists* (SBL.SBS 19; Atlanta 1988) 1-14; RICHARDS *Secretary*, 129-153, as well as the appendix on 211-216; MURPHY-O'CONNOR, *Paul the Letter-Writer*.

ines what is meant by consolation in antiquity and highlights the three elements in a letter of consolation: sympathy, consolation proper and (also) explicit exhortation[31]. He recognizes that in the church of Thessalonica there seems to have been two sources of affliction: hostility (up to persecution) and the death of some Thessalonians[32].

Chapa then gives of survey of the passages in 1 Thessalonians which could function in a letter of consolation[33]. In 2,17-18 Paul's mention of his inability to visit Thessalonica may have a consolatory purpose. In 2,2 Paul refers to his own suffering and so expresses his sympathy. In 3,3-4 Paul perhaps aims "to lessen the sorrow of those who were suffering, through the consideration of the universality and inescapability of sorrow and pain"[34]. Moreover, he stresses that suffering was to be expected. In 1,6-10 Paul praises the noble Christian conduct of the Thessalonians; such a praise can easily be regarded as a source of consolation. In 2,14-15 he refers to the sufferings of Christ and the churches of Judaea; as is well known examples of people with similar experiences of grief may have a consolatory intention. Chapa mentions that "Paul's continuous exhortation, especially in chapters 4 and 5, might be seen as a response to circumstances of sorrow and affliction, which could have put at risk the fulfilment of Christian obligations"[35]; such exhortations may possess a consolatory purpose.

For Chapa "it is clear that 1 Thessalonians contains some rhetorical strategies current in literature of consolation which seem to fit a situation of some sort of crisis caused by sorrow or affliction in the Christian community at Thessalonica, like the death of some of its members or the consequences which persecution has left among them"[36]. However, because an

---

[31] On the presence of exhortation in a letter of consolation, see CHAPA, "Letter of Consolation", 151-153: "Explicit exhortation was ... the natural connotation of consolation" (152); "... the exhortation to accept bravely the misfortune which is connatural to the human condition, not to be overcome excessively by grief and, in consequence, to neglect one's duties" (151).

[32] Ibid., 150-156. Cf., e.g., SÖDING, "Der Erste Thessalonicherbrief", 182-183. For DONFRIED, "Theology", 254-256, it is probable that persecution in Thessalonica has led to occasional deaths. He suggests that "the dead who are referred to in 1 Thess 4,13-18 are those who may have died in some mob-action type of persecution in Thessalonica" (254). The two sources of affliction are thus linked. Rightly? Donfried refers to his earlier study "The Cults of Thessalonica and the Thessalonian Correspondence", NTS 31 (1985) 336-356, esp. 349-350, and to the same conclusion of J.S. POBEE, Persecution and Martyrdom in the Theology of Paul (JSNT.S 6; Sheffield 1985) 113-114.

[33] CHAPA, "Letter of Consolation", 156-159.

[34] Ibid., 158.

[35] Ibid., 158-159.

[36] Ibid., 159.

overall linking scheme is missing he hesitates. "Is then 1 Thessalonians a letter of consolation? I do not think one can give a definite and precise answer to this question"[37]. His final word is: "If we should not formally classify 1 Thessalonians as a 'letter of consolation,' we may, nevertheless, be justified in calling it a consoling letter without intending to exclude other valid purposes"[38]. I myself wonder whether the consoling character of 1 Thessalonians is thus not overly stressed even by Chapa.

The second question is a rhetorical one. Does 1 Thessalonians belong to demonstrative (epideictic) or to deliberative speech? The first type of speech wants to praise a present situation and to confirm the addressees in their conduct[39], the second looks to the future and exhorts to new and better action[40]. To what extent can this rhetorical distinction be applied to 1 Thessalonians? It would seem to me that, because of the situation in Thessalonica, a choice between the two kinds of languages is unnecessary and should be avoided. The needs of Christians may have differed from person to person, from family to family. In his letter Paul speaks of both present and future; he wants to reaffirm good conduct as well as to bring back to the right behavior.

The Peculiar Structure of 1 Thessalonians

In an ancient letter, including the Pauline letter, one normally expects

---

[37] Ibid.

[38] Ibid., 160. Cf. also the critical approach by MURPHY-O'CONNOR, *Paul the Letter-Writer*, 95-98: "... the value of epistolary classification of whole letters must be considered extremely dubious" (98).

[39] Cf. CHAPA, "Letter of Consolation", 153-154: Chapa thinks that 1 Thess is "epideictic"; equally, e.g., JEWETT, *The Thessalonian Correspondence*, 71-72; WANAMAKER, *Thessalonians*, 47-48; HUGHES, "Rhetoric", 97 and 106-107; KIEFFER, "Eschatologie", 211-212; S. WALTON, "What Has Aristotle To Do with Paul? Rhetorical Criticism and 1 Thessalonians", *TynB* 46 (1995) 229-250. WUELLNER, "Argumentative Structure", calls the genre of 1 Thessalonians more specifically a "Paradoxical Encomium" (encomiastic = epideictic). Yet see MURPHY-O'CONNOR, 70: "However justified this [rhetorical] classification may be in theoretical terms, it is manifest that a huge abyss separates 1 Thessalonians from the classic display discourses ..." (display rhetoric = epideictic rhetoric).

[40] Cf. JOHANSON, *To All the Brethren*, 166: "... there is the future-oriented focus in the response-changing function of dissuasion from grief and incipient doubt, besides in the response-reinforcing, more general admonitions to advance in leading a life pleasing to God". Since the response-changing function is the most important of the letter, Johanson concludes: "As for the rhetorical genre, the one to which 1 Thessalonians would have the closest resemblance is the deliberative one" (189).

a salutation at the beginning and greetings at the end. 1 Thessalonians respects this rule. After the salutation the Pauline letter mostly begins with a thanksgiving and then the "body" follows. Already here the first letter to the Thessalonians goes its own way. The thanksgiving of 1 Thessalonians is scattered over the first half of the letter and certainly belongs to the "body" of this particular letter.

One may expect after the "body" of a letter and before its "closing" some requests or recommendations. Sometimes a distinction can be made between a doctrinal (dogmatic) part and an exhortative (paraenetic) part (cf. Romans 1–11 and 12–15). Again, 1 Thessalonians is different. Chapters 4 and 5 are more than paraenesis; they contain doctrine as well; these chapters, too, belong to the "body" of the letter.

The special outlook of Paul's first letter should not hinder our view on its peculiar and even artistic structure[41]. I hope that my article from 1990 and this supplementary paper be a help in detecting the structural quality of 1 Thessalonians and Paul's argumentation or, at least, in stimulating the discussion in our seminar.

---

[41] For WUELLNER, "Argumentative Structure", however, this is, I think, still the "literary" structure. He sees "Paul's rhetoric of argumentation and ... the rhetorical structure of 1 Thessalonians, as distinct from both the traditionally more familiar concern for discrete rhetorical features *in* 1 Thessalonians, and for *literary* structures" (127-128). By rhetorical criticism he means, above all, "the rhetoric, the type of persuasion, *of* 1 Thessalonians" (135). "Better than any other modern critical approach it brings to comprehension (which is more than explanation) what all exegetical methods *want* to 'explain' — the text's 'power' (G. Kennedy)" (135-136).

Additional Note

For a defense of the same metaphorical sense for the verbs "to be awake" and "to be asleep" in 5,10 as in 5,6-7 (= to be ethically or spirititualy vigilant or negligent), see recently J.P. HEIL, "Those Now 'Asleep' (not Dead) Must Be 'Awakened' for the Day of the Lord in 1 Thess 5.9-10", *NTS* 46 (2000) 464-471. If Heil's interpretation is correct, our proposed a - a' structure of 4,13-18 and 5,9-11 disappears. Yet can one assume in 5,10 the hortatory nuance: "those presently 'asleep' must be awakened for life in the Lord Jesus Christ in the future" (468)? Moreover, it would seem that the broader but not too distant context makes possible the remarkable shift in the metaphorical use of γρηγορέω and καθεύδω: from being vigilant or negligent in 5,6-7 to being still alive or already dead in 5,10 (cf. 4,13-18).

See now also A.B. MALHERBE, *The Letters to the Thessalonians* (AB; New York 2000) 300: Paul "returns again to the two groups of believers at the Parousia (4:13, 14, 16), only now he describes them with two different words.... These two verbs do not normally describe life and death ..., but their use here is suggested by their appearance in the exhortation in vv 6-8 and by the use of euphemism in consolation". For the framing similarities between 5,9-11 and 4,13-18, see pp. 299-301. 5,11 also functions as a transition to 5,12-22. Malherbe considers the whole of 4,1–5,22 as "exhortation".

Collationes 27 (1997) 227-241 (in Dutch)

23

Christ and the Church, Husband and Wife in Ephesians 5,21-33***

The so-called anti-feminist Paul writes in Gal 3,27-28: "As many of you as were baptized into Christ have clothed yourselves with Christ. There is no longer Jew or Greek, there is no longer slave or free, there is no longer male and female; for all of you are one in Christ Jesus". This text has a revolutionary ring, but an official church document warns us to be cautious in interpretation. Paul is speaking here, it is said, of the "fundamental equality of men and women, as children of God in Christ", not of church ministries[1]. The discussion on ministries occurs in 1 Corinthians 12 where in verse 13, however, the opposition male-female does not appear: "For in the one Spirit we were all baptized into one body — Jews or Greeks, slaves or free — and we were all made to drink of one Spirit". In this chapter Paul further explains the diversity of charismata and functions in the church (see vv. 14-30)[2].

*** These pages contain the English translation of the discussion paper which was read at the General Meeting of the (Flemish) *Interdiocesaan Pastoraal Beraad* at Antwerp on June 7, 1996. The footnotes are added.

[1] *On the Question of the Admission of Women to the Ministerial Priesthood (= Inter insigniores)*. Declaration of the Sacred Congregation for the Doctrine of the Faith (1977). English translation in *The Order of Priesthood. Nine Commentaries on the Vatican Decree "Inter insigniores"* (Huntington, Indiana 1978) 1-20, 9. Cf. p. 16: "... this passage [= Gal 3,28] does not concern ministries: it only affirms the universal calling to divine filiation, which is the same for all". See also the "Commentary Prepared at the Congregation's Request by a Theologian Expert", ibid., 21-50: "The Declaration also points out the defect in the argument that seeks to base the demand that the priesthood be conferred on women on the text Galatians 3.28, which states that in Christ there is no longer any distinction between man and woman. For St. Paul this is the effect of baptism. The baptismal catechesis of the Fathers often stressed it. But absolute equality in baptismal life is quite a different thing from the structure of the ordained ministry. This latter is the object of a vocation within the Church, not a right inherent in the person" (44).

[2] Cf. A. VANHOYE, "Nécessité de la diversité dans l'unité selon 1 Co 12 et Rom 12" *Unité et diversité dans l'Eglise* (Città del Vaticano 1989) 143-156: "Il est ... très important de distinguer les niveaux. Parce qu'ils ne le font pas, plusieurs auteurs tirent de certains textes pauli-

In the same letter to the Corinthians, chapter 7, Paul once more puts the woman on a par with the man: "The husband should give to his wife her conjugal rights, and likewise the wife to her husband" (v. 3)[3]. Yet even more famous is the injunction from chapter 11 that women in church meetings should cover their heads when they pray or prophesy. Paul grounds this rule as follows: "I want you to understand that Christ is the head of every man, and the husband is the head of his wife, and God the head of Christ" (v. 3)[4]. A similar saying is also found in Eph 5,23: "The husband is the head of the wife just as Christ is the head of the church"[5].

The verse from the letter to the Ephesians belongs to the unit called "the household code" which goes from 5,21 to 6,9. First husband and wife are addressed (5,22-33), then children and father (6,1-4), and, finally, slaves and masters (6,5-9)[6]. In the present discussion paper only the first part is dealt with. In 5,22-33 the relation between husband and wife is compared with that between Christ and the church; it is not only compared but also motivated and grounded by the relation between Christ and the church. The passage Eph 5,21-33 presents itself as an expansion of Col 3,18-19: "Wives, be subject to your husbands, as is fitting in the Lord. Husband, love your wives and never treat them harshly"[7].

---

niens des conclusions abusives et mettent leur lecteurs en pleine confusion. Ils confondent, par exemple, la perspective de Gal 3,28 et celle de 1 Cor 12. Le texte de Ga 3,28 proclame l'inexistence de la diversité au niveau fondamental de la foi au Christ: 'Il n'y a ni Juif ni Grec, ni esclave ni homme libre, ni mâle et femelle'. Qui ne distingue pas les niveaux applique ce texte au plan social, en y voyant une théorie révolutionnaire, ou à celui des fonctions dans l'Eglise, en affirmant qu'aucune différence entre hommes et femmes n'est admissible dans l'attribution des ministères. Mais c'est là confondre le niveau fondamental, considéré dans la lettre aux Galates, et le niveau fonctionnel, considéré en 1 Co 12. En Galates, Paul exclut la diversité, parce qu'il parle de la justification par la foi. En 1 Co 12, il démontre que, pour les ministères, la diversité est indispensable (12,28-30)" (151).

[3] See in the same chapter also vv. 4-6.10-16 and 32-34.

[4] Cf. in the same chapter vv. 7-10: "... man ... is the image and reflection of God; but woman is the reflection of man" (v. 7). But in vv. 11-12 there is again an egalitarian text: "... in the Lord, woman is not independent of man or man independent of woman. For just as woman came from man, so man comes through woman; but all things come from God". Many exegetes doubt the authenticity of 1 Cor 14,34-36: women must keep silent in the churches. In fact, this text may be a later, non-Pauline addition, a gloss.

[5] Paul sees the church as the body of Christ: "Now you are the body of Christ and individually members of it" (1 Cor 12,27; see also 12,13 and Rom 12,4-5). The author of Ephesians distinguishes between the head (Christ) and the body (the church). The church consists of Jews and Gentiles: Christ has reconciled both groups to God into one body (cf. 2,15-16); this body contains many parts which from the head receive power to reach the perfect growth in love (cf. 4,15-16).

[6] This "household" code was known in the Greco-Roman world.

[7] Cf. 1 Pet 3,1-7: "1 *Wives*, in the same way, accept the authority of your husbands, so

An exhaustive treatment of this pericope cannot be given here. Two questions will be focused upon. How precisely does the relation between Christ and the church function in the exhortations given to husband and wife, and does that comparison with Christ and the church determine the relation between husband and wife strictly and definitively? However, a few words of comment about the pericope should be offered first.

I. THE TEXT

We present here a structured translation of Eph 5,21-33 (NRSV):
21   Be subject to one another out of reverence for Christ.

I A 22   *Wives*, be subject to your husbands as you are to the Lord.
  B 23a   For the husband is the head of the wife
     b   just as Christ is the head of the church,
     c   the body of which he is the Savior.
     24a   Just as the church is subject to Christ,
     b   so also wives ought to be, in everything, to their husbands.

II A 25a   *Husbands*, love your wives,
   B b   just as Christ loved the church and gave himself up for her,
      26   in order to make her holy by cleansing her with the washing of water by the word,
      27a   so as to present the church to himself in splendor, without a spot or wrinkle or anything of the kind
      b   — yes, so that she may be holy and without blemish.
   A' 28a   In the same way, husbands should love their wives as they do their own bodies.

---

that, even if some of them do not obey the word, they may be won over without a word by their wives' conduct, 2 when they see the purity and reverence of your lives. 3 Do not adorn yourselves outwardly by braiding your hair, and by wearing gold ornaments or fine clothing; 4 rather, let your adornment be the inner self with the lasting beauty of a gentle and quiet spirit, which is very precious in God's sight. 5 It was in this way long ago that the holy women who hoped in God used to adorn themselves by accepting the authority of their husbands. 6 Thus Sarah obeyed Abraham and called him lord. You have become her daughters as long as you do what is good and never let fears alarm you. 7 *Husbands*, in the same way, show consideration for your wives in your life together, paying honor to the woman as the weaker sex, since they too are also heirs of the gracious gift of life — so that nothing may hinder your prayers".

The last verse employs the well-known expression "the weaker sex".

    b   He who loves his wife loves himself.
29a   For no one ever hates his own body,
    b   but he nourishes and tenderly cares for it,
    c   just as Christ does for the church,
30   because we are members of his body.
31a   "For this reason a man will leave his father and mother
    b   and be joined to his wife,
    c   and the two will become one flesh".
32a   This is a great mystery,
    b   and I am applying it to Christ and the church.

33a   Each of you, however, should love his wife as himself,
    b   and a wife should respect her husband[8].

The Structure

As is assumed by a great number of exegetes, the letter to the
Ephesians is presumably not written by Paul; the writing probably dates
from the nineties. For its composition the author evidently employed the
letter to the Colossians. The situation to which Ephesians is reacting is no
longer that of the early church, nor that of Colossians. Eph 5,22–6,9
belongs to the second half of the letter, its hortatory part (3,1–6,20). It
directly follows 5,15-21, a text that should also be quoted in full:

15   Be careful then how you live, not as unwise people but as
       wise,
16   making the most of the time, because the days are evil.
17   So do not be foolish, but understand what the will of God is.
18   Do not get drunk with wine, for that is debauchery; but be
       filled with the Spirit,
19   as you sing psalms and hymns and spiritual songs among
       yourselves, singing and making melody to the Lord in your
       hearts,
20   giving thanks to God the Father at all times and for everything
       in the name of our Lord Jesus Christ.
21   Be subject to one another out of reverence for Christ.

---

[8] The remaining part the household code, 6,1-9, reads as follows:
"1 *Children*, obey your parents in the Lord, for this is right. 2 'Honor your father and
mother' — this is the first commandment with a promise: 'so that it may be well with you and
you may live long on the earth'. 4 And, *fathers*, do not provoke your children to anger, but
bring them up in the discipline and instruction of the Lord.

What "to be filled with the Spirit" concretely means for husbands and wives is then elaborated by the author in 5,22-33. It should be noted that the terms "be subject"[9] and "reverence" or "respect" frame the pericope: both occur in v. 21 and return in v. 22 (be subject) and v. 33 (respect).

Within 5,22-33 first the wives twice receive a commandment (v. 22 and v. 24b), then the husbands two times also (v. 25 and v. 28a)[10]. In the closing verse 33, in reversed order, the husbands are addressed first, after that the wives. In that way, both in vv. 22-24 (I) and vv. 25-32 (II), the injunctions frame the grounding comparisons. All these features may be illustrated by pointing out the following structure:

Verse 21: introduction (injunction)
I. Verses 22-24: wives
    A: commandment (22)
    B: motivation and comparison (23-24a)
    A': commandment (24b)
II. Verses 25-32: husbands
    A: commandment (25a)
    B: motivating comparison (25b-27)
    A': commandment (28a)
    and further grounding explanation (28b-32)
Verse 33: conclusion (injunctions: husband, wife).

It must strike the readers that more verses are devoted to what must be done by the husbands (vv. 25-32) than to what is expected from the wives (vv. 22-24)[11]. Within the B-sections the author works out his doctrinal vision on Christ and the church. In the grounding explanation of vv. 28b-32 there is first a comparison with one's own body (see already the end of

---

5 *Slaves*, obey your earthly masters with fear and trembling, in singleness of heart, as you obey Christ; 6 not only while being watched, and in order to please them, but as slaves of Christ, doing the will of God from the heart. 7 Render service with enthusiasm, as to the Lord and not to men and women, 8 knowing that whatever good we do, we will receive the same again from the Lord, whether we are slaves or free. 9 And, *masters*, do the same to them. Stop threatening them, for you know that both of you have the same Master in heaven, and with him there is no partiality".

[9] In Eph 5,22 a verb is missing, but this verse is grammatically still dependent on the main verb in v. 18b. "Be subject" must be added from v. 21. In v. 24b, too, the same verb must be mentally supplied from v. 24a.

[10] In the following two sections as well the presumably "weaker" Christians are first addressed: "children" (6,1; cf. "fathers" in 6,4) and "slaves" (6,5; cf. "masters" in 6,9). See text in n. 8.

[11] In 1 Pet 3,1-7 the lack of balance is the opposite: six verses for the wives, only one (lengthy) verse for the husbands. See text in n. 7.

v. 28a and then vv. 28b-29b), but after that we have an expanded reference to Christ and the church (vv. 29c-32). This means that more or less half of the verses in this passage deal with the theme "Christ-church".

The Exegesis

A second reading of the pericope must help us better to grasp the intentions of the author. In v. 21 he urges all Ephesian Christians to reciprocal submission: ὑποτασσόμενοι ἀλλήλοις ἐν φόβῳ Χριστοῦ (literally: "in the 'fear' of Christ"). The fear-vocabulary (the verb φοβέομαι) is also used in the injunction to the wives in v. 33b: "a wife should 'fear' her husband". Of course, already in the Old Testament "to fear" is not necessarily a negative concept. Fearing God contains reverence and love. Yet if by the translation of this vocabulary by "reverence" or "respect" one wants to deny any nuance of fear, this most probably goes against the intention of the author. The Christians "fear" Christ in a religious way; analogously the author demands from the wife to "fear" her husband. Likewise, the meaning of the verb ὑποτάσσομαι ("to be subordinate", "to be subject") in vv. 21, 22 and 24 should not be softened and weakened, although through the addition of "as you are to the Lord" in v. 22 the submission is certainly qualified in a Christian manner.

In v. 23c the author says more about Christ and the church than he is able to say about husband and wife, for Christ is the Savior of "his body", the church. We note that verse 24 constitutes a comparative sentence: ὡς ... οὕτως καί ....

The readers still remembering the expression of v. 23a ("to be the head of") may expect in v. 25 a verb such as "rule over". But the author writes, rather surprisingly, "husbands, love your wives". As in v. 23c, there is also a surplus in vv. 25b-27. At great length the author describes here what Christ did for the church; again, this cannot be meant literally with regard to the husbands. "The washing of water" alludes to baptism and "the word" is the gospel that is proclaimed and confessed. Perhaps verse 26 should be understood as follows: in order to cleanse the church by the word at baptism (not the material water but the spiritual word "cleanses"). In the comparison of v. 28a the order of that in v. 24 is reversed: οὕτως ... ὡς; moreover, at the beginning that comparison has nothing to do with Christ and the church (however, see v. 29c). The "profane" comparison in v. 28a ("as they [love] their own bodies") and the elaboration of it in vv. 28b-29b surprises the readers. One gets the impression that already here the author is thinking of Gen 2,24, a text which he will cite further on, in v. 31.

By means of the clause "this is a great mystery" in v. 32a the author refers back to the quotation of v. 31. In the whole of vv. 29c-32, even in v. 31, he appears to have in mind Christ and the church. Of course, the quotation originally points to the relation between man and woman, between husband and wife, but in Ephesians it receives a metaphorical meaning (although this remains somewhat strange to us). As is explicitly indicated in v. 32b, the author relates that quotation to Christ and the church: the figurative sense pushes the literal one aside. Therefore, it would seem better not to claim that the author first, in v. 32a, has in mind marriage and then only, in v. 32b, relates that marriage reality to the relation between Christ and the church. No, the "great mystery" points to what which Christ has done and still does for his body the church. In the Latin Vulgate μυστή-ριον is translated by "sacramentum", and thus the Catholic Church was brought to the view that in this text marriage was declared to be a "sacrament"[12].

In v. 33a ("each of you should love his wife as himself") the author is possibly alluding to Lev 19,18b: "You shall love your neighbor as yourself". The partner in marriage, the wife, is the neighbor par excellence!

II. CHRIST/CHURCH AND HUSBAND/WIFE

Five observations are presented in this second part of the paper, very briefly.

All Christians are the Body of Christ. The church of Christ is his body. This body consists of all Christians, men and women. In 5,30 the author of Ephesians writes: "we [all] are members of the body" of Christ. This causes the comparison of husband/wife with Christ/church to be strained. The male Christians, too, ought to "be subject" to Christ.

"To be subject" and "to fear". The difference between "to be subordinate" and "to love" should not be discounted. It is true that in v. 21 a recip-

---

[12] From Eph 5,21-33 the Council of Trent cites two verses. By his passion Christ has earned beforehand ("promeruit") for us the sacramental grace of marriage. The Apostle suggested ("innuit") this when he wrote: "Husbands, love your wives, just as Christ loved the church and gave himself up for her" (v. 25), and further added: "This is a great mystery ('sacramentum hoc'), and I am applying it to Christ and the church" (v. 30). See the Latin text in Denzinger–Schönmetzer, no. 1799.

rocal submission is enjoined. But one could ask whether by this introductory verse the author really requires the husband's submission to his wife. What immediately follows in the text pleads against such an understanding. It is also true that the love with which Christ loved his church consisted of a total dedication and of sacrifice. Whenever that love is imitated by husbands, it will contains self-sacrifice and often submission of oneself to the wife. It is equally true that the subjection and fear which are required from the wife are not slavish at all; both attitudes are transformed in a Christian way (cf. "as to the Lord" in v. 22 and "in the fear of Christ" in v. 21). Yet, notwithstanding all this, it appears that what is asked from the wife is different from what is asked from the husband. Subjection is not simply love. That the author takes this subjection seriously appears from v. 24: "Wives ought to be, 'in everything', subject to their husbands". Such injunctions undoubtedly reflect the hierarchal relations in the patriarchal societies of those days. But, once again, exegesis of a text becomes questionable when the differences in the text are blurred or softened by translation (or by interpretation).

What Christ did (and does) for his church. It has already been stated above: what Christ has done for the church goes much farther than what can be expected from the Christian husband: see the "surplus" in v. 23c and vv. 26-27. On the other hand, when the author in v. 29b comments on the husband's love of his own body ("he nourishes it and tenderly takes care of it"), he emphasizes that the same applies to Christ's loving care of the church: see vv. 29c-30.

"As ..." and "just as ...". According to the author the manner in which Christ loves the church and the perfect submission of the church to Christ are the example for a husband to love his wife, and the example for a wife to be subject to her husband. In this pericope Christ and the church function as a comparison and are to be imitated: see with the regard to the wife v. 24 ("*as* the church is subject to Christ") and with regard to the husband v 25 ("*just as* Christ loved the church"). These two verses are explicitly comparative. Yet comparative particles often possess in themselves a grounding nuance. This seems to be the case in our text as well. The husband must love his wife also *because* Christ loved the church; and the wife ought to be subject to the husband also *because* the ideal church is subject to Christ. But recognizing a motivation in the relation between Christ and the church, again, is not enough. Although the idea is not elaborated, we may assume that to author's mind Christ has made possible the reciprocal relation between the Christian husband and his Christian wife. Therefore, in addition to *just as* and to *because*, there seems to be equally a *through*. Through the fact that Christ delivered himself and made believ-

ers holy (cf. vv. 25-27) and through the fact that they are members of his body (cf. v. 30), the Christian wife and the Christian husband are able to do what the inspired author instructs them to do.

Sacrament. In the relationship between husband and wife that between Christ and the church becomes visible. To marry is to become a visible sign of divine incarnate love. Married life lived in a Christian way means to give shape to Christ's love and the church's obedience. Christ's activity of cleansing and making holy, of nourishing and tenderly caring, as well the church's obedient responsiveness, are effective in the Christian married couple. Christian marriage is a sacrament.

III. A FIXED MODEL?

This paper is meant to introduce reflection and discussion. In the third part, therefore, I first will bring together the main data of the scriptural passage and risk some actualizing ideas. Then I will briefly summarize how an official church document, "Inter insigniores", uses the marriage symbolism within the discussion on the question of the admission of women to the ministerial priesthood. I will conclude with a few critical questions.

The Comparison

The relation between Christ and the church is seen in Eph 5,21-33 apparently in a threefold way: that between "head" and the subordinate (vv. 23b and 24), that between the husband and his body (vv. 23c and 29c-30) and, above all, that between husband and wife (vv. 25b-27 and 31-32). What strikes the readers is the fact that in this pericope these three approaches are employed, as it were, in a reverse manner. For by means of them the author does not intend to expound the relation between Christ and the church, but he uses them to admonish and instruct the married Christians. The husband is "head", man and bridegroom: he must behave as Christ. The wife is the subordinate, the body and the bride: she must behave as the ideal church. Of course, all this cannot be perfectly coherent, since the Christian husband is also a member of the subordinate church and thus belongs to the body of Christ; the Christian wife, too, is "in Christ" and Christ also lives in her.

The whole argument of the author of Ephesians is being conditioned by three factors. There is the influence of the creation narrative[13]. There is also the marriage symbolism: already in the Old Testament God is seen as the husband and Israel as his bride; the New Testament, also Paul[14], applied these images to Christ and the church. In the third place there are the anthropological views of the Jewish-hellenistic society of the author with its patriarchal structures: in the family the husband is "the head" and is in a position of authority; the wife is subject to him (often not without fear).

While listening to Eph 5,21-33 today's readers almost spontaneously introduce two modifications. First, with regard to the attitude of the wife, they mostly avoid the terms "submission" and "fear" or soften the meaning of them. Second, they emphasize that "loving" is as much the duty of the wife as it is that of the husband. They also stress that the tender and caring love of the husband will often manifest itself in forms of obedience and submission. Consequently, the reciprocity of subjection expressed in the introductory verse 21 is easily carried over into the pericope itself.

Women and Ministerial Priesthood

Since reference is made to this passage from Ephesians in the fifth part of the Declaration *Inter insigniores*, which in 1977 was promulgated by the Sacred Congregation for the Doctrine of the Faith, we had best begin with a summary of this part[15]. In the first four parts the Declaration stresses that it was not by accident that Jesus Christ was a man, that he deliberately appointed only men as the Twelve, that the Church ordained only men as bishops and priests and that this whole constant tradition is normative. These are the well-known arguments. In the fifth part the Declaration no longer deals strictly with the norm and its grounds, but indicates the appropriateness of the norm. Theology is reflection: "It is not a question here of bringing forward a demonstrative argument, but of clarifying this teaching by the analogy of faith"[16].

---

[13] Genesis 2–3. See the quotation of Gen 2,24 in Eph 5,31. With regard to Paul, see 1 Cor 11,7-12.

[14] See 2 Cor 11,2: "I feel a divine jealousy for you, for I promised you in marriage to one husband, to present you as a chaste virgin to Christ".

[15] *Inter insigniores* (see n. 1), 11-15: "The Ministerial Priesthood in the Light of the Mystery of Christ"; cf. "Commentary", 38-43. The sixth and last part of the Declaration (pp. 15-18) is entitled "The Ministerial Priesthood Illustrated by the Mystery of the Church".

[16] *Inter insigniores*, 11. See also the Apostolic Letter *Mulieris dignitatem* (1988), which in nos. 23-27 provides, it would seem, a somewhat forced explanation of Eph 5,21-33, and the Apostolic Letter *Ordinatio sacerdotalis* (1994) (no further elaboration of the analogy of faith). Cf. W. VAN SOOM, "'Ordinatio sacerdotalis' en de argumenten in het debat", *Coll* 24 (1994) 341-361.

It is stated first that the priest represents Christ, especially in the celebration of the Eucharist[17]. He "acts not only through the effective power conferred on him by Christ, but *in persona Christi*, taking the the role of Christ"[18]. "The Christian priesthood is therefore of a sacramental nature: the priest is a sign"[19]. The sign must be perceptible and a natural resemblance is required. Only a man can take the role of Christ who "himself was and remains a man"[20].

But, it could be asked, must Christ be a man, why not a woman? The Declaration states that the "Incarnation of the Word took place according to the male sex: this is indeed a question of fact, and this fact ... cannot be disassociated from the economy of salvation: it is, indeed, in harmony with the entirety of God's plan ... of which the mystery of the Covenant is the nucleus"[21]. The union between God and Israel took on, from the prophets onward, "the privileged form of a nuptial mystery: for God the Chosen People is seen as his ardently loved spouse"[22]. In the New Covenant the church is born from the side of Christ, just as Eve from Adam. Christ is now the bridegroom, and the church his bride. Along this line of reasoning Christ has to be a man. Within this context the Declaration refers to 2 Cor 11,2 and Eph 5,22-33, also to John 3,29; Rev 19,7.9; Mark 2,19; and to the parable of Matt 22,1-14. "It is through this language, all interwoven with symbols ... that there is revealed to us the mystery of God and Christ, a mystery that of itself is unfathomable"[23].

In order to respect this symbolism in the economy of Revelation, the Declaration maintains, it must be admitted that Christ should be represented by a man[24]. At the end of this fifth part, after answering some difficul-

---

[17] Cf. *Inter insigniores*, 11-12.

[18] *Inter insigniores*, 12.

[19] *Inter insigniores*, 12.

[20] *Inter insigniores*, 12.

[21] *Inter insigniores*, 12.

[22] *Inter insigniores*, 12-13. See especially the Song of Songs, Hosea 1-3 and Jeremiah 2; cf. Isa 54,4-8.10, cited in *Mulieris dignitatem*, no. 23.

[23] *Inter insigniores*, 13. Cf. "Commentary", 43: "... the whole economy of salvation has been revealed to us through essential symbols from which it cannot be separated, and without which we would be unable to understand God's design".

[24] Cf. "Commentary", 43: "by using this language, Revelation shows why the Incarnation took place according to the male gender, and makes it impossible to ignore this historical reality. For this reason, only a man can take the part of Christ, be a sign of his presence, in a word 'represent' him (that is, be an effective sign of his presence) in the essential acts of the Covenant". The expression "essential acts" refers above all to the Eucharist. The reasoning does not apply to Baptism.

ties, the Declaration adds: "If one does justice to these reflections, one will better understand how well-founded is the basis of the Church's practice"[25], i.e., to admit only men to the ministerial priesthood.

Critical Questions

A first question concerns the reasoning which mentions the sacramental order and recalls what happens in the Eucharist. As the representant of Christ the priest is a perceptible sign. Because of that sign character, a natural resemblance, i.e., the male equality with Christ, is required. But, from the point of view of the incarnation, is it really certain that "being a man" is needed, rather than simply "being a human being"?

The second critique refers to the use of the nuptial symbolism in Ephesians. Some data of 5,21-33 betray a somewhat circular reasoning. The relation between Christ and the church is first compared and depicted by means of that between husband and wife; then, for the concrete behavior of husband and wife, reference is made to that of Christ and the ideal church. This is rather odd. But the Declaration goes further than the Letter to the Ephesians does. From that comparison the appropriateness of the ordained priesthood of men is deduced. But why could women, who as baptized people no less than men are members of the body of Christ, not represent Christ? It has more than once been noted that it is in no way stranger to see a woman in the functional role of Christ[26] than to see a man, who like the woman is a member of Christ's body, in the role of bride.

Today's philosophical linguistics teach us that a metaphor is more than just illustration. A metaphor that is employed correctly is creative and provides new information. Great poets appear to be masters in this kind of speaking. "The church is the body of Christ". Through the friction between the impossibility of understanding the identification of church and body of Christ literally and the search for a metaphorical sense, the novel insight comes about: the church is most intimately connected with Christ. It has been said that certain realities can only be expressed by figurative language or metaphor.

But in our case more is involved than the metaphorical enunciation

---

[25] *Inter insigniores*, 15.

[26] When the Pope was in the United States some years ago for a Youth Day, a troupe of mimes — I am told — re-enacted the way of the cross, with a woman taking the part of Christ. She was criticized by right-wing Catholics, but defended by the Papal spokesman.

"Christ is the head, and the church is his body". There also is the comparison husband/wife with Christ/church. Does it follow from the comparison of God and Christ with a bridegroom that "in actions that demand the character of ordination and in which Christ himself ... is represented, exercising his ministry of salvation — which is in the highest degree the case of the Eucharist — his role must be taken by a man"?[27] Many are tempted to answer this question in the negative.

In order to speak of the Creator/Savior and his creatures/people Israel has used a number of other images such as sovereign and vassal (with regard to the covenant!), father and son, lord and servant, master and slave, king and subject .... Yet only the comparison of bridegroom and bride put the male half of humanity on the side of God and Christ. According to Gen 1,27, however, God created male *and* female, man *and* woman in his image. Just as the existing nuptial symbolism concerning the Lord God and Israel does not imply that God is really male and Israel only female, so also does the imagery of "bridegroom" and "bride" not determine the essential femaleness of the church nor, it would seem, the necessary maleness of Christ.

It is well known that comparative and, even more, metaphorical language is difficult to expound in clear terms. Yet hearers and commentators again and again tend to expand this kind of language allegorically and make it say more than has originally been intended. Metaphorical language should not be over-interpreted through logical deductions. One easily runs into unfounded speculation. It appears to us that this occurs where Declaration and Commentary argue by means of nuptial symbolism.

We may conclude. To the teaching authority of the Church the arguments drawn from nuptial symbolism are not the most important. They are part of "the analogy of faith" and should provide the debate with an additional motivation. Eph 5,21-33 was investigated here within this framework. Our analysis pointed out some weaknesses in the reasoning. Before that discussion we showed how the biblical passage speaks of the relation husband–wife in a way that today's Christians can no longer accept. In the pericope there is the comparison of husband–wife with Christ–church and its use with regard to the ordained ministry. It would seem that what is said in Ephesians on the relation between husband and wife by means of the existing relation between Christ and the church is better not employed to expound the convenience of the present law that only men can be allowed to the ministerial priesthood.

---

[27] *Inter insigniores*, 11-12; cf. n. 24.

Appendix

Although it was not my task to offer historical, anthropological and sociological considerations, I would like to present a personal reflection by way of appendix. This may be a sign of my own hesitant approach. As human persons man and woman are fundamentally equal. Yet a man is not the same as a woman, and the woman is different from man. This is not only a matter of biology but also of basic anthropology. The whole person is either male or female. It would seem that because of this primary diversification certain social functions and religious ministries could be more suitable to men, other to women. Yet feminism and other types of emancipation have taught us that today the social and functional division of roles is no longer fixed in a manner as it used to be.

Yet the complementarity of man and woman cannot be denied. This leaves us with intricate problems. Within the fundamental equality of the two genders, to what extent does the sexual differentiation also bring with it a man–woman hierarchy? Is a man–woman hierarchy so completely conditioned by culture as is often said nowadays or is it given by nature itself? To be sure, not a male superiority is meant here, but a (as it were matter-of-course) position of authority and leadership, which — it has to be added — from both the human and Christian points of view have to be serving and loving. Even if a form of "hierarchal order" could be regarded as belonging to nature, would this for Christians ipso facto exclude the priesthood of women? Perhaps not even then, since women will be a different type of priest (and their leadership will be complementary).

In this context another problem should be mentioned. In the early church functions and ministries came into existence necessarily, rightly and slowly. Toward the end of the first century in some regions the threefold structure of ministry became visible: deacon, priest and bishop; still later the ordained sacramental priesthood was instituted and finally universally accepted. That evolution took place certainly also under the influence of social, cultural and cultic factors. To what degree did the sacralization and sacramentalization of Christian ministry, and its consequent reservation to men, occur according to God's will and the guidance of the Spirit? To call this evolution permanent and unchangeable is still one more postulate.

Jesus was not a priest in the sense the term has today. A more biblical vision of ministry, together with new anthropological and sociological insights, could perhaps overcome the deadlock of the debate and relax the controversy. Of course, not men alone but more than ever also women must continue to reflect upon this delicate and most sensitive issue.

Ephemerides theologicae Lovanienses 76 (2000) 435-441

24

Loving God and Steadfastly Awaiting Christ
A Note on 2 Thessalonians 3,5

The New Revised Standard Version translates 2 Thess 3,5 as follows: "May the Lord direct your hearts to the love of God and the steadfastness of Christ". The Greek text is Ὁ δὲ κύριος κατευθύναι ὑμῶν τὰς καρδίας εἰς τὴν ἀγάπην τοῦ θεοῦ καὶ εἰς τὴν ὑπομονὴν τοῦ Χριστοῦ. All commentators mention the embarrassment caused by the two genitives "of God" and "of Christ". Are both subjective or objective genitives? Is there necessarily a grammatical parallelism between the expressions "the love of God" and "the steadfastness of Christ"?

Exegetes have to indicate their choices or preferences. We may quote four recent authors. In his brief comment George Soarez-Prabhu writes: Paul prays "that his readers may grow in their love of God and in their Christ-like steadfastness in persecution"[1]. The first genitive appears to be objective, while the second seems to be taken as a "Hebrew" genitive"[2]. According to Earl J. Richard the phrase 'God's love' "should be taken as a subjective genitive"[3]; this also applies to 'Christ's constancy' which refers "to Jesus' death and resurrection as exemplary" for suffering Christians[4]. Charles A. Wanamaker concludes his lengthy discussion as follows: "Thus Paul's wish-prayer is for the Lord to direct the readers' hearts to God's love for them and to the perseverance which Christ demonstrated as a basis for encouraging what Paul considers proper Christian behavior"[5], thus twice a subjective genitive. The preference of Maarten J.J. Menken goes to the acceptance of an objective genitive in both expressions, "the love for God" and "the steadfast expectation of Christ". He explains the second expres-

---

[1] G.M. SOAREZ-PRABHU, "2 Thessalonians", W.R. FARMER (ed.), *The International Bible Commentary* (Collegeville 1998) 1727.

[2] Cf. M. ZERWICK, *Biblical Greek* (Rome 1963), no. 40.

[3] E.R. RICHARD, *First and Second Thessalonians* (SP; Collegeville 1995) 376.

[4] Ibid., 372.

[5] C.A. WANAMAKER, *The Epistles to the Thessalonians* (NIGTC; Grand Rapids – Exeter 1990) 279.

sion: "the congregation is the subject of the steadfastness, and Christ has then to be its object"[6].

Can a reasonable certainty or, at least, a well-grounded probability be reached for these two prepositional phrases? As is well known 2 Thess 3,5 possesses other particularities. The verse appears to be dependent on 1 Thess 3,11. The expression "to direct the hearts" is Septuagintal language; what is its exact nuance? Moreover, 2 Thess 3,5 provides the only instance in the letter where an unqualified "Christ" occurs. All these characteristics will be dealt with in the discussion of the genitives. First an overview of the possibilities.

I. AN OVERVIEW

The two expressions, the love of God and the steadfastness of Christ, must be treated separately in this overview.

God

Three interpretations of the genitive "of God" are defended. (1) A subjective genitive understands the expression as God's love for the Thessalonian believers, God loving them[7]. (2) An objective genitive points to the love for God, the Thessalonians loving God[8]. (3) A third possibility

---

[6] M.J.J. MENKEN, 2 Thessalonians (NT Readings; London – New York 1994) 129. C. SPICQ, Theological Lexicon of the New Testament. Vol. 3 (Peabody, MA 1994) thinks that the expression "can be understood as a call to participate in the sufferings that Christ endured .... Less probably, this could be the constancy to wait for Christ, or simply hope that has Christ as its object" (420, n. 28).

[7] Cf. RICHARD in n. 3 and WANAMAKER in n. 5. See also E. VON DOBSCHÜTZ, Die Thessalonicher-Briefe (KEK; Göttingen 1909) 309; J.E. FRAME, The Epistles of St. Paul to the Thessalonians (ICC; Edinburgh 1912) 296; B. RIGAUX, Les épîtres aux Thessaloniciens (EtB; Paris–Gembloux 1956) 699-700; E. BEST, A Commentary on the First and Second Epistles to the Thessalonians (BNTC; London 1972) 330-331; F.F. BRUCE, 1 & 2 Thessalonians (WBC; Waco 1982) 201-202; I.H. MARSHALL, 1 and 2 Thessalonians (NCBC; Grand Rapids – London 1983) 317-318.

[8] Cf. MENKEN in n. 6 and also W. TRILLING, Der zweite Brief an die Thessalonicher (EKK; Zürich – Neukirchen/Vluyn 1980) 138-140; A. ROOSEN, De Brieven van Paulus aan de Tessalonicenzen (Roermond 1971) 164-165.

is the "general" genitive. In proposing this usage for expressions such as "God's love" Maximilian Zerwick writes: "... we must beware lest we sacrifice to clarity of meaning part of the fullness of the meaning"[9]. According to this view the genitive is both subjective and objective, God's love and our love together and, moreover, comprehensive[10].

Christ

What about the second expression? (1) If one assumes "of Christ" in εἰς τὴν ὑπομονὴν τοῦ Χριστοῦ to be a subjective genitive, the term ὑπομονή means endurance, steadfastness, constancy, perseverance. We may think of Christ's exemplary endurance, especially during his passion[11]. (2) Some commentators prefer "the steadfastness that comes from Christ" and, in defense of this genitive of origin, refer to Rom 15,4: "by the steadfastness and by the encouragement of the scriptures [= derived from scriptures]"[12]. (3) Taking "of Christ" as an objective genitive the term refers to a human attitude. Is it the Christians' patient and steadfast awaiting of Christ[13] or their more active enduring expectation[14]? (4) A "general" genitive is again proposed by Zerwick: Christ himself is "enduring" in the believers[15]. The endurance is that of Christ as well as that of the Thessalonians. Believers are in Christ and Christ is in them. (5) A fifth pos-

---

[9] ZERWICK, *Biblical Greek*, no. 36. Cf. the monograph by O. SCHMITZ, *Die Christus-Gemeinschaft des Paulus im Lichte seines Genitivsgebrauchs* (Gütersloh 1924).

[10] L. MORRIS, *The First and Second Epistles to the Thessalonians* (NICNT; Grand Rapids 1991) 251, refers to J.B. Lightfoot. He himself prefers "love of God for us" as the primary idea and "our love for him" as the secondary idea. Cf. W. MARXSEN, *Der zweite Thessalonicherbrief* (ZüBKNT; Zürich 1982) 97-98; Marxsen is of the opinion "dass man über die beiden (vom Verfasser offensichtlich ad hoc gebildeten) Genitive keine Spekulationen mit Hilfe der Grammatik anstellen sollte. Die ganze Aussage ist ganz allgemein".

[11] Cf. R.F. COLLINS, *Letters That Paul Did Not Write: The Epistle to the Hebrews and the Pauline Pseudepigrapha* (GNS 28; Wilmington 1988) 127, and the references in our n. 7 (not von Dobschütz). Richard explains the exemplary character to a great extent: "'Christ's constancy' is a model for those who suffer and the basis for a balanced eschatology and righteous behavior with a more proper focus on ecclesial and missionary activity (3,1)" (p. 377). See also Jas 5,11: "You have heard of the ὑπομονή Ἰώβ" (example).

[12] Cf. BEST, *2 Thessalonians*, 330 (one of the two possibilities).

[13] Cf. E. VON DOBSCHÜTZ, *Die Thessalonicher-Briefe* (KEK; Göttingen 1909) 308-309: "ὑπομονή kann wohl das geduldige, standhafte Erwarten bedeuten" (309). He notes: "auf das Tun der Leser kommt wenig an" (ibid.).

[14] Cf. MENKEN in n. 6.

[15] ZERWICK, *Biblical Greek*, no. 38. Cf. SCHMITZ, *Christus-Gemeinschaft*, 139-140.

sibility is not to be excluded, that of a "Hebrew" genitive with more or less the value of a Greek adjective, also called an attributive or qualitative genitive. The believers' attitude is then a "Christ-like" endurance[16]; it is the same attitude which was also in Christ (cf. Phil 2,5).

The mere variety of these listed proposals makes it difficult to reach a responsible choice. Moreover, the brevity of the genitive constructions, as well as the symmetric juxtaposition of ἀγάπη and ὑπομονή and of God and Christ, may heighten the doubts regarding the presumable sense of these constructions.

II. THE STEADFASTNESS OF CHRIST

It may prove better to begin with the second expression. We thus ask what the author intends to say when he prays: "May the Lord conduct your hearts ... εἰς τὴν ὑπομονὴν τοῦ Χριστοῦ". What is the significance of the last phrase? How is "to the steadfastness of Christ" to be understood?

Just as in the New Testament the verb ὑπομένω does not mean "to await"[17], so also the noun ὑπομονή by itself does not have the sense of "awaiting" or "expectation". In its 32 occurrences in the New Testament the noun means patient endurance or steadfastness, perseverance.

The Context

The examination of "the steadfastness of Christ" must, of course, take into account the immediate context. In 3,1 the parenetical section begins with a not uncommon τὸ λοιπόν[18]: "'Finally', brothers, pray for us". In 3,3 the author stresses that the Lord who is faithful will strengthen the believers and guard them from evil. In 3,4 he expresses his confidence in the Lord concerning them, namely, that they are doing and will continue to do

---

[16] Cf. SOAREZ-PRABHU in n. 1.

[17] Cf. B.C. METZGER, *A Textual Commentary on the Greek New Testament* (Stuttgart ²1994) 427: "... although the verb ὑπομένειν with object ('to await something') is rather common in the Septuagint, no example for this use can be cited from the New Testament...".

[18] 1 Cor 7,29; Phil 3,1 and 4,8. Cf. λοιπόν in 1 Cor 1,16; 4,2; 2 Cor 13,11; 1 Thess 4,1; 2 Tm 4,8; Heb 10,13; τοῦ λοιποῦ in Gal 6,17; Eph 6,10.

what he commands. The reader expects that in the wish-prayer of 3,5 the author will point to a concrete Christian behavior, to a human attitude and not to what God does or what Christ has endured. The hortatory and even commanding style goes on in 3,6 and 12-13.

The author has already used the term ὑπομονή once, at the beginning of the letter, in 1,4. He is bound to give thanks to God always for the abundance of the Thessalonians' faith and their increasing mutual love (1,3). Therefore he is able to boast of them in the churches for their "steadfastness" and faith in persecutions and tribulations (1,4). "Steadfastness" here certainly pertains to human conduct. Perhaps, without counter-indication, the same meaning can be presumed in the second usage of the term at the end of the letter.

Furthermore, as is well known, the thanksgiving of 2 Thess 1,3-4 depends on that of 1 Thess 1,2-3. "Your 'steadfastness' of hope in our Lord Jesus Christ" in 1 Thess 1,3 equally refers to a human attitude, to human enduring courage.

The Believer's Steadfast Hope

If steadfastness in 2 Thess 3,5 indicates an attitude that the believers should cultivate, what is then the function of the genitive "of Christ"? It can hardly be a subjective genitive. Yet an objective genitive is not all that easy to admit either. Of course, Christians have not to "endure" Christ. Must they manifest steadfastness towards Christ in the midst of difficulties[19] or endure tribulations for Christ? In the last two cases, however, one would expect another construction.

Although ὑπομονή is not directly expectation, the consideration of 1 Thess 1,3 and similar passages leads us to the hypothesis that the idea of "awaiting Christ" is implicitly present in 2 Thess 3,5. This thought is to be mentally supplied. In 1 Thess 1,3 the phrase ἡ ὑπομονὴ τῆς ἐλπίδος τοῦ κυρίου ἡμῶν Ἰησοῦ Χριστοῦ combines three elements: endurance, hope and Christ. "Our Lord Jesus Christ" is an objective genitive: hope in Christ. "The steadfastness of hope" means constant hope notwithstanding tribulations. The author of 2 Thess 3,5 is most probably pointing to a similar atti-

---

[19] Cf. TRILLING, *2 Thessalonicher*, 330-331; cf. J.H. MOULTON, *A Grammar of New Testament Greek. III: Syntax* by N. TURNER (Edinburgh 1963) 212: "Steadfast loyalty to Christ'? or subjective?".

tude, i.e., to a patient, enduring expectation of Christ[20]. What Paul writes in Rom 8,25 regarding hope, endurance and expectation supports this hypothesis: "If we hope for what we do not see, we 'await' it with patience (δι᾽ ὑπομονῆς ἀπεκδεχόμεθα)". One may also refer to the connection of steadfastness and hope in Rom 5,3-5, as well as in 2 Cor 1,6-7. Of course, the rather frequent Septuagintal expression ὑπομένω τὸν κύριον could also have influenced the author[21].

The Parousiac Christ

The unqualified "Christ" is used only in 3,5 in the whole of 2 Thessalonians, a letter which abounds in phrases such as "our Lord Jesus Christ", "the Lord", "the Lord Jesus" and "our Lord Jesus"[22]. Yet it would seem that no special intention is to be sought in this usage. The grammatical subject of the sentence is ὁ κύριος, the title referring to Jesus which already appeared in the immediate preceding context (3,1.3 and 4) and will also be the grammatical subject of the prayer in 3,16 (αὐτὸς δὲ ὁ κύριος). In 3,5 the author could hardly write "his" after the intervening expression "the love of God" nor repeat the term "Lord" at the end of the sentence. That "Christ" is the expected parousiac Lord is, moreover, suggested by 1,7-8. The endurance of the afflictions, mentioned in 1,4, will come to an end at the return of the Lord. God will grant rest to the believers who are afflicted, "when the Lord Jesus is revealed from heaven with his mighty angels in flaming fire" (1,7-8; cf. 1,10).

In view of 1,5-12 it can hardly be maintained that 2 Thessalonians is thoroughly anti-apocalyptic, let alone anti-eschatological. True, in chapter 2 the author rejects the false letter and corrects a false teaching: the day of the Lord has not yet come. He informs his readers that the revelation of the Lord Jesus will be preceded by the rebellion, the working of the mystery of lawlessness and the 'parousia' of the lawless one (cf. 2,1-11). But he in no way denies the ἀποκάλυψις τοῦ κυρίου ᾽Ιησοῦ (1,7), the παρουσία τοῦ κυρίου ἡμῶν ᾽Ιησοῦ Χριστοῦ (2,1), or the ἐπιφανεία τῆς παρουσίας αὐτοῦ (2,8), probably in a not too distant future. Therefore, the eschatological information in chapter 2 makes a mentioning of Christ's return in 3,5 rather likely.

---

[20] The only occurrence of the term "hope" in this letter is in 2,16, part of a wish-prayer (2,16-17), not so far from 3,5, also a wish-prayer.

[21] Cf., e.g., LXX Ps 36, 3 and 34. For more references, see F. HAUCK, *TDNT IV*, 584; SPICQ, *Lexicon 3*, 418-419.

[22] On the Christology of 2 Thessalonians, see COLLINS, *Letters*, 226-232.

Christ's Steadfastness?

Nowhere else in the New Testament ὑπομονή indicates the endurance or steadfastness of Christ himself, not even in Rev 3,10[23]. To find it in 2 Thes 3,5 would be rather strange.

Moreover, the assumption of a subjective genitive, i.e., a reference to Christ's own steadfastness, would necessitate a reasoning which is much less probable than the here presumed mental addition of hopeful awaiting. The author would pray that the Lord direct the hearts of the Thessalonians to his steadfastness, i.e., that the Lord make them attentive to Christ's exemplary way of acting in the past in order to imitate that pattern of steadfastness. While such an understanding is not impossible, it certainly is more complicated, not to say rather strained.

Some of those who consider "of Christ" to be a general genitive fill out the expression with even more and rather opposite nuances: Christ's endurance given to the believers will provide them with their own endurance (exercised for Christ?). Certainly the author could and would be in full agreement with such ideas, but the question remains whether he intended to express all of them by means of the straightforward expression in 3,5. Some may claim that the notion of Christ's example is explicit and that of the Christians' attitude implicit, or vice versa[24]. Yet we keep asking whether the author actually means both senses together. Others defend that the full sense of this genitive remains vague and comprehensive. They insist that this genitive here indicates only the appurtenance of "endurance" to "Christ" and that the nature of this appurtenance depends upon the context[25]. But this distinction between the genitive and its context appears to be uttermost strained.

---

[23] Most probably τὸν λόγον τῆς ὑπομονῆς μου means "my word of patient endurance, i.e., my call for constancy". See, however, the verb ὑπομένω in Heb 12,2-3. The wish-prayer of Rom 15,5-6 is not without interest: "May the God of steadfastness and encouragement (ὁ δὲ θεὸς τῆς ὑπομονῆς καὶ τῆς παρακκλήσεως) grant you to live in such harmony with one another, in accord with Christ Jesus, that together you may with one voice glorify God and Father of our Lord Jesus Christ". The steadfastness comes from God and appears to be a gift for the Christians. Paul does not say here that God himself is enduring.

[24] Cf. the conclusions regarding "the faith of Christ" in A. VANHOYE, "Πίστις Χριστοῦ: fede in Cristo o affidabilità di Cristo?" *Bib* 80 (1999) 1-21, esp. pp. 16-21: the first conclusion is "che non è il caso di presentare come un dilemma la scelta tra senso oggettivo e senso soggettivo, perché questi due sensi sono correlativi"; the second conclusion is "che conviene capire in modo giusto la correlatività" (p. 16: one sense is explicit while the other remains implicit).

[25] Cf. SCHMITZ, *Christus-Gemeinschaft*, passim; ZERWICK, *Biblical Greek*, nos. 36-39.

III. THE LOVE OF GOD

The difficulties explained in the preceding paragraph equally apply to the views which consider "of God" either as a subjective genitive or as a "general" genitive. The author would then pray that the Lord direct the hearts of the believers to (the gift of) a loving God. The Lord must lead the Christians to "reflection on the character of God's love".

To Direct the Heart

Does the expression κατευθύνω τὴν καρδίαν εἰς (or πρός) mean "to direct the attention to" or "to bring to reflect on"? Hardly. It is true, in Semitic anthropology "heart" refers to the core of the person, to the human center of thinking and willing. Yet the author of 2 Thessalonians most probably borrowed the verb from 1 Thess 3,11 where the direct object is τὴν ὁδόν ("to straighten the way", i.e., to prosper the journey). The metaphorical use of κατευθύνω τὴν καρδίαν (or τὰς καρδίας) is found more than once in the Septuagint, nearly always in a clearly moral sense: see 1 Chr 29,18; 2 Chr 12,14; 19,3; 20,33; Sir 49,3; Ps 77,8; Prov 21,2.

To say that one does not direct his or her heart towards God implies that one does what is evil. In 1 Chr 29,18-19, David prays the Lord God to direct the heart of the people towards God and to grant to Solomon καρδίαν ἀγαθὴν τοῦ ποιεῖν τὰς ἐντολάς σου. The "directing" brings about behavior, not reflection.

God Loving Us or We Loving God?

Most defenders of a subjective genitive refer to the wish-prayer of 2,16-17 and its qualification of God as loving us: "God our Father ὁ ἀγαπήσας ἡμᾶς and gave us eternal comfort and good hope through grace" (v. 16; cf. v. 13: ἀδελφοὶ ἠγαπημένοι ὑπὸ κυρίου). In this prayer the author asks that Christ and God may comfort the hearts of the believers and establish them in every good work and word. In 3,5, as a consequence, the author can pray to the Lord that the Christians respond to God's prior love for them (cf. 2,16) by means of their love for him[26].

---

[26] Otherwise WANAMAKER, *2 Thessalonians*, 278-279.

In 2 Thessalonians the expression ἡ ἀγάπη τοῦ θεοῦ occurs only once, namely in 3,5. It has to be conceded that elsewhere, more in particular in the letters of Paul (Rom 5,5; 8,39; 2 Cor 13,13) and the writings of John, the genitive is mostly subjective. A clear exception is 1 John 5,3: αὕτη γάρ ἐστιν ἡ ἀγάπη τοῦ θεοῦ, ἵνα τὰς ἐντολὰς αὐτοῦ τηρῶμεν. By keeping God's commandments we show that we love God. It would seem that 2 Thess 3,5 may offer a similar exception in the Pauline corpus. One should also take note of the fact that in 2,10 ἀγάπη is followed by an objective genitive (the love of truth).

Concise Parallelism

The notably composed form of the wish-prayer in 3,5, ending on two concise εἰς-constructions, may take the edge off the argument that the author should "have employed the infinitive to ἀγαπᾶν with the object τὸν θεόν", if he "had wished to call his readers to love God"[27]. In 2 Thessalonians subjective and objective genitives appear one next to the other (cf. 2,13). Therefore, the argument from parallelism, namely that in 3,5 both genitives have to be of the same class, is by itself not conclusive[28]. Yet the two εἰς-expressions depend on the same clause ὁ δὲ κύριος κατευθύναι ὑμῶν τὰς καρδίας which strongly suggests that a human activity will be mentioned. Both "loving God" and "steadfastly awaiting Christ" require the (God-given) effort on the part of Christians.

A conclusion from this analysis is that absolute certainty in the interpretation of 2 Thess 3,5 does not appear available. What has been presented in this note is, we think, a well-grounded probability that "of God" and "of Christ" are two objective genitives.

---

[27] WANAMAKER, *2 Thessalonians*, 278.

[28] Cf. TRILLING, *2 Thessalonicher*, 139; MENKEN, *2 Thessalonians*, 129. VON DOBSCHÜTZ, *Thessalonicher-Briefe*, 309, comments: "also sollen ihre Herzen gerichtet sein auf die von Gott bewiesene Liebe und auf die freudig-standhafte Erwartung des kommenden Christus". See WANAMAKER, *2 Thessalonians*, 279, for claiming a parallelism of subjective genitives and SCHMITZ, *Christus-Gemeinschaft*, 140, for twice a general genitive: "die Gottes-Liebe und das Christus-Ausharren als einheitliche in sich geschlossene pneumatische Erfahrungsgrössen".

Additional Note: A.B. MALHERBE, *The Letters to the Thessalonians* (AB; New York 2000) 447-448, prefers two subjective genitives: the love of God and the steadfastness of Christ ("which in a certain sense parallels God's faithfulness", 447). He also thinks that, as elsewhere in 2,1-5, "the Lord" refers to God, not to Christ.

(Unpublished)

25

Christian Freedom in 1 Pet 2,16
A Grammatical and Exegetical Note

In his carefully written 1998 monograph *Petrus oder Paulus* Jens Herzer discusses 1 Pet 2,13-17 in the eighth chapter: "Christliche Freiheit und weltliche Herrschaft"[1]. As in the other chapters, no dependence on Paul is assumed for the author of 1 Peter. The passage is not influenced by Rom 13,1-7. At the end of this chapter special attention is devoted to 1 Pet 2,16 and it possible connections with Rom 6,22; Gal 5,13 and 1 Cor 7,22: the mention of free (freedom) and servant, as well as the warning that freedom should not be a pretext for evil, are striking[2]. Yet notwithstanding these similarities the author of 1 Peter, according to Herzer, does not appear to be dependent on Paul. To be subject to the emperor and civil authorities is a traditional exhortation: "das traditionell bekannte Unterordnungsgebot". Moreover, the expression "servants of God" is not present in the Pauline passages and the formulation "as a pretext for evil" is different from "as an opportunity for the flesh" in Gal 5,13. The author of 1 Peter uses the notion of freedom only here, visibly because it must have been of importance to his addressees in their specific life situation. Apparently he has to admonish his fellow-Christians because they probably misuse their freedom and do not subject themselves to the civil authorities; this is the concrete evil which must be avoided, not various kinds of malice as in 2,1. In his letters, more especially in Gal 5,13, Paul points to other problems, the "works of the flesh"[3]. Can Herzer's straightforward interpretation of verse 16 be sustained?

The difficulties regarding 1 Pet 2,16 are numerous. Is there really not a contact with Paul, no Pauline influence whatsoever? How is the verse syntactically constructed in its immediate context, 2,13-17, and what is the

---

[1] J. HERZER, *Peter oder Paulus? Studien über das Verhältnis des Ersten Petrusbriefes zur paulinischen Tradition* (WUNT 103; Tübingen 1998) 227-244.

[2] Ibid., 239-243.

[3] Ibid.: "Die Gefahr bzw. der tatsächliche Missbrauch von Freiheit is hierbei anderer Art als die Probleme, mit denen sich Paulus auseinanderzusetzen hatte" (243).

precise line of thought in that pericope? How is the grammatical form of verse 16 itself, with its threefold "as", to be explained? What is the meaning of "free" and "freedom" in this verse? Is "evil" here only the absence of civil obedience or submission?

This brief note wants to address these questions. No direct discussion or criticism of Herzer is meant. I first begin with the context of 2,16 and then will consider the verse as far as its grammar is concerned; the final section of this note investigates the freedom nuances of the three interrelated clauses in 2,16.

I. UNITY, TENSIONS AND SHIFTS IN 2,13-17

A few remarks can suffice with regard to the passage[4]. The unity of 2,13-17 appears clearly from the terms and notions which frame the pericope. "Subject yourselves ... to the emperor" in v. 13 is not so different from "honor the emperor" at the end of v. 17. These two commands (imperatives) constitute the main injunction and express the basic idea of the passage. Moreover, "every human creature" in v. 13 corresponds with "all (people)" in v. 17, just as the mention of "the Lord" (probably not Christ[5]) in v. 13 with that of "God" in v. 17.

There are tensions, however, in vv. 13-14 as well as in v. 17. It is almost certain that in v. 13 the expression πάσῃ ἀνθρωπίνῃ κτίσει means "to every human creature (= being)" and not "to every human instance"[6]. But how then is the double concretizing εἴτε ... εἴτε ("whether ... or") logically to be connected? One expects either an introductory term which already points to "authorities" or, instead of "whether ... or", an expression

---

[4] Cf. S. LEGASSE, "La soumission aux authorités d'après 1 Pierre 2. 13-17: version spécifique d'une parénèse traditionelle", *NTS* 34 (1988) 378-396 (bibliography on pp. 395-396); N. BROX, *Der erste Petrusbrief* (EKK; Zürich – Neukirchen/Vluyn 1979); J.R. MICHAELS, *1 Peter* (WBC; Waco 1988); P.H. DAVIDS, *The First Epistle of Peter* (NICNT; Grand Rapids 1990); L. GOPPELT, *A Commentary on 1 Peter* (original German edition in 1978 by F. Hahn, translated and augmented by J.E. Alsup) (Grand Rapids 1993).

[5] GOPPELT, *1 Peter*, 183-184, emphasizes that the Lord here is Christ.

[6] Cf. LEGASSE, "Soumission", 380-383; GOPPELT, *1 Peter*, 182-183. Otherwise, e.g., E.G. SELWYN, *The First Epistle of St. Peter* (London 1947) 172; BROX, *Der erste Petrusbrief*, 119. Cf. also the NEB and NIV translations. After his discussion of the expression HERZER, *Petrus oder Paulus?* 229-231, prefers "Institution" and judges it "wahrscheinlich" (231).

such as "above all" or "more in particular". In v. 17 the tension is threefold. The general πάντας ("all [people]") is surprising after the specific command in vv. 13-14 and its continuation in v. 16. Moreover, the three present imperatives ἀγαπᾶτε, φοβεῖσθε and τιμᾶτε after the aorist imperative τιμήσατε are difficult to explain. Some claim that this change is not significant. Commentators may then ask how the four clauses relate to each other. Since the verb "honor" occurs at the beginning and the end, one may perhaps order the four into two chiastic pairs and interpret as follows: "honor all people, but love the Christian brothers and sisters [a crescendo]; fear God and honor the emperor [a decrescendo]"[7]. Yet, because of the tense-forms and the broader context, Scot Snyder defends the importance of the change from aorist to present and renders the verse (freely): "honour all: (yes, as was already directed) love the brethren and fear God and (also) honour the king"[8]. The aorist is merely descriptive, followed by a general object; the present is used with three specific objects, concrete instances of honoring all people[9]. It might be noted that the specification of a first general command is not unlike that of vv. 13-14.

The shifts in the line of thought are numerous. In the preceding paragraph was mentioned the move from a general imperative to a specification in vv. 13-14, and more or less similarly in v. 17, in both cases, however, not without tension. A beginning of a more general consideration may be present at the end of v. 14: the punishment of evildoers is contrasted to the praise of those who do right; this praise contains not only the officially conferred public commendations but also appraisal of good social conduct[10]. There is, moreover, a difference of nuance between that which fol-

---

[7] Cf. LEGASSE, "Soumission", 384: "une sorte de chiasme doublé d'un crescendo–descrescendo dans les verbes...", with reference to E. BAMMEL, "The Commands in I Peter ii.17", *NTS* 11 (1964-65) 279-281; BROX, *Der erste Petrusbrief*, 123; DAVIDS, *The First Epistle of Peter*, 103. See also GOPPELT, *1 Peter*, 189-190. In Prov 24,21a we read: φοβοῦ τὸν θεόν, υἱέ, καὶ βασιλέα.

[8] S. SNYDER, "1 Peter 2:17: A Reconsideration", *FilNeotest* 5 (1990) 211-215, 213. Verse 17 functions as a summary statement with regard to what precedes in the letter (cf. 1,17: God; 1,22; brothers; 2,13: emperor) (see pp. 212-213). Cf. already S.E. PORTER, *Verbal Aspect in the Greek of the New Testament, with Reference to Tense and Mood* (Stud. Bibl. Greek 1; New York 1989) 260; ID, *Idioms of the Greek New Testament*, (Sheffield ²1994) 54: "the aorist imperative [in 1 Pet 2,17] serves as a summary-term for the following specifying or particularizing present imperatives". But see also the lengthy, somewhat inconclusive discussion of the frequent aorist imperative for general precepts in 1 Peter (and 2 Peter, 1 Timothy, James and Jude) in B.M. FANNING, *Verbal Aspect in New Testament Greek* (Oxford 1990) 371-379.

[9] Cf. SNYDER, "1 Peter 2:17", 212.

[10] Cf. GOPPELT, *1 Peter*, 185-186: not only inscriptions and documents but also, in an extended sense, all civic recognition. Otherwise B.M. WINTER, "The Public Honouring of Christian Benefactors. Romans 13.3-4 and 1 Peter 2.14-15", *JSNT* 34 (1988) 87-103.

lows the first ὡς in v. 13 and that which follows the second ὡς in v. 14. In "be subject ... to the emperor as being supreme" the "as" gives the reason: because he is supreme. In "be subject ... to the governors as being sent by him (= the emperor)"[11], the "as" also points to the reason (their appointment by the emperor), but a task, a dual function, is indicated as well: to punish and to praise. "To do wrong" is to transgress the law; "to do right" refers to all good deeds, not only to benefactions and not only to deeds in compliance with an explicit law[12].

Even more shifts seem to be present in v. 15. It is not completely evident — although probable, since the article is missing before ἀγαθο-ποιοῦντας — that the grammatical subject after "it is God's will" is "you"[13]; in any case, Christians, no longer the governors of v. 14, are those who put to silence the foolish people. Furthermore, the motivating clause of this verse (ὅτι) adduces a parenthetical "missionary" reflection which, it must be conceded, does not greatly surprise the reader of 1 Peter: for it is God's will[14] that Christians by doing right put to silence the ignorance of foolish people[15]. That all of the οἱ ἄφρονες ἄνθρωποι, a rather general expression, are "people who do wrong" and do not observe the laws (v. 14) is unlikely.

Notwithstanding all tensions and shifts, verse 16, which has its own problems, clearly shows that the author has not forgotten the initial command of vv. 13-14.

II. THE SYNTAX IN 2,16

The Greek text of verse 16 consists of three nominative ὡς-clauses, the first and third being positive, the second negative:

---

[11] Sometimes "God" is taken as the implied agent, but such an interpretation seems highly improbable.

[12] Cf. the broader sense in the same verb in 2,20; 3,6 and 17, and in the noun in 4,19. For a discussion of ἀγαθοποιέω, see W.C. VAN UNNIK, "The Teaching of Good Works in I Peter", ID., *Sparsa collecta. II* (NT.S 30; Leiden 1980) 83-105 (= *NTS* 1 [1954] 92-110); GOPPELT, *1 Peter*, 177-179.

[13] Some textual witnesses insert ὑμᾶς. Cf., e.g., also the RSV: "that by doing right 'you' should put to silence the ignorance of foolish men".

[14] The introductory οὕτως is here the equivalent of an announcing τοῦτο. Otherwise E.G. SELWYN, *The First Epistle of St. Peter* (London 1947) 173 (the word is "retrospective").

[15] For the positive influence of the good Christian behavior, cf. 2,12; 3,1-2 and 16. See., e.g., BROX, *Der erste Petrusbrief,* 121.

16a ὡς ἐλεύθεροι
16b   καὶ μὴ ὡς ἐπικάλυμμα ἔχοντες τῆς κακίας τὴν ἐλευθερίαν
16c   ἀλλ' ὡς θεοῦ δοῦλοι[16].

The nominative in the first clause is an adjective (ἐλεύθεροι), in the second it is a participle (ἔχοντες) and in the third a noun (δοῦλοι). The repetition of the freedom notion in v. 16b and the antithetical correspondence between "free" and "servants" in v. 16a and c manifest that the clauses constitute a small, tight unit. There is, however, no main verb. Rather than seeing the first and third nominatives as the equivalents of imperatives or associated with the verbs in the following verse[17], a return to and grammatical dependence on the imperative ὑποτάγητε at the beginning of v. 13 appears to be preferable. Verse 16 thus forms the end of the long sentence. Yet it has to be admitted that because of the shifts in vv. 14-15 the line of thought is very strained indeed.

It should be duly noted that the three ὡς-clauses do not grammatically and syntactically function on the same level[18]. "As free (people)" qualifies the command of submission in a paradoxical way: be subject but as free people, i.e., not as slaves. The second and third ὡς-clauses want to prevent a wrong understanding of the character of freedom. The second clause contains a warning which applies directly to the first clause and, therefore, only indirectly to the imperative of v. 13. One could paraphrase v. 16b: "yet do not use that freedom as a pretext for evil"; καί thus possesses an oppositional nuance ("yet") and τὴν (ἐλευθερίαν) is somewhat anaphoric ("that"). Furthermore, it would seem that μή of v. 16b and ἀλλά of v. 16c belong together ("not ... but"), so that the positive ἀλλ' ὡς-clause completes the preceding negative (μή) and, like that second one, is connected in a direct way with the first clause, only indirectly with the imperative of v. 13. "Being free" of v. 16a, therefore, is qualified in a double manner: Christians should not misuse that freedom to perpetrate evil deeds and they must be free, paradoxically speaking, while being slaves, i.e., servants of God. The placement of the last expression "draws to that phrase the main emphasis"[19].

---

[16] The two variant readings (δοῦλοι θεοῦ and φίλοι θεοῦ) can be neglected given their weak attestation.

[17] Cf. the critical discussion by LEGASSE, "Soumission", 382, n. 2. The RSV, e.g., has: "live as free men ...; but live as servants of God". MICHAELS, *1 Peter*, 120, translates vv. 16-17: "As those who are free, without making that freedom an excuse to cause trouble, yet as God's slaves, show respect for everyone ...".

[18] Otherwise GOPPELT, *1 Peter*, 188, n. 46: "The threefold ὡς in v. 16, like the twofold ὡς in v. 14, has a causal meaning".

[19] MICHAELS, *1 Peter*, 128.

III. THE QUALIFICATIONS OF CHRISTIAN FREEDOM

In the brief first letter of Peter the terms ἐλεύθερος, ἐλευθερία and ἐπικάλυμμα of 2,16, as well as its expression θεοῦ δοῦλοι, are hapax legomena. Whether or not 2,13-17 as a whole is influenced by Rom 13,1-7[20] remains outside the discussion of this note. Yet direct (or at least mediate) Pauline influence on 2,16 can hardly be excluded. The cumulative presence of the oppositional notions free and slave (cf., e.g., Rom 6,22; 1 Cor 7,22; Gal 5,1 and 13) and the idea of a possible misuse of Christian freedom (cf. Gal 5,13) should not be explained as coincidence or through dependence on a common tradition. It would seem that a literary contact must be postulated between 2,16 and more particularly Gal 5,13: ὑμεῖς γὰρ ἐπ᾽ ἐλευθερίᾳ ἐκλήθητε, ἀδελφοί· μόνον μὴ τὴν ἐλευθερίαν ϵἰς ἀφορμὴν τῇ σαρκί, ἀλλὰ διὰ τῆς ἀγάπης δουλεύετε ἀλλήλοις. The fact that the wording, style and content in 1 Pet 2,16 are partly different from those of Paul, esp. in Gal 5,13, is easily understandable and in no way a counter-indication.

What does the author mean by his first paradox: "subject yourselves as free people"? The Pauline idea of freedom from the law as found in Galatians 5 and elsewhere is not present in 1 Peter 2. One could be tempted to refer to 1,18 and fill the notion "free" of 2,16a as free from sin: you were liberated from your former sinful conduct (cf. 1,14 and 2,10)[21]. Although the author would agree that this liberation constitutes the basis of Christian freedom, in 2,16a he rather points, it would seem, to the absence of constraint and compulsion, to spontaneity and free will. We may refer to the example of Christ in 2,21-24 ("When he was reviled, he did not revile in return", v. 23; Christ could have done otherwise). A similar freedom appears to be alluded to in what is said to the elders: "tend the flock of God μὴ ἀναγκαστῶς ἀλλὰ ἑκουσίως (not by constraint but willingly) (5,2)"[22].

The absence of a slavish submission, however, is not without danger: such a freedom can be used as a cover, a pretext for evil. The author thinks here of "evil" in its general moral significance of sin, just as the same term

---

[20] Cf. HERZER, *Petrus oder Paulus?* 227-244. But see also, e.g., G. JOSSA, "La sottomissione alle autorità politiche in 1Pt 2,13-17", *RivBib* 44 (1996) 205-211; according to Jossa, the author "rimane sostanzialmente fedele al pensiero di Paolo" (208).

[21] Cf. GOPPELT, *1 Peter*, 188; LEGASSE, "Soumission", 389-390; Légasse even comments: "C'est *parce qu*'ils ont été libérés par le Christ de leur dépravation antérieure (1. 18) que les chrétiens sont soumis à l'Etat" (p. 389; his italics).

[22] For an analogous qualification of the submission instruction in 3,1, see 3,6: μὴ φοβούμεναι.

κακία indicates in 2,1, not in a supposedly limited sense of disobedience to civic instructions[23]. By means of the expression εἰς ἀφορμὴν τῇ σαρκί in Gal 5,13, Paul appears to refer to the same danger of sin.

The second qualification of freedom occurs "in paradoxer Diktion"[24]. This may strike the reader since it occurs so soon after the first paradox of the command to be subject as free people. The author now adds: as free people, yet as servants of God. Besides the intended contrast "free–slave", the addition "as servants of God" recalls a qualification such as ὡς τέκνα ὑπακοῆς in 1,14 and is contentwise the equivalent of ὡς Χριστιανοί in 4,14.

Norbert Brox maintains that not in all circumstances (see, e.g., 3,8) but "in vielen Fällen christlichen Verhaltens liegt für den 1Petr das Ideal in einem 'Sich-Fügen', 'Sich-Unterwerfen'"[25]. The Christians' subjection, however, should be not slavish, not by compulsion; it must be shown willingly, by people who are free. Yet those people should realize that such a freedom may risk to become a cover for sinful actions. Their standard of conduct, therefore, is that of servants of God. Through qualifying the Christians' freedom by service of God, the author equally relativizes and restricts their submissive obedience to political authorities; the emperor is not divine; he is only "a human creature" (2,13)[26]. Thus civil obedience is in no way absolute, though it is said to be "for the Lord's sake" (v. 13) and though it certainly belongs to the Christian life-style according to God's will (v. 15).

---

[23] So HERZER, *Petrus oder Paulus?* 243. Cf. already GOPPELT, *1 Peter*, 189: the pretext is understood "as exemption from this obligation to civil authorities".

[24] BROX, *Der erste Petrusbrief*, 122. M.H. BOLKESTEIN, *De brieven van Petrus en Judas* (Pediking NT; Nijkerk ²1972) 104, calls this paradox a "fine oxymoron".

[25] BROX, *Der erste Petrusbrief*, 117.

[26] The qualifications of political submission remain true, even if the author of 1 Peter does not intend to write in a critical way. Cf. JOSSA, "Sottomissione": "il brano ha ... una sua precisa, e forte, pregnanza teologica" (208).

PART TWO

THE BOOK OF REVELATION

Ephemerides theologicae Lovanienses 75 (1999) 421-429

26

Jewish Slander
A Note on Revelation 2,9-10

In the message to the church of Smyrna (Rev 2:9-11) the risen Lord says (RSV):

9a   I know your tribulation and your poverty (but you are rich)

9b   and the slander of those who say that they are Jews and are not, but are a synagogue of Satan.

10a   Do not fear what you are about to suffer.

10b   Behold, the devil is about to throw some of you into prison, that you may be tested,

10c   and for ten days you will have tribulation.

10d   Be faithful unto death, and I will give you the crown of life.

"Slander" in verse 9b refers to an action done by some Jews, and the Christians of Smyrna are affected by what these Jews do. It has recently been claimed that "slander" is not the correct translation of τὴν βλασφη-μίαν in verse 9b, because this translation does not retain the nuance of "blasphemy". According to H. Lichtenberger the term here means "die Lästerung Gottes oder Jesu Christi als des Messias und Heilands der Welt"[1]. Others take for granted that "slander" here more specifically points to the denunciation of Christians before pagan authorities[2]. What exactly have some Jews of Smyrna been doing to Christians?

---

[1] H. LICHTENBERGER, "Überlegungen zum Verständnis der Johannes-Apokalypse", C. LANDMESSER – H.-J. ECKSTEIN – H. LICHTENBERGER (eds.), *Jesus Christus als die Mitte der Schrift. Studien zur Hermeneutik des Evangeliums. FS O. Hofius* (BZNW 86; Berlin – New York 1997) 603-618, 613.

[2] Cf., e.g., D.E. AUNE, *Revelation I* (WBC; Dallas 1997) 162.

I. ARE JEWS BLASPHEMING?

The main argument for a theological or/and christological understanding of τὴν βλασφημίαν in Rev 2,9b is the fact that elsewhere in the Apocalypse the noun and verb of this word group are used theologically. In addition to 2,9b the noun is used four times (13,1.5.6 and 17,3) and the verb likewise four times (13,6; 16,9.11.21). The noun always appears in connection with the beast which represents the Roman Empire. On its heads there are "names of blasphemy", i.e., blasphemous names: see 13,1[3]; in 17,3 a woman sits on a scarlet beast which is full of "names of blasphemy". These names most probably refer to the blasphemous "divine" titles of the Roman emperor god[4]. According to 13,5-6 the beast is given a mouth boasting and uttering "blasphemies"; it opens its mouth εἰς βλασφημίας, i.e., "to (utter) blasphemies" against God, and it "blasphemes" God's name and dwelling, that is, those who dwell in heaven. In 13,6 the verb βλασφημέω appears; it occurs three more times in Rev 16. At the fourth plague a bowl is poured on the sun; in 16,9 unbelieving men (οἱ ἄνθρωποι) "blaspheme" the name of God because of their suffering from the heat, but they do not repent. At the fifth plague a bowl is poured on the throne of the beast and in 16,11 men "blaspheme" the God of heaven for their pain and sores, but they do not repent. At the seventh plague a bowl is poured into the air; in 16,21 hailstones are dropped from heaven and men "blaspheme" God for the plague of the hail, "because that plague was very great indeed".

As can be seen, beast, Roman emperor and unbelieving humankind curse and blaspheme God; a christological reference is absent or, at the least, such a reference is nowhere explicit. One should ask whether those eight rather stereotyped theological uses render another use of the verb impossible. Must the Jewish βλασφημία in 2,9 be theological (or christological)? The question cannot be avoided since here it is not directly God who is cursed; the intended recipients of the Jews' action are the Smyrnean Christians.

It has to be recognized that in the New Testament the direct object of "blaspheming" is often God, Christ or the Spirit. Yet the simple secular

---

[3] In Rev 13,1 a great number of manuscripts have the singular "name". See B.M. METZGER, *A Textual Commentary on the Greek New Testament* (Stuttgart [2]1994): "On the strength of the two most important witnesses (A 2053) a majority of the Committee preferred to print ὀνόματα in the text, but to enclose the last two letters within square brackets in order to represent the opposing evidence" (673).

[4] Cf. O. HOFIUS, βλασφημέω, βλασφημία, βλάσφημος, *EDNT I*, 219-221.

meaning of slandering, defaming or speaking evil which Greek dictionaries mention is not absent[5]. We may refer to the vice lists[6] and to 2 Tim 3,2: remind the Christians "to speak evil of no one". Of course, both the secular and the religious meanings can be present at the same time. An example of this double nuance can be found, it would seem, in the list of trials in 1 Cor 4,10-13: "when slandered[7], we bless" (v. 13). It can be assumed that this slander was religiously motivated, although probably not limited to strictly Christian items.

In John 10,33 and 36 the Jews accuse Jesus of "blaspheming" because he says "I am the Son of God"; being a man, he makes himself God. O. Hofius notes appropriately: "This formulation reflects the post-Easter discussion between Church and synagogue over the Christian confession of Jesus as Messiah and Son of God"[8]. Such a post-Easter discussion can be supposed to have formed the background of the slander mentioned in Rev 2,9 as well.

In the New Testament writings the persecution of Christians by Jews is often referred to: see, e.g., John 9,22; 12,42; 16,2; 1 Thess 2,14-16; 2 Cor 11,24. Before his conversion, Paul himself was a persecutor of the church (Gal 1,13; 1 Cor 15,9). Mention can also be made of the Birkat-ha-Minim, at the end of the first century, the Jewish curse against the heretics, the Jewish Christians included[9].

For Christians God and Christ cannot be separated. For them it is blaspheming to throw doubt on the messianic claims of Jesus. According to 1 Tim 1,13, Paul recognizes that as a persecutor of Christians he has been a blasphemer: "I formerly blasphemed and persecuted and insulted him (= Christ Jesus our Lord)". Moreover, "the fate of being slandered and attacked in their basic faith passed from Christ to his community in its union with the Lord .... Suffering blasphemy is one of the sufferings laid on the community"[10]. Since in the Book of Revelation the author easily transfers divine titles and characteristics of God to Christ, it should not

---

[5] Cf. LIDDELL-SCOTT (under 2): "speak ill, speak to the prejudice of one, slander"; BAUER-ALAND (under 1): "in üblen Ruf bringen, verleumden, verunglimpfen".

[6] Cf. Mark 7,22 and Matt 15,19; Col 3,8; Eph 4,31; 1 Tim 6,4.

[7] A variant reading has δυσφημούμενοι instead of βλασφημούμενοι.

[8] HOFIUS, EDNT I, 221.

[9] See Justin, Dialogue with Trypho, 16,4; 17,6; 96,2. Cf., however, LICHENTBERGER, "Überlegungen", 615: "... ob der 'Ketzersegen' auch in Kleinasien üblich war, wissen wir freilich nicht" and: "Die Birkat ha-Minim war nicht die Wasserscheide zwischen Judentum und Christentum, zu der sie gerne gemacht wird. Sie ist eher ein Dokument als die Ursache des Auseinandergehens".

[10] BEYER, TDNT I, 623-624.

cause wonder that Jews reviling Christ could be regarded as blasphemers and their action in the final analysis as the work of Satan[11]. The fact that in a similar context, i.e., the message to Laodicea (3,7-13), Christ announces that he will make the Jews of Laodicea "come and bow down" before the feet of the Christians (v. 9) means that (at the judgment?) they will recognize that the Christians are right regarding their faith in Christ.

Yet, notwithstanding all these pertinent considerations, it remains doubtful that the term βλασφημία points to blaspheming God in Christ in Rev 2,9 when this verse is considered in its immediate context.

II. ARE JEWS DENOUNCING?

Rev 2,9 can hardly be explained without what is said in the following verse. Almost certainly ὁ διάβολος in verse 10 is not different from τοῦ σατανᾶ in verse 9. The sufferings which Christ announces in verse 10, as well as the prison (in order that some Smyrnian Christians "may be tested"), the tribulation "for ten days" and even the possibility of death: all this put forward immediately after verse 9 must probably be considered as being caused by the Jews referred to in that verse. So almost necessarily one is brought to the assumption that Jews not only revile Christians but also denounce them to the pagan magistrates. These Jews must have been "delatores"; they formulate an "accusatio"[12].

---

[11] Cf. LICHTENBERGER, "Überlegungen", 618; E. LOHSE, "Synagogue of Satan and Church of God: Jews and Christians in the Book of Revelation", in SvEÅ (1993) 105-123, 119-120: "... it is the most probable assumption that the controversy about the problem of the Messiah and the Christian confession of the church has caused refusal and contradiction from the side of the synagogues". Cf., e.g., Acts 18,5-6 and 26,11.

[12] A. YARBRO COLLINS, "Vilification and Self-Definition in the Book of Revelation", HTR 79 (1986) 308-320, esp. 312-314: "This juxtaposition [of the reference to the Jews with the prediction of detention in prison] suggests that the 'synagogue of Satan' are instigators of legal action against the persons whom John is addressing. Their blasphemy or slander then would be the charge or accusation which they made to initiate legal proceedings. The attribution of the detention to the work of the devil (2:10) links that event to the synagogue of Satan (2:9)" (p. 313). M. HENGEL, Die johanneische Frage. Ein Lösungsversuch (WUNT 67; Tübingen 1993) writes: "Dass es von jüdischer Seite zu Klagen gegen die missionarisch aktiven Christen (vgl. Apk 3,9) kam, ist nur zu gut verständlich: Die Juden mussten diese enthusiastisch-missionarische Lehre als eine gefährliche Konkurrenz betrachten, durch die sie selbst bei den staatlichen Organen in Misskredit kommen konnten" (292). Cf. AUNE, Revelation, 163, on the Roman legal system in the provinces.

Within such a context one unavoidably thinks of what happened to Jesus himself; the Jewish authorities deliver Jesus to the Roman procurator Pilate: see Mark 15,1-15 (and parallels) and John 18,28–19,15. Furthermore, the Jewish actions of denouncing Paul and Silas in Thessalonica are depicted in Acts 17,5-8; a similar procedure regarding Paul in Corinth is narrated in Acts 18,12-17. Finally, according to the "Martyrdom of Polycarp" (12,2; 13,1; 17,2 and 18,1) Jews denounced Polycarp and were participating in his execution around the middle of the second century in the very city of Smyrna[13].

D.E. Aune concludes his broad discussion of 2,9 as follows: "If Christians have suffered legal penalties at the hands of Roman authorities in Smyrna, such actions were probably initiated by local citizens, and this passage strongly suggests that the Jews actively participated in the process"[14]. The expression "this passage strongly suggests" refers to the comments on the previous page where he states that βλασφημία involves either "verbal slander" or the "denunciation of Christians before Roman or civic authorities"[15].

Is the meaning of denunciation a real possibility? Just as for the specific sense of "blasphemy" in the first paragraph, so also for "denunciation" here the question is to be raised whether βλασφημία itself can contain this nuance. It does not seem that the verb βλασφημέω which is used for the reaction of the Jews to the preaching of Paul at Antioch of Pisidia (Acts 13,45) and for that at Corinth (Acts 18,6) points by itself to "denouncing": twice, according the RSV translation, it said that the Jews "revile" Paul[16].

---

[13] AUNE, *Revelation*, 162, warns: "This account, however, is historically tendentious as well as strikingly anti-Jewish, consciously formulated in an attempt to replicate the Gospel narratives of the passion of Jesus". For a critical edition and discussion of the *Martyrdom of Polycarp*, see B. DEHANDSCHUTTER, *Martyrium Polycarpi. Een literair-kritische studie* (BETL 52; Leuven 1979).

[14] AUNE, *Revelation*, 163. See, however, LICHTENBERGER, "Überlegungen": "βλασφημία /-μεῖν bedeutet in der Johannes-Apokalypse nie die Denunziation (gegenüber Behörden o.ä), sondern immer die Lästerung Gottes oder Jesu Christi als des Messias und Heilands der Welt. Damit entfallen all die Vermutungen und Konstruktionen, die eine jüdische Beteiligung an den Leiden der kleinasiatischen Gemeinde postulieren" (613-614). W. SCHRAGE, "Meditation zu Offenbarung 2,8-11", *EvT* 48 (1988) 388-402, 391, is hesitant: "Ob speziell die 'Blasphemie' der *Joudaioi* das Leiden der Gemeinde ausgelöst hat und einige der Gemeindeglieder dadurch ins Gefängnis geworfen werden, lässt sich nicht sagen"; cf. also p. 394 and already W. BOUSSET, *Die Offenbarung Johannis* (KEK; Göttingen 1906) 209.

[15] AUNE, *Revelation*, 162.

[16] In either case the Greek verb is a participle and has no direct object. There can be no doubt that in Acts 18,6 Paul is meant. This is less clear in 13,45 (the NRSV changes to "blaspheming").

III. REVELATION 2,8-11 AND 3,7-13

At this point a reading of the context may prove useful. Not only 2,8-11 but also 3,7-13 must be considered. These are the only passages where Jews are mentioned and where it is stated that they are not real Jews but the synagogue of Satan. To a certain extent the two texts appear to provide complementary information.

a) Rev 2,8-11 contains the second message of the risen Christ (and the Spirit), that to the church of Smyrna. One immediately notes the correspondence between verses 8 and 10-11. The opposition of death and life on the one hand and (eschatological) life and death on the other is present at the beginning and the end of this message. The theme referred to in the clause "the words of the first and the last ὃς ἐγένετο νεκρὸς καὶ ἔζησεν" (v. 8; cf. 1,17-18) is taken up in "be faithful ἄχρι θανάτου and I will give you τὸν στέφανον τῆς ζωῆς"[17] (v. 10) and equally in "he who conquers shall not be hurt ἐκ τοῦ θανάτου τοῦ δευτέρου" (v. 11). Obviously, this inclusion is by no means accidental.

It would seem that the clauses of verses 9 and 10 together constitute a unity; they are mutually explanatory. Although the reference to "poverty" in verse 9a may be partly due to the social and economic situation of Christians in Smyrna[18], the "tribulation" in the same clause should almost certainly be connected with the slander of the Jews in verse 9b as well as with the suffering, the prison and its testing[19] and the "tribulation" (same term θλῖψις) which Christ announces in verse 10. Moreover, although the vocabulary varies, the "devil" in verse 10b can hardly be different from the "Satan" at the end of verse 9 (see the identification of the dragon in 12,9, who is called "the Devil and Satan"; cf. also 20,2).

It has been claimed that the term "Jews" in 2,9 (and 3,9) does not refer to non-Christian Jews but to "heretical" Christians such as the Nicolaitans or the followers of Jezebel: they claim to be "spiritual" Jews, but in fact they are not[20]. However, since specific warnings against such "spiritual"

---

[17] The last expression is not found outside the New Testament. Cf. R.H. CHARLES, *The Revelation of St. John. Vol. I* (ICC; Edinburgh 1920) 56; SCHRAGE, "Meditation", 391-392.

[18] Cf. AUNE, *Revelation*, 161: "Uncompromising Christians found it difficult to make a living in a pagan environment".

[19] Cf. CHARLES, *Revelation*, 58: "πειράζειν and πειρασμός in iii. 10 refer to the demonic attacks which are to befall all the unbelievers on the earth, but which cannot affect those who have been sealed .... But in the present verse πειράζειν is used in the sense of testing by persecution".

[20] SCHRAGE, "Meditation", 390-391.394-395, seems to prefer this identification. See H.

Jews are lacking, it is better to take the name "Jews" in its normal meaning, i.e., in its non-Christian sense and not as disignating heretical Jewish Christians[21].

The Christians' tribulation and suffering, their being in prison and tested, even "unto death", appear to be caused by Jews in Smyrna. In view of the connection between verse 9 and verse 10, especially the mention of "prison" in verse 10, one seems compelled to postulate Jews denouncing Christians before pagan authorities[22]. Jewish Christians in Smyrna may have tried to avoid the obligations of emperor worship by emphasizing their Jewish birth, but non-Christian Jews denounce them to those authorities who, therefore, persecute Christians and throw some of them into prison in order to "test" them, i.e., to force them publicly to honor the emperor. There must have been more that just all kinds of slander. There must have been Jewish denunciation and accusation. Consequently, this means the active participation of some Jews in causing tribulation, suffering and imprisonment to Christians[23].

b) The sixth message, that to the church of Philadelphia (3,7-13), is longer than the second. Besides parts of verse 9, which are very much like 2,9, one may see a reminder of that second letter in the mention of "crown" at the end of 3,11 (cf. 2,10) and perhaps also in the clause "you have but little power" in 3,8 (cf. "poverty", 2,9). Moreover, these two letters are the only ones in which no word of blame is uttered.

KRAFT, *Die Offenbarung des Johannes* (HNT; Tübingen 1974) 60-61: "Johannes ist nicht an den Juden, sondern an den Christen interessiert. Eine Satanssynagoge in seinem Sinn ist eine jüdisch-christliche Gruppe, deren Kult von ihm als Götzendienst, d.i. Satansdienst angesehen wird. Ihre 'Lästerungen' sind ihre Behauptungen über Tod und Auferstehung Christi, die sie entweder völlig, oder wenigstens in ihrem Heilswert leugnen .... Da jene Gruppe sich ausdrücklich als Juden bezeichnet, ist nicht nur zu folgern, dass den Juden in der bevorstehenden Verfolgung keine Gefahr droht, sondern auch vor allem, dass die Gruppe eben dadurch, dass sie sich als Juden bezeichnet, sich der Verfolgung entzieht" (61); see also pp. 81-82.

[21] See YARBRO COLLINS, "Vilification", esp. 310-316, and cf. LOHSE, "Synagogue of Satan", 106-107; H. GIESEN, *Die Offenbarung des Johannes* (RNT; Regensburg 1997) 107; AUNE, *Revelation*, 164; P. BORGEN, "Polemic in the Book of Revelation", C.A. EVANS – D.A. HAGNER (eds.), *Anti-Semitism and Early Christianity: Issues of Polemic and Faith* (Augsburg, 1993) 119-211; esp. 200.

[22] So, e.g., LOHSE, "Synagogue of Satan", 119-120: "... it is the most probable assumption that the controversy about the problem of the Messiah and the Christian confession of the church has caused refusal and contradiction from the side of the synagogues". Cf., e.g., Acts 18,5-6 and 26,11.

[23] For this procedure reference is very often made to the well-known letter of Pliny the Younger (*Ep.* 10.96,1-10) and the answer by Emperor Trajan (*Ep.* 10.97,1-2). Cf., e.g., CHARLES, *Revelation*, 55-56; H.-J. KLAUCK, "Das Sendschreiben nach Pergamon und der Kaiserkult in der Johannesapokalypse", *Bib* 74 (1992) 153-182, esp. 162-164.

Elements of the christological predication of verse 7 (the one "who has the key of David, who opens and no one shall shut, who shuts and no one opens") are carried over into verse 8: "an open door, which no one is able to shut". The expression "my name" at the end of verse 8 corresponds with "my own new name" at the end of verse 12; both expressions thus constitute an inclusion.

Just as in 2,9 the mention of Jews in 3,9 cannot be isolated from its immediate context. The Christians in Philadelphia have proven their faithful obedience to Christ's word (vv. 8 and 10), most probably during the tribulation and sufferings which Jews brought about. The hypothesis of the Jewish denunciation of Christians as well as the announcements of 2,9-10 have to be supplied. The sentence in the first half of 3,9 is incomplete. A verb in the infinitive (or a purpose clause) is missing after ἰδοὺ διδῶ[24]; the sentence remains incomplete but is further taken up by means of a new introduction ἰδοὺ ποιήσω[25] and completed by what follows. In contrast to 2,8-10, however, nothing explicit is said here about the activity of the Jews. Christ announces the final outcome; he will make Jews prostrate before Christians and they will learn that he has loved[26] the Christians of Philadelphia (v. 9). In verse 10 he adds that because of the Christians' faithfulness he will keep them out of the hour of trial (for both vocabulary and thought, cf. John 17,6.11-12.15). In verse 10b, however, the horizon is suddenly widened: a "trial which is coming on the whole earth, to try those who dwell upon the earth" is mentioned[27].

In verse 12 it is also announced that the conquerors will be made pillars in God's eschatological temple and receive God's name, the name of "the new Jerusalem" and also the new name of the risen Christ himself. By mentioning "the new Jerusalem which comes down from my God out of heaven" John the prophet anticipates his depiction of 21,1–22,5. The readers should interpret the symbol of that city as a reference to the eschatological future of the church. One cannot but ask how non-Christian Jews have reacted to such a Christian self-perception.

c) Just as John's statements of what the Jews are doing, so also his

---

[24] M. ZERWICK – M. GROSVENOR, *A Grammatical Analysis of the Greek New Testament* (Rome 1981) 748, explain the two words as follows: a "literal Hebrew construction 'behold me granting, that...'; i.e., 'I will bring it about that...'". The present tense points to the future; cf. the future tense of the second verb.

[25] Cf. BOUSSET, *Offenbarung*, 227: "erklärende Wiederaufname".

[26] W.J. HARRINGTON, *Revelation* (SP; Collegeville 1993) comments: "... here, for the first time in these messages, in relation to this little but faithful Church, we find explicit mention of the love of Christ" (72).

[27] For the differences in the πειράζω-terminology, cf. n. 19.

counterattack in 2,9 and 3,9 consists of words spoken by the risen Lord (cf. 2,8 and 3,7) and, at the same time, by the Spirit (cf. 2,11a and 3,13). In both letters those words contain for Jews an extremely negative content, but for Christians a positive one. The Jews who slander (and denounce) Christians are not true Jews; on the contrary, they belong to the synagogue of Satan. From this counterattack and also from 3,12 it appears that John considers the Christians as the genuine Jews.

Almost certainly the genitive in the expression "the synagogue of Satan" is subjective[28]. For this expression reference is often made to the parallel Qumran phrases "the congregation of Belial" (1QH 2,22 and 1QM 4,9). These and other Qumran passages show how bitter inner fights among Jews could lead to abuse with such dualistic pronouncements[29]. One thinks, of course, also of John 8,44, where Jesus says to the Pharisees that the devil is their father. In Revelation, the tension is also still intramural; two groups, Jews and Christians (most of them Jewish Christians) consider themselves as "Jews". There is still a Jewish context; the boundaries between them have not yet broken down completely[30]. It should, however, be noticed that in the second part of Revelation John demonizes non-Christian Gentiles to the extreme. For the mention of Satan in the message to Pergamum, see 2,13 — twice[31]. This data, of course, tends to make a parallel between Jews and Gentiles.

In contrast to Rev 3,9, where the expression "the synagogue of Satan" occurs at the beginning of the sentence ("Behold, I will make [certain ones] out of the synagogue of Satan ..."), in 2,9 it is found at the very end (they are not Jews, "but they are the synagogue of Satan"). Then, immediately afterwards, one reads in 2,10: "Do not fear what you are about to suffer. Behold, the devil is about to throw (certain ones) of you into prison ...". The close connection of these clauses suggests in its own way that at the root of the suffering as well as within the activity of the devil one must most probably see the involvement of Jews. They are instigators; they cause the suffering and are the instruments in the persecuting work of the

---

[28] In Num 16,3; 20,4; 26,9 (variant) and 31,16 the expression συναγωγὴ κυρίου is found.

[29] Cf., e.g., BORGEN, "Polemic", 204-205 and 209-210. The expression τὰ βαθέα τοῦ σατανᾶ in Rev 2,24 is used for the teaching of other (heretical) Christians. See also 2 Cor 11,14-15.

[30] Cf. BORGEN, "Polemic", 206-211; YARBRO COLLINS, "Vilification", 113-114; AUNE, *Revelation*, 164: "This phrase ('synagogue of Satan') may reflect the beginning of separation of the church from the synagogue ...".

[31] Rev 2:13: "I know where you dwell, 'where Satan's throne is'; you hold fast my name and you did not deny my faith even in the days of Antipas, my witness, my faithful one, who was killed among you 'where Satan dwells'". See KLAUCK, "Sendschreiben", esp. 156-164.

devil. The question can be asked whether that is not the main reason why the Jews are called "the synagogue of Satan".

In 2,10 the risen Lord states that the tribulation will last only ten days. If the Christians are faithful unto death, he will give them "the crown of life". In 2,11, moreover, it is said that the one who conquers will not be hurt "by the second death" (cf. 20,6 and 21,8). In 3,9, however, the reversal of the Jews' situation is indicated: "I will make them come and bow down before your feet, and learn that I have loved you". It would seem that John refers here to the Isaian motif which announces the homage of the Gentiles: "The sons of those who oppressed you shall come bending low to you; and all who despised you shall bow down at your feet" (Isa 60,14; cf. 45,14; 49,23). In the same way as the Gentiles will honor Israel, the so-called Jews will humble themselves before the Christians, the true Jews: "eine merkwürdige Umkehrung"[32].

CONCLUSION

At the end of this note a threefold conclusion can be drawn.

1. Although the background of 2,9 is definitely christological and the use of the word group elsewhere in Revelation is clearly theological, the term βλασφημία as Jewish slander against the Christians, in this particular verse, does not directly signify blasphemous utterances against God and his Christ.

2. Nor does the term by itself point to denunciation. One has to make a distinction between what is expressed and what must be postulated in a given context.

3. Several data in 2,8-11 and 3,7-13 require a hypothetical reconstruction. Most probably there is a strict connection between 2,9 and 2,10. Both the repetitions in the first part of 3,9 and the eschatological reversal which are announced in its second part lead one to presuppose in this verse the future sufferings of Christians already depicted in 2,10. Moreover, that reversal in what the Jews are going to do (3,9b) completes the overall image of 2,9-10. Now the reader knows that there is not only victory and life for the faithful Christians but also a final change in the attitude of the Jews. The announcement of prison to the Christians, as well as the appeal

---

[32] M. Rissi, "Das Judenproblem im Lichte der Johannesapokalypse", *ThZ* 13 (1957) 241-259, 258.

to faithfulness unto death, together with the heavy attack against the Jews as being not really Jews but the synagogue of Satan, leads the reader of these passages almost irresistibly to the hypothesis that those Jews not only reviled Christians but also proceeded to the legal action of denunciation. Not the term "slander" itself but the whole context of both passages appears to require this reconstruction.

One should, of course, not lose sight of the fact that at the end of the first century the non-Christian Jews in Asia constituted a majority in comparison with the still rather small number of Christians. Not so much later, Ignatius of Antioch will emphasize the Christian identity as different from that of the Jews: Christianity is no longer "Judaism".

27

Synagogues of Satan (cf. Rev 2,9 and 3,9) Anti-Judaism in the Apocalypse

No doubt the main enemy of the Christians[1] in the book of Revelation is the surrounding omnipresent paganism. Concretely speaking, behind the actions of Satan and the two Beasts who appear on the scene in chs. 12 and 13 there is the emperor cult with its political, economic and religious pro-paganda and its menacing oppression[2]. Christians in western Asia Minor are suffering; persecution, even to death, could be imminent. Some Christians are tempted to adapt to a pagan life–style and "to compromise with trade guilds and their patron deities"[3]. In the church of Sardis, Christ "who has the seven spirits of God and the seven stars" does not find the Christians' "works perfect" (3,1-2); in Laodicea, Christ who is "the Amen, the faithful and true witness, the origin of God's creation" addresses Christians as follows: "You are neither cold nor hot .... Because you are lukewarm ... I am about to spit you out of my mouth" (3,14-16). Visibly there is in more than one community lack of ardor, even of perseverance.

Moreover, the Christians of Ephesus as well as those of Pergamum are warned against the sect of the Nicolaitans "who hold the teaching of

---

[1] Most probably the majority of the Christians in the churches of Revelation are Jewish-Christians who will still have considered themselves as "Jews". In this paper the term "Christians" points to all believers in Jesus Christ in western Asia Minor.

[2] See, e.g., S.R.F. PRICE, *Rituals and Power. The Roman imperial cult in Asia Minor* (Cambridge 1984). T. SÖDING, "Heilig, heilig, heilig. Zur politischen Theologie der Johannes-Apokalypse", *ZThK* 96 (1999) 49-76, provides a brief and balanced description on pp. 50-54. Cf. A. YARBRO COLLINS, "Vilification and Self-Definition in the Book of Revelation", *HTR* 79 (1986) 308-320: "The receptive audience of Revelation would reject the symbolic universe held by many around them which had the emperor at the center" (315).

[3] G.K. BEALE, *The Book of Revelation* (NIGTC; Grand Rapids 1999) 30. On the same page Beale writes: "Homage to the emperor as divine was included along with worship of such local deities .... After all, the patron gods of the guilds together with the imperial god of Rome were purportedly responsible for the social and economic blessings that the culture had enjoyed".

Balaam, who taught Balak to put a stumbling block before the people of Israel, so that they would eat food sacrificed to idols and practice fornication" (2,14; see 2,15 and 2,6). The Christians of Thyatira appear to be tolerating "that woman Jezebel, who calls herself a prophet and is teaching and beguiling my servants to practice fornication and to eat food sacrificed to idols" (2,20; also see 2,21-24). Notwithstanding the Old Testament comparison with Balaam and the Old Testament name Jezebel, the people referred to are or represent heretic Christians, not Jews.

Yet in two letters, according to the author of Revelation, the early Christian prophet John, the risen Lord speaks of "those who say that they are Jews and are not, but are a synagogue of Satan" (2,9b; compare 3,9a). In the author's opinion not the Jews but the Christians are the real Jews. Corroborative evidence is found in the way John identifies the Christian community with Israel and depicts the eschatological future of the church as the "new Jerusalem". Because of this negative mention of the Jews as well as in view of John's almost matter-of-course presentation of the church's identity, the question cannot be avoided whether there is not a degree of anti-Judaism in the Book of Revelation.

This brief contribution will first analyze the immediate literary context of 2,9 and 3,9 and try to determine the activity of the inimical Jews[4]. In a second part, the counterattack of John the prophet will be investigated. Finally, a critical reflection must lead us to some hermeneutical conclusions[5].

I. THE JEWS IN REV 2,9 AND 3,9

Rev 2,8-11: Smyrna

8a Καὶ τῷ ἀγγέλῳ τῆς ἐν Σμύρνῃ ἐκκλησίας γράψον·
 b Τάδε λέγει ὁ πρῶτος καὶ ὁ ἔσχατος, ὃς ἐγένετο νεκρὸς καὶ ἔζησεν·

---

[4] In this study no analysis of the clause "where their Lord was crucified" in 11:8 is offered. Some commentators are or the opinion that probably there is no reference here to Jerusalem. See also n. 31.

[5] For extensive bibliographies see BEALE, *Revelation*, xxviii-lxiv, and D.E. AUNE, *Revelation* Vol. I (WBC; Dallas 1997), more particularly on pp. 106 and 238 for 2,8-11 and 3,7-13 respectively.

9a οἶδά σου τὴν θλῖψιν καὶ τὴν πτωχείαν, ἀλλὰ πλούσιος εἶ,

 b καὶ τὴν βλασφημίαν ἐκ τῶν λεγόντων Ἰουδαίους εἶναι ἑαυτοὺς καὶ οὐκ εἰσὶν ἀλλὰ συναγωγὴ τοῦ σατανᾶ.

10a μηδὲν φοβοῦ ἃ μέλλεις πάσχειν.

 b ἰδοὺ μέλλει βάλλειν ὁ διάβολος ἐξ ὑμῶν εἰς φυλακὴν ἵνα πειρασθῆτε

 c καὶ ἕξετε θλῖψιν ἡμερῶν δέκα.

 d γίνου πιστὸς ἄχρι θανάτου, καὶ δώσω σοι τὸν στέφανον τῆς ζωῆς.

11a Ὁ ἔχων οὖς ἀκουσάτω τί τὸ πνεῦμα λέγει ταῖς ἐκκλησίαις.

 b Ὁ νικῶν οὐ μὴ ἀδικηθῇ ἐκ τοῦ θανάτου τοῦ δευτέρου.

8a And to the angel of the church in Smyrna write:
 b These are the words of the first and the last, who was dead and came to life.
9a I know your affliction and your poverty, even though you are rich.
 b I know the slander on the part of those who say that they are Jews, and are not, but are a synagogue of Satan.
10a Do not fear what your are about to suffer.
 b Beware, the devil is about to throw some of you into prison so that you may be tested,
 c and for ten days you will have affliction.
 d Be faithful until death, and I will give you the crown of life.
11a Let anyone who has an ear listen to what the Spirit is saying to the churches.
 b Whoever conquers will not be harmed by the second death.
 (NRSV-translation)

The first occurrence of the name Ἰουδαῖοι is to be found in the letter or message to the church of Smyrna, the second in the series of seven: 2,8-11. One immediately notes the correspondence between verses 8 and 10-11. The opposition of death and life on the one hand and eschatological life and death on the other is present at the beginning and the end of the letter. The theme referred to in the clause "the words of the first and the last ὃς ἐγένετο νεκρὸς καὶ ἔζησεν" (v. 8b; cf. 1,17-18) is taken up in "be faithful ἄχρι θανάτου and I will give you τὸν στέφανον τῆς ζωῆς"[6] (v. 10d)

---

[6] The last expression is not found outside the New Testament. Cf. R.H. CHARLES, *The Revelation of St. John. Vol. I* (ICC; Edinburgh, 1920) 56; W. SCHRAGE, "Meditation zu Offenbarung 2,8-11", *EvT* 48 (1988) 388-402, 391-392.

and equally in "whoever conquers will not be harmed ἐκ τοῦ θανάτου τοῦ δευτέρου" (v. 11b). Obviously, this inclusion referring to both Christ and Christians is by no means accidental.

It would seem that the clauses of verses 9 and 10 together constitute a unity; they explain one another. Although the reference to "poverty" in verse 9a may be partly due to the social and economic situation of Christians in Smyrna, the "affliction" in the same clause should almost certainly be connected with the slander of the Jews in verse 9b as well as with the suffering, the prison, the testing[7] and the "affliction" (same term θλῖψις) mentioned in verse 10abc. Moreover, although the vocabulary varies, the "devil" in verse 10b can hardly be different from the "Satan" at the end of verse 9b (see the identification of the dragon in 12,9, who is called "the Devil and Satan"; cf. also 20,2).

It has been claimed that the term "Jews" in 2,9b (and 3,9a) does not refer to non-Christian Jews but to "heretical" Christians such as the Nicolaitans or the followers of Jezebel: they claim to be "spiritual" Jews, but in fact they are not[8]. However, since specific warnings against such "spiritual" Jews are lacking, it is better to take the name "Jews" in its normal meaning, i.e., in its non-Christian sense and not pointing to Jewish Christians[9].

The Christians' affliction and suffering, their being in prison and being tested appear to be caused by the βλασφημία of the Jews of Smyrna[10]. Elsewhere in the Book of Revelation, this term, as well as the verb βλασφημέω, signify the insult of God and hence plausibly also the denial of Jesus as his Messiah[11]. However, in view of the connection between verse

---

[7] Cf. CHARLES, *Revelation*, 58.

[8] Cf. SCHRAGE, "Meditation", 390-391 and 394-395; see H. KRAFT, *Die Offenbarung des Johannes* (HNT; Tübingen 1974) 60-61 and 81-82.

[9] See YARBRO COLLINS, "Vilification", esp. 310-316; cf. E. LOHSE, "Synagogue of Satan and Church of God: Jews and Christians in the Book of Revelation", *SvEÅ* 58 (1993) 105-123, esp. 106-107; H. GIESEN, *Die Offenbarung des Johannes* (RNT; Regensburg 1997) 107; AUNE, *Revelation*, 164; P. BORGEN, "Polemic in the Book of Revelation", C.A. EVANS – D.A. HAGNER (eds.), *Anti-Semitism and Early Christianity: Issues of Polemic and Faith* (Augsburg 1993) 119-211, esp. 200.

[10] Otherwise AUNE, *Revelation*, 166: "There is no explicit connection between the βλασφημία of the Jews mentioned in v. 9 and impending imprisonment, though the work of Satan or the Devil is seen behind both". SCHRAGE, "Meditation", 391, is hesitant: "Ob speziell die 'Blasphemie' der *Joudaioi* das Leiden der Gemeinde ausgelöst hat und einige der Gemeindeglieder dadurch ins Gefängnis geworden werden, lässt sich nicht sagen"; cf. also p. 394 and already W. BOUSSET, *Die Offenbarung Johannis* (KEK; Göttingen 1906) 209.

[11] So, e.g., LOHSE, "Synagogue of Satan", 119-120. Cf., e.g., Acts 18,5-6 and 26,11. In Rev 13,1.5.6; 16,9.11.21 and 17,3 the terminology is employed in the usual sense of blaspheming against God, cursing (the name of) God.

9 and verse 10, especially the mention of prison (v. 10b), the term most likely means here "slander", not "blasphemy"; the context makes that it probably points here to the denunciation of Christians before Roman or civic authorities[12]. Jewish Christians in Smyrna may have tried to avoid the obligations of emperor worship by emphasizing their Jewish birth, but non-Christian Jews must have denounced them to those authorities who, therefore, persecuted Christians and threw some of them into prison in order to "test" them, i.e., to force them publicly to honor the emperor. Slander thus contains Jewish accusation or denunciation; in this sense it contains active participation of some Jews in causing affliction, suffering and imprisonment to Christians[13].

Rev 3,7-13: Philadelphia

7a Καὶ τῷ ἀγγέλῳ τῆς ἐν Φιλαδελφείᾳ ἐκκλησίας γράψον·

b Τάδε λέγει ὁ ἅγιος, ὁ ἀληθινός, ὁ ἔχων τὴν κλεῖν Δαυίδ, ὁ ἀνοίγων καὶ οὐδεὶς κλείσει καὶ κλείων καὶ οὐδεὶς ἀνοίγει·

8a οἶδά σου τὰ ἔργα,

b ἰδοὺ δέδωκα ἐνώπιόν σου θύραν ἠνεῳγμένην, ἣν οὐδεὶς δύναται κλεῖσαι αὐτήν,

c ὅτι μικρὰν ἔχεις δύναμιν καὶ ἐτήρησάς μου τὸν λόγον καὶ οὐκ ἠρνήσω τὸ ὄνομά μου.

---

[12] Cf. J. LAMBRECHT, "Jewish Slander. A Note on Revelation 2,9-10", in *ETL* 75 (1999) 421-429; also in this volume, pp. 329-339. For the procedure of denunciation reference is very often made to the well-known letter of Pliny the Younger (*Ep.* 10.96,1-10) and the answer by Emperor Trajan (*Ep.* 10.97,1-2).

[13] Cf., e.g., CHARLES, *Revelation*, 55-56; BEALE, *Revelation*, 29-32 and 239-241; H.-J. KLAUCK, "Das Sendschreiben nach Pergamon und der Kaiserkult in der Johannesapokalypse", *Bib* 74 (1992) 153-182, esp. 162-164; YARBRO COLLINS, "Vilification", 312-314.

Jews who persecute Christians are, of course, mentioned in Acts and the Pauline letters. In Acts 17,5-8 and 18,12-17 Jews accuse Christians before pagan authorities. Mention must also be made of the so-called *Birkat-ha-Minim* at the end of the first century, the Jewish curse against the heretics, Jewish Christians included (cf. Justin, *Dialogue with Trypho*, 16,4; 17,6; 96,2). Cf., however, H. LICHTENBERGER, "Überlegungen zum Verständnis der Johannes-Apokalypse", C. LANDMESSER – H.-J. ECKSTEIN – H. LICHTENBERGER (eds.), *Jesus Christus als die Mitte der Schrift. Studien zur Hermeneutik des Evangeliums. FS. O. Hofius* (BZNW 86; Berlin – New York 1997) 603-618: "... ob der 'Ketzersegen' auch in Kleinasien üblich war, wissen wir freilich nicht" and "Die Birkat ha-Minim war nicht die Wasserscheide zwischen Judentum und Christentum, zu der sie gerne gemacht wird. Sie is eher ein Dokument als die Ursache des Auseinandergehens" (615).

In the *Martyrium Policarpi* 12,2; 13,1; 17,2 and 18,1 Jews are said to have participated in Polycarp's execution in Smyrna (ca 155). According to AUNE, *Revelation*, 162, this may be "historically tendentious".

9a ἰδοὺ διδῶ ἐκ τῆς συναγωγῆς τοῦ σατανᾶ τῶν λεγόντων
    ἑαυτοὺς ᾿Ιουδαίους εἶναι, καὶ οὐκ εἰσὶν ἀλλὰ ψεύδονται.
 b ἰδοὺ ποιήσω αὐτοὺς ἵνα ἥξουσιν καὶ προσκυνήσουσιν ἐνώ-
    πιον τῶν ποδῶν σου καὶ γνῶσιν ὅτι ἐγὼ ἠγάπησά σε.
10a ὅτι ἐτήρησας τὸν λόγον τῆς ὑπομονῆς μου,
 b κἀγώ σε τηρήσω ἐκ τῆς ὥρας τοῦ πειρασμοῦ τῆς μελλούσης
    ἔρχεσθαι ἐπὶ τῆς οἰκουμένης ὅλης πειράσαι τοὺς κατοικοῦν-
    τας ἐπὶ τῆς γῆς.
11a ἔρχομαι ταχύ·
 b κράτει ὃ ἔχεις, ἵνα μηδεὶς λάβῃ τὸν στέφανόν σου.
12a ῾Ο νικῶν ποιήσω αὐτὸν στῦλον ἐν τῷ ναῷ τοῦ θεοῦ μου καὶ
    ἔξω οὐ μὴ ἐξέλθῃ ἔτι
 b καὶ γράψω ἐπ᾿ αὐτὸν τὸ ὄνομα τοῦ θεοῦ μου καὶ τὸ ὄνομα
    τῆς πόλεως τοῦ θεοῦ μου, τῆς καινῆς ᾿Ιερουσαλὴμ ἡ κατα-
    βαίνουσα ἐκ τοῦ οὐρανοῦ ἀπὸ τοῦ θεοῦ μου, καὶ τὸ ὄνομα
    μου τὸ καινόν.
13 ῾Ο ἔχων οὖς ἀκουσάτω τί τὸ πνεῦμα λέγει ταῖς ἐκκλησίαις.

7a And to the angel of the church in Philadelphia write:
 b These are the words of the holy one, the true one, who has the key
    of David, who opens and no one will shut, who shuts and no one
    opens.
8a I know your works.
 b Look, I have set before you an open door, which no one is able to
    shut.
 c I know that you have but little power, and yet you have kept my
    word and have not denied my name.
9a I will make those of the synagogue of Satan who say that they are
    Jews and are not, but are lying —
 b I will make them come and bow down before your feet, and they
    will learn that I have loved you.
10a Because you have kept my word of patient endurance,
 b I will keep you from the hour of trial that is coming on the whole
    world to test the inhabitants of the earth.
11a I am coming soon;
 b hold fast to what you have, so that no one may seize your crown.
12a If you conquer, I will make you a pillar in the temple of my God;
    you will never go out of it.
 b I will write on you the name of my God, and the name of the city
    of my God, the new Jerusalem that comes down from my God out
    of heaven, and my own new name.

13   Let anyone who has an ear listen to what the Spirit is saying to
     the churches.
     (NRSV-translation)

The sixth letter, that to the church in Philadelphia (3,7-13), is longer than the second. Besides parts of 3,9, which are very much like 2,9, one may see a remainder of that second letter in the mention of "crown" at the end of 3,11b (cf. 2,10d) and perhaps also in the clause "you have but little power" in 3,8c (cf. "poverty", 2,9a). Moreover, these two letters are the only ones in which no word of blame is uttered against the churches[14].

Elements of the christological predication of 3,7b (the one "who has the key of David, who opens and no one will shut, who shuts and no one opens") are carried over into verse 8b: "an open door, which no one is able to shut"[15]. The expression "my name" at the end of verse 8c corresponds with "my own new name" at the end of verse 12b; both expressions thus constitute an inclusion.

Just as in 2,9b the mention of the Jews in 3,9a cannot be isolated from its immediate context. The Christians in Philadelphia have proven their faithful obedience to Christ's word (3,8c and 10a), most probably during the affliction and sufferings which the Jews brought about. The hypothesis of the Jewish denunciation as well as the announcements of 2,9-10 have to be supplied. The sentence in 3,9a is incomplete. A verb in the infinitive (or a purpose clause) is missing after ἰδοὺ διδῶ[16]; this unfinished statement is further taken up by means of the new introduction ἰδοὺ ποιήσω in verse 9b[17] and completed by what follows. In contrast to 2,9-10, however, nothing explicit is said here about the activity of the Jews. Christ announces the final outcome; he will make Jews prostrate before Christians and they will learn that "he has loved"[18] the Christians of Philadelphia (v. 9).

---

[14] It must strike the reader of the *Martyrium Policarpi*, 19,1, that Philadelphia is mentioned as the place where, as in Smyrna, Christians have been martyred.

[15] The expression "open door" probably refers to favorable opportunities for missionary work. Cf. CHARLES, *Revelation*, 87.

[16] M. ZERWICK – M. GROSVENOR, *A Grammatical Analysis of the Greek New Testament* (Rome 1981) 748, explain the two words as follows: a "literal Hebrew construction 'behold me granting, that...'; i.e. 'I will bring it about that...'". The present tense points to the future; cf. the future tense of the second verb. The positive comment on 3,9 by BEALE, *Revelation*, 286-288, can hardly be correct: "behold, I will give" of v. 9a echoes "behold I have given" of v. 8b; "Christ will continue to empower his church to witness by opening the door of salvation for the unbelieving Jews in their community" (286).

[17] Cf. BOUSSET, *Offenbarung*, 227: "erklärende Wiederaufname".

[18] An aorist indicative with a perfective value. Cf. G. MUSSIES, *The Morphology of Koine Greek as Used in the Apocalypse of St. John. A Study in Bilingualism* (NT.S 27; Leiden 1971) 338.

In verse 10 he adds that because of the Christians' faithfulness he will keep them out of the hour of trial (for both vocabulary and thought, cf. John 17,6.11-12.15). In verse 10b, however, the horizon is suddenly widened: a "trial that is coming on the whole earth, to test the inhabitants of the earth"[19].

In verse 12 it is also announced that the conquerors will be made pillars in God's eschatological temple[20] and receive God's name, the name of "the new Jerusalem" and also the new name of the risen Christ himself. By mentioning "the new Jerusalem that comes down from my God out of heaven" John the prophet anticipates his depiction of 21,1–22,5. The readers should interpret the symbol of that city as a reference to the eschatological future of the church universal. One cannot but ask how non-Christian Jews could react to such a Christian self-perception.

II. THE COUNTERATTACK OF JOHN

Just as John's statements of what the Jews are doing, so also his counterattack in 2,9 and 3,9 consists of words spoken by the risen Lord (cf. 2,8b and 3,7b) and, at the same time, by the Spirit (cf. 2,11a and 3,13). In both letters those words contain a negative and a positive content. The Jews who slander and denounce Christians are not true Jews; on the contrary, they belong to synagogues of Satan. Moreover, from this counterattack and also from 3,12 it appears that John considers the Christians as the genuine Jews.

They Are Not (Real) Jews

In 2,9b the text reads τῶν λεγόντων Ἰουδαίους εἶναι ἑαυτοὺς καὶ οὐκ εἰσὶν ἀλλά .... (3,9a has ἑαυτούς after λεγόντων). The καί here

---

[19] For the πειράζω-terminology ("to try, trial"), cf. CHARLES, *Revelation*, 58.

[20] Notwithstanding the fact that John is directly dependent on Ezekiel 40-48 (new temple) for his description of the new Jerusalem, he explicitly states in 21,22: "And I saw no temple in the city, for its temple is the Lord God the Almighty and the Lamb". Yet in 3,12, as well as in 11,1-2, passages which are equally influenced by Ezekiel, the temple is mentioned. See for an excellent discussion J.M. VOGELGESANG, *The Interpretation of Ezekiel in the Book of Revelation* (unpublished Ph.D. Diss. Harvard 1985), 39-40 and 76 ("each utilization represents a *different* interpretation of the Ezekiel-traced material"). Cf. also p. 113.

possesses an adversative sense: "but", in reality, they are not Jews. Then, in 2,9b the even stronger adversative ἀλλά-clause indicates what they really are, "a synagogue of Satan". In 3,9a this last expression stands at the beginning of the sentence; an ἀλλά-clause is equally present; it stresses the Jews' insincerity: but, as a matter of fact, they lie[21]. This qualification applies, it would seem, to all Jews in Smyrna and Philadelphia, not only to those who slander Christians.

One should duly note that in 3,9a the partitive ἐκ-construction manifests that not all Jews in Philadelphia are involved. The indefinite pronoun τινες must be mentally supplemented before the ἐκ-construction: "(certain ones) out of the synagogue of Satan"[22]. This construction, however, does not imply that not all Jews belong to that synagogue of Satan. In 2,9b the ἐκ-construction grammatically depends on τὴν βλασφημίαν: I know the slander 'proceeding from' those who say .... Here the preposition ἐκ most probably indicates the agents, those who slander. One may refer to 2,11b in the same pericope for a similar ἐκ after a passive verb: "Whoever conquers will not be harmed 'by' the second death". Yet, notwithstanding these different grammatical functions of the preposition, the nuance of "certain ones" can be assumed to be present in 2,9b as well: not all those in Smyrna who say that they are Jews, but only some of them are denouncing the Christians.

Synagogues of Satan

Almost certainly the genitive "of Satan" in 2,9b and 3,9a is subjective. For the expression "synagogue of Satan"[23] reference is often made to the parallel Qumran phrase "the congregation of Belial" (1QH 2,22 and 1QM 4,9). One thinks, of course, also of John 8,44, where Jesus says to the Pharisees that the devil is their father: ὑμεῖς ἐκ τοῦ πατρὸς τοῦ διαβόλου ἐστέ. These expressions and other Qumran passages show how bitter inner fights between Jews could lead to abuse with such dualistic pronouncements[24]. In Revelation, the tension is perhaps still somewhat intra-

---

[21] For the complex expression, compare 2,2: "... how you cannot bear evil men but have tested 'those who call themselves apostles but are not, and found them to be false (ψευδεῖς)'"; see also 2,20: "... the woman Jezebel, who calls herself a prophetess ..."). For the grammar of such clauses, see MUSSIES, *Morphology*, 327.

[22] According to MUSSIES, *Morphology*, 96, n. 1, such a partitive ἐκ, is used in 2,7.10; 3,9; 5,9 and 11,9.

[23] In Num 16,3; 20,4; 26,9 (variant) and 31,16 the expression συναγωγὴ κυρίου is found.

[24] Cf., e.g., BORGEN, " Polemic", 204-205 and 209-210. The expression τὰ βαθέα τοῦ σατανᾶ in Rev 2,24 is employed for the teaching of other (heretical) Christians. See also 2 Cor 11,14-15.

mural; there is still a Jewish context. Yet the boundaries between Jews and Christians are breaking down almost completely[25]. It should be noticed that in the second part of his work John the prophet demonizes non-Christian Gentiles to the extreme. For the mention of Satan in the letter to Pergamum, see 2,13[26]. This data, of course, tends to make a parallel between Jews and Gentiles.

In both messages John appears to refer concretely to the local communities of Jews. In Smyrna, they are not Jews, "but are a synagogue of Satan" (2,9b: no article). In Philadelphia, John uses the article: (in a more literal translation) "Behold, I will make [certain ones] out of 'the' synagogue of Satan ..." (3,9a); by means of the article he points to the Jewish community in that city.

In contrast to Rev 3,9a, where the expression the "synagogue of Satan" occurs almost at the beginning of the sentence, in 2,9b the expression is found at the very end. Then, immediately afterwards, one reads in 2,10a: "Do not fear what you are about to suffer. Beware, the devil is about to throw some of you into prison ...". The close connection of these clauses suggests in its own way that at the root of the suffering as well as within the activity of the devil one must most probably see the involvement of Jews. They are instigators; they cause the suffering and are the instruments in the persecuting work of the devil. The question cannot but be asked whether that is not the main reason why the Jews are called a "synagogue of Satan"[27].

---

[25] Cf. BORGEN, "Polemic", 206-211; YARBRO COLLINS, "Vilification", 113-114; VOGELGESANG, *Interpretation*, 385, n. 106; AUNE, *Revelation*, 164. Not so much later, Ignatius of Antioch will emphasize the Christian identity as different from that of the Jews: Christianity is no longer "Judaism". Cf. YARBRO COLLINS, "Vilification", 311-312.

[26] Twice: "I know where you are living, 'where Satan's throne is' [ὅπου ὁ θρόνος τοῦ Σατανᾶ]. Yet you are holding fast to my name and you did not deny your faith in me even in the days of Antipas, my witness, my faithful one, who was killed among you 'where Satan dwells' [ὅπου ὁ Σατανᾶς κατοικεῖ]". See KLAUCK, "Sendschreiben", esp. 156-164.

[27] Cf. also the different approach by J.N. KRAYBILL, *Imperial Cult and Commerce in John's Apocalypse* (JSNT.S 132; Sheffield 1996) 169-172: "Vituperative language about a 'synagogue of Satan' might stem from a belief that Jews helped persecute Christians. John's larger use of symbolism, however, suggests that he mentions Satan here as a way of highlighting commercial or political relationships some Jews had with Rome .... By using the epithet 'synagogue of Satan' in his letter to Smyrna and Philadelphia, John implies that certain Jews in those cities are in the same category as Rome — that is, in league with Satan" (170).
Still another hypothesis is proposed by LICHTENBERGER, "Überlegungen": since in Revelation there is "die Übertragung von Gottesprädikate auf Jesus Christus", one can understand "dass die 'Schmähungen' gegen das Bekenntnis zu Christus vom Verfasser der Apokalypse wie der Gemeinden in Analogie zur Lästerung Gottes verstanden werden mussten.

In 2,10c the risen Lord states that the affliction will last only ten days. If the Christians are faithful unto death, he will give them "the crown of life" (v. 10d). In 2,11b, moreover, it is said that the one who conquers will not be hurt "by the second death" (cf. 20,6 and 21,8). In 3,9b, however, the reversal of the Jews' situation is indicated: "I will make them come and bow down before your feet, and they will learn that I have loved you". It would seem that John refers here to the Isaian motif which announces the homage of the Gentiles: "The descendants of those who oppressed you shall come bending low to you, and all who despised you shall bow down at your feet" (Isa 60,14; cf. 45,14; 49,23). In the same way as the Gentiles will honor Israel, the so-called Jews will humble themselves before the Christians, the true Jews[28]. Perhaps John mentally adds the rest of Isa 60,14: the Jews "shall call you the City of the Lord, the Zion of the Holy One of Israel" (cf. Rev 3,12b).

The Christians Are the True Jews

The term "Jews" in 2,9b and 3,9a is certainly to be understood positively[29]. The fact that John so strongly denies that the Jews are genuine Jews implicitly proves that in his opinion the Christians are the true Jews. This seizure of the Jewish identity, its denial to the Jews and use for themselves must have appeared to the Jews as "anti-judaistic" to the extreme[30].

Und auch nur so ist die Heftigkeit des Vorwurfs, 'Synagoge Satans' zu sein, begreifbar, macht sich doch die jüdische Gemeinde durch die Ablehnung, d.h. Lästerung Christi, in den Augen des Verfassers der Gotteslästerung schuldig und verwirkt damit den Anspruch auf den Ehrentitel 'Jude'" (618). Yet see LAMBRECHT, "Jewish Slander".

[28] Cf. CHARLES, Revelation, 89: "The homage that the Jews expected from the Gentiles, they were themselves to render to the Christians". See also, e.g., LOHSE, "Synagogue of Satan", 122; AUNE, Revelation, 238. Recently G.K. BEALE, John's Use of the Old Testament in Revelation (JSNT.S 166; Sheffield 1998) 122-123, and Revelation, 288, calls this procedure an "inverted" use of the Old Testament. John here shows an "ironic understanding" of a major theme in Isaiah 40–66. To explain Rev 3,9b as pointing to Jews becoming Christians would force, it would seem, the text.

[29] BORGEN, "Polemic", 198; P. TOMSON, "The Names Israel and Jew in Ancient Judaism and in the New Testament", in Bijdr 47 (1986) 120-140 and 266-289, esp. 286. RISSI, Das Judenproblem, 42, writes: it is evident "dass 'Ιουδαῖος für den christlichen Apokalyptiker [= the author John the prophet] höchstes Ehrenprädikat bedeutet ...". Cf. also CHARLES, Revelation, 57: "The fact that our author attaches a spiritual significance of the highest character to the name 'Ιουδαῖος shows that he is himself a Jewish Christian. In such a connection the Fourth Evangelist would have used the term 'Ισραηλίτης (cf. i. 47), whereas he represents the 'Ιουδαῖοι as specifically and essentially the opponents of Christianity". Cf. BOUSSET, Offenbarung, 209 and 227.

[30] Cf. Rom 2,28-29; 9,6-9 and Phil 3,3: ἡμεῖς γάρ ἐσμεν ἡ περιτομή.

That our making explicit what remains inherent in 2,9 and 3,9 is correct is corroborated by what is stated in 3,12. The conquering Christians will be part of the new Jerusalem[31] which comes down out of heaven; they have the name of that city written on them. From 21,1–22,5 it will become evident that this city is nothing other than the eschatological church, "the bride, the wife of the Lamb" (21,9). The Christians are that city. The same already appeared from 7,4-8: in John's self-perception the Christians are the "one hundred forty-four thousand sealed", the twelve tribes of Israel[32]. They are the new, true Israel (cf. 14,3 and 21,12-14).

Throughout the whole Book of Revelation, thus, those who believe in Jesus are to be considered at the same time as the real Jews, the new Jerusalem and the true Israel. This third aspect of John's counterattack is by no means the least severe and the least damaging to the Jews' honor and what would seem to be their righteous pride.

III. CRITICAL REFLECTION

The language of the author of Revelation in 2,9 and 3,9 is not moderate, not objective. It is a language of aggression and vilification. Much has been written about the sad and dreadful *Wirkungsgeschichte* expressions such as a or the "synagogue of Satan" have had. One poignant example may be given: "In 1988 in Germany we had to draw the attention of our people to the awful events that had taken place fifty years ago. On November 9 in 1938 hundreds of synagogues all over Germany were burnt and destroyed, many Jewish people were arrested, some of them were killed — a terrible foreboding sympton of the holocaust which took place

---

[31] Can a somewhat hidden but scathing counterattack also be assumed in 11,8 where the unnamed Jerusalem would be pointed to by the clause "where the Lord was crucified"? Like Rome, the old historical Jerusalem then is "the great city which is allegorically called Sodom and Egypt". Cf. BORGEN, "Polemic", 205. RISSI, *Das Judenproblem*, 244-250, detects Jerusalem (and Israel) polemic in the whole of Rev 11. But see, e.g., BEALE, *Revelation*: "... the 'great city' where the bodies lie is best identified as the ungodly world and not the earthly city of Jerusalem" (591); that world-city "is spiritually like Jerusalem, which had become like other ungodly nations, and even worse, by killing Christ" (592).

[32] On Rev 7,1-8 (*ecclesia in via*) and 7,9-17 (*ecclesia triumphans*) — not two different groups! — see J. LAMBRECHT, "The Opening of the Seals (Rev 6,1-8,6)", *Bib* 79 (1998) 198-220, esp. 210-212; also in this volume, esp. 368-370. This church consists of Jewish Christians and (a minority of) Gentile Christians. Cf. BORGEN, "Polemic", 209.

some years later. In 1988 we had to explain what had been done at that time, we had to show how dreadful the consequences of antisemitism are .... Accidentally it happened to be that the pericope given for the following Sunday service was Revelation 2,8-11 .... All of you who will look to the text will be frightened finding the sentence: that the Jews from whom the congregation was separated are in fact the Synagogue of Satan (Rev 2,9)"[33]. In order to redress the anguish caused by the content of these verses it would seem that three hermeneutical considerations should be made.

Generalization

In defense of John the prophet and his view of the Jews many commentators emphasize that the Jews are mentioned in only two of the seven messages. Therefore, it is said, the Jewish anti-Christian activity appears to have been limited locally. Moreover, the ἐκ-construction in 3,9a points to "some", and not all of the Jews living in Philadelphia. The direct object of ἰδοὺ διδῶ, contained in the ἐκ-expression (3,9a) and taken up by αὐτούς after ἰδοὺ ποιήσω (3,9b), restricts their number in Philadelphia. The limiting nuance of the partitive ἐκ ("some") should be fully recognized. Furthermore, as already stated, one is allowed to suppose that a similar restriction applies to Smyrna although the ἐκ-construction in 2,9b is grammatically different.

There certainly is, however, a generalization in John's attack. We must assume that not some but all non-Christian Jews in Smyrna and Philadelphia say that they are Jews but, according to John, are not, and that in John's opinion not some but all Jews in both cities belong to those synagogues of Satan. Exceptions are not mentioned and should not be imported into the text.

It may also be questioned if John would qualify the Jews of other cities in the province Asia differently[34]. If pressed, he might even have included not only those in western Asia Minor but all non-Christian Jews. Local synagogues then become "the synagogue of Satan". One can hardly escape the conclusion that John is generalizing, indeed.

---

[33] This is the beginning of LOHSE's conference; see "Synagogue of Satan", 105. Cf. SCHRAGE, "Meditation", esp. 388-389 and 397.

[34] AUNE, Revelation, 162 , writes: in Rev 2,9 and 3,9 "the author is not condemning Jews generally but only those associated with synagogues in Smyrna and Philadelphia". As a matter of fact, this statement may be too exclusive as far as John is concerned.

Demonization

As has been explained above the twofold sharp outburst "synagogue of Satan"[35] should most probably not be interpreted in isolation from its context in 2,9-10 as well as in 3,8-10. It is because of vile, presumably denouncing actions of some Jews that the Jewish communities of Smyrna and Philadelphia are called "synagogues of Satan" by John the prophet[36]. In 3,9b it is stated that by way of retribution the risen Lord will prostrate the persecuting Jews before the feet of the Christians and thus the Jews will learn that Christ has loved the Christians. The author of Revelation detects behind the Jewish accusing slander Satan as the instigator. This is part of what can be called "the sad overkill of polemic"[37].

Of course, this sample of identification of Satan is but a part of the major demonization in the Book of Revelation. The persecution of the church which manifests itself through forms of imperial worship and an idolatrous trade system, is for John in the last analysis the work of the dragon, "that ancient serpent, who is called the Devil and Satan, the deceiver of the whole world" (12,9). The dragon gives authority to the first (political) beast (cf. 13,4) and the first beast gives authority to the (religious) second, the false prophet (cf. 13,12). To John diabolizing the Jews is but a detail of that worldwide scenery which seems to be governed by demonic forces. Confronted with such a deep conviction one may tend to excuse John for his lack of love of the human enemy.

Christian Minority

It is rightly held that the author of Revelation is a Jewish Christian. The major part of the church in western Asia Minor must have been Jewish Christian. The Jewish Christians considered themselves still as ethnic Jews. As Jews they, too, are the heirs of the promises to Israel and the legitimate owners of the Jewish traditions. But the separation of the church

---

[35] BOUSSET, *Offenbarung*, 209, notes: "Das Wort συναγωγή (nicht ἐκκλησία) is wohl mit Absicht gewählt".

[36] One should perhaps point out a more profound theological reason. See, e.g., J. ROLOFF, *Die Offenbarung des Johannes* (ZüBKNT; Zürich 1984) 52: Since the Jews reject Christ, they no longer belong to God's people. "Wer sich ... der Herrschaft Jesu Christi und damit Gottes nicht unterstellt, der gibt sich, gemäss der zum Dualismus tendierenden Geschichtsschau der Apokalypse, der Herrschaft des dämonischen Widersachers Gottes anheim".

[37] So HARRINGTON, *Revelation*, 58.

from the synagogue by that time had almost become an irreversible fact.

Guesses about numbers are extremely tentative. At the end of the first century the Roman empire is estimated to have had a population of sixty million; there may have been four to five million Jews and presumably not many more than fifty thousand Christians[38]. Not only in the midst of a Gentile society but confronted with the unbelieving Jews, the followers of Christ could not have failed to grasp how small a minority they were.

One should try to realize the painful experience of a vulnerable minority of Christians who, lost as they are in a pagan society, happened sometimes to be accused by fellow Jews. They must have felt betrayed. Therefore, one can hardly be surprised at their fierce reaction. Those Jews who are accusing us, they say, and all the non-Christian Jews are not true Jews; they are the synagogue of Satan. More and more, as days go on, that counterattack is being founded in their own conviction and claim: we are the true Israel and new Jerusalem, we are the real Jews[39].

This type of anti-Judaism, to be sure, took its origin in people who as Christians were for the most part still Jews and as weak and poor minority people were persecuted not only by Gentiles but eventually also by fellow Jews. In the message to the church in Philadelphia Jesus says: "I am coming soon" (3,11a; cf. 22,7.12.20). This can no longer be understood in a directly temporal way. The parousia is delayed and the situations later in history have been very different. Christian majorities persecuted Jewish minorities. It is extremely sad that New Testament texts, also Rev 2,9 and 3,9, have been used to justify what in no way could and can be justified.

---

[38] AUNE, *Revelation*, 164; LOHSE, "Synagogue of Satan", 108; P.W. VAN DER HORST, "Jews and Christians in the Light of their Relations in Other Cities of Asia Minor", *NTT* 43 (1989) 106-121. With particular attention to Aphridisias and Sardis, the last author deals with the impressive position of Judaism in Asia Minor, especially in the fourth and fifth centuries AD. For the diaspora Jews in Asia, see now P.R. TREBILCO, *Jewish Communities in Asia Minor* (MS.SNTS 69; Cambridge 1991); KRAYBILL, *Imperial Cult*; J.M.G. BARCLAY, *Jews in the Mediterranean Diaspora. From Alexander to Trajan (323 BCE – 117 CE)* (Edinburgh 1996) esp. 259-281: "The Province Asia". In note 50 (p. 279) Barclay remarks: "It is possible to interpret ... the opposition of the synagogues to the churches in Rev 2.9 ... and 3.9 ... as attempts to dissociate the Jews from the more socially subversive Christians".

[39] Cf. YARBRO COLLINS, "Vilification", 319-320: "John's polemic was part of the struggle of Christians in western Asia Minor to survive physically and to establish an identity as legitimate heirs to the heritage of Israel. Christians were an extreme minority and in a very precarious position".

Appendix

After the completion of this paper I read the excellent monograph *Das eschatologische Israel. Untersuchungen zum Gottesvolkverständnis der Johannesoffenbarung* by Peter HIRSCHBERG (WMANT 84; Neukirchen/Vluyn 1999). The author devotes a substantial part of his work to Rev 2,9 and 3,9 (pp. 31-127) and two major sections to chapters 7 and 21-22. In Hirschberg's opinion the expression "synagogue of Satan" most probably is "eine Reaktion auf die jüdischen Distanzierungsmassnahmen ..., die für Christen verhängnisvolle Folgen hatten. In der Sicht des Sehers werden die Synagogen zu Handlangern des gottfeindlichen Rom" (123). The accusation of βλασφημία refers to "das konkrete gesellschaftliche Verhalten der Juden den Christen gegenüber", as well as to "die darin implizierte Gotteslästerung" (ibid.). John, a Jew who believes in Jesus, blames other Jews.

Hirschberg stresses that the separation between Jews and Christians was not yet definitive. Part of historical Israel (= Jewish Christians) as well as Gentile believers belong to God's eschatological people. "Heilsgeschichtlich unterscheidet der Seher also zwischen Juden und Heiden, soteriologisch ist jeder Unterschied aufgehoben" (194). Therefore, the later theological category of the substitution of Jews by Christians should be avoided with regard to the Book of Revelation. John's emphasis on the twelve tribes of Israel — "die eschatologische Fülle" — may even point to an "eschatologische Hoffnung für Israel" (286-287).

Biblica 79 (1998) 198-220

28

The Opening of the Seals
(Revelation 6,1–8,6)

In 1996 Giancarlo Biguzzi published a remarkable study in Italian on the septets in the structure of the book of Revelation[1]. In this work, the four evident series of "seven" are investigated: letters, seals, trumpets and bowls, the last three in much more detail. As the subtitle indicates, a history of the exegesis is provided, the texts are analyzed and their interpretation is offered. The problem of the connection between seals, trumpets and bowls is carefully examined. Biguzzi asks whether one can speak of progression and climax, or rather should choose between recapitulation and encompassing technique. Moreover, the question is asked what these terms exactly mean.

Biguzzi's thorough acquaintance with the scholarly literature on Revelation is admirable. With great perspicacity and an astounding familiarity with earlier interpretations as well as modern research, Biguzzi composes his surveys and thereafter presents his own well-considered views. Not only does he, as is common practice, distinguish between the letters in chapters 1–3 and the other three septets, he also strongly defends the difference between the seals (chs. 4–7) on the one hand and the trumpets and bowls (chs. 8–9 and 15–16) on the other. In the section of the seals the Lamb only "reveals"; in the sections of the trumpets and bowls seven angels "bring about" God's medicinal punishments and plagues. Rev 4,1–7,17 is a separate section; the passages 7,13-17 and 5,4-5 constitute an inclusion. In 8,1 a different register commences: no longer revelation but action.

The present article will attempt to investigate again, in dialogue with Giancarlo Biguzzi, the "story-line" in chapters 4–8, more specifically in

---

[1] G. BIGUZZI, *I settenari nella struttura dell'Apocalisse. Analisi, storia della ricerca, interpretazione* (RivBiv.S 31; Bologna 1996). See, e.g., the recension by P. Prigent in *Bib* 78 (1997) 294-297.

6,1–8,6[2]. In the first section the main ingredients of Biguzzi's position will be explained. The second section will examine his views in a critical way. Finally the hopefully justified insights will be gathered and reflected upon. The reader should bear in mind that only one section of Revelation is dealt with explicitly; other texts are brought into the discussion in so far as they advance the understanding of 6,1–8,6.

I. BIGUZZI ON REV 6,1-8,6

Chapters 4–7 of Revelation can be divided into two parts: the Introductory Vision of the Scroll (chs. 4–5) with the One sitting on the throne in chapter 4 and the Lamb taking the scroll sealed with the seven seals in chapter 5; and the First Six Seals (chs. 6–7) with the opening of these seals in chapter 6 and in chapter 7 the pericopes on those sealed on earth (7,1-8), as well as on the great multitude of martyrs in heaven (7,9-17). After the "interruption" of chapter 7 the text continues with the seventh seal, rather mysteriously: "When the Lamb opened the seventh seal, there was silence in heaven for about half an hour" (8,1).

Specific Views

The Lamb. Biguzzi very much emphasizes that in the opening of the seven seals the Lamb is the unique agent (pp. 108-109). The Lamb is the protagonist in chapter 6 and 8,1. In chapter 5 a mighty angel had proclaimed with a loud voice: "Who is worthy to open the scroll and break its seals?" (v. 2). The Lion of the tribe of Judah, the Root of David, the one who has conquered is the only one who can open the scroll and its seven seals. The Lamb stands as if it has been slaughtered. The Lamb has seven horns and seven eyes "which are the seven spirits of God sent out into all

---

[2] Cf. J. LAMBRECHT, "A Structuration of Revelation 4,1–22,5", ID. (ed.), *L'Apocalypse johannique et l'Apocalyptique dans le Nouveau Testament* (BETL 53; Leuven 1980) 77-104. This study tried to "visualize" a great many of the results found in U. VANNI, *La struttura letteraria dell'Apocalisse* (Aloisiana 8; Roma 1971). For crictical discussions of my proposal, see the second and enlarged edition of Vanni's book (Roma 1980) 274-280, and also F.D. MAZZAFERRI, *The Genre of the Book of Revelation from a Source-critical Perspective* (BZNW 54; Berlin 1989) 356-363.

the earth" (v. 6). The Lamb takes the scroll from the right hand of the one who is seated on the throne. Then follows the liturgy of the four living creatures and the twenty-four elders. Their new song is heard: "You are worthy to take the scroll and to open its seals ..." (v. 9). This song is more or less repeated by the many angels surrounding the throne: "Worthy is the Lamb ..." (v. 12). Finally, every creature in heaven and on earth and under the earth as well as in the sea, and all that is in them, give glory to God and to the Lamb.

After this most solemn inauguration one reads the equally stately beginning of the opening: "Then I saw the Lamb open one of the seven seals, and I heard one of the living creatures call out, as with a voice of thunder, 'Come!'" (6,1). Four times this scene is more or less repeated and four times a horse and its rider appear. But also for the three remaining seals it is the Lamb who opens them. Biguzzi concludes that the reader cannot but pay attention to the absolutely primary role of the Lamb as unique subject of the action. Moreover, the reader is greatly impressed by the emphasis given to this fact by the author of Revelation[3].

A comparison with the trumpets and the bowls underscores the importance of this first remark. In both these series the action is carried out by seven angels; they are numbered and form a group; they are ministers of God and received their task from God (cf. the passive "was given" and, with regard to a command, 9,13-14: "I heard a voice from the four horns of the golden altar before God, saying to the sixth angel ..."). No doubt is possible: because of their number and their lower rank as angels, and also because of the way John introduces them, these protagonists are clearly inferior to the Lamb[4].

Positive an Negative Description. The introductory formulae in chapter 6 (the seals) are less stereotyped than those of the trumpets and the bowls: see those of the fifth seal (6,9) and the sixth seal (6,12; cf. also 8,1) (pp. 105-105). With horse and rider in each seal the first four seals (6,1-8) undoubtedly constitute a quartet. Yet the first seal ends with the clause: (the rider) "came out conquering and to conquer" (6,2); such an execution is not mentioned for the other three riders. As many other commentators, Biguzzi emphasizes the positive character of the first rider: white color, the crown,

---

[3] See BIGUZZI, *Settenari*, 109: "All'attenzione del lettore ... si impone il ruolo di assoluto primo piano svolto dall'Agnello: egli è non solo soggetto unico nella formula d'introduzione di ogni sigillo, ma quel ruolo è preconizzato con emfasi unica".

[4] Not only the number but "si introvvede l'inferiorità dei sette angeli tribicini nei confronti dell'Agnello, sia per dignità, che per autorità e ruolo" (BIGUZZI, *Settenari*, 113). For the trumpets, cf. 109-110 and 113; for the bowls, cf. 114-115.

the verb "to conquer" and the parallel 19,11 where the rider is Christ. Although nothing in 6,1-2 points to Christ and the rider should, therefore, not be taken as Christ, the first seal is most probably different from the other three: positive *versus* negative[5]. Furthermore, these first four seals do not point to events which are taking place. In Biguzzi's opinion they are characterized by "non-episodicità e a-istoricità"[6]. The first is not a blessing; the other three are not plagues. By means of them John points to a conflicting and already existing and permanent situation on earth.

The Christian Martyrs. The fifth seal (6,9-11), too, cannot be a plague or a punishment. In a rather unexpected way John speaks here of those who have been slaughtered for the word of God and are already in heaven ("under the altar"). They are the Christian martyrs who have died during the persecution. Biguzzi emphasizes a twofold emergence. It is no longer the Lamb who directs his riders to the earth; no, in the fifth seal the martyrs pray to God. It is no longer an a-historical qualification of contrast; in the fifth seal the time dimensions come to the forefront: the text refers to the past and imminent persecution of the Christians and the martyrs' prayer for God's judgment and vindication ("how long will it be before ...?" 6,10). God's answer is that the number of the fellow servants must be completed first. As can be seen, the fifth seal is very different from the foregoing seals. A thematic progression and a continuous narration are not to be expected[7].

The End of a Narrative Cycle. According to Biguzzi the content of the sixth seal goes from 6,12 to 7,17 and contains three pericopes (pp. 134-146). The first pericope (6,12-17) depicts a cosmic upheaval which causes the panic of sinful humankind; it announces the imminent wrath of God and the Lamb: "the great day of their wrath has come, and who is able to stand?" (6,17). Visibly this is already the beginning of the divine answer to the prayers of the martyrs in the preceding seal. The second pericope (7,1-8), however, explains that the actual punishment cannot take place yet; the servants of God must first be marked with a seal. John narrates this sealing; the twelve tribes and the number of people, 144,000, symbolize the whole

---

[5] BIGUZZI, *Settenari,* 121-130. Cf. also, e.g., M. BACHMANN, "Der erste apokalyptische Reiter und die Anlage des letzten Buches der Bibel", *Bib* 67 (1986) 240-275.

[6] BIGUZZI, *Settenari,* 130; cf. 147: "L'autore nei primi quattro sigilli pare dunque interessato a presentare una situazione o condizione continuata e permanente, caratterizzata dalla non-episodicità. In altre parole sembra predisporre una scenografia sul cui sfondo proietterà la vicenda, essa sì fatta di eventi unici, che ha in programma di raccontare".

[7] BIGUZZI, *Settenari,* 130-134; cf. the interesting study of J.P. HEIL, "The Fifth Seal (Rev 6,9-11) as a Key to the Book of Revelation", *Bib* 74 (1993) 220-243.

of Israel, which in this context, no doubt, refers to the Christian church on earth (pp. 137-140). The third pericope (7,9-17) is suddenly eschatological: the great multitude represents the same Christian church, but now as triumphant and situated in heaven. A comparison with chapters 21–22 confirms the end-time character of this scene (p. 215).

Together with the fifth seal the whole of history is presented: past, present and future persecution of the church, sealing of the servants, (announced) divine vengeance and punishment, and final salvation[8]. The historical range is even wider than that of trumpets and bowls in chapters 8–16 which deals only with medicinal punishments and plagues[9]. One has to assume that according to John between 7,8 and 7,9 both the medicinal and the final punishments as well as God's victory take place. The expression μετὰ ταῦτα in 7,9 (plural; compare μετὰ τοῦτο in 7,1, singular) appears to suggest that judgments have intervened[10].

In 7,13 one of the elders addresses John and says: "Who are these, robed in white, and where have they come from?" This is the start of an informative, interpretative dialogue; the revelation proper has ended at 7,12. Biguzzi compares the dialogue of 7,13-17 with that in 5,4-5, the only two texts where an elder gives explanation to John; they possess a very similar vocabulary, and twice also there is the context of a liturgy. Therefore, the two passages appear to function as an inclusion; they "frame" the revelation of chapters 6–7 and at the same time they indicate that chapters 4–7 constitute a complete narrative cycle[11].

Revelation. Biguzzi does not accept the view that the content of the scroll can only be revealed after the opening of the seventh seal. A comparison with trumpets/bowls, where each blast of a trumpet and each pouring of a bowl is followed by a plague, as well as due attention given to the close grammatical connection of each vision with the opening of the seal,

---

[8] Biguzzi, *Settenari*, 134: "Mentre l'Autore scrive, la persecuzione è già fatto del passato, e nello stesso tempo è temuta per un futuro imminente. Oltre quel supplemento di persecuzione, infine, si intravvedono giudizio e 'vendicazione', e quindi anche premio e ricompensa. Attraverso il tema della persecuzione dunque si innesca nella trama del libro tutto l'arco temporale che va dalla storia contemporanea all'escatologia". See also 148-149.

[9] See the correspondences and differences which are graphically set out in Biguzzi, *Settenari*, 213.

[10] Biguzzi, *Settenari*, 145-146: "... giudizio e vittoria sono da supporre tra la sigillazione dei 144.000 e la gloria della folla innumerevole" (146).

[11] Biguzzi, *Settenari*, 217-220: "... estendosi dall'interrogativo dell'Angelo Forte su chi sia degno d'aprire il rotolo fino alla sua più esauriente risposta, Ap 4–7 risulta essere un ciclo narrativo completo, e una vera e propria 'apocalisse', in se stessa compiuta e autosufficiente" (220).

should overcome the so-called "archeological" difficulty. The symbolic world does not always obey the rules of the historical reality, i.e., that a scroll cannot be read before all its seals are broken. No, in Revelation after each opening there is a manifestation of part of the scroll's content (pp. 188-191).

Yet what occurs through the Lamb's opening of the seals is revelation, not realization. The opening of the book by the Lamb causes visions and auditions of God's fixed plan of history, of what is and what will be; they are not indications that (in John's mystical experience) events are already taking place. This can be compared with the beginning of the book: "The revelation of Jesus Christ which God gave him to show his servants what must soon take place; he made it known by sending his servant John ..." (1,1-2). Biguzzi repeatedly stresses that the series of seals is different from the trumpets and bowls where events really occur. In the seals one remains in the sphere of knowledge, publication, manifestation, prophecy; the realization has no yet begun (see, e.g., pp. 191-193 and 210).

The Silence. The opening of the seventh seal (8,1) is decidedly different from the opening of the previous ones. It has already been said that the revelation proper ends at 7,12[12]. The introductory formula in 8,1 contains a ὅταν instead of the six times repeated ὅτε in chapter 6 (vv. 1.3.5.7.9 and 12) and — what is much more important — the opening is not immediately followed by a verb of seeing or hearing but by ἐγένετο, which indicates an event[13]. In 8,1 the text reads: "When the Lamb opened the seventh seal, there was silence in heaven for about half an hour".

According to Biguzzi, the silence is a time period of intense positive expectation of God's intervention, just that. One is not permitted to put the content of 8,2-6 into it. The apparition of the seven angels (v. 2), the liturgy of incense and prayer (vv. 3-4), the throwing of the fire on the earth (v. 5), the preparatory activity of the angels (v. 6): all this is in no way simultaneous with the silence and, therefore, not to be placed within the "half hour". Those events presumably occur after the revelation by the Lamb and also after the period of the expectation (p. 226).

For Biguzzi 8,1 constitutes the vertex, the intersection between the

---

[12] Cf. BIGUZZI, *Settenari*, 221: because of the dialogue in 7,13-17 "... l'apertura del settimo sigillo (8,1) è sorprendentemente e incredibilmente fuori della rivelazione, nonostante che aprire un sigillo di per sé significhi rivelare".

[13] Cf. BIGUZZI, *Settenari*, 221-222: the seventh seal "non parla più di visioni o di audizioni, ma di accadimenti. Dopo l'apertura del settimo sigillo dunque *non* vien detto che Giovanni 'vede' o 'ode' alchunché, come era dal primo al sesto sigillo, ma — solo al settimo — che qualcosa 'accade'".

first cycle and what follows, the caesura between revelation and action, between promise and execution, between word and history[14].

Conclusions and Questions

The main conclusions from the above mentioned data can be summarized as follows. (1) Otherwise than in the sections of the trumpets and the bowls, in that of the seals (6,1–8,1) the Lamb is the unique protagonist. In the first six seals the Lamb "reveals" (see p. 214). (2) The series of seals does not contain plagues or punishments. Only the first pericope of the sixth seal announces them. (3) In 6,1–7,12 a survey of the situation in the world, of the history of persecution and of the final vindication of the martyrs is sketched. (4) Chapters 8–22 present a (partial) repetition of what is merely announced is chapters 6–7[15], but in order to call this a "recapitulation" one has to note, with Biguzzi, that there is first only promise and then in the "recapitulation" execution, thus first prophecy and then action. The classic understanding of recapitulation, on the contrary, assumes a repetition in the narrating of events[16]. (5) The seventh seal (8,1) does not encompass the rest of the book. The silence of half an hour possesses its own content, that of eager expectation. (6) Moreover, those who propose an encompassment can hardly explain how an eschatological passage (7,9-17) comes before the pre-eschatological trumpets and bowls[17].

Without any doubt the attention given by Biguzzi to the particular characteristics of the fifth seal, as well as to the "not yet" aspect present in 6,11; 6,12-17 and 7,1 and 3, must be duly recognized. Yet three clusters of critical questions arise. The first cluster concerns the series of seven. Have the seals in Biguzzi's interpretation after all not become too divergent? This applies not only to the members of the initial quartet, but also to the

---

[14] Cf. BIGUZZI, *Settenari*, 226: "... il silenzio di 8,1 non è solo un'indimenticabile invenzione letteraria di Giovanni, ma in Ap svolge il ruolo strutturale e strategico di chiave di volta. E vertice narrativo per il ciclo del rotolo, e segna il trapasso tra rivelazione dell'Agnello da una parte e azione di Dio dall'altra, tra promessa ed esaudimento della promessa, tra parola e storia".

[15] BIGUZZI, *Settenari*, 215: "... gli stessi eventi sono narrati due volte ma accadono una volta soltanto ...".

[16] BIGUZZI, *Settenari*, 216: "... si tratta di una ricapitolazione in qualche modo anomala e non del tutto corrispondente alla definizione classica .... Qui ... c'è prima il racconto prolettico e poi la descrizione degli accadimenti".

[17] See, e.g., BIGUZZI, *Settenari*, 260-261: The Italian term for "encompassing" is "inglobante"; cf. the noun "inglobamento".

identity of fifth and sixth seals and, of course, to that of the seventh seal. What of the climax which one is justified to expect at the end of a series of seven? And what about the function of the seventh "open" seal in view of the following series of seven trumpets (and seven bowls)? A second cluster of questions is connected with the concept of "revelation". That antithesis enables Biguzzi to declare that the narrative cycle of seals is complete and closed. Yet is the opening of seals no more than simply communication or, perhaps better, can "revelation" in chapters 6–7 be restricted to vision and audition without realization? The third cluster contains questions regarding such matters as the line of thought, the story-line, the progression of the narrative and the linear sequence, all this not only in chapters 4–7 and 8–22 separately, but also in the visionary second part of the Book of Revelation as a whole, i.e., chapter 4–22. More specifically, to what degree is 8,1 a break between two so-called independent cycles? These questions, it would seem, necessitate a new analysis.

II. ANALYSIS

Some brief preliminary remarks may be helpful in clarifying the way for the subsequent analysis. (1) Often a narrative tells the story of past events. Apocalyptic literature also provides visions of the future. More than once the "seer" begins the report of his vision(s) by first narrating past and contemporaneous facts: the exactitude of their detailed description should increase the credibility of the ensuing prophecies[18]. It is not always easy to determine where on the time-line the seer exactly stands. Furthermore, the linear progression of the story can be interrupted by flash-backs, repetitions or anticipations (i.e., proleptic scenes) or even by bringing in foreign materials. In the last case the story-line is as it were doubly interrupted[19]. (2) In his dealing with the "woes" in Revelation (see 8,13; 9,12 and 11,14) Biguzzi distinguishes between time-moment and time-duration. The breaking of a seal, the blowing of a trumpet and the pouring

---

[18] Cf., recently the remarks by C.R. SMITH, "The Structure of the Book of Revelation in Light of Apocalyptic Conventions", *NT* 36 (1994) 373-393, 390.

[19] Cf. LAMBRECHT, "Structuration", 99. For a thorough treatment of narrative terminology, see J.L. SKA, *"Our Fathers Have Told us". Introduction to the Analysis of Hebrew Narratives* (Subsidia biblica 13; Rome 1990).

of a bowl are actions which need but a moment of time. A "woe", on the other hand, by its nature points to duration, to a time period (pp. 263-263). Since in this article the terms seal, trumpet and bowl are also employed broadly for what occurs after the breaking, blowing or pouring and for what is announced by those actions, the distinction, by itself valid, becomes less significant. (3) It would seem that one should respect as much as possible the logic of the grouping in a series of seven. The sequence within the series may be increasing or simply cumulative, yet the seventh element must have to do with completion or the end, and hence it constitutes a climax. Abstractly and generally speaking, when the trumpets and the bowls are punishments, the same should perhaps be supposed with regard to the seals. Or when the first five bowls are plagues, it is probably that the sixth and the seventh will be plagues as well or, at least, will be connected with plagues. The creative liberty of the author, real as it may appear, is not absolute[20].

(4) Biguzzi devotes a brief paragraph to what he calls "a book in the book" (p. 216). By "a book" he means the scroll of chapters 4–7 which finds its place within the book of Revelation. However, the question may be asked whether the revelation of the scroll ends at 7,12. Can it not be argued that all that follows in chapters 8–16 (or even chs. 8–22) is the content of that book in the book?[21] (5) Biguzzi distinguishes between a "weak" and a "strong" revelation (pp. 191-192). The "weak" revelation is only the giving of information. "Weak" revelation makes known and communicates, while "strong" revelation assumes that God's speaking equals God's acting (present or future). As has been seen, Biguzzi considers the revelation in 6,1–7,12 as weak. Is this view correct?

Chapter Six

It would seem that not much can be deduced from the small differences within the introductory formulae of the seals: e.g., the presence or absence of εἶδον and/or ἤκουσα, the presence of "as with a voice of thun-

---

[20] Yet Smith, "Structure", 382, agrees with D.E. Aune, "The Apocalypse of John and the Problem of Genre", *Semeia* 36 (1986) 65-86, who emphasizes that an apocalyptic writer often somewhat conceals his message (also by muddying "structural indicators", Smith) so that the reader, by decoding it, may participate in the original revelatory experience. For lack of clarity, cf. also R.E. Brown, *An Introduction to the New Testament* (New York 1997) 796-797.

[21] The identity and function of the "little book" of chapters 10–11 (one more "book in the book"?) are not discussed in this article.

der" in 6,1, the ordinal number after or before the noun (seal or living creature), ἄλλος in verse 4 and ὅτε in ch. 6 (over against ὅταν in 8,1)[22]. They probably are not more than stylistic variations.

Since the term "plague" is not present in chapter 6 and since, in opposition to both trumpets and bowls, no literary influence from the Exodus plagues manifests itself, it is indeed better not to refer to the seals as "plagues". Yet by opening the seals the Lamb announces *God's punishments* for sinful humankind. This may very well also apply to the first seal. Notwithstanding color and terms, as well as the white horse and its rider (Christ) in 19,11-13, in view of the quite strict parallelism between this first and the three other seals of the quartet[24], it is most probable that the irresistible conquering power of the rider on the white horse will bring punishment (cf. the bow). Within the context the final clause "and he came out conquering and to conquer" (6,2) hardly adds a significant element in comparison to the other three where a similar clause is absent.

The prayer of the fifth seal, of course, is not a punishment. Yet those who have been slaughtered ask for justice and vengeance; they are told to wait "a little longer", which implies that vengeance will be carried out later. So in its own way the fifth seal announces God's punitive intervention against "the inhabitants of the earth" (6,10) and should therefore not be considered as too great a disturbing factor in the series of punishments.

Twice it is explicitly stated that the catastrophe will *not* be *complete*. There is a restriction. For the famine, see v. 6: "a quart of wheat for a day's pay, and three quarts of barley for a day's pay, but do not damage the olive and the wine" (24); for the killing power of Death and Hades, see v. 8: "they

---

[22] BIGUZZI, *Settenari*, 104-109, 121-149, and M. BACHMANN, "Noch ein Blick auf den ersten apokalyptischen Reiter (von Apk 6.1-2)", *NTS* 44 (1998) 257-278, esp. 260-265, may be exaggerating the significance of these variations.

[23] Cf., e.g., recently, H. GIESEN, *Die Offenbarung des Johannes* (RNT; Regensburg 1997): "Die ersten vier Visionen weisen durch einen streng parallelen Aufbau und ihre Motivverwandtschaft eine grosse Geschlossenheit auf" (184). A. KERKESLAGER, "Apollo, Greco-Roman Prophecy, and the Rider on the White Horse in Rev 6:2", *JBL* 112 (1993) 116-121: "... the similarities of form in each of the first four seals imply that the seals must be viewed as a unity made up of parallel members" (116; cf. 117: "a unified group"). However, the identification of the first rider by Kerkeslager as the false messiah is hardly acceptable. See now the remarks by BACHMANN, "Noch ein Blick", 274-276. One may ask, however, whether Bachmann himself does not exaggerate the positive character of the first rider needlessly. What for the addressees of Revelation is positive consists in the avenging of the martyrs' blood "on the inhabitants of the earth" (6,10).

[24] Cf. U. VANNI, "Il terzo 'sigillo' dell'Apocalisse (Ap 6,5-6): simbolo dell'ingiustizia sociale?" ID., *L'Apocalisse. Ermeneutica, esegesi e teologia* (RivBiv.S 17; Bologna 1988) 193-213.

were given authority over a fourth of the earth, to kill with sword, famine, and pestilence, and by the wild animals of the earth"[25].

From the fifth seal it appears that the actual vengeance has *not yet* taken place: the martyrs are told "to rest a little longer", until the number be complete of both the fellow servants and the brothers and sisters who are soon to be killed as they themselves have been killed (6,11; cf. 7,1-3). Although in the sixth seal the cosmic disturbances commence, the punishment of humankind is not yet being carried out. The people flee and hide themselves "from the one seated on the throne and from the wrath of the Lamb; for the great day of their wrath has come, and who is able to stand?" (6,16-17). The day has come; the wrath is imminent! One can conclude from this that the riders of the first four seals are made ready, but that they are not yet active and carrying out their punitive task; they too are waiting (cf. again 7,1-3: the four winds are withheld until the marking of the servants is done).

Chapter 6 contains *more than informative prophecy*. It appears that John is shown the preparation of the imminent punishment. True, the judgment is not yet carried out; the preparation, however, has really begun. This is action, not just publication. The distinction between "weak" and "strong" revelation does not apply here. What is manifested by the prophetic visions after the opening of the seals is not only "word" or "knowledge", not just a preview, not simply a reading of the book (cf. 5,4), but the commencement of the eschatological event itself. "The opening of the seals does not reveal events; it causes events"[26] or, better, the revelation by the Lamb is already an initial realization and enactment.

The *pivotal function of the fifth seal* cannot be denied. In 6,9 John sees those killed during the difficult days of persecution in which he himself

---

[25] Most likely the expression "they were given authority over a fourth of the earth" (6,8) applies to Death and Hades of the fourth seal alone, not to the whole quartet, as the ensuing specification "and to kill with sword, famine, and pestilence, and by the wild animals of the earth" could seem to suggest.

[26] R.H. GUNDRY, "Angelomorphic Christology in the Book of Revelation" (*SBL 1994 Seminar Papers*, Atlanta 1994) 662-678, 666, n. 15. Would it make much difference for our approach if one does not take each breaking of a seal as a progressive revelation (so Biguzzi) but sees the real opening of the scroll only after the breaking of the seventh seal? See Gundry, ibid.: "With the opening of each seal certain events take place, to be sure. But these events do not make up the contents of the scroll, for it is not open for reading of its contents till all seven seals are opened". Cf. R. BAUCKHAM, *The Climax of Prophecy. Studies on the Book of Revelation* (Edinburgh 1993) 250: "The progressive opening of the scroll is a literary device which John has created in order to narrate material which prepares us for and is presupposed by the content of the scroll itself".

lives. One could say that John and his persecuted fellow Christians on earth, like the martyrs in heaven, are asking for God's intervention. God's message is that they must wait ἔτι χρόνον μικρόν (6,11)[27]. Already in the sixth seal that intervention begins: the cosmic upheaval announces God's final vengeance; there is a great earthquake and chaos in the whole creation. Because of the close connection between the fifth and sixth seals and because of the temporal sequence, one is justified in considering the first four seals as preparatory operations as well. The riders are made ready for action but not yet acting. The prayer of the martyrs (6,10) takes place, as it were, during the preparation which is depicted in the first four seals (6,1-8). It should be stressed that, notwithstanding the compositional importance of the fifth seal, the eschatological drama already starts with the Lamb's taking of the scroll (5,8) and, more properly, the opening of the first seal (6,1).

Chapter Seven

With the introductory μετὰ τοῦτο εἶδον (7,1) and μετὰ ταῦτα εἶδον (7,9) John adds two pericopes in chapter 7. Do these passages in the strict sense belong to the sixth seal or do they constitute intercalations?

Verses 1-8. The content connections of the first pericope with the preceding seals are evident. There is not only the linking expression "after this I saw", but also the fact that the four angels and four winds in verses 1-3 almost certainly remind the reader of the four horses and the four riders in the quartet of chapter 6; all of them are meant for damaging the earth and punishing its inhabitants. Still more important, however, is the fact that the passage provides an explanation why the martyrs in heaven have to wait and rest a little longer (cf. 6,11) and why the wrath itself has not yet broken loose: the servants of God must first be marked with a seal.

The number 144,000 and the twelve tribes of Israel symbolize the church on earth, the *ecclesia in via*, it would seem, the church in its completeness. One should, however, pay attention to 14,4 where that same number of servants, now in heaven, is called ἀπαρχή: "they have been redeemed from humankind a 'firstfruits' for God and the Lamb"[28]. That

---

[27] Cf. 10,6: χρόνος οὐκέτι ἔσται, and 10,7: "... in the days when the seventh angel is to blow his trumpet, the mystery of God will be fulfilled ...".

[28] The "firstfruits" may be the martyrs. See now D.C. OLSON, "'Those Who Have Not Defiled Themselves with Women': Revelation 14:4 and the Book of Enoch", *CBQ* 59 (1997)

qualification should perhaps dissuade the reader from a straightforward identification of the "counted" number with the great multitude that no one could "count" of 7,9.

Notwithstanding its numerous connections with 6,12-17, the passage 7,1-8 most likely does not belong to the sixth seal as such[29]. Not only does the phrase μετὰ τοῦτο introduce a new vision, different from the preceding one, but the passage contains no punishment. If this view is correct, it follows that John interrupts the Lamb's action of opening. This does not mean, however, that the story-line is broken. No, the actual "sealing" of the servants must take place before the judgment of the inhabitants of the earth is carried out. The "sealing" precisely clears the way for the expected judgment and vindication.

Verses 9-17. The plural ταῦτα in the phrase μετὰ ταῦτα (7,9) could point to the longer period of time which the marking of the servants demands. Yet one wonders whether the expression μετὰ ταῦτα εἶδον in verse 9 is really different in sense from μετὰ τοῦτο εἶδον in 7,1 and whether by it John indicates an extended time[30]. Perhaps the phrase just introduces another vision.

The pericope 7,9-17 offers a proleptic vision of the final victory of the servants of God: their standing forever before the throne and before the Lamb. The multitude cannot be counted; it is really universal: every nation, all tribes, peoples and languages. Those present have come out of the great tribulation; they have washed their robes in the blood of the Lamb. They now worship God day and night. They will hunger and thirst no more. The Lamb will guide them to the springs of the water of life; God will wipe away every tear from their eyes. No doubt, the correspondence of this passage with chapters 21–22 regarding both vocabulary and themes confirms its eschatological character[31]. In an anticipatory way John depicts the *ecclesia triumphans.*

492-510. Olson sees in 14,4a a conscious literary allusion to the Book of Watchers in Enoch (chs. 6–19) which narrates the famous tale of the angelic "sons of God" who defile themselves with the "daughters of men" (cf. Gen 6,1-4). The redeemed 144,000 constitute the church as a "kingdom of priests" replacing the fallen angelic priesthood.

[29] Just as 10,1–11,13 does not belong to the sixth trumpet (9,13-21) and the second woe (cf. 9,12b and 11,14), so also chapter 7 is not part of the sixth seal.

[30] The clause μετὰ ταῦτα εἶδον is used by John only two more times, in 15,5 and 18,1. In these passages, too, no specific reference to a longer period is present.

[31] See BIGUZZI, *Settenari,* 144. Five items are mentioned: (1) the verb λατρεύω which occurs only in 7,15 and 22,3; (2) the theme of God's "sheltering" expressed by means of the verb σκηνόω, present only in 7,15 and 21,3; (3) the removal of all evil expressed by οὐ ... ἔτι in 7,16 and 21,4; (4) the themes of "thirst" (7,16) and "water of life" (7,17) which recur together in 21,6 (cf. 21,1); and (5) "God who will wipe away every tear" in 7,17 and 21,4. I defended the non-eschatological character of the passage in "Structuration", 95, n. 48.

Not only is the reader confronted here at this point with an interruption of the punishment as in 7,1-8, i.e., a shift from seals of judgment to sealing for protection and likewise a shift from the inhabitants of the earth to the servants of God, but the pericope of 7,9-17 also interrupts the linear progression of the story. Suddenly John has a proleptic vision of the eschaton; he introduces the very end of time. According to the logic of his narration a great many things have yet to occur: medicinal punishments, the fall of Babylon, the judgment of the Beast and of the false prophet, the defeat of Satan, the judgment of the dead, the annihilation of Death and Hades, the appearance of the new heaven and earth and of the new Jerusalem. For a moment, as it were, John forgets the story-line and pays attention here to the final enduring celebration.

It would appear that the dialogues of 7,13-17 and 5,4-5 cannot be taken as an inclusion. To be sure, 7,9-17 reminds the reader of chapter 5: the throne, the Lamb, the angel, the elders and the four living creatures, the liturgy and, more specifically, the fact that one of the elders provides an explanation. Yet, as already said, 7,9-17 is strictly eschatological and, therefore, an anticipation of chapters 21–22. Moreover, in no way is 7,9-17 the closing passage of a so-called first revelatory cycle (chs. 4–7). The vision of 7,9-17 and that of 7,1-8 are both interruptions, be it each in its own way. The seventh seal must still come. The story is not yet finished; the narrative has not yet been completed.

The Seventh Seal

Rev 8,1-6 contains a number of seemingly disparate elements. In verse 1 the opening of the seventh seal is mentioned as well as the silence of half an hour which follows that opening. Then, in verse 2, John sees seven angels who stand before God, and also the giving of trumpets to them. Verses 3-5 depict the vision of a liturgy: another angel with a golden censer comes and stands before the altar; a great quantity of incense is given to him to put on the altar, together with the prayers of all the saints. John sees that the smoke of incense with prayers rises before God. After that, the same angel fills the censer with fire from the altar and throws it on the earth: "and there were peals of thunder, rumblings, flashes of lightning, and an earthquake". In verse 6 attention is again given to the seven angels with the trumpets: they prepare themselves to blow the trumpets. The readers of Revelation ask themselves what the content of the seventh seal might be (only silence?) and whether verses 1-6 are somehow interrelated and linked together.

Verse 1. It would seem that both the silence and the duration of it (half an hour) function in the first place as an indication of positive expectation which is full of tension. The mention of such a silence certainly is intended to emphasize the importance of the last seal. God's servants are waiting. Yet does it not mean anything more?

Verse 2. The phrase καὶ εἶδον introduces a complex vision which goes at least to verse 6: the seven angels and their trumpets; the other angel and his double action with the censer; the getting ready of the seven trumpet angels (and perhaps even what follows in chs. 8–9: the blowing of the trumpets). All this is part of the vision, indeed. What is more, there appears to be no valid reason to hold that what is seen occurs only after the silence. No μετὰ τοῦτο or μετὰ ταῦτα is present in verse 2.

One of the reasons for silence in heaven might be precisely that the prayers of the saints (v. 4) could be heard[32]. According to such an understanding verses 1-6 are closely connected; together they form a text unit.

Because of the limited time of half an hour, the blowing of the first six trumpets (8,7–9,21) must most probably be seen as taking place after that silence. After all, John may have taken the blowing itself of the trumpets as the breaking of the silence, its unavoidable end and the deafening beginning of the plagues[33].

Verses 3-5. What is narrated about the "other angel" is part of what occurs during the half hour of silence. John now tells how his vision shows that the prayers of all the saints — not only those of the martyrs in heaven who are mentioned in the fifth seal (6,9-11), but also those of the servants of God still on earth (cf. 7,1-8) — are very pleasing to God. At the same time that vision indicates that these prayers are heard. By throwing the censer now filled with fire on the earth, the angel, in a somewhat proleptic manner, enacts God's "fiery" punishment[34]. The text is clearly connected with verses 2 and 6 in which the seven punishing angels are mentioned.

Verse 6. There is a progression in time between verse 2 and verse 6. In verse 2b the seven angels were given their trumpets; in verse 6 they make

---

[32] Cf., e.g., VANNI, *Struttura*, 123-125 and 222-223; BAUCKHAM, *The Climax of Prophecy*, 71: At the climax of history, heaven is silent so that the prayers of the saints can be heard, and the final judgment occurs in response to them (v. 5)"; see pp. 70-83, where a discussion of this idea in apocalyptic and rabbinic traditions is provided.

[33] According to BROWN, *Introduction*, 788, "the half hour silence that begins the vision creates a contrast with the trumpet blasts to follow".

[34] Cf. BAUCKHAM, *The Climax of Prophecy*, 82: "To indicate that the prayers of the saints are answered by the eschatological judgment of God on the earth, the angel takes fire, symbolizing judgment, from the altar and throws it on the earth".

themselves ready to blow them. The two verses, moreover, constitute an inclusion and "frame" the events of verses 3-5. If the view that καὶ εἶδον of verse 2 introduces the vision which takes place during the silence is correct, then the whole of verses 2-6 "fills" that silence. Because of all this, a further conclusion becomes almost unavoidable: John uses the technique of encompassing. The seventh seal not only leads to but also contains the seven trumpets[35].

Data from 11,15-19 and 15,1-16,1. The absence of repentance and conversion referred to in 9,20-21 clearly marks the end of the sixth trumpet. The intercalation of 10,1–11,13 (the open little book and its contents) follows. In 11,14 one reads: "The second woe has passed. The third woe is coming very soon" (cf. 8,13 and 9,12); and in 11,15a: "The seventh angel blew his trumpet". In 11,15-19 John appears to return to the trumpets of chapters 8–9. After another lengthy intercalation (chs. 12–14) there is the section which introduces the pouring of the seven bowls: 15,1–16,1. Between 8,1-6 on the one hand and 11,15-19 and 15,1–16,1 on the other, remarkable similarities exist. They seem to confirm the approach of 8,1-6 as a unit which is being defended in this article.

First of all to be noted is the presence of interruptions both after the sixth seal (ch. 7) and the sixth trumpet (10,1–11,13), i.e., before the opening of the seventh seal (8,1) and the blowing of the seventh trumpet (11,15). One should further compare:

8,1b (silence)	11,5b (loud voices)
8,2a (7 angels)	15,1 (7 angels with plagues)
8,2b (trumpets given)	15,5-8 (bowls given)
8,3-5abc (liturgy)	11,15c-18 (liturgy) and
	15,2-4 (liturgy)
8,5d (earthquake)	11,19 (earthquake)
8,6 (preparation)	16,1 (preparation).

The clause καὶ ἐγένοντο φωναὶ μεγάλαι ἐν τῷ οὐρανῷ (11,15b) antithecally corresponds to the clause ἐγένετο σιγὴ ἐν τῷ οὐρανῷ (8,1b). The silence symbolizes expectation and tension; it is filled with the actions of the angels in 8,3-5abc. The loud voices already celebrate God's immi-

---

[35] Cf. LAMBRECHT, "Structuration", 87-88. See also VANNI, *Struttura*, e.g., 125: the seventh seal "ha, come suo contenuto specifico, un altro settenario annunciato in 8,2: il settenario degli angeli con le trombe"; BAUCKHAM, *The Climax of Prophecy*, 70: "The seven angels with their trumpets are introduced in the midst of the account of the opening of the seventh seal in order to indicate that the account ... of the seven trumpet blasts is in some sense included in the events that follow the opening of the seventh seal"; cf. p. 250, be it in a less clear way.

nent victory; silence would here be out of place: see 11,15c-19ab (cf. also the song of Moses in 15,3-4). In 8,5d the actions of the "other angel" are accompanied by "thunder, rumblings, flashes of lightning, and an earthquake". In 11,19 the celebration is followed by the opening of God's temple and the presentation of the ark of the covenant within it (v. 19ab); this is accompanied by "flashes of lightning, rumblings, peals of thunder, an earthquake, and heavy hail" (v. 19c)[36]. In 8,6 the seven angels make themselves ready to blow the trumpets, in 16,1 a loud voice orders the seven angels to pour out on the earth the bowls of the anger of God[37].

The numerous similarities between 8,1-6 and 11,15-19/15,1–16,1 regarding content and vocabulary, as well as their position within the respective series of seals and trumpets — together with the progression of 11,15-19/15,1–16,1 on the story-line — should confirm one's conviction that 8,2-6 is intimately connected with 8,1 and the whole of 8,1-6 constitutes a tight unity. From all this it again appears that the seventh seal encompasses the seven trumpets[38].

III. CONCLUSION AND REFLECTION

By way of summary five main conclusions are drawn from the preceding brief analysis of the texts. Some final remarks will be added; they are intended as a means to confront the results of this study with those in the major and valuable work of Giancarlo Biguzzi.

---

[36] In comparison with 4,5 "earthquake" is added in 8,5d; and in 11,19c the formula is even more expanded by means of "heavy hail"; in 16,18-21 the formula will break: no longer accompanying phenomena but the destroying events themselves are depicted by terms taken from that formula. Cf. BAUCKHAM, *The Climax of Prophecy*, 199-209: "The Eschatolgocial Earthquake" (the O.T. influences are studied); BIGUZZI, *Settenari*, 241-244.

[37] For more details see LAMBRECHT, "Structuration", 93-95 (the earthquakes) and 100-103 (11,15-19 and 15,1–16,1).

[38] One is probably also justified to expect that John will use the same encompassing technique for the seventh trumpet as well. Cf. LAMBRECHT, "Structuration", 85-88; VANNI, *Struttura*, passim; BAUCKHAM, *The Climax of Prophecy*, 7-9. L.L. THOMAS, *Revelation 1–7* (Chicago 1992) 43: "'telescopic' arrangement"; ID., "The Structure of the Apocalypse: Recapitulation or Progression?" *The Master's Seminary Journal* 4 (1993) 45-66 (this technique is also called "dove-tailing"); D.E. AUNE, *Revelation.* Vol. I (WBC; Dallas 1997) xciv-xcv and c-cv.

Five Conclusions

The series of the seals is a series of *punishments*. In this general respect seals are not different from trumpets and bowls. The punishment character applies to all four seals of horse and rider, thus also to the first seal. The fifth seal, itself not a punishment, nevertheless appears to be, through the martyrs' prayer and God's answer, very much connected with judgment and vengeance. The sixth seal ends at 6,17. In its depiction of the cosmic upheaval this seal shows the circumstantial onset of the day of imminent wrath. The opening of the seventh seal by the Lamb has to be considered as the climax of God's vengeance, or, perhaps better, as the beginning of its climactic realization.

The seals, however, are but *the actual preparation* of God's punitive intervention. As such they are decidedly more than verbal prophecy or pure notification, more than Biguzzi's "weak" revelation. In the vision of John, after each opening of a seal something occurs. The riders in heaven are made ready; they are prepared to go into action on earth (cf. 6,1-8). The whole creation is shaken by the great earthquake; in their fear of God's wrath the inhabitants of the earth flee to the caves in the mountains (cf; 6,12-17). Such an onset, such an actual beginning is, of course, at the same time an effective announcement of future catastrophes[39]. It may surprise the reader that the first four seals as well as the sixth seal remain without precise continuation. After 8,1 they simply disappear from the scene. Another series of seven, the trumpets, begins.

Strictly speaking the two visions or scenes of chapter 7 do not belong to the sixth seal. They constitute *an interruption*. In this and similar interruptions John pays attention to the persecuted Christians who are or will be saved. The intercalated passages are meant to console and encourage the servants of God. Although the visions of chapter 7 are not properly included in the series of seven seals, they must in one way or another be part of the scroll which is taken and opened by the Lamb, and as such they belong integrally to the revelation which the scroll contains. The author, however,

---

[39] Cf. BIGUZZI, *Settenari*, 177, where he refers to commentators who "restando su di un piano generale e vago, definiscono i sigilli come 'annuncio' o 'preparazione' differenziandoli da trombe e coppe che vengono invece definite 'realizzazione'", with reference in note to, "per tutti", E.-B. Allo, A. Feuillet and U.B. Müller. These commentators, however, may be right. C. GIBLIN, "Recapitulation and the Literary Coherence of John's Apocalypse", *CBQ* 56 (1994) 81-95, defines 4,1–8,6 as the "beginning", yet at the same time — less correctly, I think — as "an overview of what is now under way", "a suspenseful, oracle-like preface", and "a preview"; moreover, Giblin does not consider 7,1-17 to be an interlude (85-86).

does not explain how he sees the junction of consoling visions with those of punishing seals, how he sees that integration concretely.

The second scene (7,9-17) is *a proleptic vision*. In an eschatological anticipation John leaves the basic story-line of his prophetical report of future events, a line which goes from chapter 4 to chapter 22. For a moment he neglects, as it were, the logical progression in time; he leaps forwards immediately to the eschaton. In apocalyptic literature, however, one should not in the least be surprised by such proleptic procedures.

A climactic event is justly expected after the opening of the seventh seal in 8,1. The events which John describes in 8,2-6 most probably occur during the silence of half an hour which is mentioned in 8,1b. Seven angels appear and receive seven trumpets. The prayers of the Christians rise to heaven; the throwing of fire on the earth indicates that these prayers are heard. The angels with the trumpets prepare themselves to blow. The whole of 8,1-6 constitutes an introduction to the punitive actions of the seven trumpet angels in chapters 8–9. The narrative commences again with a series of seven, but the position on the story-line is advanced; there is a "chronological progression of some sort"[40]; from preparation to partial, medicinal punishments, i.e., to plagues. In composing Revelation in this rather strange and intricate way John appears to be using *the encompassing technique*. The seventh seal includes and envelops the subsequent seven trumpets.

Critical Reflection

The major difference between the reading of chapters 4–8 by Giancarlo Biguzzi and the one presented and defended in this study concerns the view of "revelation". It is our firm belief that by breaking the seals and opening the book the Lamb not only communicates the fixed purposes of God's eschatological plan; this revelation is also and at the same time visionary "realization". No doubt, one has to add with much emphasis that the realization is far from being complete. Only the preparation of God's punitive intervention is taking place in heaven or in creation; the day has come but its wrath is still checked. However, for John this preparation, which proclaims and guarantees the fulfilment, is already a commencing enactment, not merely an announcing word, not a prophetical preview or advance showing. Therefore, as far as "action" is concerned the first series

---

[40] THOMAS, *Revelation 1-7*, 43, and ID., "Structure", 52-56 and 58-63.

of the seals is not different from the other series, i.e., the trumpets and the bowls.

It would seem that John considers the three septets as three series of punishment[41]. To be sure, Rev 4–22 is much more than judgment and catastrophe. Most probably, however, the intervening chapters 7 and 10–14 as well as chapters 17–22 do not properly belong to the threefold series of seven. The materials of chapter 7, of 10,1–11,13 and of chapters 12–13 and 14 are best seen as intercalations *vis-à-vis* the main "seven" structure suggested by the opening of the scroll. It is also true that the seventh element of a series is always open-ended and, therefore, leading up to the climactic final stage of judgment (19,11–20,15). This judgment, however, prepares the way for its positive counterpart and outcome: the appearance of the new Jerusalem (21,1–8)[42]. These remarks must unavoidably remain somewhat bold and provocative, since no critical analysis of the trumpets and bowls, no investigation of the interrupting and final passages could be carried out in this study.

The presence of repetitions is evident in the book of Revelation, especially in its proleptic visions, the hymnic materials and the intercalations[43]. A comparison, e.g., of the bowls with the trumpets, as well as structural similarities, would indicate that a kind of repetition is also to be found in the septets[44]. However, repetition and, more specifically, "recapitulation"[45] do not appear to be the most appropriate terms for the three series of seven. Between the second and the first series (and equally, it would seem, between the third and the second) there is progression in time, there is a new start on a more advanced point of the story-line, not pure repetition. With regard to the seventh seal, some form of encompassment or envelopment has to be assumed: that seal encloses the seven trumpets. It could well be that this equally applies to the seventh trumpet and the ensuing seven bowls.

---

[41] For BIGUZZI the sixth and the seventh bowls cannot strictly be called plagues: see the lenghty discussion in *Settenari*, 235-244.

[42] SMITH, "Structure", 387, calls 17,1–19,10 the Babylon Vision and 21,9–22,5 the Jerusalem Vision: "Unlike the surrounding sections, they have no plot motion but are rather 'tableaus,' symbol-rich emblems whose meaning is expounded and meditated upon".

[43] For the intercalations, see THOMAS, "Structure", 63-65.

[44] Cf. LAMBRECHT, "Structuration", 89; see p. 104 for a possible explanation for the frequency of the punishments and their somewhat repetitive character: John "warns as it were his readers that future historical realization will not necessarily follow his artificial prophecy".

[45] The classic understanding of "recapitulation" is meant here, not the one modified by Biguzzi. See p. 363 and n. 16 of this study.

The emphasis on punishment (i.e., on the specific content of the three series) should not prevent a correct understanding of Rev 4–22 as a whole. To be sure, "what must soon take place" (1,1) is in the first place God's punitive action against the sinful "inhabitants of the earth". One should, however, not forget that this vindication functions as a somewhat delayed but positive answer to the martyrs' prayer for vengeance, that the servants of God still on earth, those marked with God's seal, will be redeemed and, above all, that all punishments, except the last absolutely eschatological condemnation, are intended to bring about the conversion of the enemies[46]. At the end of John's book, the so impressive vision of punishments and plagues gives way to the vision of the new heaven and new earth and that of the new Jerusalem. It is no doubt mainly because of that future reality — the city with the throne of God and the Lamb and with all God's servants — that both John and his readers pray "Come, Lord Jesus" (22,20).

---

[46] This is defended with great emphasis by BAUCKHAM, *The Climax of Prophecy*, in the lengthy chapter "The Conversion of the Nations", 238-337. See, e.g., 258: "God's kingdom will come, not simply by the deliverance of the church and the judgment of the nations, but primarily by the repentance of the nations as a result of the church's witness".

29

The People of God in the Book of Revelation***

The author of the book of Revelation calls himself "John". His position is the fourth on a vertical line of five, from above downward: God, Christ, the angel, God's "servant John" (1,1) and the believers. He appears to have been a charismatic prophet, probably an itinerant missionary. He refers to his writing as "the words of the prophecy" (1,3; cf. 22,18). John's birthplace may have been Palestine, which he, together with other Jewish Christians, left after the fall of Jerusalem. Those Christians are now living in the western part of Asia Minor. John has been exiled or is still in exile "on the island called Patmos because of the word of God and the testimony of Jesus" (1,9). According to what is fairly generally accepted, he must have composed his so-called apocalyptic writing during the reign of the Roman Emperor Domitian, possibly around 95.

The first and second parts of Revelation (chs. 1–3 and 4–22) are very different from each other, not only regarding length. Just as in 1,10, so also in 4,2 John receives a vision: ἐγενόμην ἐν πνεύματι. In the first part, however, he remains on earth. Jesus Christ, "one like the Son of Man" (1,13), appears. In his right hand Christ holds seven stars (1,16.20 and 2,1) and he walks among seven golden lampstands (2,1): "the seven stars are the angels of the seven churches and the seven lampstands are the seven churches" (1,20). John must write a letter of Christ (and the Spirit) to each of these seven churches; they are explicitly named. Nothing more occurs.

In the second part, however, John is taken up to heaven where a door stands open (4,1). In heaven he sees God, "one seated on the throne"; that throne is surrounded by the four living creatures and the twenty-four

---

*** This article is the translation of the Dutch contribution to *Vroegchristelijke gemeenten tussen werkelijkheid en ideaal* (= Early Christian Churches: Reality and Ideal), the Jubilee Volume of the "Studiosorum Novi Testamenti Conventus", which in 2001 celebrates its fifty years of existence. Each article of this volume describes a specific Christian community by analyzing a New Testament writing. — The translation of the biblical texts is that of the NRSV.

elders, and myriads and myriads of angels who all bring honor and thanks to God. Between the throne and the four living creatures stands the Lamb which receives the sealed scroll. "What must take place after this" (4,1; cf. 22,6: "what must soon take place") is written in this scroll. God and the Lamb will strike the devil and the sinful "inhabitants of the earth" (6,10 and elsewhere) by means of terrible cosmic punishments; then a new heaven and a new earth will be manifested and the new Jerusalem will come down from heaven (21,1-2). Thus the whole future, in all its details and its final outcome, is announced. The overcrowded narrative, however, is more than once interrupted by short visions, by liturgies and not a few exhortations.

How did "the servant John", both in the messages of the first part and in the expanded "prophecies" of the second, regard those who believe in Christ. We call them "Christians. Yet it would seem that in the days of John and in the regions where he lived one could hardly already speak of churches which were completely separated from the Jewish communities. Therefore preference is given by some to the expression "the eschatological people of God". What kind of image of these Christian groups in Asia Minor is provided by John? Does his description correspond to reality or is it perhaps a somewhat distorted picture? Also, we must consider that two images present themselves, that of the first part of the Apocalypse and that of the second part. Are they merely juxtaposed, one next to the other, without internal link or connection? Which is the true one? Or does John aim at a more subtle understanding by means of this strange composition? These questions lead to the division of our contribution into three sections: the opposite images, the connections between these images, John's compositional aim.

I. TWO OPPOSITE IMAGES

Differently from what happens in the first part of the Apocalypse, the addressees in the second are not named. Yet just as in the first, the second part is evidently meant for the Christians of the Roman province "Asia". But the horizon of this part is extremely wide. John speaks of the whole universe: heaven, sea and earth. He alludes to the enmity of the Roman empire and its threat to the Christians. Two "camps" are clearly distinguished: on the one hand the sinners who dwell on the earth together with the corrupted Babylon and the dragon or devil and the two beasts, on the other hand "the souls of those who have been slaughtered for the word of God and the testimony they had given" (6,9, in heaven), the hundred and forty-four thousand sealed (7,4-8, on earth) and, by way of a prophetic vision of the future, the great heavenly multitude which nobody can count (9,9; cf. 14,1-5), furthermore also the two witnesses (ch. 11), the woman clothed with the sun, her male child and the rest of her offspring (ch. 12). Nowhere in this second part of Revelation does one see that people or individuals move from one camp to the other. True, in 11,13 John mentions that the rest of those who have reviled the two witnesses are terrified after the earthquake and its catastrophe: they give "glory to the God of heaven". But does John mean by this remark a repentance followed by conversion and faith in Christ? Most probably not. It is equally far from certain that the call "fear God and give him glory ..." in 14,7 is intended as an appeal to the unbelievers. To be sure, it has also to be recognized that in this second part implicit as well as explicit warnings and exhortations are addressed to the believers. Obviously, sin remains possible. Yet in this second part John hardly points to apostasy (see, however, 14,9-11). The Christians are faithful Christians. Conversely, the enemies are "demonized"; there seems to be no possibility of conversion. The readers are no doubt confronted with a "dualistic" depiction, although, of course, no radical dualism with its two autonomous and opposing principles can be intended.

The global image of the believers in the first part appears thoroughly different. John writes to small local communities each of which possesses its own particular identity. However, differing political or social characteristics are of little interest. John focuses on the religious and moral integrity or the lack of it and on the discord and divisons within the communities. In the same church John perceives good and evil people (2,2). In Pergamum the martyr Antipas, a "faithful witness" (2,13), has been killed; but in the same church the poisonous teaching of the Nicolaitans (2,14-15; cf. 2,5) is spreading. In Laodicea believers do not realize that they are "wretched, pitiable, poor, blind, and naked" (3,17), and in Thyatira the woman Jezebel, who calls herself a prophetess, finds a number of followers (2,20-23). Evidently, in John's view, there is sin in several communities. John also fears that persecution might cause apostasy. In Ephesus the love which the believers had at first is abandoned (2,4) and in Laodicea the believers are neither cold nor hot; they are miserably lukewarm (3,15). John writes to the church of Smyrna that the believers will be tested and have tribulation, and that they must be "faithful unto death" (2,10). Many Christians must repent and come back to a better life (2,5.16; 2,21; 3,3.19). Apparently, eating food sacrificed to idols, probably also immorality (2,14.20-22), and the temptations of riches (3,17) are real dangers. All letters end on the same appeal: "Let anyone who has an ear listen to what the Spirit is saying to the churches". From those messages in the first part of Revelation concrete and realistic churches emerge. If possible, their fidelity is praised, yet often weakness and sin are strongly rebuked. Those diverging images of churches which John depicts in the first part of his book seem to be realistic, true to life.

The Actual Communities of the First Part

John reminds Christians that Jesus Christ loves them and has redeemed them from their sins; he made them "a kingdom, priests serving his God and Father" (1,5-6). Yet the picture of them which the letters of the first part gives us is not so bright. The following seven items can be pointed out.

(1) Christ is acquainted with everything regarding the situation in the churches. He knows the deeds of the Christians, their steadfastness but also their weakness or unfaithfulness (cf., e.g., 2,2-4 and 3,15-17). Christ searches minds and hearts (2,23).

(2) Enemies, corruptive people and apostates are present in the communities: the Jews in Smyrna (2,9) and Philadelphia (3,9); the Nicolaitans in Ephesus (2,6) and Pergamum (2,14-15); the so-called prophetess Jezebel and her followers in Thyatira (2,20-24). Satan or the devil is at work (for Satan see 2,9.13.24, for the devil 2,10). Moreover riches in Laodicea have caused relaxation and conceitedness, half-heartedness and a tendency to compromises (3,15-17).

(3) Christ announces his imminent parousia, not without warning and threat: besides the introductory verses (1,7-8) see above all 2,16 ("I will come to you soon"; cf. 3,11 and also 1,3 and 22,12: "the time is near"). He will come like a thief; one does not know at what hour (3,3; cf. 16,25).

(4) Christ repeatedly emphasizes that he will punish both apostates and enemies: see 2,5.16.22; 3,9.19. He is the judge; he will give to each of the Christians what their deeds deserve (2,23; cf. 22,12: "to repay according to everyone's work").

(5) Each letter contains exhortations to steadfastness or a better moral conduct ("repent, and do the works you did at first", 2,5), to conversion after immorality and idolatry (2,21; the verb μετανοέω occurs in 2,5.16.21.22; 3,3.19). One should not fear future suffering and tribulation; one should remain faithful unto death (2,10).

(6) All messages also admonish the readers to listen carefully: ὁ ἔχων

οὓς ἀκουσάτω τί τὸ πνεῦμα λέγει ταῖς ἐκκλησίαις. This appeal is either preceded or followed by a promise. But the condition is clear: the believers must be victorious; they must "conquer": see 2,7.11.17.26-29; 3,5-6.12-13.21-22 (cf. also 21,7). The promise is formulated by means of a variety of images which all refer to lasting salvation and eternal life, to deliverance from the second death (2,11), or to an abiding stay in the city of God, the new Jerusalem which comes down from God (3,12).

(7) The one who guarantees both promise and punishment is the risen Christ. At the beginning of each letter he introduces himself by means of qualifications which each time are different. But all qualifications come from the solemn presentation of the one who is like the Son of Man at the occurrence of the vision (1,12-20).

Some commentators are of the opinion that the first part of the Apocalypse has been written last. John would have thus intended to make his cosmic visions of the second part subservient to the actual situation of his fellow-believers. Yet one can claim equally well that John, by means of his appeals to perseverance in the first part, wanted to spiritually prepare the seven churches for the extravagant and strange cosmic scene he was about to develop in the second part. Most probably the first part has not been composed after the second. Furthermore, the number "seven" is not accidental. As a symbol of completeness it stands for all communities in this Asian region with its many cities and their varying situations. All Christians there must listen to what the Spirit is saying to the seven churches.

The "Dualistic" Vision of the Second Part

In chapters 12 and 13 the readers of Revelation are confronted quite suddenly with three apocalyptic figures: the dragon, the beast which rises out of the sea, and another beast which rises out of the earth. The great red dragon with the seven heads is "that ancient serpent, who is called the Devil and Satan, the deceiver of the whole world" (12,9). He persecutes the woman who has brought forth the male child (cf. 12,13). This woman most probably is the people of God. The Devil makes war on the rest of her children, on "those who keep the commandments of God and hold the testimony of Jesus" (12,17).

To whom or what does the symbol of the first beast point (13,1-10; cf. also 17,7-14)? There can hardly be any doubt that it refers to the powerful Roman empire in the days of Domitian, or to the emperor himself. In 13,3 an allusion to the return of Nero is present. Nero's return was hoped for or, more often, feared; stories about it were going around and pseudo-Neros made their appearance. John tells his readers that the whole earth followed the beast with wonder. To it the dragon has given political power and great authority. John's description of the beast is meant as a parody of the Messiah:

> And the beast was given a mouth uttering haughty and blasphemous words, and it was allowed to exercise authority for forty-two months. It opened its mouth to utter blasphemies against God, blaspheming his name and his dwelling, that is, those who dwell in heaven. Also it was allowed to make war on the saints and to conquer them. It was given authority over every tribe and people and language and nation, and all the inhabitants of the earth will worship it, everyone whose name has not been written from the foundation of the world in the book of life of the Lamb that was slaughtered (13,5-8).

The second beast (13,11-18) speaks like the dragon. It exercises the power of the first beast and functions as its servant. The second beast makes the earth and its inhabitants worship the first beast. The second beast works great signs; it deceives those who dwell on earth, bidding them to make an image for the first beast. The second beast is the false prophet (see 16,13; 19,20; 20,20); in all probability it symbolizes the oppressive religious and social structures of the Roman empire, its worldwide intolerant cult of the god-emperor.

In 16,3-4 dragon, first beast and false prophet are mentioned together: their spirits go abroad to the kings of the whole world, to assemble them for the battle against God on the great day. They appear as it were as a satanic "trinity"; some interpreters even claim that John saw them as a counter-image of God, Christ (the Lamb) and the Spirit. Those satanic "three" are present on earth and dangerously active. The inhabitants of the world cannot but experience their baleful influence.

The three mythological figures are not alone. One should not forget the concrete evil on earth, the corruptive and pernicious "Babylon":

> Then one of the seven angels who had the seven bowls came and said to me, "Come, I will show you the judgment of the great whore who is seated on many waters, with whom the kings of the earth have committed fornication, and with the wine of whose fornication the inhabitants of the earth have become drunk". So he carried me away in the spirit into a wilderness, and I saw a woman sitting on a scarlet beast that was full of blasphemous names, and it had seven heads and ten horns. The woman was clothed in purple and scarlet, and adorned with gold and jewels and pearls, holding in her hand a golden cup full of abominations and the impurities of her fornication; and on her forehead was written a name, a mystery: "Babylon the great, mother of whores and of earth's abominations". And I

saw that the woman was drunk with the blood of the saints and the blood
of the witnesses to Jesus (17,1-6).

Hardly any doubt is possible: "Babylon" which is depicted here as a
whore, is meant by John to signify the powerful, anti-Christian Rome. That
city is seen as the center of riches, idolatry and fornication. That great city
exercises power over the kings of the world. Just as the authority of the
satanic "three", so also the ungodly power of Rome is very much at work
on earth. Christians experience it as a threat and temptation. Many will be
deceived and will take part in Babylon's sins. All nations have drunk the
wine of the harlot's impure passion; the kings of the earth have committed
fornication with her; the merchants have grown rich with the wealth of that
city: see 18,2-5. What can a poor Christian do in the face of such religious
power and socio-economic pressure?

It can be safely assumed that the broad and cosmic descriptions of all
those enemies ultimately go back to real experiences of the author. Of
course, he stylized them, magnified evil by means of apocalyptic figures
and Babylonian references. He traced back the cause and root of all evil to
Satan and his satellites. He presented evil as a demonic power, a threat for
his Christians. Thus he also intended to point to a future with still greater
and even more dangerous evil: the last, insane assault against God (cf.
16,13-14; 19,19-21; 20,7-10). In his own world, however, evil was a concrete reality. Christians were surrounded by it. Some were already killed by
enemies, all suffered the negative influence of the pagan society;
Christians were in grave danger. This pessimistic view of actual life in Asia
appears to have been John's deeply conviction though many today question
its basis in fact.

In the second part of the Apocalypse (4,1–22,5), believers and their
numerous enemies are diametrically opposed. John speaks of the martyrs'
souls who are under the altar in heaven. They receive a "white robe" (6,9-
11). In a proleptic vision John sees the great multitude "which no one can
count"; they will stand before the Lamb (7,9-13); already now he sees the
eschatological hundred and forty-four thousand who are sealed on earth
(7,1-8) and remain undefiled (14,4-5); they will stand before the throne of
God and sing the new song (14,1-3). Surely, Babylon will fall; the first
beast and the false prophet and the Satan too will be conquered (chs.
17–20). Everyone whose name is not found written in the book of life will
be thrown into the lake of fire: the cowardly, the faithless, the polluted, the
murderers, fornicators, sorcerers, idolaters and all liars. That lake of fire is
the second death (20,15 and 21,8). Nothing unclean shall enter the city of

God, only those who are written in the Lamb's book of life (21,27), for they are the "peoples" of God (21,3).

How can one explain these two contrasting images of the Christian community in the book of Revelation? Is the church "unblemished", without sin, or is she a "mixed body" with good and less good members? Can one find lines of connection between the two parts of John's Apocalypse? Should these two differing images not be put together and reconciled? Are they perhaps in some sense complementary?

II. INTRINSICALLY RELATED PARTS

In its main division the structure of the Apocalypse is clear and evident. To the prologue (1,1-3) corresponds the epilogue (22,6-21). The letter proper commences with the address "John to the seven churches that are in Asia" (1,4) and ends with the solemn words "the Lord God will be their light, and they will reign forever and ever" (22,5). The passage 1,4-8 constitutes the beginning and contains the salutation, the praise of Jesus Christ and the announcement of his return. This passage ends with "'I am the Alpha and the Omega', says the Lord God, who is and who was and who is to come, the Almighty" (1,8). The lengthy letter itself consists of two main parts, a rather brief first part, that is, one sole vision with the hortatory messages to the seven churches (1,9–3,22), and the extensive and deeply apocalyptic second part (4,1–22,5).

No doubt, the beatitude of the prologue is not without a hidden exhortation: blessed are those who hear the prophecy and "who keep what is written in it; for the time is near" (1,3). Yet what follows in 1,3-8 is rather "dualistic". In 1,5b-6 we learn what Jesus Christ means for the believers: he loves them; he redeemed them from their sins by his blood; he made them a kingdom, priests to his God and Father. And after these indications of what Christ has done for the faithful in the past and still does in the present, a reference to the future and to the enemy occurs in 1,7: "Look, he is coming with the clouds"; this coming will bring a judgment. "All the tribes of the earth" are for John all the unbelievers, people who refuse to acknowledge Christ and persecute the believers. They will be condemned.

The epilogue, too, contains admonishment for the Christians; again, this is somewhat discreetly hidden in beatitudes: see 21,7 and 14. Yet the readers also come across the "dualistic" separation of sinners and saints: see 21,11 and 14. So the question arises: is this double feature of exhortation to recovery and dualist fixation also present in the two main parts. How then are these parts linked together?

"Dualism" Also in the First Part

In 1,9-20 John narrates the introductory vision of "one like the Son of Man" (1,13), that is the glorified Christ. This figure holds in his right hand seven stars and out of his mouth comes a two-edged sword (1,16). The stars are the angels; they represent the churches of which Christ will take care during the approaching difficult times. The sword symbolizes the imminent judgment: with the sharp sword he will strike down the nations (cf. 19,15 and 19,21). The churches are protected; they are separated from the world which is going to be severely punished.

In the initial vision the seven churches are still seen as a whole, but the letters address each community individually. The final word of each letter, however, is the same: "Let anyone who has an ear listen to what the Spirit is saying to 'the churches'" (plural). The world outside the Christian community hardly plays a part in the letters. Yet a beginning of demonization already appears in expressions such as "the throne of Satan" in 2,13, "the deep things of Satan" in 2,24 and, in regard to the Jews, "synagogue of Satan" in 2,9 and 3,9. Moreover, in 2,26-28 John mentions the power that the conquering Christians will receive to destroy the nations. But a consistent dualistic opposition of believer and unbeliever cannot be found in these letters. For the enemy is present within the communities themselves: the heretic Nicolaitans and/or the followers of Jezebel, and those Christians whose faith is dangerously weakened and threatened. According to John Christ will war against the heretics, just as he will fight against the nations, with the sword of his mouth (2,16). Yet Christ and the Spirit in Revelation 1–3 exert themselves, as it were, by means of praise and blame, appeal and promise, as well as urgent calls to conversion and perseverance, to bring the Christian community to victory and final salvation.

It would seem that, notwithstanding their evident parenetic character, both the initial vision and the realistic messages contain elements of a somewhat "dualistic" approach.

Exhortation Also in the Second Part

The parenetic impact of the first three chapters will remain to some extent with the readers of the second part of the Apocalypse. Although the impression cannot be avoided that according to this lengthy second part the course of history is as it were already definitely fixed, they will detect a hidden but no less insistent exhortation. Not everything appears to be decided. The ungodly power is frightening in all its dimensions; evil remains at work until the very end; Christians are killed and so become qualified witnesses. The readers might think that John by his depictions in chapters 4–21 only wants to prophecy God's vengeance of the martyrs' blood; but no, he simultaneously warns his fellow-believers.

This takes place indirectly in the four beatitudes of the second part: "And I heard a voice from heaven saying, 'Write this: Blessed are the dead who from now on die in the Lord'. 'Yes', says the Spirit, 'they will rest from their labors, for their deeds follow them'" (14,13; cf. 16,15; 19,9 and 20,6). Each time in pronouncing a beatitude John for a moment forgets the thread of his narrative and addresses his readers. Anyone who wants to become blessed must labor (14,13), be vigilant and awake and clothed (16,15), take care that he or she might share in the first resurrection (20,6) and be invited to the marriage supper of the Lamb (19,9). Over that kind of believers only will the second death have no power (20,6).

Moreover, the second part of the Apocalypse contains four sentences introduced by the adverb ὧδε ("now"): see 13,10.18; 14,12; 17,9. Two of these sentences are clearly hortatory. Immediately before 14,13, a verse that is cited above, we read: "Here (or: now) is a call for the endurance of the saints, those who keep the commandments of God and hold fast to the faith of Jesus" (14,12). And at the end of 13,10 John writes: "Here (or: now) is a call for the endurance and faith of the saints". Just before it, in 13,9, comes the appeal: "Let anyone who has an ear, listen".

Both these beatitudes and ὧδε-sentences bring the readers back to the parenetic first part. Notwithstanding the impression of determinism which is left by the second part, in John's opinion the Christian struggle is not yet completely won. The elaborate apocalyptic visions must emphasize the critical character of that situation and prompt the readers to vigilance. The second part needs the first as a key to its correct interpretation. The two parts of the Apocalypse should be read together. The Christian who listens to the many explicit appeals of the first part, as well as the more implicit parenesis of the second, will get spiritually ready to confront the attacks of the enemy and endure with courage the inevitable persecution.

The Real Israel

The unity of Revelation becomes evident not only through the presence of "dualism" as well as exhortation in the two parts. A number of terms and expressions equally appear in both parts, such as "the second death" in 2,1 and 20,6.14 and 21,8, or "to everyone who conquers ..." in all the letters to the churches and also in 21,7, or "an iron rod" (referring to Ps 2,9) in 2,27 as well as in 12,5 and 19,15.

Still more important, however, is the fact that the theocentrism of John, his christology and ecclesiology, are identical in the two parts. By way of self-definition "the Lord God, who is and was and who is to come, the Almighty" says: "I am the Alpha and the Omega" (1,8; the term παντο-κράτωρ, "the Almighty", is a frequent title in Revelation). The Lord God, the Almighty sits on the throne for judgment. The risen Christ is God's Messiah (see 11,15; 12,10; cf., e.g., 5,5), the Son of Man (see 14,14 and cf. 1,13), but above all the Lamb that was slaughtered (cf. 5,9 and often). In the first vision Christ speaks of himself: "I am the first and the last, and the living one. I was dead, and see, I am alive forever and ever; and I have the keys of Death and of Hades" (1,17-18). He is "the firstborn of the dead, and the ruler of kings of the earth" (1,5).

The people of God is the new Jerusalem and the true Israel. As is well known, Revelation nowhere cites the Old Testament; yet allusions to it and free uses of scriptural images and concepts are numerous. Thus it becomes evident to the readers that in this writing of John the believers constitute the true and real Israel. These believers are Jewish Christians, but "a great multitude that no one could count, from every nation, from all tribes and peoples and languages" is added (7,9; cf; 5,9-10 and 21:3: "the home of God is among mortals ... they will be his peoples" [note the plural "peoples"]. All these Christians will sing "the song of Moses" which is no longer different from "the song of the Lamb" (15,3-4). The woman from chapter 12, the mother of the Messiah, is also the mother of Israel and at the same time the mother of rest of her persecuted offspring (12,17).

Twice, in 2,9 (Smyrna) and 3,9 (Philadelphia), Christ reproaches inimical Jews that they are "a synagogue of Satan". Twice he adds that they keep claiming to be Jews but, as a matter of fact, they are not real Jews. One can hypothesize that some Jews in those cities have accused the Christians before the pagan authorities and that in this way they have caused suffering and imprisonment to Christians. Now John implicitly reserves the honorific title "Jews" to the Christians; they are the true Jews and the real Israel. In 3,9 Christ announces: the Jews "are lying — I will make them come and bow down before your feet ...". In a free way John here employs the text of Isa 60,14: "the descendants of those who oppressed you shall come bending low to you, and all who despised you shall bow down at your feet; they shall call you the City of the Lord, the Zion of the

Holy One of Israel". In Rev 3,9, however, it is not the Gentiles who will honor the Israelites, but the so-called Jews will recognize the Christians as the true Jews. From this daring reversal one learns the revolutionary idea the believers have regarding their identity. According to John the Christians are "a kingdom", they are "priests" serving God (1,5; 5,10; cf. Exod 19,9); they are the real Israel.

The polemical tone also indicates that John does not renounce his Jewish past. Jews who believe in Christ remain Israel, an Israel, however, which has opened her doors to the Gentiles. Believing Jews and believing Gentiles together constitute the eschatological people of God. Perhaps, through his emphasis on Israel's completeness ("one hundred and forty-four thousand", 7,4; cf. 14,1.3; "all tribes", 7,4; "the twelve tribes", 21,12), John suggests that he himself and with him all Jewish Christians keep hoping for the salvation of the whole of Israel.

III. AN EXTREME POSITION?

As already stated, a majority of exegetes assume that the Book of Revelation was composed about 95 and addressed to the Christians of the province "Asia". In those days there does not seem to have been an acute persecution such as that of Nero at Rome in 64. Yet, especially in the Near East, the emperor cult was vigorously propagated and this went hand in hand with the repression of those who resisted that spread. The emperor cult was more than a purely inner religious affair; it influenced much of the public political and socio-economic life. The Christians experienced the temptation to join in and to do as the others and so to yield to all kinds of pressure. Eventually Roman governors seem to have executed some Christians, but probably not without an official accusation of fellow-citizens. The claim of some commentators that there was no persecution at all is no longer accepted nowadays. The situation of John's time can be characterized as follows: not (or not) yet a general persecution of Christians by the central state authorities, but often a local oppression and harassment. In such circumstances more than one Christian may have been faced with difficult choices.

Dangers and Temptations

In 2,14 and 20 the Christians are warned against eating food sacrificed to idols and practicing immorality. Did John connect these sins with the teaching of the Nicolaitans at Pergamum and Jezebel at Thyatira? Rightly so?

Paul too deals extensively with food sacrificed to idols in 1 Corinthians 8–10. His position is put forward very clearly. Christians must know that idols have no real existence and that therefore they are allowed to eat every kind of food (8,4-8; 10,25-27). Yet, though knowledge and freedom are thus highly valued, love of the weaker Christians — i.e., not wounding their weak conscience — can require renouncing one's liberty (8,7-12; 10,28). "If food is a cause of their falling, I will never eat meat, so that I may not cause one of them to fall" (8,13). Yet it would seem, more exactly, that Paul recognizes a twofold danger: not only the lack of love through despising the scrupulous fellow-Christian, but also the danger of idolatry. Of course, idols are nothing, but demons really exist, and participation in a pagan cult is idolatry; such participation means becoming partners with demons (10,14-30). In the Book of Revelation Pauline liberty is not referred to; only the danger of idolatry is treated. John's more radical position cannot have been without consequences for the socio-economic life of Christians. As far as we can guess, his fellow-Christians were not allowed to participate in meals where food offered to idols was eaten. Could it be that in this matter the so-called "heretics" were closer to the practice and ideas of Paul than John? They, too, seem to have founded their conduct on a teaching (cf. Rev 2,14-15 and 20).

We know that in Scripture "immorality" is quite often a metaphor for idolatry. The question, however, can be asked whether in Revelation that term points to idolatry (and connected immorality) alone and not also to all kinds of loose sexual behavior. Moreover, it would seem that in the enumeration of 9,21 "immorality" is not identical with idolatry. This may also apply to the lists of 21,8 and 22,15. According to John both idolatry and sexual sins most probably go hand in hand with the dangerous moral weakening which itself is seen by him as a consequence of wealth and riches.

The accusation which Christ directs against the Christians of Laodicea draws the attention of western Christians as well: "I know your works; you are neither cold nor hot. I wish that you were either cold or hot! So, because you are lukewarm, and neither cold nor hot, I am about to spit you out of my mouth" (3,15-16). That lack of fervor evidently is caused by material comfort:

> You say, "I am rich, I have prospered, and I need nothing". You do not realize that you are wretched, pitiable, poor, blind, and naked. Therefore I counsel you to buy from me gold refined by fire so that you may be rich;

and white robes to clothe you and to keep the shame of your nakedness from being seen; and salve to anoint your eyes so that you may see (3,17-18).

In 18,2 the angel calls out with a mighty voice: "Fallen, fallen is Babylon the great". In 18,3 it is said that "all nations have drunk of the wine of the wrath of her fornication; the kings of the earth have committed fornication with her, and the merchants of the earth have grown rich with the power of her luxury". In the extensive passage further in this chapter (18,11-19) the merchants weep and mourn and wail, and the seafaring people stand far off. Wares are named and listed. Merchants of these wares gained their wealth; all who have had ships at sea have become rich. In Asia the attraction of Rome's riches must have been intoxicating. Most probably the temptation of that wealth caused some Christians to adapt their standards to those of the society in which they lived and so to risk part of their moral integrity and religious identity.

The Radicalism of John

In the Book of Revelation certain data (or absence of data) remain mysterious. After all, why did John put his prophecy of the second part ("what is to take place after this", 1,19; cf. 4,1) into such extravagant images and why this strange climactic and encompassing repetition? Or how can it be explained that in Revelation no mention is made of a church hierarchy of presbyters and bishops, which is to be postulated in view of other writings from roughly the same time and region? Is John, as the brother who shares with the addressees the tribulations (cf. 1,9), perhaps decidedly egalitarian or does he keep silence about ministries, except that of prophet, for some other reason? One cannot but suppose that John's expectation of Christ's return and of the near end (cf., e.g., 1,3; 22,7.12 and 20) influenced the content and formulation of the message. The question is: in what sense and to what degree?

Over against the first part the second strikes the readers through its "cosmic, mythological" widening, its "dualistic" vision and its "demonization" of evil. Yet none of these characteristics is completely absent in the first part. Nor, on the other hand, is John's pastoral concern about the communities with its appeals to faithfulness, so typical for the first part, completely missing in the second.

John is convinced that the situation is critical. The end is imminent; a last attack of the Satan and his allies is to be expected. John sees that

Christians, too, risk being suffocated in a society of wealth, idolatry and immorality. He is convinced that every compromise is misguided, utterly sinful. In the final analysis his main message is that of the voice from heaven: "Come out of her [= Babylon], my people, so that you do not take part in her sins, and so that you do not share in her plagues" (18,4). To be sure, he also encourages his fellow believers. He repeats that there should be no fear, but his entire writing is pervaded with an anxious radicalism. The apocalyptic genre, the threatening language and the "dualism" are no doubt connected with a kind of over-anxiety. All these items belong to his rhetorical strategy.

Exaggerated Strictness?

The command of 18,4 reminds us of the similar command in 2 Cor 6,17 where Isa 52,11 is quoted: "Therefore come out from them, and be separate from them, says the Lord, and touch nothing unclean". This last verse belongs to 2 Cor 6,14–7,1, a passage which many commentators consider to be an interpolation. In 6,17 the text is not asking for a literal exodus or a real separation from the Gentiles or ritual purity. But then, as soon as the quotation is understood in a metaphorical way, it can no longer be taken as a parallel of Rev 18,4.

Above we pointed to Paul's opinion regarding food sacrificed to idols in 1 Corinthians 8–10. Another passage from the same letter comes to mind here. In 5,9-11 Paul corrects the Corinthians' wrong understanding of an earlier writing:

> I wrote to you in my letter not to associate with sexually immoral persons — not at all meaning the immoral of this world, or the greedy and robbers, or idolaters, since you would then need to go out of the world. But now I am writing to you not to associate with anyone who bears the name of brother or sister who is sexually immoral or greedy, or is an idolater, reviler, drunkard, or robber. Do not even eat with such a one.

Again we meet a Paul who certainly requires an authentic Christian lifestyle but declares at the same time that his Christians cannot leave this concrete world, a Paul who cannot ban daily contacts with immoral pagans.

According to Acts Paul remained some time at Philippi during his second mission journey (Acts 16,12-40). One day he himself and Silas went out to the riverside, to a place of prayer. Among the women who had come together there was also Lydia, a woman originally from the city of Thyatira, one of the seven cities in Asia with a Christian community addressed by John (see Rev 2,18-29). Lydia happened to be a seller of "purple goods", a ware also mentioned in Rev 18,12. The woman and her household were baptized and Paul and Silas came to her house and stayed there. We may assume that Lydia, as a Christian now, remained a seller of purple, a commerce which according to the appeal of Rev 18,4 would hardly have been acceptable.

Once more the question cannot be avoided: were the "demonized" Nicolaitans and followers of Jezebel not precisely those Christians who (sincerely) tried to adjust to the culture and socio-economic life of their places? Have they perhaps become the victims of John's radicalism? A clear, reliable answer to this question cannot be given. Yet Paul's principles and later church adaptions lead one to suspect that John's "dualistic" and radical reasoning is not offering the right solution for the future, certainly not when it becomes apparent that the end has not yet come and Christ's return may still be far away. In the meantime the eschatological people of God need not go out of the world.

Bibliography

Some recent publications on Revelation which were used in this contribution:

BAUCKHAM, R., *The Theology of the Book of Revelation* (NTT; Cambridge 1993).

BIGUZZI, G., *I settenari nella struttura dell'Apocalisse. Analisi, storia della ricerca, interpretazione* (RivBib.S 31; Bologna 1996).

HIRSCHBERG, P., *Das eschatologische Israel. Untersuchungen zum Gottesvolkverständnis der Johannesoffenbarung* (WMANT 84; Neukirchen-Vluyn 1999).

KLAUCK, H.-J., "Das Sendschreiben nach Pergamon und der Kaiserkult in der Johannesoffenbarung", *Bib* 73 (1992) 153-182.

LAMBRECHT, J., "Rev 13,9-10 and Exhortation in the Apocalypse", A. DENAUX (ed.), *FS J. Delobel* (Leuven 2001).

SATAKE, A., "Kirche und feindliche Welt. Zur dualistischen Auffassung der Menschenwelt in der Johannesapokalypse", D. LÜHRMANN and G. STRECKER (eds.), *Kirche. FS G. Bornkamm* (Tübingen 1980) 329-349.

YARBRO COLLINS, A., "Vilification and Self-Definition in the Book of Revelation", *HTR* 79 (1986) 308-320.

The most recent major commentaries on Revelation are those by H. GIESEN, *Die Offenbarung des Johannes* (RNT; Regensburg, 1997), D.E. AUNE, *Revelation* (WBC; Dallas 1997-99) and G.H. BEALE, *Revelation* (NIGTC; Grand Rapids 1998).

Biblica 81 (2000) 362-385

30

Final Judgments and Ultimate Blessings
The Climactic Visions of Revelation 20,11–21,8

Rev 20,11–21,8 can hardly be called a self-contained pericope, nor even a text unit. Within the major section 16,17–22,5 (seventh bowl and completion) the passage 20,11-15 concludes the text unit of the final judgment which deals with the destruction of the beast, the false prophet and the dragon, and with the judgment of the dead (19,11–20,15), while the new Jerusalem passage 21,1-8 is clearly connected with the description and explanation given by the interpreting angel in 21,9–22,5. These two passages, however, can be taken together. They constitute the final two visions of John the prophet in which something happens to "mortals", one rather negative (the judgment of the dead) and the other very positive (the appearance of the new Jerusalem, the bride)[1].

Moreover, the two passages — each with a twofold καὶ εἶδον (20,11.12 and 21,1.2) — are also linked by themes and vocabulary: see "death" in 20,14 and 21,4; the identification of "the second death" in 20,14 and 21,8. "The lake of fire" in 20,14 and 15 corresponds to "the lake that burns with fire and sulphur" in 21,8. The disappearance of the (first) heaven and the (first) earth is spoken of in 20,11 as well as in 21,1. "Sea" in 21,1 refers to "sea" in 20,13 (sea, Death and Hades giving up the dead) but also proves that the author has not forgotten its absence in 20,14 (only personified Death and Hades are punished). Moreover, the theme of "life" in

---

[1] Cf. D.E. AUNE, *Revelation 17–22* (WBC; Nashville 1998) ix and 1040-113, who considers the whole of 19,11–21,8 as belonging together and divides this section into 19,11-21; 20,1-10; 20,11-15 (Vision of the Judgment of the Dead) and 21,1-8 (The Transition to the New Order). In "The Millennium (Rev 20.4-6) is Heaven", *NTS* 45 (1999) 553-570, C.H. GIBLIN takes 20,11-15 and 21,1-8 together as one narrative (see pp. 568 and 570). In n. 41 he argues: "Dividing integral narratives merely by the occurrence of 'I saw' is short-sighted here as elsewhere in Revelation". Applied to 20,11–21,8 this remark might be too sweeping. Cf. in an earlier study: C.H. GIBLIN, *The Book of Revelation* (GNS 34; Collegeville 1991), 177 and 190-196.

the "book of life" (20,12 and 15) reappears in the "fountain of the water of life" in 21,6. Some of those whose "name was not found written in the book of life" in 20,15 are specified in the list of 21,8 ("the cowardly ..."); their place is the lake of fire and this is the second death[2].

The text of Rev 20,11–21,8 is not without its difficulties and uncertainties. Does 20,11-15 depict a general judgment of all the dead, good and bad, or only the final judgment of the sinners? Is the lot of those condemned annihilation or eternal torment? Does the mention of a first resurrection in 20,5 announce a second resurrection to be found in 20,13? Are the "new heaven" and the "new earth" in the second passage (21,1) a completely new creation or should one rather assume a renewal, a transformation of the first heaven and the first earth as 21,5 ("See, I am making all things new") seems to suggest? Furthermore, to what extent is the author dependent on Old Testament Scriptures and/or Jewish as well as extrabiblical traditions? Last but not least, can one detect a really climactic conclusion in these final visions and what is the trustworthy content, negative and positive, hidden in their wealth of images and allusions?

A close reading of 20,11-15 (I) and 21,1-8 (II) will gather elements for answering those questions. For each pericope three aspects will be focused upon: the line of thought (the narrative), the influence of the main Old Testament passages, and the function of the text within its context. In the concluding part of this study (III) special attention will be given to the last double question, i.e., the climactic character of 20,11–21,8, more in particular 21,1-8, and the contemporary hermeneutical approach.

I. THE FINAL JUDGMENT AND THE SECOND DEATH (20,11-15)

This is the translation of Rev 20,11-15 given in the New Revised Standard Version:

11a Then I saw a great white throne and the one who sat on it;
  b the earth and the heaven fled from his presence,
  c and no place was found for them.
12a And I saw the dead, great and small, standing before the throne,

---

[2] The connection between 20,11-15 and 21,1-8 is duly emphasized by, e.g., U. MELL, *Neue Schöpfung. Eine traditionsgeschichtliche und exegetische Studie zu einem soteriologischen Grundsatz paulinischer Theologie* (BZNW 56; Berlin – New York 1989) 127-129.

b and books were opened.

c Also another book was opened, the book of life.

d And the dead were judged according to their works, as recorded in the books.

13a And the sea gave up the dead that were in it,

b Death and Hades gave up the dead that were in them,

c and all were judged according to what they had done.

14a Then Death and Hades were thrown into the lake of fire.

b This is the second death, the lake of fire;

15a and anyone whose name was not found written in the book of
life

b was thrown into the lake of fire.

The Narrative

The report of John's vision in 20,11-15 is not straightforward. A reconstruction of the logical sequence of what happened would only select the
following facts: John sees the great white throne and the one who sat on it
(v. 11a); earth and heaven flee from God's presence (v. 11b); then John sees
the dead standing before the throne (v. 12a); books are opened (v. 12b);
also the book of life is opened (v. 12c); all are judged according to their
works, as written in the books mentioned first (v. 12d); anyone whose
name is not in the book of life (v. 15a) is thrown into the lake of fire (v.
15b).

One immediately sees that v. 12c, which adds another book and its
opening, interrupts as it were the opening of the books (v. 12b) and the
judgment proper (v. 12d). Yet the "book of life" had to be mentioned
because of what is stated in v. 15a: the absence of one's name in that book
indicates the criterion for the punishment[3]. Furthermore, in vv. 11-12 two
details are rather illustrative: see v. 11c (no place is found for earth and heav-
en) and v. 12a (great and small).

The inserted verses 13-14 provide the readers with postponed explicative information and new data, but also repetition. In vv. 13a and
13b John explains how the dead can be present before God's throne: the
sea, Death and Hades have given up their dead; then v. 13c repeats the

---

[3] G.K. BEALE, *The Book of Revelation* (NIGTC; Grand Rapids – Cambridge 1999) 1033,
appropriately notes: "As in 13:8 and 17:8 the 'book of life' is introduced to bring attention to
those excluded from it".

judgment[4]. In v. 14a John describes personified Death and Hades being thrown into the lake of fire; v. 14b adds the explanation that this lake of fire is "the second death". The insertion of v. 14a makes the punishment of the sinners in v. 15 become a replica of that of Death and Hades; consequently; verse 15 is no longer the climax of the narrative[5].

The Old Testament

As is well known Revelation must be interpreted by reference to the Old Testament and Jewish traditions. We omit a discussion of the intricate problem of which OT text and/or Greek translation John has been dependent. Nor can attention be given here to the number, age and interconnection of the Jewish (apocalyptic) traditions and to possible extrabiblical motifs[6]. Moreover, only the main Old Testament passages will be dealt with. Regarding 20,11-15 John is certainly influenced by the books of Ezekiel, Daniel and Isaiah.

Ezekiel. In Revelation 20–22 John appears to follow the order of Ezekiel 37–48[7]. A fourfold structural parallelism can be noted[8]:

for the resurrection of the martyrs (and all Christians?) in 20,4a,
cf. the revival of the dry bones in Ezek 37,1-14;
for the messianic kingdom in 20,4b-6,
cf. the reunited kingdom governed by the messianic king David in Ezek 37,15-28;
for the final battle against Gog and Magog in 20,7-10,

---

[4] Cf. AUNE, *Revelation*, 1081: "The composition of this pericope is problematic". On the order of vv. 12-13 see also pp. 1102 and 1124.

[5] Not so BEALE, *Revelation*, 1037: (on v. 15) "The note of final judgment is rung once more for emphasis". For AUNE, *Revelation*, v. 15 is an "appended clause", a "redactional insertion into the final text" (p. 1103).

[6] For ample information and discussion of the Jewish traditions see, e.g., the recent major commentaries by AUNE and BEALE.

[7] For the influence of Ezekiel on Revelation see A. VANHOYE, "L'utilization du livre d'Ezéchiel dans l'Apocalypse", *Bib* 43 (1962) 436-473, and, especially for Rev 1; 4–5; 10 and 21–22, J.M. VOGELGESANG, *The Interpretation of Ezekiel in the Book of Revelation* (Unpublished Ph.D. dissertation, Harvard University 1985). Vogelgesang highlights John's direct dependence on Ezekiel and, moreover, maintains that John modeled his work on that of Ezekiel (see, e.g., pp. 71-72).

[8] Cf. J. LUST, "The Order of the Final Events in Revelation and in Ezekiel", in J. LAMBRECHT (ed.), *L'Apocalypse johannique et l'Apocalyptique dans le Nouveau Testament* (BETL 53; Leuven 1980) 179-183; ID., "Ezekiel 36–40 in the Oldest Greek Manuscript", *CBQ* 43 (1981) 517-533; VOGELGESANG, *Interpretation*, 64-66; BEALE, *Revelation*, 1012.

cf. the final battle against Gog of Magog in Ezekiel 38–39;
for the descent of the new Jerusalem in 21,1–22,5,
  cf. the vision of the new Temple and the new Jerusalem in
  Ezekiel 40–48.

John's dependence on Ezekiel cannot be denied, even though no parallel can be found for the passage 20,11-15. However, not only in 20,7-10, but also already in chapter 19, John refers to Ezekiel's oracles against Gog. J. Lust notes that most probably the order of Ezekiel 37–39 was not yet stabilized during the period in which the book of Revelation was being composed. In the oldest manuscript of Ezekiel, i.e., the recently discovered Greek Papyrus 967 (late 2d or early 3rd cent.), as well as in the best manuscript of the Vetus Latina, the Codex Wirceburgensis, chapter 37 follows chapters 38–39. This arrangement would provide an even more striking general parallelism between Rev 19,17–20,10 (battle against the two beasts and the dragon) and Ezekiel 38–39 (final battle against Gog of Magog), and between Rev 20,11-15 (judgment after resurrection) and Ezekiel 37 (revival of the dry bones)[9]. Yet even without an appeal to this different order, John's dependence on Ezekiel remains certain[10]. The discrepancies, more specifically the distinction between a first and second resurrection and the millennial kingdom in Revelation 20, may be due to John's dependence on later traditions and to his own creativity.

Daniel. The throne and the one who sits on it have already been mentioned in Rev 4,2 and 5,7. In 20,11 the adjectives "great and white" are added. The throne here is the majestic judgment seat and without a doubt, like in 4,2 and 5,7, it is God who sits on it (not the Lamb). In 20,11a and 12b (12d) a reference to Dan 7,9-10 must be assumed: in both instances a throne is spoken of; God (in Daniel: "an Ancient One") takes his throne; in Daniel the throne is qualified by "fiery flames", in Rev 20,11 by "great white"; the books are opened. The presence of these three parallels (or four, if the resemblance between "fiery flames" and "great white" is accepted) cannot be accidental.

Moreover, in Dan 12,1 the author says that "everyone who is found written in the book" will be delivered and in 12,2 a resurrection is dealt

---

[9] Cf. LUST, "Final Events", 181-183. Lust guesses that John knew both editions of Ezekiel. See the balanced evaluation of this hypothesis by VOGELGESANG *Interpretation*, 65, n. 87.

[10] One more reason is given by AUNE, *Revelation*, 1104: "Since the names God and Magog occur only rarely in Jewish apocalyptic literature, John has very likely derived these code names directly from Ezekiel".

with: many will awake, "some to everlasting life, and some to shame and everlasting contempt". The conjunction of these two elements in Rev 20,12c.15a (book) and 13ab (resurrection) points to a conscious allusion on the part of John. The book in Dan 12,1 becomes "the book of life" in Rev 20,12c.15a (cf. the same phrase in 3,5; 13,8 and 17,8). "The books in Daniel 7 [v. 10] focus on the evil deeds of the end-time persecutor of God's people for which he will be judged. The book in Dan 12,1-2 also concerns the end time, but is an image of redemption: those written in that book will be given life, but those excluded from it will suffer final judgment"[11].

Isaiah. The description in Rev 20,11bc ("the earth and the heaven fled from his presence and no place was found for them") announces what will become the main theme of 21,1-8 (see especially vv. 1ab.4d and 5b). The new creation motif in Revelation 21 clearly refers to texts of the Deutero- and Trito-Isaiah, mainly to Isa 65,17-20. What is said in Rev 20,11bc functions as a preparation to this utilization of Isaiah.

Text in Context

Climax. The passage Rev 20,11-15 forms the third and last part of the final judgment. In 19,11-21 Christ's victory over the beast and the false prophet is narrated; the two are thrown into the lake of fire (19,20). In 20,1-10 the victory over the dragon — "who is the Devil and Satan" (20,2) — is indicated after the millennial kingdom. It is the outcome of the final battle of Satan together with Gog and Magog; the devil is thrown into the lake of fire. In 20,11-15 the dead are judged according to their works; Death and Hades are thrown into the lake of fire, as well as anyone whose name is not found written in the book of life.

The climactic nature of this vision should not go unnoticed: the great white throne and God himself as judge (v. 11a); the cosmic dissolution (v. 11bc); the "general" resurrection (v. 13ab); the standing of the dead, great and small, before the throne (v. 12); the judgment itself (vv. 12bcd and 13c); the removal of Death and Hades (v. 14a); the outcome of the judgment (v. 15). G.K. Beale's comment on 20,11a (cf. 4,2 and 5,7) is to the point: "The scene [of chs. 4–5] is repeated here to signify the consummate judgment, to which all previous judgments pointed and which is the climax of them all"[12].

---

[11] BEALE, *Revelation*, 1032. On the different categories of heavenly books in apocalyptic literature, see VOGELGESANG, *Interpretation*, 318-323.

[12] *Revelation*, 1031.

Annihilation? The expression "lake of fire" occurs six times in Revelation: see 19,20 (first scene: beast and false prophet); 20,10 (second scene: dragon); 20,14a (third scene: Death and Hades); 20,14b (third scene: this lake is the "second death"); 20,15b (third scene: unbelieving mortals); 21,8 (sinners). One could be tempted to interpret the throwing of Death and Hades into the lake of fire as pointing to their complete annihilation, all the more so since 21,4b says that "death will be no more". Does then the same perhaps apply to the sinners who are thrown into the lake of fire? For that lake is called the "second death" and one might argue that by definition death means non-existence[13]. Most probably, however, this is not what John is thinking.

In 19,20 we read: "These two (= beast and false prophet) were thrown alive into the lake of fire that burns with sulphur" and in 20,10 the portrayal becomes even more explicit: "And the devil ... was thrown into the lake of fire and sulphur, where the beast and the false prophet were, and they will be tormented day and night forever and ever". There seems to be no reason to believe that according to John the lake of fire for unbelievers means annihilation rather than the permanent torment experienced by the devil. Moreover, it is not to be excluded that personified Death and Hades suffer that identical judgment, since they may be taken as evil spirits, agents of the devil. What is indicated in 20,15 about unbelievers is expanded in 21,8 by means of a list of sinners. John concludes: "their place will be in the lake that burns with fire and sulphur, which is the second death". No mention is made of the end of the burning fire and no mention of the annihilation of those who are in the lake. A passage such as 14,9-11 no doubt reveals John's conviction regarding the eternal punishment of "those who worship the beast and its image" (v. 9): "the smoke of their torment goes up forever and ever. There is no rest day or night" for those people (v. 11).

General Judgment? A first impression could be that the vision in 20,11-15 deals with the general judgment. The dead are present, "great and small". Since "all" (ἕκαστος: each person) are judged according to their deeds, one thinks of the books in which the good and evil works of all mortals are recorded. Before the judgment a resurrection has taken place: sea,

---

[13] On second death see P.-M. BOGAERT, "La 'seconde mort' à l'époque des *Tannaïm*", in *Vie et survie dans les civilisations orientales* (Acta orientalia Belgica; Leuven 1983) 199-207; AUNE, *Revelation*, 1091-93: "The Egyptian significance of second death and the lake of fire, i.e., complete and total destruction, cannot be meant in Revelation, as Rev 14:9-11 and 20:10 make clear. Rather ... *eternal torment* is signified, so that what we have is an adaptation of Egyptian underworld mythology to Judeo-Christian tradition" (p. 1093).

Death and Hades have given up their dead[14]. One almost spontaneously thinks of a "neutral" resurrection like the one mentioned in Dan 12,1-2, a resurrection of the dead as a precondition to be present at the judgment. Eternal life and eternal punishment are the alternatives after the judgment according to anyone's works[15].

Yet text and context force us to correct this initial picture. If with 20,11-15 John means the "second resurrection" — but the expression is not used — one must not forget what he has written in 20,4-6: the martyrs (cf. 6,9-10), probably all Christians, come to life before the millennium; this is the first resurrection. The rest of the dead do not come to life before the end of the millennium. Are, in John's opinion, the still living future martyrs (and other Christians) also standing before the throne of judgment (v. 12a)? This is not evident.

The question arises whether the second resurrection of v. 13, suggested by the first mentioned in vv. 5-6, could be that of the unbelievers alone and whether the books (v. 12b) only contain their evil works[16] and have to be properly distinguished from the book of life (v. 12c) in which the names of the believers are written (v. 15a). This view is supported by the fact that in 20,11-15 attention appears to be given to punitive judgment alone, not to reward and salvation[17]. What John narrates here seems to be different from

---

[14] Cf. R. BAUCKHAM, "Resurrection as Giving Back: A Traditional Image of Resurrection in the Pseudepigrapha and the Apocalypse of John", J.H. CHARLESWORTH – C.A. EVANS (eds.), *The Pseudepigrapha and Early Biblical Interpretation* (JSP.S 14; Sheffield 1993) 269-291. Not so, e.g., H. GIESEN, *Die Offenbarung des Johannes* (RNT; Regensburg 1997) 448: "Von einer Auferstehung ist aber auch hier keine Rede". According to J. ROLOFF, "Weltgericht und Weltvollendung in der Offenbarung des Johannes", H. KLAUCK (ed.), *Weltgericht und Weltvollendung. Zukunftsbilder im Neuen Testament* (QD 150; Freiburg-Basel-Wien 1994) 106-127, John avoids the mention of a resurrection in 20,14, because some enthusiastic believers proclaim that the resurrection has already taken place (cf. 2 Tim 2,17-18). But such a supposition cannot but remain highly hypothetical.

[15] Cf. BEALE, *Revelation*, 1032: "That John sees 'the dead, great and small, standing before the throne' assumes that the last, great resurrection of the unrighteous *and* the righteous has finally taken place".

[16] The expression "according to ... works" of vv. 12d and 13c is also present in 2,23 and equally refers to evil works. Yet see AUNE, *Revelation*, 1102: "The plural [books] in both Dan 7:10 and here [Rev 20,12b and d] probably reflects the early Jewish tradition of *two* heavenly books, one for recording the deeds of the righteous and the other for recording the deeds of the wicked...". One may doubt that this is still so in 20,12b and d.

[17] Cf. ROLOFF, *Weltgericht und Weltvollendung*, 126: "Im Gegensatz zur sonstigen urchristlichen Tradition spricht die Offenbarung nicht von einer Konfrontation der Glieder der Heilsgemeinde mit Gott bzw. Christus im Weltgericht. Vor allem die Richterfunktion des Parusie-Christus gegenüber den Seinen fällt aus". The explanation by AUNE, *Revelation*, 1104, does not focus on this problem.

the twofold judgment mentioned in 11,18: "... the time for judging the dead, for rewarding your servants ..., both small and great, and for destroying those who destroy the earth"[18].

II. THE NEW CREATION AND NEW JERASALEM (21,1-8)

This is the NRSV translation of Rev 21,1-8:
1a Then I saw a new heaven and a new earth;
 b   for the first heaven and the first earth had passed away,
 c   and the sea was no more.
2a And I saw the holy city, the new Jerusalem,
 b   coming down out of heaven from God,
 c   prepared as a bride adorned for her husband.
3a And I heard a loud voice from the throne saying,
 b   "See, the home of God is among mortals.
 c   He will dwell with them as their God,
 d   they will be his peoples,
 e   and God himself will be with them.
4a he will wipe every tear from their eyes.
 b   Death will be no more;
 c   mourning and crying and pain will be no more,
 d   for the first things have passed away".
5a And the one who was seated on the throne said,
 b   "See, I am making all things new".
 c   Also he said,
 d   "Write this, for these words are trustworthy and true".
6a Then he said to me,
 b   "It is done!
 c   I am the Alpha and the Omega, the beginning and the end.
 d   To the thirsty I will give water as a gift from the spring of the water of life.
7a Those who conquer will inherit these things,
 b   and I will be their God

---

[18] This means that the expression τοὺς μικροὺς καὶ τοὺς μεγάλους in 11,18 points to the servants while in 20,12a the similar expression τοὺς μεγάλους καὶ τοὺς μικρούς indicates those thrown in the fire (cf. 20,15b).

c   and they will be my children.

8a   But as for the cowardly, the faithless, the polluted, the murderers, the fornicators, the sorcerers, the idolaters, and all liars, their place will be in the lake that burns with fire and sulphur,

b   which is the second death".

The Narrative

In 21,1 John continues his report of visions by means of καὶ εἶδον: see 20,11.12 (cf. also, e.g., 19,11.17.19; 20,1.4). In 21,2 this verbal form is repeated again, but no longer at the beginning of the sentence. The opposition between 20,11-15 and 21,1-8 is complete: definitive judgment on the one hand and new creation (or creation's renewal) on the other. Yet literary connections can easily be shown: the throne (21,3) and the one who is seated on it (21,5) are still there in this new vision (cf. 20,11a for the previous vision). Moreover, the content of 21,1b (heaven and earth) reminds the reader of 20,11bc, and that of 21,8 (lake of fire, second death) refers back to 20,14 and 15b.

The passage is best divided into two units: vv. 1-4 and vv. 5-8[19]. In the first unit John reports what he sees (twice καὶ εἶδον in vv. 1-2) and what he hears (vv. 3-4; καὶ ἤκουσα). Verse 4d ("for the first things have passed away: ἀπῆλθαν") forms an inclusion with verse 1b ("for the first heaven and the first earth had passed away: ἀπῆλθαν"). In vv. 5-8 God ("the one who was seated on the throne") speaks in the first person singular. This second unit does not begin with "I heard"; God takes the initiative. The end of this unit (v. 8b) repeats the identification of the lake of fire with the "second death", which was already emphasized in 20,14b. As stated above, the whole of 21,8 recalls 20,15.

John sees a new cosmos; the dimensions point to completeness: heaven and earth and also what they contain (v. 1a; cf. "all" in v. 5b). The repetitive character of v. 1b and the additional note on the sea[20] of v. 1c have

---

[19] A. VÖGTLE, *Das Buch mit den sieben Siegeln. Die Offenbarung des Johannes in Auswahl gedeutet* (Freiburg–Basel–Wien 1981) 163, divides the passage into a *Vision* (21,1-2) and an *Audition* (21,3-8); cf. MELL, *Neue Schöpfung*, 129-130; AUNE, *Revelation*, 1112-13: vv. 1-2.3-4.5-8. P. HIRSCHBERG, *Das eschatologische Israel. Untersuchungen zum Gottesvolkverständnis der Johannesoffenbarung* (WMANT 84; Neukirchen/Vluyn 1999), pp. 205.223-224, sees a concentric structure in 21,1-5 of which verses 2-3 constitute the center.

[20] For John the "sea" seems to symbolize a demonic realm of evil. For other possible nuances, cf. BEALE, *Revelation*, 1042-43.

already been pointed out. John's attention, however, is not so much cosmic. The focus lies on the "holy city, the new Jerusalem" (v. 2a) which comes down "out of heaven from God" (v. 2b). One wonders whether in John's vision much space is left for any reality that is not the holy city. Perhaps the new heaven and the new earth are just the background for Jerusalem[21]. The holy city has been prepared "as a bride adorned for her husband" (v. 2c). She represents the universal church of the end time. The "loud voice from the throne" (v. 3a) explains what the "coming down" of Jerusalem means. Is this voice that of one of the elders or one of the four living creatures (cf. ch. 5)? Or is it perhaps the voice of God who, in the third person singular, reflects upon his own actions? This remains uncertain.

A more literal translation of v. 3bcde may be helpful here:

3b   Behold, the tent of God [will be] with men,

c   and he will put up his tent with them,

d   and they will be his peoples[22]

e   and God himself will be with them, their God[23].

In what the voice announces in 21,3-4 no more attention is given to the comparison of v. 2c ("prepared as a bride..."). Three elements can be distinguished: (1) that city is God's tent (σκηνή) among "men" (ἄνθρωποι); God will put up his tent (σκηνώσει) among them (v. 3bc); (2) this divine dwelling results in a reciprocal relationship: they will be God's peoples (λαοί) and God himself will be with them as their God (v. 3de: the covenant formula); (3) the whole of verse 4 then indicates what God through this "newness" will bring about; he will take away all suffering and even death.

In v. 5a "the one who is seated" renders the same Greek term as "the one who sat" in 5,1 (καθήμενον). Three times a verb of "saying" introduces a direct speech of God: καὶ εἶπεν (v. 5a), καὶ λέγει (v. 5c) and καὶ εἶπέν μοι (v. 6a)[24]. The third and last time God's speaking is much longer

---

[21] Cf. VÖGTLE, *Das Buch mit den sieben Siegeln*, 172; D. GEORGI, "Die Visionen vom himmlischen Jerusalem in Apk 21 und 22", D. LÜHRMANN – G. STRECKER (eds.), *Kirche. FS G. Bornkamm* (Tübingen 1980) 351-372, 354-355.

[22] One could hesitate between plural and singular of this word, both readings being supported by good manuscripts. Yet "peoples" should be given preference because it is the more difficult reading.

[23] For a discussion of the numerous variants regarding "their God", see AUNE, *Revelation*, 1110-11, and B.M. METZGER, *A Textual Commentary on the Greek New Testament* (Stuttgart ²1994) 688-689: "... After considerable discussion the Committee concluded that the least unsatisfactory procedure was to print the text of A, but to enclose the words αὐτῶν θεός within square brackets" (p. 689).

[24] Cf. BEALE, *Revelation*, 1057: "The fluctuation of tenses in vv. 5-6 from 'he said' to 'he

(see vv. 6b-8b)²⁵. Therefore, verses 5-8 are best divided into v. 5ab, v. 5cd and vv. 6-8.

(1) V. 5ab. By means of "see, I am making all things new" in v. 5b God refers to the new things mentioned in vv. 1-4 and highlights his personal involvement (cf. v. 2b: "from God"). The prophetic present "I am making" refers to the end time.

(2) V. 5cd. By his command to write as well as by its motivation in v. 5d God underscores the validity of what he said in v. 5b (and, through v. 5b, of course, of the entire content in vv. 1-4)²⁶.

(3) VV. 6-8. The perfect tense in the exclamation "it is done!" (γέγο-ναν) in v. 6b confirms that the prophecies will certainly be fulfilled. Then, in v. 6c, God defines himself and in this solemn way points to his enduring sovereignty: "I am the Alpha and the Omega, the beginning and the end". While using the plural in vv. 3b-4a ("men", "peoples", "'their' eyes") God does not use it in vv. 6d-7abc; he speaks of the believer in the singular. In v. 6d, just as in v. 4abc, the blessings of salvation are pointed out figuratively: the thirsty person will receive living water from God without payment. The term δωρεάν — "by way of gift" — at the end of the sentence is clearly not without emphasis (cf. 22,17). The inclusive NRSV translation has eliminated the singular in v. 7. A literal rendering is needed for the discussion:

7a   He who conquers will inherit these things,
 b   and I will be his God
 c   and he will be my son.

It is possible that in "he who conquers" the necessary condition is alluded to: one has to conquer in order to get the inheritance, i.e., the whole newness. In the concluding promise of all seven letters that condition of "conquering" has been repeated (2,7.11.17.26; 3,5.12.21). In v. 7bc the well-known adoption formula (cf. 2 Sam 7,14) is quoted freely. Then, in v.

---

says' and back again to 'he said' is a feature of John's visionary style, in which he can refer to what he has heard in a past vision but then, at the same time, use the present tense in the narration for the purpose of vividness". According to GEORGI, "Visionen", 359, n. 32, v. 5cd constitutes a later addition which had its origin "als eine bewundernde Bemerkung eines Abschreibers oder Lesers". This is hardly convincing.

²⁵ Vv. 6b-8b are better taken as one coherent speech-unit and not, with AUNE, Revelation, 1114, as part of a collection of seven sayings to be found in vv. 5-8.

²⁶ Rev 21,5d functions much like 19,9 ("Write this ... These are true words of God"), a verse that is a formal confirmation of the marriage passage 19,7-8 (cf. 21,2c). AUNE, Revelation, 1126, comments: Rev 21,5d "... is the last of several commands to write that apparently have the entire composition in view (Rev 1:11, 19; 21:5; cf. 10:4) rather than just partial texts that are the objects of the commands to write in 14:13 and 19:9". But can such a comprehensive reference be assumed for 21,5d?

8 God's last words rather unexpectedly return to the exclusion from salvation (cf. 20,15). "All liars"[27] comes last and concludes the preceding seven categories. Does this list, therefore, in the first place refer to cowardly, unfaithful, compromising, insincere believers? If so, verse 8 contains an impressive warning since "their lot will be in the lake that burns with fire and sulphur, which is the second death". Yet this is not certain; all kinds of pagan unbelievers could be meant as well.

The Old Testament

It would seem that the main Old Testament impact on John in 21,1-8 comes from three different writings: Ezekiel, Isaiah and 2 Samuel.

Ezekiel. John's dependence on Ezekiel 37–48 regarding the order in Revelation 20–22 has already been discussed on pp. 398-399. His creative modification of Ezekiel concerning God's presence in the new Jerusalem will be dealt with in the following paragraph. For his use of the covenant fomula in Rev 21,3 John is most probably directly influenced by Ezek 37,27[28]. Ezek 37,27 (LXX) reads:

27a   My dwelling place (κατασκήνωμα) shall be with (ἐν) them;
b   and I will be their God,
c   and they shall be my people.

The fact that Ezekiel 37–48 influences John in the global structuring of his last chapters as well as the presence of the term κατασκήνωμα in 37,27a (cf. σκηνή in Rev 21,3b and σκηνώσει in 21,3c)[29] should convince us that John depends on this particular rendering of the often quoted formula and not on Lev 26,12 or Zech 2,14-15[30]. What are the changes effected by John? He duplicates the first clause (Ezek 37,27a): "Behold, the tent of God [will be] with men, and he will put his tent with them" (v. 3bc).

---

[27] According to BEALE, *Revelation*, 1060, the expression points to "those whose Christian profession is betrayed by compromising behavior and false doctrine". The lists in 21,8.27 and 22,15 are all three concluded with "liars".

[28] Cf. VOGELGESANG, *Interpretation*, 81-86.

[29] The only other place in the book of Revelation where noun and verb occur together (and in the same order) is 13,6: the beast utters blasphemies against God, "his name and his dwelling, that is, those who dwell in heaven".

[30] Zech 2,15 has the plural: "and many nations shall join themselves to the Lord in that day, and shall be my people; and I will dwell in the midst of you [= daughter of Zion]". Cf. AUNE, *Revelation*, 1123-24. Recently HIRSCHBERG, *Israel*, 235-243, defends John's dependence in 21,2-3.23-25 on Zech 2,5-17. Yet in Zechariah the covenant formula is less clear; moreover, John may have taken the plural λαοί from 7,9 (cf. also σκηνώσει in 7,15).

Then John adds: "and they will be his peoples and God himself will be with them, their God" (v. 3de). For John the new Jerusalem is not only a restored Israel but comprises all Christians: see "men" (v. 3b), the plural "peoples" (v. 3d; compare with "my people" in Ezek 37,27c)[31] and "they, them, they" (v. 3de). This rewriting in v. 3bc may have caused the inversion in v. 3d and e as well as the stylistically less happy alterations in v. 3e: first "they will be his peoples" and then "God himself will be with them, their God" (compare Ezek 37,27b and c)[32]. The "covenant of peace" or "everlast-ing cove-nant" of Ezek 37,26 is not mentioned nor, of course, the "sanctuary in the midst of them" of 37,26.28. Yet the covenant formula of 37,27 is prominent, in its edited form, i.e., without any particularism.

Isaiah. Two specific passages of the book of Isaiah appear to have influenced John in 21,1-8, namely Isa 65,17-20[33] and 25,7-8. In the first passage five parallelisms can be pointed out; they stand, moreover, in the same sequence: (1) "I am about to create new heavens and a new earth" (65,17a[34]; cf. Rev 21,1a; in 21,5b God himself radicalizes and universalizes this vision: ἰδοὺ καινὰ ποιῶ πάντα); (2) "the former things shall not be remembered or come to mind" (65,17b; cf. Rev 21,1b); (3) Jerusalem is mentioned in 65,18-19 (cf. Rev 21,2); (4) "no more shall the sound of weeping be heard in it or the cry of distress" (65,19a; cf. Rev 21,4a); (5) (possible) "no more shall there be" (65,20a; cf. Rev. 21,4b and c)[35].

The second passage contains two allusions: (1) "he (= the Lord) will swallow up death forever" (25,8a; cf. Rev. 21,4b); (2) "then the Lord God will wipe away the tears from all faces" (25,8b; cf. Rev 21,4a). Here, the

---

[31] Cf. VOGELGESANG, *Interpretation*, 84: the plural "peoples" is "a slight change in detail creating a major difference in interpretation". In his comment on Rev 7,15-17 BEALE, *Revelation*, 440-441, writes: "The application of Ezek. 37:27 to the church is striking .... Ezekiel 37 was a prophecy uniquely applicable to ethnic or theocratic Israel in contrast to the nations, yet now John understands it as fulfilled in the church". BEALE calls this a "reversed application of OT prophecy". Compare Rev 21,3bc with 7,15c; 21,4a with 7,17c; and 21,6d with 7,16a.17b.

[32] U. VANNI, "Linguaggio, simboli ed esperienza mistica nel libro dell'Apocalisse. II", *Greg* 79 (1998) 473-501, translates 21,3e: "ed egli, Iddio con loro, sarà il loro Dio" (p. 478), "con una punteggiatura che salvi il valore dell'espressione e il parallelismo con quella che precede" (note 14). But see also our note 23.

[33] Cf. J. VAN RUITEN, "The Intertextual Relationship between Isaiah 65,17-20 and Revelation 21,1-5b", *EstBib* 51 (1993) 473-510.

[34] The Septuagint translates: "For there will be the new heaven and the new earth". Both here and in Rev 21,1a the verb "create" is absent. However, according to MELL, *Neue Schöpfung*, 133-134, John does not directly depend on this version. A "traditionsgeschichtlicher Zusammenhang zu äthHen 91,16" is postulated (p. 133). Such a possible dependence, however, remains difficult to prove.

[35] For this last possible parallelism, see BEALE, *Revelation*, 1050: the formula "is derived from Isa. 65:19-20".

order is inverted, yet in both Isaiah and Revelation the texts are found together. The disappearance of sorrow is brought about by the abolition of death. As usual John does not quote literally; but in v. 4ab, too, his dependence on both Isa 25,8 and 65,19-20 can hardly be doubted[36].

2 Samuel. In Rev 21,7bc the adoption formula is cited. In 2 Samuel 7, the Lord, through the prophet Nathan, explains to David that not he but his son will build "a house for his name", a temple. God will establish the throne of his kingdom forever (cf. 7,13). Then comes the adoption promise: "I will be a father to him, and he shall be a son to me" (7,14). One can hardly prove that John directly depends on this passage from 2 Samuel. The adoption formula is too familiar for that. The rewriting of "a father to him" (αὐτῷ εἰς πατέρα) and "a son to me" (μοι εἰς υἱόν) into a nominative without εἰς does not yield much of a difference in sense. Instead of "father" in v. 7b John writes "God". This may be under the influence of v. 3 where "God" is repeated in the covenant formula three times. Some authors, moreover, assume that John avoids "father" which noun he reserves for use by the unique son Jesus (cf. 1,6; 2,28; 3,5.21; 14,1)[37].

Text in Context

Creation? In Rev 21,1-8 God's initiative is very much emphasized. The language surely suggests a completely new beginning and no continuity with what existed in the past. The first things have passed away; the new reality comes from heaven, from God. Yet what appears is a new "heaven", a new "earth"; what comes down is a new "Jerusalem". The terms themselves seem to betray a persisting relation between old and new. The new is "an identifiable counterpart" of the old and "a renewal of it"[38]. According to 21,5b God is not replacing the old but "making all things new". This points to transformation rather than to an outright new creation of a totally different reality[39]. It would seem that by the symbolic language

---

[36] Cf. VAN RUITEN, "Intertextual Relationship" for more possible allusions, e.g., Isa 43,19 (a new thing); 52,1 (Jerusalem holy city); 49,18 and 61,10 (bride). See his conclusions on pp. 508-510 regarding the lexical and thematical level of the Old Testament influence.

[37] See GIESEN, *Offenbarung*, 458 (with reference to other authors); BEALE, *Revelation*, 1058.

[38] BEALE, *Revelation*, 1040: "Indeed, καινός ... refers predominantly to a change in quality or essence rather than something new that has never previously been in existence".

[39] Cf. G.Z. HEIDE, "What is New about the New Heaven and the New Earth? A Theology of Creation from Revelation 21 and 2 Peter 3", *JETS* 40 (1997) 37-56.

of 21,1-2 John above all refers to the so-called preexistent salvation which he "sees" as coming down from heaven. By preexistence and heavenly origin he emphasizes the certainty of God's eschatological salvation and thus encourages his endangered addressees[40].

The New Jerusalem. The holy city comes down out of heaven from God (21,2ab; cf. 21,10 and already 3,12). The cube form of the city, her enormous dimensions and the precious stones as building materials underline the grandiose character of that Jerusalem from above (cf. 21,11-21).

Jerusalem is prepared as a bride adorned for her husband[41]. That husband is the Lamb (see 21,9: the interpreting angel will show him [= John] "the bride, the wife of the Lamb"). In 19,7-9 the marriage of the Lamb and his bride is announced. The "bride has made herself ready; to her it has been granted to be clothed with fine linen, bright and pure" (19,7c-8a). John explains: "for the fine linen is the righteous deeds of the saints" (19,8b). The perfect bride is the church of the end time, the new Israel, represented by the twelve apostles of the Lamb (21,13-14), as well as consisting of "the peoples" (21,3), "the nations" (21,24-26 and 22,2; and cf. ch. 7)[42]. In his recent monograph Peter Hirschberg shows convincingly, it would seem, how the eschatological people of God preserves its continuity with the historical Israel, and how it is open to all peoples. In Revelation one should not find the idea of substitution of Israel by the church[43].

Through her magnitude the new Jerusalem fills, one would say, the new heaven and the new earth. There seems to be no room for anything else. God's presence in that city is emphasized (21,3bc)[44]. In the new

---

[40] See MELL, *Neue Schöpfung*, 134-135.

[41] Cf. K.E. MILLER, "The Nuptial Eschatology of Revelation 19–22", *CBQ* 60 (1998) 301-318.

[42] Cf. A. VÖGTLE, "'Dann sah ich einen neuen Himmel und eine neue Erde...' (Apk 21,1. Zur kosmischen Dimension neutestamentlicher Eschatologie", E. GRÄSSER – O. MERK (eds.), *Glaube und Eschatologie. FS W.G. Kümmel* (Tübingen 1985) 303-333: a "geradezu provizierende Identifizierung von Frau und Stadt" functions "als Sinnbild der vollerlösten Heilsgemeinde" (pp. 327-328).

[43] Cf. HIRSCHBERG, *Israel*. Besides 2,9 and 3,9 chapters 7 and 21–22 are analyzed. He coins his basic insight as follows: "Heilsgeschichtlich unterscheidet der Seher ... zwischen Juden und Heiden, soteriologisch ist jeder Unterschied aufgehoben" (p. 194). Moreover, John's emphasis on the twelve tribes (see 7,4-8 and 21,12-13) may point to his hope of the salvation of the whole of Israel.

[44] Cf. R.H. GUNDRY, "The New Jerusalem: People as Place, not Place for People", *NT* 29 (1987) 254-264: "The New Jerusalem is a dwelling place, to be sure; but it is God's dwelling place in the saints rather than their dwelling place on earth. The new earth ... is the saints' dwelling place" (p. 256).

Jerusalem there will be no temple, "for its temple is the Lord God and the Lamb" (21,22). Ezekiel's new temple is, as it were, replaced by the whole of the new Jerusalem. "The city has no need of sun or moon to shine on it, for the glory of God is its light, and its lamp is the Lamb" (21,23; cf. 22,5). God's dwelling "with men" cannot but produce a covenantal relationship: they are his peoples, he is their God (21,3de).

This eschatological salvation is further explained negatively: no more grief and groaning, no more death (21,4abc and cf. the exclusion sayings of 21,8.27; 22,3a), but then also positively: the gift of water (21,6d), inheritance (21,7a), sonship (21,7bc) and, of course, God's radiant glory itself (21,22-26), as well as the river of the water of life (22,1-5ab). The believers "will reign forever and ever" (22,5c; cf., e.g., 20,6: they are "priests of God and of Christ" and they "will reign")[45].

Covenant and Adoption. Are the covenant formula (21,3de) and the adoption formula (21,7bc) without a mutual connection? Just as in the alleged fragment 2 Cor 6,14–7,1, so also in Rev 21,1-8 both formulae are employed in the same context and in a similar interrupted sequence. The two formulae appear to be intended as complementary promises; they interpret one another, but adoption appears to be more than covenant. Compare 2 Cor 6,16d with Rev 21,3de (covenant), and 2 Cor 6,17d-18b with Rev 21,7bc (adoption). In 2 Cor 6 Paul inserts allusions to other Old Testament texts; he uses introductory expressions which show that he wants to cite; the covenant formula is most probably cited from Lev 26,12, not from Ezek 37,27; in 6,18 he expands the last clause of the adoption formula: "and you will be sons *and daughters* to me"[46].

John does not formally introduce his references; as a matter of fact he does not quote properly. Within the context of 21,1-8 the adoption formula of v. 7bc probably has a climactic function. No longer the voice and the third person as for the covenant formula, but God himself speaks in the first person singular. Moreover, the collective plural of "men" and "peoples" gives way to a seemingly more direct and engaging singular: the individual is addressed. Not only divine presence and gifts and inheritance are offered, not only overwhelming riches, but a filial relationship with God.

God and Lamb. The passage 21,1-8 is remarkably theocentric. In vv. 1-4 God is explicitly mentioned three times. He is the only agent; he makes

---

[45] In 7,14-17 a number of motifs are anticipated. See especially v. 15: "the one who is seated on the throne" (cf. 21,5a) and σκηνώσει (cf. 21,3c); v. 17: the "springs of the water of life" (cf. 21,6d) and "God will wipe away every tear from their eyes" (cf. 21,4a).

[46] Cf. J. LAMBRECHT, *Second Corinthians* (SP; Collegeville 1999) 123-125.

all things new (cf. v. 5b). This is highlighted by the words of the voice in vv. 3b-4d. Moreover, in vv. 5-8 the Lord God himself proceeds to speak in the first person[47]. He does it three times with much decision and authority and in a solemn, climactic way. He points out his identity and sovereignty. One can scarcely avoid the impression that this intentional theocentrism might have caused the somewhat strange absence of the Lamb in vv. 1-8.

Nevertheless, "husband" in 21,2c contains a reference to the Lamb. Moreover, immediately after 21,1-8 the Lamb is mentioned several times: "the bride, the wife of the Lamb" (21,9); "the twelve apostles of the Lamb" (21,14); "its temple is the Lord God the Almighty and the Lamb" (21,22); "the glory of God is its light and its lamp is the Lamb" (21,23); "the throne of God and of the Lamb" (22,1). These five references appear to be a conscious clarification, almost a corrective[48]. In 22,13 Christ applies to himself God's identification of 21,6c: "I am the Alpha and the Omega, ..., the beginning and the end".

III. THE LAST TWO VISIONS

Why can Rev 20,11-15 and 21,1-8 be called the last two visions? What about 21,9–22,5? Just as in 17,1-3 one of the seven angels who had the bowls carries John away in the spirit into the wilderness, so also in 21,9-10 one of the seven angels who had the seven bowls full of the seven last plagues carries John away in the spirit to a great high mountain. In 17,3 John sees a woman sitting on a scarlet beast (Babylon, Rome) and in 21,10 he sees the holy city Jerusalem (the bride, the wife of the Lamb) coming down out of heaven from God. Just as in 17,4-18 so also in 21,11–22,5 the interpreting angel provides the explanation of what is seen by John. Strictly

---

[47] Cf. GIESEN, *Offenbarung*, 456; AUNE, *Revelation*, 1125; BEALE, *Interpretation*, 1055: "Verses 5 and 6 are only the second time in the Apocalypse where God is explicitly quoted. The first was in 1:8. Both there and here the title 'the Alpha and the Omega' occurs. That this title appears at the beginning and end of the book is fitting and cannot be coincidence. The placement heightens further the figurative point of the divine title, which mentions two polar opposites (first and last) to underscore that everything between the opposites is included: all the events narrated and portrayed between 1:8 and 21:6 lie under God's absolute sovereignty, as has all history prior to the writing of Revelation".

[48] Compare also the role of Christ in the battle of 19,11-21: he is the "King of kings and Lord of lords" (v. 16).

speaking, both passages, 17,1-18 and 21,9–22,5 are not visions; the first does not carry forward God's judgment of his enemies nor does the second complete the definitive salvation of the saints[49]. The last two visions in 20,11–21,8 contain the outcome of both the final judgment and victory which are depicted in 19,11–22,5[50].

What remains to be done is to summarize the main data of this climactic outcome and to present some hermeneutical reflections.

The Final Outcome

a) Rev 20,11-15 contains the last scene of God's victory over his enemies. John sees the great white judgment seat and the one who is seated on it; the dead, great and small, are standing before the throne; the books are opened. Earth and heaven have fled from God's presence. Sea, Death and Hades have given up their dead. Then Death and Hades are thrown into the lake of fire; the same happened with those whose name is not written in the book of life.

In vv. 11-13 one spontaneously imagines a general resurrection or, if one takes into account the first resurrection mentioned in 20,5-6, at least the resurrection of the rest of the dead so that all the dead can be judged. One expects, therefore, the separation of the saints from the sinners; one looks for both reward and punishment. But the judgment in vv. 14-15 is one-sidedly negative; the focus is on "the inhabitants of the earth, whose names have not been written in the book of life from the foundation of the world" (17,8). For all of them it is the ultimate catastrophe, the second death. This is, of course, not just information for the Christians; a hidden warning is also present. Yet the reader is tempted to ask: what happens to those whose names are written in that book? After all, that momentous throne pericope of 20,11-15 remains somewhat strange.

This reminds us of the compositional irregularities which are discussed above. After John has depicted the lot of the dragon, the beast and the false prophet, he does not want to omit the same destiny for Death and Hades. What in vv. 13-14 is said about sea, Death and Hades appears to be an insertion.

b) The start of 21,1-8 is brusque. There is a kind of suspense at the end

---

[49] Cf., e.g., BEALE, *Interpretation*, 1062: "21:9–22:5 is a recapitulation of the immediately preceding section of 21:1-8 that amplifies the picture there of God's consummate communion with his people and their consummate safety in the new creation".

[50] Moreover, an inclusion is formed by 19,9-10 and 22,6-9.

of 20,11-15. The final judgments took place, but what happened to the believers? Their resurrection does not seem alluded to; their reward is not depicted. The negative punitive vision of 20,11-15 requires, as it were, a positive victorious counterpart. In 21,1, without any form of transition, the vision of the new heaven and the new earth is introduced, utterly positive. A judgment of the righteous which would result in a just reward is not described. One has to wait until v. 3 before "men" and "peoples" are mentioned, but even then they are not called by one of their known names, e.g., "those written in the book of life", "followers of the Lamb" (cf. 14,4) or "servants of God with a seal on their foreheads" (cf. 7,3). Yet the holy city which comes down out of heaven from God in 21,2 is the new Jerusalem; she is the bride. It would seem, however, that in 21,3-4 John does not further reflect on the marital image (in contrast with 19,7-8; Isa 52,10; 62,3-5). Attention goes to God's covenantal presence, not to the intimate marriage relationship. Jerusalem is the home of God; God dwells with "men". These "men" are the inhabitants of that city. They are his "peoples", the renewed Israel consisting of Jew and Gentile alike. The holy city, the new Jerusalem, is a metaphor for the church universal. In the eschaton the saints will be the bride adorned for her husband, the Lamb. In a climactic way, the definitive future is announced. The message has divine authentication. First a voice from the throne proclaims the universalistic covenant of God with the redeemed humankind. This means God's covenantal presence and, at the same time, the absence of mourning and pain, the immunity to first and second death.

Then, in 21,5-8, three times the Lord God himself validates the absolute victory that is announced. (1) He emphasizes that he is making all things new. (2) He stresses that his words are trustworthy and true. (3) He affirms that "it is done!"[51] and refers to his sovereign, authoritative identity: he is the Alpha and the Omega, the beginning and the end (cf. 1,8). He confirms the free gift of living water and of the inheritance for the conqueror. And, at the very peak of this brief discourse, to the individual faithful servant God promises adoption, i.e., divine sonship: I will be his God and he will be my son. This is hardly only a metaphor which refers to God's special protection and care. No, in Christ, God's Son, his followers become sons and daughters of God, divinely renewed and transformed.

---

[51] The perfect γέγοναν (plural) reminds the reader of γέγονεν (singular) in 16,17: "The seventh angel poured his bowl into the air, and a loud voice came out of the temple, from the throne, saying, "it is done!" The creation of new Jerusalem comes after the destruction of great Babylon (see 16,18-21).

Such an attractive, triumphant view of the eschatological future must bring encouragement to those who still suffer on earth. God himself, however, in a rather astonishing way, at once adds a severe warning: the place of the compromising unfaithful, the lot of sinners, will be in the lake of fire, which is the second death.

The compact vision of 21,1-8 is then further elaborated in 21,9–22,5 by the angel's expansive interpretation which, of course, maintains and even further heightens the climax.

Hermeneutical Reflections

There is hopefully no longer any need today to warn the alert reader against a literal, fundamentalist interpretation of the whole imagery of the last two visions. In this concluding paragraph attention will be given to three problematic items: the lake of fire, theocentrism and the expectation of an imminent end.

a) In 21,4b it is said that (physical) death will be no more. This means its definitive disappearance and annihilation. The same may apply to the misery mentioned in v. 4a and 4c and to the inimical sea of v. 1c. But this is likely not the case as far as the first heaven and the first earth in v. 1b are concerned. John possibly sees the new heaven and new earth (v. 1a) as a renewal of the old, not as a completely new creation (cf. v. 5b). And what about all those thrown into the lake of fire: false prophet, beast and devil, as well as the people not written in the book of life? According to Revelation they do not appear to be annihilated. They will be tormented in hell forever; their damnation is eternal.

A number of apocalyptic data should be interpreted in due manner. Hell is not to be localized. Fire and bodily pain are not to be taken as real. Hell must be thought of as a state of complete frustration, absence of love, definite separation from God. Should hermeneutics go further? Nowadays, more than before and notwithstanding the traditional creed, critical Christians not only doubt the existence of devil and demons but also seriously ask themselves whether total lack of love in a human being will not end in his or her non-existence, a "second death", and, moreover, how one can imagine a merciful God who in his justice condemns human beings, his creatures, to an everlasting doom. However, a study of Revelation alone can hardly endorse such radical criticisms[52].

b) Both the severe judgment in 20,11-15 and the extreme theocentrism in 21,1-8 could wrongly suggest the absence of human action and responsibility. As elsewhere in Revelation, the radical separation between bad and good appears to be fixed. One might suspect a sort of determinism, a certain predestination, in these visions. Moreover, in the Book of Revelation little or nothing is said about the conversion of "the inhabitants of the earth". Time and again the absence of repentance is recorded[53]. "Let the evildoer still do evil, and the filthy still be filthy, and the righteous still do right, and the holy still be holy" (22,11).

John, however, is more nuanced. First of all, one should remember that in 20,11–21,8 John describes the end of history, i.e., final damnation and eternal salvation. Then changes will no longer be possible. Moreover, significant details in the text certainly point to human accountability. The dead will be judged according to their works (20,12d and 13c). One has to remain faithful and to conquer in order to receive the inheritance (21,7a). Before the end compromise, infidelity and all sorts of sin remain possible.

John's addressees are the Christians in Asia. The depiction of the future judgment is certainly also intended as warning and encouragement, as threat and exhortation during the present life on earth.

c) What John announces in 20,11–21,8 — final judgments and ultimate blessings — is not seen in a distant future. After 21,9–22,5 the interpreting angel says to John: "Do not seal up the words of the prophecy of this book; for the time is near" (22,10). In 22,12 Jesus speaks of his return: "See, I am coming soon; my reward is with me, to repay according to everyone's work" (cf. 22,20). As is commonly assumed, in the book of Revelation the linear time-line of the prophecies is more than once interrupted by proleptic scenes (cf., e.g., 7,9-17; 11,16-18; 16,5-7). The future thus becomes present to some extent, all the more so since the very announcement of a near future by itself heightens its impact on the present. But above all there is the Christ-event; Christ has become "the firstborn of the dead, and the ruler of the kings of the earth" (1,6; cf. the Lamb in 5,6-14). Salvation is an already present reality in history, on earth. The servants of God in Asia experience not only the "not yet" but without a doubt also this "already"[54].

---

[52] A conclusion such as that of T.F. GLASSON, "The Last Judgment — in Rev. 20 and Related Writings" *NTS* 28 (1982) 528-539, cannot be rejected: "The conviction remains valid, that finally wrong will be righted, realities seen in their true light, the mysteries of life made plain; the conviction that we are responsible to God, and that his purpose to sum up all things in Christ will be fulfilled" (p. 528).

[53] R. BAUCKHAM, *The Climax of Prophecy: Studies in the Book of Revelation*, Edinburgh 1963, contends — in a rather forced way, it would seem — that John hopes for the conversion of the Gentiles: see the long chapter "The Conversion of the Nations", 238-337.

[54] Cf. VÖGTLE, *Das Buch mit den sieben Siegeln*, 169: "Schon in ihrer irdischen Existenz verstand sich ja die Urkirche ihrem Wesen nach als eine vorwegnehmende Realisierung des 'oberen', des 'himmlischen' Jerusalem (Gal 4,25f; Hebr 12,22f)".

Modern Christians no longer look forward to the imminent return of their Lord; most of them cannot be convinced that the end is unmistakably near. But they can and should look forward to their personal encounter with the Lord at the moment of their own death. Perhaps, in a sense different from that in Revelation, this encounter may be called a "first resurrection". Like the souls of those "who have been slaughtered for the word of God and for the testimony they have given" we, too, hope to find ourselves "under the altar" in heaven (cf. 6,9), at death to enter immediately and safely "the city by the gates" (22,14) and become inhabitants of the new Jerusalem. All this does not, of course, exclude the parousia of the Lord and the final judgment — whatever it means — and the gathering in of all the saints, the end of the age and the consummate fulfillment of history.

No annihilation perhaps but a transformation of the cosmos, not only God's intervention but also human responsible activity, and most probably not a near end but a still open future for human beings whose life span in world history is but a brief breathing space: the conclusion to each of these reflections refers to the need of daily care for this earth and its inhabitants, as well as to the testimony to Jesus and the proclamation of the word of God (cf. 20,4).

Index of Biblical References

Index of Authors

Finito di stampare
nel mese di aprile 2001

presso la tipografia
"Giovanni Olivieri" di E. Montefoschi
00187 Roma - Via dell'Archetto, 10,11,12

136. MANZI, Franco: *Melchisedek e l'angelologia nell'Epistola agli Ebrei e a Qumran.* 1997, pp. XVIII-434.

137. TREMOLADA, Pierantonio: *«E fu annoverato fra iniqui». Prospettive di lettura della Passione secondo Luca alla luce di Lc 22,37 (Is 53,12d).* 1997, pp. 288.

48. LYONNET, Stanislas - SABOURIN, Léopold: *Sin, Redemption, and Sacrifice. A Biblical and Patristic Study.* First Reprint. 1998, pp. XVI-352.

138. GIURISATO, Giorgio: *Struttura e teologia della Prima Lettera di Giovanni. Analisi letteraria e retorica, contenuto teologico.* 1998, pp. IV-720 + pieghevole.

139. BARTHOLOMEW, Craig G.: *Reading Ecclesiastes. Old Testament Exegesis and Hermeneutical Theory.* 1998, pp. VIII-322.

140. MILER, Jean: *Les citations d'accomplissement dans l'Évangile de Matthieu. Quand Dieu se rend présent en toute humanité.* 1999, pp. 424.

73/74. DE LA POTTERIE, Ignace: *La vérité dans Saint Jean.* Deuxième édition revue et corrigée. 1999, pp. XXX-1132.

141. NAY, Reto: *Jahwe im Dialog. Kommunikationsanalytische Untersuchung von Ez 14,1-11 unter Berücksichtigung des dialogischen Rahmens in Ez 8-11 und Ez 20.* 1999, pp. XII-428.

142. NORTH, Robert: *Medicine in the Biblical Background and Other Essays on the Origins of Hebrew.* 2000, pp. 196.

143. BECHARD, Dean P.: *Paul outside the Walls: A Study of Luke's Socio-geographical Universalism in Acts 14:8-20.* 2000, pp. 544

144. HEIL, J. Paul: *The Transfiguration of Jesus: Narrative Meaning and Function of Mark 9:2-8, Matt17:1-8 and Luke 9:28-36.* 2000, pp. 368.

145. NORTH, Robert: *The Biblical Jubilee ... after fifty years.* 2000, pp. 168.

146. PRASAD, Jacob: *Foundations of the Christian Way of Life according to 1 Peter 1, 13-25. An Exegetico-theological study.* 2000, pp. XX-468.

147. LAMBRECHT, Jan: *Collected Studies on Pauline Literature and on The Book of Revelation.* 2001, pp. XVI-438.

For the other volumes see the GENERAL CATALOGUE of the publisher

For further informations, orders and payments write to:

EDITRICE PONTIFICIO ISTITUTO BIBLICO
Piazza della Pilotta, 35 – 00187 Roma, Italia
Tel.06/678.15.67 – Fax 06/678.05.88

ISBN 88-7653-147-5

Most of these thirty collected studies were written in Rome. Two are translations from the Dutch; three have not been published previously. Some few studies address philological problems, but most try to explain the thought of the biblical text. There are full-fledged articles and also brief notes. Bringing them together in one volume will prove useful to students of Paul, of Pauline Literature and of The Book of Revelation. These essays are the result of years of teaching experience and extensive research.

The reader will find not only analyses of various passages but also broad syntheses of biblical thought. This book consists of two parts: "Pauline and Deutero-Pauline Letters", the larger one, and "The Book of Revelation", the smaller. The first part considers Paul's view of the law, his eschatological convictions and his reasoning regarding the resurrection of Christ and of the Christians. The second part examines the ecclesiology and the climatic composition of The Book of Revelation. The movement from judgments to blessings is carefully investigated.

JAN LAMBRECHT, S.J., is Professor Emeritus of New Testament and Biblical Greek at the Catholic University of Leuven, Belgium. From 1996 to 2001 he was also Visiting Professor at the Pontifical Biblical Institute of Rome. He is an internationally known scholar and was a member of the Pontifical Biblical Commission from 1985 to 1995.

His books in English include *Once More Astonished: The Parables of Jesus* (New York: Crossroad, 1981); *The Sermon on the Mount: Proclamation and Exhortation* (GNS 14; Wilmington, Del.: Glazier, 1985); (together with Richard W. Thompson) *Justification by Faith: The Implications of Romans 3:27-31* (Zacchaeus Studies; Wilmington, Del.: Glazier, 1989); *Out of the Treasure: The Parables in the Gospel of Matthew* (Leuven: Peeters, 1992); *The Wretched 'I' and Its Liberation: Paul in Romans 7 and 8* (Leuven: Peeters, 1992); and the commentary *Second Corinthians* (Sacra Pagina; Collegeville, Min.: The Liturgical Press, 1999).

€ 25.00